Archaeological Science

This book provides an up-to-date introduction to the exciting but complex new scientific methodologies that are increasingly used in archaeological study. Written by an international team of specialists, it provides clear and engaging overviews of a wide array of approaches, including DNA and proteomics, dating methods, materials analysis, stable isotope analysis and the scientific study of human, plant and animal remains, among other topics. Each technique is explored through the use of real archaeological examples, which both explain the methods and highlight their potential applications. The work is carefully illustrated with useful charts, graphs and other images, which complement the detail in the text and help articulate the case studies explored as well as the underlying principles of the techniques involved. Tables in many of the chapters highlight selected research on each topic, providing useful summaries of the current state and scope of the field for the reader. This volume will serve as a handy reference tool for scholars, as well as a key textbook for courses on archaeological science.

Michael P. Richards is an archaeological scientist who applies methods such as isotopic analysis to determine past human and animal diets and adaptations. He is a professor of archaeology and Canada Research Chair in archaeological science at the Department of Archaeology, Simon Fraser University in Vancouver, Canada, and is a Fellow of the Society of Antiquaries of London and a Fellow of the Royal Society of Canada. He has published over 250 research papers in journals such as *Nature*, *Science* and *PNAS*.

Kate Britton is a senior lecturer in archaeological science at the University of Aberdeen and an associate research scientist at the Max Planck Institute for Evolutionary Anthropology, Leipzig, and is a Fellow of the Society of Antiquaries of Scotland. An archaeological scientist, she studies the relationship between lifetime behaviours, diets and movements and the stable isotope chemistry of body tissues.

Archaeological Science

An Introduction

Edited by

Michael P. Richards
Simon Fraser University

Kate Britton
University of Aberdeen

TABLES

CONTRIBUTORS

Richard M. Bailey
University of Oxford, United Kingdom

Simon Blockley
Royal Holloway, University of London, United Kingdom

Kate Britton
University of Aberdeen, United Kingdom and Max Planck Institute for Evolutionary Anthropology, Germany

Matthew Collins
University of Cambridge, United Kingdom and Natural History Museum of Denmark, University of Copenhagen, Denmark

Oliver E. Craig
University of York, United Kingdom

A. Catherine D'Andrea
Simon Fraser University, Canada

Patrick Degryse
Katholieke Universiteit Leuven, Belgium

Keith Dobney
University of Liverpool, United Kingdom

Nienke van Doorn
University of York, United Kingdom

Philipp Gunz
Max Planck Institute for Evolutionary Anthropology, Germany

Jessica Hendy
University of York, United Kingdom

Panagiotis Karkanas
The American School of Classical Studies, Greece

Greger Larson
University of Oxford, United Kingdom

Liisa Loog
University of Oxford, United Kingdom, University of Cambridge, United Kingdom and University of Manchester, United Kingdom

Marcello A. Mannino
Aarhus University, Denmark

Shannon P. McPherron
Max Planck Institute for Evolutionary Anthropology, Germany

Thilo Rehren
The Cyprus Institute, Cyprus

Michael P. Richards
Simon Fraser University, Canada

Hayley Saul
Western Sydney University, Australia

Andrew J. Shortland
Cranfield University, United Kingdom

Tanya M. Smith
Griffith University, Australia

Cynthianne Spiteri
Eberhard Karls Universität Tübingen, Germany

Beth Upex
Durham University, United Kingdom

Darlene A. Weston
University of British Columbia, Canada

ACKNOWLEDGEMENTS

We would first most like to thank each of our authors in this volume for their contributions, hard work and patience as we brought this volume together. Thanks also to our proof-readers and copy-editors for their valuable inputs. We are very pleased with the resulting book, and especially the high quality of all of the chapters. Our hope is that this volume will be of help to both archaeology professionals and students, to give them a starting point for the new methods of archaeological science that are increasingly being used in archaeology today.

Part I

Introduction

Introducing Archaeological Science

Kate Britton and Michael P. Richards

An introduction to the field of archaeological science and to this volume, including a brief history of the subject and a look to the future.

1 INTRODUCTION

As the study of the past through its material remains, archaeology has a long tradition of drawing on the sciences, especially the natural sciences. The multifaceted approach required in the study of human societies, and the focus on the material – artefacts and 'ecofacts', manufactured and natural – means that, perhaps more than any other academic subject, archaeology relies heavily on a diverse range of fields outside of the discipline (Pollard and Heron 2008). The plethora of scientific techniques used in modern archaeological science reflects the varied aspects of life in the past they are utilised to investigate (Brothwell and Pollard 2001: xviii). The demands of inferring of activities, motivations, behaviours, ideas and beliefs of individuals in the past requires multistranded, complementary approaches. As a consequence, archaeological science enters into many areas of the study of the past and is a fundamental component of the investigation of past societies and human behaviours.

The aim of this chapter is to introduce the field of archaeological science and the purpose and scope of this volume. This chapter will also briefly explore the development of archaeological science and provide a brief history of the field.

2 WHAT IS ARCHAEOLOGICAL SCIENCE?

Defining archaeological science, and the ways in which it differs as a subfield from the larger field of archaeology, has been a subject of great debate and is perhaps even reflected in indecision in what exactly to call it. 'Archaeological science', 'science in archaeology' and 'archaeometry' are all used to varying extents (McGovern et al. 1995: 79), with archaeological science being perhaps the most common term (especially in the United Kingdom).

Archaeologists would variously describe their research as falling within humanities, social sciences and/or natural sciences, and it is certainly a broad enough field that it can easily include research in all three. Perhaps many of the debates over the nature of archaeology are the result of different practitioners themselves identifying more with one of these three areas than the others. The differences between those who feel their research is in the humanities, and those that identify with the natural sciences are the most striking, and perhaps the root of some scepticism and suspicion about the area of archaeological science from some in other areas of archaeology. Those who believe in a relative view of knowledge even question the nature of the scientific method and knowledge, which conflicts directly with archaeological scientists who are often trained in the natural sciences. It is perhaps a fault of some in archaeological science that they argue that their methods can produce something approximating the 'truth' (or at least hard, irrefutable facts) in the past, without considering the differing theoretical frameworks their colleagues may use.

While committed to investigating social phenomena, unlike other social scientists, archaeologists start with surviving physical remains of human actions, and must use these to infer human behaviours and beliefs (Trigger 1988: 1). The application of diverse scientific technologies and techniques to analyse those physical remains thus forms a core part of 'the logical-positivist pursuit of understanding peoples through their material remains' (Rich 2015: 532). While some have argued that archaeological science is merely an 'assemblage of techniques', and 'is not science as it would be recognised in the natural sciences' (Thomas 1991: 31), others have argued this cross-disciplinary lack of purity is, in fact, the strength of the diverse subfield we know today (Brothwell and Pollard 2001: xviii).

For this edited volume, we are defining 'Archaeological Science' as a term that encompasses the application of techniques and approaches from the full range of natural sciences (biology, chemistry, physics) to archaeological materials – the 'active participation of the physical and natural sciences in the study of the past' (Bayley and Heron 1998: 137).

3 A (VERY) BRIEF HISTORY OF ARCHAEOLOGICAL SCIENCE

The practice of modern archaeology, and what we now conceive of as the field, has its origins in the eighteenth and nineteenth centuries and we would argue, at its heart, is intrinsically related to the natural sciences. After all, one of the fundamental frameworks of archaeological investigation is that of stratigraphy – a concern for the order and relative position of deposits or strata – an approach also fundamental to the field of geology. The tentative beginnings of laboratory analysis applied to archaeological materials, incorporating the expertise of chemists, metallurgists and mineralogists, can also be traced to the nineteenth century, such as the work overseen by metallurgist John Percy on the analysis of Assyrian bronzes and glass in Austen Henry Layard's 'Discoveries in the Ruins of Ninevah and Babylon' published in 1853, and Heinrich Schielmann's 'Mycenae' published in 1878 (Pollard and Heron 2008: 5).

While the relationship between mainstream archaeology and the sciences spans more than two centuries, the modern subfield of archaeological science is rooted in the blossoming of ecological and environmental-based approaches to archaeology, and particularly advances in chronometric dating, in the decades of the mid-twentieth century (Brothwell and Pollard 2001; Pollard 2007; Pollard and Heron 2008). This period saw an influx of new methodologies but also saw perceptions shift on the potential of physical archaeological evidence through its systematic and scientific study – the so-called New Archaeology (Killick 2015; Marciniak and Rączkowski 2001). Not without its critics, the position (and even the legitimacy) of archaeological science within the broader field of archaeology was called into question over the following decades (e.g., Thomas 1991). Critics of the subfield, and its practitioners, enjoyed a heyday in the 1980s and 1990s as the processual paradigm of the 'New Archaeology' was rejected by the post-processualist movement. Post-processualism was rooted in interpreting rather than explaining the archaeological record, and saw the rejection of the systematic views of human lifeways and social relationships that processualism and, by extension, archaeological scientists, envisaged (Marciniak and Rączkowski 2001: 11).

Despite the latter half of the last century being 'punctuated by papers criticising the lack of understanding between "science" and "archaeology"' (Pollard and Bray 2007: 246), the field of archaeological science has flourished and there are few archaeologists who would now deny the contribution scientific approaches make to using them is essential for all archaeologists. Beyond that, the ability to be able to interpret and assimilate archaeological science literature and data into their work should be a priority (Killick and Young 1997: 523).

5 PURPOSE AND STRUCTURE OF THE VOLUME

The purpose of this book is to further the integration of archaeological science within archaeology, and to increase understanding of the subfield. We are hopeful that this volume may serve as reference text, useful for archaeologists, who want know more about a new and unfamiliar method or even archaeological scientists who may be unfamiliar with research areas outside their own specific fields. Perhaps most consciously, we aim this book at the growing number of undergraduate students worldwide who are increasingly becoming interested in learning about, and working in, the field of archaeological science.

With this book we chose to include what are, at the time of writing, the newest archaeological science methods alongside more established methods. As explored in this introduction, our interpretation of archaeological science includes any area of archaeology that applies methods originally developed in the so-called natural sciences including biology, chemistry and physics. We include well-established research fields such as zooarchaeology and human osteoarchaeology, as well as methods related specifically to materials analysis of archaeological samples, and genetic and isotopic analysis of them. We of course also include absolute dating methods, which are so crucial to our understanding of archaeology.

Many of the methods explained here have derived originally from other fields, but are now research areas in their own right, and have, in turn, influenced the original fields that they were borrowed from. For example, ancient DNA research into how DNA degrades is now used widely outside of archaeology, including in forensic research. Isotope analysis, which was largely refined within archaeology, is now widely used in ecology and medicine. The same can be said for most of the other areas of research included in this book, as archaeological science has developed into a mature research field.

For this volume we have grouped the chapters into five broad areas, which of course do not reflect the considerable overlap between these areas, and the methods themselves. The first section is in the area of 'Biomolecular Archaeology', which we have interpreted as the application of the study of ancient biomolecules in archaeological materials. This includes ancient DNA (Loog and Larson), ancient proteins, or more specifically proteomics (Hendy, van Doorn and Collins), as well as lipids and other adsorbed organic residues (Craig, Saul and Spiteri). We have also included the two chapters on isotope analysis of human (and animal) remains, separating them into isotopes largely used to look at migration and movements (Britton) and diet (Richards). The next section is the broader category of 'Bioarchaeology', which concerns the analysis (especially morphological) of human remains. This section contains an introduction to the field of human osteoarchaeological analysis (Weston), teeth (Smith) and geometric morphometrics (Gunz). Then we have grouped papers that fit more generally into the area of 'Environmental Archaeology' together. This includes reviews of vertebrate zooarchaeology (Dobney and Upex), invertebrate zooarchaeology (Mannino), palaeoethnobotany (D'Andrea) and geoarchaeology (Karkanas). Then we have grouped together applications of materials science to inorganic archaeological artefacts as 'Materials Analysis'. This includes ceramics (Shortland and Degryse), glass (Shortland and Rehren), metals (Rehren) and lithics (McPherron). Lastly, we have included two chapters on the most commonly used chronometric dating techniques as 'Absolute Dating Methods', including radiocarbon dating (Blockley) and luminescence dating (Bailey).

We were extremely fortunate to be have been able to draw on the considerable expertise and knowledge of our contributors, and we are very grateful to all of them for their contributions to this book. Of course, with such a dynamic and growing field, we were not able to cover all areas that might be called archaeological science, but we hope that this volume will give the specialist and student the tools they need to understand newly published research in archaeological science, as well as the large existing body of literature. Finally, we are hopeful that this introductory volume will also encourage some to start research themselves in the challenging, but also very rewarding, field of archaeological science.

REFERENCES

Bayley, J. and Heron, C. 1998. Archaeological science in the UK: Current trends and future prospects. *Revue d'Archéométrie* 22(1):137–140.

Britton, K. 2017. A stable relationship: Isotopes and bioarchaeology are in it for the long haul. *Antiquity* 91(358):853–864.

Brothwell, D. R. and Pollard, A. M. 2001. Archaeological science: A current perspective. In: Brothwell, D. R. and Pollard, A. M. (eds.) *Handbook of Archaeological Sciences*, pp. xvii–xx. Chichester: Wiley.

Killick, D. 2015. The awkward adolescence of archaeological science. *Journal of Archaeological Science* 56:242–247.

Killick, D. and Young, S. M. 1997. Archaeology and archaeometry: From casual dating to a meaningful relationship? *Antiquity* 71(273):518–524.

Marciniak, A. and Rączkowski, W. 2001. Archaeology and archaeological science: Past, present and future. *Archaeologia Polona* 39:5–16.

McGovern, P. E., Sever, T. L., Myers, J. W., Myers, E. E., Bevan, B., Miller, N. F., Bottema, S., Hongo, H., Meadow, R. H., Kuniholm, P.I., Bowman, S. G. E., Leese, M. N., Hedges, R. E. M., Matson, F. R., Freestone, I. C., Vaughan, S.J., Henderson, J., Vandiver, P. B., Tumosa, C. S., Beck, C. W., Smith, P., Child, A. M., Pollard, A. M., Thuesen, I., Sease, C., 1995. Science in Archaeology: A Review. *American Journal of Archaeology* 99:79–142.

Pollard, A. M. 2007. *Analytical Chemistry in Archaeology*. Cambridge: Cambridge University Press.

Pollard, A. M. and Bray, P. 2007. A bicycle made for two? The integration of scientific techniques into archaeological interpretation. *Annual Review of Anthropology* 36:245–259.

Pollard, A. M. and Heron, C. 2008. *Archaeological Chemistry*. Cambridge: RSC Publishing.

Rich, L. E. 2015. 'Leapin' lizards, Mr. Science': Old reflections on the new archaeology (and musings on anthropology, art, bioethics, and medicine). *Journal of Bioethical Inquiry* 12(4):531–535.

Szpak, P., Metcalfe, J. Z. and Macdonald, R. A. 2017. Best practices for calibrating and reporting stable isotope measurements in archaeology. *Journal of Archaeological Science: Reports* 13:609–616.

Thomas, J. 1991. Science versus anti-science? *Archaeological Review from Cambridge* 10(1):27–36.

Torrence, R., Martinón-Torres, M. and Rehren, Th. 2015. Forty years and still growing: *Journal of Archaeological Science* looks to the future. *Journal of Archaeological Science* 56:1–8.

Trigger, B. G. 1988. Archaeology's relations with the physical and biological sciences: A historical review. In: Farquhar, R. M., Hancock, R. G. V. and Pavlish, L. A. (eds.) *Proceedings of the 26th International Archaeometry Symposium*. Toronto: University of Toronto.

Wood, R. 2015. From revolution to convention: The past, present and future of radiocarbon dating. *Journal of Archaeological Science* 56:61–72.

Part II

Biomolecular Archaeology

2

Ancient DNA

Liisa Loog and Greger Larson

The analysis of genetic information in archaeology, from both humans and animals, including extracted ancient DNA and the analysis of modern DNA.

1 INTRODUCTION

Genetic sequences have traditionally been generated solely from modern individuals. Advances in laboratory and sequencing techniques, however, have made it possible to retrieve genetic information from fossil, archaeological, museum, or otherwise dead and degraded specimens. Genetic material derived from ancient specimens is referred to as ancient DNA (aDNA). The main advantage of ancient DNA is that it allows researchers to study past genetic diversity directly, rather than having to rely on modern genetic patterns to infer past population processes.

Genetic sequences generated from ancient samples have been successfully employed to tackle long-standing questions in the fields of archaeology and genetics. Ancient DNA has been especially important for reconstructing population histories, for example, to study past population interactions and relationships between past and present populations and species; to quantify past levels of movement and identify major migration episodes; as well as to investigate where and when different plant and animal species were domesticated. Ancient DNA has also been used to calibrate molecular clocks that measure the rates of evolution in different species (e.g., Palkopoulou et al. 2015; Rieux et al. 2014; Skoglund et al. 2015) and to date past demographic events, such as population splits, expansions, and fluctuations in population size (particularly in the recent past), as well as to generate date estimates for previously undated specimens. Ancient DNA can also be used for species identification (e.g., Horsburgh 2008); for establishing the biological sex of ancient individuals (Skoglund et al. 2013); and for reconstructing past environments and past diets.

The ability to extract data from archaeological specimens opens inroads to research areas previously inaccessible. For example, ancient DNA has allowed researchers to directly estimate past phenotypes and to study the effect of changing environments on genetic variation (e.g., Girdland Flink et al. 2014; Krause et al. 2007; Lalueza-Fox et al. 2007; Ludwig et al. 2009; Olalde et al. 2014) and, by measuring changes in the frequency of adaptive genetic variants over time, researchers have been able to directly estimate the strength of natural selection at different genetic loci (genes) (Loog et al. 2017; Ludwig et al. 2009; Sverrisdóttir et al. 2014; Wilde et al. 2014).

The retrieval of ancient DNA does not come without challenges. After the death of an organism, the DNA in their cells starts rapidly degrading due to internal and external factors, inevitably resulting in a complete lack of recoverable DNA. In favorable conditions, however, DNA can survive up to hundreds of thousands of years (e.g., Orlando et al. 2013). Nevertheless, the recovered ancient DNA molecules tend to be fragmented, damaged, and at risk of contamination by modern-day sources. This reduction in quantity and quality requires specific techniques to retrieve and analyse ancient DNA.

2 ANCIENT DNA MATERIALS AND TECHNIQUES

Materials

DNA can be extracted from a wide range of archaeological or fossil material. What specimen is most suitable for extracting DNA depends on the research question and the availability of material. Ancient DNA is commonly extracted from bones, teeth, or seeds of an organism of interest, as these are frequently preserved in the archaeological record. Retrieval of genetic material from hair (e.g., Rasmussen et al. 2011), skins, eggshells, (Oskam et al. 2010) or pollen (e.g., Parducci et al. 2005) can also be viable. While DNA from bones and teeth can be used to glean insights into past population dynamics, movements, interactions, and phenotypes, DNA from dental calculus (e.g., Adler et al. 2013), and mummified stomach contents (e.g., Rollo et al. 2002) or coprolites (e.g., Poinar et al. 2003) can be used to study past diet. DNA that was once in the cells of animals, plants, bacteria, and fungi can even be retrieved from soil, sediments, and ice cores and used to reconstruct past environments in the absence of macrofossils or archaeological remains (e.g., Haile et al. 2009).

Challenges

Following the death of an organism, DNA repair mechanisms cease and the DNA begins breaking down due to hydrolysis, the action of endogenous enzymes and microorganisms, as well as physical factors such UV light (Collins et al. 2002; Lindahl 1993). These processes are amplified by and additional damage can result from heat, humidity, soil acidity, air, and water flow and fluctuations in temperature (Allentoft et al. 2012; Bollongino and Vigne 2008; Collins et al. 2002; Smith et al. 2003).

After the death of an organism, DNA degrades exponentially until there is no endogenous DNA molecules left to be extracted and sequenced (Lindahl 1993). The time since death of a specimen is a strong predictor of the quantity and quality of recoverable DNA (Allentoft et al. 2012). It is well understood that the geographical and environmental and climatic conditions in which the specimen is preserved also play a large role in the process of DNA degradation (Collins et al. 2002; Smith et al. 2003).

The oldest and best preserved genetic data has usually been recovered from permafrost and high altitude caves, where conditions are dry and cool, but also stable, with small fluctuations around the annual mean (e.g., Reich et al. 2010). The oldest DNA molecules currently isolated are from an approximately 700,000-year-old horse preserved in Siberian permafrost (Orlando et al. 2013). However, DNA molecules preserved in less cold or less stable conditions are unlikely to survive even half of that period (Allentoft et al. 2012). Temperate regions have yielded relatively good quality data from time periods up to the Upper Palaeolithic. Despite a few successful attempts (Llorente et al. 2015; Pinhasi et al. 2015; Prendergast et al. 2019; Schlebusch et al. 2017; Skoglund et al. 2017), ancient DNA researchers are struggling to produce DNA from remains preserved in hot or humid conditions, such as those in Africa or the Middle East.

The observations above tend to be true when comparing samples that differ greatly in their age and geographic origin. Variation in factors such as the season of the death, burial depth, local pH and water saturation levels, and thickness and structure of the bones analysed, can also cause large variations in DNA survival, resulting in a situation where variable results can be obtained within single sites, layers, and even within individual specimens (Collins et al. 2002). DNA degradation in archaeological contexts remains a poorly understood process. As a result, and since the isolation of DNA is a destructive process, it is important to assess the likelihood of presence of endogenous DNA molecules in specimens prior to attempting DNA extraction, especially when dealing with valuable archaeological or fossil material.

Contamination

Due to the low concentration of endogenous DNA in archaeological samples relative to DNA from the surrounding environments, ancient samples are highly prone to contamination from modern-day sources. This leads to a situation where contamination instead of endogenous DNA from archaeological material of interest is extracted and sequenced. To make matters worse, it is often difficult to distinguish DNA from exogenous sources (especially conspecifics) from authentic, endogenous DNA. As a result, working with archaeological samples requires special precautions to avoid contamination, especially when dealing with ancient humans or pathogens since these sources of DNA are ubiquitous in most excavation and laboratory environments.

It has been shown that post-excavation handling, as well as improper storage of samples, can often be a source of contamination and may lead to further DNA degradation (Bollongino et al. 2008). Therefore, to avoid contamination and preserve DNA molecules, it is important that samples are excavated quickly and placed directly into separate clean bags to avoid sample cross-contamination. The excavated samples should then be stored in cool, dark, and dry conditions. Especially old, valuable, or poorly preserved material may call for a full body suit, a facemask and gloves that are changed between handling different samples. Tools and surfaces that are likely to be in contact with samples should be cleaned with diluted bleach. It is also important that the samples are not washed, since even purified water often contains DNA from exogenous sources that can permeate the excavated sample (Yang and Watt 2005).

DNA extraction should be carried out in facilities uniquely dedicated to ancient DNA work. For an example plan of an ancient DNA laboratory see Figure 2.1. Strict protocols regarding the equipment, dress, and laboratory procedures minimise the contamination potential (Cooper and Poinar 2000; Gilbert et al. 2005).

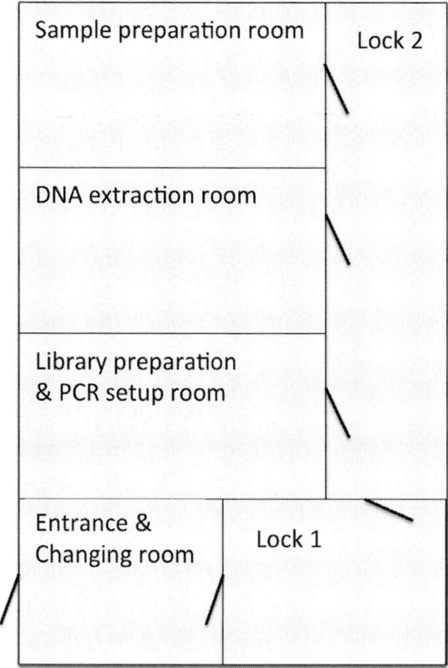

FIGURE 2.1 A typical ancient DNA laboratory setup.

Sanger Sequencing vs. High Throughput Sequencing (Next Generation Sequencing)

The essence of any bimolecular research is the ability to generate and analyse genetic sequences. The most commonly used techniques in the field of archaeogenetics are Sanger sequencing, introduced in the late 1970s, and high throughput or next generation sequencing (NGS), which has been developed only in the past few decades.

In Sanger sequencing, a fragment of DNA is initially amplified using the polymerase chain reaction (PCR) method. This method works though cyclical amplification of DNA fragments, which allows for exponential growth of the target sequence (in each cycle the amount of target fragment is doubled). The PCR cycles generate fragments of different lengths, all ending in radioactively or fluorescently labeled nucleotides (the building blocks of DNA), with different labels for different nucleotides (A, C, G, or T). The fragments are then sorted and read in the order of their length. This allows for a straightforward determination of the order of DNA bases in the sequenced fragment since differently coloured labels can be detected automatically.

The underlying principle of next generation sequencing (NGS) is similar to Sanger sequencing in that bases of a DNA fragment are sequentially identified based on the signals they emit. A key difference between Sanger sequencing and NGS is that the latter technology allows billions of short DNA fragments to be sequenced in parallel. This means that entire genomes of archaeological or ancient individuals can be sequenced to high coverage, or the genomes of multiple individuals can be sequenced at lower coverage on a single run. Whole genomes can then be reconstructed by mapping the resulting sequence fragments (known as reads) to reference genomes. Alternatively, genomes can be *de novo* reconstructed using overlapping ends of reads, allowing for determination of genetic sequence for species without an existing reference genome. NGS enables laboratories to produce data faster and in larger quantities, resulting in a much lower cost per each sequenced DNA base.

Sanger sequencing requires a minimum of around thirty good quality bases to specify the target locus, but ancient DNA is often too fragmented or damaged for this to be the case. Because NGS technology allows the sequencing of much shorter fragments, a much higher proportion of endogenous DNA from old specimens can be recovered (Knapp and Hofreiter 2010).

Additionally, NGS reduces the problem of contamination by providing means to detect it (Knapp and Hofreiter 2010). First, reads that do not map back to the organism of interest can be assumed to be exogenous DNA and therefore removed from the analyses. In this way it may also be possible to identify the source of the exogenous DNA (contamination). However, this approach only deals with contamination that comes from a species different from that of the target of the sequencing. Secondly, researchers can use the DNA damage patterns characteristic to ancient DNA to differentiate between modern and degraded ancient DNA (Skoglund et al. 2014a). Also, the next generation sequencing process itself can discriminate against longer fragments that modern contaminating DNA is characterized by. Nevertheless, care should be taken, as old contamination from conspecifics still remains virtually undetectable.

Despite the proliferation of NGS technologies, Sanger sequencing remains a common approach in many laboratories as it is appropriate for smaller scale projects. Sanger sequencing is also a more accurate approach for sequencing repetitive regions (largely due to the problem of uniquely mapping reads to the reference in such regions).

The challenges associated with ancient DNA research do not end once the sequencing is complete. The billions of reads generated by high throughput sequencing also pose significant computational and analytical challenges. In order to accommodate the large sets of raw sequence data, laboratories specialized in ancient DNA work require considerable data processing power and storage solutions. Ancient DNA work also requires non-standard bioinformatics tools that can deal with damage and other features associated with ancient DNA (Korneliussen et al. 2014; Pickrell and Reich 2014).

Capture Data vs. Whole Genome Sequences

Whole genome sequences are important in population genetics as they enable detection of previously uncharacterized variation. Complete genome sequences from ancient individuals or extinct species are therefore of especially high value. Because the majority of DNA recovered from ancient samples is not endogenous to the organism of interest but instead comes from bacteria and fungi of the surrounding environment, sequencing whole genomes may not always be the most cost-efficient method of accessing ancient genetic data. A more cost-efficient option for sequencing samples with low content of endogenous DNA might be targeted enrichment approach (Knapp and Hofreiter 2010; Carpenter et al. 2013; Pickrell and Reich 2014). In this approach specially designed "baits" are used to capture small fragments of endogenous DNA so that the exogenous content can be excluded before sequencing. This approach enables researchers to focus their resources on generating high quality information about specific loci.

How to best design the baits depends on the research question. In some cases researchers have targeted organelle genomes, the exome (the coding part of the genome), or regions that are known to be polymorphic in modern samples. Though attractive, this latter strategy possesses a potential ascertainment bias that could complicate the analysis. If the targeted loci are selected based on a small number of or closely related populations some variation may go undetected, resulting in a situation where differences between individuals can be artificially deflated or inflated depending what populations were included in the ascertainment of polymorphic loci (Nielsen 2004).

CASE STUDY 1: MITOCHONDRIAL CAPTURE FROM A 300,000-YEAR-OLD HOMININ FROM SIMA DE LOS HUESOS

Meyer and colleagues took up the challenge of attaining genetic information from a >300,000-year-old hominin from Sima de los Huesos cave in Spain

(Meyer et al. 2014). They isolated DNA from the specimen and performed next generation sequencing without any enrichment. Unsurprisingly, the specimen contained very little endogenous DNA. On average, only 0.1 per cent of the reads that were not contamination from modern humans mapped to a human genome, insufficient for most genetic analyses. One option would have been to perform more sequencing, but that would have been exorbitantly expensive, and required destruction of a lot of the fossil material, while discarding approximately 99.9 per cent of the generated data. Instead, they created baits based on human and Denisovan (an extinct hominin from Siberia, closely related to Neanderthals) mitochondrial genomes. The enriched libraries then yielded a sufficient number of mitochondrial sequences to reconstruct a full mitochondrial genome of this ancient hominin.

3 ANALYSES OF (ANCIENT) GENETIC DATA

Modern vs. Ancient DNA

Evolutionary processes are fueled by genetic variation generated by novel mutations, which are passed down to subsequent generations. Different demographic processes shape genetic variation in distinct ways, resulting in different patterns of genetic variation within populations and individuals. Thus, using mathematical models it is possible to study population history by comparing (i.e., fitting) the patterns of genetic variation expected from different demographic processes to empirical data.

CASE STUDY 2: THE SERIAL FOUNDER EFFECT MODEL

The serial founder effect refers to a reduction in diversity that occurs during range expansions. This is due to random subsampling of source populations during the founding of new populations. In other words, each subsequent population is founded by small subset of individuals, carrying only fraction of the genetic diversity present in the parent population.

The serial founder effect has been used (in combination with data from modern-day populations) to test hypotheses about the origins of domesticated plants (Molina et al. 2011) and animals (Pang et al. 2009; Warmuth et al. 2011, 2012);

modern humans (Linz et al. 2007; Prugnolle et al. 2005; Ramachandran et al. 2005); as well as to explore language expansions (Atkinson 2011).

For example, before the widespread use of genetic data in archaeological and palaeontological research, two competing models of modern human origins existed based on the fossil findings. Firstly, according to the multiregional evolution (MRE) hypotheses (Weidenreich 1940), anatomically modern humans evolved independently at various parts of the world from archaic hominins. The close similarity between all modern human populations today was explained by continuous gene flow between the populations (Wolpoff 1989). Alternatively, the recent African origins (RAO) hypothesis (Stringer 1974) argued for a single origin of anatomically modern human features in Africa. These individuals subsequently spread to Eurasia and the rest of the world without significant interbreeding between the resident archaic homo species and newly arrived anatomically modern humans (Stringer and Andrews 1988).

These two hypotheses were addressed using genetic data from multiple present-day human populations. The results demonstrated that the genetic diversity within modern human populations decreased with increasing distance from Eastern or Southern Africa (Prugnolle et al. 2005; Ramachandran et al. 2005). Assuming the serial founder effect model, this pattern fits with the RAO hypotheses but not the MRE model. This suggested that that majority of human variation arose in Africa ~200,000 years ago and was subsequently carried to other parts of the world through migration.

Inferring the past from modern genetic data is not always straightforward since population histories are composed of multiple demographic processes each having separate affects on the patterns of genetic variation. Different demographic scenarios can result in very similar genetic patterns in present-day populations. Furthermore, more recent demographic processes can override signals of past events so the effects of the latter are more difficult or impossible to detect. As a result, large-scale migrations and population replacements may lead to a situation where present-day populations are not representative of the populations that once occupied the same geographic locations, as has been demonstrated by several pioneering ancient DNA studies (Bramanti et al. 2009; Malmström et al. 2009; Ottoni et al. 2013).

Ancient DNA has a unique advantage in that it can provide information about individuals with no present-day descendants, such as extinct species or populations (e.g., "lost cultures"), impossible using data from modern sources alone. It also allows direct characterisation of genetic variation within past populations and individuals, thereby avoiding many of the problems outlined above.

Mitochondrial vs. Genomic Data

For the purpose of retrieval and analysis, ancient DNA can be divided into genomic DNA (found in the cell nucleus), and DNA from the mitochondria in the cells (organelles involved in the production of chemical energy within cells). Early ancient DNA studies focused exclusively on mitochondrial DNA and it remains a popular target locus for ancient DNA studies. Mitochondrial DNA is more likely to survive in ancient remains, because each cell contains a number of mitochondria, each with an identical copy of the mitochondrial genome, whereas a cell usually contains a single nucleus, home to just two homologous copies of each chromosome. Thus, the use of mitochondrial DNA can greatly benefit the demographic inference since it can provide information about samples with wider range of temporal and geographic contexts. The faster mutation rate of the mitochondrial genome also helps to increase the temporal resolution.

A key characteristic of mitochondrial DNA (as well as Y chromosome DNA) is that it does not recombine. Each individual inherits its mitochondria from their mother who has, in turn, inherited it from their mother. The analogous pattern occurs for the Y chromosome in the male line. This simple inheritance mechanism makes the analyses of mitochondrial DNA deceptively straightforward: analyses of mitochondrial data often lack the statistical power to disentangle complex population histories (Ballard and Whitlock 2004; Balloux 2010; Nielsen and Beaumont 2009; Rosenberg and Nordborg 2002).

In contrast, genetic variation in the nuclear genome gets shuffled in every generation between individuals' chromosomes in a process called recombination. In this case, each of the two homologous chromosomes possess a mix of the individual's maternal and paternal grandparents' chromosomes respectively, while each of their chromosomes, in turn, contains a mix of their maternal and paternal grandparents' chromosomes. As a consequence, different parts of individuals' chromosomes come from different ancestors. Loci sufficiently far apart in the nuclear genome are statistically independent, and can be analysed as different stochastic outcomes of an unknown population history. Because the resolution at which population history can be reconstructed increases with the number of loci included in the analyses, the statistical independence of genome-wide loci means that researchers greatly benefit from including several loci in the analyses when inferring population history.

CASE STUDY 3: INCOMPLETE LINAGE SORTING IN NEANDERTHALS, HUMANS AND DENISOVANS

In early 2010, researchers published a complete mitochondrial genome sequence retrieved from a hominin excavated from the Denisova cave in Siberia (Krause et al. 2010). They compared the mitochondrial sequence to a large sample of mitochondrial sequences from modern humans and six Neanderthals. The results demonstrated that the Denisovan linage diverged early from modern humans and Neanderthals. As a result, it was concluded that the ancestors of the Denisovan hominin must have split off from the ancestors of modern humans and Neanderthals relatively early and independently migrated out of Africa prior to modern humans and Neanderthals. The split was dated to ~1 million years ago. Later that same year, however, a complete nuclear genome of the Denisovan individual was also published (Reich et al. 2010). Using multiple loci the scientists demonstrated that, in fact, Neanderthals and Denisovans formed a clade to the exclusion of modern humans. In other words, they were much more closely related to each other than either one is to modern humans. This situation arose as a result of incomplete linage sorting (ILS). Closely related populations or species share many genetic linages that extend beyond the population split or speciation event. As a consequence, individual gene trees may have a topology different from the population (species) trees (see Figure 2.2).

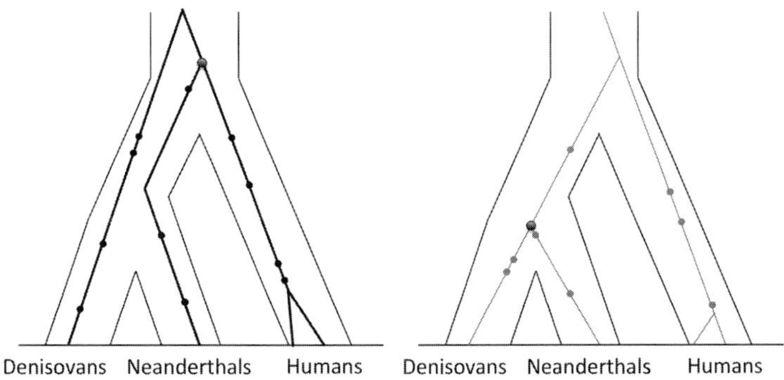

FIGURE 2.2 Incomplete lineage sorting between Neanderthals, Denisovans and humans.

4 DEMOGRAPHIC INFERENCE FROM ANCIENT DNA

Phylogeographic inference is an approach to reconstruct population histories that was especially popular in the early days of ancient DNA research (e.g., Oppenheimer 2012; Secher et al. 2014). Here a phylogenetic tree is constructed based on the mutations in a non-recombining part of the genome (e.g., mtDNA or the Y chromosome). All sampled individuals are assigned to haplogroups and haplotypes, which are the branches and sub-branches, or lineages, on the phylogenetic tree. Inferences about the past are based on the phylogenetic relationship between different haplotypes or haplogroups, their estimated splitting times, and their distribution in space and time.

The main problem with inferring the past from these constructed trees lies in that, on the level of individuals, demographic scenarios are highly stochastic, and therefore so are the phylogenetic trees of any single loci (such as mtDNA or the Y chromosome). As a consequence, events in the phylogenetic trees do not generally correspond directly to population-level events but are simply stochastic outcomes of given population histories. Furthermore, often there are different population history scenarios that can give rise to similar gene trees and distribution of haplotypes. Although ancient DNA provides additional resolution by enabling the researchers to exclude less likely scenarios (e.g., Larson et al. 2007; Thalmann et al. 2013; Valdiosera et al. 2007), the conclusions can still be easily steered by the subjective biases of a particular researcher (Nielsen and Beaumont 2009).

A second popular approach, using nuclear genetic markers, is to analyse the patterns in summary statistics such as the F-statistic, D-statistic, principal components, or related statistics to quantify the genome-wide levels of genetic similarity between individuals and to cluster individuals according to shared genetic patterns (e.g., Fu et al. 2014; Prüfer et al. 2014; Reich et al. 2009; Seguin-Orlando et al. 2014). Frameworks such as TreeMix (Pritchard et al. 2000), AdmixtureGraph (Patterson et al. 2012) and qpGraph (Castelo and Roverato 2012) build on these statistics to construct taxonomic trees, using genome wide data and bootstrap analysis to assess the significance of population splits. However, although ancient DNA can offer extra resolution to population genetic analyses, care should be taken when using such genetic statistics and tools. Under certain idealised conditions these statistics can be used to study past population interactions and exchange of genes, but they are also influenced by a large number of potentially confounding factors (such as geographic structure and population size changes through time) (Eriksson and Manica 2012; McVean 2009; Skoglund et al. 2014b).

A third approach employs coalescent theory to simulate patterns of genetic data under range of hypothesised demographic parameters (e.g., Gerbault et al. 2012;

Warmuth et al. 2012). Inference consists of finding the parameter values where the patterns generated by the simulation model most closely match those observed in real data. A powerful way to do this formally is to calculate the probability of obtaining the observed data for a particular set of parameter values (full likelihood). For more complex models, this is often not possible, but can be estimated by comparing descriptive statistics of simulated and observed data (approximate Bayesian computation or ABC) (Rosenberg and Nordborg 2002; Sunnåker et al. 2013).

Simulation methods make assumptions explicit, and can accommodate very complex demographic scenarios, and can incorporate information from various sources (such as climatic and geographic information, and archaeological and linguistic data). The flip side of this flexibility is that such simulation methods can be complicated to set up and computationally demanding to perform. Unless parameters can be constrained using independent data (e.g., historical or archaeological information), it is usually necessary to consider a very large number of combinations of values for each parameter in order to make reliable inferences about the past, which can be computationally expensive. When different scenarios may give rise to similar genetic patterns, large amounts of genetic data are required to distinguish between them. In these situations it is very important that all the scenarios that could have generated the data are considered. Modelling, in contrast to the approaches mentioned above, provides a formal means to make assumptions explicit and to compare the goodness of fit of different scenarios.

Finally, several specialised, coalescent-based approaches like PSCM (Li and Durbin 2011), MSMC (Schiffels and Durbin 2014), and GPhoCS (Gronau et al. 2011) have been developed recently to infer past population dynamics. As a single recombining genome contains information about the combined history of its ancestors, the advantage of these methods is that only a single gemone or a few good quality genomes are required to reconstruct the history of entire populations. All of these approaches, however, require high-quality full genomes as well as good estimates of other parameters such as the mutation rates.

CASE STUDY 4: MAMMOTH GENOMES

In 2015, a study published two high quality woolly mammoth complete genome sequences (Palkopoulou et al. 2015). One of the individuals dated to the Late Pleistocene (44,800 years old) and the other, one of the last surviving individuals of this species, dated to 4,300 years ago. By using the complete genomes and the

PSMC, the authors were able to reconstruct the demographic history of this extinct species. They inferred several contractions in population size including one just before its extinction. Using the difference in age between the two specimens the researchers were able to recalibrate the mammoth molecular clock and date the events in population history. They were able to show that the younger individual had significantly reduced genetic diversity and that the population size at this point was low. This study, along with other previously published ancient DNA studies demonstrated that alongside fragmented or reduced geographic range, low genetic diversity and small population sizes are the hallmarks of populations in danger of extinction.

5 GLOSSARY OF TERMS

Allele: An allele is a genetic variant at a given locus. Because most mammals have two copies of homologous chromosomes, they have two alleles at each genetic locus, each allele inherited from each of its parents.

Ascertainment bias: Ascertainment bias results from selection of genetic markers in a nonrepresentative subset of a population or species. For example, if genetic markers are chosen on the basis of that they are highly polymorphic in one subpopulation, the genetic variability of this subpopulation might be artificially inflated compared to other subpopulations included in the study, potentially biasing downstream analysis.

Chromosome: A chromosome is a bundle of tightly coiled DNA. Organisms vary in the number of chromosomes they carry but most eukaryotes have two homologous copies of each chromosome (apart from the sex chromosomes), one inherited from each of its parent.

Copy number variation (CNV): Copy number variation is genetic variation that arises if members of a species are carrying a variable number of copies of the same gene (or other section of DNA). For example, an individual's ability to digest starch has been found to be partially determined by the number AMY1 gene copies the individual carries.

DNA: Deoxyribonucleic acid (DNA) is a molecule that carries genetic information. The DNA molecule consists of two strands, composed of nucleotides that are tightly coiled around each other and form a double helix. Each nucleotide is composed of a sugar (called deoxyribose), a phosphate group, and a nucleotide base – either cytosine (C), guanine (G), adenine (A), or thymine (T).

Endogenous DNA: Endogenous DNA is DNA originating from within an organism whose remains the DNA is extracted from.

Exogenous DNA: Exogenous DNA is DNA originating from outside an organism whose remains the DNA is extracted from. Most commonly exogenous DNA originates from the soil or other environment in which the remains are found, or from contamination, that is, from organisms that have directly or indirectly been in contact with the remains.

Gene: A gene is a genetic locus that contains information to build proteins.

Genetic locus or (pl. loci): A genetic locus is a specific location within a genome.

Genetic marker: A genetic marker is a chosen site in a genome that is known to be variable within a population or species of interest.

Genome: A genome is a complete set of an organism's DNA. An organism's genome contains essentially all the information needed for building and maintaining an organism. Whole genome sequence refers to genetic sequence that contains information about the great majority, if not all, of loci within the given genome. Genome-wide data refers to data that contains information about several loci across the entire genome.

Genotype: The genotype is the genetic makeup of an individual.

Mitochondrial genome: The mitochondrial genome is circular and composed of ~16,000 base pairs of DNA. It is found within organelles involved in the production of chemical energy within cells, called mitochondria. Mitochondrial DNA does not recombine and is inherited as a whole through the maternal line.

Molecular clock: A molecular clock is the concept that mutations accumulate at an average rate through time. Thus, by calculating the genetic distance, a divergence time between two populations or species can be calculated.

Mutation: A mutation is a permanent change in the DNA sequence of an organism. Mutations can be substitutions, where a base-pair is replaced with a different base-pair, or insertions and deletions, where some proportion of the DNA sequence is deleted or inserted into or from the existing sequence. Mutations can also be large structural changes like rearrangement of chromosomes.

NGS read: A NGS read is a short fragment of DNA sequence produced by high throughput (next generation) sequencing. Reads are assembled into longer sequences using overlapping ends of the reads (*de novo* assembly) or by mapping reads to a reference genome.

Phenotype: A phenotype is a set of observable characteristics of an individual, determined by the individual's genotype as well as the environment, such as an individual's size or height. Phenotypic characteristics such as coat, hair, eye, or skin colour or ability to digest lactose, as well as certain diseases that are known to be under strong genetic control, can be inferred from an individual's genotype.

Polymerase chain reaction (PCR): The polymerase chain reaction (PCR) is a technology in molecular biology used to amplify fragments of DNA. PCR consists of cycles of temperature changes allowing different reactions necessary for DNA amplification to take place: First the two strands of the DNA fragment are physically separated. Each strand is then copied using an enzyme called DNA polymerase. At each cycle the number of generated copies of the fragment doubles, resulting in millions of copies of a particular DNA sequence.

Population history: Population history is the demographic history of a population or subpopulation through time. It is composed of events such as changes in population size, expansions, admixture between subpopulations and movements in space.

REFERENCES

Adler, C. J., Dobney, K., Weyrich, L. S., Kaidonis, J., Walker, A. W., Haak, W., Bradshaw, C. J. A., Townsend, G., Sołtysiak, A., Alt, K. W., and Parkhill, J. 2013. Sequencing ancient calcified dental plaque shows changes in oral microbiota with dietary shifts of the Neolithic and Industrial Revolutions. *Nature Genetics* 45(4):450–455.

Allentoft, M. E., Collins, M., Harker, D., Haile, J., Oskam, C. L., Hale, M. L., Campos, P. F., Samaniego, J. A., Gilbert, M. T. P., Willerslev, E., and Zhang, G. 2012. The half-life of DNA in bone: Measuring decay kinetics in 158 dated fossils. *Proceedings of the Royal Society B: Biological Sciences* 279(1748):4724–4733.

Atkinson, Q. D. 2011. Phonemic diversity supports a serial founder effect model of language expansion from Africa. *Science* 332(6027):346–349.

Ballard, J. W. O. and Whitlock, M. C. 2004. The incomplete natural history of mitochondria. *Molecular Ecology* 13(4):729–744.

Balloux, F. 2010. The worm in the fruit of the mitochondrial DNA tree. *Heredity* 104(5):419.

Bollongino, R., Tresset, A., and Vigne, J.-D. 2008. Environment and excavation: Pre-lab impacts on ancient DNA analyses. *Comptes Rendus Palevol* 7(2–3):91–98.

Bollongino, R. and Vigne, J.-D. 2008. Temperature monitoring in archaeological animal bone samples in the Near East arid area, before, during and after excavation. *Journal of Archaeological Science* 35(4):873–881.

Bramanti, B., Thomas, M. G., Haak, W., Unterlaender, M., Jores, P., Tambets, K., Antanaitis-Jacobs, I. I., Haidle, M. N., Jankauskas, R., Kind, C. J., and Lueth, F. 2009. Genetic discontinuity between local hunter-gatherers and Central Europe's first farmers. *Science* 326(5949):137–140.

Carpenter, M. L., Buenrostro, J. D., Valdiosera, C., Schroeder, H., Allentoft, M. E., Sikora, M., Rasmussen, M., Gravel, S., Guillén, S., Nekhrizov, G., and Leshtakov, K. 2013. Pulling out the 1%: Whole-genome capture for the targeted enrichment of ancient DNA sequencing libraries. *The American Journal of Human Genetics* 93(5):852–864.

Castelo, R., and Roverato, A. 2012. Inference of regulatory networks from microarray data with R and the bioconductor package qpgraph. *Methods Molecular Biology.* 802:215–233.

Collins, M. J., Nielsen-Marsh, C. M., Hiller, J., Smith, C. I., Roberts, J. P., Prigodich, R. V., Wess, T. J., Csapo, J., Millard, A. R., and Turner-Walker, G. 2002. The survival of organic matter in bone: A review. *Archaeometry* 44(3):383–394.

Cooper, A. and Poinar, H. N. 2000. Ancient DNA: Do it right or not at all. *Science* 289(5482):1139.

Eriksson, A. and Manica, A. 2012. Effect of ancient population structure on the degree of polymorphism shared between modern human populations and ancient hominins. *Proceedings of the National Academy of Sciences* 109(35):13956–13960.

Fu, Q., Li, H., Moorjani, P., Jay, F., Slepchenko, S. M., Bondarev, A. A., Johnson, P. L. F., Aximu-Petri, A., Prüfer, K., de Filippo, C., and Meyer, M. 2014. Genome sequence of a 45,000-year-old modern human from Western Siberia. *Nature* 514(7523):445–449.

Gerbault, P., Leonardi, M., Powell, A., Weber, C., Benecke, N., Burger, J., and Thomas, M. G. 2012. Domestication and migrations: Using mitochondrial DNA to infer domestication processes of goats and horses. In: Kaiser, E., Burger, J., and Schier, W. (eds.) *Population Dynamics in Prehistory and Early History*, pp. 17–30. Berlin, Boston: De Gruyter.

Gilbert, M. T. P., Bandelt, H.-J., Hofreiter, M., and Barnes, I. 2005. Assessing ancient DNA studies. *Trends in Ecology and Evolution* 20(10):541–544.

Girdland Flink, L., Allen, R., Barnett, R., Malmström, H., Peters, J., Eriksson, J., Andersson, L., Dobney, K., and Larson, G. 2014. Establishing the validity of domestication genes using DNA from ancient chickens. *Proceedings of the National Academy of Sciences* 111(17):6184–6189.

Gronau, I., Hubisz, M. J., Gulko, B., Danko, C. G., and Siepel, A. 2011. Bayesian inference of ancient human demography from individual genome sequences. *Nature Genetics* 43(10):1031–1034.

Haile, J., Froese, D. G., MacPhee, R. D. E., Roberts, R. G., Arnold, L. J., Reyes, A. V., Rasmussen, M., Nielsen, R., Brook, B. W., Robinson, S., and Demuro, M. 2009. Ancient DNA reveals late survival of mammoth and horse in Interior Alaska. *Proceedings of the National Academy of Sciences* 106(52):22352–22357.

Horsburgh, K. A. 2008. Wild or domesticated? An ancient DNA approach to canid species identification in South Africa's Western Cape Province. *Journal of Archaeological Science* 35(6):1474–1480.

Knapp, M. and Hofreiter, M. 2010. Next generation sequencing of ancient DNA: Requirements, strategies and perspectives. *Genes* 1(2):227–243.

Korneliussen, T.S., Albrechtsen, A., and Nielsen, R., 2014. ANGSD: Analysis of Next Generation Sequencing Data. BMC Bioinformatics 15:356.

Krause, J., Fu, Q., Good, J. M., Viola, B., Shunkov, M. V., Derevianko, A. P., and Pääbo, S. 2010. The complete mitochondrial DNA genome of an unknown hominin from Southern Siberia. *Nature* 464(7290):894–897.

Krause, J., Lalueza-Fox, C., Orlando, L., Enard, W., Green, R. E., Burbano, H. A., Hublin, J.-J., Hänni, C., Fortea, J., De La Rasilla, M., and Bertranpetit, J. 2007. The derived FOXP2 variant of modern humans was shared with Neandertals. *Current Biology* 17(21):1908–1912.

Lalueza-Fox, C., Römpler, H., Caramelli, D., Stäubert, C., Catalano, G., Hughes, D., Rohland, N., Pilli, E., Longo, L., Condemi, S., and De La Rasilla, M. 2007. A melanocortin 1 receptor allele suggests varying pigmentation among Neanderthals. *Science* 318(5855):1453–1455.

Larson, G., Albarella, U., Dobney, K., Rowley-Conwy, P., Schibler, J., Tresset, A., Vigne, J.-D., Edwards, C. J., Schlumbaum, A., Dinu, A., and Bălăçsescu, A. 2007. Ancient DNA, pig domestication, and the spread of the Neolithic into Europe. *Proceedings of the National Academy of Sciences* 104(39):15276–15281.

Li, H. and Durbin, R. 2011. Inference of human population history from individual whole-genome sequences. *Nature* 475(7357):493–496.

Lindahl, T. 1993. Instability and decay of the primary structure of DNA. *Nature* 362(6422):709–715.

Linz, B., Balloux, F., Moodley, Y., Manica, A., Liu, H., Roumagnac, P., Falush, D., Stamer, C., Prugnolle, F., van der Merwe, S. W., and Yamaoka, Y. 2007. An African origin for the intimate association between humans and Helicobacter pylori. *Nature* 445(7130):915–918.

Llorente, M. G., Jones, E. R., Eriksson, A., Siska, V., Arthur, K. W., Arthur, J. W., Curtis, M. C., Stock, J. T., Coltorti, M., Pieruccini, P., and Stretton, S. 2015. Ancient Ethiopian genome reveals extensive Eurasian admixture in Eastern Africa. *Science* 350(6262):820–822.

Loog, L., Thomas, M. G., Barnett, R., Allen, R., Sykes, N., Paxinos, P. D., Lebrasseur, O., Dobney, K., Peters, J., Manica, A., and Larson, G. 2017. Inferring allele frequency trajectories from ancient DNA indicates that selection on a chicken gene coincided with changes in medieval husbandry practices. *Molecular Biology and Evolution* 34(8):1981–1990.

Ludwig, A., Pruvost, M., Reissmann, M., Benecke, N., Brockmann, G. A., Castanos, P., Cieslak, M., Lippold, S., Llorente, L., Malaspinas, A. S., and Slatkin, M. 2009. Coat color variation at the beginning of horse domestication. *Science* 324(5926):485.

Malmström, H., Gilbert, M. T. P., Thomas, M. G., Brandström, M., Storå, J., Molnar, P., Andersen, P. K., Bendixen, C., Holmlund, G., Götherström, A., and Willerslev, E. 2009. Ancient DNA reveals lack of continuity between Neolithic hunter-gatherers and contemporary Scandinavians. *Current Biology* 19(20):1758–1762.

McVean, G. 2009. A genealogical interpretation of principal components analysis. *PLoS Genetics* 5(10):e1000686.

Meyer, M., Fu, Q., Aximu-Petri, A., Glocke, I., Nickel, B., Arsuaga, J.-L., Martínez, I., Gracia, A., de Castro, J. M. B., Carbonell, E., and Pääbo, S. 2014. A mitochondrial genome sequence of a hominin from Sima de Los Huesos. *Nature* 505(7483):403–406.

Molina, J., Sikora, M., Garud, N., Flowers, J., Rubinstein, S., Reynolds, A., Huang, P., Jackson, S., Schaal, B. A., Bustamante, C. D., and Boyko, A. R. 2011. Molecular evidence for a single evolutionary origin of domesticated rice. *Proceedings of the National Academy of Sciences* 108(20):8351–8356.

Nielsen, R. 2004. Population genetic analysis of ascertained SNP data. *Human Genomics* 1(3):218.

Nielsen, R. and Beaumont, M. A. 2009. Statistical inferences in phylogeography. *Molecular Ecology* 18(6):1034–1047.

Olalde, I., Allentoft, M. E., Sánchez-Quinto, F., Santpere, G., Chiang, C. W. K., DeGiorgio, M., Prado-Martinez, J,. Rodríguez, J. A., Rasmussen, S., Quilez, J., and Ramírez, O. 2014. Derived immune and ancestral pigmentation alleles in a 7,000-year-old Mesolithic European. *Nature* 507(7491):225–228.

Oppenheimer, S. 2012. Out-of-Africa, the peopling of continents and islands: Tracing uniparental gene trees across the map. *Philosophical Transactions of the Royal Society of London B: Biological Sciences* 367(1590):770–784.

Orlando, L., Ginolhac, A., Zhang, G., Froese, D., Albrechtsen, A., Stiller, M., Schubert, M., Cappellini, E., Petersen, B., Moltke, I., and Johnson, P. L. 2013. Recalibrating Equus evolution using the genome sequence of an Early Middle Pleistocene horse. *Nature* 499(7456):74–78.

Oskam, C. L., Haile, J., McLay, E., Rigby, P., Allentoft, M. E., Olsen, M. E., Bengtsson, C., Miller, G. H., Schwenninger, J. L., Jacomb, C., and Walter, R. 2010. Fossil avian eggshell preserves ancient DNA. *Proceedings of the Royal Society of London B: Biological Sciences* 277(1690):1991–2000.

Ottoni, C., Girdland Flink, L., Evin, A., Georg, C., De Cupere, B., Van Neer, W., Bartosiewicz, L., Linderholm, A., Barnett, R., Peters, J., and Decorte, R. 2013. Pig domestication and human-mediated dispersal in Western Eurasia revealed through ancient DNA and geometric morphometrics. *Molecular Biology and Evolution* 30(4):824–832.

Palkopoulou, E., Mallick, S., Skoglund, P., Enk, J., Rohland, N., Li, H., Omrak, A., Vartanyan, S., Poinar, H., Götherström, A., and Reich, D. 2015. Complete genomes reveal signatures of demographic and genetic declines in the woolly mammoth. *Current Biology* 25(10):1395–1400.

Pang, J.-F., Kluetsch, C., Zou, X.-J., Zhang, A. B., Luo, L.-Y., Angleby, H., Ardalan, A., Ekström, C., Sköllermo, A., Lundeberg, J., and Matsumura, S. 2009. mtDNA data indicate a single origin for dogs south of Yangtze River, less than 16,300 years ago, from numerous wolves. *Molecular Biology and Evolution* 26 (12):2849–2864.

Parducci, L., Suyama, Y., Lascoux, M., and Bennett, K. D. 2005. Ancient DNA from pollen: A genetic record of population history in Scots Pine. *Molecular Ecology* 14 (9):2873–2882.

Patterson, N., Moorjani, P., Luo, Y., Mallick, S., Rohland, N., Zhan, Y., Genschoreck, T., Webster, T., and Reich, D. 2012. Ancient Admixture in Human History. *Genetics* 192:1065–1093.

Pickrell, J. K. and Reich, D. 2014. Toward a new history and geography of human genes informed by ancient DNA. *Trends in Genetics* 30(9):377–389.

Pinhasi, R., Fernandes, D., Sirak, K., Novak, M., Connell, S., Alpaslan-Roodenberg, S., Gerritsen, F., Moiseyev, V., Gromov, A., Raczky, P., and Anders, A. 2015. Optimal ancient DNA yields from the inner ear part of the human petrous bone. *PLoS One* 10(6):e0129102.

Poinar, H., Kuch, M., McDonald, G., Martin, P., and Pääbo, S. 2003. Nuclear gene sequences from a Late Pleistocene sloth coprolite. *Current Biology* 13(13):1150–1152.

Prendergast, M.E., Lipson, M., Sawchuk, E.A., Olalde, I., Ogola, C.A., Rohland, N., Sirak, K. A., Adamski, N., Bernardos, R., Broomandkhoshbacht, N., Callan, K., Culleton, B.J., Eccles, L., Harper, T.K., Lawson, A.M., Mah, M., Oppenheimer, J., Stewardson, K., Zalzala, F., Ambrose, S.H., Ayodo, G., Gates, H.L., Gidna, A.O., Katongo, M., Kwekason, A., Mabulla, A.Z.P., Mudenda, G.S., Ndiema, E.K., Nelson, C., Robertshaw, P., Kennett, D.J., Manthi, F.K., and Reich, D., 2019. Ancient DNA reveals a multistep spread of the first herders into sub-Saharan Africa. Science 365: eaaw6275.

Pritchard, J.K., Stephens, M., and Donnelly, P. 2000. Inference of Population Structure Using Multilocus Genotype Data. *Genetics* 155:945–959.

Prüfer, K., Racimo, F., Patterson, N., Jay, F., Sankararaman, S., Sawyer, S., Heinze, A., Renaud, G., Sudmant, P. H., De Filippo, C., and Li, H. 2014. The complete genome sequence of a Neanderthal from the Altai Mountains. *Nature* 505(7481):43–49.

Prugnolle, F., Manica, A., and Balloux, F. 2005. Geography predicts neutral genetic diversity of human populations. *Current Biology* 15(5):R159–160.

Ramachandran, S., Deshpande, O., Roseman, C. C., Rosenberg, N. A., Feldman, M. W., and Cavalli-Sforza, L. L. 2005. Support from the relationship of genetic and geographic distance in human populations for a serial founder effect originating in Africa. *Proceedings of the National Academy of Sciences of the United States of America* 102(44):15942–15947.

Rasmussen, M., Guo, X., Wang, Y., Lohmueller, K. E., Rasmussen, S., Albrechtsen, A, Skotte, L., Lindgreen, S., Metspalu, M., Jombart, T., and Kivisild, T. 2011. An Aboriginal Australian genome reveals separate human dispersals into Asia. *Science* 334(6052):94–98.

Reich, D., Green, R. E., Kircher, M., Krause, J., Patterson, N., Durand, E. Y., Viola, B., Briggs, A. W., Stenzel, U., Johnson, P. L., and Maricic, T. 2010. Genetic history of an archaic hominin group from Denisova Cave in Siberia. *Nature* 468(7327):1053–1060.

Reich, D., Thangaraj, K., Patterson, N., Price, A. L., and Singh, L. 2009. Reconstructing Indian Population History. *Nature* 461(7263):489–494.

Rieux, A., Eriksson, A., Li, M., Sobkowiak, B., Weinert, L. A., Warmuth, V., Ruiz-Linares, A., Manica, A., and Balloux, F. 2014. Improved calibration of the human mitochondrial clock using ancient genomes. *Molecular Biology and Evolution* 31(10):2780–2792.

Rollo, F., Ubaldi, M., Ermini, L., and Marota, I. 2002. Ötzi's last meals: DNA analysis of the intestinal content of the Neolithic glacier mummy from the Alps. *Proceedings of the National Academy of Sciences* 99(20):12594–12599.

Rosenberg, N. A. and Nordborg, M. 2002. Genealogical trees, coalescent theory and the analysis of genetic polymorphisms. *Nature Reviews Genetics* 3(5):380–390.

Schiffels, S. and Durbin, R. 2014. Inferring human population size and separation history from multiple genome sequences. *Nature Genetics* 46(8):919–925.

Schlebusch, C. M., Malmström, H., Günther, T., Sjödin, P., Coutinho, A., Edlund, H., Munters, A. R., Vicente, M., Steyn, M., Soodyall, H., Lombard, M., and Jakobsson, M., 2017. Southern African ancient genomes estimate modern human divergence to 350,000 to 260,000 years ago. Science 358: 652–655.

Secher, B., Fregel, R., Larruga, J. M., Cabrera, V. M., Endicott, P., Pestano, J. J., and González, A. M. 2014. The history of the North African mitochondrial DNA haplogroup U6 gene flow into the African, Eurasian and American continents. *BMC Evolutionary Biology* 14(1):109.

Seguin-Orlando, A., Korneliussen, T. S., Sikora, M., Malaspinas, A.-S., Manica, A., Moltke, I., Albrechtsen, A., Ko, A., Margaryan, A., Moiseyev, V., and Goebel, T. 2014. Genomic structure in Europeans dating back at least 36,200 years. *Science* 346(6213):1113–1118.

Skoglund, P., Ersmark, E., Palkopoulou, E., and Dalén, L. 2015. Ancient wolf genome reveals an early divergence of domestic dog ancestors and admixture into high-latitude breeds. *Current Biology* 25(11):1515–1519.

Skoglund, P., Northoff, B. H., Shunkov, M. V., Derevianko, A. P., Pääbo, S., Krause, J., and Jakobsson, M. 2014a. Separating endogenous ancient DNA from modern day contamination in a Siberian Neandertal. *Proceedings of the National Academy of Sciences* 111(6):2229–2234.

Skoglund, P., Sjödin, P., Skoglund, T., Lascoux, M., and Jakobsson, M. 2014b. Investigating population history using temporal genetic differentiation. *Molecular Biology and Evolution* 31(9):2516–2527.

Skoglund, P., Storå, J., Götherström, A., and Jakobsson, M. 2013. Accurate sex identification of ancient human memains using DNA shotgun sequencing. *Journal of Archaeological Science* 40(12):4477–4482.

Skoglund, P., Thompson, J. C., Prendergast, M. E., Mittnik, A., Sirak, K., Hajdinjak, M., Salie, T., Rohland, N., Mallick, S., Peltzer, A., and Heinze, A. 2017. Reconstructing prehistoric African population structure. *Cell* 171(1):59–71.

Smith, C. I., Chamberlain, A. T., Riley, M. S., Stringer, C. B., and Collins, M. J. 2003. The thermal history of human fossils and the likelihood of successful DNA amplification. *Journal of Human Evolution* 45(3):203–217.

Stringer, C. B. 1974. *A Multivariate Study of Cranial Variation in Middle and Upper Pleistocene Human Populations.* Doctoral thesis, Universiy of Bristol.

Stringer, C. B. and Andrews, P. 1988. Genetic and fossil evidence for the origin of modern humans. *Science* 239(4845):1263–1268.

Sunnåker, M., Busetto, A. G., Numminen, E., Corander, J., Foll, M., and Dessimoz, C. 2013. Approximate Bayesian computation. *PLoS Comput Biol* 9(1):e1002803.

Sverrisdóttir, O. Ó., Timpson, A., Toombs, J., Lecoeur, C., Froguel, P., Carretero, J. M., Arsuaga Ferreras, J. L., Götherström, A., and Thomas, M. G. 2014. Direct estimates of natural selection in Iberia indicate calcium absorption was not the only driver of lactase persistence in Europe. *Molecular Biology and Evolution* 31(4): 975-983.

Thalmann, O., Shapiro, B., Cui, P., Schuenemann, V. J., Sawyer, S. K., Greenfield, D. L., Germonpré, M. B., Sablin, M. V., López-Giráldez, F., Domingo-Roura, X., and Napierala, H. 2013. Complete mitochondrial genomes of ancient canids suggest a European origin of domestic dogs. *Science* 342(6160):871–874.

Valdiosera, C. E., García, N., Anderung, C., Dalén, L., Crégut-Bonnoure, E., Kahlke, R.-D., Stiller, M., Brandström, M., Thomas, M. G., Arsuaga, J. L., and Götherström, A. 2007. Staying out in the cold: Glacial refugia and mitochondrial DNA phylogeography in ancient European brown bears. *Molecular Ecology* 16(24):5140–5148.

Warmuth, V., Eriksson, A., Bower, M. A., Barker, G., Barrett, E., Hanks, B. K., Li, S., Lomitashvili, D., Ochir-Goryaeva, M., Sizonov, G. V., and Soyonov, V. 2012. Reconstructing the origin and spread of horse domestication in the Eurasian Steppe. *Proceedings of the National Academy of Sciences* 109(21):8202–8206.

Warmuth, V., Eriksson, A., Bower, M. A., Cañon, J., Cothran, G., Distl, O., Glowatzki-Mullis, M.-L., Hunt, H., Luís, C., do Mar Oom, M., and Yupanqui, I. T. 2011. European domestic horses originated in two Holocene refugia. *PLoS One* 6(3):e18194.

Weidenreich, F. 1940. Some problems dealing with ancient man. *American Anthropologist* 42(3):375–383.

Wilde, S., Timpson, A., Kirsanow, K., Kaiser, E., Kayser, M., Unterländer, M., Hollfelder, N., Potekhina, I. D., Schier, W., Thomas, M. G., and Burger, J. 2014. Direct evidence for positive selection of skin, hair, and eye pigmentation in Europeans during the last 5,000 Y. *Proceedings of the National Academy of Sciences* 111(13):4832–4837.

Wolpoff, M. H. 1989. Multiregional evolution: The fossil alternative to Eden. In: Mellar, P. and Stringer, C. (eds.) *The Human Revolution*, pp. 62–108. Princeton, NJ: Princeton University Press.

Yang, D. Y. and Watt, K. 2005. Contamination controls when preparing archaeological remains for ancient DNA analysis. *Journal of Archaeological Science* 32(3):331–336.

3

Proteomics

Jessica Hendy, Nienke van Doorn, and Matthew Collins

The study of preserved proteins in archaeology, including the extraction, sequencing and analysis of proteins from a range of archaeological and palaeontological contexts.

1 INTRODUCTION AND THEORETICAL BACKGROUND

All the inheritable material possessed by an organism, the *genome*, is stored as DNA, the study of which has made an enormous impact upon archaeological science. The *proteome* is the suite of proteins produced by the genome at any one time. The field of *proteomics* is the study of this proteome, and uses mass spectrometry to identify proteins by their amino acid sequence.

Archaeologists will most commonly encounter proteins, especially the most common bone protein, collagen, as targets for radiocarbon dating or stable isotope analyses. These techniques and applications have had a long life in archaeology. In contrast, the analysis of amino acid sequences is a more recent development, stemming from technological advances in mass spectrometric technology in the early 2000s.

Amino Acids: The Building Blocks of Proteins

Proteins are composed of chains of *amino acids*. Twenty amino acids are responsible for all protein sequences (Table 3.1). A chain of amino acids is termed a *peptide*. Each amino acid has the same general structure, containing a central carbon atom (the 'α-carbon'), a hydrogen atom (H), a carboxyl group (COOH), an amino group (NH_2) and a variable side chain (R) (Figure 3.1).

Peptides, Epitopes and Proteins

Proteins are made of chains of amino acids folded into characteristic forms which govern their function (Figure 3.1). However, these higher order structures are prone to deterioration, termed denaturing.[1] Initial attempts to recover peptide sequences using Edman degradation sequencing was met with almost no success, apart from the first 16 residues of the bone protein osteocalcin in New Zealand moa (Huq et al. 1990). However, even short sequences can be useful to identify the origin of a protein. There are 20 amino acids as compared to 4 DNA bases, making for much greater potential sequence variability.

In addition to identification by their general amino acid composition or amino acid sequence, proteins can also be detected using antibody-based (also called immunological) approaches. Antibodies are proteins that bind to a small, accessible region of a target protein (an antigen). This target region, called an epitope, typically spans about 6 amino acid residues. Antibody-antigen binding is highly specific, so the binding of an antibody can be used to positively identify the presence of a particular protein (acting as the antigen). Whilst antibodies are widely used to identify proteins in the medical, environmental and food industries, it is noted that many kits fail to detect samples that have been denatured. In archaeological contexts, there is a myriad of physical, chemical and biological processes acting upon the protein, making the survival of these small regions highly variable. In addition, given the presence of other biomolecules present in archaeological contexts, cross-reactivity can generate false positive identifications. It can also be difficult to find a single unique peptide 'biomarker' and consequently one has to judge the full pattern of results and use archaeological knowledge of the target to assess the findings. Thus, the application of antibody-based methods to detect ancient proteins remains controversial (Cattaneo et al. 1992; Lowenstein 1981; Loy and Hardy 1992; Tuross et al. 1996) but has been used in a variety of archaeological applications, recently reviewed in Malainey (2011).

Degradation and Post-Translational Modifications

We have already touched on the idea that the degradation of proteins means that we have to be selective about what approach we take with ancient protein analysis

[1] There is some evidence that collagen fibrils may survive. Microscopic detail of collagen was detected by (Doborenz and Wyckoff 1967) and (Towe 1972).

(i.e., that denaturing of higher order protein structures means that we must focus on amino acid sequences, and that protein degradation often prevents success with immunological approaches). Understanding patterns of degradation, and how they can be detected, is integral for assessing the validity of ancient protein techniques and applications. One such controversy, the detection of blood on stone tools, will be highlighted below.

Peptide bonds (the bonds that join amino acids together) undergo bond cleavage through the addition of water, a process termed hydrolysis (Bada 1991). Enzymes called proteases catalyse hydrolysis. Archaeological material is particularly susceptible to attack from microbial proteases from the decompositional or burial environment. But even if an intact protein is not present it may be still possible to recover some of the more robust peptides (Demarchi et al. 2016).

DNA sequencing is able to detect DNA damage patterns that authenticate the age of the sample. Similarly, analysis of proteins using mass spectrometry is also able to detect patterns of protein degradation. The chemical changes that occur to amino acids after protein synthesis are termed post-translational modifications (often shortened to PTMs). These changes may be the result of a biological process integral to protein function. One of the most widely encountered of this type of post-translation in archaeology is hydroxylation of proline, a PTM common in collagen (and also in plant cell wall proteins). More recently, another modification, hydroxylysine glucosylgalactosylation, was detected in collagen extracted from 120,000-year-old extinct bison (Hill et al. 2015). But for archaeology, particular modifications that result from external chemical, physical or biological processes acting on the protein can also be detected and used to indicate authentically old proteins. Deamidation, the removal of an amino group as ammonium, is one of the most common modifications in proteins and is one of the most rapid on the geological timescale (Bada and Miller 1968). Asparagine and glutamine are the amino acids most commonly affected, but the rate of deamidation of asparagine can be up to ten times faster than for glutamine (Daniel et al. 1996; Terwilliger and Clarke 1981). The deamidation of glutamine can be used as an indicator of collagen degradation in bone (van Doorn et al. 2012; Wilson et al. 2012) and keratin degradation in textiles (Solazzo et al. 2014).

Protein Survival Into the Pleistocene and Beyond

Reports of collagen peptides from both *Tyrannosaurus rex* (~68 Ma) (Asara et al. 2007) and a Hadrosaur (~80 Ma) (Schweitzer et al. 2009) have proved controversial

(Buckley et al. 2017; Pevzner et al. 2008), although have received some support (Bern et al. 2009). Despite these controversies, there is no doubt the collagen survives in palaeontological samples (Wang et al. 2012). Perhaps more conclusive is the detection of collagen in fossilised bone of mastodon (160–600 ka) (Asara et al. 2007; Buckley et al. 2008a), mammoth and straight-tusked elephant (20–200 ka) (Buckley et al. 2011), a mammoth of 43 ka (Cappellini et al. 2012) and a 560–780 ka Late Pleistocene horse (Orlando et al. 2013).

In a non-mineralised context, collagen (skin, leather) is easily hydrolysed and degraded by the enzyme collagenase (Collins et al. 1995; Lees 1989). The survival of mineralised collagen in ancient samples is linked to its intimate association with hydroxyapatite, the mineral component of bone (Collins et al. 2002), and consequently collagen is one of the most easily accessible protein in the archaeological record. Mineralised tissues may also protect other non-collagenous proteins (NCPs) from degradation. Improved extraction methods and increasing mass spectrometry instrument resolution (see below) has enabled the detection of other less abundant NCPs and the characterisation of the bone proteome. Bone proteomes were recently extracted from a 1 ka Moa (Cleland et al. 2015), a 43 ka mammoth (Cappellini et al. 2012), 150 ka bison (Hill et al. 2015) and 700 ka horse bone (Orlando et al. 2013).

Survival of DNA and Proteins

Proteins are generally more robust than DNA and RNA, and have often been detected in samples that have failed to yield usable DNA. For example, in the analysis of bone remains of Toxodon and Macrauchenia (Buckley 2015; Welker et al. 2015a), as well as the Malagasy aardvark (Buckley 2013), DNA analysis was not successful for accessing phylogenetic information, although analysis of collagen sequences enabled the taxonomic placement of these extinct species. However, the relationship between DNA and protein survival in the same samples is still poorly understood (Buckley et al. 2008b).

2 MASS SPECTROMETRY

Essential Principles of Mass Spectroscopy

Mass spectrometry (MS) is used for protein identification, having been first developed in the late nineteenth century, based on the principle that molecules of

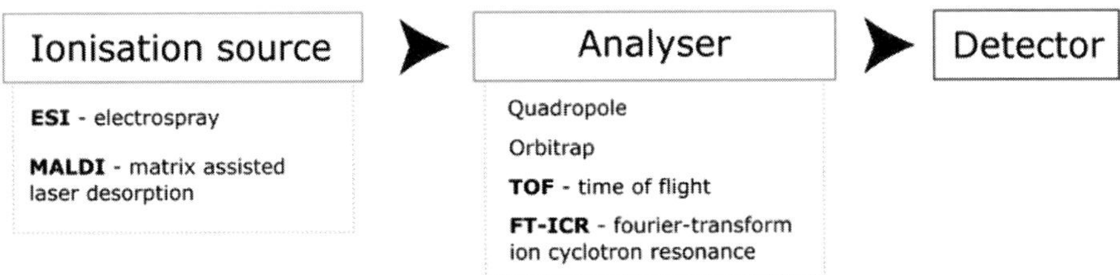

FIGURE 3.2 Simplification of the three major components of a protein mass spectrometry workflow.

different masses can be detected by observing the behaviour of ions (charged molecules) in electric or magnetic fields. Differences in behaviour reflect the difference in the mass and charge of different ions. The following section will describe the broad principles involved in mass spectrometry and the subsequent downstream processes that are required for protein identification.

Proteins can be very large biomolecules; for instance, the main protein in silk, fibroin, is composed of more than 5000 amino acids. However, mass spectrometers can only measure rapidly and accurately across a relatively narrow range. Therefore, during sample preparation, prior to MS/MS analysis, proteases, often the enzyme trypsin, are typically used to cleave the protein into peptide fragments. Peptides are then separated, typically using (reverse phase) liquid chromatography, before being introduced into the mass spectrometer and detected on the basis of mass and fragmentation pattern (Figure 3.2).

Ionisation

To analyse the mass of a molecule, it necessary to ionise it (i.e., to create a charged molecule) so that it can be mobilised and detected in the mass spectrometer. 'Soft ionisation' methods, such as electrospray ionisation (ESI) and matrix assisted laser desorption ionisation (MALDI) have been developed to introduce fragile molecules like peptide and nucleotide ions into the vacuum of a mass spectrometer.

MALDI (Hillenkamp et al. 1991) ionises a dried sample where the sample is dried together with a highly absorbing matrix as spots on a target plate. A laser bombards parts of each spot in turn and some of the energy absorbed by the matrix is transferred to the co-crystallised peptides, with sufficient energy transferred to cause the peptide to be charged and sputter off the surface as singly charged molecular ions. MALDI ionisation tends to generate singly charged ions, making spectra easier to interpret. Because MALDI uses a solid substrate the samples can be analysed multiple times, stored and re-analysed. Hundreds of spots can be placed on a single MALDI target plate, and the technique is ideal for peptide mass fingerprinting (discussed below). However, if the sample is complex (i.e., contains a large variety of peptides), abundant peptides can mask more interesting but less abundant ones, and masses of <800 Da are often obscured by peaks from the matrix.

Electrospray ionisation (ESI) directly ionises peptides from the liquid phase by stripping a volatile solvent from tiny droplets of (polar) liquid (Yamashita and Fenn 1984). The ions are retained in the droplet and as the droplet size decreases, electrostatic repulsion causes it to eventually explode into even smaller charged droplets. The electrostatic repulsion becomes so high that the peptide ions are stripped of solvent in the gas phase and they enter into the vacuum of the mass spectrometer. Ionised peptides may carry only a single charge, but most are multiply charged. Proteins tend to be analysed as positive ions by the addition of protons (H+) to an amine groups, to form ammonium ions. ESI is well suited to interfacing with liquid chromatography. Analyses are conducted in real time and, unlike MALDI, it is not possible to revisit the analyte if insufficient spectra were acquired. However, because ions are multiply charged, peptides of a larger mass are able to be identified. It is also easier to modify the chemistry in electrospray and introduce a range of chemical ionisation methods. For more details of ESI and MALDI see useful reviews by Domon and Aebersold (2006) and El-Aneed et al. (2009).

Detection

Once the ion is in the vacuum, it can be manipulated by electric or magnetic fields and propelled into a mass analyzer that resolves each ion according to its m/z (mass/charge) ratio. A mass of 2000 daltons (Da)[2] carrying a double charge (i. e., 2000 Da/2+) will behave the same way in a field as a mass of 1000 carrying single charge as they share the same mass-to-charge ratio (m/z)

[2] Da (Dalton) is the mass of one atomic unit, the approximate mass of a hydrogen atom, hydrogen ion (H^+) proton or neutron. 1000 daltons is a kilodalton kDa, the typical mass of a protein is about 30,000 Da, 30 kDa. Thomson (Th) is sometimes used in mass spectrometry as the unit of mass-to-charge ratio.

(i.e., 2000/2+ = 1000/1+). Note that the molecular mass includes that of the analyte (the analysed molecule) *plus* the protons, given that the peptides have been ionised.

Different instruments use a variety of different strategies to detect ions, but the typical behaviour is to increase the velocity of the molecule and measure the mass as a function of behaviour after acceleration. In a time-of-flight analyzer (TOF) ions are accelerated by application of a constant voltage, with the time taken for an ion to reach the detector is determined by its mass, the smaller the mass the faster it flies. Other types of detection include manipulating the ions in a radio frequency quadrupole field, which involves separating ions as they flux in a field of four electromagnetic rods or an Orbitrap, in which ions are electrostatically trapped in an orbit around a central, spindle shaped electrode. Fourier transform ion cyclotron resonance (FT-ICR) mass spectrometry measures mass by detecting the image current produced by ions cyclotroning in the presence of a magnetic field. This technique is extremely accurate but the large magnets used need to be super-cooled. The mass range, speed and accuracy (defined as the ability to distinguish between two peaks of similar *m/z* ratio) vary between detectors. Different analysers can be combined together to improve resolution and mass accuracy.

Tandem Mass Spectrometry (MS/MS)

MALDI-TOF is fast, inexpensive and a useful identification tool or screening method. However, sequence analysis and a more detailed interrogation of complex samples can be achieved by tandem mass spectrometry (MS/MS), where individual peptides identified by the first mass spectrometer (MS1) can be further fragmented and analysed in a second mass spectrometer (MS2). After identification of the precursor peptide in MS1, this peptide is further fragmented and it's constituent parts detected in MS2 (Figure 3.3). This secondary fragmentation can be achieved by a number of approaches, such as collision induced dissociation (CID), electron capture dissociation (ECD) or electron transfer dissociation (ETD).

These masses can be used to identify the sequence of the original ionised peptide (termed the precursor ion) since each amino acid has its own unique mass (with the exception of leucine and isoleucine) (Figure 3.3 and 3.4). Hydroxyproline differs only slightly from these two amino acids, and it requires a high resolution instrument to discriminate it from leucine and isoleucine.

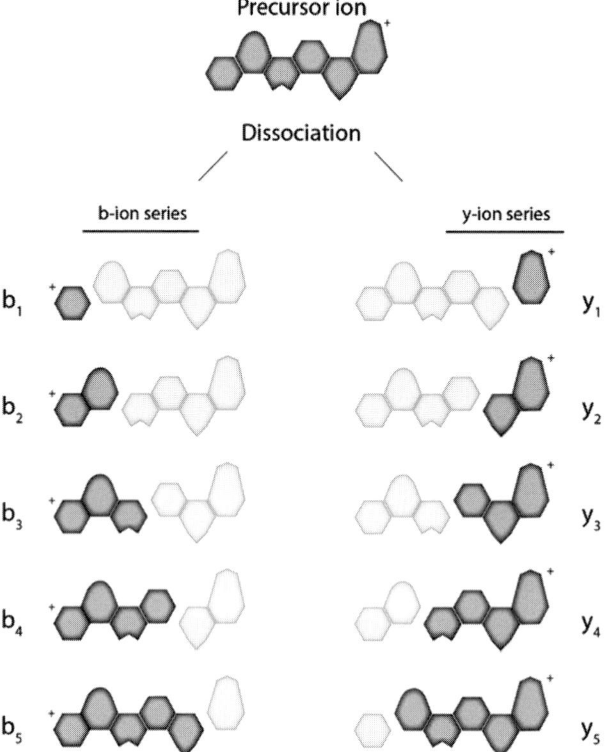

FIGURE 3.3 A highly idealised example of how dissociation leads to peptide identification in tandem mass spectrometry. Dissociation of the precursor ion leads to two fragments, one of which retains the charge. If this charge is retained on the N-terminal fragment the ion is classified as the a, b or c ion-series. If the charge is retained on the C-terminus the ion is classified as the x, y or z ion series. A b-ion and y-ion series is shown here as an example. During sample preparation, prior to MS/MS analysis, the enzyme trypsin is typically used to cleave the protein into peptide fragments. This results in lysine or arginine as the C-terminal residue, both of which are electrophiles, so the charge tends to reside at the C-terminus.

Mass Spectrometry and the Detection of Degradation

Patterns of degradation (the importance of which was outlined above) can be detected by mass spectrometry, another reason why this technique is so useful for archaeological applications. Characteristic changes to the masses of particular amino acids are reflective of distinct post-translational modifications (see Figure 3.5). For example, a mass shift of 1 Da is characteristic of the deamidation of asparagine or glutamine

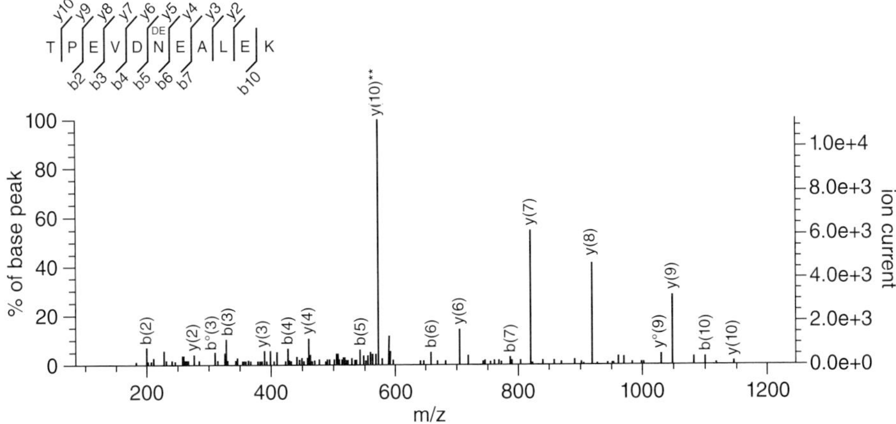

FIGURE 3.4 An example of how an MS/MS spectrum generates a peptide sequence. Each *m/z* present in the spectrum corresponds to a dissociated peptide fragment (Figure 3.3). Masses are reported as mass over charge (i.e., *m/z*), because they are measured by their behaviour in a field; thus a mass with twice the charge will be indistinguishable from a peptide with half that mass but half the charge (i.e., 250/2 = 500/1). Data are from Warinner et al. (2014a,b)

Interpretation

Once peptide masses have been detected (either through MS or MS/MS), resulting spectra need to be analysed in order to make meaningful interpretations. Two broad approaches commonly applied in ancient proteomics are discussed here; the use of peptide mass fingerprinting (MS), and database spectral matching from MS/MS spectral data.

Peptide Mass Fingerprinting (ZooMS)

Peptide mass fingerprinting (PMF, also known as peptide mass mapping, PMM) (Henzel et al. 2003) is a rapid and simple system to compare peptide sequences between samples. When samples are relatively simple (e.g., a purified protein or a sample dominated by a single protein such as collagen in bone) PMF is a useful method, and it is the approach adopted for “ZooMS” (discussed below). The method is of limited value in complex mixtures of proteins as numerous peptides may have similar masses.

Peptide mass fingerprinting does not involve direct identification of the amino acid sequence. Instead, it involves the comparison of the distribution pattern of peptide masses (the mass spectra) between an unknown sample and a reference

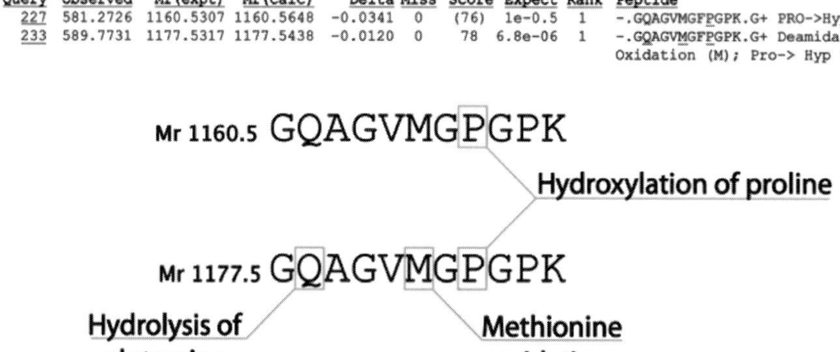

FIGURE 3.5 Example of degradation detected in a peptide sequence. This example is a collagen sequence extracted from archaeological leather.

library of known spectra. The peptide mass distribution acts as a fingerprint or barcode, since differences in amino acid sequences result in different peptide masses. Simplified examples of such spectra from collagen are shown in Figure 3.6.

M/MS Sequence Queries

Peptide mass fingerprinting enables the identification of peptides through a fingerprint-matching approach. However, the actual sequence of amino acids in each peptide itself can be identified using tandem mass spectrometry (MS/MS). Often, a sequence is identified by pattern matching, between the *m/z* values detected in a MS/MS experiment and all the theoretical *m/z* values potentially generated by peptides in a set reference database. In the case of an organism for which the complete genome is known, pattern matching is a powerful approach. Even if there are multiple variants of a protein there should be a number of clearly recognisable peptides.

Peptide identification via pattern matching from LC-MS/MS data involves the following steps;

1. Protein sequences (typically translated from genomic data) are broken *in silico* into theoretical peptide sequences, based on the known cleavage patterns of protease enzymes, such as trypsin.

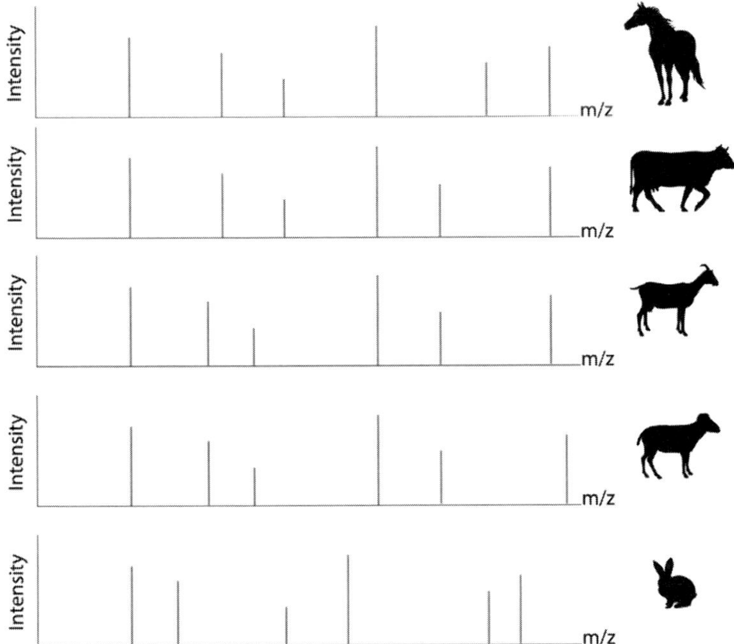

FIGURE 3.6 A simplified example of peptide mass fingerprints deriving from different animal species. Each of the vertical lines represents a different detected mass (*x*-axis) whose height (*y*-axes) is a measure of the number of times that mass was detected in the experiment. Differences in the masses of the peptide fingerprints typically reflect differences in the sequence composition, but can also represent biologically directed or diagenetic modifications of the peptide, which has resulted in a change of mass. Note in ZooMS experiments all masses only carry one charge.

2. For every *in silico* peptide all possible dissociation ions are generated. All *in silico* peptides with masses identical to the precursor ion (see Figure 3.3) are included in this approach (within defined error). Additional peptides can be considered, for example, those containing post-translational modifications, if the combined mass matches the mass of the precursor ion. However, the larger the number of possible *in silico* peptides, which may match the precursor ion, the slower the downstream bioinformatic search and the greater the chance of false-positive matches.
3. Masses generated via MS/MS are compared to masses generated from these digested *in silico* peptides, and ranked according to the correspondence between observed and prediction.

4. Identifications may be improved by narrowing down the search space of possible peptides by taking into account the nature of the sample. For example, if the organism (or taxonomic family) in question is known then the *in silico* peptides can be restricted to proteins from this organism.

Peptide identifications are expressed as a probability of the match between the MS/MS generated and theoretical *m/z* ions, but this probability is strongly influenced by the size of the database and the quality of the spectra. A useful approach to assess the likelihood of false positive matches is to estimate a false discovery rate (FDR) by additionally matching the MS/MS generated *m/z* ions against a so-called *decoy database*, which contains all of the sequences in the target databases, but either reversed or randomly jumbled. An FDR of 1 per cent means that one in 100 peptide identifications may be incorrect. Despite the large size of databases, they only contain a very small fraction of proteins that exist from all forms of life and may have a bias towards pathogenic or commercially relevant species.

Some useful rules of thumb for generating valid results are:

1. Avoid reliance on 'one-hit-wonders', proteins only identified from a single peptide.
2. If the peptide is matched based upon a post-translational modification, does the modification make sense in terms of the history and treatment of the sample?
3. If the peptide displays evidence of degradation (e.g., deamidation), is the undamaged version also present?
4. In the case of unusual or rare samples it may be necessary to make (or confirm) an identification by *de novo* sequencing. *De novo* sequencing involves building a peptide sequence via analysis of masses of the ion series (see Figure 3.3), rather than via matching against *in silico* generated masses.

Useful Tools

A number of portals exist for resources, databases and software tools, notable examples include ExPASy (formerly the Expert Protein Analysis System), NCBI (National Center for Biotechnology Information) and UniProtKB.

3 ARCHAEOLOGICAL APPLICATIONS

The following section will discuss the archaeological applications of ancient proteins; from studies. These case studies are not exhaustive, but give an overview of the past, current and future applications of ancient protein research. Selected case studies are summarised in Table 3.2.

Targeted Single Proteins

The term proteomics is used to describe studies that explore the range and diversity of proteins found in particular tissues. However, more often than not, studies of archaeological and fossil proteins have been focused on identification of a single protein, from early studies of the bone protein osteocalcin in bison (Nielsen-Marsh et al. 2002) to collagen in Pleistocene camel (Rybczynski et al. 2013) or South American ungulates (Buckley 2015; Welker et al. 2015a).

Archaeologists may target single proteins of interest to address specific questions. Perhaps the most well-known case of this approach is the attempt to characterise proteins found as residues on tools, in order to understand tool use, as well as the biological origin of any identified proteins.

The use of proteins to detect blood on stone tools was first reported by Loy (1983), who argued that the crystallisation pattern of hemoglobin was specific to different animal species. The principle behind this is that species-specific sequence differences in the four peptide chains that constitute hemoglobin (i.e., its quaternary structure) create different crystal shapes when the protein is precipitated. This approach has been criticised for a number of reasons, including that a) hemoglobin is unlikely to survive as a pure and intact (and hence crystallisable) protein, b) the formation of crystals would not be suitable for species-specific identifications (Smith and Wilson 1992), c) the crystals are contaminants from the environment (Hyland et al. 1990), and d) it has proved challenging to replicate. Criticisms and responses can be found in Remington (1994) and Loy (1994).

Immunological approaches (discussed in section 1) were subsequently adopted as an alternative method to explore protein residues on lithics. However, these have also met with substantial controversy, mainly owing to problems of cross-reactivity

Table 3.2 *Selected case studies in ancient protein research.*

Material	Age	Proteins Identified	Method	References
Pottery	AD 1200–1400	Myoglobin	nanoLC, nanoESI, FT ICR, MALDI-TOF	Solazzo et al. 2008
Food residues	1980 BC–seventh century	Food derived proteins	LC-MS/MS	Cappellini et al. 2010; Hong et al. 2012; Shevchenko et al. 2014; Yang et al. 2014
Binding material/ Glue	AD 1300–1400	Ovotransferrin Ovalbumin Ovamucoid Phosvitin Lipovitellin	MALDI-TOF, NanoLC/nanoESI/ Q-q-TOF	Tokarski et al. 2006
	AD 1800	Ovalbumin Casein	MALDI-TOF	Kuckova et al. 2007; Kuckova et al. 2005
	AD 1300–1600	Gelatin Albumin Ovalbumin Casein	ESI-MS	Peris-Vicente et al. 2005
Bone	Modern and archaeological	Collagen	MALDI-TOF	Buckley et al. 2009; Buckley and Kansa 2011; Richter et al. 2011
	Late Quaternary	Collagen	nanoLC-MS/MS	Buckley 2015; Welker et al. 2015a,b
	800–53 ka BP	Osteocalcin	MALDI-TOF	Ostrom et al. 2000; Nielsen-Marsh et al. 2005
	43,000 BP	Bone proteome (NCPs)	nanoLC-MS/MS	Cappellini et al. 2012
	7500 BC – recent	Various NCPs	2D-PAGE, LC-MS/MS	Schmidt-Schultz and Schultz 2007

Mummified tissue	5,300 BP, 500 BP	Immune proteins, Brain proteome,	LC-MS/MS	Corthals et al. 2012; Maixner et al. 2013
Eggshell	Tenth–seventh century AD	Intra-crystalline proteins	MALDI-TOF	Stewart et al. 2013; Stewart et al. 2014
	3.8 mya	Intra-crystalline peptides	LC-MS/MS	Demarchi et al. 2016
Dental calculus	Modern and archaeological	Oral proteome, dietary proteins	nanoLC-MS/MS	Warinner et al. 2014a,b
Dentine	Medieval, nineteenth century AD	Dentine proteome	nanoLC-MS/MS	Warinner et al. 2014a
Dental pulp	Modern and archaeological	Collagen and NCPs	MALDI-TOF	Tran et al. 2011
Antler	Fifth–tenth centuries AD	Collagen	MALDI-TOF	von Holstein et al. 2014
Wool, baleen, porcupine quill, horn and hoof	Modern and archaeological	Keratin	MALDI-TOF, nanoLC-MS/MS	Solazzo et al. 2013b
Hair/Textile	5300 y	Keratin	MALDI-TOF	Solazzo et al. 2015; Solazzo et al. 2011; Solazzo et al. 2013a; Hollemeyer et al. 2008
Lithics/ Ceramics/ Glass/Flint	Modern, artificial, experimental	Albumin, Casein, Myoglobin, Ovalbumin (artificially applied)	DESI-MS	Heaton et al. 2009
Mortars	AD 1100	Casein, Haemoglobin	MALDI-TOF	Kuckova et al. 2009a
Metal (Patina)	AD 1100-1300, AD 1900	Haemoglobin	TOF-SIMS	Mazel et al. 2007

and false-positive results. Although reports detecting blood residues from stone tools have included success rates of up to 25–30 per cent in the assemblage (Kooyman et al. 1992), different immunological approaches that have been compared and blind tested have often yielded cautionary results (e.g., Downs and Lowenstein 1995; Leach and Mauldin 1995). A refined version using radioimmunoassay (pRIA) has been developed to species discriminate bone fragments and residues (Potter et al. 2010: 910) that, although a valuable tool for forensics, should be applied only with caution to archaeological remains because cross-reactions still occur when proteins are diagenetically altered. As is clear from this example, at the heart of these controversies is the nature of protein survival. Thus, understanding protein survival is crucial for assessing the validity of these approaches.

Enrichment Methods

The first analysis of single proteins using mass spectrometry was completed using enrichment methods, using ion exchange resin to selectively extract the negatively charged small protein osteocalcin from bone extracts (Ostrom et al. 2000). This was able to concentrate sufficiently to obtain sequence data, enabling the sequence identification of osteocalcin against the relatively much higher quantity of bone collagen peptides.

Wadsworth and Buckley (2014) observed that collagen tends to dominate in ancient bone, and although a number of recent studies (Cappellini et al. 2012; Cleland et al. 2015; Hill et al. 2015) have extracted proteomes that were dominated with collagen, detecting lower abundance proteins in these proteomes can be challenging. Potential enrichment approaches could include the use of antibodies (Whiteaker et al. 2007) to target specific proteins or peptides present in lower concentrations, capturing the majority of the low abundance proteins (e.g., ProteoMiner Protein Enrichment Kit).

Single Proteins: Detection with Mass Spectrometry

Single proteins are routinely targeted in archaeological applications, typically collagen, which is abundant in skeletal material where it is often well preserved. However, in contrast to the techniques described above, such as immunological approaches, increasing resolving power of instruments allows much more detailed sequence information to be uncovered.

Keratins

Natural fibres consist mostly of keratin, a mostly insoluble and sulfur-rich protein formed primarily of alpha-helical domains. These chemical and structural properties mean that keratinous fibres are relatively resistant to biodegradation, preserving in frozen (Rasmussen et al. 2010), waterlogged (Frei et al. 2015) and dry environments (Wilson et al. 2013). Using PMF (Altmeyer et al. 2002) and more detailed sequence information obtained by MS/MS, it is possible to identify the biological origin of many keratinous materials (Hollemeyer et al. 2002). For example, keratins were detected in the analysis of the clothing of Oetzi – the Tyrolean iceman – where it was found that his coat was made from sheep and his moccasins from cattle (Hollemeyer et al. 2008), and his other clothing made from red deer, goat and chamois and canid species (Hollemeyer et al. 2012). In textiles from the Pacific Northwest coast, it was found that dog hair, as well as sheep wool, was incorporated into textiles – a finding that corroborated local, oral traditions (Solazzo et al. 2011).

As well as animal fibres, keratin is also present in other organic materials, such as skins, horns, hooves, baleen and quills (O'Connor et al. 2015). Using a database of selected peptides, Solazzo et al. (2013b) discovered it is possible to distinguish α-keratins from different taxa. Keratin and collagen were also used to identify the species composition of skin garments from Danish peat bogs. In this study, foetal haemoglobin was identified, indicating skin production from a young calf (Brandt et al. 2014).

Silk

Silk is traditionally made from the single fibres produced by insects, made primarily of antiparallel beta sheet (a form of secondary structure) domains. This material has been identified archaeologically through the extraction of proteins from burial soil underneath a fibre imprint (Zhu et al. 2014). Amino acid profiling (Becker et al. 1995) and proteomic analysis (Becker et al. 1995; Solazzo et al. 2012) have been used to understand silk textile degradation, whist racemisation has also been used to date historical silk fibres (Moini et al. 2011).

Collagen

Collagen is the most abundant protein in skin, teeth and bone, with an atypical triple helix structure, unlike the more common alpha helix and beta sheet secondary structures found in wool and silk respectively. ZooMS, short for zooarchaeology by mass spectrometry, is a low cost, minimally destructive identification method that uses PMF to discriminate between collagen sequences from bones (Buckley et al. 2009b; van Doorn 2014). The archaeological record is littered with the debris of human-animal interactions (Sykes 2014). However, in many cases, this material may be fragmented and degraded, meaning that determining species from bone morphology may be difficult or impossible (Steele 2015).

ZooMS has been applied to many archaeological contexts and is used to understand dietary patterns, or reconstruct local ecology (Barker 2011; Buckley and Kansa 2011; Vaiglova et al. 2014), even into the middle to upper Palaeolithic (Welker et al. 2015b). One particular application is in the distinction between ovid (sheep) and caprid (goat) species that are morphologically similar and therefore difficult to identify by faunal skeletal remains alone. Unique collagen sequences, which result in characteristic mass fingerprints, enable bone fragments from these species to be uniquely identified (Buckley et al. 2010). ZooMS has been applied not only for identifying common domesticates, but for the identification of the fragmentary remains of other animals including fish (Richter et al. 2011), marine mammals (Buckley et al. 2014), and giant tortoises (Van der Sluis et al. 2014).

As well as bone, the ZooMS approach has also been applied to other collagenous materials, such as parchment (Fiddyment et al. 2015; Kirby et al. 2013; Toniolo et al. 2012), and antler combs (von Holstein et al. 2014), as well as bird eggshell (Stewart et al. 2013; Stewart et al. 2014). In this case the target is not collagen, but elements of the bird's uterine proteome (Mann and Mann 2013). Fortunately for many species there is good coverage of high-quality genomes (Eöry et al. 2015), which enables adequate database sequence information to make the technique feasible.

Simple Protein Mixtures

The analysis of single proteins, especially ZooMS, is becoming a familiar part of the archaeologist's toolkit. However, many archaeological materials constitute a mixture of different proteins. For example, proteins derived from animal products such as blood and milk have been identified as plasticisers in building mortars and plasters (Krizkova et al. 2014; Kuckova et al. 2009b), whilst collagen, flour and blood have all been identified in wooden buildings (Chamberlain et al. 2011; Rao et al. 2015) and animal glue detected in the polychrome terracotta army of Qin Shihuang (Yan et al. 2014). Understanding these compositions is valuable for exploring past building practices and has repercussions in restoration and conservation practices. Proteins were also commonly used as binding materials for pigments, the most common being egg yolk or milk. The sensitivity of MALDI-TOF MS is so high that it was possible to distinguish between the presence of egg yolk or whole egg in paint (Kuckova et al. 2007). In addition, proteomics is able to identify organic colouring in artworks (Kuckova et al. 2005), identify the use of egg as a binder in ink (Rasmussen et al. 2012) and as binding medium in murals (Chambery et al. 2009). Furthermore, especially in the case of paintings or other painted artefacts, mass spectrometry is able to facilitate minimal sample size (Tokarski et al. 2006) and proteomics could contribute greatly towards investigations on biodeterioration (Leo et al. 2011; Vanden Berghe 2012) and the preservation of cultural heritage and archaeological artefacts (Solazzo et al. 2013a).

Complex Protein Mixtures and Proteomes

The high resolving power and sensitivity of mass spectrometry enables the characterisation even more complex archaeological materials, including plant remains, food residues, and microbial systems. In particular, these are giving insights into two long-standing archaeological concepts; understanding past dietary patterns and foodstuffs, and exploring ancient health and disease. Many of these recent applications represent the use of proteomics in its strictest sense, as the study of protein expression and quantification.

Seeds

Detecting plant tissues in the archaeological record using proteomic approaches can be challenging given that most plant tissues are relatively protein poor. However, as far back as 1977 Derbyshire and colleagues, investigating 700-year-old maize kernels, made a prescient comment that archaeological seed proteins may be useful in studies of plant domestication and evolution (Derbyshire et al. 1977). As Shewry et al. (1982) highlights, seeds are under strong selective pressure and therefore the phenotypic analysis of seed proteins would be a valuable new source of information for archaeobotanical research. Shewry et al. (1982) compared the protein profile of barley grains, generated using a combination of sequential extraction and gel electrophoresis, from ancient Egypt and historical samples, and were able to generate different proteomic profiles for these two sources. Cappellini et al. (2010) analyzed preserved grape seeds from medieval York using amino acid analysis, revealing that approximately 80 per cent of the protein content of was lost, and mass spectrometry approaches also identified degraded peptides.

Pottery

The detection of proteins from pottery has proven challenging (Barker et al. 2012; Craig and Collins 2000; Evershed and Tuross 1996;), although improved extraction methods (Craig and Collins 2000) have, for example, enabled the immunological detection of milk proteins in Iron Age ceramics (Craig et al. 2000). Using soft ionisation mass spectrometry (Solazzo et al. 2008) identified seal myoglobin in an Alaskan potsherd dating to AD 1200–1400. (Buckley et al. 2013) identified casein, a milk protein, in a preserved food residue inside a vessel dating to over 4000 years ago. In addition, the same method was able to detect that the stitching comprising the vessel was made from animal sinews. Dallongeville et al. (2011) used ecological replicas to develop methods for detecting fish residues in ceramic vessels.

Food Residues

Proteomics has been used to uncover the composition of food residues and to study past food preparation. For example Hong et al. (2012) were able to demonstrate cattle and sheep/goat dairying in Western China by at least 2300 BP on the basis of immunological and proteomic detection of milk proteins in a ceramic bowl from an Early Iron Age burial at Subeixi. Yang et al. (2014) were able to identify food residues adjacent to a mummy from Xinjiang, China, identifying the earliest preserved cheese (1980–1450 BC). They were also able to identify fermentation bacteria, uncovering some of the mechanisms behind the production of a digestible dairy product. Similarly, analysis of cereal and cereal food, also from China, has provided insight into the composition of sourdough bread, revealing the use of barley and broomcorn millet as well as yeast and fermentation bacteria (Shevchenko et al. 2014).

Bone and Dentine

Beyond bone collagen, tandem mass spectrometry has also been applied to identifying the bone proteome. This has been characterised in a 1 ka Moa (Cleland et al. 2015), a 43 ka mammoth (Cappellini et al. 2012), a 150 ka bison (Hill et al. 2015), a 700 ka horse bone (Orlando et al. 2013), as well as in medieval human dentine (Warinner et al. 2014a) and human bone (Sawafuji et al. 2017) These approaches have focused on the recovery of proteins expressed in archaeological bone and dentine and understanding which of these persist in the oldest samples (Buckley and Wadsworth 2014). As the field matures it is likely that this proteome may identify more phylogenetic information proteins than collagen alone (e.g., A2HSG protein) (Wadsworth and Buckley 2014). The preservation of the proteome and the constituent peptides could also be used as a proxy for DNA preservation (Orlando et al. 2013). Furthermore it may prove possible to understand physiological changes and disease states (Cappellini et al. 2012), although profiles may be skewed by preservation biases.

Dental Calculus

Ancient dental calculus, or mineralised dental plaque (also known as tartar or dental calculus), is another complex proteomic substrate receiving archaeological attention. Proteomic analysis of this deposit, which forms on the tooth surface during life, has revealed the preservation of proteins derived from oral and respiratory bacteria, as well as proteins expressed in the human mouth (Warinner et al. 2014b). This is giving insight into the nature of the ancient oral microbiome, and into past oral diseases. As well as identifying the suite of proteins preserved in dental calculus, the characterisation of single proteins within this complex mixture is also informative, such as those linked to diet. For example, Warinner et al. (2014a) identified the milk whey protein, beta-lactoglobulin, a species-specific biomarker enabling the study of dairy consumption directly from human remains.

Mummified Remains

Analysis of mummified remains is also revealing that a diverse range of proteins can survive through time. For example, analysis of buccal swabs from 500-year-old mummified individuals from the Andes revealed a suite of proteins associated with the immune system, suggesting that an active anti-bacterial response was present at the time of death (Corthals et al. 2012). Analysis of the brain proteome of the Tyrolean Iceman revealed expression of proteins related to wound healing, suggesting a possible head injury (Maixner et al. 2013).

4 CONCLUSION

A diverse range of proteins exist in nature, found in human tissues, plants, animals and microorganisms. Proteins can be extracted from archaeological sources, such as human bone, teeth and dental calculus, as well as material artefacts, such as well-preserved food remains and cultural heritage objects. This data can be used to reconstruct a range of aspects on the past, such the phylogenetic reconstruction of extinct species, the species identification of bone remains, the reconstruction of past foodways, as well as patterns of disease and health.

A variety of different techniques can be applied to study ancient proteins. Immunological approaches target a single protein of interest and detect its presence or absence, although this technique can be hampered by false positive results. Peptide mass fingerprinting (PMF), a mass spectrometry based technique, enables the rapid and inexpensive detection of archaeological proteins. This technique forms the basis of Zooarchaeology by Mass Spectrometry, ZooMS, which enables the species identification of archaeological collagen, due to differences in the collagen amino acid sequence between different animal taxa. Another mass spectrometric technique is tandem mass spectrometry, which facilitates the reconstruction of peptide sequences. This technique enables the identification of multiple different proteins in a sample, such as a bone proteome, and can also detect evidence of protein degradation.

Since the 1990s, ancient protein research has been expanding on the back of technological developments in mass spectrometry, making it possible to detect degraded peptides within complex proteomes. No doubt further technological advances will have implications on ancient protein analysis. Firstly, increasing instrument sensitivity allows sample sizes to be reduced (van der Werf et al. 2012). For rare samples or valuable museum exhibits, minimal destruction is of paramount importance. Secondly, increasing instrumental resolution allows highly complex proteomes to be analysed, including proteins derived from multiple species (the 'metaproteome').

REFERENCES

Abelson, P. H., 1954. Amino acids in fossils. *Science* 119(3096):576.

Altmeyer, W. et al. 2002. Method for qualitative and/or quantitative determination of gender, species, race and/or geographical origin of biological materials. Patent. Available at: http://google.com/patents/CA2452851A1?cl=zh (accessed June 29, 2019).

Asara, J. M. et al. 2007. Protein sequences from mastodon and Tyrannosaurus rex revealed by mass spectrometry. *Science* 316(5822):280–285.

Bada, J. L. 1991. Amino acid cosmogeochemistry. Philosophical transactions of the Royal Society of London. Series B, *Biological sciences* 333(1268):349–358.

Bada, J. L. and Miller, S. L. 1968. Ammonium ion concentration in the primitive ocean. *Science* 159(3813):423–425.

Barker, A. 2011. Archaeological protein residues: New data for conservation science. *Ethnobiology Letters* 1:58–65.

Barker, A., Venables, B., Stevens, S. M., Jr., Seeley, K. W., Wang, P., and Wolverton, S. 2012. An optimized approach for protein residue extraction and identification from ceramics after cooking. *Journal of Archaeological Method and Theory* 19(3):407–439.

Becker, M. A., Willman, P., and Tuross, N. C. 1995. The U.S. First Ladies' gowns: A biochemical study of silk preservation. *Journal of the American Institute for Conservation* 34(2):141–152.

Bern, M., Phinney, B. S., and Goldberg, D. 2009. Reanalysis of Tyrannosaurus rex mass spectra. *Journal of Proteome Research* 8(9):4328–4332.

Brandt, L. Ø., Schmidt, A. L., Mannering, U., Sarret, M., Kelstrup, C. D., Olsen, J. V., and Cappellini, E. 2014. Species identification of archaeological skin objects from Danish bogs: Comparison between mass spectrometry-based peptide sequencing and microscopy-based methods. *PloS One* 9(9):e106875.

Buckley, M. 2013. A molecular phylogeny of Plesiorycteropus reassigns the extinct mammalian order "Bibymalagasia." *PloS One* 8(3):e59614.

Buckley, M. 2015. Ancient collagen reveals evolutionary history of the endemic South American "ungulates." *Proceedings of the Royal Society B-Biological Sciences* 282(1806):20142671.

Buckley, M., Anderung, C., Penkman, K., Raney, B. J., Gotherstrom, A., Thomas-Oates, J., and Collins, M. J. 2008b. Comparing the survival of osteocalcin and mtDNA in archaeological bone from four European sites. *Journal of Archaeological Science* 35:1756–1764.

Buckley, M., Collins, M., Thomas-Oates, J., and Wilson, J. C. 2009. Species identification by analysis of bone collagen using matrix-assisted laser desorption/ionisation time-of-flight mass spectrometry. *Rapid Communications in Mass Spectrometry* 23:3843–3854.

Buckley, M., Fraser, S., Herman, J., Melton, N. D., Mulville, J., and Palsdottir, A. H. 2014. Species identification of archaeological marine mammals using collagen fingerprinting. *Journal of Archaeological Science* 41:631–641.

Buckley, M. and Kansa, S. W. 2011. Collagen fingerprinting of archaeological bone and teeth remains from Domuztepe, South Eastern Turkey. *Archaeological and Anthropological Sciences* 3(3):271–280.

Kansa, S. W., Howard, S., Campbell, S., Thomas-Oates, J., and Collins, M. 2010. Distinguishing between archaeological sheep and goat bones using a single collagen peptide. *Journal of Archaeological Science* 37:13–20.

Buckley, M., Larkin, N., and Collins, M. 2011. Mammoth and mastodon collagen sequences: Survival and utility. *Geochimica et Cosmochimica Acta* 75(7):2007–2016.

Buckley, M., Melton, N. D., and Montgomery, J. 2013. Proteomics analysis of ancient food vessel stitching reveals >4000-year-old milk protein. *Rapid Communications in Mass Spectrometry* 27(4):531–538.

Buckley, M. and Wadsworth, C. 2014. Proteome degradation in ancient bone: Diagenesis and phylogenetic potential. *Palaeogeography, Palaeoclimatology, Palaeoecology* 416:69–79.

Buckley, M., Walker, A., Ho, S. Y. W., Yang, Y., Smith, C., Ashton, P., Oates, J. T., Cappellini, E., Koon, H., Penkman, K., Elsworth, B., Ashford, D., Solazzo, C., Andrews, P., Strahler, J., Shapiro, B., Ostrom, P., Gandhi, H., Miller, W., Raney, B., Zylber, M. I., Gilbert, M. T. P., Prigodich, R. V., Ryan, M., Rijsdijk, K. F., Janoo, A., and Collins, M. J. 2008a. Comment on "protein sequences from mastodon and Tyrannosaurus rex revealed by mass spectrometry." *Science* 319:33.

Buckley, M., Warwood, S., Van Dongen, B., Kitchener, A. C., and Manning, P. L. 2017. A fossil protein chimera: Difficulties in discriminating dinosaur peptide sequences from modern cross-contamination. *Proceedings of the Royal Society B-Biological Sciences* 284:20170544.

Cappellini, E., Gilbert, M. T. P., Geuna, F., Fiorentino, G., Hall, A., Thomas-Oates, J., Ashton, P. D., Ashford, D. A., Arthur, P., Campos, P. F., Kool, J., Willerslev, E., and Collins, M. J. 2010. A multidisciplinary study of archaeological grape seeds. *Naturwissenschaften* 97:205–217.

Cappellini, E., Jensen, L. J., Szklarczyk, D., Ginolhac, A., Da Fonseca, R. a. R., Stafford, T. W., Holen, S. R., Collins, M. J., Orlando, L., Willerslev, E., Gilbert, M. T. P., and Olsen, J. V. 2012. Proteomic analysis of a Pleistocene mammoth femur reveals more than one hundred ancient bone proteins. *Journal of Proteome Research* 11:917–926.

Cattaneo, C., Gelsthorpe, K., Phillips, P., and Sokol, R. J. 1992. Detection of human proteins in buried blood using Elisa and monoclonal-antibodies – Towards the reliable species indentification of blood stains on buried material. *Forensic Science International* 57:139–146.

Chamberlain, P., Drewello, R., Korn, L., Bauer, W., Gough, T., Al-Fouzan, A., Collins, M., Van Doorn, N., Craig, O., and Heron, C. 2011. Construction of the Khoja Zaynuddin mosque: Use of animal glue modified with urine. *Archaeometry* 53:830–841.

Chambery, A., Di Maro, A., Sanges, C., Severino, V., Tarantino, M., Lamberti, A., Parente, A., and Arcari, P. 2009. Improved procedure for protein binder analysis in mural painting by LC-ESI/Q-q-TOF mass spectrometry: Detection of different milk species by casein proteotypic peptides. *Analytical and Bioanalytical Chemistry* 395:2281–2291.

Cleland, T. P., Schroeter, E. R., and Schweitzer, M. H. 2015. Biologically and diagenetically derived peptide modifications in moa collagens. *Proceedings of the Royal Society B-Biological Sciences* 282:20150015.

Collins, M. J., Nielsen-Marsh, C. M., Hiller, J., Smith, C. I., Roberts, J. P., Prigodich, R. V., Weiss, T. J., Csapo, J., Millard, A. R., and Turner-Walker, G. 2002. The survival of organic matter in bone: A review. *Archaeometry* 44:383–394.

Collins, M. J., Riley, M. S., Child, A. M., and Turnerwalker, G. 1995. A basic mathematical simulation of the chemical degradation of ancient collagen. *Journal of Archaeological Science* 22:175–183.

Corthals, A., Koller, A., Martin, D. W., Rieger, R., Chen, E. I., Bernaski, M., Recagno, G., and Davalos, L. M. 2012. Detecting the immune system response of a 500 year-old Inca mummy. *PLoS One* 7(7):e41244.

Craig, O. E. and Collins, M. J. 2000. An improved method for the immunological detection of mineral bound protein using hydrofluoric acid and direct capture. *Journal of Immunological Methods* 236(1–2):89–97.

Craig, O., Mulville, J., Pearson, M. P., Sokol, R., Gelsthorpe, K., Stacey, R., and Collins, M. 2000. Detecting milk proteins in ancient pots. *Nature* 408:312.

Dallongeville, S., Garnier, N., Casasola, D. B., Bonifay, M., Rolando, C., and Tokarski, C. 2011. Dealing with the identification of protein species in ancient amphorae. *Analytical and Bioanalytical Chemistry* 399:3053–3063.

Daniel, R. M., Dines, M., and Petach, H. H. 1996. The denaturation and degradation of stable enzymes at high temperatures. *Biochemical Journal* 317(Pt 1):1–11.

Demarchi, B. and Collins, M., 2014. Amino acid racemisation dating. In: Rink, W. J and Thompson, J. (eds.) *Encyclopedia of Scientific Dating Methods*, pp. 1–22. Springer Netherlands.

Demarchi, B., Hall, S., Roncal-Herrero, T., Freeman, C. L., Woolley, J., Crisp, M. K., Wilson, J., Fotakis, A., Fischer, R., Kessler, B. M., Jersie-Christensens, R. R., Olsen, J. V., Haile, J., Thomas, J., Marean, C. W., Parkington, J., Presslee, S., Lee-Thorp, J., Ditchfield, P., Hamilton, J. F., Ward, M. W., Wang, C. M., Shaw, M. D., Harrison, T., Dominguez-Rodrigo, M., Macpheel, R. D. E., Kwekason, A., Ecker, M., Horwitz, L. K., Chazan, M., Kroger, R., Thomas-Oates, J., Harding, J. H., Cappellini, E., Penkman, K., and Collins, M. J. 2016. Protein sequences bound to mineral surfaces persist into deep time. *Elife* 5: e17092.

Demarchi, B., O'Connor, S., Ponzoni, A. D., Ponzoni, R. D. R., Sheridan, A., Penkman, K., Hancock, Y., and Wilson, J. 2014. An integrated approach to the taxonomic identification of prehistoric shell ornaments. *PLoS One* 9(6):e99839.

Derbyshire, E., Harris, N., Boulter, D., and Jope, E. M. 1977. The extraction, composition and intra-cellular distribution of protein in early maize grains from an archaeological site in NE Arizona. *New Phytologist* 78:499–504.

Doberenz, A. R. and Wyckoff, R. W. 1967. Fine structure in fossil collagen. *Proceedings of the National Academy of Sciences of the United States of America* 57(3):539–541.

Domon, B. and Aebersold, R. 2006. Mass spectrometry and protein analysis. *Science* 312 (5771):212–217.

Downs, E. F. and Lowenstein, J. M. 1995. Identification of archaeological blood proteins: A cautionary note. *Journal of Archaeological Science* 22(1):11–16.

El-Aneed, A., Cohen, A., and Banoub, J. 2009. Mass spectrometry, review of the basics: Electrospray, MALDI, and commonly used mass analyzers. *Applied Spectroscopy Reviews* 44(3):210–230.

Eöry, L., Gilbert, M. T. P., Li, C., Li, B., Archibald, A., Aken, B. L., Zhang, G. J., Jarvis, E., Flicek, P., and Burt, D. W. 2015. Avianbase: A community resource for bird genomics. *Genome Biology* 16:21.

Evershed, R. P. and Tuross, N. 1996. Proteinaceous material from potsherds and associated soils. *Journal of Archaeological Science* 23(3):429–436.

Fiddyment, S., Holsinger, B., Ruzzier, C., Devine, A., Binois, A., Albarella, U., Fischer, R., Nichols, E., Curtis, A., Cheese, E., Teasdale, M. D., Checkley-Scott, C., Milner, S. J., Rudy, K. M., Johnson, E. J., Vnoucek, J., Garrison, M., Mcgrory, S., Bradley, D. G., and Collins, M. J. 2015. Animal origin of 13th-century uterine vellum revealed using non-invasive peptide fingerprinting. *Proceedings of the National Academy of Sciences of the United States of America* 112:15066–15071.

Heaton, K., Solazzo, C., Collins, M. J., Thomas-Oates, J., and Bergstrom, E. T. 2009. Towards the application of desorption electrospray ionisation mass spectrometry (DESI-MS) to the analysis of ancient proteins from artefacts. *Journal of Archaeological Science* 36(10):2145–2154.

Henzel, W. J., Watanabe, C., and Stults, J. T. 2003. Protein identification: The origins of peptide mass fingerprinting. *Journal of the American Society for Mass Spectrometry* 14 (9):931–942.

Hill, R. C., Wither, M. J., Nemkov, T., Barrett, A., D'alessandro, A., Dzieciatkowska, M., and Hansen, K. C. 2015. Preserved proteins from extinct bison latifrons identified by tandem mass spectrometry: Hydroxylysine glycosides are a common feature of ancient collagen. *Molecular and Cellular Proteomics* 14:1946–1958.

Hillenkamp, F., Karas, M., Beavis, R. C., and Chait, B. T. 1991. Matrix-assisted laser desorption/ionization mass spectrometry of biopolymers. *Analytical chemistry* 63(24):1193A–1203A.

Hollemeyer, K., Altmeyer, W., and Heinzle, E. 2002. Identification and quantification of feathers, down, and hair of avian and mammalian origin using matrix-assisted laser desorption/ionization time-of-flight mass spectrometry. *Analytical Chemistry* 74(23):5960–5968.

Hollemeyer, K., Altmeyer, W., Heinzle, E., and Pitra, C. 2008. Species identification of Oetzi's clothing with matrix-assisted laser desorption/ionization time-of-flight mass spectrometry based on peptide pattern similarities of hair digests. *Rapid Communications in Mass Spectrometry* 22(18):2751–2767.

Hollemeyer, K., Altmeyer, W., Heinzle, E., and Pitra, C. 2012. Matrix-assisted laser desorption/ionization time-of-flight mass spectrometry combined with multidimensional scaling, binary hierarchical cluster tree and selected diagnostic masses improves species identification of Neolithic keratin sequences from furs of the Tyrolean Iceman Oetzi. *Rapid Communications in Mass Spectrometry* 26(16):1735–1745.

Hong, C., Jiang, H. G., Lu, E. G., Wu, Y. F., Guo, L. H., Xie, Y. M., Wang, C. S., and Yang, Y. M. 2012. Identification of milk component in ancient food residue by proteomics. *PLoS One* 7(5):e37053.

Huq, N. L., Tseng, A., and Chapman, G. E. 1990. Partial amino acid sequence of osteocalcin from an extinct species of ratite bird. *Biochemistry International* 21(3):491–496.

Hyland, D. C., Tersak, J. M., Adovasio, J. M., and Siegel, M. I. 1990. Identification of the species of origin of residual blood on lithic material. *American Antiquity* 55(1):104–112.

Kirby, D. P., Buckley, M., Promise, E., Trauger, S. A., and Holdcraft, T. R. 2013. Identification of collagen-based materials in cultural heritage. *The Analyst* 138(17):4849–4858.

Kooyman, B., Newman, M. E., and Ceri, H. 1992. Verifying the reliability of blood residue analysis on archaeological tools. *Journal of Archaeological Science* 19(3):265–269.

Krizkova, M. C., Kuckova, S. H., Santrucek, J., and Hynek, R. 2014. Peptide mass mapping as an effective tool for historical mortar analysis. *Construction and Building Materials* 50:219–225.

Kuckova, S., Crhova, M., Vankova, L., Hnizda, A., Hynek, R., and Kodicek, M. 2009b. Towards proteomic analysis of milk proteins in historical building materials. *International Journal of Mass Spectrometry* 284:42–46.

Kuckova, S., Hynek, R., and Kodicek, M. 2007. Identification of proteinaceous binders used in artworks by MALDI-TOF mass spectrometry. *Analytical and Bioanalytical Chemistry* 388(1):201–206.

Kuckova, S., Hynek, R., and Kodicek, M., 2009a. Application of peptide mass mapping on proteins in historical mortars. *Journal of Cultural Heritage* 10(2):244–247.

Kuckova, S., Nemec, I., Hynek, R., Hradilova, J., and Grygar, T. 2005. Analysis of organic colouring and binding components in colour layer of art works. *Analytical and Bioanalytical Chemistry* 382(2):275–282.

Leach, J. D. and Mauldin, R. P. 1995. Additional comments on blood residue analysis in archaeology. *Antiquity* 69(266):1020–1022.

Lees, S. 1989. Some characteristics of mineralised collagen. In: *Calcified Tissue*, pp. 153–173. Topics in Molecular and Structural Biology. London: Macmillan.

Leo, G., Bonaduce, I., Andreotti, A., Marino, G., Pucci, P., Colombini, M. P., and Birolo, L. 2011. Deamidation at asparagine and glutamine as a major modification upon deterioration/aging of proteinaceous binders in mural paintings. *Analytical Chemistry* 83 (6):2056–2064.

Lowenstein, J. M. 1981. Immunological reactions from fossil material. Philosophical Transactions of the Royal Society of London. *Series B, Biological sciences* 292(1057):143–149.

Loy, T. H. 1983. Prehistoric blood residues: Detection on tool surfaces and identification of species of origin. *Science* 220(4603):1269–1271.

Loy, T. H. 1994. Response. *Science* 266(5183):299–300.

Loy, T. H. and Hardy, B. L. 1992. Blood residue analysis of 90,000-year-old stone tools from Tabun Cave, Israel. *Antiquity* 66(250):24–35.

Maixner, F., Overath, T., Linke, D., Janko, M., Guerriero, G., Van Den Berg, B. H. J., Stade, B., Leidinger, P., Backes, C., Jaremek, M., Kneissl, B., Meder, B., Franke, A., Egarter-Vigl, E., Meese, E., Schwarz, A., Tholey, A., Zink, A., and Keller, A. 2013. Paleoproteomic study of the Iceman's brain tissue. *Cellular and Molecular Life Sciences* 70 (19):3709–3722.

Malainey, M. E. 2011. Blood and protein residue analysis. In: Malainey, M. E. (ed.) *A Consumer's Guide to Archaeological Science*. Manuals in Archaeological Method, Theory and Technique, pp. 219–236. Springer New York.

Mann, K. and Mann, M. 2013. The proteome of the calcified layer organic matrix of turkey (Meleagris gallopavo) eggshell. *Proteome Science* 11(1):40.

Frei, K. M., Mannering, U., Kristiansen, K., Allentoft, M. E., Wilson, A. S., Skals, I., Tridico, S., Nosch, M. L., Willerslev, E., Clarke, L., and Frei, R. 2015. Tracing the dynamic life story of a Bronze Age female. *Scientific Reports* 5:10431.

Mazel, V., Richardin, P., Debois, D., Touboul, D., Cotte, M., Brunelle, A., Walter, P., and Laprevote, O. 2007. Identification of ritual blood in African artifacts using TOF-SIMS and synchrotron radiation microspectroscopies. *Analytical Chemistry* 79 (24):9253–9260.

Moini, M., Klauenberg, K., and Ballard, M. 2011. Dating silk by capillary electrophoresis mass spectrometry. *Analytical Chemistry* 83(19):7577–7581.

Nielsen-Marsh, C. M., Ostrom, P. H., Gandhi, H., Shapiro, B., Cooper, A., Hauschka, P. V., and Collins, M. J. 2002. Sequence preservation of osteocalcin protein and mitochondrial DNA in bison bones older than 55 ka. *Geology* 30(12):1099–1102.

Nielsen-Marsh, C. M., Richards, M. P., Hauschka, P. V., Thomas-Oates, J. E., Trinkaus, E., Pettitt, P. B., Karavanic, I., Poinar, H., and Collins, M. J. 2005. Osteocalcin protein sequences of Neanderthals and modern primates. *Proceedings of the National Academy of Sciences of the United States of America* 102(12):4409–4413.

O'Connor, S., Solazzo, C., and Collins, M. 2015. Advances in identifying archaeological traces of horn and other keratinous hard tissues. *Studies in Conservation* 60(6):393–417.

Orlando, L., Ginolhac, A., Zhang, G. J., Froese, D., Albrechtsen, A., Stiller, M., Schubert, M., Cappellini, E., Petersen, B., Moltke, I., Johnson, P. L. F., Fumagalli, M., Vilstrup, J. T.,

Raghavan, M., Korneliussen, T., Malaspinas, A. S., Vogt, J., Szklarczyk, D., Kelstrup, C. D., Vinther, J., Dolocan, A., Stenderup, J., Velazquez, A. M. V., Cahill, J., Rasmussen, M., Wang, X. L., Min, J. M., Zazula, G. D., Seguin-Orlando, A., Mortensen, C., Magnussen, K., Thompson, J. F., Weinstock, J., Gregersen, K., Roed, K. H., Eisenmann, V., Rubin, C. J., Miller, D. C., Antczak, D. F., Bertelsen, M. F., Brunak, S., Al-Rasheid, K. a. S., Ryder, O., Andersson, L., Mundy, J., Krogh, A., Gilbert, M. T. P., Kjaer, K., Sicheritz-Ponten, T., Jensen, L. J., Olsen, J. V., Hofreiter, M., Nielsen, R., Shapiro, B., Wang, J., and Willerslev, E. 2013. Recalibrating Equus evolution using the genome sequence of an early Middle Pleistocene horse. *Nature* 499(7456):74–78.

Ostrom, P. H., Schall, M., Gandhi, H., Shen, T. L., Hauschka, P. V., Strahler, J. R., and Gage, D. A. 2000. New strategies for characterizing ancient proteins using matrix-assisted laser desorption ionization mass spectrometry. *Geochimica et Cosmochimica Acta* 64 (6):1043–1050.

Palmqvist, P., Grokke, D. R., Arribas, A., and Farina, R. A. 2003. Paleoecological reconstruction of a lower Pleistocene large mammal community using biogeochemical (δ13C, δ15N, δ18O, Sr: Zn) and ecomorphological approaches. *Paleobiology* 29(2):205–229.

Penkman, K. E. H., Kaufman, D. S., Maddy, D., and Collins, M. J. 2008. Closed-system behaviour of the intra-crystalline fraction of amino acids in mollusc shells. *Quaternary Geochronology* 3(1–2)2–25.

Penkman, K. E. H., Preece, R. C., Bridgland, D. R., Keen, D. H., Meijer, T., Parfitt, S. A., White, T. S., and Collins, M. J. 2013. An aminostratigraphy for the British Quaternary based on Bithynia opercula. *Quaternary Science Reviews* 61(C):111–134.

Peris-Vicente, J., Simo-Alfonso, E., Adelantado, J. V. G., and Carbo, M. T. D. 2005. Direct infusion mass spectrometry as a fingerprint of protein-binding media used in works of art. *Rapid Communications in Mass Spectrometry* 19(23):3463–3467.

Pevzner, P. A., Kim, S., and Ng, J. 2008. Comment on "Protein sequences from mastodon and Tyrannosaurus rex revealed by mass spectrometry." *Science* 321(5892):1040.

Potter, B. A., Reuther, J. D., Lowenstein, J. M., and Scheuenstuhl, G. 2010. Assessing the reliability of pRIA for identifying ancient proteins from archaeological contexts. *Journal of Archaeological Science* 37(5):910–918.

Rao, H. Y., Li, B., Yang, Y. M., Ma, Q. L., and Wang, C. S. 2015. Proteomic identification of organic additives in the mortars of ancient Chinese wooden buildings. *Analytical Methods* 7(1):143–149.

Rasmussen, M., Li, Y. R., Lindgreen, S., Pedersen, J. S., Albrechtsen, A., Moltke, I., Metspalu, M., Metspalu, E., Kivisild, T., Gupta, R., Bertalan, M., Nielsen, K., Gilbert, M. T. P., Wang, Y., Raghavan, M., Campos, P. F., Kamp, H. M., Wilson, A. S., Gledhill, A., Tridico, S., Bunce, M., Lorenzen, E. D., Binladen, J., Guo, X. S., Zhao, J., Zhang, X. Q., Zhang, H., Li, Z., Chen, M. F., Orlando, L., Kristiansen, K., Bak, M., Tommerup, N., Bendixen, C., Pierre, T. L., Gronnow, B., Meldgaard, M., Andreasen, C., Fedorova, S. A., Osipova, L. P., Higham, T. F. G., Ramsey, C. B., Hansen, T. V. O., Nielsen, F. C., Crawford, M. H., Brunak, S., Sicheritz-Ponten, T., Villems, R., Nielsen, R., Krogh, A.,

Wang, J., and Willerslev, E. 2010. Ancient human genome sequence of an extinct Palaeo-Eskimo. *Nature* 463(7282):757–762.

Rasmussen, K. L., Tenorio, A. L., Bonaduce, I., Colombini, M. P., Birolo, L., Galano, E., Amoresano, A., Doudna, G., Bond, A. D., Palleschi, V., Lorenzetti, G., Legnaioli, S., Van Der Plicht, J., and Gunneweg, J. 2012. The constituents of the ink from a Qumran inkwell: New prospects for provenancing the ink on the Dead Sea Scrolls. *Journal of Archaeological Science* 39(9):2956–2968.

Remington, S. J. 1994. Identifying species of origin from prehistoric blood residues. *Science* 266(5183):298–300.

Richter, K. K., Wilson, J., Jones, A. K. G., Buckley, M., van Doorn, N., and Collins, M. J. 2011. Fish'n chips: ZooMS peptide mass fingerprinting in a 96 well plate format to identify fish bone fragments. *Journal of Archaeological Science*, 38(7):1502–1510.

Rybczynski, N., Gosse, J. C., Harington, C. R., Wogelius, R. A., Hidy, A. J., and Buckley, M. 2013. Mid-Pliocene warm-period deposits in the high Arctic yield insight into camel evolution. *Nature Communications* 4:1550.

Sawafuji, R., Cappellini, E., Nagaoka, T., Fotakis, A. K., Jersie-Christensen, R. R., Olsen, J. V., Hirata, K., and Ueda, S. 2017. Proteomic profiling of archaeological human bone. *Royal Society Open Science* 4(6):161004.

Schmidt-Schultz, T. H. and Schultz, M. 2007. Well preserved non-collagenous extracellular matrix proteins in ancient human bone and teeth. *International Journal of Osteoarchaeology* 17(1):91–99.

Schroeter, E. R. and Cleland, T. P. 2016. Glutamine deamidation: An indicator of antiquity, or preservational quality? *Rapid Communications in Mass Spectrometry* 30 (2):251–255.

Schweitzer, M. H., Zheng, W. X., Organ, C. L., Avci, R., Suo, Z. Y., Freimark, L. M., Lebleu, V. S., Duncan, M. B., Heiden, M. G. V., Neveu, J. M., Lane, W. S., Cottrell, J. S., Horner, J. R., Cantley, L. C., Kalluri, R., and Asara, J. M. 2009. Biomolecular characterization and protein sequences of the Campanian hadrosaur B. canadensis. *Science* 324(5927):626–631.

Shevchenko, A., Yang, Y. M., Knaust, A., Thomas, H., Jiang, H. E., Lu, E. G., Wang, C. S., and Shevchenko, A. 2014. Proteomics identifies the composition and manufacturing recipe of the 2500-year-old sourdough bread from Subeixi cemetery in China. *Journal of Proteomics* 105:363–371.

Shewry, P. R., Kirkman, M. A., Burgess, S. R., Festenstein, G. N., and Miflin, B. J. 1982. A comparison of the protein and amino acid composition of old and recent barley grain. *The New Phytologist* 90(3):455–466.

Smith, P. R. and Wilson, M. T. 1992. Blood residues on ancient tool surfaces: A cautionary note. *Journal of Archaeological Science* 19(3):237–241.

Solazzo, C., Clerens, S., Plowman, J. E., Wilson, J., Peacock, E. E., and Dyer, J. M. 2015. Application of redox proteomics to the study of oxidative degradation products in archaeological wool. *Journal of Cultural Heritage* 16:896–903.

Solazzo, C., Dyer, J. M., Clerens, S., Plowman, J., Peacock, E. E., and Collins, M. J. 2013a. Proteomic evaluation of the biodegradation of wool fabrics in experimental burials. *International Biodeterioration and Biodegradation* 80:48–59.

Solazzo, C., Dyer, J. M., Deb-Choudhury, S., Clerens, S., and Wyeth, P. 2012. Proteomic profiling of the photo-oxidation of silk fibroin: Implications for historic tin-weighted silk. *Photochemistry and Photobiology* 88(5):1217–1226.

Solazzo, C., Fitzhugh, W. W., Rolando, C., and Tokarski, C. 2008. Identification of protein remains in archaeological potsherds by proteomics. *Analytical Chemistry* 80(12):4590–4597.

Solazzo, C., Heald, S., Ballard, M. W., Ashford, D. A., Depriest, P. T., Koestler, R. J., and Collins, M. J. 2011. Proteomics and Coast Salish blankets: A tale of shaggy dogs? *Antiquity* 85(330):1418–1432.

Solazzo, C., Wadsley, M., Dyer, J. M., Clerens, S., Collins, M. J., and Plowman, J. 2013b. Characterisation of novel α-keratin peptide markers for species identification in keratinous tissues using mass spectrometry. *Rapid Communications in Mass Spectrometry* 27(23):2685–2698.

Solazzo, C., Wadsley, M., Dyer, J. M., Clerens, S., Collins, M. J., and Plowman, J. 2014. Modeling deamidation in sheep α-keratin peptides and application to archeological wool textiles. *Analytical Chemistry* 86(1):567–575.

Steele, T. E. 2015. The contributions of animal bones from archaeological sites: The past and future of zooarchaeology. *Journal of Archaeological Science* 56:168–176.

Stewart, J. R. M., Allen, R. B., Jones, A. K. G., Kendall, T., Penkman, K. E. H., Demarchi, B., O'connor, T., and Collins, M. J. 2013. ZooMS: Making eggshell visible in the archaeological record. *Journal of Archaeological Science* 40(4):1797–1804.

Stewart, J. R. M., Allen, R. B., Jones, A. K. G., Kendall, T., Penkman, K. E. H., Demarchi, B., O'Connor, T., and Collins, M. J. 2014. Walking on eggshells: A study of egg use in Anglo-Scandinavian York based on eggshell identification using ZooMS. *International Journal of Osteoarchaeology* 24(3):247–255.

Sykes, N., 2014. *Beastly Questions: Animal Answers to Archaeological Issues.* London: Bloomsbury Academic.

Terwilliger, T. C. and Clarke, S. 1981. Methylation of membrane proteins in human erythrocytes. Identification and characterization of polypeptides methylated in lysed cells. *The Journal of Biological Chemistry* 256(6):3067–3076.

Tokarski, C., Martin, E., Rolando, C., and Cren-Olive, C. 2006. Identification of proteins in renaissance paintings by proteomics. *Analytical Chemistry* 78(5):1494–1502.

Towe, K. M. 1972. Collagen-like structures in Ordovician graptolite periderm. *Nature* 237:443–445.

Tran, T. N. N., Aboudharam, G., Gardeisen, A., Davoust, B., Bocquet-Appel, J. P., Flaudrops, C., Belghazi, M., Raoult, D., and Drancourt, M. 2011. Classification of ancient mammal individuals using dental pulp MALDI-TOF MS peptide profiling. *PLoS One* 6(2):e17319.

Tuross, N., Barnes, I., and Potts, R. 1996. Protein identification of blood residues on experimental stone tools. *Journal of Archaeological Science* 23(2):289–296.

Toniolo, L., D'amato, A., Saccenti, R., Gulotta, D., and Righetti, P. G. 2012. The Silk Road, Marco Polo, a Bible and its proteome: A detective story. *Journal of Proteomics* 75 (11):3365–3373.

Vaiglova, P., Bogaard, A., Collins, M., Cavanagh, W., Mee, C., Renard, J., Lamb, A., Gardeisen, A., and Fraser, R. 2014. An integrated stable isotope study of plants and animals from Kouphovouno, southern Greece: A new look at Neolithic farming. *Journal of Archaeological Science* 42:201–215.

Vanden Berghe, I. 2012. Towards an early warning system for oxidative degradation of protein fibres in historical tapestries by means of calibrated amino acid analysis. *Journal of Archaeological Science* 39(5):1349–1359.

Van Der Sluis, L. G., Hollund, H. I., Buckley, M., De Louw, P. G. B., Rijsdijk, K. F., and Kars, H. 2014. Combining histology, stable isotope analysis and ZooMS collagen fingerprinting to investigate the taphonomic history and dietary behaviour of extinct giant tortoises from the Mare aux Songes deposit on Mauritius. *Palaeogeography, Palaeoclimatology, Palaeoecology* 416:80–91.

van Der Werf, I. D., Calvano, C. D., Palmisano, F., and Sabbatini, L. 2012. A simple protocol for Matrix Assisted Laser Desorption Ionization-time of flight-mass spectrometry (MALDI-TOF-MS) analysis of lipids and proteins in single microsamples of paintings. *Analytica Chimica Acta* 718:1–10.

van Doorn, N. L. 2014. Zooarchaeology by Mass Spectrometry (ZooMS). In: *Encyclopedia of Global Archaeology*, pp. 7998–8000. New York: Springer.

van Doorn, N. L., Wilson, J., Hollund, H., Soressi, M., and Collins, M. J. 2012. Site-specific deamidation of glutamine: A new marker of bone collagen deterioration. *Rapid Communications in Mass Spectrometry* 26:2319–2327.

von Holstein, I. C. C., Ashby, S. P., van Doorn, N. L., Sachs, S. M., Buckley, M., Meiri, M., Barnes, I., Brundle, A., and Collins, M. J. 2014. Searching for Scandinavians in pre-Viking Scotland: Molecular fingerprinting of Early Medieval combs. *Journal of Archaeological Science* 41:1–6.

Wadsworth, C. and Buckley, M. 2014. Proteome degradation in fossils: Investigating the longevity of protein survival in ancient bone. *Rapid Communications in Mass Spectrometry* 28(6):605–615.

Wang, S.-Y., Cappellini, E., and Zhang, H.-Y. 2012. Why collagens best survived in fossils? Clues from amino acid thermal stability. *Biochemical and Biophysical Research Communications* 422(1):5–7.

Warinner, C., Hendy, J., Speller, C., Cappellini, E., Fischer, R., Trachsel, C., Arneborg, J., Lynnerup, N., Craig, O. E., Swallow, D. M., Fotakis, A., Christensen, R. J., Olsen, J. V., Liebert, A., Montalva, N., Fiddyment, S., Charlton, S., Mackie, M., Canci, A., Bouwman, A., Ruhli, F., Gilbert, M. T. P., and Collins, M. J. 2014a. Direct evidence of milk consumption from ancient human dental calculus. *Scientific Reports* 4:7104.

Warinner, C., Rodrigues, J. F. M., Vyas, R., Trachsel, C., Shved, N., Grossmann, J., Radini, A., Hancock, Y., Tito, R. Y., Fiddyment, S., Speller, C., Hendy, J., Charlton, S.,

Luder, H. U., Salazar-Garcia, D. C., Eppler, E., Seiler, R., Hansen, L. H., Castruita, J. a. S., Barkow-Oesterreicher, S., Teoh, K. Y., Kelstrup, C. D., Olsen, J. V., Nanni, P., Kawai, T., Willerslev, E., Von Mering, C., Lewis, C. M., Collins, M. J., Gilbert, M. T. P., Ruhli, F., and Cappellini, E. 2014b. Pathogens and host immunity in the ancient human oral cavity. *Nature Genetics* 46(4):336–344.

Welker, F., Collins, M. J., Thomas, J. A., Wadsley, M., Brace, S., Cappellini, E., Turvey, S. T., Reguero, M., Gelfo, J. N., Kramarz, A., Burger, J., Thomas-Oates, J., Ashford, D. A., Ashton, P. D., Rowsell, K., Porter, D. M., Kessler, B., Fischer, R., Baessmann, C., Kaspar, S., Olsen, J. V., Kiley, P., Elliott, J. A., Kelstrup, C. D., Mullin, V., Hofreiter, M., Willerslev, E., Hublin, J. J., Orlando, L., Barnes, I., and Macphee, R. D. E. 2015a. Ancient proteins resolve the evolutionary history of Darwin's South American ungulates. *Nature* 522(7554):81–84.

Welker, F., Soressi, M., Rendu, W., Hublin, J. J., and Collins, M. 2015b. Using ZooMS to identify fragmentary bone from the Late Middle/Early Upper Palaeolithic sequence of Les Cottés, France. *Journal of Archaeological Science* 54:279–286.

Whiteaker, J. R., Zhao, L., Zhang, H. Y., Feng, L. C., Piening, B. D., Anderson, L., and Paulovich, A. G. 2007. Antibody-based enrichment of peptides on magnetic beads for mass-spectrometry-based quantification of serum biomarkers. *Analytical Biochemistry* 362(1):44–54.

Wilson, A. S., Brown, E. L., Villa, C., Lynnerup, N., Healey, A., Ceruti, M. C., Reinhard, J., Previgliano, C. H., Araoz, F. A., Diez, J. G., and Taylor, T. 2013. Archaeological, radiological, and biological evidence offer insight into Inca child sacrifice. *Proceedings of the National Academy of Sciences of the United States of America* 110(33):13322–13327.

Wilson, J., van Doorn, N. L., and Collins, M. J. 2012. Assessing the extent of bone degradation using glutamine deamidation in collagen. *Analytical Chemistry* 84(21):9041–9048.

Yamashita, M. and Fenn, J. B. 1984. Electrospray ion source. Another variation on the free-jet theme. *The Journal of Physical Chemistry* 88(20):4451–4459.

Yan, H. T., An, J. J., Zhou, T., Xia, Y., and Rong, B. 2014. Identification of proteinaceous binding media for the polychrome terracotta army of Emperor Qin Shihuang by MALDI-TOF-MS. *Chinese Science Bulletin = Kexue tongbao* 59(21):2574–2581.

Yang, Y. M., Shevchenko, A., Knaust, A., Abuduresule, I., Li, W. Y., Hu, X. J., Wang, C. S., and Shevchenko, A. 2014. Proteomics evidence for kefir dairy in Early Bronze Age China. *Journal of Archaeological Science* 45:178–186.

Zhu, Z. Y., Chen, H. F., Li, L., Gong, D. C., Gao, X., Yang, J. C., Zhao, X. C., and Ji, K. Z. 2014. Biomass spectrometry identification of the fibre material in the pall imprint excavated from Grave M1, Peng-state Cemetery, Shanxi, China. *Archaeometry* 56(4):681–688.

4

Residue Analysis

Oliver E. Craig, Hayley Saul, and Cynthianne Spiteri

The extraction and characterisation of organic residues that survive on archaeological artefacts and in archaeological contexts.

1 INTRODUCTION AND THEORETICAL BACKGROUND

Residue analysis, as used in archaeology, is a generic term used to describe the characterisation of traces of organic products from the past. This chapter is concerned with organic residues that are commonly encountered bound to, adhered to or absorbed within a mineral artefact, such as a ceramic vessel or a stone tool. Methods of analysis are varied and range from microscopic identification of remnant tissue fragments to chemical and structural analysis of the major classes of biomolecules, such as lipids, proteins and DNA. This chapter aims to provide the reader with a broad overview of the composition of residues associated with artefacts, their formation and preservation, the principal methods of analysis and to demonstrate the impact that this field has made for understanding the use of artefacts in the past. For more detailed overviews of the occurrence and analysis of specific biomolecules in archaeology, readers are directed to Evershed et al. (2001), Evershed (2008a) and Pollard and Heron (2008) for lipids; Hendy et al. (Chapter 3) for proteins; and Loog and Larson (Chapter 2) for DNA. Evershed et al. (2001), Pollard and Heron (2008), Colombini and Modugno (2009) and Regert (2011) also provide a comprehensive description of lipid residue analysis of artefacts.

Why Study Residues?

First and foremost, the analysis of organic residues associated with an archaeological artefact provides direct evidence for the use of that artefact. Thus whilst the identification of organic materials, attributable say to a particular foodstuff, may help our understanding of food procurement strategies and even diet, the principal inference relates to the artefact's use and its technological function. This point is crucial when assessing the archaeological implications of residue analysis studies and highlights the need for closely integrating residue analysis with other forms of artefact analysis.

2 WHICH ARTEFACTS PRODUCE RESIDUES?

Residues may be found on any inorganic artefact, such as stone or metallic tools or ceramic or glass vessels that have come into contact with an organic substance, be it a plant or animal tissue, or a transformed natural product such as a resin or tar. Factors that affect residue formation are:

1. Physical properties of the artefact (porosity, surface area, mineral composition)
2. Physical and chemical properties of the organic component (e.g., solid, liquid, size, hardness)
3. Mode of contact between artefact and organic component (time, temperature, pressure applied, repetition of contact)

Variability in the factors listed above is reflected by the myriad of ways that artefacts may have been used in the past. This severely limits our ability to securely identify artefacts that routinely produce residues. However, some general principles can be followed. For example, it is reasonable to assume that an unglazed pot used repeatedly to stew meat over many years is likely to accumulate a greater organic residue than a wine glass used once or twice. Note here it is not only the length of use that is important but also the difference in the porosity of the mineral surfaces, as well as the composition of the material processed and the probability of it leaving a residue. As we shall see, past studies have tended to focus on unglazed ceramic vessels, whereas residue analysis of less porous glass and metallic artefacts has received comparatively little attention (see Table 4.1). It is noteworthy that the large number of analyses carried out on nonporous cryptocrystalline lithic tools (Table 4.1), thought to be used for hunting and butchery, are disproportional to their expected ability to produce residues.

Table 4.1 *A list of selected published reports of the occurrence of residues on archaeological artefacts.*

Type of Artefact	Type of Residues Detected	Reference
Visible Residues		
Ceramic vessels	Phytoliths, starches	Lusteck and Thompson 2007; Saul et al., 2012, 2013; Zarrillo et al. 2008
Stone tools	Phytoliths, starches, blood, muscle tissue	Chandler Ezell 2006; Kealhofer et al. 1999; Loy 1983, 1993;
Bone tools	Starch	Hardy et al. 2009
Lipids		
Ceramic vessels	Fatty acids, cholesterol, phytosterols; wax esters, mono-, di- and triacylglycerols, terpenoids, *n*-alkanes, ketones, *n*-alcohols, isoprenoids, ω-(-*o*-alkylphenyl) alkanoic acids, dicarboxylic acids, hydroxy acids	Charters et al. 1993a,b; Charters et al. 1995; Craig et al. 2011; Cramp et al. 2014; Dunne et al. 2012; Evershed et al. 1991; Evershed 2008a,b; Evershed et al. 2008a; Gregg et al. 2009; Guasch-Jané et al. 2004; Hansel et al. 2004; Hansel and Evershed 2009; Heron et al. 2013; McGovern et al. 2013; Mirabaud et al. 2007; Raven et al. 1997; Reber and Evershed 2004; Regert et al. 1998; Salque et al. 2013; Stern et al. 2008
Stone	Fatty acids, diterpnoids, triterpenoids	Buonasera 2007; Colombini et al. 2009
Glass vessels	Fatty acids, hydroxy-acids, *n*-alkanols, alkandiols, *n*-alkanes, long-chain monoesters, phytosterols, diterpenoid acids, α, ω -dicarboxylic acids, hydroxycarboxylic fatty acids	Ribechini 2008a,b
Metal vessels	Fatty acids, triterpenoids	Dudd and Evershed 1999; Evershed et al. 2004

Table 4.1 (*cont.*)

Type of Artefact	Type of Residues Detected	Reference
Proteins		
Ceramics	bovine caseins, human myoglobins, seal myoglobins	Barnard et al. 2007; Craig et al., 2000, 2003; Solazzo et al. 2008
Stone tools	blood 'proteins' (haemoglobins)	Loy and Dixon 1998; Loy 1983, 1993; Newman and Julig 1989; Newman et al. 1996
DNA		
Ceramics	Yeast ribosomal DNA, chloroplast DNA	Cavalieri et al. 2003; Hansson and Foley 2008
Stone tools	Mammalian mitochondrial DNA	Hardy et al. 1997; Shanks et al. 2005

3 WHAT ARE ARCHAEOLOGICAL RESIDUES COMPOSED OF?

The composition of a residue reflects the original organic component that was bound, absorbed or adhered to the artefact during the artefact's use-life and any changes that occurred after its last use. The latter includes the intentional physical removal of residues prior to deposition, post-depositional physical, microbial and chemical degradation of organic matter and the leaching of components in the burial environment. Residues are therefore complex mixtures; potentially they can be formed from a range of different uses and modified by a range of different post-use processes.

The composition of an organic residue can also be classified on a range of nested scales from the preservation of whole organisms (e.g., microorganisms), to tissues (e.g., muscle, connective tissue), to cells (e.g., plant epidermis, mammalian blood cells), to macromolecules (e.g., starch or collagen), to biomolecules (e.g., fatty acids or amino acids) and finally to elements (e.g., carbon, oxygen). However, extensive degradation of organic residues that occurs through use and during exposure to the post-depositional environment, usually limits survival to the macromolecular level at best. Therefore, most studies have focused on characterising the degradation products of intact lipids and proteins (i.e., at the biomolecular level).

Residue composition is also governed by the mechanism of stabilisation/preservation, of which a distinction can be made between surface deposits and absorbed residues. Surface deposits reflect accumulations of organic residues that have built up on the surface of an artefact but are not necessarily closely associated or protected by the mineral surface itself. They are usually visible and often charred. Absorbed residues are not usually visible and have either accumulated directly on the mineral surface or have accumulated within the artefact's accessible internal volume (e.g., pores, micro-cracks). Both types of residues preserve biomolecules; however, the limited number of studies aimed at classifying tissue or cell structures have only focused on visible surface residues (Table 4.1).

4 THE PRESERVATION OF BIOMOLECULES IN ORGANIC RESIDUES

Lipids

The majority of organic residue studies, including nearly all the work on residue analysis of ceramics, has focused on the characterisation of lipids, that is, fats, oils and waxes. Lipids are more robust and less soluble in water than most other biomolecules. They are abundant in a diverse range of foodstuffs and natural products, and are readily absorbed or bound to mineral surfaces through a wide range of activities. For example, experimental studies have shown that appreciable amounts of lipids (ca. 20 mg g^{-1}) were transferred to the interior rim of an unglazed ceramic vessel used to boil lamb (Evershed 2008b). This value is probably close to the lipid capacity of potsherds and substantially greater than the capacity of other artefacts with less porous fabrics and smaller surface areas (such as glass or metallic implements). Lipids have been recovered from a wide range of archaeological artefacts (Table 4.1), but at much lower concentrations than their capacity, indicating that a substantial proportion is lost during burial; for example, the mean value recovered from archaeological potsherds is ca. 0.1 mg g^{-1} (e.g., Evershed et al. 2008a).

Lipids become modified during degradation. The most common lipid class that has been studied are fatty acids, a name given to a range of compounds with a hydrocarbon chain and a terminal carboxyl group. Fatty acids are commonly found free or esterified to glycerol, as triacylglycerols (TAGs), in a wide range of animal fats and plant oils. Whilst intact TAGs are sometimes found in residues, they readily decompose through chemical and microbial processes (Dudd et al. 1998;

Evershed 2008a). Decomposition products include diacylglycerols (DAGs), monoacylglycerols (MAGs) and free fatty acids. The latter are the most commonly encountered and studied lipids associated with archaeological artefacts. Fatty acids are more soluble than their parent acyl lipids (TAGs, DAGs, MAGs), and are eventually lost through exposure to the burial environment. Other changes to the distribution of fatty acids can also occur. Most notably, oxidation of any carbon double bonds in the hydrocarbon chain leads to a relative increase in the loss of unsaturated acids over saturated acids. Several experiments have been carried out to study these degradation processes, a synthesis of which can be found in Evershed (2008b). Nevertheless, fatty acids have the potential to survive many thousands of years, for example, saturated fatty acids have been recovered from the interior of 15,000-year-old ceramic vessels (Craig et al. 2013), allowing further characterisation. Many other classes of lipids are also commonly recovered from artefacts. These include sterols, alkanes, alcohols, ketones and wax esters.

Proteins

Although they hold more information, proteins degrade more easily and are generally more soluble than lipids. The peptide bond is readily hydrolysed, and amino acid side chains become damaged (e.g., deamidation) or modified (e.g., glycation). Proteins are also particularly susceptible to hydrolysis by bacterial proteases; enzymes that are abundant in soils and sediments. The general mechanisms for survival are akin to those described for bone (e.g., Collins et al. 2002). As with bone, the survival of protein on artefacts is reliant on close association with a mineral surface, in this case the artefact itself. This is achieved either through direct bonding (Craig and Collins 2002) or through encapsulation in the porous structure that may exclude large bacterial enzymes. Another potential mechanism of protein preservation is polymerisation with other biomolecules, such as lipids and sugars. Condensation reactions (browning or Maillard reactions) that link sugars and proteins are known to occur through many methods of food preparation (Nursten 2005). Protein polymerisation during use will increase and tend to lead to a less soluble and a more recalcitrant residue capable of surviving for many thousands of years (Collins et al. 1992). However, all mechanisms of survival come at a price, such as irreversible damage or modification to the intact protein. Loss of protein quaternary and tertiary structure should be anticipated by all residue analysts and methods need to be targeted at the recovery of modified peptides. Furthermore, one of the major challenges facing this field is to develop methods to effectively extract highly polymerised or tightly bound proteinaceous materials from artefacts (Craig and Collins 2000; Craig and Collins 2002). Table 4.1 lists the types of artefacts that have been subjected to protein residue analysis.

DNA

The extraction of DNA from archaeological residues has only rarely been attempted (Table 4.1). DNA is highly susceptible to degradation, even more so than proteins. Paradoxically, DNA is the most informative biomolecule and offers the greatest potential for residue identification. The mechanism for DNA survival in organic residues is poorly understood but may share many features in common with proteins, as described above.

5 DESCRIPTION OF EQUIPMENT USED

The strategy for organic residue analysis invariably involves the extraction of organic matter from the artefact. Molecules in the extract are then usually separated and characterised structurally, isotopically or distributions of molecules are compared to provide a 'chemical fingerprint'. An obvious drawback of this approach is that only the 'extractable' portion of the residue is analysed, with the potential loss of information. Methods for analysing the entire residues are able to get around this and have been widely applied to organic rich surface deposits and involve combusting the samples and identifying the molecule or atoms that are released by mass spectrometry. These include bulk isotope ratio mass spectrometry (EA-IRMS) to determine the stable isotope ratios of carbon and nitrogen atoms (e.g., Craig et al. 2007; McGovern et al. 2004; Morton and Schwarcz 2004), pyrolysis mass spectrometry (PyMS) (Asperger et al. 1999; Beverly et al. 1995; Buckley et al. 1999; Buckley ct al. 2014; Hardy ct al. 2012; Hardy ct al. 2015; Jones et al. 2014; Oudemans and Boon 1991) and direct temperature resolved mass spectrometry (DTMS; Oudemans et al. 2007b). Fourier transform infrared spectroscopy (FTIR) and nuclear magnetic resonance (NMR) spectroscopy have also been used to provide chemical fingerprints of residue in their solid state (Oudemans et al. 2007a). As organic residues are complex mixtures of different biomolecules in various states of decay, the data obtained by these techniques broadly classifies residues, either by their chemical

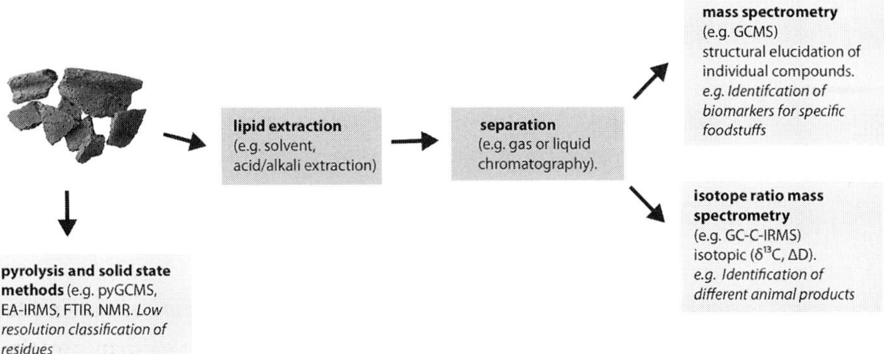

FIGURE 4.1 Schematic diagram of methodological approaches taken for the identification of organic residues associated with archaeological pottery.

composition (e.g., to identify lipid, protein or carbohydrate markers), or isotopic composition (to identify carbon from C_4 plants or marine animals). They are generally not suitable to identify more specific biomarkers. As such they are useful tools for screening samples prior to more lengthy methods that require extraction.

Lipid Analysis

Methods for lipid analysis are well established and equally well described in the literature (Evershed et al. 1990; Evershed et al. 1999; Evershed et al. 2001; Pollard and Heron 2008; Pollard et al. 2007; Regert 2011). Figure 4.1 shows a schematic diagram of the approach. Lipids are usually extracted from powdered samples with a mixture of organic solvents (e.g., dichloromethane and methanol). More severe acid and alkali extractions (e.g., Correa-Ascencio and Evershed 2014; Regert et al. 1998) have also been used to recover more tightly bound lipids. Lipids are separated on capillary columns by gas chromatography (GC) and identified by mass spectrometry (MS). In GC, volatile components of samples are partitioned between a mobile (carrier gas) and a stationary liquid phase bonded onto the inside of the column, and separation depends on how these components interact with the two phases. Structural information about individual molecules is obtained by combining the GC with an MS detector, which is useful for the identification of complex samples. GC and GC-MS allow the analysis of intact lipids with a wide range of molecular weights (Evershed 1992). High temperature GC-MS (HT-GCMS) is used to identify high molecular weight (intact) lipids such as triacylglycerols (TAGs) and wax esters (Evershed et al. 1990). Arrays of TAGs can also be further resolved using liquid chromatography MS (LC-MS) (Guasch-Jané et al. 2004), GC chemical ionisation-MS (CI-MS; Aichholz and Lorbeer 2000), or electrospray ionisation-MS (ESI-MS; Mirabaud et al., 2007; Regert et al. 2003). Stable isotope analysis of lower molecular weight compounds is achieved by a method known as gas chromatography combustion isotope ratio mass spectrometry (GC-c-IRMS). Here, individual compounds are separated by GC, combusted individually to produce CO_2, which is then passed into an IRMS to measure the carbon isotope ratio (i.e., $^{13}C/^{12}C$) (see Evershed et al. 1994, and Meier-Augenstein 2002 for review). Examples of how this technique has been applied to archaeology are given below.

Protein Extraction, Separation and Analysis

Despite the widespread application of protein residue analysis, particularly applied to the analysis of 'blood' residues on stone tools (Table 4.1), there has been no consensus on the most effective extraction method and a wide range of techniques have been used (see Craig and Collins 2002). A range of immunological methods have been widely applied in protein residue analysis (Table 4.1). A major and important goal of these studies has been to identify the species of blood serum proteins on lithic artefacts (e.g., Hogberg et al. 2009; Loy and Hardy 1992; Newman and Julig 1989; Newman et al. 1996; Nolin et al. 1994; Shanks et al. 1999). Exact methodologies have varied but more recently the cross-over immunoelectrophoresis method of Newman and Julig (1989) has been preferred (Hogberg et al. 2009; Shanks et al. 1999). This relies on the specificity of commercial anti-sera, which contain a series of (polyclonal) antibodies, each of which will recognise structural features of blood proteins (known as antigens) from a particular species of animal. Residue extracts are migrated against a range of these anti-sera by gel-electrophoresis, if any antigens specific for the anti sera are present in the extract they will precipitate in the gel allowing identification. For example, Hogberg tested extracts from a range of Early Neolithic Scandinavian stone tools against anti-sera raised against 27 different types of animal, including 10 fish (2009). They found that several stone tool extracts reacted against the fish anti-sera but not the other animal species. A major criticism of this approach is lack of specificity, as anti-sera can cross-react with antigens from a range of related species and also against a range of totally unrelated degraded protein (Tuross et al. 1996). Coupled with the finding that immunologically blood residues are lost incredibly quickly from stone tools during burial (Cattaneo et al. 1993) the field of blood residue analysis of stone tools has been left lacking any serious credibility.

Further immunological work has targeted proteins on ceramics using more specific monoclonal antibodies raised against degraded proteins and thoroughly tested for cross-reactivity (Craig et al. 2000; Craig and Collins 2002; Evershed and Tuross 1996). Whilst this approach has had some success, the use of expensive immunological reagents, which have a limited ability to detect all but the specific antigens they were designed to target, has largely been overtaken by approaches using protein mass spectrometry (Barnard et al. 2007; Hendy et al. in Chapter 3; Solazzo et al. 2008). This approach has the clear advantage of theoretically being able to sequence all the proteins in the extract, including degraded protein and shorter peptides. Extraction of proteins, especially mineral-bound protein, still remains a challenge and new methods, which aim to directly analyse mineral bound protein by mass spectrometry, perhaps hold the answer (Heaton et al. 2009).

DNA Extraction and Analysis

The study of DNA in organic residues has received only scant attention (Table 4.1), and, considering the fragility of this molecule, perhaps rightly so. Nevertheless, the occurrence of ancient DNA in sediments (e.g., Willerslev et al. 2003) suggests that investigations of artefacts from exceptionally well preserved deposits may be possible. Methods of analysis are not well developed and have involved simple extraction with guanidinium chloride (Hardy et al. 1997) or ammonia (Shanks et al. 2005) followed by PCR amplification of mitochondrial sequences containing species-specific polymorphisms. Further challenges will involve optimizing the extraction and purification of DNA from highly degraded bound organic matter and ruling out contamination of exogenous DNA moving through the burial environment. Previous studies that have claimed to have amplified mitochondrial DNA by PCR from a range of middle Palaeolithic stone tools (Hardy et al. 1997) need to be independently replicated. Similar criticisms may also be levelled at more modest claims using essentially the same approach (e.g., Hansson and Foley 2008; Shanks et al. 2005) even though serious attempts to consider mechanisms for preservation and contamination have been made (e.g., Shanks et al. 2001; Shanks et al. 2004).

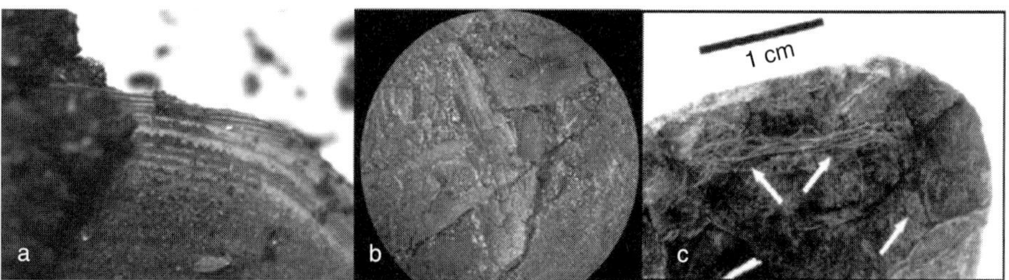

FIGURE 4.2 a. A well-preserved fish scale embedded in a carbonised deposit, magnification x40; b. Mistletoe leaves adhering to a vessel from Ronæs Skov, Denmark, magnification x25; c. Hairs embedded in a blood residue on a stone tool, arrows point to the edges of the most recent blood residues. (Adapted from Karg 2008 and Loy 1993)

6 GENERAL EXAMPLES

Finding Fossil Artefacts in Visible Deposits

Residues that are observable with the naked eye and investigable using low powered microscopy are documented on many artefact types including stone, bone and ceramic (Table 4.1). The term 'visible residue' masks a diversity of micro-environments for the preservation of fossilised evidence of artefact use. With a large enough sample number it is possible to categorise the deposit appearance, and relate these categories to subsequent organic geochemical results (Regert 2007). Low-powered microscopy is sometimes sufficient to identify well-preserved animal and plant tissues (see Figure 4.2). The identification of red blood cells on stone tools is more controversial and, as with all these studies, analysis of control samples (e.g., soils, unused surfaces) and more specific chemical tests are generally needed to confirm a non-contaminator source. Isolated discoveries such as the mistletoe leaves adhering to a Stone Age ceramic vessel (Figure 4.2) are a tantalising novelty, and this remains a challenging area of research.

The systematic study of plant microfossils such as starches and phytoliths, in carbonised ceramic deposits is an emerging research area. The process of carbonisation through heating can lead to the destruction of microfossils, or their alteration beyond recognition. However, some microfossils such as phytoliths are more thermally stable and robust than starches, spores and pollens. Silica phytoliths can retain their morphology up to 600°C (Piperno 2006), whilst starches begin to alter and gelatinise above 50°C (Gott et. al. 2006), although the process of starch degradation is poorly understood (Barton and Matthews 2006). Crucially, if plant microfossils are identified within the carbonised surface residues it is likely that they derive from vessel use (Crowther 2005). Lusteck and Thompson (2007) identified maize phytoliths from late prehistoric ceramics in North Dakota and Minnesota to show that maize lineages have a much longer and more complex history than previously thought. The use of starches as dietary indicators from carbonised pottery foodcrusts is increasing in microfossil research (Saul et al. 2012), although applications to archaeological problems have been limited, with debates about New World maize (*Zea mays*) agriculture (Boyd et al. 2006; Boyd et al. 2008), Australasian taro (*Colocasia esculenta*) domestication (Crowther 2005) spearheading research.

Distinguishing Animal Fats by GC-c-IRMS

Traces of lipid, particularly fatty acids, are encountered in such high frequency on prehistoric ceramic vessels that attempts have been made to determine statistically meaningful 'patterns of use' by analysing and comparing lipid distributions from many different pots (e.g., Malainey et al. 1999). This approach opens new exciting possibilities for the comparison of pottery use through time, at different sites, within different contexts at individual sites and by vessel typology. However, differential preservation and selective loss of fatty acids during burial has severely hampered these efforts. It is often impossible to tell with any certainty whether observed differences in fatty acid profiles relate to pottery use or merely to preservational circumstance. Isotope analysis of individual lipids by GC-c-IRMS circumvents this problem since the degree of preservation is not important, provided the original isotope ratios are preserved in the organic component that remains. Most lipid isotope studies have targeted the two most frequently encountered and most abundant fatty acids; palmitic acid ($C_{16:0}$ fatty acid or *n*-hexadecanoic acid) and stearic acid ($C_{18:0}$ fatty acid or *n*-octadecanoic acid). When found together in high abundance, these acids are broadly indicative of degraded animal fats. However, by measuring the isotopic composition of each acid it is possible to determine their origin at much greater resolution.

The resolving power of this isotope approach is related to the way different animals synthesise fatty acids, as well as their diets. Most animals synthesise both fatty acids from dietary carbohydrate, thus the values of each fatty acid are usually similar and reflect the dietary source of carbohydrate carbon. As with collagen, the $\delta^{13}C$ values of fatty acids of terrestrial animals with C_3 diets tend to be more

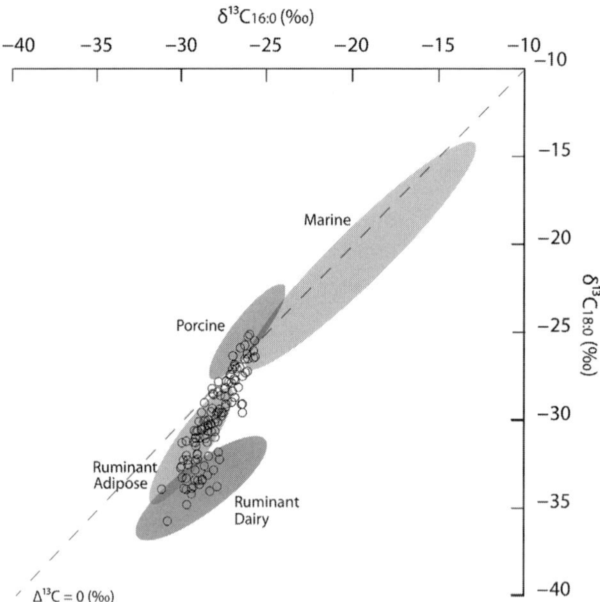

FIGURE 4.3 Scatter plot showing the δ^{13}C values of $C_{16:0}$ and $C_{18:0}$ fatty acids measured from extracts of Neolithic Grooved Ware pottery from Durrington Walls, Wiltshire, UK (Craig et al. 2015) by GC-c-IRMS. The ranges and means for some common modern reference fats are also shown. (Adapted from Copley et al. 2003 and Craig et al. 2011)

negative (i.e., isotopically lighter) than fish and terrestrial animals with C_4 diets. However, ruminant animals (including sheep, goat, cattle, deer and antelope) may also obtain a portion of their stearic acid ($C_{18:0}$ fatty acid) directly from ingested plant lipid. Fatty acids from this source are isotopically lighter than those synthesised *de novo* by the animal itself (Copley et al. 2004), resulting in an isotopic difference between stearic and palmitic acid (Figure 4.3). This relative depletion of ^{13}C in stearic acid compared to palmitic acid (Δ^{13}C) is even more pronounced in ruminant dairy fats, as the mammary gland is unable to synthesise any stearic acid. Crucially, this has allowed dairy fats to be discriminated from ruminant carcass fats and other animal fats (e.g., Figure 4.3), providing unique avenues for investigating dairying (see below).

One of the first applications of GC-c-IRMS to archaeological pottery was by Dudd and Evershed (1998), who showed that dairy products, ruminant carcass fats, non-ruminant carcass fats and pig fats could be discriminated from a range of Iron Age to medieval British pottery. The research team had thought that there might be differences in the types of animal fats used in these pots due to different distributions of TAGs, which in this case, were often preserved. The application of GC-c-IRMS not only supported their original inference but also allowed the residues to be characterised when no TAGs were present. This latter point means that GC-c-IRMS is applicable to pots even with generally poor lipid preservation, allowing a much greater number of samples to be compared (see example in Figure 4.3). GC-c-IRMS can also be used to measure the deuterium isotope value (δD) of the major fatty acids (Cramp and Evershed 2014). As hydrogen isotopes values vary widely with precipitation, they can be used to distinguish the season the fats were synthesised, especially in parts of the world where there are large differences in seasonal precipitation or temperature. Using this rationale, Outram et al. (2009) were able to distinguish horse carcass fats from horse dairy fats in Copper Age pottery from Kazakhstan, as the dairy fats could only have been produced in the drier summer months. Notably, as horses are non-ruminants, their carcass and dairy fats would not be distinguishable from the $\delta^{13}C$ value of the fatty acids.

Towards Species Identification

GC-c-IRMS of fatty acids is a powerful tool but it does not have the capacity to discriminate lipid residues derived from different species. Discriminating ruminant fats is obviously important, especially to discern the preparation of wild from domestic ruminant products, but also to investigate specific husbandry practices in the past (e.g., cattle from sheep dairying). Analysis of the complex mixtures of preserved TAGs associated with archaeological pottery has been attempted with soft ionisation mass spectrometry, such as nanoelectrospray ionisation time of flight mass spectrometry (e.g., Mirabaud et al. 2007). This allowed the discrimination of ruminant adipose and dairy fats to species on a range of Neolithic vessels from the French Jura. Whilst an important advance, this approach is only applicable to well-preserved residues, that is, when appreciable amounts of TAGs are preserved. Another approach, again using soft ionisation mass spectrometry, but this time aimed at proteins, succeeded in identifying peptides of muscle tissue protein (myoglobin), with sequences corresponding to Harbour Seal (*Phoca vitulina*) from a ca. 700-year-old Alaskan Inuit potsherd (Solazzo et al. 2008). Again, the success of this study is in part due to exceptional protein preservation at this high-latitude site. The degree of protein/peptide preservation at much older and warmer sites is not yet known; consequently this area presents a significant analytical challenge.

What about Plant Lipid Residues?

Unlike animal products, the lack of biomolecular evidence for plant residues is still a concern in residue analysis. Plants generally have a lower lipid content compared to animal tissues, therefore less is transferred to ceramic vessels during cooking and their survival potential over archaeological timescales is lower. Nevertheless, some plants with high abundances of epicuticular leaf waxes (e.g., Brassicas) or oil rich seeds have been identified using GC-MS (Charters et al. 1997; Dunne et al. 2016; Evershed et al. 1991). Starchy grains, such as barley, wheat, maize and rice, on the other hand, with lower lipid content are often masked by oilier/fattier foodstuffs making their identification extremely difficult (Reber and Evershed 2004). Similarly, reliable immunological detection of plant proteins looks to be equally problematic (Leach 1998). The identification of specific compounds (biomarkers) attributable to cereals offers the best hope for the future. For example, miliacin, a pentacyclic triterpene methyl ether, found at high concentration in broomcorn millet (*Panicum miliaceum*), has been identified at very low concentration in Bronze Age pottery from Korea and Poland (Heron et al. 2016). Similarly, a series of phenolic lipids, (alkylresorcinols) found in wheat or barley have been identified in a visible residue associated with a wooden container from an alpine glacier, dating to the early Bronze Age (Colonese et al. 2017). The finding was corroborated by the recovery of ancient protein sequences from the residue that were attributable to wheat (*Triticum spp.*) and barley/rye (Hordeinae) using a shotgun proteomic approach. The extent to which these cereal lipid biomarkers and proteins can be routinely recovered from archaeological artefacts is unknown. More work in this area is certainly called for considering that biomolecular evidence for starchy cereal grains is crucial for studying the emergence of agriculture and pre-agricultural plant exploitation.

7 CASE STUDIES

Organic residue analysis is expensive relative to many other forms of artefact analysis and is usually at least partially destructive. Therefore, deciding when to use this approach needs to be commensurate with the potential to gain new or unique information. Often, the question is focused around identification of a particular commodity of interest, of which there is only very limited scope for any other method of identification. For example, the identification of cocoa residue on preclassical Mayan vessels (Hurst et al. 2002), which pushed back the data for the earliest consumption of this product. Similarly, the identification of wine residues within Egyptian amphorae (Guasch-Jané et al. 2006) not only confirmed the use of the amphorae investigated but the identity of a previously unknown commodity often referred to in Egyptian texts. Whilst the scientific literature is awash with similar examples, especially claims of the first or the oldest, whether these studies have made a lasting impact in archaeology is debatable.

The two case studies reviewed below have started to generate genuine interest from archaeologists, but not necessarily because of the novelty of the approach. Rather they potentially allow independent corroboration and integration with existing methods and are applicable to a wide range of archaeological contexts. Both integrate with the broader studies of food in the past; whether that is to look at economies of production, cuisine or diet.

The Origins of Dairying

It is pointless to study dairying alone, as until very recently, dairying always existed as part of the larger integrated pastoralist economy where the decision to kill an animal for its meat or save it for its milk, or other secondary products, was taken year by year and maybe even animal by animal. Nevertheless, attempts to understand the development, scale and significance of dairying have reinvigorated the broader study of early animal production strategies and contributed to our understanding of domestication. Whilst dairying is often inferred from faunal kill-patterns, as we saw with the early application of GC-c-IRMS, direct evidence such as milk lipids residues on pots is considered to be stronger (e.g., Dudd and Evershed 1998). Dairy lipid residues have been identified on pottery produced by some of the earliest farming communities of Europe (Copley et al. 2003; Craig et al. 2005) and Southwest Asia (Evershed et al. 2008a), corresponding to the Early Neolithic period. These studies have far reaching implications; notably dairying was practiced as soon as domestic animals were introduced to many parts of Europe and Asia and perhaps within a millennium of the first domesticate species (ca. 10,000 years ago) and before populations were lactose tolerant (Itan et al. 2009). In fact, ancient DNA studies suggest that the genes for lactase persistence were probably not under selection in Europe at least until the late Neolithic or early Bronze Age (Allentoft et al., 2015), meaning that milk must have been initially processed into low-lactose dairy products, such as yoghurts or cheeses. The identification of dairy lipids on 8,000-year-old ceramic sieves (Salque et al. 2013), interpreted as cheese-strainers, from Northern Europe supports the DNA evidence although questions remain as to why the consumption of raw milk gave such a selective advantage, if such technological solutions to remove lactose were already in place much earlier.

Although organic residue analysis provides a useful way of identifying dairy products, it is important to be aware of the biases. Firstly, fat saturated milk has a propensity to form organic residues over many other commodities. Secondly, ceramics are not always implicated in all forms of food preparation and processing; in fact the function of ceramics is culturally controlled and may change through space or time, irrespective of the wider economy. Therefore the frequency of occurrence of organic residues on pottery is a rather weak proxy for overall food production strategies. More recent and detailed analysis of faunal kill patterns (see Helmer and Vigne 2007 for review), identification of ancient cattle stock selectively bred for high milk yields (Beja-Pereira et al. 2003), calcium isotope analysis of human remains (Reynard et al. 2008), and the identification of milk proteins in human dental calculus (Warinner et al. 2014) offer new opportunities to more effectively address the scale of dairy production and details of their consumption. Combining residue analysis within a wider framework of approaches is clearly desirable.

Identification of Marine Foods

The degree to which ancient populations relied on the sea for food is often questioned and notoriously hard to study. This question is no less pertinent when considered in relation to the shift to terrestrial food production and the possible arrival of 'farmers' that lacked the necessary maritime culture to exploit marine food resources. Due to their small size and friability, fish bones are underrepresented in the archaeological record, especially smaller species (e.g., Nicholson 1998), and artefacts unambiguously associated with fishing are rare. Stable isotope analysis of human remains has been widely applied to tackle this question. For example, carbon and nitrogen isotope analysis describes an apparent dietary shift from a wholly marine diet to a fully terrestrial one during the Mesolithic-Neolithic transition in the UK and Scandinavia (e.g., Richards et al. 2003; Schulting and Richards 2002;). Whilst, these findings have been debated (Lidén et al. 2004; Milner et al. 2004; Milner et al. 2006; Richards et al. 2006), analysis of organic residues in ceramic vessels found at prehistoric coastal sites is beginning to provide important corroborative evidence (see Cramp and Evershed 2014 for review).

There is a relatively long history of attempts using organic residue analysis to detect marine components in archaeological residues (Copley et al. 2004; Craig et al. 2007; Craig et al. 2011; Craig et al. 2013; Cramp et al. 2014; Hansel et al. 2004; Hansel and Evershed 2009; Heron et al. 2013; Morgan et al. 1983; Morgan et al. 1984; Morgan et al. 1992; Olsson and Isaksson 2008; Patrick et al. 1985; Taché and Craig 2015). The fatty acid composition of fish oils is very complex. They comprise relatively little saturated fatty acids ($C_{14:0}$, $C_{16:0}$ and $C_{18:0}$), and consist mainly of long chain unsaturated fatty acids containing 20 to 22 carbon atoms, with up to six double bonds (deMan 1999). They are therefore susceptible to degradation, especially by oxidation (Aillaud 2001), which has hampered early attempts to detect them in pottery and sediments. However, experiments have been successful in relating several degradation products of marine oils/fats to their precursor compounds, including ω-(-*o*-alkylphenyl)alkanoic acids of carbon length C_{18}, C_{20} and C_{22}, isoprenoid fatty acids (phytanic, pristanic and 4, 8, 12-tetramethyltridecanoic acid) and dihydroxy acids (Evershed et al. 2008b; Hansel et al. 2004; Hansel and Evershed 2009). These more stable compounds serve as excellent biomarkers for marine oils and have been identified in a range of ceramics dating to ca. 4000 cal BC (Craig et al. 2007; Hansel et al. 2004) and have been combined with GC-c-IRMS to identify ^{13}C enriched marine derived fatty acids (Craig et al. 2011; Craig et al. 2013; Cramp et al. 2014; Taché and Craig 2015).

Using these approaches, analysis of late Mesolithic and early Neolithic ceramics from a number of Northern German and Danish sites (Craig et al. 2007; Craig et al. 2011) provides strong evidence for continued exploitation of aquatic resources across the transition to agriculture (Craig et al. 2011). Whilst an extensive analysis of pottery coastal British sites found no evidence for marine products until the Iron Age (Cramp et al. 2014), some 3000 years after the arrival of farming. These studies point to considerable variation in the Neolithisation process across Europe. Again it is important to point out that the interpretation of such evidence needs to be considered in relation to the changing use of pottery and cuisine not just to changes in subsistence. As Olsson and Isaksson (2008) point out, pottery use does not necessarily reflect everyday diet and there are many ways to process fish, other than cooked in a pot. Nevertheless, the ubiquity of pottery at archaeological sites with lipids preserved, coupled with the fact that analyses are becoming more routine and less expensive, has prompted a move to a quantitative approach to residue analysis within major programs of research. These new programs aim to determine, not just vessel use, but patterns of use both spatially across a site or a landscape and temporally, through seasons, generations and major economic transitions. Only by applying residue analysis at these scales can we truly have a glimpse into the culinary world of our ancestors.

REFERENCES

Aichholz, R. and Lorbeer, E. 2000. Investigation of combwax of honeybees with high-temperature gas chromatography and high–temperature gas chromatography-chemical ionization mass spectrometry II. High-temperature gas chromatography-chemical ionization mass spectrometry. *Journal of Chromatography A* 883:75–88.

Aillaud, S. 2001. *Field and laboratory studies of diagenetic reactions affecting lipid residues absorbed in unglazed archaeological pottery vessels.* Doctoral thesis, University of Bristol, UK.

Allentoft, M. E., Sikora, M., Sjögren, K.-G., Rasmussen, S., Rasmussen, M., Stenderup, J., Damgaard, P. B., Schroeder, H., Ahlström, T., Vinner, L., Malaspinas, A.-S., Margaryan, A., Higham, T., Chivall, D., Lynnerup, N., Harvig, L., Baron, J., Della Casa, P., Dąbrowski, P., Duffy, P. R., Ebel, A. V., Epimakhov, A., Frei, K., Furmanek, M., Gralak, T., Gromov, A., Gronkiewicz, S., Grupe, G., Hajdu, T., Jarysz, R., Khartanovich, V., Khokhlov, A., Kiss, V., Kolář, J., Kriiska, A., Lasak, I., Longhi, C., McGlynn, G., Merkevicius, A., Merkyte, I., Metspalu, M., Mkrtchyan, R., Moiseyev, V., Paja, L., Pálfi, G., Pokutta, D., Pospieszny, L., Price, T. D. Saag, L., Sablin, M., Shishlina, N., Smrčka, V., Soenov, V. I., Szeverényi, V., Tóth, G., Trifanova, S. V., Varul, L., Vicze, M., Yepiskoposyan, L., Zhitenev, V., Orlando, L., Sicheritz-Pontén, T., Brunak, S., Nielsen, R., Kristiansen K. and Willerslev, E. 2015. Population genomics of Bronze Age Eurasia. *Nature* 522:167–172.

Asperger, A., Engewald, W. and Fabian, G. 1999. Analytical characterization of natural waxes employing pyrolysis-gas chromatography-mass spectrometry. *Journal of Analytical and Applied Pyrolysis* 50:103–115.

Barnard, H., Shoemaker, L., Rider, M., Craig, O. E., Parr, R. E., Sutton, M. Q. and Yohe II, R. M. 2007. Introduction to the analysis of protein residues in archaeological ceramics. In: Barnard, H. and Eerkens, J. (eds.) *Theory and Practice of Archaeological Residue Analysis.* BAR International Series 1650, pp. 216–231. Oxford: Archaeopress.

Barton, H. and Matthews, P. J. 2006. Taphonomy. In Torrence, R. and Barton, H. (eds.) *Ancient Starch Research.* California: Left Coast Press.

Beja-Pereira, A., Luikart, G., England, P. R., Bradley, D. G. Jann, O.C., Bertorelle, G., Chamberlain, A. T., Nunes, T. P., Metodiev, S., Ferrand, N. and Erhardt, G. 2003.

Gene-culture coevolution between cattle milk protein genes and human lactase genes. *Nature Genetics* 35(4):311–313.

Beverly, M. B., Kay, P. T. and Voorhees, K. J. 1995. Principal component analysis of the pyrolysis-mass spectra from African, Africanized hybrid, and European beeswax. *Journal of Analytical and Applied Pyrolysis* 34:251–263.

Boyd, M., Surette, C. and Nicholson, B. A. 2006. Archaeobotanical evidence of prehistoric maize (Zea mays) consumption at the northern edge of the Great Plains. *Journal of Archaeological Science* 33(8):1129–1140.

Boyd, M., Varney, T., Surette, C. and Surrette, J. 2008. Reassessing the northern limit of maize consumption in North America: Stable isotope, plant microfossil, and trace element content of carbonised food residue. *Journal of Archaeological Science* 35:2545–2556.

Buckley, S. A., Stott, A. W. and Evershed, R. P. 1999. Studies of organic residues from ancient Egyptian mummies using high temperature gas chromatography mass spectrometry and sequential thermal desorption gas chromatography mass spectrometry and pyrolysis gas chromatography mass spectrometry. *Analyst* 124(4):443–452.

Buckley, S., Usai, D., Jakob, T., Radini, A. and Hardy, K. 2014. Dental calculus reveals unique insights into food items, cooking and plant processing in prehistoric Central Sudan. *PLoS One* 9:e100808.

Buonasera, T. 2007. Investigating the presence of ancient absorbed organic residues in ground stone using GC-MS and other analytical techniques: A residue study of several prehistoric milling tools from central California. *Journal of Archaeological Science* 34:1279–1390.

Cattaneo, C., Gelsthorpe, K., Phillips, P. and Sokol, R. J. 1993. Blood residues on stone tools — indoor and outdoor experiments. *World Archaeology* 25(1):29–43.

Cavalieri, D., McGovern, P. E., Hartl, D. L., Mortimer, R. and Polsinelli, M. 2003. Evidence for S-cerevisiae fermentation in ancient wine. *Journal of Molecular Evolution* 57: S226–S232.

Chandler Ezell, K., Pearsall, D. M. and Zeidler, J. A. 2006. Root and tuber phytoliths and starch grains document manioc (*Manihot esculenta*) arrowroot (*Maranta arundinacea*) and ilerén (*Calathea* sp.) at the real Alto site Ecuador. *Economic Botany* 60(2):103–120.

Charters, S., Evershed, R. P., Blinkhorn, P. W. and Denham, V. 1995. Evidence for the mixing of fats and waxes in archaeological ceramics. *Archaeometry* 37(1):113–127.

Charters, S., Evershed, R. P., Goad, L. J., Heron, C. and Blinkhorn, P. 1993a. Identification of an adhesive used to repair a Roman jar. *Archaeometry* 35(1):91–101.

Charters, S., Evershed, R. P., Goad, L. J., Leyden, A., Blinkhorn, P. W. and Denhem, V. 1993b. Quantification and distribution of lipid in archaeological ceramics: Implications for sampling potsherds for organic residue analysis and the classification of vessel use. *Archaeometry* 35(2):211–223.

Charters, S., Evershed, R. P., Quye, A., Blinkhorn, P. W. and Reeves, V. 1997. Simulation experiments for determining the use of ancient pottery vessels: The behaviour of epicuticular leaf wax during boiling of leafy vegetable. *Journal of Archaeological Science* 24:1–7.

Collins, M. J., Nielsen-Marsh, C. M., Hiller, J., Smith, C. I., Roberts, J. P., Prigodich, R. V., Wess, T. J., Csapò, J., Millard, A. R. and Turner-Walker, G. 2002. The survival of organic matter in bone: A review. *Archaeometry* 44:383–394.

Collins M. J., Westbroek P., Muyzer G. and deLeeuw J. W. 1992. Experimental evidence for condensation reactions between sugars and proteins in carbonate skeletons. *Geochimica et Cosmochimica Acta* 56:1539–1544.

Colombini, M. P., Giachi, G., Iozzo, M. and Ribechini, E. 2009. An Etruscan ointment from Chiusi (Tuscany, Italy): Its chemical characterisation. *Journal of Archaeological Science* 36:1488–1495.

Colombini, M. P. and Modugno, F. 2009. *Organic Mass Spectrometry in Art and Archaeology*. Chichester: Wiley.

Colonese, A. C., Hendy, J., Lucquin, A., Speller, C. F., Collins, M. J., Carrer, F., Gubler, R., Kühn, M., Fischer, R., Craig, O. E., 2017. New criteria for the molecular identification of cereal grains associated with archaeological artefacts. *Scientific Reports* 7:6633.

Copley, M. S., Berstan, R., Dudd, S. N., Docherty, G., Mukherjee, A. J., Straker, V., Payne, S. and Evershed, R. P. 2003. Direct chemical evidence for widespread dairying in prehistoric Britain. *Proceedings of the National Academy of Sciences of the United States of America* 100(4):1524–1529.

Copley, M. S., Hansel, F. A., Sadr, K. and Evershed, R. P. 2004. Organic residue evidence for the processing of marine animal products in pottery vessels from the pre-colonial archaeological site of Kasteelberg D east, South Africa. *South African Journal of Science* 100:279–283.

Correa-Ascencio, M. and Evershed, R. P. 2014. High throughput screening of organic residues in archaeological potsherds using direct acidified methanol extraction. *Analytical Methods* 6:1330–1340.

Craig, O. E. and Collins, M. J. 2000. An improved method for the immunological detection of mineral bound protein using hydrofluoric acid and direct capture. *Journal of Immunological Methods* 236(1–2):89–97.

Craig, O. E. and Collins, M. J. 2002. The removal of protein from mineral surfaces: Implications for residue analysis of archaeological materials. *Journal of Archaeological Science* 29(10):1077–1082.

Craig, O. E., Chapman, J., Figler, A., Patay, P., Taylor, G. and Collins, M. J. 2003. 'Milk jugs' and other myths of the Copper Age of Central Europe. *European Journal of Archaeology* 6(3):251–265.

Craig, O. E., Chapman, J., Heron, C., Willis, L. H., Bartosiewicz, L., Taylor, G., Whittle, A. and Collins, M. 2005. Did the first farmers of central and eastern Europe produce dairy foods? *Antiquity* 79(306):882–894.

Craig, O. E., Forster, M., Anderson, S. H., Koch, E., Crombé, P., Miller, N. J., Stern, B., Bailey, G. N. and Heron, C. P. 2007. Molecular and isotopic demonstration of the processing of aquatic products in Northern European prehistoric pottery. *Archaeometry* 49(1):135–152.

Craig, O. E, Mulville, J., Pearson, M. P., Sokol, R., Gelsthorpe, K., Stacey, R. and Collins, M. 2000. Archaeology – Detecting milk proteins in ancient pots. *Nature* 408(6810):312–312.

Craig, O. E., Saul, H., Lucquin, A., Nishida, Y., Tache, K., Clarke, L., Thompson, A., Altoft, D. T., Uchiyama, J., Ajimoto, M., Gibbs, K., Isaksson, S., Heron C. P. and Jordan, P. 2013. Earliest evidence for the use of pottery. *Nature* 496:351–354.

Craig, O. E., Shillito, L.-M., Alberella, U., Chan, B., Cleal, R., Ixer, R., Jay, M., Marshall, P., Wright, E. and Parker Pearson, M. 2015. Feeding Stonehenge: Cuisine and consumption at the Late Neolithic site of Durrington Walls. *Antiquity* 89(347):1–14.

Craig, O. E., Steele V. J., Fischer A., Hartz S., Andersen S. H., Donohoe P., Glykou A., Saul H., Jones D. M., Koch E. and Heron C. P. 2011. Ancient lipids reveal continuity in culinary practices across the transition to agriculture in Northern Europe. *Proceedings of the National Academy of Sciences of the United States of America* 108:17910–17915.

Cramp, L. and Evershed R. P. 2014. Reconstructing aquatic resource exploitation in human Prehistory using lipid biomarkers and stable isotopes. In: H. D. H. K. Turekian (ed.) *Treatise on Geochemistry*, 2nd ed., pp. 319–339. Oxford: Elsevier.

Cramp, L., Jones, J., Sheridan, A., Smyth, J., Whelton, H., Mulville, J., Sharples N. and Evershed R. P. 2014. Immediate replacement of fishing with dairying by the earliest farmers of the Northeast Atlantic archipelagos. *Proceedings of the Royal Society. Biological Sciences* 281:20132372.

Crowther, A. 2005. Starch residues on undecorated Lapita pottery from Anir, New Ireland. *Archaeology in Oceania* 40:62–66.

deMan, J. M. 1999. *Principles in Food Chemistry* (3rd edn). Maryland: Aspen Publishers Inc.

Dudd, S. N. and Evershed, R. P. 1998. Direct demonstration of milk as an element of archaeological economies. *Science* 282(5393):1478–1481.

Dudd, S. N. and Evershed, R. P. 1999. Unusual triterpenoid fatty acyl ester components of archaeological birch bark tars. *Tetrahedron Letters* 40:359–362.

Dudd, S. N., Regert M. and Evershed, R. P. 1998. Assessing microbial lipid contributions during laboratory degradations of fats and oils and pure triacylglycerols absorbed in ceramic potsherds. *Organic Geochemistry* 29: 1345–1354.

Dunne, J., Evershed, R. P., Salque, M., Cramp, L., Bruni, S., Ryan, K., Biagetti, S. and Di Lernia, S. 2012. First dairying in green Saharan Africa in the fifth millennium BC. *Nature* 486:390–394.

Dunne, J., Mercuri, A. M., Evershed, R. P., Bruni, S., di Lernia, S., 2016. Earliest direct evidence of plant processing in prehistoric Saharan pottery. *Nature Plants* 3:16194.

Evershed, R. P. 1992. Gas chromatography of lipids. In: Hamilton, R. J. and Hamilton, S. (eds.) *Lipid Analysis: A Practical Approach*, pp. 113–151. Oxford: Oxford University Press.

Evershed, R. P. 2008a. Organic residue analysis in archaeology: The archaeological biomarker revolution. *Archaeometry* 50:895–924.

Evershed, R. P. 2008b. Experimental approaches to the interpretation of absorbed organic residues in archaeological ceramics. *World Archaeology* 40(1):26–47.

Evershed, R. P., Arnot, K. I., Collister, J., Eglinton, G. and Charters, S. 1994. Application of isotope ratio monitoring gas chromatography-mass spectrometry to the analysis of organic residues of archaeological origin. *Analyst* 119:909–914.

Evershed, R. P., Berstan, R., Grew, F., Copley, M. S., Charmant, A. J. H., Barham, E., Mottram, H. R. and Brown, G. 2004. Formulation of a Roman cosmetic. *Nature* 432:35–36.

Evershed, R. P., Copley, M. S., Dickson, L. and Hansel, F. A. 2008b. Experimental evidence for the processing of marine animal products and other commodities containing polyunsaturated fatty acids in pottery vessels. *Archaeometry* 50(1):101–113.

Evershed, R. P., Dudd, S. N., Charters, S., Mottram, H. A., Stott, A. W., Raven, A. van Bergen, P. F. and Bland, H. A. 1999. Lipids as carriers of anthropogenic signals from prehistory. *Philosophical Transactions of the Royal Society of London Series B-Biological Sciences* 354:19–31.

Evershed, R. P., Dudd, S., Lockheart, M. J. and Jim, S. 2001. Lipids in archaeology. In: Brothwell, D. R. and Pollard, A. M. (eds.) *Handbook of Archaeological Sciences*, pp. 331–349. Chichester: Wiley.

Evershed, R. P., Heron, C. and Goad, L. J. 1990. Analysis of organic residues of archaeological origin by high temperature gas chromatography and gas chromatography/mass spectrometry. *Analyst* 115:1339–1342.

Evershed, R. P., Heron, C. and Goad, L. J. 1991. Epicuticular wax components preserved in potsherds as chemical indicators of leafy vegetables in ancient diets. *Antiquity* 65:540–544.

Evershed, R. P., Payne, S., Sherratt, A. G., Copley, M. S., Coolidge, J., Urem-Kotsu, D., Kotsakis, K., Ozdogan, M., Ozdogan, A. E., Nieuwenhuyse, O., Akkermans, P., Bailey, D., Andeescu, R. R., Campbell, S., Farid, S., Hodder, I., Yalman, N., Ozbasaran, M., Bicakci, E., Garfinkel, Y., Levy, T. and Burton, M. M. 2008a. Earliest date for milk use in the Near East and southeastern Europe linked to cattle herding. *Nature* 455 (7212):528–531.

Evershed, R. P. and Tuross, N. 1996. Proteinaceous material from potsherds and associated soils. *Journal of Archaeological Science* 23(3):429–436.

Gott, B., Barton, H., Samuel, D. and Torrence, R. 2006. Biology of starch. In: Torrence, R. and Barton, H. (eds.) *Ancient Starch Research*, pp. 35–46. California: Left Coast Press.

Gregg, M. W., Banning, E. B., Gibbs, K. and Slater, G. F. 2009. Subsistence practices and pottery use in Neolithic Jordan: Molecular and isotopic evidence. *Journal of Archaeological Science* 36:937–946.

Guasch-Jané, M.R., Andres-Lacueva, C., Jauregui, O. and Lamuela-Raventos, R. M. 2006. The origin of the ancient Egyptian drink Shedeh revealed using LC/MS/MS. *Journal of Archaeological Science* 33(1):98–101.

Guasch-Jané, M. R., Ibern-Gomez, M., Andres-Lacueva, C., Jauregui, O. and Lamuela-Raventos, R. M. 2004. Liquid chromatography with mass spectrometry in tandem mode applied for the identification of wine markers in residues from ancient Egyptian vessels. *Analytical Chemistry* 76(6):1672–1677.

Hansel, F. A., Copley, M. S., Madureira, L. A. S. and Evershed, R. P. 2004. Thermally produced ω-(-o-alkylphenyl) alkanoic acids provide evidence for the processing of marine products in archaeological pottery vessels. *Tetrahedron Letters* 45:2999–3002.

Hansel, F. A. and Everhsed, R. P. 2009. Formation of dihydroxy acids from Z-monounsaturated alkenoic acids and their use as biomarkers for the processing of marine commodities in archaeological pottery vessels. *Tetrahedron Letters* 50:5562–5564.

Hansson, M. C. and Foley, B. P. 2008. Ancient DNA fragments inside Classical Greek amphoras reveal cargo of 2400-year-old shipwreck. *Journal of Archaeological Science* 35:1169–1176.

Hardy, K., Blakeney, T., Copeland, L., Kirkham, J., Wrangham, R. and Collins, M. 2009. Starch grains, dental calculus and new perspectives on ancient diet. *Journal of Archaeological Science* 36(2):248–255.

Hardy, K., Buckley, S., Collins, M. J., Estallrich, A., Brothwell, D., Copeland, L., García-Tabernero, A., García-Vargas, S., Rasilla, M., Lalueza-Fox, C., Huguet, R., Bastir, M., Santamaría, D., Madella, M., Wilson, J., Cortés, Á. and Rosas, A. 2012. Neanderthal medics? Evidence for food, cooking, and medicinal plants entrapped in dental calculus. *Naturwissenschaften* 99:617–626.

Hardy, K., Radini, A., Buckley, S., Sarig, R., Copeland, S., Gopher, A. and Barkai, R. 2015. Dental calculus reveals potential respiratory irritants and ingestion of essential plant-based nutrients at Lower Palaeolithic Qesem Cave Israel. *Quaternary International* 398:129–135.

Hardy, B. L. Raff, R. A. and Raman, V. 1997. Recovery of mammalian DNA from Middle Paleolithic stone tools. *Journal of Archaeological Science* 24(7):601–611.

Heaton, K., Solazzo, C., Collins, M. J., Thomas-Oates, J. and Bergstrom, E. T. 2009. Towards the application of desorption electrospray ionisation mass spectrometry (DESI-MS) to the analysis of ancient proteins from artefacts. *Journal of Archaeological Science* 36 (10):2145–2154.

Helmer, D. and Vigne, J.-D. 2007. Was milk a 'secondary product' in the Old World Neolithisation process? Its role in the domestication of cattle, sheep and goats. *Anthropozoologica* 42(2):9–40.

Hendy, J., van Doorn, N. and Collins, M. in press. Proteomics. In: Richards, M. P. and Britton, K. (eds.) *Archaeological Science.* Cambridge: Cambridge University Press.

Heron, C., Andersen, S., Fischer, A., Glykou, A., Hartz, S., Saul, H., Steele, V. and Craig, O. 2013. Illuminating the Late Mesolithic: Residue analysis of 'blubber' lamps from Northern Europe. *Antiquity* 87:178–188.

Heron, C., Shoda, S., Breu Barcons, A., Czebreszuk, J., Eley, Y., Gorton, M., Kirleis, W., Kneisel, J., Lucquin, A., Müller, J., Nishida, Y., Son, J.-H., Craig, O. E. 2016. First molecular and isotopic evidence of millet processing in prehistoric pottery vessels. *Scientific Reports* 6:38767.

Hogberg, A., Puseman, K. and Yost, C. 2009. Integration of use-wear with protein residue analysis – a study of tool use and function in the south Scandinavian Early Neolithic. *Journal of Archaeological Science* 36(8):1725–1737.

Hurst, W. J., Tarka, S. M., Powis, T. G., Valdez, F. and Hester, T. R. 2002. Archaeology: Cacao usage by the earliest Maya civilization. *Nature* 418(6895):289–290.

Itan, Y., Powell, A., Beaumont, M. A., Burger, J. and Thomas M. G. 2009. The origins of lactase persistence in Europe. *PLoS Computational Biology* 5(8):e1000491.

Jones, J., Higham, T. F. G., Oldfield, R., O'Connor, T. and Buckley, S. A. 2014. Evidence for prehistoric origins of Egyptian mummification in Late Neolithic burials. *PLoS One* 9:1–13.

Karg, S. 2008. På Karrets Bund. *SKALK* 4:32.

Kealhofer, L., Torrence, R. and Fullager, R. 1999. Integrating phytoliths within use-wear/residue studies of stone tools. *Journal of Archaeological Science* 26:527–547.

Leach, J. D. 1998. A brief comment on the immunological identification of plant residues on prehistoric stone tools and ceramics: Results of a blind test. *Journal of Archaeological Science* 25:171–175.

Lidén, K., Eriksson, G., Nordqvist, B., Götherström, A. and Bendixen, A. 2004. The wet and the wild followed by the dry and the tame – or did they occur at the same time? Diet in Mesolithic-Neolithic southern Sweden. *Antiquity* 78:23–33.

Loog, L.and Larson, G. in press. Ancient DNA. In: Richards, M. P. and Britton, K. (eds.) *Archaeological Science*. Cambridge: Cambridge University Press.

Loy, T. H. 1983. Prehistoric blood residues: Detection on tool surfaces and identification of species of origin. *Science* 220(4603):1269–1271.

Loy, T. H. 1993. The artifact as site – an example of the biomolecular analysis of organic residues on Prehistoric tools. *World Archaeology* 25(1):44–63.

Loy, T. H. and Dixon, J. E. 1998. Blood residues on fluted points from Eastern Beringia. *American Antiquity* 63:21–46.

Loy, T. H. and Hardy, B. L. 1992. Blood residue analysis of 90,000-year-old stone tools from Tabun Cave, Israel. *Antiquity* 66(250):24–35.

Lusteck, R. K. and Thompson, R. G. 2007. Residues of maize in North American pottery: What phytoliths can add to the story of maize. In: Barnard, H. and Eerkens, J. W. (eds.) *Theory and Practice of Archaeological Residue Analysis*. BAR International Series 1650, pp. 8–16. Oxford: Archaeopress.

Malainey, M. E., Przybylski, R. and Sherriff, B. L. 1999. Identifying the former contents of late precontact period pottery vessels from western Canada using gas chromatography. *Journal of Archaeological Science* 26(4):425–438.

McGovern, P. E., Luley, B. P., Rovira, N., Mirzoian, A., Callahan, M. P., Smith, K. E., Hall, G. R., Davidson, T. and Henkin, J. M. 2013. Beginning of viniculture in France. *Proceedings of the National Academy of Sciences* 110(25):10147–10152.

McGovern, P. E., Zhang, J. H., Tang, J. G., Zhang, Z. Q., Hall, G. R., Moreau, R. A., Nunez, A., Butrym, E. D., Richards, M. P., Wang, C. S., Cheng, G. S., Zhao, Z. J. and

Wang, C. S. 2004. Fermented beverages of pre- and proto-historic China. *Proceedings of the National Academy of Sciences of the United States of America* 101:17593–17598.

Meier-Augenstein, W. 2002. Stable isotope analysis of fatty acids by gas chromatography-isotope ratio mass spectrometry. *Analytica Chimica Acta* 465(1–2):63–79.

Milner, N., Craig, O. E., Bailey, G. N. and Andersen, S. H. 2006. A response to Richards and Schulting. *Antiquity* 80:456–458.

Milner, N., Craig, O. E., Bailey, G. N., Pedersen, K. and Andersen, S. H. 2004. Something fishy in the Neolithic? A re-evaluation of stable isotope analysis of Mesolithic and Neolithic coastal populations. *Antiquity* 78:9–22.

Mirabaud, S., Rolando, C. and Regert, M. 2007. Molecular criteria for discriminating adipose fat and milk from different species by NanoESI MS and MS/MS of their triacylglycerols: Application to archaeological remains. *Analytical Chemistry* 79:6182–6192.

Morgan, E. D., Edwards, C. and Pepper, S. A. 1992. Analysis of the fatty debris from the wreck of a Basque whaling ship at Red Bay, Labrador. *Archaeometry* 34(1):129–133.

Morgan, E. D., Titus, L., Small, R. J. and Edwards. C. 1983. The composition of fatty materials from a Thule Eskimo site on Herschel Island. *Arctic* 36(4):356–360.

Morgan, E. D., Titus, L., Small, R. J. and Edwards. C. 1984. Gas chromatographic analysis of fatty material from a Thule Midden. *Archaeometry* 26(1):43–48.

Morton, J. D. and Schwarcz, H. P. 2004. Palaeodietary implications from stable isotopic analysis of residues on prehistoric Ontario ceramics. *Journal of Archaeological Science* 31:503–517.

Newman, M. E., Ceri, H. and Kooyman, B. 1996. The use of immunological techniques in the analysis of archaeological materials: A response to Eisele; with report studies at Head-Smashed-In Buffalo Jump. *Antiquity* 70:677–682.

Newman, M., and Julig, P. 1989. The identification of protein residues on lithic artefacts from a stratified boreal forest site. *Canadian Journal of Archaeology* 13:119–132.

Nicholson, R. A. 1998. Fishing for facts: A preliminary view of the fish remains from Old Scatness Broch. In: Nicholson, R. A. and Dockrill, S. J. (eds.) *Old Scatness Broch, Shetland: Retrospect and Prospect*, pp. 97–110. Bradford: Department of Archaeological Sciences.

Nolin, L. Kramer, J. K. G. and Newman, M. 1994. Detection of animal residues in humus samples from a prehistoric site in the Lower Mackenzie River Valley, Northwest Territories. *Journal of Archaeological Science* 21:403–412.

Nursten H. E. 2005. *The Maillard Reaction: Chemistry, Biochemistry, and Implications.* London: Royal Society of Chemistry.

Olsson, M. and Isaksson, S. 2008. Molecular and isotopic traces of cooking and consumption of fish at an Early Medieval manor site in eastern middle Sweden. *Journal of Archaeological Science* 35:773–780.

Oudemans, T. F. M. and Boon, J. J. 1991. Molecular archaeology: Analysis of charred (food) remains from prehistoric pottery by pyrolysis-gas chromatography/mass spectrometry. *Journal of Analytical and Applied Pyrolysis* 20:197–227.

Oudemans, T. F. M., Boon, J. J. and Botto, R. E. 2007a. FTIR and solid-state C-13 CP/MAS NMR spectroscopy of charred and non-charred solid organic residues preserved in Roman Iron Age vessels from the Netherlands. *Archaeometry* 49:571–594.

Oudemans, T. F. M., Eijkel, G. B. and Boon, J. J. 2007b. Identifying biomolecular origins of solid organic residues preserved in Iron Age Pottery using DTMS and MVA. *Journal of Archaeological Science* 34:173–193.

Outram, A. K., Stear, N. A., Bendrey, R., Olsen, S., Kasparov, A., Zaibert, V., Thorpe, N. and Evershed, R. P. 2009. The earliest horse harnessing and milking. *Science* 323 (5919):1332–1335.

Patrick, M., de Koning, A. J. and Smith, A. B. 1985. Gas liquid chromatographic analysis of fatty acids in food resides from ceramics found in the Southwestern Cape, South Africa. *Archaeometry* 27(2):231–236.

Piperno, D. 2006. *Phytoliths. A Comprehensive Guide for Archaeologists and Paleoecologists.* Lanham: Alta Mira Press.

Pollard, A. M., Batt, C., Stern, B. and Young, S. M. M. 2007. *Analytical Chemistry in Archaeology.* Cambridge: Cambridge University Press.

Pollard, A. M. and Heron C. 2008. *Archaeological Chemistry*, 2nd ed. Cambridge: Royal Society of Chemistry.

Raven, A. M., van Bergen, P. F., Stott, A. W., Dudd, S. N. and Evershed, R. P. 1997. Formation of long-chain ketones in archaeological pottery vessels by pyrolysis of acyl lipids. *Journal of Analytical and Applied Pyrolysis* 40–41:267–285.

Reber, E. A. and Evershed, R. P. 2004. Identification of maize in absorbed organic residues: A cautionary tale. *Journal of Archaeological Science* 31:399–410.

Regert, M. 2007. Elucidating pottery function using a multi-step analytical methodology combining infrared spectroscopy, chromatographic procedures and mass spectrometry. In: Barnard, H. and Eerkens, J. W. (eds.) *Theory and Practice of Archaeological Residue Analysis.* BAR International Series 1650, pp. 61–76. Oxford: Archaeopress.

Regert, M. 2011. Analytical strategies for discriminating archaeological fatty substances from animal origin. *Mass Spectrometry Reviews* 30:177–220.

Regert, M., Bland, H. A., Dudd, S. N., van Bergen, P. F. and Evershed, R. P. 1998. Free and bound fatty acid oxidation products in archaeological ceramic vessels. *Proceedings of the Royal Society of London B* 265:2027–2032.

Regert, M., Garnier, N., Decavallas, O., Cern-Olivé, C. and Ronaldo, C. 2003. Structural characterization of lipid constituents from natural substances preserved in archaeological environments. *Measurement Science and Technology* 14:1620–1630.

Reynard, L. M. Hedges, R. E. M. and Henderson, G. M. 2008. Stable calcium isotope ratios (delta Ca-44/42) in bones and teeth for the detection of dairying by ancient humans. *Geochimica et Cosmochimica Acta* 72(12):A790–A790.

Ribechini, E., Modugno, F., Baraldi, C., Baraldi, P. and Colombini, M. P. 2008a. An integrated analytical approach for characterizing an organic residue from an archaeological glass bottle recovered in Pompeii (Naples, Italy). *Talanta* 74:555–561.

Ribechini, E., Modugno, F., Colombini, M.P. and Evershed, R. P. 2008b. Gas chromatographic and mass spectrometric investigations of organic residues from Roman glass uguentaria. *Journal of Chromatography A* 1183:158–169.

Richards, M. P., Price, T. D. and Koch, E. 2003. Mesolithic and Neolithic subsistence in Denmark: New stable isotope data. *Current Anthropology* 44:288–295.

Salque, M., Bogucki, P. I., Pyzel, P. I., Sobkowiak-Tabaka, I., Grygiel, R., Szmyt, M. and Evershed, R. P. 2013. Earliest evidence for cheese making in the sixth millennium BC in northern Europe. *Nature* 493:522–525.

Saul, H., Madella, M., Fischer, A., Glykou, A., Hartz, S. and Craig, O. E. 2013. Phytoliths in pottery reveal the use of spice in European prehistoric cuisine. *PLoS One* 8:e70583, 1–5.

Saul, H., Wilson, J., Heron, C., Glykou, A., Hartz, S. and Craig, O. E. 2012. A systematic approach to the recovery and identification of starches from carbonised deposits on ceramic vessels. *Journal of Archaeological Science* 39:3483–3492.

Schulting, R. and Richards, M. 2002. Finding the coastal Mesolithic in southwest Britain: AMS dates and stable isotope results on human remains from Caldey Island, south Wales. *Antiquity* 76(294):1011–1025.

Shanks, O. C., Bonnichsen, R., Vella, A. T. and Ream, W. 2001. Recovery of protein and DNA trapped in stone tool microcracks. *Journal of Archaeological Science* 28 (9):965–972.

Shanks, O. C., Hodges, L., Tilley, L., Kornfeld, M., Larson, M. L. and Ream, W. 2005. DNA from ancient stone tools and bones excavated at Bugas-Holding, Wyoming. *Journal of Archaeological Science* 32(1):27–38.

Shanks, O. C., Kornfeld, M. and Hawk, D. D. 1999. Protein analysis of Bugas-Holding tools: New trends in immunological studies. *Journal of Archaeological Science* 26(9):1183–1191.

Shanks, O. C., Kornfeld, M. and Ream, W. 2004. DNA and protein recovery from washed experimental stone tools. *Archaeometry* 46:663–672.

Solazzo, C., Fitzhugh, W. W., Rolando, C. and Tokarski, C. 2008. Identification of protein remains in archaeological potsherds by proteomics. *Analytical Chemistry* 80 (12):4590–4597.

Stern, B., Heron, C. C., Tellefsen, T. and Serpico, M. 2008. New investigations into the Uluburun resin cargo. *Journal of Archaeological Science* 35:2188–2203.

Taché, K. and Craig, O. E. 2015. Cooperative harvesting of aquatic resources and the beginning of pottery production in north-eastern North America. *Antiquity* 89:177–190.

Tuross, N., Barnes, I. and Potts, R. 1996. Protein identification of blood residues on experimental stone tools. *Journal of Archaeological Science* 23(2):289–296.

Warinner, C., Hendy, J., Speller, C., Cappellini, E., Fischer, R., Trachsel, C., Arneborg, J., Lynnerup, N., Craig, O. E., Swallow, D. M., Fotakis, A., Christensen, R. J., Olsen, J. V., Liebert, A., Montalva, N., Fiddyment, S., Charlton, S., Mackie, M., Canci, A., Bouwman, A., Rühli, F., Gilbert, M. T. P. and Collins M. J. 2014. Direct evidence of milk consumption from ancient human dental calculus. *Scientific Reports* 4:7104.

Willerslev, E., Hansen, A. J., Binladen, J., Brand, T. B., Gilbert, M. T. P., Shapiro, B., Bunce, M., Wiuf, C., Gilichinsky, D. A. and Cooper, A. 2003. Diverse plant and animal genetic records from Holocene and Pleistocene sediments. *Science* 300(5620):791–795.

Zarrillo, S., Pearsall, D. M., Raymond, J. S., Tisdale, M. A. and Quon, D. J. 2008. Directly dated starch residues document early formative maize (Zea mays L.) in tropical Ecuador. *Proceedings of the National Academy of Sciences* 105(13):5006–5011.

5

Isotope Analysis for Mobility and Climate Studies

Kate Britton

The use of radiogenic and stable isotope analysis of human and animal bioapatites to reconstruct past movement patterns and climates.

1 INTRODUCTION

Isotope studies in archaeology are often concerned with the analysis of preserved proteins for the reconstruction of past diets, but isotopic signatures in the mineral phase of archaeological skeletons can also be used to reconstruct place of residence and even the contemporary local climate. These applications are based upon the premise of a relationship between underlying local geology/local soils (strontium) and ingested water (oxygen) to the body isotope chemistry of the individuals in question (see reviews in Bentley 2006, and Pederzani and Britton 2019). Where the distribution of isotope signatures within and across different ecosystems varies predictably, these methods can be used to source human and animal remains to specific regions or to identify non-local outliers or migrants (e.g., Bentley 2013; Müldner et al. 2009).

Human mobility is interesting from an archaeological perspective as, through its study, not only are we able to reconstruct the life histories of ancient individuals but we can also gain valuable insight into the demographic, economic, social and cultural conditions of the past. Strontium and oxygen isotope studies can be used to infer immigration and emigration (e.g., Knudson et al. 2004); to investigate population diasporas and dispersals (e.g., Leach et al. 2009); to reveal social systems and conventions, such as matri- or patrilocality (e.g., Bentley et al. 2005) or transhumance (e.g., Bentley and Knipper 2005); and to explore trade and exchange networks (e.g., Laffoon et al. 2013; Thornton 2011).

As well as identifying non-local outliers from the analysis of 'bulk' tissues, incrementally developed tissues (such as tooth enamel) can be used to reconstruct movements made during life. These methods can be applied to wild or domestic zooarchaeological remains as well as to human samples. The analysis of domesticates allows the investigation of trade and exchange networks (e.g., Evans et al. 2007), and the investigation of transhumance, animal husbandry and herding practices (e.g., Balasse et al. 2002; Bentley and Knipper 2005). The analysis of wild species can be used to investigate animal palaeobiogeography, and to explore prey-species movements and seasonality (e.g., Pellegrini et al. 2008). These can, in turn, be used to better understand the movement patterns, landscape use and subsistence decisions of the human hunter-gatherers that depended on these animals (e.g., Britton et al. 2011; Price et al. 2017). The isotope analysis of human or animal remains may also provide information about the contemporary climate, including seasonal climatic variability (e.g., Bernard et al. 2009; Fabre et al. 2011) or, inversely, isotopes that serve as climatic indicators (e.g., oxygen) can be used to infer geographical origin (e.g., Leach et al. 2009).

The inorganic component of bone and tooth – often referred to as bioapatite – is most commonly analysed in archaeological studies utilising strontium and oxygen isotope analysis, although organic materials can also be used in some instances (e.g., Kirsanow et al. 2008). In mammals, bioapatite is found and commonly sampled from three materials: bone, dentine and enamel. Some skeletal materials, such as bone, remodel during life and can provide longer-term evidence for isotopic inputs. Other tissues, such as teeth, form and mineralise incrementally (progressively) and do not undergo significant remodelling during life. These tissues are important as they can reveal variations in isotopic composition within a temporal context. In many species, different teeth within the jaw will form at different times, and often in sequence, providing time-series isotopic data for that fixed period of development. Furthermore, individual teeth form incrementally, permitting the elucidating of finer resolution isotopic information. Depending on the species in question, a single tooth can take anything between a few months to a few years to fully form, providing evidence for seasonal and even inter-annual variations (Sharp and Cerling 1998).

Focusing on the analysis of bioapatites, this chapter will explore the theory, methods and key applications of the two isotope systems that are most commonly used to explore mobility and migrations, and even ancient climate, through the analysis of animal and human skeletal remains – strontium (Sr) and oxygen (O).

2 STRONTIUM ISOTOPE ANALYSIS

Basic Principles

Strontium applications are based on the principle that processes of radioactive decay produce strontium isotope variations in rocks of different ages and type. These signatures undergo no further modification through fractionation in the biosphere (as strontium moves from soil, to plant and ultimately to animals and humans) and therefore these methods can be used to determine geological provenance (and subsequently geographical origins) by comparing the strontium isotope value in the biological tissue of interest with known strontium isotope ratios from different localities. Originally developed by geologists to age rocks, these methods have been used by archaeologists, anthropologists and ecologists for over 30 years to map the geographical origins of environmental materials (e.g., Åberg 1995; Capo et al. 1998); modern and archaeological faunal species (e.g., Britton et al. 2009; Britton et al. 2011; Evans et al. 2007; Hoppe et al. 1999; Koch et al. 1992; Pellegrini et al. 2008;); and humans (e.g., Bentley et al. 2004; Bentley 2013; Budd et al. 2004; Chenery et al. 2010; Ericson 1985; Evans et al. 2006; Ezzo et al. 1997; Montgomery et al. 2003; Montgomery et al. 2005; Montgomery et al. 2007; Schweissing and Grupe 2003).

Strontium has four naturally occurring stable isotopes: ^{88}Sr is the most abundant (82.53 per cent), followed by ^{86}Sr (9.87 per cent), ^{87}Sr (7.04 per cent) and ^{84}Sr (0.56 per cent) (values from Capo et al. 1998: 199). The radiogenic daughter-isotope ^{87}Sr is formed from the β-decay of ^{87}Rb (rubidium). The decay of ^{87}Rb to ^{87}Sr has a half-life of approximately 4.88×10^{10} years (Faure 1986: 119), leading to different abundances of ^{87}Sr (relative to the non-radiogenic or 'stable' ^{86}Sr) in rocks of different ages. Strontium isotope compositions are therefore most commonly expressed as the ratio, $^{87}Sr/^{86}Sr$. Given the long half-life of ^{87}Rb, there is insignificant change in isotope ratios of $^{87}Sr/^{86}Sr$ over archaeological time scales and therefore this system is commonly referred to as 'stable' for the purposes of archaeological applications (Bentley 2006).

Strontium in the Environment and 'Bioavailablity'

Chemical weathering is the primary mechanism by which strontium is released from rocks. As fractionation (i.e., alteration of the isotope ratio) is negligible, the isotope ratios that characterise a specific geology theoretically pass from the source rocks, into soil, groundwater and plants and eventually up the food chain into animal feeders (Bentley 2006; Capo et al. 1998). Despite this anticipated relationship between local surficial geology and the strontium isotope ratios of local food chains, several secondary factors may influence the 'bioavailable' strontium isotope signature of an area (i.e., that which is transferred to soils, plants and further up the food chain). These issues are very important to consider as they could potentially result in the values measured in these materials not being the same as that of the underlying solid lithology. The mineral content of the rock itself can be especially important. Certain rock types can include a range of different minerals that themselves may have different $^{87}Sr/^{86}Sr$ ratios. The proportion of these different minerals within different rocks may vary and some minerals may weather more rapidly than others, again influencing the isotopic signature of local bioavailable strontium. Therefore weathering may lead to strontium isotope signatures representative of bulk samples of the underlying lithology, or perhaps only to values characteristic (but not wholly replicating that) of the rock-type in question.

As well as the mineral composition of the rock-type, another important consideration is the isotopic mixing that may occur within environments where there are different 'inputs'. Underlying lithologies themselves may be of different age or rock-type, but also material bearing non-local strontium isotope signatures may be introduced to the region through weathering products, such as those that are airborne (aeolian) or waterborne (fluvial). Other local inputs may include ground waters (e.g., Graustein and Armstrong 1983); river/stream water; Sr cycling in soils (e.g., Dijkstra and Smits 2002; Morgan et al. 2001); atmospheric sources (e.g., Gosz and Moore 1989; Kennedy et al. 1998; Vitousek et al. 1999); surficial geological movement (e.g., Steele and Pushkar 1973: 338); precipitation, irrigation and sea-spray (e.g., Chadwick et al. 1999; Green et al. 2004; Hartman and Richards 2014; Xin and Hanson 1994); and fertilisers (e.g., Németh et al. 2006).

'Outputs' within any particular area may also influence local $^{87}Sr/^{86}Sr$, for example, the removal of certain types of material through the weathering of soils. As a result, the local bioavailable strontium within any area must be viewed as the sum of a number of different contributing factors – including the (primary) local lithologically driven inputs, as well as other potentially non-local inputs, and possibly also outputs (Bentley 2006).

Despite these varied influences, it has been observed that in most environments, the weathering of local geology remains the most significant Sr contribution – especially in pre-modern times (Bentley 2006: 153). Furthermore, averaging effects observed in plant values (e.g., Blum et al. 2000; Sillen et al. 1998) and up the food chain to herbivore feeders, carnivores and humans (e.g., Burton et al. 1999; Price et al. 2002) have been demonstrated to widely eliminate local variation, demonstrating values in organisms more closely align to underlying geology and soil values. In turn, vegetation is dominated by the isotopic composition of labile Sr in the soil (Åberg et al. 1990; Capo et al. 1998; Graustein and Armstrong 1983). Although the isotope signature of bioavailable strontium in a region is therefore primarily determined by underlying lithology, and geological maps can provide a guide for such estimates, 'bioavailiability' studies provide the best estimates of bioapatite values of local fauna. Bioavailability studies can include the analysis of local soils (Evans et al. 2010), local soils and plants (Willmes et al. 2014) or microfauna (Copeland et al. 2008) for example, and may involve the integration of such data into powerful predictive models of spatial isotopic variability or 'isoscapes' (e.g. Bataille et al. 2018).

Strontium Isotopes in Animals and Humans

Unlike calcium (Ca), strontium is considered a non-essential element but is also found in living organisms. Strontium has a valency of +2 and an ionic radius of 1.32 Å, which is only slightly larger than that of calcium (Ca^{2+} = 1.18 Å), its biological uptake occurring as a substitution for the chemically similar Ca (Bentley 2006; Capo et al. 1998). Sr^{2+} substitutes for Ca^{2+} in many minerals including biological hydroxyapatite or bioapatite, the major component of the mineral phase of mammalian bone and tooth (Capo et al. 1998). Therefore, the strontium isotope ratios of terrestrial herbivores reflect the isotopic composition of the strontium taken up by the plants they consume and therefore underlying rocks. Generally, animals living on older lithologies will have higher $^{87}Sr/^{86}Sr$ values; animals living on younger geologies will have lower values. Strontium is incorporated in significant concentrations during bioapatite formation (in bone, enamel and dentine), as a substitute for calcium. The amount of total strontium in enamel is between 25 and 600ppm (parts per million), but can be greater, with concentrations dependent on the local environmental concentrations, dietary choices and extent of mineralisation (Iyengar et al. 1978; Steadman et al. 1958).

The Issue of Diagenesis

Early applications of strontium isotope analysis within archaeology often made use of bone bioapatite (e.g., Ericson 1985). However, it has since been demonstrated that archaeological bone bioapatite is often contaminated or chemically altered during burial – a process known as diagenesis. During diagenesis, original chemical signatures can be substituted, replaced or contaminated with those of the surrounding burial environment. Given the small crystal size, high porosity and organic content of bone, it is highly susceptible to diagenesis (Nielsen-Marsh et al. 2000; Nielsen-Marsh and Hedges 2000b; Nielsen-Marsh and Hedges 2000a; Price et al. 1992; Tuross et al. 1989). Acid leaching, often undertaken in the laboratory to remove diagenetic contaminants from bone, is insufficient to remove all contaminating strontium (e.g., Hoppe et al. 2003; Koch et al. 1992; Nelson et al. 1986; Trickett et al. 2003) and as much as 80 per cent of diagenetic strontium can remain in samples (Hoppe et al. 2003: 26). It must be noted that acid treatments do not isolate diagenetic strontium, and *in situ* biogenic strontium may also be leached out and lost (Hoppe et al. 2003).

Although dentine is denser than bone and surrounding enamel affords it some protection in the burial environment, it has a similar crystal size to bone and is not a reliable reservoir of original *in vivo* strontium isotope composition. In turn, however, it can be a useful indictor of local soil strontium values in its diagenetically altered state (e.g., Britton et al. 2011). Enamel, however, is considered far less susceptible to such alteration or contamination and is now the preferred analyte in archaeological, palaeontological and palaeoecological studies (Hoppe et al. 2003; Montgomery 2002). Furthermore, the analysis of intra-tooth samples of enamel (formed sequentially over a number of months) can be utilised to reconstruct time-series isotopic profiles and therefore annual and potentially seasonal geographical histories (e.g., Hoppe et al. 1999; Pellegrini et al. 2008).

Analysing Strontium Isotope Ratios in Bioapatites

Analysis of strontium isotope ratios from bioapatites normally first involves the dissolving of the sample in a strong acid. The resulting solution is then purified to chemically isolate the strontium (normally using cation exchange columns) and then measured using thermal ionisation mass spectrometry (TIMS) or multicollector inductively coupled plasma mass spectrometry (MC-ICP-MS). $^{87}Sr/^{86}Sr$ measurements are standardised through the analysis of the international strontium isotope standard NIST SRM987. SRM987 is a highly pure carbonate with a published $^{87}Sr/^{86}Sr$ value of 0.710240 (e.g., Johnson et al. 1990; Terakado et al. 1988).

Strontium isotope ratios in biogenic and geological materials can also be measured directly *in situ* using laser ablation MC-ICP-MS (e.g., Richards et al. 2008a). There is no need for chemical preparation or sample destruction, with a laser path typically around 250 × 750μm (Copeland et al. 2008). However, this method is also less precise and may be susceptible to molecular interference due to the inadvertent creation (and subsequent measurement) of Ca-P-O molecules during the laser ablation process (Copeland et al. 2008; Horstwood et al. 2008; Nowell and Horstwood 2009; Simonetti et al. 2007).

3 OXYGEN ISOTOPE ANALYSIS

Basic Principles

Oxygen isotope studies in bioarchaeology are based on the correlation between the oxygen isotope composition of mineralised animal tissues and that of the water they consumed in life, which, in turn, reflects local temperatures and climatic conditions (Longinelli 1965; Longinelli 1966; Longinelli and Nuti 1968, 1973; Longinelli 1984). There are three naturally occurring isotopes of oxygen, the most abundant being ^{16}O (99.755 per cent), as well as ^{17}O (0.039 per cent) and ^{18}O (0.206 per cent) (Schoeller 1999: 668). The ratio of ^{18}O to ^{16}O (or $\delta^{18}O$) in local meteoric water is the product of natural environmental processes that occur as part of the hydrological cycle, which influence the ratios of these isotopes through fractionation (where there is a separation of the heavier and lighter isotopes). This gives precipitation in a particular area its local oxygen isotopic 'signature'. These signatures are influenced by local temperature, but also by other factors such as altitude, humidity and distance from the coast. Given the correlation with temperature, this means the oxygen isotope values of precipitation vary geographically and can also vary seasonally in the same location. Therefore, the oxygen isotope analysis of mammalian bioapatite can be used as a secondary indicator of provenance (along with isotope systems such as sulphur or strontium), and also to reconstruct contemporary climatic conditions (palaeotemperatures) and seasonality.

Oxygen Isotopes in the Hydrosphere – from the Ocean to the Water We Drink

Ultimately, the water that falls as rain or other types of precipitation originates from the ocean. The average annual worldwide isotope composition of precipitation is depleted in the heavier isotope (^{18}O) compared to ocean water as evaporation serves to initially deplete the evaporating water, making it isotopically lighter than the source. Global and local meteoric processes then continue to bring about further depletions (Dansgaard 1964). Fractionation, like many reactions, is energy dependent, bringing about a strong relationship between temperature and the $\delta^{18}O$ of precipitation, with elevated $\delta^{18}O$ values of water increasing with increasing temperature (Dansgaard 1964). There are also correlations between local rainwater $\delta^{18}O$ values and latitude, altitude and season. The latitude effect shows an increased depletion of ^{18}O with latitude, for example, 0.5‰ $\delta^{18}O$ per degree latitude over North America (Dansgaard 1964; Yurtsever 1975). Furthermore, at mid- and high-latitudes precipitation will demonstrate seasonal variations with precipitation depleted in the heavier isotope (^{18}O) in winter months relative to the warmer seasons (Dansgaard 1964). This effect is amplified at higher latitudes, where seasonal temperature differences are exaggerated. There is also an altitudinal effect, resulting in lower $\delta^{18}O$ values with higher altitudes (Clark and Fritz 1997; Dansgaard 1964; Gat 1980) and gradients of 0.15–0.5‰ $\delta^{18}O$ per 100m are typical (Gat 1980). Coastal proximity is also known to influence the $\delta^{18}O$ values of local precipitation. As water vapour moves inland from the ocean, condenses and falls, the resultant precipitation is isotopically enriched relative to the water vapour. However, as water moves inland there is a progressive depletion of ^{18}O. This is known as the 'continental effect', as the heavier isotope is 'rained out' (Clark and Fritz 1997; Cuntz et al. 2002; Dansgaard 1964;).

There are additional processes that can influence the isotopic composition of local environmental water after rain has fallen, such as the evaporation process that occur in surface water causing ^{18}O enrichment. Lakes, rivers and other bodies (including the ocean itself) may have a lower degree of seasonal isotopic variability than meteoric water. There may be other local processes such as water mixing or water movement that could influence the oxygen isotope composition of drinking water. Water source is an especially important consideration when looking at archaeological human samples. The use of, for example, spring water, melt-water streams, or seasonally rain-filled wells would all influence human bioapatite values and lead to drinking water values that are not necessarily representative of local seasonal or mean annual meteoric isotope values (see Pederzani and Britton 2019 for an overview).

Oxygen Isotopes in Animal and Human Bioapatite

Oxygen is found in mammalian bioapatite, the structural component of mineralised tissues such as bone and tooth. These biogenic phosphates also incorporate carbonate (CO_3) components, including structural CO_3 (which substitutes for phosphate (PO_4) and hydroxyl (OH) groups in bioapatite), as well as other nonstructural mobile CO_3 components. The isotopic composition of oxygen in bioapatite (both phosphate and carbonate fractions) depends on the isotopic composition of body water and the temperature at which it is precipitated. The isotopic composition of body water is directly related to that of drinking water, along with other contributions from food and other sources within the body (Bryant and Froelich 1995; Kohn 1996; Podlesak et al. 2008). As mammals are thermoregulators, their body temperatures are relatively constant and therefore their tissue oxygen isotope composition varies systematically with the water they consume (Longinelli 1984; Luz et al. 1984). This, and the premise that ingested water is the same or very similar to oxygen isotope composition of precipitation, has allowed the application of oxygen isotope analysis to archaeological and fossil bone and teeth in order to reconstruct palaeoclimate, palaeotemperatures and – when combined with the serial-sampling of incrementally formed teeth (see Figure 5.1) – seasonal temperature variations (Bryant et al. 1994; Bryant et al. 1996a; Fricke et al. 1998; Hoppe et al. 2004). These techniques are therefore capable of producing valuable *terrestrial* palaeoclimate proxy data. For example, at the late Middle Pleistocene cave site of Coudoulous (southwestern France), the stacked phosphate oxygen isotope analysis of nine bison teeth revealed a mean annual temperature around 4°C lower than present, and increased seasonality compared to today (Bernard et al. 2009).

Fractionation occurs between ingested water and body water, although this appears to be broadly linear and predictable, with a consistent offset between the $\delta^{18}O$ of body water and PO_4 in mineralised tissues (~18‰) (cited in Kohn and Cerling 2002: 464). There is a further offset between PO_4 and CO_3 of ~9‰, although values have been reported ranging from ~8 to ~12‰ (e.g., Bryant et al. 1996b; Iacumin et al. 1996; Longinelli and Nuti 1973; Martin et al. 2008). Some interspecific differences have been observed, and these have been attributed to differences in food source, water source, water volume, local humidity and metabolic differences between species (e.g., Ayliffe et al. 1992; Bryant and Froelich 1995; Kohn 1996; Kohn et al. 1996; Longinelli 1984; Luz et al. 1984). These modern studies are very

FIGURE 5.1 A sequentially sampled archaeological horse tooth. This sampling approach, combined with oxygen isotope analysis, can reveal past seasonal temperature variations. (Photo: Kate Britton)

important, as species-specific equations are required to most accurately calculate original drinking water $\delta^{18}O$ inputs and estimate contemporary air temperatures from archaeological mammalian bioapatite $\delta^{18}O$ values.

Archaeological applications of oxygen isotope analyses thus largely focus on climatic reconstructions and the investigation of mobility in past human populations, and these are therefore the focus of this chapter. However, cultural and biological processes can also lead to changes in the oxygen isotopic composition of fluids consumed and are now also being investigated by some archaeologists. For example, due to isotopic fractionation between mother's body milk and breast milk, $\delta^{18}O$ values of tissues forming in childhood can be used to investigate past breastfeeding and weaning practices (Britton et al. 2015; Wright and Schwarcz 1998). Culturally mediated processes can also serve to modify the oxygen isotope content of fluids intended for consumption, including stewing, boiling, fermentation and distillation (Brettell et al. 2012), highlighting the potential of these methods to investigate the culinary preparation of drinking water in the past (e.g., Lamb et al. 2014). It should also be noted that water ingested can originate from food as well as liquids consumed, and that these too can be influenced by different cooking methods (e.g., Daux et al. 2008; Royer et al. 2017)

Carbonate or Phosphate Oxygen?

Oxygen isotope ratios are analysed in both the phosphate and carbonate portions of bioapatite. Due to the strength of the P-O bonds within the PO_4 component of bioapatite, it has been suggested that phosphate has a greater resistance to diagenetic alteration than carbonate components of the same sample (Kohn et al. 1999; Kolodny et al. 1983; Luz et al. 1984). As with strontium, tooth enamel is often the preferred analyte and the highly packed, dense structure of enamel even affords the structural CO_3 a degree of diagenetic resistance. However, when preparing carbonate samples, it can be necessary to remove the mobile nonstructural CO_3 with an acid pretreatment (e.g., Garvie-Lok et al. 2004; Koch et al. 1997).

It has also been demonstrated that, although carbonate components are often diagenetically altered through frequently occurring chemical contamination in the burial environment, less common biological and enzymatic attack is more likely to affect the phosphate component (e.g., Sharp et al. 2000). However, bacterial action on bones (and teeth) can normally be determined visibly or using light microscopy and samples can be avoided as necessary.

Analysing Oxygen Isotope Ratios in Bioapatite

The carbonate (CO_3) component of bioapatite (in bone and teeth) is normally analysed by dissolution in phosphoric acid (H_3PO_4), sometimes following pretreatment to remove labile carbonates (e.g., Garvie-Lok et al. 2004; Koch et al. 1997). The carbon dioxide (CO_2) evolved from the reaction with phosphoric acid is analysed for its carbon and oxygen isotope composition using a mass spectrometer. In order to analyse the phosphate component, the PO_4 must first be separated from other O-containing structures. This is normally done through dissolving the sample in acid (such as hydrofluoric acid, or HF) followed by chemical processing to produce silver phosphate (Ag_3PO_4) (e.g., Britton et al. 2015; Crowson et al. 1991; Dettman et al.

2001). This is then combusted in the presence of carbon, producing CO_2, which is then measured for its oxygen isotope composition using mass spectrometry.

The standard originally used in the first applications of oxygen isotope analysis to palaeoclimatology was PDB (Pee Dee Belemnite) – a fossil belemnite from the Pee Dee Formation of South Carolina, USA (e.g., Urey et al. 1951). This standard is now exhausted, leading to the expression of $\delta^{18}O$ values relative to two other notations – V-PDB (Vienna Pee Dee Belemnite, based on the value of standard, NBS19 carbonate, relative to PDB) or the more commonly used V-SMOW (Vienna Standard Mean Ocean Water, a recalibration of an actual ocean water sample) (see Coplen 1995).

4 COMBINING STRONTIUM AND OXYGEN ISOTOPE ANALYSIS IN MOBILITY STUDIES

As with other isotopic techniques (such as carbon and nitrogen), strontium and oxygen isotope analyses are particularly effective when used in tandem. Despite the connection to local environmental conditions, used in isolation, oxygen is not a reliable indicator of lifetime movement in archaeological teeth as a variety of factors *may* influence the oxygen isotope ratios of human tooth enamel. These include the seasonality of tooth growth and mineralisation (see discussion in Britton et al. 2015); culinary preparation techniques of food and water (Brettell et al. 2012; Daux et al. 2008; Lamb et al. 2014; Royer et al. 2017) and even an individual's physiology (Reitsema 2013; see review in Pederzani and Britton 2019). However, used alongside strontium, oxygen can be extremely useful in mobility studies, particularly in areas of very mixed or (conversely) homogenous lithology and can aid in pinpointing likely geographical origins. For example, the combined use of strontium and oxygen isotope analysis helped to identify possible geographical areas of origin for the medieval Bishops of Whithorn in lithologically varied Scotland (Müldner et al. 2009). A similar approach also helped identify first-generation immigrants to Roman York, possibly from North Africa, from where similar strontium values to those in the UK can be found but where oxygen isotope values of drinking water are markedly higher than anywhere in Europe (Leach et al. 2009). The integration of oxygen isotope analyses into intra-tooth strontium studies can allow the placing of movements in a seasonal context, for example, when reconstructing the migratory behaviours of important prey-species.

5 CASE STUDY: EXPERIMENTAL AND ANCIENT STUDIES OF CARIBOU/ REINDEER MIGRATION USING STRONTIUM AND OXYGEN ISOTOPE ANALYSIS

This case study explores the application of strontium and oxygen isotope analysis to the reconstruction of modern and Palaeolithic caribou/reindeer migrations (published in Britton et al. 2009; Britton et al. 2011). Understanding the migratory behaviours of archaeologically important prey-species, such as reindeer, is key to understanding the landscape use, subsistence choices and hunting behaviours of prehistoric hunter-gatherers (Britton 2018). In light of the relationships between underlying geology and climate, and the strontium and oxygen isotope ratios of mineralised biological tissues (explored above) it follows that the sequential sampling and subsequent isotope analysis of incrementally developed tissues should reflect movements made during the period in which those tissues grew. Where movements are regular, reflecting a true seasonal migration, such as that seen in modern North American barren-ground caribou (*Rangifer tarandus granti*), these behaviours should be documented in incremental tissues as recurrent isotopic signals.

Reindeer/caribou have low-crowned (hypsodont) teeth, and it is predicted that a full unworn molar would represent between 6 and 12 months of growth (Wu et al. 2012). Posteruptive wear would shorten this time period, although the use of the second (M2) and third molars (M3) together – which form sequentially – can extend the time-series isotopic information. Based on the formation times of fallow deer teeth, as well as radiographs of caribou jaws taken during tooth formation and eruption, it is likely that the M2 forms between the ages of <3.5 and 9-12 months, and the M3 forms between the ages of 9-12 and <24 months (Brown and Chapman 1991a: 373; Brown and Chapman 1991b; Wu et al. 2012: 556). Intra-tooth sampling methods for isotope studies are based on the idea that tooth enamel forms sequentially from cusp to cervix: these assumptions are only partially correct. Differences in the phasing and direction of enamel mineralisation, and the homogenising nature of transverse sampling, can all contribute to attenuating (or dampening) effects in isotope signals and have to be borne in mind when interpreting this type of data.

In order to explore whether these methods are applicable to archaeological materials, it was first necessary to test these methods on modern animals of known migration route, and migratory caribou from Western Alaska were selected (first presented in Britton et al. 2009; Britton 2010). The Western Arctic Herd undertakes a regular, bi-annual (seasonal) migration, which spans an area of around 360,000 km^2, incorporating areas of older underlying lithology in the summer months and more recent lithologies in winter months (Beikman 1980; Dau 2003). As a high latitude area, oxygen isotope ratios of water in the region vary seasonally, with higher values in summer and lower values in winter. Sequential strontium and oxygen (carbonate) isotope analysis of molars from several caribou from the Western Arctic Herd reveals isotope variations consistent with their movement patterns and the contemporary seasonal temperature variability (Figures 5.2a,b,c, below, based on those in Britton et al. 2009; Britton 2010). In Figure 5.2c, strontium isotope values from four migratory Alaskan caribou are compared to that of a non-migratory bison (*Bison bison*) from Utah. Compared to the Alaskan caribou, the non-migratory bison from Utah demonstrates little intra-tooth variation.

The application of these methods to a modern migratory caribou herd demonstrated their potential for investigating migratory behaviour amongst Pleistocene reindeer populations in Europe. Given the differences in climate, topography and environment between modern North America and Pleistocene Europe, along with the variety of caribou and reindeer ecotypes found today, it cannot be assumed that *Rangifer* living in Europe during the last glacial period behaved like their modern Alaskan counterparts.

The site of Jonzac is a Neanderthal butchery site in the Charente-Maritime region of France. The site is rich in faunal material and the assemblage is dominated by reindeer. Zooarchaeological analyses have suggested that the Quina Mousterian portions of this site appear to be the product of seasonal hunting activity (Jaubert et al. 2008; Richards et al. 2008b). Intra-tooth strontium isotope analysis was used to investigate whether or not reindeer (*Rangifer tarandus* sp.) and bison (*Bison* cf. *priscus*) were local or migratory at Jonzac, and to explore the implications for our understanding of Neanderthal hunting strategies. A single bison sampled from the site demonstrated very little intra-tooth variability (see Figure 5.3a) and exhibited strontium isotope values similar to the local strontium isotope 'signature' of rocks and soils (Kelly 2007), indicating this species was likely both local and non-migratory (Britton et al. 2011).

As demonstrated in Figure 5.3a and 5.3b, however, reindeer do show intra-tooth strontium isotope variability consistent with seasonal migratory behaviour – as they move between areas of different strontium isotope 'signatures'. Interestingly, none of these values match the local strontium isotope values of Jonzac soil and rock (Kelly 2007), indicating that the reindeer did not spend a significant period of time in the vicinity of Jonzac. It is instead suggested that the reindeer passed through the area on their annual migrations, with their calving/ summer and over-wintering grounds elsewhere. This new evidence for the

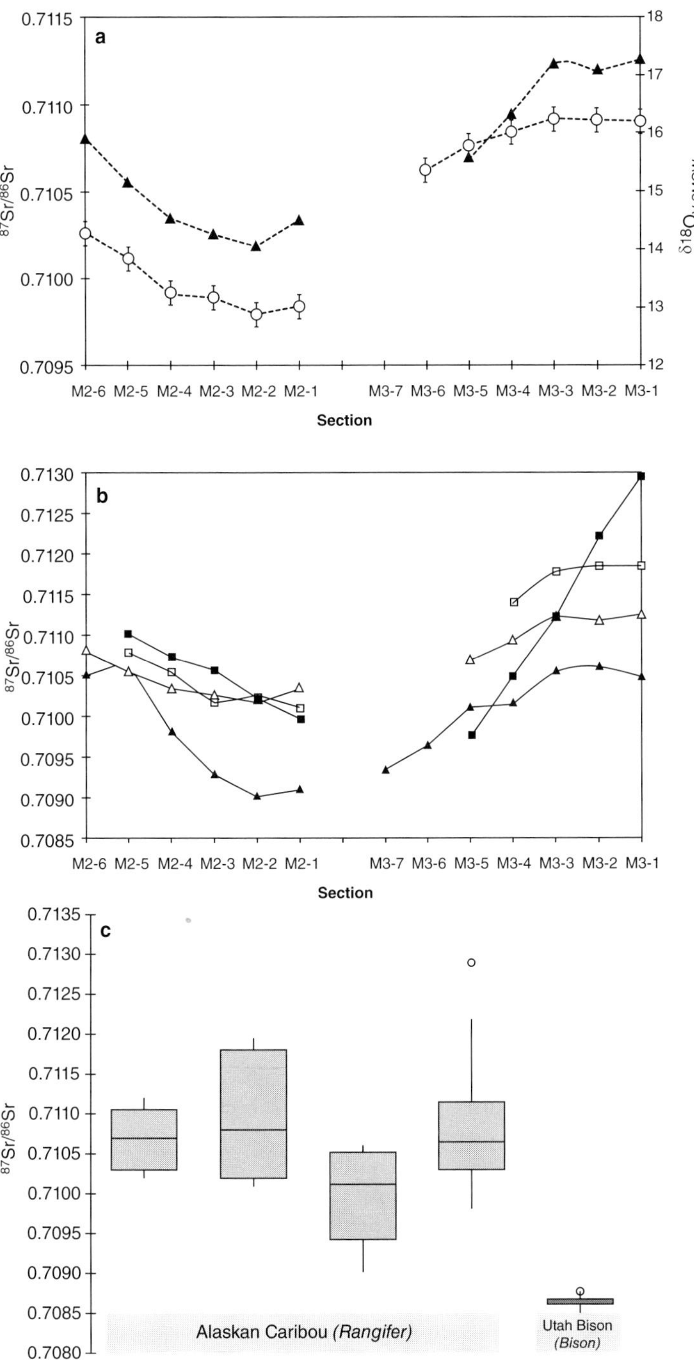

FIGURE 5.2 a. Plot of intra-tooth isotope values of $^{87}Sr/^{86}Sr$ (solid symbols) and $\delta^{18}O$ (open symbols) for the M2 and M3 of one migratory Alaskan caribou from the Western Arctic Herd. (Adapted from Britton et al. 2009: 1169, figure 4a); b. Plot of strontium isotope data ($^{87}Sr/^{86}Sr$) from intra-tooth sections from four migratory Alaskan caribou from the Western Arctic Herd. Open symbols are female and solid symbols are male. (Adapted from Britton et al. 2009: 1168, figure 2); c. Sequential $^{87}Sr/^{86}Sr$ data from four Alaskan caribou from the Western Arctic Herd and a single free-roaming bison from Utah. Box plots display the first and third quartile, median, minimum and maximum values, including outliers. (Data from Britton 2010)

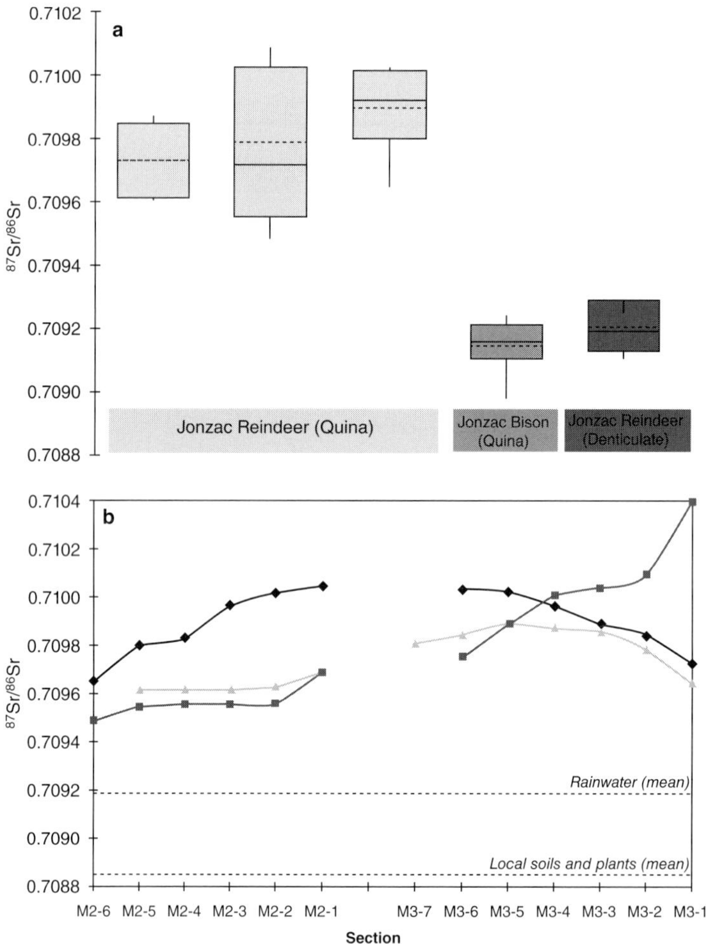

FIGURE 5.3 a. Sequential $^{87}Sr/^{86}Sr$ data from three reindeer and a bison from Quina Mousterian levels at Jonzac, and a reindeer from Denticulate Mousterian levels at Jonzac. Box plots display the first and third quartile, median, minimum and maximum values. (Adapted from Britton et al. 2011: 182, figure 3 and Britton 2018: 359, figure 20.4); b. Sequential $^{87}Sr/^{86}Sr$ data from three Quina Mousterian reindeer from Jonzac. The strontium isotope ratios of rainwater and local environmental samples (Kelly, 2007) are shown. (Adapted from Britton et al. 2011: 182, figure 2)

migratory behaviour of this species, combined with the seasonally restricted nature of hunting at the site, suggests Neanderthals used the site deliberately to target reindeer during their seasonal migrations. A single reindeer tooth was also analysed from the more recent Denticulate Mousterian cultural phase of the

Jonzac site. The lower (local) values and decreased intra-tooth variation (suggesting a lack of movement) in the Denticulate individual (Figure 5.3a) may provide the first tentative evidence for changes in reindeer migratory behaviour through time, and may indicate that this species was more 'local' and less vagile during this later, warmer period (Britton 2010; Britton 2018). This case study demonstrates not only the potential for these methods to explore animal biogeography and palaeoecology, but also shows how these data can be used to better understand hominin predation behaviour, landscape use and site selection (Britton et al. 2011).

ACKNOWLEDGEMENTS

The content of this chapter is based on a series of chapters from the doctoral thesis of the author (Britton 2010) and associated publications (Britton et al. 2009; Britton et al. 2011). This work was funded by the Max Planck Society, University of Durham, and the UK Natural Environment Research Council (ref: NER/S/A/2006/14004), with thanks to the University of Aberdeen for professional and financial support during the preparation of this chapter.

REFERENCES

Åberg, G. 1995. The use of natural strontium isotopes as tracers in environmental studies. *Water, Air and Soil Pollution* 79:309–322.

Åberg, G., Jacks, G., Wickman, T. and Hamilton, P. J. 1990. Strontium isotopes in trees as an indicator for calcium availability. *Catena* 17:1–11.

Ayliffe, L. K., Lister, A. M. and Chivas, A. R. 1992. The preservation of glacial-interglacial climatic signatures in the oxygen isotopes of elephant skeletal phosphate. *Palaeogeography, Palaeoclimatology, Palaeoecology* 99:179–191.

Balasse, M., Ambrose, S. H., Smith, A. B. and Price, T. D. 2002. The seasonal mobility model for prehistoric herders in the South-western Cape of South Africa assessed by isotopic analysis of sheep tooth enamel. *Journal of Archaeological Science* 29:917–932.

Bataille, C. P., von Holstein, I. C. C., Laffoon, J. E., Willmes, M., Liu, X. -M. and Davies, G. R., 2018. A bioavailable strontium isoscape for Western Europe: A machine learning approach. *PLoS ONE* 13:e0197386.

Beikman, H. M. 1980. *Geologic Map of Alaska*, 1:2 500 000. US Geological Survey.

Bentley, R. A. 2006. Strontium isotopes from the earth to the archaeological skeleton: A review. *Journal of Archaeological Method and Theory* 13:135–187.

Bentley, R. A. 2013. Mobility and the diversity of Early Neolithic lives: Isotopic evidence from skeletons. *Journal of Anthropological Archaeology* 32:303–312.

Bentley, R. A. and Knipper, C. 2005. Transhumance at the early Neolithic settlement at Vaihingen (Germany). *Antiquity 79 (December. Online Project Gallery).*

Bentley, R. A., Pietrusewsky, M., Douglas, M. T. and Atkinson, T. C. 2005. Matrilocality during the prehistoric transition to agriculture in Thailand? *Antiquity* 79:865–881.

Bentley, R. A., Price, T. D. and Stephen, E. 2004. Determining the 'local' $^{87}Sr/^{86}Sr$ range for archaeological skeletons: A case study from Neolithic Europe. *Journal of Archaeological Science* 31:365–375.

Bernard, A., Daux, V., Lécuyer, C., Brugal, J.-P., Genty, D., Wainer, K., Gardien, V., Fourel, F. and Jaubert, J. 2009. Pleistocene seasonal temperature variations recorded in the $\delta^{18}O$ of *Bison priscus* teeth. *Earth and Planetary Science Letters* 283:133–143.

Blum, J. D., Taliaferro, E. H., Weisse, M. T. and Holmes, R. T. 2000. Changes in Sr/Ca, Ba/Ca and $^{87}Sr/^{86}Sr$ ratios between trophic levels in two forest ecosystems in the northeastern U.S.A. *Biogeochemistry* 49:87–101.

Brettell, R., Montgomery, J. and Evans, J. 2012. Brewing and stewing: The effect of culturally mediated behaviour on the oxygen isotope composition of ingested fluids and the implications for human provenance studies. *Journal of Analytical Atomic Spectrometry* 27:778–785.

Britton, K. 2010. *Multi-isotope analysis and the reconstruction of prey species palaeomigrations and palaeoecology.* Doctoral thesis, Durham University.

Britton K. 2018. Prey species movements and migrations in ecocultural landscapes: Reconstructing late Pleistocene herbivore seasonal spatial behaviours. In: Pilaar-Birch, S. (ed.) *Multi-Species Archaeology*, pp. 347–367. London: Routledge.

Britton, K., Fuller, B. T., Tutken, T., Mays, S. and Richards, M. P. 2015. Oxygen isotope analysis of human bone phosphate evidences weaning age in archaeological populations. *American Journal of Physical Anthropology* 157:226–241.

Britton, K., Grimes, V., Dau, J. and Richards, M. P. 2009. Reconstructing faunal migrations using intra-tooth sampling and strontium and oxygen isotope analyses: A case study of modern caribou (*Rangifer tarandus granti*). *Journal of Archaeological Science* 36:1163–1172.

Britton, K., Grimes, V., Niven, L., Steele, T., McPherron, S., Soressi, M., Kelly, T. E., Jaubert, J., Hublin, J.-J. and Richards, M. P. 2011. Strontium isotope evidence for migration in late Pleistocene Rangifer: Implications for Neanderthal hunting strategies at the Middle Palaeolithic site of Jonzac, France. *Journal of Human Evolution* 61:176–185.

Brown, W. A. B. and Chapman, N. G. 1991a. Age assessment of fallow deer (*Dama dama*): From a scoring scheme based on radiographs of developing permanent molariform teeth. *Journal of Zoology, London* 224:367–379.

Brown, W. A. B. and Chapman, N. G. 1991b. The dentition of red deer (*Cervus elaphus*): A scoring scheme to assess age from wear of the permanent molariform teeth. *Journal of Zoology, London* 224:519–536.

Bryant, J. D. and Froelich, P. N. 1995. A model of oxygen isotope fractionation in body water of large mammals. *Geochimica et Cosmochimica Acta* 59:4523–4537.

Bryant, J. D., Froelich, P. N., Showers, W. J. and Genna, B. J. 1996a. Biologic and climatic signals in the oxygen isotopic composition of Eocene-Oligocene equid enamel phosphate. *Palaeogeography, Palaeoclimatology, Palaeoecology* 126:75–89.

Bryant, J. D., Koch, P. L., Froelich, P. N., Showers, W. J. and Genna, B. J. 1996b. Oxygen isotope partioning between phosphate and carbonate in mammalian apatite. *Geochimica et Cosmochimica Acta* 60:5145–5148.

Bryant, J. D., Luz, B. and Froelich, P. N. 1994. Oxygen isotopic composition of fossil horse tooth phosphate as a record of continental paleoclimate. *Palaeogeography, Palaeoclimatology, Palaeoecology* 107:303–316.

Budd, P., Millard, A., Chenery, C., Lucy, S. and Roberts, C. 2004. Investigating population movement by stable isotope analysis: A report from Britain. *Antiquity* 78:127–141.

Burton, J. H., Price, T. D. and Middleton, W. D. 1999. Correlation of bone Ba/Ca and Sr/Ca due to biological purification of calcium. *Journal of Archaeological Science* 26:609–616.

Capo, R. C., Stewert, B. W. and Chadwick, O. A. 1998. Strontium isotopes as tracers of ecosystem processes: Theory and methods. *Geoderma* 82:197–225.

Chadwick, O. A., Derry, L. A., Vitousek, P. M., Huebert, B. J. and Hedin, L. O. 1999. Changing sources of nutrients during four million years of ecosystem development. *Nature* 397:491–497.

Chenery, C., Muldner, G., Evans, J., Eckardt, H. and Lewis, M. 2010. Strontium and stable isotope evidence for diet and mobility in Roman Gloucester, UK. *Journal of Archaeological Science* 37:150–163.

Clark, I. and Fritz, P. 1997. *Environmental Isotopes in Hydrogeology*. New York: Lewis Publishers.

Copeland, S. R., Sponheimer, M., le Roux, P. J., Grimes, V., Lee-Thorp, J. A., de Ruiter, D. J. and Richards, M. P. 2008. Strontium isotope ratios ($^{87}Sr/^{86}Sr$) of tooth enamel: Comparison of solution and laser ablation multicollector inductively coupled plasma mass spectrometry methods. *Rapid Communications in Mass Spectrometry* 22:3187–3194.

Coplen, T. B. 1995. New manuscript guidelines for the reporting of stable hydrogen, carbon, and oxygen isotope-ratio data. *Geothermics* 24:707–712.

Crowson, R. A., Showers, W. J., Wright, E. K. and Hoering, T. C. 1991. Preparation of phosphate samples for oxygen isotope analysis. *Analytical Chemistry* 63:2397–2400.

Cuntz, M., Ciais, P. and Hoffmann, G. 2002. Modelling the continental effect of oxygen isotopes over Eurasia. *Tellus B* 54:895–911.

Dansgaard, W. 1964. Stable isotopes in precipitation. *Tellus* 16:436–468.

Dau, J. 2003. Units 21D, 22A, 22B, 23, 24, 26A. In: Healy, C. (ed.) *Caribou survey-inventory management report, July 1 2000–June 30 2002*. Juneau: Alaska Department of Fish and Game.

Daux, V., Lécuyer, C., Héran, M.-A., Amiot, R., Simon, L., Fourel, F., Martineau, F., Lynnerup, N., Reychler, H. and Escarguel, G. 2008. Oxygen isotope fractionation between human phosphate and water revisited. *Journal of Human Evolution* 55:1138–1147.

Dettman, D. L., Kohn, M. J., Quade, J., Ryerson, F. J., Ojha, T. P. and Hamindullah, S. 2001. Seasonal stable isotope evidence for a strong Asian monsoon throughout the past 10.7 m.y. *Geology* 29:31–34.

Dijkstra, F. A. and Smits, M. M. 2002. Tree species effects on calcium cycling: The role of calcium uptake in deep soils. *Ecosystems* 5:385–398.

Ericson, J. E. 1985. Strontium isotope characterization in the study of Prehistoric human ecology. *Journal of Human Evolution* 14:503–514.

Evans, J. A., Montgomery, J., Wildman, G. and Boulton, N. 2010. Spatial variations in biosphere 87Sr/86Sr in Britain. *Journal of the Geological Society* 167:1–4.

Evans, J. A., Stoodley, N. and Chenery, C. 2006. A strontium and oxygen isotope assessment of a possible fourth-century immigrant population in a Hampshire cemetery, southern England. *Journal of Archaeological Science* 33:265–272.

Evans, J. A., Tatham, S., Chenery, S. R. and Chenery, C. A. 2007. Anglo-Saxon animal husbandry techniques revealed though isotope and chemical variations in cattle teeth. *Applied Geochemistry* 22:1994–2005.

Ezzo, J. A., Johnson, C. M. and Price, T. D. 1997. Analytical perspective on prehistoric migration: A case study from east-central Arizona. *Journal of Archaeological Science* 24:447–466.

Fabre, M., Lécuyer, C., Brugal, J. P., Amiot, R., Fourel, F. and Martineau, F. 2011. Late Pleistocene climatic change in the French Jura (Gigny) recorded in the delta O-18 of phosphate from ungulate tooth enamel. *Quaternary Research* 75:605–613.

Faure, G. 1986. *Principles of Isotope Geology*. New York: Wiley.

Fricke, H. C., Clyde, W. C., O'Neil, J. R. and Gingerich, P. D. 1998. Evidence for rapid climate change in North America during the latest Paleocene thermal maximum: Oxygen isotope compositions of biogenetic phosphate from Bighorn Basin (Wyoming). *Earth and Planetary Science Letters* 160:193–208.

Garvie-Lok, S. J., Varney, T. and Katzenberg, M. A. 2004. Preparation of bone carbonate for stable isotope analysis: The effects of treatment time and acid concentration. *Journal of Archaeological Science* 31:763–776.

Gat, J. R. 1980. The isotopes of hydrogen and oxygen in precipitation. In: Fritz, P. and Fontes, J.-C. (eds.) *Handbook of Environmental Isotope Geochemistry*, Vol. 1: *The Terrestrial Environment*, pp. 21–42. Amsterdam: Elsevier.

Gosz, J. R. and Moore, D. I. 1989. Strontium isotope studies of atmospheric inputs to forested watersheds in New Mexico. *Biogeochemistry* 8:115–134.

Graustein, W. C. and Armstrong, R. 1983. The use of $^{87}Sr/^{86}Sr$ ratios to measure atmospheric transport into forested watersheds. *Science* 219:289–292.

Green, G. P., Bestland, E. A. and Walker, G. S. 2004. Distinguishing sources of base cations in irrigated and natural soils: Evidence from strontium isotopes. *Biogeochemistry* 68:199–225.

Hartman, G. and Richards, M. 2014. Mapping and defining sources of variability in bioavailable strontium isotope ratios in the Eastern Mediterranean. *Geochimica et Cosmochimica Acta* 126:250–264.

Hoppe, K. A., Amundson, R., Vavra, M., McClaran, M. P. and Anderson, D. L. 2004. Isotopic analysis of tooth enamel carbonate from modern North American feral horses: Implications for palaeoenvironmental reconstructions. *Palaeogeography, Palaeoclimatology, Palaeoecology* 203:299–311.

Hoppe, K. A., Koch, P. L., Carlson, R. W. and Webb, D. S. 1999. Tracking mammoths and mastodons: Reconstruction of migratory behaviour using strontium isotope ratios. *Geology* 27:439–442.

Hoppe, K. A., Koch, P. L. and Furutani, T. T. 2003. Assessing the preservation of biogenic strontium in fossil bones and tooth enamel. *International Journal of Osteoarchaeology* 13:20–28.

Horstwood, M. S. A., Evans, J. and Montgomery, J. 2008. Determination of Sr isotopes in calcium phosphates using laser ablation inductively coupled plasma mass spectrometry and their application to archaeological tooth enamel. *Geochimica et Cosmochimica Acta* 72:5659–5674.

Iacumin, P., Bocherens, H., Mariotti, A. and Longinelli, A. 1996. Oxygen isotope analyses of co-existing carbonate and phosphate in biogenic apatite: A way to monitor diagenetic alteration of bone phosphate? *Earth and Planetary Science Letters* 142:1–6.

Iyengar, W. E., Kollmer, W. E. and Bowen, H. J. M. 1978. *The Elemental Composition of Human Tissues and Body Fluids*. New York: Verlag Chemie.

Jaubert, J., Hublin, J.-J., McPherron, S. P., Soressi, M., Bordes, J.-G., Claud, E., Cochard, D., Delagnes, A., Mallye, J.-B., Michel, A., Niclot, M., Niven, L., Park, S.-J., Rendu, W., Richards, M., Richter, D., Roussel, M., Steele, T. E., Texier, J.-P. and Thiébaut, C. 2008. Paléolithique moyen récent et Paléolithique supérieur ancien a Jonzac (Charente-Maritime): premiers résultats des campagnes 2004-2006. In: Jaubert, J., Bordes, J.-G. and Ortega, I. (eds.) *Les Sociétés du Paléolithique dans un Grand Sud-ouest de la France: nouveaux gisements, nouveaux résultats, nouvelles méthods*. Paris: Mémoire de la Société Préhistorique Française.

Johnson, C. M., Lipman, P. W. and Czamanske, G. K. 1990. H, O, Sr, Nd, and Pb isotope geochemistry of the Latir volcanic field and cogenetic intrusions, New Mexico, and the relations between evolution of a continental magmatic center and modifications of the lithosphere. *Contributions to Mineralogy and Petrology* 104:99–124.

Kelly, T. E. 2007. *Strontium isotope tracing in animal teeth at the Neanderthal site of Les Pradelles, Charente, France*. B.Sc. Thesis, The Australian National University.

Kennedy, M. J., Chadwick, O. A., Vitousek, P. M., Derry, L. A. and Hendricks, D. M. 1998. Changing sources of base cations during ecosystem developement, Hawaiian Islands. *Geology* 26:1015–1018.

Kirsanow, K., Makarewicz, C. and Tuross, N. 2008. Stable oxygen (δ18O) and hydrogen (δD) isotopes in ovicaprid dentinal collagen record seasonal variation. *Journal of Archaeological Science* 35:3159–3167.

Knudson, K. J., Price, T. D., Buikstra, J. E. and Blom, D. E. 2004. The use of strontium isotope analysis to investigate Tiwanaku migration and mortuary ritual in Bolivia and Peru. *Archaeometry* 46:5–18.

Koch, P. L., Halliday, A. N., Walter, L. M., Stearley, R. F., Huston, T. J. and Smith, G. R. 1992. Sr isotopic composition of hydroxyapatite from recent and fossil salmon: The record of lifetime migration and diagenesis. *Earth and Planetary Science Letters* 108:277–287.

Koch, P. L., Tuross, N. and Fogel, M. L. 1997. The effects of sample treatment and diagenesis on the isotopic integrity of carbonate in biogenic hydroxylapatite. *Journal of Archaeological Science* 24:417–429.

Kohn, M. J. 1996. Predicting animal $\delta^{18}O$: Accounting for diet and physiological adaptation. *Geochimica et Cosmochimica Acta* 60:4811–4829.

Kohn, M. J. and Cerling, T. E. 2002. Stable isotope compositions of biological apatite. In: Kohn, M. J., Rakovan, J. F. and Hughes, J. M. (eds.) *Phosphates: Geochemical, Geobiological, and Materials Importance*, pp. 455–488. Washington, DC: Mineralogical Society of America.

Kohn, M. J., Schoeninger, M. J. and Barker, W. W. 1999. Altered states: Effects of diagenesis on fossil tooth chemistry. *Geochimica et Cosmochimica Acta* 63:2737–2747.

Kohn, M. J., Schoeninger, M. J. and Valley, J. W. 1996. Herbivore tooth oxygen isotope compositions: Effects of diet and physiology. *Geochimica et Cosmochimica Acta* 60:3889–3896.

Kolodny, Y., Luz, B. and Navon, O. 1983. Oxygen isotope variations in phosphate of biogenic apatites. 1. Fish bone apatite – rechecking the rules of the game. *Earth and Planetary Science Letters* 64:398–404.

Laffoon, J. E., Plomp, E., Davies, G. R., Hoogland, M. L. P. and Hofman, C. L. 2013. The movement and exchange of dogs in the Prehistoric Caribbean: An isotopic investigation. *International Journal of Osteoarchaeology* 25:454–465.

Lamb, A. L., Evans, J. E., Buckley, R. and Appleby, J. 2014. Multi-isotope analysis demonstrates significant lifestyle changes in King Richard III. *Journal of Archaeologial Science* 50:559–565.

Leach, S., Lewis, M., Chenery, C., Müldner, G. and Eckardt, H. 2009. Migration and diversity in Roman Britain: A multidisciplinary approach to the identification of immigrants in Roman York, England. *American Journal of Physical Anthropology* 140:546–561.

Lee-Thorp, J. A. 2008. On isotopes and old bones. *Archaeometry* 50:925–950.

Longinelli, A. 1965. Oxygen isotopic composition of orthophosphate from shells of living marine organisms. *Nature* 207:716–719.

Longinelli, A. 1966. Ratios of Oxygen-18: Oxygen-16 in phosphate and carbonate from living and fossil marine organisms. *Nature* 211:923–927.

Longinelli, A. 1984. Oxygen isotopes in mammal bone phosphate: A new tool for paleohydrological and paleoclimatological research? *Geochimica et Cosmochimica Acta* 48:385–390.

Longinelli, A. and Nuti, S. 1968. Oxygen-isotope ratios in phosphate from fossil marine organisms. *Science* 160:879–882.

Longinelli, A. and Nuti, S. 1973. Oxygen isotope measurements of phosphate from fish teeth and bones. *Earth and Planetary Science Letters* 20:337–340.

Luz, B., Kolodny, Y. and Horowitz, M. 1984. Fractionation of oxygen isotopes between mammalian bone-phosphate and environmental drinking water. *Geochimica et Cosmochimica Acta* 48:1689–1693.

Martin, C., Bentaleb, I., Kaandorp, R., Iacumin, P. and Chatri, K. 2008. Intra-tooth study of modern rhinoceros enamel delta O-18: Is the difference between phosphate and carbonate delta O-18 a sound diagenetic test? *Palaeogeography, Palaeoclimatology, Palaeoecology* 266:183–187.

Montgomery, J. 2002. *Lead and strontium isotope compositions of human dental tissues as an indicator of ancient exposure and population dynamics: The application of isotope source-tracing methods to identify migrants among British archaeological burials and a consideration of ante-mortem uptake, tissue stability and post-mortem diagenesis.* Doctoral thesis, University of Bradford.

Montgomery, J., Evans, J. and Cooper, R. E. 2007. Resolving archaeological populations with Sr-isotope mixing models. *Applied Geochemistry* 22:1502–1514.

Montgomery, J., Evans, J. A. and Neighbour, T. 2003. Sr isotope evidence for population movement within the Hebridean Norse community of NW Scotland. *Journal of the Geological Society* 160:649–653.

Montgomery, J., Evans, J., Powlesland, D. and Roberts, C. A. 2005. Continuity or colonization in Anglo-Saxon England? Isotope evidence for mobility, subsistence practice and status at West Heslerton. *American Journal of Physical Anthroplogy* 126:123–138.

Morgan, J. E., Richards, S. P. G. and Morgan, A. J. 2001. Stable strontium accumulation by earthworms: A paradigm for radiostrontium interactions with its cationic analogue, calcium. *Environmental Toxicology and Chemistry* 20:1236–1243.

Müldner, G., Montgomery, J., Cook, G., Ellam, R., Gledhill, A. and Lowe, C. 2009. Isotopes and individuals: Diet and mobility among the medieval Bishops of Whithorn. *Antiquity* 83:1119–1133.

Nelson, D. E., DeNiro, M. J., Schoeninger, M. J., DePaolo, D. J. and Hare, P. E. 1986. Effects of diagenesis on strontium, carbon, nitrogen, and oxygen concentration and isotopic composition of bone. *Geochimica et Cosmochimica Acta* 50:1941–1949.

Németh, T., Kiss, Z., Kismányoky, T. and Lehoczky, E. 2006. Effect of long-term fertilization on the strontium content of soil. *Communications in Soil Science and Plant Analysis* 37:2751–2758.

Nielsen-Marsh, C. M., Gernaey, A., Turner-Walker, G., Hedges, R. E. M., Pike, A. and Collins, M. 2000. The chemical degradation of bone. In: Cox, M. and Mays, S. (eds.) *Human Osteology in Archaeology and Forensic Science*, pp. 439–454. London: GMM.

Nielsen-Marsh, C. M. and Hedges, R. E. M. 2000a. Patterns of diagenesis in bone II: Effects of acetic acid treatment and removal of diagenetic CO_3. *Journal of Archaeological Science* 27:1151–1159.

Nielsen-Marsh, C. M. and Hedges, R. E. M. 2000b. Patterns of diagenesis in bone I: The effects of site environments. *Journal of Archaeological Science* 27:1139–1150.

Nowell, G. M. and Horstwood, M. S. A. 2009. Comments on Richards et al. Journal of Archaeological Science 35, 2008 'Strontium isotope evidence of Neanderthal mobility at the site of Lakonis, Greece using laser-ablation PIMMS'. *Journal of Archaeological Science* 36:1334–1341.

Pederzani, S. and Britton, K., 2019. Oxygen isotopes in bioarchaeology: Principles and applications, challenges and opportunities. *Earth-Science Reviews* 188, 77–107.

Pellegrini, M., Donahue, R. E., Chenery, C., Evans, J., Lee-Thorp, J., Montgomery, J. and Mussi, M. 2008. Faunal migration in late-glacial central Italy: Implications for human resource exploitation. *Rapid Communications in Mass Spectrometry* 22:1714–1726.

Podlesak, D. W., Torregrossa, A.-M., Ehleringer, J. R., Dearing, M. D., Passey, B. H. and Cerling, T. E. 2008. Turnover of oxygen and hydrogen isotopes in the body water, CO_2, hair, and enamel of a small mammal. *Geochimica et Cosmochimica Acta* 72:19–35.

Price, T. D., Blitz, J., Burton, J. H. and Ezzo, J. A. 1992. Diagenesis in prehistoric bone: Problems and solutions. *Journal of Archaeological Science* 19:513–529.

Price, T. D., Burton, J. H. and Bentley, R. A. 2002. The characterization of biological available strontium isotope ratios for the study of prehistoric migration. *Archaeometry* 44:117–135.

Price, T. D., Meiggs, D., Weber, M.-J. and Pike-Tay, A. 2017. The migration of Late Pleistocene reindeer: Isotopic evidence from northern Europe. *Archaeological and Anthropological Sciences* 9:371–394.

Reitsema, L. J. 2013. Beyond diet reconstruction: Stable isotope applications to human physiology, health, and nutrition. *American Journal of Human Biology* 25:445–456.

Richards, M. P., Harvati, K., Grimes, V., Smith, C., Smith, T., Hublin, J. J., Karkanas, P. and Panagopoulou, E. 2008a. Strontium isotope evidence of Neanderthal mobility at the site of Lakonis, Greece using laser-ablation PIMMS. *Journal of Archaeological Science* 35:1251–1256.

Richards, M. P., Taylor, G., Steele, T., McPherron, S. P., Soressi, M., Jaubert, J., Orschiedt, J., Mallye, J. B., Rendu, W. and Hublin, J. J. 2008b. Isotopic dietary analysis of a Neanderthal and associated fauna from the site of Jonzac (Charente-Maritime), France. *Journal of Human Evolution* 55:179–185.

Royer, A., Daux, V., Fourel, F. and Lécuyer, C. 2017. Carbon, nitrogen and oxygen isotope fractionation during food cooking: Implications for the interpretation of the fossil human record. *American Journal of Physical Anthropology* 163:759–771.

Schoeller, D. A. 1999. Isotope fractionation: Why aren't we what we eat? *Journal of Archaeological Science* 26:667–673.

Schweissing, M. M. and Grupe, G. 2003. Stable strontium isotopes in human teeth and bone: A key to migration events of the late Roman period in Bavaria. *Journal of Archaeological Science* 30:1373–1383.

Sharp, Z. D., Atudorei, V. and Furrer, H. 2000. The effect of diagenesis on oxygen isotope ratios of biogenic phosphate. *American Journal of Science* 300:222–237.

Sharp, Z. D. and Cerling, T. E. 1998. Fossil isotope records of seasonal climate and ecology: Straight from the horse's mouth. *Geology* 26:219–222.

Sillen, A., Hall, G., Richardson, S. and Armstrong, R. 1998. $^{87}Sr/^{86}Sr$ ratios in modern and fossil food-webs of the Sterkfontein Valley: Implications for early hominid habitat preference. *Geochimica et Cosmochimica Acta* 62:2463–2478.

Simonetti, A., Buzon, M. R. and Creaser, R. A. 2007. In-situ elemental and Sr isotope investigation of human tooth enamel by laser ablation-(MC)-ICP-MS: Successes and pitfalls. *Archaeometry* 50:371–385.

Steadman, L. T., Brudevold, F. and Smith, F. A. 1958. Distribution of strontium in teeth from different geographic areas. *Journal of the American Dental Association* 57:340–344.

Steele, J. D. and Pushkar, P. 1973. Strontium isotope geochemistry of the Scioto River basin and the $^{87}Sr/^{86}Sr$ ratios of the underlying lithologies. *The Ohio Journal of Science* 73:331–338.

Terakado, Y., Shimizu, H. and Masuda, A. 1988. Nd and Sr isotopic variations in acidic rocks formed under a peculiar tectonic environment in Miocene Southwest Japan. *Contributions to Mineralogy and Petrology* 99:1–10.

Thornton, E. K. 2011. Reconstructing ancient Maya animal trade through strontium isotope (87Sr/86Sr) analysis. *Journal of Archaeological Science* 38:3254–3263.

Trickett, M. A., Budd, P., Montgomery, J. and Evans, J. 2003. An assessment of solubility profiling as a decontamination procedure for the $^{87}Sr/^{86}Sr$ analysis of archaeological human skeletal tissue. *Applied Geochemistry* 18:653–658.

Tuross, N., Behrensmeyer, A. K. and Eanes, E. D. 1989. Strontium increases and crystalinity changes in taphonomic and archaeological bone. *Journal of Archaeological Science* 16:661–672.

Urey, H. C., Lowenstam, H. A., Epstein, S. and McKinney, C. R. 1951. Measurement of paleotemperatures and temperatures of the Upper Cretaceous of England, Denmark, and the southeastern United States. *Bulletin of the Geological Society of America* 62:399–416.

Vitousek, P. M., Kennedy, M. J., Derry, L. A. and Chadwick, O. A. 1999. Weathering versus atmospheric sources of strontium in ecosystems on young volcanic soils. *Oecologia* 121:255–259.

Willmes, M., McMorrow, L., Kinsley, L., Armstrong, R., Aubert, M., Eggins, S., Falguères, C., Maureille, B., Moffat, I. and Grün, R. 2014. The IRHUM (Isotopic Reconstruction of

Human Migration) database – bioavailable strontium isotope ratios for geochemical fingerprinting in France. *Earth System Science Data* 6:117–122.

Wright, L. E. and Schwarcz, H. P. 1998. Stable carbon and oxygen isotopes in human tooth enamel: Identifying breastfeeding and weaning in prehistory. *American Journal of Physical Anthropology* 106:1–18.

Wu, J. P., Veitch, A., Checkley, S., Dobson, H. and Kutz, S. J., 2012. Linear enamel hypoplasia in caribou (Rangifer tarandus groenlandicus): A potential tool to assess population health. *Wildlife Society Bulletin* 36:554–560.

Xin, G. and Hanson, G. N. 1994. *Strontium isotope study of the Peconic river watershed, Long Island, New York.* MSc thesis, State University of New York at Stony Brook.

Yurtsever, Y. 1975. *Worldwide survey of stable isotopes in precipitation. Report Section Isotope Hydrology.* Vienna: IAEA.

6

Isotope Analysis for Diet Studies

Michael P. Richards

Stable isotope analysis of humans and animals from archaeological sites as a means of constructing past diets (palaeodiet).

1 INTRODUCTION

Bone collagen carbon and nitrogen isotope analysis is a powerful tool for providing direct measures of past human diets (Lee-Thorp 2008; Macarewicz and Sealy 2015). Since it was first applied to archaeological bone samples in the late 1970s and early 1980s it has grown into a well-established and now widely applied method (Britton 2017).

The interpretations of past human diets using this method are limited, telling us only about long-term dietary sources of protein, and then only being able to discriminate between marine and terrestrial resources, C_3 and C_4 plants and plant and animal foods. However, when linked to the appropriate question they can be extremely useful in understanding past human diets. Indeed, they have been instrumental in our understanding of dietary change at many important points in archaeology, and especially in prehistory. These include the Mesolithic/Neolithic transition in Europe (Bonsall et al. 1997; Lubell et al. 1994; Richards et al. 2003; Tauber 1981); the spread of maize agriculture in North America (Schoeninger 2009; van der Merwe and Vogel 1978; Vogel and van der Merwe 1977); the introduction of millet into human diets in Neolithic China (Hu et al. 2008; Pechenkina et al. 2005), and the dietary adaptations of Neanderthals and Upper Palaeolithic humans in Europe (Bocherens 2009; Richards and Trinkaus 2009).

In this chapter the methods of extracting collagen from bone and measuring the isotope values is discussed in detail, along with how and what the carbon and nitrogen isotopes can tell us about past diets.

2 WHY BONE COLLAGEN?

Carbon and nitrogen isotope measurements of bone collagen were first used not as a dietary indicator but instead as part of the radiocarbon dating process for determining the age of bone. To effectively calibrate ^{14}C dates it is necessary to measure the ^{12}C and ^{13}C ratio of the material being dated, and in the late 1970s and early 1980s radiocarbon dating researchers in South Africa (Vogel and van der Merwe 1977), Denmark (Tauber 1981) and Canada (Chisholm et al. 1982) noticed that there was a pattern in the isotope data produced as part of the dating process. Specifically, they observed that bone collagen carbon isotope values from humans that had consumed marine foods or C_4 photosynthetic-pathway plants like maize in their diets had distinct $^{13}C/^{12}C$ bone collagen isotope ratios (e.g., Chisholm et al. 1982; Tauber 1981; Vogel and van der Merwe 1977). Since then, isotope measurements of bone collagen has become a research field in its own right, widely applied to sites around the world, although there are still strong links to radiocarbon dating, with isotope measurements of bone collagen to determine preservation quality often undertaken as the first step in radiocarbon dating.

Collagen itself has become the preferred substrate for isotope analysis also because of this link to radiocarbon dating. Early radiocarbon researchers attempted to date whole bone, and various bone constituents like carbonate in bone mineral, but soon realised that bones were often contaminated with carbon from other sources (such as soil). Longin (1971) proposed that it was better to extract the protein collagen from the bone, as it was believed to have been better preserved and less altered, in terms of carbon, than whole bone or the more abundant bone mineral. Subsequently, tests on collagen quality showed that there was a range of preservation factors that could be applied to the extracted collagen to determine if it was contaminated, or intact, original collagen (Ambrose 1990; DeNiro 1985). This is discussed in more detail in the next section.

3 BONE COLLAGEN EXTRACTION AND QUALITY CONTROL METHODS

Modern bone is composed of approximately 20 per cent collagen by weight (Simkiss and Wilbur 1989). The collagen molecules form a structural base for bone mineral (the main bone component). In order to use collagen for palaeodietary studies it is necessary to extract the collagen, and ensure that other bone constituents that contain carbon such as mineral or lipids, and post-mortem contaminants that contain carbon and nitrogen are all removed. There are essentially two methods for extracting collagen from archaeological bone samples (pretreatment). The first, and most widely used, method is derived from the original 1971 Longin paper, which describes how to extract collagen for radiocarbon dating, as discussed above. This method, and others related to it, uses a weak hydrochloric (HCl) acid treatment to dissolve away the bone mineral and then through various rinses and filters leaves behind the insoluble (in HCl) fraction, which is largely composed of bone collagen (although not entirely, therefore many researchers refer to the extracted material as 'collagen' indicating that it may also contain other molecules). More recent refinements of the method include pretreatment at cold (ca. 5°C) temperatures (as opposed to the more usual room temperature) (Collins and Galley 1998; Richards and Hedges 1999). Other modifications include the use of sodium dilute sodium hydroxide (NaOH) to remove contaminating humic acids following demineralisation (e.g., Ambrose 1990), and the use of an ultrafiltration step to extract collagen fragments of particular sizes (with >30,000 kDa being the most used size) (Brown et al. 1988). The second method involves the use of Ethylenediaminetetraacetic acid (EDTA) to dissolve the bone mineral (Tuross et al. 1988), however, as EDTA contains both carbon and nitrogen care must be taken to effectively rinse away the EDTA after pretreatment. Due to this complication, EDTA is only rarely used for archaeological samples.

There are a number of quality indicators that have been proposed as a means to test whether the extracted collagen is well preserved, or has been contaminated or altered (Ambrose 1990; DeNiro 1985; van Klinken 1999). The first of these is simply the collagen yield, which is the percentage, by weight, of collagen extracted from the total bone weight. Further measurements are often undertaken as part of the isotope measurement process. They are the measurement, using an elemental analyser, of the carbon and nitrogen contents of the extract. Modern collagen has approximately 46 per cent carbon and 16 per cent nitrogen, and therefore has a carbon to nitrogen ratio of 3.21. There is a widely accepted recognition that most archaeological collagen has been altered in some way after deposition, so a range of accepted values has been proposed (Ambrose 1990; DeNiro 1985) for well-preserved collagen. These are a C:N ratio of between 2.9 and 3.6, and collagen yield of greater than 1 per cent. With the use of filtration methods such as ultrafiltration, the collagen yields are lower than the total collagen yields, as only a specific size fraction of collagen is extracted, so if these filter are used it is possible to have acceptable collagen with yields lower than 1 per cent, if the C:N ratios are within the range of 2.9 to 3.6.

4 HOW TO MEASURE THE STABLE ISOTOPE RATIOS OF CARBON AND NITROGEN

Once collagen has been extracted the isotope values are most commonly measured using an elemental analyser (EA) attached ('coupled') to a gas isotope ratio mass spectrometer (together colloquially called a 'continuous flow isotope ratio mass spectrometer', or cf-irms) (Hoefs 2008). The collagen sample is combusted at high temperature in an elemental analyser, which results in the production of various gases, including the two of primary interest, N_2 and CO_2, and then these gases pass through a gas chromatograph, which separates the various gases based on their mass. The separated gases are then introduced into a gas mass spectrometer where the isotope ratios of the various gases are measured. Previous to the use of continuous flow mass spectrometers linked to elemental analysers, collagen was combusted 'off-line' in a vacuum and then the various gases of interest were collected – a method still used in some laboratories and for specific types of samples (i.e., very small samples). In this method the gas is then introduced directly into a mass spectrometer (usually a 'dual-inlet' mass spectrometer) (Hoefs 2008).

There are various types of elemental analysers, the first step in the continuous flow process, and these are routinely used in chemistry, biology and earth science as a means of measuring the relative amounts of elements such as C, N and S in a sample (e.g., soils, foodstuffs). Elemental analysers were first joined to mass spectrometers in the 1980s (Preston and Owens 1983), and the essential design of them has not changed. Indeed, as they are mostly used for non-isotope related research, there can be a number of problems and issues in the coupling of the elemental analyser to a gas isotope-ratio mass spectrometer. The main one issue is that the EAs are not designed (at least the standard ones) for very small samples, so collagen sizes used for measurement tend to be between 0.5 and 1 mg. However, the gas isotope mass spectrometers are capable of measuring very small gas samples, so theoretically it should be possible to measure much smaller samples, but currently this requires custom-built or modified elemental analysers, or off-line combustion of samples. However, for most archaeological samples (especially Holocene material from temperate climates) collagen preservation is such that it is relatively easy to extract enough collagen for carbon and nitrogen analysis using the standard elemental analyser-gas isotope mass spectrometer configuration.

Elemental analysers need to be set up specifically (especially the gas chromatography column, if the EA uses one) to measure the element, or elements of interest. To achieve the best precision in isotope measurements, it is therefore best practice to focus on measuring just one element at the time, setting up the EA and mass spectrometer for just carbon measurements, for example. This is because the mass spectrometers need to be optimised to a specific amount of gas from the sample compared to a known standard. Therefore, as there is approximately three times more carbon than nitrogen in a collagen samples (as can be seen by the C:N ratio of 3.21), it can cause problems in the mass spectrometer with much more CO_2 than N_2 being introduced during the same sample run. Also, the mass spectrometers are set to measure specific masses (e.g., 45, and 44 for measuring $^{13}C^{16}O_2$, compared to $^{12}C^{16}O^2$) and switching the setting to measure different masses during a sample run (e.g., to 30, 29 and 28 to measure $^{15}N^{15}N_2$, $^{15}N^{14}N_2$ and $^{14}N^{14}N_2$) is disruptive and introduces the possibility of inaccurate measurements of the second elements if the magnet settings of the mass spectrometer do not switch to the new masses adequately.

However, despite this issue, it is now common practice in carbon and nitrogen collagen isotope measurements to measure both C and N in the same sample in the same sample run. After the initial measurements of N_2 (it is the lighter gas, so comes through the gas chromatography column first) the magnet settings of the mass spectrometer are changed to then be able to measure the heavier CO_2. This results in a loss of precision for both elements, with errors on carbon isotope ratios being on the order of ±0.1 per mil (‰), and ±0.2 ‰ for nitrogen. However, for palaeodietary studies this is not usually a problem, as the questions that are being addressed rely on differences between samples of over 1 per mil (‰), which is much greater than the precision differences between measuring each element individually.

One advantage of the use of the EA is to measure of total elemental composition in the sample when collagen is combusted, which is then used to measure the %C and % N in a sample, and C:N ratio. However, many researchers do not use the built-in capabilities of the EA for these measurements and instead rely on the measurements (peak intensity) of the amount of CO_2 and N_2 in the mass spectrometer, compared to a known standard sample with known C and N amounts, which is then combusted in the same sample sequences as the unknown samples. Indeed an essential part of the process of determining isotope ratios is the use of standards that are measured alongside the unknown samples. These standards should be matrix-matched (meaning they are composed of the same material as the unknown, so a collagen standard for measuring collagen). In addition, there are a number of internationally used standards that are available for isotope laboratories to use. When reporting isotope data in a publication is it important to include the information on what standards were used, and how the isotope values of the unknown samples were determined in relation to these known-isotope ratio standards.

5 INTERPRETING THE ISOTOPE RATIO MEASUREMENTS OF CARBON AND NITROGEN IN BONE COLLAGEN

The first isotope studies of bone collagen for dietary analysis were undertaken using primarily carbon isotopes, with a more limited number of applications of nitrogen isotope analysis (e.g., DeNiro and Epstein 1981; Epstein 1982; Schoeninger et al. 1983; Tauber 1981; Vogel and van der Merwe 1977). In the 1990s it became technically easier to measure nitrogen isotopes in collagen (using continuous-flow elemental analysers coupled to gas isotope ratio mass spectrometers, discussed above), which led to a significant increase in the number of papers that measured both carbon and nitrogen isotopes together in archaeological bone collagen samples. However, even today relatively little is known about exactly how nitrogen isotope ratios fractionate in the body, so unlike carbon, which is fairly well understood, there are still debates about the interpretation of bone collagen nitrogen isotope ratio values. However, in the appropriate contexts, and when addressing appropriate questions, nitrogen isotopes can be a powerful palaeodietary tool, especially when measured alongside carbon.

Carbon Isotopes

The best understood, and best established, element used for bone collagen palaeodiet studies is carbon. There are a number of stable and unstable isotopes of carbon, and the two stable isotopes that are used for palaeodietary studies are carbon 13 (^{13}C) and carbon 12 (^{12}C). ^{12}C is the most abundant, representing approximately 98.89 per cent of the total carbon in the biosphere, while the more rare ^{12}C represents approximately 1.11 per cent (Hoefs 2008). Carbon isotopes are measured using the delta notation (δ), and the isotope ratio of ^{13}C to ^{12}C in a sample is called the $\delta^{13}C$ value, and is expressed in parts per thousand (per mil, ‰) and is defined as:

$$\delta^{13}C = [[(^{13}C/^{12}C)sample/(^{13}C/^{12}C)standard] - 1] \times 1000$$

The original standard used in the above equation was a marine fossil shell, called Pee Dee Belemnite, which has now been replaced with a more abundant standard called Vienna Pee Dee Belemnite (vPDB) (Coplen 1994). As this marine shell was the first carbon isotope standard, the $\delta^{13}C$ value was set, arbitrarily, to a value of 0 ‰. Atmospheric carbon has slightly less ^{13}C than in ocean seawater (the main source of carbon in the Pee Dee Belemnite standard) and when compared to the

PDB standard it has a $\delta^{13}C$ value of approximately −7 ‰. This difference of approximately 7 ‰ between the average seawater carbon value and the average atmosphere value is important when we look at differences in diets between marine and terrestrial foods, as this difference is maintained through the food chains in both ecosystems. Also, as a marine shell was chosen as the standard, it means that most reported terrestrial $\delta^{13}C$ values are negative in relation to the standard, which is why most reported human $\delta^{13}C$ collagen values are negative.

There are differences in the carbon isotope values of plants that use different photosynthetic pathways (O'Leary 1981). In the terrestrial ecosystem, plants use atmospheric CO_2 in photosynthesis, and take in this gas through their stomata. These stomata open and close throughout the day and night, as the plants balance out the benefits of absorbing CO_2 when the stomata is open with the loss of water from the plants that also occurs during this process (see Marshall et al. 2007 for a review of this process). C_3 (the most common pathway) plants are typically found in temperate environments. In these temperate climates there is limited loss of water from evaporation when their stomata is open, so they can open for longer periods of time than plants that follow other photosynthetic pathways, and discriminate against (block) the heavier isotope ^{13}C, in favour of the lighter ^{12}C. This is because it requires less energy by the plant to process ^{12}C than ^{13}C. Therefore, there is fractionation between the atmosphere and the CO_2 that is taken into the plant, which leaves more of the ^{13}C behind in the atmosphere, resulting in C_3 plant tissues having $\delta^{13}C$ values that are much lower than the atmosphere values. This process is called kinetic fractionation, and results in C_3 plants in temperate environments having an average of approximately −26 ‰, compared to the atmospheric value of ca. 7 ‰. This average C_3 plant $\delta^{13}C$ value also includes fractionations that occur during biological physiological processes of building plant tissues, which also discriminates against the heavier ^{13}C isotope.

Plants that use the less common C_4 photosynthetic pathway (i.e., millet, maize) are usually found in arid environments, where water loss from evaporation can be detrimental to the plants, and they therefore they open their stomata for much shorter periods than C_3 plants. This means that there is much less time to discriminate against the heavier ^{13}C atoms, therefore, there is less of a fractionation between the atmospheric CO_2 and the plant tissues compared to C_3 plants (Marshall et al. 2007). This results in C_4 plants having an average $\delta^{13}C$ value of −13 ‰.

Even more uncommon are plants that use the CAM (Crassulean acid metabolism) photosynthetic pathway (e.g., bromeliads such as pineapples) and they can greatly vary their uptake of CO_2 and discrimination against atmospheric ^{13}C (Marshall et al. 2007). Therefore, they can have plant tissue $\delta^{13}C$ values that fall between the C_3 to the C_4 plant values.

In oceans, similar fractionations occur within food webs as in terrestrial ecosystems, and there is also a discrimination against the heavier ^{13}C by marine plants, most of which also use the C_3 photosynthetic pathway (Michener et al. 2007). Marine plant tissues have $\delta^{13}C$ values that are just as fractionated from their source (ocean carbonate) as terrestrial plants are from theirs (atmospheric carbon). However, their starting points are different, as marine ocean carbon values are approximately 7 ‰ more positive than atmospheric carbon, so marine plants have, on average, tissue $\delta^{13}C$ values of approximately −19 ‰, compared to atmospheric C_3 plants with a value of −26 ‰.

When animals consume either marine or terrestrial plants they use the carbon for many purposes, including building their body tissues such as muscle tissue and bone collagen (see Koch 2007 for a review of carbon isotopes in vertebrate body tissues). Herbivores will use some of the plant amino acids directly (with some fractionation during the process) to form their body tissues (these are traditionally called essential amino acids) and for other amino acids (non-essential) they construct these from various sources of dietary carbon and from carbon resulting from the normal breakdown and turnover of existing body tissues. The carbon in each amino acid that is found in body tissue has its own history of either being directly incorporated in collagen (or more accurately, mostly composed of the same carbon from amino acids from when that amino acid was ingested) or formed using dietary carbon from various sources. There are many steps in both of these processes that result in fractionation (discriminating against the heavier ^{13}C) between the carbon that was consumed and the final amino acid that is used to make bone collagen. The sum total of all of these fractionations is that herbivore muscle tissue (flesh) has an average value that is approximately 3 ‰ heavier (i.e., with more ^{13}C) than the average plant tissue $\delta^{13}C$ value. Herbivore bone collagen, which of course is the material that we extract and study for isotope palaeodietary research, is less heavy (with less ^{13}C) than herbivore flesh, with an average bone collagen $\delta^{13}C$ value that is approximately 5 ‰ heavier than the average plant tissue $\delta^{13}C$ values (Ambrose and Norr 1993; Kellner and Schoeninger 2007). Omnivores and carnivores that consume herbivore flesh also make their body tissues using some of the dietary amino acids taken directly from the herbivore tissue and others assembled within their bodies. Omnivore and carnivore flesh is then fractionated compared to the herbivore flesh they consume, and their bone collagen, after all of the fractionations, ends up being only slightly fractionated compared to the herbivore average collagen value (1–2 ‰), but 5 ‰ compared to herbivore tissue values.

There are many caveats to the above explanations. First, there are variations in marine and atmospheric $\delta^{13}C$ values in different regions of the world. Plant tissue $\delta^{13}C$ values also vary according to climate, partial pressure and aridity. And indeed these values have also changed and varied through time. Also, some organisms, when they have a high protein diet, route non-essential amino acids from their diets to their bone collagen and so it if far less fractionated than when that same type of amino acid is formed by the body. Freshwater ecosystems can have multiple sources of carbon, including carbon from terrestrial plants as well as carbon originating from the underlying bedrock. In extreme cases where the bedrock is limestone (and therefore past ocean floor sediments), freshwater organisms can have $\delta^{13}C$ values that resemble marine ecosystems. And indeed, marine ecosystems can also have significant freshwater input that can alter the starting plant $\delta^{13}C$ values to result in values that may appear to be more like typical terrestrial values. Also, unusual ecosystems like marine reefs or terrestrial rainforests also have effects on the $\delta^{13}C$ values of plants (e.g., the so-called canopy effect in forests with heavy tree cover and poor CO_2 circulation; van der Merwe and Medina 1991). Much work still needs to be done on understanding the processes of how carbon moves through the food chain and is used to form bone collagen. However, for much of the world and for most time periods, bone collagen carbon isotope values have proven to be a very robust and reliable method for determining the dietary source of carbon for mammals.

Nitrogen Isotopes

While the carbon in bone collagen can derive from dietary protein, carbohydrates and fats (lipids), the nitrogen in bone collagen can only come from nitrogen in dietary protein, as lipids and carbohydrates do not contain nitrogen (Koch 2007). However, although there is only a single source of nitrogen it is still poorly understood how and where nitrogen isotope fractionation occurs in the body between consuming dietary protein and the formation of bone collagen. As discussed above, dietary protein is composed of individual amino acids and there is some evidence that some of these amino acids (called essential, or indispensable) that the body cannot produce itself are then routed fairly directly after digestion into bone collagen with little or no fractionation of the nitrogen isotope values. This means that for many organisms the bone collagen essential amino acids have the same, or similar, nitrogen isotope ratios as the dietary protein. The majority of bone collagen, however, is composed of non-essential (also called dispensable) amino acids, which can be formed by the organism. The nitrogen in these non-essential amino acids can come from a variety of body sources, including digested nitrogen from proteins, as well as from the breakdown and turnover of existing body proteins. Therefore, the non-essential amino acids often have a nitrogen isotope ratio that is very different from the nitrogen isotope ratio of dietary protein. To confuse matters further, in cases of high protein diets there is also some evidence that non-essential amino acids can also be directly routed to bone collagen, so in those cases they actually would have similar nitrogen isotope values to dietary protein.

Despite all of the possible complications in nitrogen fractionation in non-essential amino acids and direct routing of essential and non-essential amino acids, there is a remarkably consistent offset between the overall nitrogen isotope value of dietary protein and an organism's total body protein nitrogen isotope value. In many organisms, from plankton, to insects, to mammals, the fractionation is approximately 3 ‰ (Schoeninger and DeNiro 1984). This points to a source of the fractionation that is fundamental to all organisms, likely related to the similar processes of forming non-essential amino acids.

For humans, the fractionation between dietary protein and bone collagen is not as clear, but also not extremely variable. It has been reported to be between 3 and 6 ‰, with many studies that have both human and animal bone collagen values (with the animals indicating the dietary nitrogen isotope value) having a fractionation closer to 4.5 ‰ (Hedges and Reynard 2007).

Nitrogen isotope values are expressed in a similar way to carbon isotopes, also using the delta notation. The $\delta^{15}N$ value is defined as the ratio of the rarer (0.366 per cent of biosphere nitrogen) nitrogen 15 (^{15}N) to the more abundant (99.634 per cent of biosphere nitrogen) nitrogen 14 (^{14}N) in a sample (Hoefs 2008), expressed in parts per thousand (per mil, ‰) using this equation:

$$\delta^{15}N = [[(^{15}N/^{14}N)\text{sample}/(^{15}N/^{14}N)\text{standard}] - 1] \times 1{,}000$$

The standard used for $\delta^{15}N$ measurements is AIR, which is the Ambient Inhalable Reservoir, the average value of atmospheric nitrogen, and is set at a value of 0 ‰, although the observed value of atmospheric nitrogen is closer to 1.6 ± 1.4 ‰ (Owens 1987).

Plants obtain nitrogen from either the atmosphere directly (legumes) or from biologically available nitrogen in the soil. Therefore, legumes (such as pulses) have

$\delta^{15}N$ values close to the atmospheric value of 0 ‰, whereas most other plants have $\delta^{15}N$ values that are linked to the values of the soil N. Environmental and climatic effects such as temperature, soil pH and salinity also influence the $\delta^{15}N$ values of plants. In warmer environments the available N has a higher $\delta^{15}N$ value than in more temperate environments, for reasons that are poorly understood, and likely relate to the soil bacterial breakdown of organic nitrogen (Szpak 2014).

In archaeological studies, nitrogen isotopes are primarily used as indicators of the source of dietary protein, as discussed above. The usual way of employing them is to first establish the baseline, food-web values of nitrogen by measuring the bone collagen nitrogen isotope values of herbivores, omnivores and carnivores ideally from the same site and time period as the humans of interest (Koch 2007; Makarewicz and Sealy 2015). Then when the baseline values are established, we can see how the humans compare to other mammals of known diets to then determine if their values are more similar to herbivores, indicating a mostly plant-based diet, carnivores, indicating a mostly animal protein (meat and milk) diet, or most like omnivores, somewhere between the herbivore and carnivore values.

In human palaeodietary studies the baseline herbivore values are important to establish first. This is because, as mentioned above, due to temperature and soil effects, the absolute values of the nitrogen isotopes in plants in different regions can vary significantly. In hot and arid environments plants have more elevated $\delta^{15}N$ values than in colder climates. As the interpretation of human nitrogen values are dependent on comparisons to the local food-web values one can see how erroneous interpretations could be made if one just measured the humans from a hot and arid environment, for example, and compared these directly to humans from a colder environment as they would have much higher $\delta^{15}N$ values due to the differences in ecosystem baseline $\delta^{15}N$ values, not necessarily due to differences in diets. Indeed, in some cases herbivores like cattle, from arid environments can have nitrogen isotope values of 9–10 ‰ (e.g., Egypt, see Thompson et al. 2005), which is a similar value observed for carnivores like wolves in temperate environments (e.g., Europe). This does not mean, of course, that the cattle were carnivorous, just that the baseline starting point of the plant $\delta^{15}N$ values were much higher in the arid environment. In this example the carnivores from the arid environment would then have $\delta^{15}N$ values of 12 or 13 ‰, and in the temperate environment herbivores would have $\delta^{15}N$ values of 5 or 6 ‰.

In establishing the baseline $\delta^{15}N$ values, carnivores will show the fractionation difference resulting from consuming herbivores, and they are almost always 3 ‰ higher than the local herbivores, but it is important to measure as wide a range of herbivores and carnivores (and omnivores) to measure to establish as best as possible the palaeo-food web and the dietary relationships between them. For example, this may be important at a site where there are both wild and domestic herbivores. Wild herbivores, like deer for example, may originate from a colder location and higher latitude where the plant $\delta^{15}N$ values are lower than the plant $\delta^{15}N$ values at the site. Domestic herbivores like cattle that consume plants at the site with higher $\delta^{15}N$ values would then have higher $\delta^{15}N$ values than the deer. Both are herbivores, but are from different environments with different baseline plant $\delta^{15}N$ values and therefore different bone collagen $\delta^{15}N$ values. This may be important in understanding and interpreting the human $\delta^{15}N$ values from the same site. In addition, human herd management and feeding strategies for domestic animals can also influence their isotope values, including grazing or foddering animals on saltmarshes (Britton et al. 2008) or seaweed (Balasse et al. 2009)

An additional complicating factor in interpreting nitrogen isotope values is when humans are consuming foods from an aquatic ecosystem, in addition to foods from a terrestrial ecosystem. As discussed above, there is a ca. 3 ‰ increase in body $\delta^{15}N$ values at each stop in the food chain. In aquatic ecosystems, top level consumers like seals, which have consumed higher trophic level fish, which in turn have consumed smaller, lower trophic level fish, can end up with very high $\delta^{15}N$ values of 18–20 ‰, simply because there are many more steps in these ecosystems, which each trophic level leading to an increase of approximately 3 ‰ in nitrogen isotope ratio values (Fry 1991; Owens 1987). This is much higher than the usual top-level consumer values for temperate ecosystem of 9 to 10 ‰. Therefore, it may be confusing to find humans at a coastal site with nitrogen isotope values of 14 or 15 ‰, when herbivores from the same site have values of 5 or 6 ‰ and carnivores have values of 9 or 10 ‰. This points again to the need, where possible, to measure the isotope values of all the available food sources, as in this example if the fish from the site had a value of 11 or 12 ‰ then they would be the best candidate for the main dietary protein source of the humans.

In addition, there are physiological effects, and particularly disease, that can have an effect on human $\delta^{15}N$ values (Katzenberg and Lovell 1999; Richards and Montgomery 2012). And breastfeeding infants have $\delta^{15}N$ values that are higher than their mother, as their bodies process the mother's milk and fractionate the values by 3–5 ‰. There have been a number of studies that have used this phenomenon to explore the weaning ages of children in different societies (Beaumont et al. 2015; Richards et al. 2002; Schurr 1998).

Finally, as climate has changed through time, and we know the baseline $\delta^{15}N$ values are linked to temperature and environment (van Klinken et al.

2000), there are variations in the $\delta^{15}N$ values of the same species of herbivores from the same region that are directly related to the climate and environmental changes in the past (Drucker et al. 2003; Richards and Hedges 2003). Therefore, it is particularly important to make sure that the humans of interest are compared to herbivores from the same time period, as well as region, especially for Pleistocene material.

6 TYPICAL VALUES OF CARBON AND NITROGEN ISOTOPE MEASUREMENTS OF HUMANS CONSUMING A RANGE OF DIETS

In interpreting the human carbon and nitrogen isotope values from an archaeological site there are a number of important issues that need to be considered. First, the human bone collagen values likely only tell us about the sources of dietary protein. This is of course the case for nitrogen, as dietary protein is the only source of body nitrogen. However, carbon can come from dietary lipids, carbohydrates and proteins, yet most studies have indicated that bone collagen carbon is almost always from dietary protein, when there is sufficient protein in the human diets. Secondly, bone collagen turns over (is replaced) throughout life, so the collagen extracted is composed of collagen formed over many years. The turnover rate of collagen varies between bones, as well as between individuals (Hedges et al. 2007; Koch 2007; Stenhouse and Baxter 1976). Generally speaking, collagen from long bones such as femurs in adults probably reflects 10–20 years of diet, or more, whereas smaller bones like ribs may represent closer to an average of 5 years of diet.

Most palaeodietary isotope studies of bone collagen use both carbon and nitrogen measurements simultaneously to better interpret the past diets of humans. As can be seen above, there may be a number of cases where the interpretation of the carbon or nitrogen isotope values alone may be ambiguous. A human bone collagen $\delta^{13}C$ value of −12 ‰ could indicate the consumption of either C_4 plants (or animals that consumed C_4 plants) or marine foods. And a human $\delta^{15}N$ value of 15 ‰ could mean that the humans were consuming proteins from a very warm environment, or aquatic (marine and freshwater) foods. Indeed, the best way to determine if a human $\delta^{13}C$ value of −12 ‰ is from marine or C_4 plant sources is to also measure the $\delta^{15}N$ value. If there is a relatively low $\delta^{15}N$ value it is most likely that the source of dietary protein was then C_4 plants. As marine ecosystems generally have much higher $\delta^{15}N$ values than terrestrial

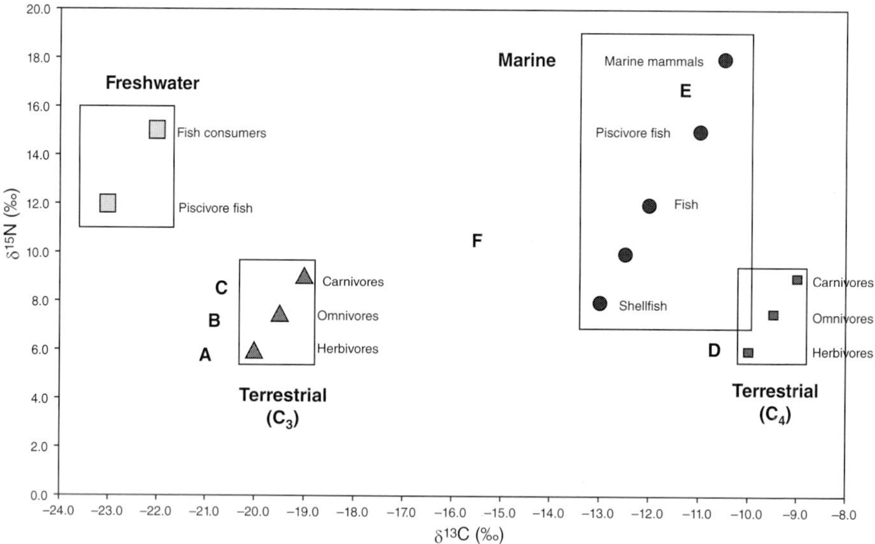

FIGURE 6.1 Typical bone collagen isotope values for a temperate ecosystem with human values indicated by individual letters (A to F) as discussed in the text.

ones, then a human with a δ^{13}C of −12 ‰ from consuming marine foods will also have a correlated high (usually over 15 ‰) δ^{15}N value. Therefore, the measurements of both δ^{13}C and δ^{15}N from the humans and as many classes of associated animals from the site is important.

To best interpret the human and animal carbon and isotope values from a site, they are usually plotted on an *x-y* graph with carbon on the *x*-axis and nitrogen on the *y*-axis. This allows a simple visual representation of the relative isotope values between classes of consumers (herbivores, omnivores, carnivores) and humans.

Typical human and animal bone collagen carbon and nitrogen isotope values from a temperate ecosystem are given in Figure 6.1. In this example, human A has a diet where their dietary protein came from terrestrial C_3 plant resources, human B had a mix of both terrestrial C_3 plant and animal foods, while human C consumed mostly animal protein (meat or milk) from a C_3 ecosystem. Human D consumed mostly plants from a C_4 ecosystem, as they have relatively low δ^{15}N values, whereas human E, with much higher δ^{15}N values, consumed mostly marine protein. Human F, plotting halfway between the terrestrial omnivore (human B) and marine carnivore (human E) had a diet of approximately 50 per cent marine and 50 per cent terrestrial foods.

7 SUMMARY

Bone collagen carbon and nitrogen isotopes are now a routine measure of past human diets, and work in concert with zooarchaeological and palaeobotanical studies of diet at archaeological sites. Despite the limitations in the method, it can tell us about the sources of dietary protein in human diets over the long-term. It has been useful in looking at long-term human dietary changes in a region, animal husbandry methods, weaning ages, social differences in diets, to name just a very few of the now hundreds of applications of this method to humans and animals from archaeological sites. In the future, more work on looking at the isotope values of individual amino acids in collagen will continue to contribute to our understanding of how collagen isotope values are linked to diets (see Evershed et al. 2007 for a review). And combining carbon and nitrogen bone collagen values with measurements of the isotope ratios of other elements, including hydrogen (Reynard and Hedges 2008) and sulphur (Nehlich 2015) in collagen and calcium (Reynard et al. 2013) and zinc (Jaouen et al. 2016) in bone and tooth mineral will allow us to much better refine and interpret the isotope record of diets from human bones.

REFERENCES

Ambrose, S. H. 1990. Preparation and characterization of bone and tooth collagen for stable carbon and nitrogen isotope analysis. *Journal of Archaeological Science* 17:431–451.

Ambrose S. H. and Norr, L. 1993. Experimental evidence for the relationship of the carbon isotope ratios of whole diet and dietary protein to those of bone collagen and carbonate. In: Lambert, J. and Grupe, G. (eds.) *Prehistoric Human Bone: Archaeology at the Molecular Level*, pp. 1–37. New York: Springer-Verlag.

Balasse, M., Mainland, I. and Richards, M. P. 2009. Stable isotope evidence for seasonal consumption of marine seaweed by modern and archaeological sheep in the Orkney archipelago (Scotland). *Environmental Archaeology* 14:1–14.

Beaumont, J., Montgomery, J., Buckberry, J. and Jay, M. 2015. Infant mortality and isotopic complexity: New approaches to stress, maternal health, and weaning. *American Journal of Physical Anthropology* 157:441–457.

Bocherens, H. 2009. Neanderthal dietary habits: Review of the isotopic evidence. In: Hublin, J.-J. and Richards, M. P. (eds.) *The Evolution of Hominin Diets*, pp. 241–250. Springer Netherlands.

Bonsall, C., Lennon, R., McSweeney, K., Stewart, C., Harkness, D., Boronean, V., Bartosiewicz, L., Payton, R. and Chapman, J. 1997. Mesolithic and early neolithic in the iron gates: A paiaeodietary perspective. *Journal of European Archaeology* 5:50–92.

Britton, K. 2017. A stable relationship: Isotopes and bioarchaeology are in it for the long haul. *Antiquity* 91(358):853–864.

Britton, K., Muldner, G. and Bell, M. 2008. Stable isotope evidence for salt-marsh grazing in the Bronze Age Severn Estuary, UK: Implications for palaeodietary analysis at coastal sites. *Journal of Archaeological Science* 35:2111–2118.

Brown, T. A., Nelson, D. E, Vogel, J. S. and Southon, J. R. 1988. Improved collagen extraction by modified Longin method. *Radiocarbon* 30:171–177.

Chisholm, B. S., Nelson, D. E. and Schwarcz, H. P. 1982. Stable carbon ratios as a measure of marine versus terrestrial protein in ancient diets. *Science* 216:1131–1132.

Collins, M. J. and Galley, P. 1998. Towards an optimal method of archaeological collagen extraction: The influence of pH and grinding. *Ancient Biomolecules* 2:209–222.

Coplen, T. B. 1994. Reporting of stable hydrogen, carbon and oxygen isotopic abundances. *Pure and Applied Chemistry* 66:273–276.

DeNiro, M. J. 1985. Post-mortem preservation and alteration of in vivo bone collagen isotope ratios in relation to paleodietary reconstruction. *Nature* 317:806–809.

DeNiro, M. and Epstein, S. 1978. Influence of diet on the distribution of carbon isotopes in animals. *Geochimica et Cosmochimica Acta* 42:495–506.

DeNiro, M. and Epstein, S. 1981. Influence of diet on the distribution of nitrogen isotopes in animals. *Geochimica et Cosmochimica Acta* 45:341–351.

Drucker D., Bocherens H. and Billiou, D. 2003. Evidence of shifting environmental conditions in Southwestern France from 33,000 to 15,000 years ago derived from carbon-13 and nitrogen-15 natural abundances in collagen of large herbivores. *Earth and Planetary Science Letters* 216:163–173.

Evershed, R., Bull, I., Corr, L., Crossman, Z., van Dongen, B., Evans, J., Jim, S., Mottram, H., Mukherjee, A. and Pancost, R. 2007. Compound-specific stable isotope analysis in ecology and paleoecology. In: Michener, R. and Lajtha, K. (eds.) *Stable Isotopes in Ecology and Environmental Science*, 2nd ed., pp. 480–540. Chichester: Wiley.

Fry, B. 1991. Stable isotope diagrams of freshwater food webs. *Ecology* 72:2293–2297.

Hedges, R. E. M., Clement, J. G., Thomas, D. L. and O'Connell, T. C. 2007. Collagen turnover in the adult femoral mid-shaft: Modeled from anthropogenic radiocarbon tracer measurements. *American Journal of Physical Anthropology* 133:808–816.

Hedges, R. E. M. and Reynard, L. 2007 Nitrogen isotopes and the trophic level of humans in archaeology. *Journal of Archaeological Science* 34:1240–1251.

Hoefs, J. 2008. *Stable Isotope Geochemistry*. Springer Science and Business Media.

Hu, Y., Wang, S., Luan, F., Wang, C. and Richards, M. P. 2008. Stable isotope analysis of humans from Xiaojingshan site: Implications for understanding the origin of millet agriculture in China. *Journal of Archaeological Science* 35:2960–2965.

Jaouen, K., Szpak, P. and Richards, M. P. 2016. Zinc isotope ratios as indicators of diet and trophic level in arctic marine mammals. *PLoS One* 11:e0152299.

Katzenberg, M. A. and Lovell, N. C. 1999. Stable isotope variation in pathological bone. *International Journal of Osteoarchaeology* 9(5):316–324.

Kellner, C. M. and Schoeninger, M. J. 2007. A simple carbon isotope model for reconstructing prehistoric human diet. *American Journal of Physical Anthropology* 133:1112–1127.

Koch, P. L. 2007. Isotopic study of the biology of modern and fossil vertebrates. *Stable Isotopes in Ecology and Environmental Science* 2:99–154.

Lee-Thorp, J. A. 2008. On isotopes and old bones. *Archaeometry* 50:925–950.

Longin, R. 1971. New method of collagen extraction for radiocarbon dating. *Nature* 230:241–242.

Lubell, D., Jackes, M., Schwarcz, H., Knyf, M. and Meiklejohn, C. 1994. The Mesolithic-Neolithic transition in Portugal: Isotopic and dental evidence of diet. *Journal of Archaeological Science* 21(2):201–216.

Macarewicz, C. and Sealy, J. 2015. Dietary reconstruction, mobility, and the analysis of ancient skeletal tissues: Expanding the prospects of stable isotope research in archaeology. *Journal of Archaeological Science* 56:146–158.

Marshall, J. D., Brooks, J. R. and Lajtha, K. 2007. Sources of variation in the stable isotopic composition of plants. *Stable Isotopes in Ecology and Environmental Science* 2:22–60.

Michener, R. H., Kaufman, L., Michener, R. and Lajtha, K. 2007. Stable isotope ratios as tracers in marine food webs: An update. *Stable Isotopes in Ecology and Environmental Science* 2:238–282.

Nehlich, O. 2015. The application of sulphur isotope analyses in archaeological research: A review. *Earth-Science Reviews* 142:1–17.

O'Leary, M. 1981. Carbon isotopic fractionation in plants. *Phytochemistry* 20:553–567.

Owens, N. 1987. Natural variations in 15N in the marine environment. *Advances in Marine Biology* 24:389–451.

Pechenkina, E. A., Ambrose, S. H., Xiaolin, M. and Benfer, R. A. 2005. Reconstructing northern Chinese Neolithic subsistence practices by isotopic analysis. *Journal of Archaeological Science* 32:1176–1189.

Preston, T. and Owens, N. J. 1983. Interfacing an automatic elemental analyser with an isotope ratio mass sepectrometer: The potential for fully automated total nitrogen and nitrogen-15 analysis. *Analyst* 108:971–977.

Reynard, L. M. and Hedges, R. E. M. 2008. Stable hydrogen isotopes of bone collagen in palaeodietary and palaeoenvironmental reconstruction. *Journal of Archaeological Science* 35:1934–1942.

Reynard, L. M., Pearson, J. A., Henderson, G. M. and Hedges, R. E. M. 2013. Calcium isotopes in juvenile milk-consumers. *Archaeometry* 55: 946–957.

Richards, M. P. and Hedges, R. E. M. 1999. Stable isotope evidence for similarities in the types of marine foods used by late Mesolithic humans at sites along the Atlantic coast of Europe. *Journal of Archaeological Science* 26:717–722.

Richards, M. P. and Hedges, R. E. M. 2003. Variations in bone collagen delta C-13 and delta N-15 values of fauna from Northwest Europe over the last 40 000 years. *Palaeogeography Palaeoclimatology Palaeoecology* 193:261–267.

Richards, M. P., Mays, S. and Fuller, B. T. 2002. Stable carbon and nitrogen isotope values of bone and teeth reflect weaning age at the Medieval Wharram Percy site, Yorkshire, UK. *American Journal of Physical Anthropology* 119:205–210.

Richards, M. P. and Montgomery, J. 2012. Isotope analysis and paleopathology: A short review and future developments. In: Buikstra, J. and Roberts, C. (eds.) *The Global History of Paleopathology: Pioneers and Prospects*, pp. 718–731. New York, NY, Oxford University Press.

Richards, M. P., Schulting, R. J. and Hedges, R. E. 2003. Archaeology: Sharp shift in diet at onset of Neolithic. *Nature* 425:366.

Richards, M. P. and Trinkaus, E. 2009. Isotopic evidence for the diets of European Neanderthals and early modern humans. *Proceedings of the National Academy of Sciences* 106:16034–16039.

Schoeninger, M. J. 2009. Stable isotope evidence for the adoption of maize agriculture. *Current Anthropology* 50:633–640.

Schoeninger, M. and DeNiro, M. 1984. Nitrogen and carbon isotopic composition of bone collagen from marine and terrestrial animals. *Geochimica et Cosmochimica Acta* 48:625–639.

Schoeninger, M., DeNiro, M. and Tauber, H. 1983. Stable nitrogen isotope ratios of bone collagen reflect marine and terrestrial components of prehistoric human diet. *Science* 220:1381–1383.

Schurr, M. R. 1998. Using stable nitrogen-isotopes to study weaning behavior in past populations. *World Archaeology* 30(2):327–342.

Simkiss, K. W. and Wilbur, K. M. 1989. *Biomineralization: Cell Biology and Mineral Deposition*. San Diego: Academic Press.

Stenhouse, M. J. and Baxter, M. S. 1976. The uptake of bomb ^{14}C in humans. In: Berger, R. and Suess, H. E. (eds.) *Radiocarbon Dating*, pp. 324–341. Berkeley: University of California Press.

Szpak, P. 2014. Complexities of nitrogen isotope biogeochemistry in plant-soil systems: Implications for the study of ancient agricultural and animal management practices. *Frontiers in Plant Science* 5:288.

Tauber, H. 1981. ^{13}C evidence for dietary habits of prehistoric man in Denmark. *Nature* 292:332–333.

Thompson, A. H., Richards, M. P., Shortland, A. and Zakrzewski, S. R. 2005. Isotopic palaeodiet studies of ancient Egyptian fauna and humans. *Journal of Archaeological Science* 32:451–463.

Tuross, N., Fogel, M. L. and Hare, P. E. 1988. Variability in the preservation of the isotopic composition of collagen from fossil bone. *Geochimica et Cosmochimica Acta* 52:929–935.

Van Klinken, G. J. 1999. Bone collagen quality indicators for palaeodietary and radiocarbon measurements. *Journal of Archaeological Science* 26:687–695.

Van Klinken, G. J., Richards, M. P. and Hedges, R. E. M. 2000. An overview of causes for stable isotopic variations in past European human populations: Environmental, ecophysiological, and cultural effects. In: Ambrose, S. and Katzenberg, A. (eds.) *Biogeochemical Approaches to Palaeodietary Analysis*, pp. 39–63. New York: Kluwer Academic/Plenum publishers.

van der Merwe, N. J. and Medina, E. 1991. The canopy effect, carbon isotope ratios, and foodwebs in Amazonia. *Journal of Archaeological Science* 18:249–259.

van der Merwe, N. J. and Vogel, J. C. 1978. ^{13}C Content of human collagen as a measure of prehistoric diet in Woodland North America. *Nature* 276:815–816.

Vogel, J. C. and van der Merwe, N. J. 1977. Isotopic evidence for early maize cultivation in New York State. *American Antiquity* 42:238–242.

Part III

Bioarchaeology

7

Human Osteology

Darlene A. Weston

Methods of analysis used in human osteoarchaeology, including ageing and sexing methods.

1 INTRODUCTION

The osteological study of human remains from archaeological contexts can provide a wealth of information on past peoples, principally because it involves examining the primary data: the people themselves. Human osteologists use the physical remains of the human body to reconstruct behaviour, demography, growth and development, and health at both the individual and the population level, working from a biocultural perspective (Goodman and Leatherman 1998).

The human skeleton can provide insight into past lifeways and the human life course at both the macroscopic and microscopic level, and numerous techniques have been developed to extract this information. As the specific methods a human osteologist uses will be dictated by their individual research agendas, for example, the detailed recording of specific pathological lesions, skeletal asymmetries, bone measurements, bone morphology and histomorphology, here the methods traditionally used for the *initial* analysis of a human skeletal population will be outlined: methods involved in the determination of biological skeletal age, sex, stature and morbidity (health and disease).

2 SKELETAL INVENTORY

The first question human osteologists ask themselves is 'are these remains human'? With a good grounding in the anatomy of the human skeleton, it is not difficult for an experienced osteologist to distinguish animal from human remains when bone or tooth elements are complete, but occasionally fragmentary remains can present a challenge. Differences in bone and tooth cross-sections, cortical bone texture (human bone is often less dense and more porous than faunal bone) and cortical bone microstructure (e.g., Haversian canal diameter) can all help to distinguish between human and animal bone, as can access to a good zooarchaeological reference collection (Hillier and Bell 2007; Roberts 2009).

The next step is the compilation of individual skeletal inventories. Whether analysing hundreds of skeletons from a large cemetery or a single isolated burial, it is of paramount importance to identify exactly which skeletal elements are present. There are many good human osteology texts that can help with bone and tooth identification and siding for adult (e.g., Bass 2005; Steele and Bramblett 1988; Van Beek 1983 [for teeth]; White and Folkens 2000; White and Folkens 2005) and juvenile remains (e.g., Scheuer and Black 2000; Scheuer and Black 2004). Bones and teeth present for each skeleton are typically recorded both visually and numerically. The visual inventory typically consists of an outline drawing of a skeleton (infant, child, adolescent or adult) with the elements that are present coloured in (Figure 7.1).

It is necessary to have the appropriate skeletal outline relating to the life stage of the individual being analysed, as the life stage will determine the number of skeletal elements present. For example, an infant's skull will have many more unfused elements than that of an adult, a child's skeleton will have many unfused long bone epiphyses, and an adolescent may have bone epiphyses in various states of fusion. In the visual inventory it is important to differentiate between intact whole bones and bones that have been broken via postmortem damage. The numerical inventory records the specific details of the bones present, for example, number of fragments per bone element, number of preserved joint surfaces (Fig 7.2).

While recording the skeletal inventory, taphonomic alterations to the skeleton should be noted as skeletal preservation has a crucial impact on the ability of an osteologist to determine age and sex and record pathological lesions. Erosion of the cortical bone surface can be caused by overly acidic or alkaline soil and root/fungal action, while abrasion can be caused by exposure, repeated deposition and movement of the bones above the ground surface (McKinley 2004). The degree of taphonomic alteration to the cortical surface can be scored according to stages outlined by Behrensmeyer (1978) or McKinley (2004), though the latter is more applicable to bones that have undergone surface weathering. It should always be remembered that differential preservation can occur throughout a skeleton and even on an individual bone. Additionally, other taphonomic changes should be

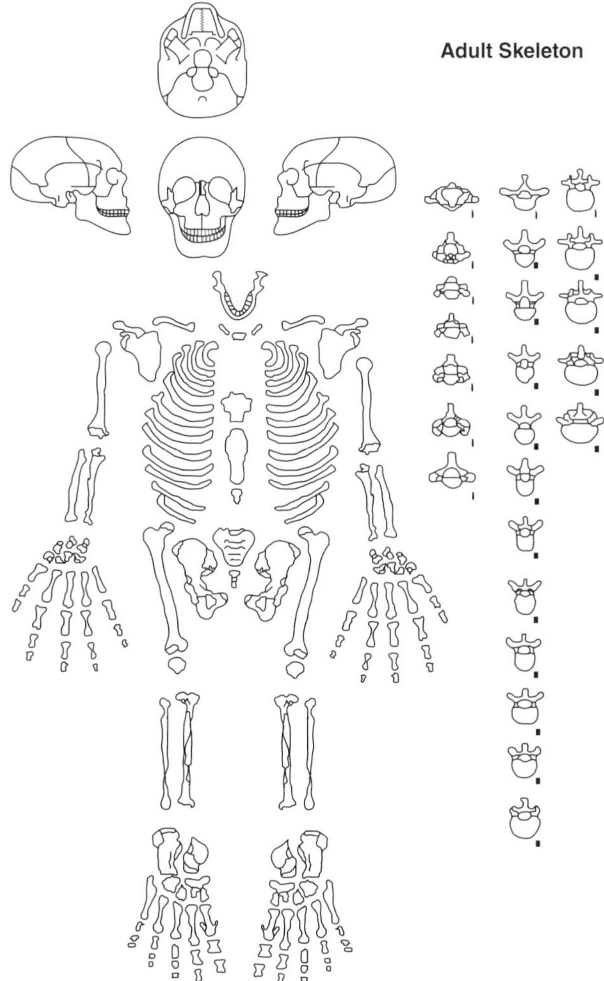

FIGURE 7.1 Adult skeleton outline drawing for visual inventory.

noted, including discolouration caused by mineral staining, sun bleaching or bacterial action; evidence of carnivore or rodent gnawing; evidence of alteration caused by insects, worms or microfauna; and 'excavation trauma'.

The final step of the inventory should be an assessment of overall skeletal completeness, recorded as the percentage of the skeleton present: 0–25 per cent, 25–50 per cent, 50–75 per cent, 75–100 per cent. Whether individual bones are present or absent will give insight into factors associated with skeletal preservation as well as possible postmortem manipulation of the corpse (Duday 2009).

Site Name:
Skeleton No:

SKELETAL INVENTORY

CRANIUM: Articulated: yes / no / partially (circle)

Single Bones	**Complete**	**Fragmentary**	**No. Fragments**	
Frontal				
Occipital				
Sphenoid				
Ethmoid				
Vomer				
Mandible				
Hyoid				
	Complete		**No. Fragments**	
Paired Bones	**Left**	**Right**	**Left**	**Right**
Parietal				
Temporal				
Maxilla				
Zygomatic				
Nasal				
Lacrimal				
Palatine				
Inferior Nasal Concha				
Auditory Ossicles				
Unidentifiable				

Upper Limb

	Complete		**No. Fragments**	
	Left	**Right**	**Left**	**Right**
Humerus				
Radius				
Ulna				
Clavicle				
Scapula				
Unidentifiable				

Hands

	Complete		**No. Fragments**	
Carpals	**Left**	**Right**	**Left**	**Right**
Total				
Scaphoid				
Lunate				
Triquetral				
Pisiform				
Trapezium				
Trapezoid				
Capitate				
Hamate				
Metacarpals				
Total				
MC1				
MC2				
MC3				
MC4				
MC5				
Proximal phalanges				
Intermediate phalanges				
Distal phalanges				
Unidentifiable				

Torso

	Complete	Fragmentary	No. Fragments
Manubrium			
Stemum			
Cervical Vertebrae			
Total			
C1			
C2			
C3			
C4			
C5			
C6			
C7			
Thoracic Vertebrae			
Total			
T1			
T2			
T3			
T4			
T5			
T6			
T7			
T8			
T9			
T10			
T11			
T12			
Lumbar Vertebrae			
Total			
L1			
L2			
L3			
L4			
L5			
Unidentifiable Vertebrae			

	Left	Right
Complete Ribs		
Rib Head Fragments		
Rib Shaft Fragments		
Unidentifiable Ribs		

Lower Limb

	Complete		No. Fragments	
	Left	Right	Left	Right
Os Coxa				
Sacrum				
Coccyx				
Femur				
Tibia				
Fibula				
Patella				
Unidentifiable				

Feet

	Complete		No. Fragments	
Tarsals	Left	Right	Left	Right
Total				
Talus				
Calcaneus				
Navicular				
Cuboid				
1st Cuneiform				
2nd Cuneiform				
3rd Cuneiform				
Metatarsals				
Total				
MT1				
MT2				
MT3				
MT4				
MT5				
Proximal phalanges				
Intermediate phalanges				
Distal phalanges				
Unidentifiable				

FIGURE 7.2 Numerical skeleton inventory.

3 PALAEODEMOGRAPHIC DATA

The palaeodemographic profile of an archaeological population is composed of information such as the minimum number of individuals (MNI) present, the numbers of adults (18+ years) and children (<18 years), the numbers of males and females and their approximate ages. Age, sex and MNI should be recorded for each burial context.

Minimum Number of Individuals

As each adult individual has 206 bones and 32 teeth (children have slightly more bones and slightly fewer teeth), if a burial has more than one example of the same bone or tooth, it means that more than one person is being represented by the skeletal assemblage. This could be indicative of a burial with multiple individuals or the encroachment of bone or tooth elements from a nearby interment. This occurs frequently in cemeteries experiencing long-term use with the intercutting of graves. When determining MNI, the biological age and sex of individual bones and teeth must also be taken into consideration. For example, a burial may contain a right and a left humerus, but one may belong to an adolescent and the other to an infant. MNI is typically calculated using a table to record the number of various skeletal and dental elements.

Age

The human life cycle consists of several stages: prenatal, which begins with conception and ends with birth; infancy, which ends when weaning starts; childhood, from weaning to puberty; adolescence, from puberty to the end of growth; and adulthood, when growth is completed and senescence begins. Though age may appear to be a simple concept, it is multifaceted when applied to human skeletal remains, as individuals have a chronological age, a biological age and a sociocultural age. Chronological age is based on calendar years, biological age is based on biological changes in the body and sociocultural age is based on sociocultural definitions. When trying to determine the age of a skeleton, our aim is to obtain the chronological age, our objective is to estimate the biological age and our goal is to gain some insight into an individual's sociocultural age, though the latter is almost always elusive.

A variety of methods are used to determine the age at death of an individual. Juvenile skeletons can be aged based on bone length and width (Fazekas and Kosa 1978 [foetal remains]; Maresh 1970; Sundick 1978; Ubelaker 1989) and the degree of epiphyseal fusion (Scheuer and Black 2000; Scheuer and Black 2004), while juvenile teeth can be aged according to the stage of development (Smith 1991) or eruption (Ubelaker 1989). Because skeletal development, growth and maturation occurs at known rates, juvenile bones and teeth can be aged with a good degree of accuracy, though caution deems that age ranges spanning two or three years (in the case of juveniles older than one year) be used. Juveniles under the age of two are frequently assigned ages spanning six month intervals. Foetal remains are aged in terms of lunar months or weeks *in utero*.

Adult bones can be aged based on senescent morphological variation in the pubic bone (Katz and Suchey 1986; Todd 1920; Todd 1921), the auricular surface of the pelvis (Buckberry and Chamberlain 2002; Falys et al. 2006; Lovejoy et al. 1985b;) and the sternal ends of the ribs (Işcan and Loth 1986a,b). Additional methods include dental attrition (Brothwell 1981; Miles 1963), the degree of cranial suture closure (Meindl and Lovejoy 1985), the amount of epiphyseal fusion seen on the sternal ends of the clavicles and the level of fusion between the first and second sacral vertebrae and among the sternabrae (McKern and Stewart 1957; Scheuer and Black 2000; Scheuer and Black 2004). As the accuracy of these ageing methods varies, many recommend as best practice to use a number of ageing methods in combination (Acsádi and Nemeskéri 1970; Boldsen et al. 2002; Lovejoy et al. 1985a).

As differences in lifestyle, health, environment and genetics will influence individual and population skeletal ageing patterns and affect method accuracy (Algee-Hewitt 2013), ascribing an exact chronological age to an individual based on morphological changes to the skeleton and teeth is not possible, and adult and juvenile skeletons are usually assigned to age groups. For adults, typical age groups consist of young adult (20–35 years), middle adult (36–49 years) and older adult (50+ years) (Buikstra and Ubelaker 1994). Some researchers prefer finer divisions: young adult (18–25 years), young middle adult (26–35 years), old middle adult 36–45 years and mature adult (46+ years) (Powers 2008). Adult skeletons that cannot be more precisely aged are put into the category of Adult: 18+ years.

Histological methods can be used to age bones and teeth, but of course require permission for destructive sampling and access to the necessary laboratory equipment. It should be noted that the preparation of simple ground bone thin-sections does not need to be overly complicated, as straightforward, low-tech methods have been developed (Maat et al. 2006). Bone histomorphometry, typically osteon counting in cortical bone (Ahlqvist and Damsten 1969; Kerley 1965; Kerley and

Ubelaker 1978; Singh and Gunberg 1970), is the most practiced histological ageing method for bone. Caution is advised for researchers when applying this method as reliability and accuracy can be affected by observer experience as well as genetic and environmental factors affecting bone remodelling rates (Stout 1992).

Arguably, the most utilised histological ageing method applied to teeth is apical root translucency (Vasiliadis et al. 1983a,b), followed by the Gustafson technique and its variants (Burns and Maples 1976; Gustafson 1950; Johanson 1971), which scores dental attrition, periodontosis, secondary dentine deposition, cement apposition, root resorption and root transparency. As dental histological ageing techniques are time-consuming and require specialised training, they are not commonly applied to archaeological materials (Hillson 1996).

Sex

It must be remembered that when human osteologists determine the sex of an individual, it is purely the biological qualities that differentiate males and females that are being identified – essentially phenotypical traits determined by either the presence of two X chromosomes (female) or an X and Y chromosome (male) (Mays and Cox 2000). Biological sex must be differentiated from gender, how a society perceives biological sex. Gender is a cultural construct that can be inferred from biological sex, however, it must be interpreted cautiously, as it not necessarily a binary concept and its cultural definition through space and time is extremely variable (Moore 1994).

Because the morphological skeletal traits that help to differentiate the sexes are largely a result of the hormone-related changes of puberty, it is extremely difficult to assign a biological sex to juvenile remains (Scheuer and Black 2000). Methods have been developed to determine sex based on the morphology of the pelvis and mandible (Schutkowski 1993) and the dimensions of deciduous tooth crowns (Black 1978; DeVito and Saunders 1990). These methods are based on the appearance of subtle sex differences, which appear from the fifth month *in utero* due to variation in testosterone levels. At approximately eight weeks *in utero*, testosterone levels in the male foetus rise and remain high until birth, after which levels fall and remain low until puberty (Schutkowski 1990). Juvenile sexing methods are not widely used as they are difficult to apply, appear to be population-specific and intra- and interobserver error is high (Vlak et al. 2008).

Determining the biological sex of an adult skeleton is a more straightforward proposition, with the most sexually dimorphic bone elements being the skull

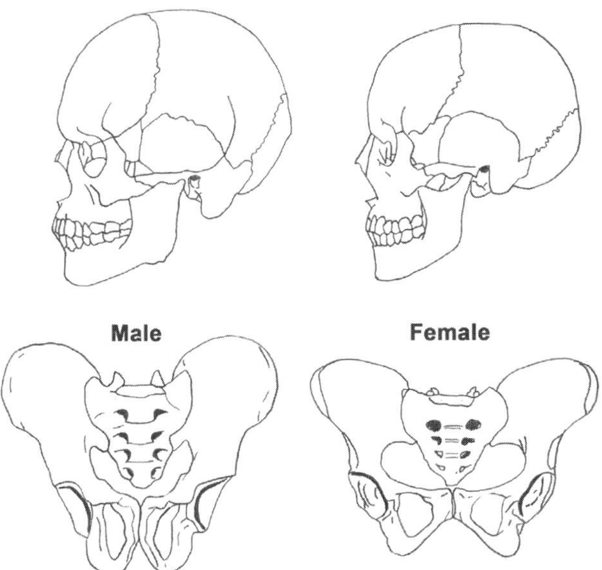

FIGURE 7.3 Male and female skull and pelvis.

(Acsádi and Nemeskéri 1970; Buikstra and Ubelaker 1994) and pelvis (Buikstra and Ubelaker 1994; Phenice 1969). Cranial traits are primarily correlated with sex differences associated with robusticity (males are more robust), while differences in pelvic traits are largely due to the obstetric demands placed on the female pelvis (Mays and Cox 2000) (Figure 7.3). When the skull and pelvis are analysed in combination, the accuracy rates for sex determination can reach as high as 98 per cent (Molleson and Cox 1993).

The metric characteristics of the clavicle (Jit and Singh 1966), scapula (Iordanidis 1961), humerus (Stewart 1979), radius (Singh et al. 1973) and femur (Pearson and Bell 1917/1919; Stewart 1979) can also be used for adult sex determination, though these measurements tend to be population specific. Additional adult sexing methods include the morphology of the distal humerus (Falys et al. 2005; Rogers 1999) and discriminant functions based on measurements of the skull (Giles and Elliot 1963) and pelvis (Schulter-Ellis et al. 1983; Schulter-Ellis et al. 1985). With the exception of methods based on discriminant functions, which have a sectioning point delineating males and females, sexing methods assign individual adult skeletons to the categories of male (M), possible male (M?), indeterminate (I), female (F) and possible female (F?).

Palaeodemographic data provides information regarding the total number of individuals present in the burial assemblage, their sex distribution and their approximate ages at death. These data can be used to construct life tables that illustrate population mortality and investigate the outcomes that age-specific probabilities of death have on survivorship (Chamberlain 2006).

Palaeodemographic data can be compared with other cemetery populations to see if mortality rates have changed through time or location. Additionally, the palaeodemographic data can be linked to mortuary practices and grave goods to determine patterns in cultural behaviour.

The palaeodemographic analysis of archaeological skeletal remains is not without its challenges (cf. Acsádi and Nemeskéri 1970; Bocquet-Appel and Masset 1982; Wood et al. 1992), but keeping in mind biases in samples and methods and problems with age and sex determination, researchers should not be discouraged from drawing cautious conclusions from the available evidence (Chamberlain 2000).

4 METRIC AND NONMETRIC SKELETAL TRAITS

Metric traits consist of measurements derived from bones and teeth. There are hundreds of potential measurements a researcher can record when analysing a skeleton, and individual research questions may dictate which specific measurements are required. Convention dictates that roughly 25 adult cranial measurements and 25 adult postcranial measurements are taken (Brothwell and Zakrzewski 2004; Buikstra and Ubelaker 1994). Dental metrics tend not to be routinely recorded unless required by specific research agendas. When recording juvenile cranial and postcranial measurements, usually only those measurements that contribute to age determination (see above) are taken.

Nonmetric skeletal traits are variable, non-pathological features in the skeleton that are usually recorded on a presence/absence basis. Again, there is a wide variety of traits that can be documented, with research programmes driving their selection. Convention dictates that roughly 30 cranial and 20 postcranial nonmetric traits are recorded (Brothwell and Zakrzewski 2004; Buikstra and Ubelaker 1994). Standards for the recording of dental nonmetric traits are provided by Turner et al. 1991.

Metric Traits

Bone measurements consisting of single measurements, indices (indicators of shape) or multivariate statistics can be used to characterise individuals and make group comparisons (Buikstra and Ubelaker 1994). Traditionally, measurements are taken using instruments such as spreading and sliding callipers, a mandibulometer, measuring tape and an osteometric board. Traditional methods of measurement have been augmented by computer-based methods such as laser scanning or digitisation, particularly for use in geometric morphometric analyses.

Measurements of the skull (craniometrics) have been shown to be influenced by genetic and environmental factors, and cranial variation can be studied at a global, regional, ethnic or intragroup level (Howells 1973; Howells 1989). Postcranial metrics are influenced by genetics, age, sex, behaviour and nutrition and can be used to determine stature, age and sex (see above), activity patterns and health (Buikstra and Ubelaker 1994). Measurements of both the skull and postcranial elements can be used to investigate such things as fluctuating asymmetry (Storm and Knüsel 2005), handedness (Steele 2000) and body proportions (Holliday and Hilton 2010; Ruff 2002).

Skeletal measurements are usually based on point to point measurements taken from specific landmarks. Definitions of skeletal landmarks and methods of measurement can be found in Bass (2005), Bräuer (1988), Martin and Saller (1957) and White and Folkens (2000).

Stature determination is one of the most common applications of skeletal measurements. The most widespread method for stature estimation involves the use of regression formulae based on long bone length (Trotter 1970). As the length of the femur and tibia contribute the most to an individual's stature, these two bones should be preferentially used. Other methods include Fully's (1956) anatomical method, which has recently been revised (Raxter et al. 2006), and involves measuring every part of the skeleton that contributes to height (the cranium, vertebral column, leg and foot), or stature estimation based on the measurements of various combinations of vertebral elements (Tibbetts 1981). It is even possible to estimate stature based on the measurement of incomplete long bones (Steele 1970), though it must be remembered that the standard error on these estimates will be high.

Skeletal measurements play an essential role in assessing growth and development. In juvenile skeletons, one method of evaluating skeletal growth involves measuring long bone shaft length and correlating it with dental age. These data can be used to construct skeletal growth profiles for the juvenile population in question by plotting mean long bone lengths against the midpoints of the dental age categories. The skeletal growth profile can then be compared to a modern standard, that is, the growth profiles of the children of the Denver Growth Study (Maresh

1970), or growth profiles from other archaeological populations (e.g., Mays 1999; Merchant and Ubelaker 1977; Saunders et al. 1993; Sundick 1978). Juvenile growth profiles can also be constructed as a percentage of attained mean adult long bone length (Saunders et al. 1993).

The main premise of juvenile growth studies is that child health and nutritional status is reflected in attained growth and development, which in turn reflects on the health and well-being of the population (Eveleth and Tanner 1990). Juvenile growth can be influenced by many factors, with genetics, environment and sociocultural factors all playing a complex, interconnected role. Children from low socioeconomic backgrounds are more commonly affected by poor living conditions, resulting in increased rates of malnutrition, infection, early death, small average stature and a slower rate of physical development (Bogin 1998). Conversely, children of higher socioeconomic status have discernibly greater height and weight (Susanne 1980).

In adults, skeletal growth is usually studied in the form of attained stature. Average attained adult stature for males and females in an archaeological population can be compared to modern standards in various geographic locations and to other archaeological populations. There is a strong relationship between growth cessation/retardation in childhood and terminal adult height: growth-retarded juveniles should be short-statured adults (Larsen 1997). The premise is largely the same as in juveniles, with short adult stature equating with poor health and nutrition. Individuals who have a healthy diet tend to attain their genetic growth potential, while those with poor health and nutrition do not (Larsen 1997).

Nonmetric Traits

Skeletal nonmetric traits, also known as epigenetic or discrete traits, usually take the following forms: 1) small bones or ossicles found within cranial sutures; 2) proliferative ossifications, for example, bony spurs, bridges; 3) ossification failures resulting in defects or 4) variation in foramen number and location (Buikstra and Ubelaker 1994). Dental nonmetric traits commonly take the form of accessory ridges and cusps, variation in groove and fissure patterns, enamel extensions and pearls and variation in root number (Hillson 1996; Scott and Turner 1997; Turner et al. 1991).

Data on nonmetric traits may provide insights into the processes of assortative mating, levels of interbreeding, gene flow, genetic drift and population dissimilarity (Tyrell 2000), though problems such as population-specific asymmetry, age/sex associations and inter-trait correlations must be taken into consideration (Buikstra and Ubelaker 1994). It should also be noted that due to their polymorphic nature and the degree of uncertainty that environmental factors play in their expression, nonmetric traits cannot be used to determine the degree of relatedness between individuals (Tyrell 2000), though dental nonmetric traits appear to be more buffered to environmental factors (Bailey 2008; Jackes et al. 2001).

5 SKELETAL AND DENTAL HEALTH

The health of an individual can be inferred by doing a palaeopathological investigation of their skeletal and dental remains. Bone can only react two ways to disease or injury: either more bone is added or bone is taken away. By looking at the patterning of bony reactions throughout the skeleton, it is possible to differentially diagnose the origins of these bone lesions. Sometimes it is possible to diagnose a specific pathological condition, but more frequently only a pathological disease category can be identified: vascular, infection, trauma, metabolic, neoplastic, congenital or joint disease (Weston 2008; Weston 2012).

When recording pathological lesions on the skeleton, it is extremely important to be anatomically precise, as different diseases may affect different bones, and even different aspects of a bone. Noting exactly where a lesion is located and being very clear and precise with the terms used to describe it may be the key to unlocking its aetiology. Lovell (2000: 221) provides examples of standard terms used to describe pathological lesions, while Grauer (2007) outlines the basic principles involved in the macroscopic recording of pathological bone lesions. There are a number of texts that deal exclusively with palaeopathology (Aufderheide and Rodriguez-Martin 1998; Ortner 2003; Roberts and Manchester 1995; Steinbock 1976; Waldron 2009), but medical texts, specifically those dealing with orthopaedic conditions and bone diseases, may also need to be consulted (see Resnick 2002).

When analysing individual skeletons for signs of disease, it is important to remember that the frequencies of pathological lesions in individuals and populations may be influenced by factors such as biological age, sex, population group or ethnicity, geographic location, and archaeological or historical time period (Ortner 2003). For example, signs of osteoporosis in the bones of a young child would be an extremely rare and unusual finding as would be the occurrence of destructive bone lesions suggestive of breast cancer in the skeleton of adult male.

It is not usual for individual skeletons to exhibit no signs of pathology on their bones or teeth. Ortner (2003) estimates that in archaeological populations, only

15 per cent of the skeletons will exhibit significant pathological lesions. This may be due to individuals dying from conditions that only affected the soft tissues or as a result of an individual's immune system not having sufficient time to mount a bony response before death occurs. Some researchers have suggested that individuals who died without any signs of disease may in fact be unhealthier than those with chronic skeletal lesions. This concept, termed the 'osteological paradox', argues that these latter individuals had stronger immune systems that were able to mount and sustain a long-term response to the disease in question (Wood et al. 1992; Wood and Milner 1994).

Infectious Disease

Infectious disease refers to illnesses caused by organisms (e.g., bacteria, viruses, parasites) that enter into the body. Not all infectious diseases leave marks on the skeleton, as bony lesions are primarily produced by chronic diseases (e.g., tuberculosis, leprosy, syphilis). Acute diseases, such as plague, smallpox or malaria, frequently kill the individual before the skeleton has a chance to respond. The presence of chronic infectious disease in a population can tell us a great deal about past living conditions. For instance, in order for chronic infections to take hold in a community, a number of conditions must be present, including: a population size that is large enough to continuously harbour disease, a permanent/semi-permanent settlement with close individual contact that facilitates disease transmission, and contact with other communities allowing introduction/reintroduction of disease (Roberts and Manchester 1995).

There are a number of texts that deal with specific infectious diseases and how these diseases manifest on the skeleton and they may be helpful to consult when trying to interpret lesions of these types. For tuberculosis, see Roberts and Buikstra (2003); for treponemal disease, see Hackett (1976) and Powell and Cook (2005); for leprosy, see Roberts et al. (2002).

Trauma

Trauma involves any injury or wound to the body and can include fractures, dislocations, disruptions to nerve or blood supplies (e.g., haematomas), amputation, trephination and artificially induced bone deformation (e.g., head or foot binding). The types of trauma found in a population can provide a great deal of information about lifestyle. For example, trauma patterns can tell us about the physical environment (urban/rural), economy (agriculture/hunter-gatherer), individual occupations, degree of interpersonal violence in the society, existence of warfare and types of weaponry. The state of healed or unhealed injuries can provide information regarding an individual's general health and nutritional status and can tell us about a population's medical knowledge and access to treatment (Roberts and Manchester 1995). Recommendations for recording fractures and weapons trauma can be found in Lovell (1997) and Boylston (2004), respectively.

Metabolic Disease

Metabolic disease refers to illnesses that interfere with the processes of bone modelling and remodelling (Brickley and Ives 2008). Many, but not all, of these illnesses are caused by dietary or hormonal deficiencies or excesses. Examples include scurvy, rickets, Paget's disease, fluorosis and osteoporosis. The presence of many of these diseases in a population, especially those caused by nutritional deficiencies, can provide information about diet, dietary practices, and even cultural practices (Roberts and Manchester 1995). For more detailed information on metabolic diseases see Brickley and Ives (2008).

Joint Disease

Joint disease refers to pathological changes in the various joints of the skeleton, including the spine, shoulders, elbows, hips, knees, ankles, hands and feet. Most joint disease is neuromechanical in nature, and involves age-related degeneration (i.e., osteoarthritis) (Rogers and Waldron 1995). Joint disease can also have other aetiologies, and may be caused by inflammation (e.g., septic arthritis), problems with the immune system (e.g., rheumatoid arthritis) or may be of metabolic origin (e.g., gout) (Rogers et al. 1987). The presence of osteoarthritis in certain joints may be used in infer activity, though interpretation of this nature must be cautious, as modern studies have not been able to correlate joint degeneration with specific occupations (Waldron 1994). For a guide to diagnosing joint disease see Rogers and Waldron (1995).

Dental Disease

Dental disease refers to pathological lesions and abnormalities affecting the teeth and jaws. Common dental pathological lesions include caries; abscesses and granulomas; periodontal disease; attrition and enamel hypoplasia. Teeth and jaws can also suffer trauma, congenital defects and cultural modification. The investigation of dental health can provide insights into individual and population diet; oral hygiene; knowledge of dentistry; cultural behaviour; subsistence; occupation and amount of physiological stress (Roberts and Manchester 1995). Information on recording dental disease can be found in Hillson (1996) and Ogden (2008).

Population Health

The appearance of specific pathological conditions in individual skeletons is always of value, and individual osteobiographies help to build up a picture of community health. However, of greater value is what the overall health of a population can tell us about past lifeways, environment and means of subsistence. The prevalence rates of various illnesses and pathological conditions can be compared with the rates seen in other archaeological populations to map skeletal health patterns and see changes through time. Additionally, comparisons of the health status of males and females and those from high status or low status burials can be used to determine if gender or high status buffered individuals from different illnesses.

6 SUMMARY

The osteological analysis of skeletal populations can provide a wealth of information. Demographics can be determined by calculating the age and sex structure of the population. Metric and nonmetric traits may be used to determine biological relationships. The analysis of skeletal growth and development can provide information about health and nutrition in childhood. Finally, the analysis of skeletal and dental health can inform about the health of a population, but can also provide information regarding population size, the degree of sedentism and contact with other communities, the nature of the physical environment, climate, economy, warfare patterns, material culture, medical knowledge, diet, dietary and other cultural practices and possibly occupations. All of this information can be compared and contrasted with other skeletal populations to build a better picture of what life was like in the past.

REFERENCES

Acsádi G. and Nemeskéri, J. 1970. *History of Human Life Span and Mortality*. Budapest: Akadémiai Kiadó.

Ahlqvist J. and Damsten, O. 1969. Modification of Kerley's method for the microscopic determination of age in human bone. *Journal of Forensic Sciences* 14:205–212.

Algee-Hewitt, B. F. B. 2013. Age estimation in modern forensic anthropology. In: Tersigni-Tarrant, M. T. A. and Shirley, N. R. (eds.) *Forensic Anthropology: An Introduction*, pp. 181–230. Boca Raton: CRC Press.

Aufderheide A. C. and Rodriguez-Martin, C. 1998. *The Cambridge Encyclopedia of Human Paleopathology*. Cambridge: Cambridge University Press.

Bailey, S. E. 2008. Inter- and intra-specific variation in *Pan* crown tooth morphology: Implications for Neandertal taxonomy. In: Irish, J. D. and Nelson, G. C. (eds.) *Technique and Application in Dental Anthropology*, pp. 293–316. Cambridge: Cambridge University Press.

Bass, W. M. 2005. *Human Osteology: A Laboratory and Field Manual*, 5th ed. Columbia: Missouri Archaeological Society.

Behrensmeyer, A. K. 1978. Taphonomic and ecological information from bone weathering. *Paleobiology* 4:150–162.

Black, T. K. 1978. Sexual dimorphism in the tooth-crown diameters of deciduous teeth. *American Journal of Physical Anthropology* 48:77–82.

Bocquet-Appel, J. and Masset, C. 1982. Farewell to paleodemography. *Journal of Human Evolution* 11:321–333.

Bogin, B. 1998. Social and economic class. In: Ulijaszek, S. J., Johnston, F. E., and Preece, M. A. (eds.) *Cambridge Encyclopedia of Human Growth and Development*, pp. 399–401. Cambridge: Cambridge University Press.

Boldsen, J. L., Milner, G. R., Konigsberg, L. W. and Wood, J. W. 2002. Transition analyses: A new method for estimating age from skeletons. In: Hoppa, R. D. and Vaupel, J. W. (eds.) *Paleodemography: Age Distributions from Skeletal Samples*, pp. 73–106. Cambridge: Cambridge University Press.

Boylston, A. 2004. Recording of weapon trauma. In: Brickley, M. B. and McKinley, J. I. (eds.) *Guidelines to the Standards for Recording Human Remains*, pp. 40–42. IFA Paper No. 7. Reading: Institute of Field Archaeologists.

Bräuer, G. 1988. Osteometrie. In: Knussmann, R. (ed.) *Anthropologie: Handbuch der Vergleichenden Biologie des Menschen*, pp. 160–232. Stuttgart: Fischer.

Brickley, M. and Ives, R. 2008. *The Bioarchaeology of Metabolic Bone Disease*. Oxford: Elsevier.

Brothwell, D. R. 1981. *Digging Up Bones: The Excavation, Treatment, and Study of Human Skeletal Remains*. Ithaca, NY: Cornell University Press.

Brothwell, D. and Zakrzewski, S. 2004. Metric and non-metric studies of archaeological human bone. In: Brickley, M. B. and McKinley, J. I. (eds.) *Guidelines to the Standards for Recording Human Remains*, pp. 14–17. IFA Paper No. 7. Reading: Institute of Field Archaeologists.

Buckberry, J. L. and Chamberlain, A. T. 2002. Age estimation from the auricular surface of the ilium: A revised method. *American Journal of Physical Anthropology* 119:231–239.

Buikstra, J. E. and Ubelaker, D. H. 1994. *Standards for Data Collection from Human Skeletal Remains*. Fayetteville: Arkansas Archaeological Survey.

Burns, K. R. and Maples, W. R. 1976. Estimation of age from individual adult teeth. *Journal of Forensic Sciences* 21:343–356.

Chamberlain, A. T. 2000. Problems and prospects in palaeodemography. In: Cox, M. and Mays, S. (eds.) *Human Osteology in Archaeology and Forensic Science*, pp. 101–115. London: Greenwich Medical Media.

Chamberlain, A. T. 2006. *Demography in Archaeology*. Cambridge: Cambridge University Press.

DeVito, C. and Saunders, S. R. 1990. A discriminant function analysis of deciduous teeth to determine sex. *Journal of Forensic Sciences* 35:845–858.

Duday, H. 2009. *The Archaeology of the Dead: Lectures in Archaeothanatology*. Oxford: Oxbow.

Eveleth, P. B. and Tanner, J. M. 1990. *Worldwide Variation in Human Growth*, 2nd ed. Cambridge: Cambridge University Press.

Falys, C. G., Schutkowski, H. and Weston, D. A. 2005. The distal humerus – a blind test of Rogers' sexing technique using a documented skeletal collection. *Journal of Forensic Sciences* 50:1–5.

Falys, C. G., Schutkowski, H. and Weston, D. A. 2006. Auricular surface ageing – worse than expected? Results from a blind test using a documented skeletal collection. *American Journal of Physical Anthropology* 130:508–513.

Fazekas, I. G. and Kosa, F. 1978. *Forensic Fetal Osteology*. Budapest: Akadémiai Kiadó.

Fully, G. 1956. Une nouvelle méthode de détermination de la taille. *Annales de Médecine Légale* 36:266–273.

Giles, E. and Elliot, O. 1963. Sex determination by discriminant function analysis of crania. *American Journal of Physical Anthropology* 21:53–68.

Goodman, A. H. and Leatherman, T. L. (eds.) 1998. *Building a New Biocultural Synthesis: Political-Economic Perspectives on Human Biology*. Ann Arbor: University of Michigan Press.

Grauer, A. L. 2007. Macroscopic analysis and data collection in palaeopathology. In: Pinhasi, R. and Mays, S. (eds.) *Advances in Human Palaeopathology*, pp. 57–76. Chichester: John Wiley and Sons.

Gustafson G. 1950. Age determination on teeth. *Journal of the American Dental Association* 41:45–54.

Hackett, C. J. 1976. *Diagnostic Criteria of Syphilis, Yaws and Treponarid (Treponematoses) and of Some Other Diseases in Dry Bones (for Use in Osteo-Archaeology)*. Berlin: Springer.

Hillier, M. L. and Bell, L. S. 2007. Differentiating human bone from animal bone: A review of histological methods. *Journal of Forensic Sciences* 52:249–263.

Hillson, S. 1996. *Dental Anthropology*. Cambridge: Cambridge University Press.

Holliday, T. W. and Hilton, C. E. 2010. Body proportions of circumpolar peoples as evidenced from skeletal data: Ipiutak and Tigara (Point Hope) versus Kodiak Island Inuit. *American Journal of Physical Anthropology* 142:287–302.

Howells, W. W. 1973. *Cranial Variation in Man: A Study by Multivariate Analysis of Patterns of Difference among Recent Human Populations*. Papers of the Peabody Museum 67. Cambridge, Mass: Peabody Museum, Harvard University.

Howells, W. W. 1989. *Skull Shapes and the Map: Craniometric Analyses in the Dispersion of Modern Homo. Papers of the Peabody Museum of Archaeology and Ethnology*, Vol. 79. Cambridge, Mass: Peabody Museum, Harvard University.

Iordanidis, P. 1961. Détermination du sexe par les os du squelette (atlas, axis, clavicule, omoplate, sternum). *Annales de Médecine Légale* 41:280–291.

Işcan, M. and Loth, S. 1986a. Determination of age from the sternal rib in white males: A test of the phase method. *Journal of Forensic Science* 31:122–132.

Işcan, M. and Loth, S. 1986b. Determination of age from the sternal rib in white females: A test of the phase method. *Journal of Forensic Science* 31:990–999.

Jackes, M., Silva, A. M. and Irish, J. 2001. Dental morphology: A valuable contribution to our understanding of prehistory. *Journal of Iberian Archaeology* 3:97–119.

Jit, I. and Singh, S. 1966. The sexing of adult clavicles. *Indian Journal of Medical Research* 54:551–571.

Johanson G. 1971. Age determination from human teeth. *Odontologisk Revy* 22:1–126.

Katz, D. and Suchey, J. M. 1986. Age determination of the male os pubis. *American Journal of Physical Anthropology* 69:427–435.

Kerley, E. R. 1965. The microscopic determination of age in human bone. *American Journal of Physical Anthropology* 23:149–164.

Kerley, E. R. and Ubelaker, D. H. 1978. Revisions in the microscopic method of estimating age at death in human cortical bone. *American Journal of Physical Anthropology* 49:545–546.

Larsen, C. S. 1997. *Bioarchaeology*. Cambridge: Cambridge University Press.

Lovejoy, C. O., Meindl, R. S., Mensforth, R. P. and Barton, T. J. 1985a. Multifactorial determination of skeletal age at death: A method and blind test of its accuracy. *American Journal of Physical Anthropology* 68:1–14.

Lovejoy, C. O., Meindl, R. S., Pryzbeck, T. R. and Mensforth, R. P. 1985b. Chronological metamorphosis of the auricular surface of the ilium: A new method for the determination of age at death. *American Journal of Physical Anthropology* 68:15–28.

Lovell, N. 1997. Trauma analysis in paleopathology. *Yearbook of Physical Anthropology* 40:139–170.

Lovell, N. 2000. Paleopathological description and diagnosis. In: Katzenberg, M. A. and Saunders, S. R. (eds.) *Biological Anthropology of the Human Skeleton*, pp. 217–248. New York: Wiley Liss.

Schutkowski, H. 1993. Sex determination of infant and juvenile skeletons: 1. Morphognotic features. *American Journal of Physical Anthropology* 90:199–205.

Scott, G. R. and Turner, C. G. II. 1997. *The Anthropology of Modern Human Teeth: Dental Anthropology and its Variation in Recent Human Populations.* Cambridge: Cambridge University Press.

Singh, G., Singh, S. P. and Singh, S. 1973. Identification of sex from the radius. *Journal of the Indian Academy of Forensic Sciences* 13:10–16.

Singh, I. J. and Gunberg, D. L. 1970. Estimation of age at death in human males from quantitative histology of bone fragments. *American Journal of Physical Anthropology* 33:373–382.

Smith, B. H. 1991. Standards of human tooth formation and dental age assessment. In: Kelley, M. A and Larsen, C. S. (eds.) *Advances in Dental Anthropology*, pp. 143–168. New York: Wiley-Liss.

Steele, D. G. 1970. Estimation of stature from fragments of long limb bones. In: Stewart, T. D. (ed.) *Personal Identification in Mass Disasters*, pp. 85–97. Washington, DC: Smithsonian Institution.

Steele, D. G. and Bramblett, C. A. 1988. *The Anatomy and Biology of the Human Skeleton.* College Station: Texas AandM University Press.

Steele, J. 2000. Skeletal indicators of handedness. In: Cox, M. and Mays, S. (eds.) *Human Osteology in Archaeology and Forensic Science*, pp. 307–323. London: Greenwich Medical Media.

Steinbock, R. T. 1976. *Paleopathological Diagnosis and Interpretation: Bone Diseases in Ancient Human Populations.* Springfield: Charles C. Thomas.

Stewart, T. D. 1979. *Essentials of Forensic Anthropology Especially as Developed in the United States.* Springfield: Charles C. Thomas.

Storm, R. A. and Knüsel, C. J. 2005. Fluctuating asymmetry: A potential osteological application. In: Zakrzewski, S. R. and Clegg, M. (eds.) *Proceedings of the Fifth Annual Conference of the British Association for Biological Anthropology and Osteoarchaeology*, pp. 113–118. BAR Report S1383. Oxford: Archaeopress.

Stout, S. D. 1992. Methods of determining age at death using bone microstructure. In: Saunders, S. R. and Katzenberg, M. A. (eds.) *Skeletal Biology of Past Peoples*, pp. 21–35. New York: Wiley.

Sundick, R. I. 1978. Human skeletal growth and age determination. *Homo* 29:228–249.

Susanne, C. 1980. Socioeconomic differences in growth patterns. In: Johnston, F. E., Roche, A. F. and Susanne, C. (eds.) *Human Physical Growth and Maturation: Methods and Factors*, pp. 329–356. New York: Plenum Press.

Tibbetts, G. L. 1981. Estimation of stature from the vertebral column in American Blacks. *Journal of Forensic Sciences* 26:715–723.

Todd, T. W. 1920. Age changes in the pubic bone I: The male white pubis. *American Journal of Physical Anthropology* 3:285–334.

Todd, T. W. 1921. Age changes in the pubic bone. III: The pubis of the white female. IV: The pubis of the female white-negro hybrid. *American Journal of Physical Anthropology* 4:1–70.

Trotter, M. 1970. Estimation of stature from intact limb bones. In: Stewart, T. D. (ed.) *Personal Identification in Mass Disasters*, pp. 71–84. Washington, DC: National Museum of Natural History.

Turner, C. G. II, Nichol, C. R. and Scott, G. R. 1991. Scoring procedures for key morphological traits of the permanent dentition: The Arizona State University dental anthropology system. In: Kelley, M. A. and Larsen, C. S. (eds.) *Advances in Dental Anthropology*, pp. 13–31. New York: Wiley.

Tyrell, A. 2000. Skeletal non-metric traits and the assessment of inter- and intra-population diversity: Past problems and future potential. In: Cox, M. and Mays, S. (eds.) *Human Osteology in Archaeology and Forensic Science*, pp. 289–306. London: Greenwich Medical Media.

Ubelaker, D. H. 1989. *Human Skeletal Remains: Excavation, Analysis, Interpretation*, 2nd ed. Washington, DC: Taraxacum.

Van Beek, G. C. 1983. *Dental Morphology: An Illustrated Guide.* Bristol: Wright PSG.

Vasiliadis, L., Darling, A. I. and Levers, B. G. H. 1983a. The amount and distribution of sclerotic human root dentine. *Archives of Oral Biology* 28:645–649.

Vasiliadis, L., Darling, A. I. and Levers, B. G. H. 1983b. The histology of sclerotic human root dentine. *Archives of Oral Biology* 28:693–700.

Vlak, D., Roksandic, M. and Schillaci, M. A. 2008. Greater sciatic notch as a sex indicator in juveniles. *American Journal of Physical Anthropology* 137:309–315.

Waldron, T. 1994. *Counting the Dead.* New York: Wiley.

Waldron, T. 2009. *Palaeopathology.* Cambridge: Cambridge University Press.

Weston, D. A. 2008. Investigating the specificity of periosteal reactions in pathology museum specimens. *American Journal of Physical Anthropology* 137:48–59.

Weston, D. A. 2012. Non-specific infection in palaeopathology: Interpreting periosteal reactions. In: Grauer, A. L. (ed.) *Companion to Paleopathology*, pp. 492–512. New York: Wiley-Blackwell.

White, T. D. and Folkens, P. A. 2000. *Human Osteology.* London: Academic Press.

White, T. D. and Folkens, P. A. 2005. *The Human Bone Manual.* London: Academic Press.

Wood, J. and Milner G. 1994. *Reply. Current Anthropology* 35:631–637.

Wood, J., Milner, G., Harpending, H. and Weiss, K. 1992. The osteological paradox. *Current Anthropology* 33:343–370.

8

Dental Histology

Tanya M. Smith

Methods of dental histology as applied in archaeological science, including sample preparation and analysis.

1 INTRODUCTION

Because they are highly mineralised, teeth are one of the best preserved and most commonly recovered elements in archaeological and fossil assemblages. They have inspired more than a century of comparative studies of hominin tooth size and shape (e.g., Bailey 2002; Brace et al. 1991; Dubois 1892; Hanihara 2008; Hanihara and Ishida 2005; Hooijer 1948; Irish and Guatelli-Steinberg 2003; Keith 1913; Le Gros Clark 1950; Weidenreich 1937; Wolpoff 1971; Wood et al. 1991). Additional valuable information is recorded on outer surfaces and inner aspects of the dental hard tissues (enamel, dentine, and cementum) that make up tooth crowns and roots, providing a permanent record of growth. Initial study of dental histology, or microscopic tooth structure, predates the fields of archaeology and evolutionary biology by several centuries. The innovative microscopist Anthony Leeuwenhoeck first described the structure of enamel in the 1600s, noting that it was made of longitudinal "pipes" (enamel prisms) that appeared as "globules" when viewed end-on (Leeuwenhoeck 1677–1678). During the 1800s and early 1900s, microscopic investigations revealed the tubular nature of dentine and the presence of successive temporal lines in enamel and dentine (reviewed in Dean 1995; Smith 2006). By the 1940s, American and Japanese teams had experimentally demonstrated the presence of circadian structural features, as well as the neonatal (birth) line, which allows one to relate developmental time to chronological (calendar) age in juvenile dentitions. These *incremental features* form the basis of a growing area of anthropological study that is illuminating aspects of human evolutionary developmental biology, as well as the health and demography of past human populations.

Tooth development in humans begins before birth and continues throughout adolescence. Like many biological systems, the formation of dental hard tissue is characterised by a circadian rhythm, which manifests in the enamel and dentine and remains unchanged in these tissues for millions of years after death. Enamel is secreted by cells known as ameloblasts, which differentiate at the enamel-dentine junction and migrate outward toward what becomes the surface of the crown. The tracks left by these individual cells are known as *enamel prisms*. These prisms show *cross-striations* that result from the circadian rhythm of enamel secretion (Figure 8.1) (Bromage 1991; Smith 2006). The successive positions of the advancing front of forming enamel are preserved as long-period incremental structures termed *Retzius lines*, which contact the enamel surface and form circumferential rings known as *perikymata* (illustrated below). Cross-striations and Retzius lines are also frequently referred to as short- and long-period structures due to their respective 24-hour and greater than 24-hour rhythms. An important relationship exists between these types of internal lines, since the long-period line *periodicity* (repeat interval or number of days between long-period lines) can be determined only by counting cross-striations between Retzius lines. This value is believed to be the same for all teeth in an individual's dentition, although it may vary among individuals (FitzGerald 1995; FitzGerald 1998). Modern human and fossil hominin periodicities range from 6–12 days (Antoine et al. 2009; FitzGerald 1998; Smith 2008); tentative evidence suggests that fossil hominin ranges were once as wide as 5–13 days (Smith et al. 2015). Dentine is produced by cells known as odontoblasts that generate *dentine tubules*, and shows daily incremental lines known as *von Ebner's lines* (equivalent to cross-striations), long-period structures known as *Andresen lines* (equivalent to Retzius lines) and *periradicular bands* (equivalent to perikymata) (reviewed in Dean 1995; Smith 2008; Smith and Reid 2009). Tooth cementum shows annual incremental features known as *cementum annulations* (e.g., Kay et al. 1984; Lieberman 1994; Wittwer-Backofen et al. 2004), but due to the difficulty of accurately identifying a full series of these lines in adult teeth (Renz and Radlanski 2006; Wittwer-Backofen et al. 2008), they are rarely used in archaeological studies.

Counts and measurements of incremental features have been used to determine the timing of tooth formation, stress experienced during development, and the age at death in juvenile fossil humans and apes (reviewed in Dean 2006; Hillson 2014; Smith 2008). Archaeological applications, which are reviewed below, have mainly

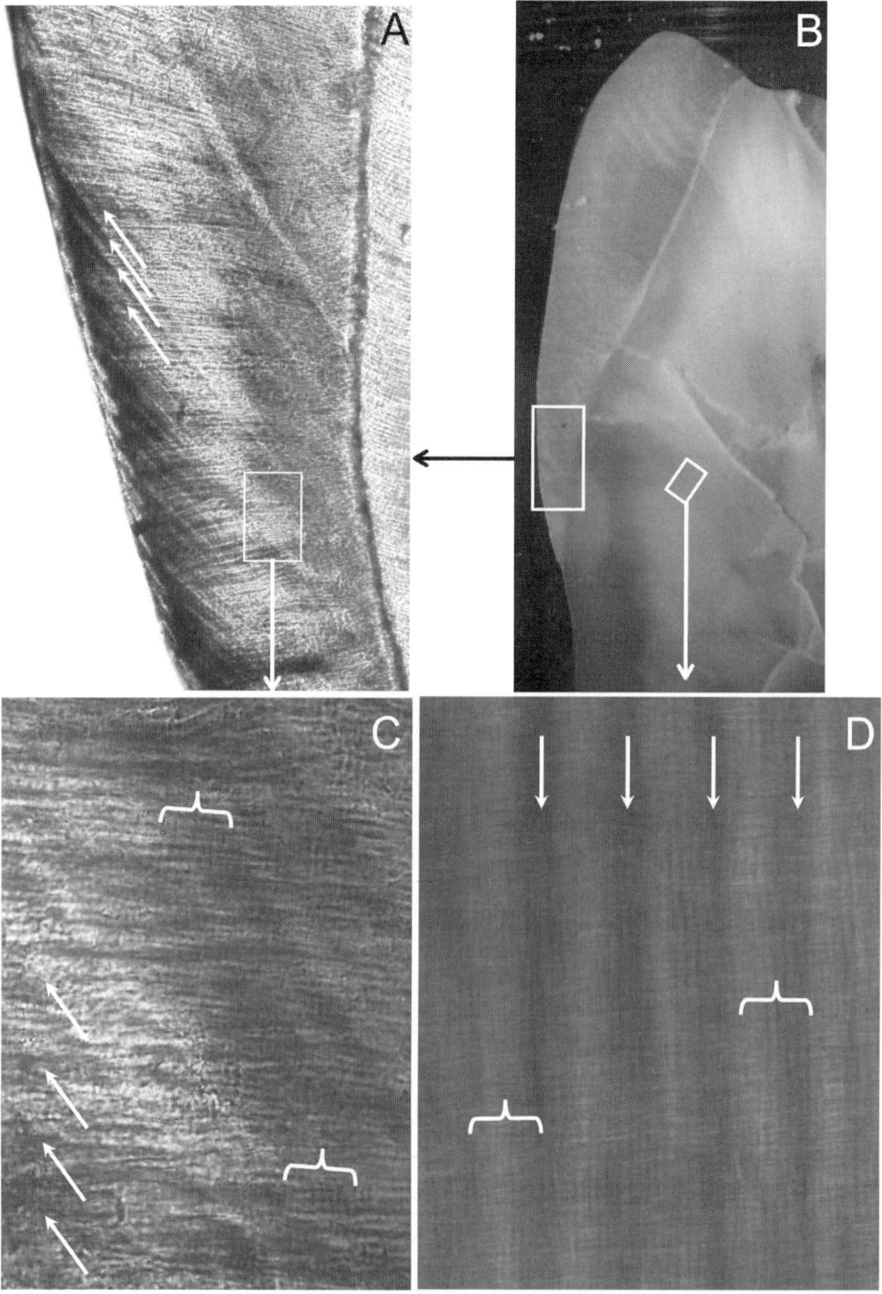

FIGURE 8.1 Polarised light images of enamel and dentine microstructure in the Scladina Neanderthal upper first molar. A. long-period Retzius lines in enamel (arrowed); B. overview of the embedded block (prior to reconstruction) showing the position of higher magnification images in A and D; C. Retzius lines (arrowed) and cross-striations in enamel (light and dark bands indicated by brackets); D. Andresen lines (arrowed) and von Ebner's lines in dentine (light and dark bands indicated by brackets). (Adapted from Smith et al. 2014)

focused on aspects of human developmental variation, determinations of age at death and defects of enamel formation. These data may provide insight into population-level developmental variation, mortality rates/demographic structure and living conditions of prehistoric cultures, respectively. Dental microstructure analyses also hold promise for the integration of temporal and chemical information locked inside teeth (e.g., Austin et al. 2013; Humphrey et al. 2007; Humphrey et al. 2008a,b; Richards et al. 2008; Sponheimer et al. 2006). In the subsequent sections, common methods of histological preparation and analysis are presented (Table 8.1), followed by a review of archaeological applications of dental histology and a case study illustrating how these methods may be used to detail the dental development, weaning process, and age at death of a juvenile Belgian Neanderthal.

2 METHODS OF STUDY

Impressions and Casts

Histological study typically requires careful preparation of high-resolution impressions of external tooth surfaces, along with physical sectioning and generation of thin (histological) sections. In both cases, high-resolution microscopy (with optical magnification factors of 200–500X) is needed to image and quantify incremental features on tooth surfaces or from histological sections. Recently, a new non-destructive approach (*virtual histology*) has been developed using synchrotron phase-contrast X-ray imaging (Figure 8.2; reviewed in Le Cabec et al. 2015; Smith and Tafforeau 2008; Tafforeau and Smith 2008), which is currently possible at the European Synchrotron Radiation Facility in Grenoble, France, the Swiss Light Source in Villigen, Switzerland and Elettra in Trieste, Italy. In the following section, aspects of conventional sample preparation are reviewed, followed by descriptions and illustrations of the various imaging techniques commonly used to assess microscopic tooth structure.

Initial analytical steps consist of macroscopic or stereoscopic photography, followed by micro-computed tomography (micro-CT) of particularly valuable samples. It is advisable to create a careful record prior to physical sectioning; micro-CT provides a means of digitally archiving a sample in three dimensions, which can be virtually sectioned in advance to guide physical sectioning, or quantified volumetrically and physically reproduced with a 3D printer (e.g., Macchiarelli et al. 2006; Olejniczak et al. 2007; Smith et al. 2007a; Smith and Tafforeau

Table 8.1 *Methods for studying tooth growth and development.*

Technique	Application	Exemplars
Preparation		
High-resolution Impressions	Replicate surface microstructure (perikymata, hypoplasias from molds or casts)	Beynon 1987; Hillson 1992a
Thin Sectioning	Prepare samples (~0.1 mm thick) for light microscopy	Antoine et al. 2009; Reid et al. 1998a
Imaging		
Transmitted Light Microscopy	Image dental thin sections from a controlled section plane	Gustafson 1959; Schmidt and Keil 1971
Stereomicroscopy	Image surface microstructure with focal depth	Smith et al. 2007a
Scanning Electron Microscopy		
- Secondary Electrons (SE)	Same as stereomicroscopy, higher resolution possible	Boyde et al. 1988; Hillson and Bond 1997 King et al. 2002
- Backscattered Electrons (BSE)	Image cut and polished internal surfaces based on density differences and interfaces	Boyde and Jones 1983; Witzel et al. 2008
Confocal Microscopy	Image subsurface microstructure to approx. 0.1 mm depth	Boyde and Martin 1987; Dean 2004
Fluorescent Light Microscopy	Illuminate experimental labels or fluorescent antibiotics	Bromage 1991; Dean et al. 1993
Profileometer	Register variation in surface topography at microscopic scale	Hillson and Jones 1989; King et al. 2002
Radiography		
- Flat Plane Radiography	Image internal tissues based on density differences	Beynon et al. 1998; Moorrees et al. 1963
- Micro-computed Tomography		
Absorption Based	Image density differences in 3D w/ near-micron resolution, quantitative mineralisation w/synchrotron	Hayakawa et al. 2000; Smith and Tafforeau 2008

Table 8.1 (*cont.*)

Technique	Application	Exemplars
Synchrotron Phase Contrast	Image internal interfaces based on phase contrast effect	Tafforeau et al. 2006; Tafforeau and Smith 2008
	Image external surfaces with Phong's algorithm and lighting effects	Le Cabec et al. 2015

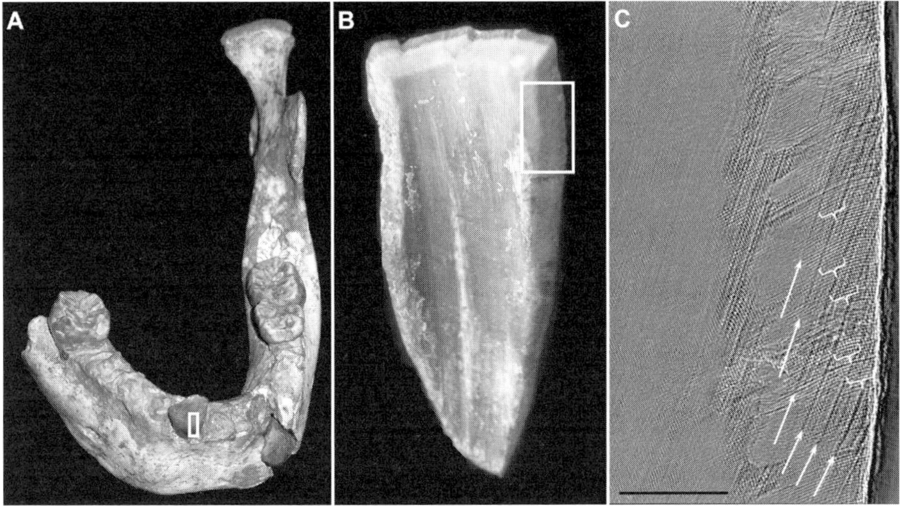

FIGURE 8.2 The first fossil hominin assessed with virtual phase-contrast X-ray imaging: the Jebel Ihroud 3 mandible. A. The North African juvenile fossil mandible showing the location of the incisor tooth enamel (white box) sampled with the Grenoble synchrotron. B. Close up of enamel fragment, with the area of interest (on right) shown in the white box. C. Synchrotron image showing Retzius lines (white arrows) with 10 daily cross-striations between them (white brackets). The scale bar is 0.2 mm. (Adapted from Smith et al. 2007c)

2008; Smith et al. 2009; Tafforeau 2004). Original tooth crown surfaces are often difficult to image directly due to the transparency of enamel; light tends to reflect poorly, complicating the resolution of fine surface details (Hillson 1992a). Marks et al. (1996) detail a method whereby tooth surfaces can be temporarily enhanced by coating with ammonium chloride (performed within a fume hood). Alternatively, tooth surfaces can be cleaned with ethanol or acetone, and molded with high-resolution dental impression materials, such as Struers' (Struers Inc., Westlake,

Ohio) Repliset or Coltène Whaledent's (Coltène/Whaledent Inc., Cuyahoga Falls, Ohio) light body systems (polyvinyl silicone). This facilitates production of epoxy replicas (casts) for preserving a copy and for efficiently visualizing hypoplasias, fine external growth lines (perikymata), and microwear.

Impression materials can be administered via a handheld dispenser (or gun) with disposable tips that mix the base and catalyst, or via a two-stage process (termed the *Beynon technique* by Hillson [1992a] after oral biologist David Beynon). In the latter case, a first impression is made with a "coarse" impression material (such as Coltène Whaledent's soft body putty), which serves after hardening as a template for a finer impression made by lightly coating the tooth with Coltène's light body, and rapidly placing it inside the soft body impression to polymerise. Guatelli-Steinberg and Mitchell (2003) note that an advantage of the Repliset system over the use of Coltène is the stability of impressions (or molds) under an electron beam, rendering them directly useful for scanning electron microscopy. These authors also demonstrate that the Repliset impression material has a slight advantage in resolution over the Coltène Whaledent light body impressions.

After dental impressions have hardened, replicas can be produced with the use of slow curing low viscosity resin. Various resins (e.g., Epo-Tek 301 resin: Rose 1983; Spurr resin: Beynon 1987; Araldite resin: Hillson 1992a) that have been employed have similar properties, including stability under an electron beam. Replicas can be coloured by the addition of commercially available resin or acrylic paint colouring agents, or their surfaces can be coated with ammonium chloride, graphite, gold, silver, or palladium to enhance the appearance of hypoplasias and incremental features (reviewed in Beynon 1987; Hillson 1992a). Often an electron microscopy sputter-coater is used to lay down a very thin coating of carbon or metal, which reduces the transparency of epoxy casts, and facilitates either stereomicroscopy or scanning electron microscopy (detailed below).

Physical Sectioning

When permissible, additional developmental information can be obtained by thin sectioning via cutting, grinding, and polishing, yielding a thin slice (approx. 0.1 mm) that allows transmission of light and visualisation of internal features. Archaeological dental remains, especially the dentine and cementum, are particularly vulnerable to diagenetic alteration (e.g., Bell et al. 1991). These tissues may appear

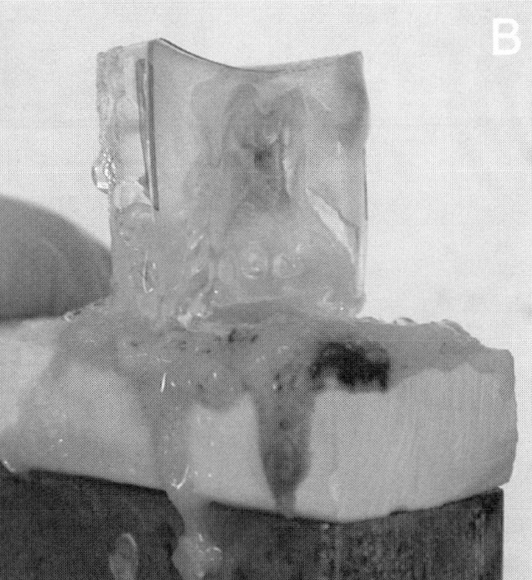

FIGURE 8.3 Preparation of the initial thick section of the Scladina Neanderthal upper first molar. A. The embedded tooth mounted to the cutting arm of the Logitech APD1 annular saw prior to the initial cut. B. Sectioned tooth showing the "thick section" still attached to the distal half of the embedded block. (Adapted from Smith et al. 2014)

very brittle or soft and chalk-like (Hillson 1996), and are liable to fragment when force is applied. In order to protect samples during the sectioning process, teeth are typically coated with successive layers of cyanoacrylate (super-glue) or embedded in a slow-curing epoxy resin or methylmethacrylate polymer. Methylmethacrylate (MMA) has been lauded for its ability to penetrate and fill very small spaces within samples (Boyde 1989), including dentine tubules that are approximately 0.001 mm in diameter. It can be removed by soaking samples in a dichloromethane, which will soften and eventually dissolve the MMA. However, epoxy resins may be preferable for embedding since they are less toxic than MMA and do not require the use of a fume hood.

Once coated or embedded, dental samples are slowly cut with a diamond-tipped blade mounted on a peripheral or annular saw. The sample is then advanced approximately 0.5 to 1.0 mm, and a second cut is made (Figure 8.3). This method results in a "thick section" of approximately 0.2–0.7 mm, which is bonded to a microscope slide, slowly ground down to a final thickness of approximately 0.1 mm, lapped or polished with a fine-grain suspension solution (e.g., 1.0 micron Alumina), cleaned with an ultrasonicator, dehydrated in an alcohol series, cleared in xylene, and covered with a cover slip and mounting medium (typically xylene-based, such as DPX [Fluka Chemicals]). After the mount dries, the thin section is ready for

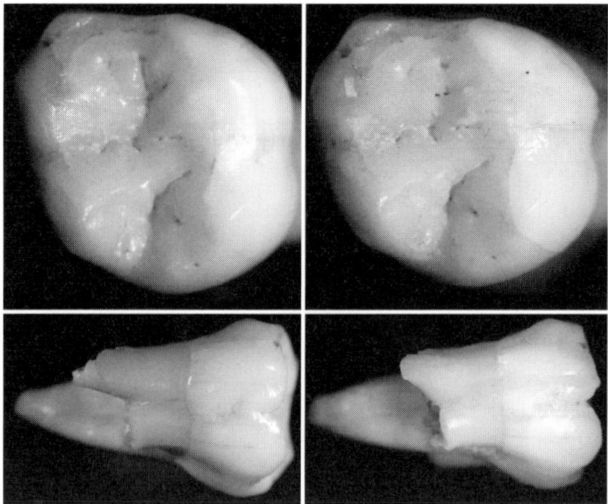

FIGURE 8.4 Image of the Scladina Neanderthal first molar before (left) and after (right) sectioning. Note a small portion of the root was removed prior to sectioning for ancient DNA analysis; this was not lost due to the physical sectioning process.
(Adapted from Smith et al. 2014)

microscopic imaging. Additional descriptions of histological preparation procedures may be found in Caropreso et al. (2000), Füsun et al. (2005), Hillson (1996), Marks et al. (1996), and Reid et al. (1998a,b); and details of ultrathin section preparation may be found in Gray and Opdyke (1962), Murphy and McNeil (1964), and Neal and Murphy (1969). An illustrated description of the sectioning process using Logitech equipment is also available in PDF format (by permission of Logitech Ltd, Glasgow, Scotland, UK) at https://www.drtanyamsmith.com/wp-content/uploads/2019/09/thin_section_prep_0.pdf.

An added advantage of sectioning teeth is the potential to sample internal surfaces for light or heavy isotopes, trace elements, enamel proteins, or preserved DNA in concert with analyses of dental development (e.g., Lakonis Neanderthal molar: Nielsen-Marsh et al. 2009; Richards et al. 2008; Smith et al. 2009; Scladina Neanderthal molar: Austin et al. 2013; Smith et al. 2007a; Nielsen-Marsh et al. 2009). Sectioned teeth are of great value for these complimentary approaches, since the internal aspects of tooth crowns, particularly the enamel portion, are subject to less diagenetic modification than are external surfaces (Schoeninger et al. 2003). Following sectioning, the tooth can be reconstructed using colour-matched dental restorative materials (Figure 8.4; also see Smith et al. 2009: 114, figure 4) or dental sticky wax (e.g., Schwartz and Dean 2001: 273, figure 1).

Microscopic Imaging

Incremental features in histological sections have traditionally been assessed with polarised (transmitted) light microscopy. This technique is ideal for revealing the birefringent (optically varied) properties of enamel and dentine, and it often enhances microstructure clarity (Figure 8.1; also see Boyde 1989; Schmidt and Keil 1971). Modern image analysis systems include transmitted light microscopes (outfitted with polarisers and analysers) coupled via high-resolution digital cameras to workstations with image analysis software. Most commercially available software packages include tools for performing linear measurements and manual counts of incremental features. Unfortunately, it has not yet been possible to automate incremental feature analysis because of subtle inhomogeneities of dental microstructure (which is also true for virtual histology).

Additional forms of incremental feature analysis include stereomicroscopy and scanning electron microscopy (SEM), which are particularly effective for visualizing features such as hypoplasias and perikymata on tooth surfaces (Figure 8.5). Scanning electron microscopy is also useful for imaging microstructure in sectioned and polished teeth (Figure 8.6) or on developing enamel surfaces (e.g., Boyde and Jones 1983; Boyde et al. 1988; Boyde 1989). An advantage of SEM over traditional stereoscopic imaging is the improved depth of focus at high resolution in secondary electron mode. Furthermore, back-scattered SEM yields density-dependent images of a single plane, as opposed to the optical averaging of light microscopic imaging of 0.1 mm sections (roughly the thickness of 20 prisms stacked longitudinally). Another technique that has been applied to human and ape dental material is confocal microscopy (Figure 8.7; also see Boyde and Martin 1987; Dean 2004), which is particularly valuable for naturally fractured teeth that are nearly flat, facilitating sub-surface microstructure imaging. Confocal microscopy has been applied to the study of hominin enamel secretion rates, periodicities, crown formation times (e.g., Lacruz et al. 2006; Lacruz et al. 2008), and enamel-prism packing patterns (e.g., Boyde and Martin 1987).

3 ARCHAEOLOGICAL APPLICATIONS

Crown Formation Time and Estimation of Age at Death

Bullion (1987) completed the first doctoral dissertation on the study of incremental enamel structures in an archaeological population, followed by

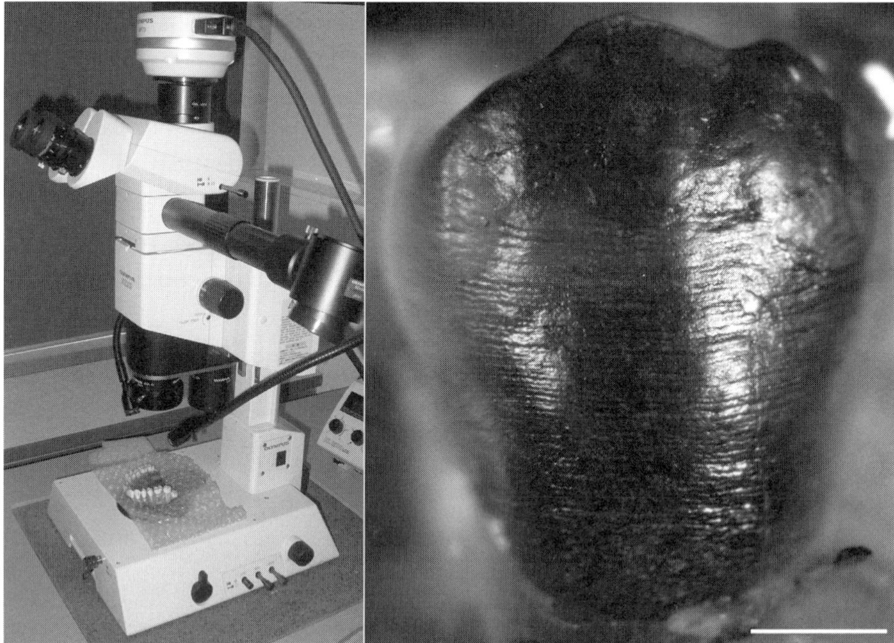

FIGURE 8.5 Stereomicroscopic imaging of dental material. Left – the Le Moustier palate on the base of the Olympus SZX 9 stereomicroscope. Right – image of a sputter-coated epoxy cast of a premolar viewed with stereomicroscopy. Note the horizontal long-period perikymata encircling the tooth crown. The scale bar is 2 mm long. (Photo: Tanya M. Smith)

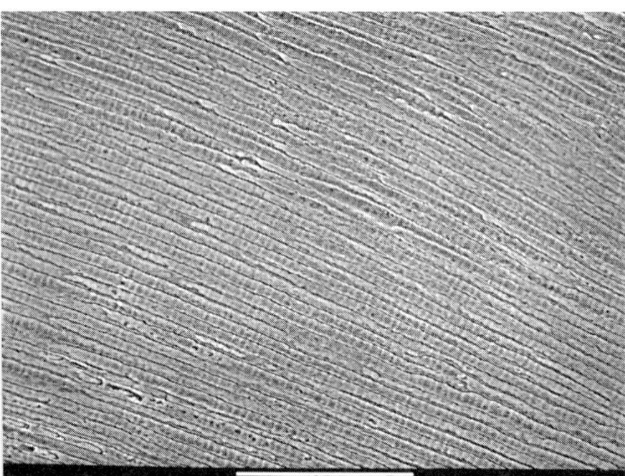

FIGURE 8.6 Scanning electron micrograph of cut, etched and polished fossil ape enamel. Note the relatively straight course of enamel prisms from the bottom right of the image toward the tooth surface (beyond the top left of field), and the fine light and dark bands that represent daily cross-striations spaced 4.1 microns (0.0041 mm) apart on average. The scale bar is 0.1 mm long. (Adapted from Smith et al. 2004)

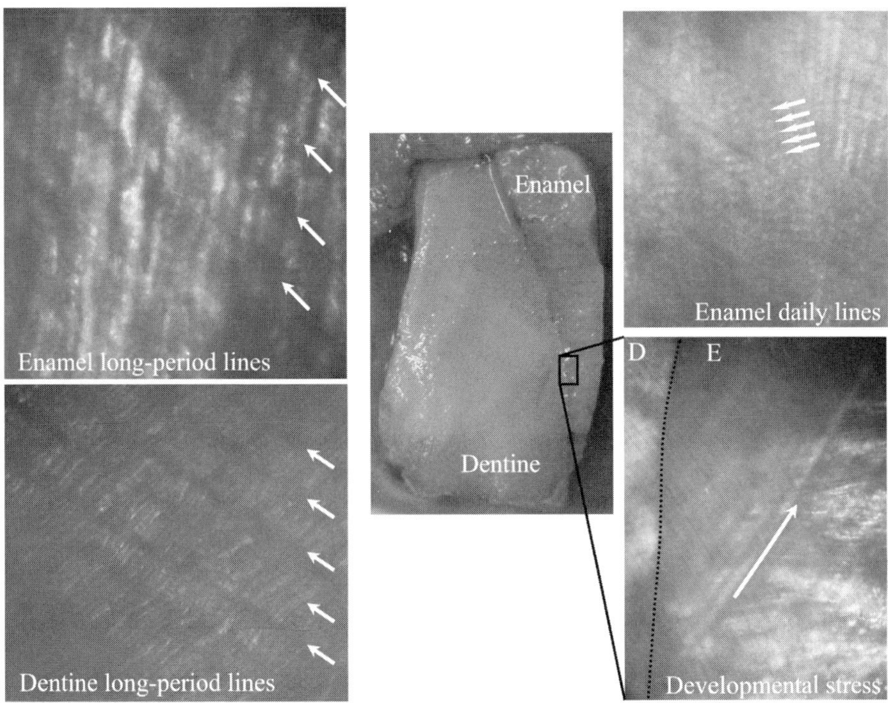

FIGURE 8.7 Spinning-disk white light confocal images of Neanderthal enamel and dentine, illustrating various incremental features and growth disturbances in a naturally fractured sample (shown in the center of image). (Photos: Tanya M. Smith)

FitzGerald (1995), Antoine (2000), and Thomas (2003), who detailed aspects of incremental growth and the prevalence of developmental stress. Several other studies have focused on the age of individuals at death, which may provide insight into the mortality rates, demography, and living conditions of ancient cultures. Archaeological applications of tooth histology include studies of the British Spitalfields collection (Antoine et al. 1999; Antoine 2000; Antoine et al. 2009; Dean and Beynon 1991; Dean et al. 1992; Hillson et al. 1999; Stringer et al. 1990;), as well as other medieval British collections (Boyde 1963; Bullion 1987; FitzGerald 1995; Huda and Bowman 1995), medieval French individuals (Reid et al. 1998b), medieval Danish individuals (Reid and Ferrell 2006; Smith et al. 2007b; Thomas 2003), imperial Roman children (FitzGerald et al. 1999; FitzGerald and Saunders 2005; FitzGerald et al. 2006), ancient Greek infants (FitzGerald and Hillson 2009) and prehistoric Native Americans (e.g., Goodman et al. 1980; FitzGerald 1995; Rose at al. 1978; Simpson 1999).

These studies provide information on human developmental variation, which is critical for consideration of individual dentitions or isolated teeth from living or fossil hominins. Currently it appears that crown formation times do not differ greatly between modern and recent archaeological European populations (e.g., Antoine 2000; Reid et al. 1998b; Smith et al. 2007b). Smith et al. (2007b) compared molar crown formation times among three modern populations and medieval Danish individuals, and found few differences between the modern and medieval specimens. No differences were found between crown formation times in the Danish and northern European samples. Less is known about histological development in non-European archaeological populations. Given developmental variation among modern northern European and southern African anterior and premolar teeth (Reid and Dean 2006; Reid et al. 2008), it is likely that additional archaeological samples will demonstrate similar regional variation. In a study of the oldest-known *Homo sapiens* juvenile from northern Africa, Smith et al. (2007c) reported long crown formation times and dental eruption ages that were quite similar to those of modern European children. Current evidence suggests that the slow-growing modern developmental condition is unique to *Homo sapiens*; recent data on a second fossil *Homo sapiens* individual and several juvenile Neanderthals supports this conclusion (reviewed below and in Smith et al. 2010).

Permanent first molars in apes and humans begin forming a few weeks before birth, permanently recording the birth process as an accentuated line known as the neonatal line (Rushton 1933; Schour 1936). Identification of the neonatal line in first molars, or calculation of postnatal delay in other teeth, allows age at death to be estimated in juveniles whose dental development is incomplete. This approach has been applied most often to fossil hominins (reviewed in Smith 2008: 218, Table 3, also see Smith et al. 2015), and also to humans from recent archaeological contexts in limited cases (e.g., Antoine 2000; Boyde 1963; Huda and Bowman 1995). FitzGerald and Hillson (2009) examined the postnatal survivorship of Greek infants in a cemetery population based on the presence and position of the neonatal line in deciduous teeth (which begin forming several months before birth). Similarly, Schwartz et al. (2010) analysed the presence or absence of the neonatal line in 50 deciduous teeth from Carthage in order to assess whether individuals were likely to have been sacrificed. It appeared that roughly half the sample died before one to two weeks after birth, leading the authors to conclude that other factors likely contributed to the death of perinatal individuals in this particular cemetery.

Studies of age at death in the known-age Spitalfields material have also been used to demonstrate the high degree of accuracy (+/− 2 per cent) of histological methods

(Antoine 2000; Antoine et al. 2009; Stringer et al. 1990). Although there are potential applications of tooth histology for forensic identification, very few published cases exist (likely because pinpointing age at death is time-consuming and technically demanding). Katzenberg et al. (2005) present a case study where the remains of an unknown infant were assessed through dental histology, historical records and DNA analysis. Histology yielded an age at death of 4.8–5.1 months, supporting putative historical identification of a 5-month-old female (see also a similar study by Skinner and Anderson 1991). Precise reconstruction of juvenile age at death represents one of the most valuable applications of dental histology, particularly when compared to other commonly employed anthropological aging methods.

Developmental Stress

The most frequent application of tooth histology in archaeology is the detection of developmental stress. External manifestations of stress are known as *hypoplasias* on tooth crowns (Berten 1895; reviewed in Hillson 2014; Hillson and Bond 1997; Simpson 1999) and *accentuated rings* on tooth roots (Smith and Reid 2009). Internal manifestations of developmental stress in enamel and dentine are termed *accentuated lines* (or, less commonly, Wilson bands in enamel [see FitzGerald and Saunders 2005] and lines of Owen in dentine [see Dean 1995]). Numerous studies have reported on the frequency and timing of hypoplasias in archaeological populations and fossil hominins, a subject beyond the scope of this review (see references in Goodman and Rose 1990; Guatelli-Steinberg 2004; Hillson 1992b; Hillson 1996; Hillson 2014; Hillson and Bond 1997; Katzenberg et al. 1996; King et al. 2002; Skinner 1996). Relatively less attention has been paid to the frequency or causation of internal accentuated lines (but see references in FitzGerald and Saunders 2005; Smith and Boesch 2015; Thomas 2003; Witzel et al. 2008;).

Unfortunately, both hypoplasias and accentuations arise from nonspecific stresses experienced during development, limiting the utility of these features for reconstructions of past environments and population health. Numerous studies have posited relationships between these features and vitamin D deficiency (rickets), hypothyroidism (hypocalcemia), acute dehydration, starvation, exanthematous fevers, or other systematic disturbances, severe trauma, weaning, parturition, psychological disorders, seasonal resource availability, disease cycles, or rainfall patterns (e.g., Bowman 1991; Boyde 1970; Bracha 2004; Nikiforuk and Fraser 1979; Schwartz et al. 2006; Simpson 1999; Skinner 1986; Skinner and Hopwood 2004;

reviewed in Dirks et al. 2002; FitzGerald and Saunders 2005; Goodman and Rose 1991; Guatelli-Steinberg 2001; Guatelli-Steinberg and Benderlioglu 2006; Hillson 2014; Katzenberg et al. 1996; Smith and Boesch 2015). This area of study would benefit from additional systematic or experimental studies of defect expression from a range of pre- and postnatal conditions in order to provide a framework for interpreting the significance of these features in archaeological and fossil populations.

A substantial debate has ensued in the archaeological literature about the most appropriate approach to determining the timing or age of hypoplasia formation (reviewed in Goodman and Rose 1991; Goodman and Song 1999; Hillson and Bond 1997; Martin et al. 2008; Reid and Dean 2000; Ritzman et al. 2008). The standard approach for much of the past century has been to divide the tooth crown into equally spaced and equally timed divisions (assuming constant linear growth rates). However, it is clear that primate teeth do not grow at a constant rate, as evidenced by varying extension rates along the enamel-dentine junction and changing perikymata spacing along the tooth surface. Furthermore, the first-formed enamel in the cuspal regions, which forms over several months to more than a year, is not represented by perikymata on the tooth surface, complicating attempts to assign ages to positions on the tooth surface without knowledge of internal development.

In contrast to decades of previous archaeological studies, Reid and Dean (2000) have shown that no relationship exists between tooth crown height and the total time of formation. They initially proposed a set of developmental standards from 115 northern European anterior teeth for approximate ages of crown surface deciles from the cusp tip to the cervix (Reid and Dean 2000: 138, figure 1). This was followed by standards for southern African anterior teeth and molars from both populations (Reid and Dean 2006). It is important to note that since anterior tooth development varies among human populations (Reid and Dean 2006), histological information will be most effectively applied to the populations from which the standards are derived. Recent studies have explored differences in the timing of defects using traditional models and histological information (Martin et al. 2008; Ritzman et al. 2008), showing deviations from several months to more than a year among methods.

A number of studies have used patterns of enamel hypoplasias or accentuated lines to match teeth forming at the same time (e.g., Boyde 1963; Gustafson 1955; King et al. 2002; Schwartz et al. 2006; Smith et al. 2007a). This aspect of hard tissue registry allows for more precise estimates of the timing of crown initiation and completion than dissection or radiographic techniques and is also critical for estimates of age at death in older juvenile material (detailed in the case study below). Kelley (2008) illustrates an interesting application of enamel hypoplasia matching in a potential birth cohort of the (presumably) rare ape species *Griphopithecus* from the Miocene locality of Paşalar (Turkey). Based on similar perikymata counts and the presence of an identical pattern of linear enamel hypoplasias on nine incisors, he suggested that the individuals attributed to this taxon were all at the same maturational stage, and that they experienced the same two stressful episodes simultaneously. From this, he inferred that these animals were part of the same cohort, that they experienced birth seasonality, and that they all died at the same time (based on identical amounts of wear). This elegantly demonstrates how incremental features can be used to reconstruct not only the "intimate history of the individual," as Gysi (1931) notes, but also the history of a group of individuals and the environmental conditions they experienced.

4 CASE STUDY: SCLADINA JUVENILE NEANDERTHAL

This case study documents the determination of crown formation time in the 127,000-year old female juvenile Neanderthal from Scladina, Belgium (Toussaint and Pirson 2006; Peyregne et al. 2019), in addition to identification of developmental stress, leading to an estimate of the age at death (originally published in Smith et al. 2007a) as well as the age at weaning (Austin et al. 2013). Following the preparative methods detailed above (photography, micro-CT scanning, molding, and casting), the upper first molar of an associated dentition was cut and a histological section prepared (Figures 8.1, 8.3, and 8.4). This tooth was sectioned to determine the long-period line periodicity and to register chronological and developmental time via the neonatal line. Birth occurred approximately 13 days after cusp initiation, and crown formation time was determined by tracking days of growth along enamel prisms (according to the procedure described in Boyde [1963; 1990]) and adding this to the number of Retzius lines multiplied by their periodicity (Figure 8.8). The formation time of this first molar cusp is approximately 872 days, and subtraction of the prenatal enamel yields an age at crown completion of 2.35 years. A record of postnatal developmental stress was also determined; a particularly marked accentuated line formed at approximately 435 days of age, followed by a second accentuated line at 875 days of age in the root dentine of both mesial cusps.

All associated teeth were molded and cast, allowing counts of long-period incremental features on tooth crowns and roots, and micro-CT scanned for

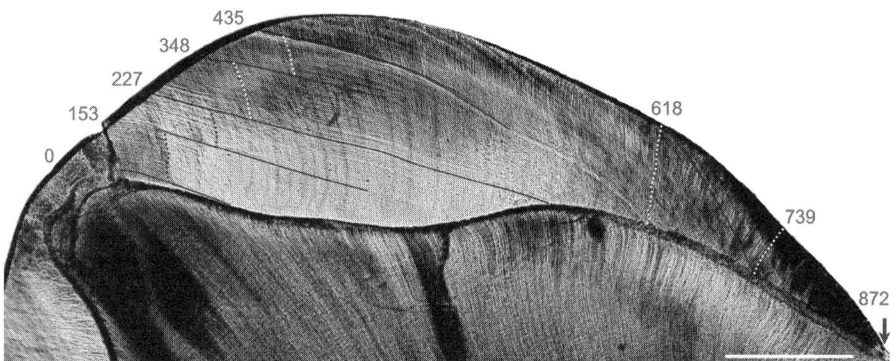

FIGURE 8.8 Case study: Scladina Neanderthal dental development. The neonatal line is indicated by the first drawn line on the lower left (0), with subsequently calculated time indicated for a series of stress events as 153 days, 227 days, 348 days, and 435 days postnatal age. The stress event at 435 days (1.2 years) was the most marked until later stressors at 875 and 1779 days of age (not shown). The scale bar is 1 mm long. (Adapted from Smith et al. 2007a; Smith et al. 2014)

quantification of the cuspal enamel thickness. Crown formation times were calculated from these variables and the long-period line periodicity of 8 days from the sectioned molar (Smith et al. 2007a; Smith et al. 2014). These data were compared with incremental development in modern humans from northern England and southern Africa, as well as a large sample of Neanderthals (Guatelli-Steinberg and Reid 2008; Reid et al. 2008; Reid and Dean 2006; Smith et al. 2007b;), revealing particularly short post-canine crown formation times in the Scladina individual. This pattern is due to thin cuspal enamel and rapid rates of crown extension in Neanderthals (Smith et al. 2007a; Smith et al. 2010), yielding teeth similar in size to those of living humans that form more rapidly. Finally, a sequence of developmental stress was mapped across the dentition, which allowed registry of teeth forming at the same time, and estimation of the age at death.

Developmental stress in the enamel and dentine of the first molar at approximately 435 and 875 days of age was matched to hypoplasias on anterior teeth (Smith et al. 2007a: 20,222, figure 1). A third developmental stress event was identified and matched at 1,779 days of age in the developing lower third premolar and upper canine, and subsequent developmental time was added to establish that the individual was approximately 8 years old at death (~2,939 days). This registry of stress across the dentition allowed the establishment of crown initiation and completion ages, yielding an overall developmental chronology for this young Neanderthal (Smith et al. 2007a: 20,223, figure 2).

When the Scladina juvenile is compared to modern humans, its tooth calcification stages and eruption status appear to be advanced by several years over modern juveniles at the same chronological age (Liversidge 2003; Smith 1991). For example, the Scladina second molar had advanced beyond clinical (gingival) occlusion by 8 years of age; second molar eruption occurs on average at 10–13 years of age in global human populations. It is clear that from these data and other studies that age at death in Neanderthals should not be assessed by comparison with modern human standards, particularly those derived from European populations. Furthermore, this individual has shed light on the on-going debate about Neanderthal life history, illustrating a developmental pattern that appears to be intermediate between that of fossil *Homo sapiens* and *Homo erectus* (Smith et al. 2007a). More recent studies employing virtual histology have confirmed this pattern of rapid dental development in other Neanderthals (Smith et al. 2010), implying that the prolonged childhood and slow developmental schedule of modern humans is, in fact, unique to our species.

Finally, the Scladina juvenile also represents the first fossil hominin for which a precise age at weaning has been reported (Austin et al. 2013). By integrating information on the timing of first molar incremental growth with patterns of the incorporation of barium, a trace element enriched in breast milk, Austin et al. (2013) demonstrated barium/calcium patterns in enamel that appear to coincide with periods of placental nutrition, exclusive breastfeeding for 7 months, and supplementation followed by an abrupt cessation of nursing at 1.2 years of age. While this fossil is particularly well preserved, having yielded enamel proteins (Nielsen-Marsh et al. 2009) and DNA (Peyrégne et al. 2019), biogenic elemental patterns and diagenetic indicators suggest that tooth histology and elemental mapping can be employed to document the timing of early life diet transitions in fossil enamel. A recent study has shown what appears to be a more normative Neanderthal weaning age at 2.5 years, as well as the seasons of birth and weaning (Smith et al. 2018). Importantly, this approach may be extended to test theories about changes in the timing of human weaning (reviewed in Reynard and Tuross 2015; Smith 2013; also see Beaumont et al. 2015).

ACKNOWLEDGEMENTS

Fossil samples were provided by Jean-Jacques Hublin, Shannon McPherron, Michel Toussaint, Louis de Bonis, Almut Hoffmann, and Debbie Guatelli-Steinberg. Comments on the text were kindly provided by JP Zermeno, Christina Warinner, Don Reid, Karola Kirsanow, and Janet Fink. This work was funded by the Max Planck Society and Harvard University.

REFERENCES

Antoine, D. 2000. *Evaluating the periodicity of incremental structures in dental enamel as a means of studying growth in children from past human populations.* Doctoral thesis, University College London.

Antoine, D., Dean, C., and Hillson, S. 1999. The periodicity of incremental structures in dental enamel based on the developing dentition of post-medieval known-age children. In: Mayhall, J. T. and Heikkinen, T. (eds.) *Dental Morphology '98: Proceedings of the 11th International Symposium on Dental Morphology*, pp. 48–55. Oulu: Oulu University Press.

Antoine, D., Hillson, S., and Dean, M. C. 2009. The developmental clock of dental enamel: A test for the periodicity of prism cross-striations in modern humans and an evaluation of the most likely sources of error in histological studies of this kind. *Journal of Anatomy* 214:45–55.

Austin, C.*, Smith, T. M.*, Bradman, A., Hinde, K., Joannes-Boyau, R., Bishop, D., Hare, D. J., Doble, P., Eskenazi, B., and Arora, M. 2013. Barium distributions in teeth reveal early life dietary transitions in primates. *Nature* 498:216–219. *These authors contributed equally to this work.

Bailey, S. E. 2002. *Neandertal dental morphology: Implications for modern human origins.* Doctoral thesis, Arizona State University.

Beaumont, J., Montgomery, J., Buckberry, J., and Jay, M. 2015. Infant mortality and isotopic complexity: New approaches to stress, maternal health, and weaning. *American Journal of Physical Anthropology* 157:441–457.

Bell, L. S., Boyde, A., and Jones, S. J. 1991. Diagenetic alteration to teeth in situ illustrated by backscattered electron imaging. *Scanning* 13:173–183.

Berten, J. 1895. Hypoplasie des Schmelzes (Congenitale Schmelzdefecte; Erosionen). *Deutsche Monatsschrift für Zahnheilkunde* 13:425–439, 483–498, 533–548, 587–606.

Beynon A. D. 1987. Replication technique for studying microstructure in fossil enamel. *Scanning Microscopy* 1:663–669.

Beynon, A. D., Clayton, C. B., Ramirez Rozzi, F. V., and Reid, D. J. 1998. Radiographic and histological methodologies in estimating the chronology of crown development in modern humans and great apes: A review, with some applications for studies on juvenile hominids. *Journal of Human Evolution* 35:351–370.

Bowman, J. E. 1991. *Life history, growth and dental development in young primates: A study using captive rhesus macaques.* Doctoral thesis, Cambridge University.

Boyde, A. 1963. Estimation of age at death of young human skeletal remains from incremental lines in the dental enamel. *Excerpta Medica International Congress Series* 80:36–46.

Boyde, A. 1970. The surface of the enamel in human hypoplastic teeth. *Archives of Oral Biology* 15:897–898.

Boyde, A. 1989. Enamel. In: Oksche, A. and Vollrath, L. (eds.) *Handbook of Microscopic Anatomy, Vol. V/6: Teeth*, pp. 309–473. Berlin: Springer-Verlag.

Boyde, A. 1990. Developmental interpretations of dental microstructure. In: De Rousseau, C. J. (ed.) *Primate Life History and Evolution*, pp. 229–267. New York: Wiley-Liss.

Boyde, A., Fortelius, M., Lester, K. S., and Martin, L. B. 1988. Basis of the structure and development of mammalian enamel as seen by scanning electron microscopy. *Scanning Microscopy* 2:1479–1490.

Boyde, A. and Jones, S. J. 1983. Backscattered electron imaging of dental tissues. *Anatomy and Embryology* 168:211–226.

Boyde, A. and Martin, L. 1987. Tandem scanning reflected light microscopy of primate enamel. *Scanning Microscopy* 1:1935–1948.

Brace C. L., Smith, S. L., and Hunt, K. D. 1991. What big teeth you had grandma! Human tooth size, past and present. In: Kelly and Larsen (eds.) *Advances in Dental Anthropology*, pp. 33–57. New York: Wiley-Liss.

Bracha, H. S. 2004. Can premorbid episodes of diminished vagal tone be detected via histological markers in patients with PTSD? *International Journal of Psychophysiology* 51:127–133.

Bromage, T. G. 1991. Enamel incremental periodicity in the pig-tailed macaque: A polychrome fluorescent labeling study of dental hard tissues. *American Journal of Physical Anthropology* 86:205–214.

Bullion, S. K. 1987. *Incremental structures of enamel and their applications to archaeology*. Doctoral thesis, University of Lancaster.

Caropreso, S., Bondioli, L. Capannolo, D., Cerroni, L., Macchiarelli, R., and Condò, S. G. 2000. Thin sections for hard tissue histology: A new procedure. *Journal of Microscopy* 199:244–247.

Dean, M. C. 1995. The nature and periodicity of incremental lines in primate dentine and their relationship to periradicular bands in OH 16 (*Homo habilis*). In: Moggi-Cecchi, J. (ed.) *Aspects of Dental Biology: Paleontology, Anthropology and Evolution*, pp. 239–265. Florence: International Institute for the Study of Man.

Dean, M. C. 2004. 2D or not 2D, and other interesting questions about enamel: Reply to Macho et al. (2003). *Journal of Human Evolution* 46:633–640.

Dean, M. C. 2006. Tooth microstructure tracks the pace of human life-history evolution. *Proceedings of the Royal Society B-Biological Sciences* 273:2799–2808.

Dean, M. C. and Beynon, A. D. 1991. Histological reconstruction of crown formation times and initial root formation times in a modern human child. *American Journal of Physical Anthropology* 86:215–228.

Dean, M. C., Beynon, A. D., and Reid, D. J. 1992. Microanatomical estimates of rates of root extension in a modern human child from Spitalfields, London. In: Smith, P. and Tchernov, E. (eds.) *Structure, Function and Evolution of Teeth*, pp. 311–333. London: Freund.

Dean, M. C., Beynon, A. D., Reid, D. J., and Whittaker, D. K. 1993. A longitudinal study of tooth growth in a single individual based on long- and short-period incremental markings in dentine and enamel. *International Journal of Osteoarchaeology* 3:249–264.

Dirks, W., Reid, D. J., Jolly, C. J., Phillips-Conroy, J. E., and Brett, F. L. 2002. Out of the mouths of baboons: Stress, life history, and dental development in the Awash National Park hybrid zone, Ethiopia. *American Journal of Physical Anthropology* 118:239–252.

Dubois, E. 1892. Palaeontologische onderzoekingen op Java. *Extra bijvoegsel der Javasche Courant, Verslag van het Mijnwezen over het 3e kwartaal 1891*:12–14.

FitzGerald, C. M. 1995. *Tooth crown formation and the variation of enamel microstructural growth markers in modern humans*. Doctoral thesis, University of Cambridge.

FitzGerald, C. M. 1998. Do enamel microstructures have regular time dependency? Conclusions from the literature and a large-scale study. *Journal of Human Evolution* 35:371–386.

FitzGerald, C. M. and Hillson, S. 2009. Deciduous tooth growth in an ancient Greek infant cemetery. In: Koppe, T., Meyer, G. and Alt, A. W. (eds.) *Comparative Dental Morphology*, pp. 178–183. Basel: Karger.

FitzGerald, C. M. and Saunders, S. R. 2005. Test of histological methods of determining chronology of accentuated striae in deciduous teeth. *American Journal of Physical Anthropology* 127:277–290.

FitzGerald, C. M., Saunders, S. R., Bondioli, L., and Macchiarelli, R. 2006. Health of infants in an imperial Roman skeletal sample: Perspective from dental microstructure. *American Journal of Physical Anthropology* 130:179–189.

FitzGerald, C. M., Saunders, S. R., Macchiarelli, R., and Bondioli, L. 1999. Large scale assessment of deciduous crown formation. In: Mayhall, J. T. and Heikkinen, T. (eds.) *Dental Morphology '98: Proceedings of the 11th International Symposium on Dental Morphology*, pp. 92–101. Oulu: Oulu University Press.

Füsun, A., Füsun, Ö., Sema, B., and Solen, K. 2005. Acetate peel technique: A rapid way of preparing sequential surface replicas of dental hard tissues for microscopic examination. *Archives of Oral Biology* 50:837–842.

Goodman, A. H., Armelagos, G. F., and Rose, J. C. 1980. Enamel hypoplasias as indicators of stress in three prehistoric populations from Illinois (AD 950–1300). *Human Biology* 52:515–528.

Goodman, A. H. and Rose, J. C. 1990. Assessment of systemic physiological perturbations from dental enamel hypoplasias and associated histological structures. *Yearbook of Physical Anthropology* 33:59–110.

Goodman, A. H. and Song, R.-J. 1999. Sources of variation in estimated ages at formation of linear enamel hypoplasias. In: Hoppa, R. D. and FitzGerald, C. M. (eds.) *Human Growth in the Past: Studies from Bones and Teeth*, pp. 210–240. Cambridge: Cambridge University Press.

Gray, J. A. and Opdyke, D. L. 1962. A device for thin sectioning of hard tissues. *Journal of Dental Research* 41:172–181.

Guatelli-Steinberg, D. 2001. What can developmental defects of enamel reveal about physiological stress in nonhuman primates? *Evolutionary Anthropology* 10:138–151.

Guatelli-Steinberg, D. 2004. Analysis and significance of linear enamel hypoplasia in Plio-Pleistocene hominins. *American Journal of Physical Anthropology* 123:199–215.

Guatelli-Steinberg, D. and Benderlioglu, Z. 2006. Brief communication: Linear enamel hypoplasia and the shift from irregular to regular provisioning in Cayo Santiago rhesus monkeys (*Macaca mulatta*). *American Journal of Physical Anthropology* 131:416–419.

Guatelli-Steinberg, D. and Mitchell J. 2003. Repliset: High resolution impressions of the teeth of human ancestors. *Structure: Struers Journal of Materialography* 40:9–12.

Guatelli-Steinberg, D. and Reid, D. J. 2008. What molars contribute to an emerging understanding of lateral enamel formation in Neandertals vs. modern humans. *Journal of Human Evolution* 54:236–250.

Gustafson, A.-G. 1955. The similarity between contralateral pairs of teeth. *Odontologisk Tidskrift* 63:245–248.

Gustafson, A.-G. 1959. A morphologic investigation of certain variations in the structure and mineralization of human dental enamel. *Odontologisk Tidskrift* 67: 366–472.

Gysi, A. 1931. Metabolism in adult enamel. *Dental Digest* 37:661–668.

Hanihara T. 2008. Morphological variation of major human populations based on nonmetric dental traits. *American Journal of Physical Anthropology* 136:169–182.

Hanihara T. and Ishida H. 2005. Metric dental variation of major human populations. *American Journal of Physical Anthropology* 128:287–298.

Hayakawa, T., Mishima, H., Yokota, I., Sakae, T., Kozawa, Y., and Nemoto, K. 2000. Application of high resolution microfocus X-ray CT for the observation of human tooth. *Dental Materials Journal* 19:87–95.

Hillson, S. W. 1992a. Impression and replica methods for studying hypoplasia and perikymata on human tooth crown surfaces from archeological sites. *International Journal of Osteoarchaeology* 2:65–78.

Hillson, S. W. 1992b. Dental enamel growth, perikymata and hypoplasia in ancient tooth crowns. *Journal of the Royal Society of Medicine* 85:460–466.

Hillson, S. W. 1996. *Dental Anthropology*. Cambridge: Cambridge University Press.

Hillson, S. W. 2014. *Tooth Development in Human Evolution and Bioarchaeology*. Cambridge: Cambridge University Press.

Hillson, S. W., Antoine, D. M., and Dean, M. C. 1999. A detailed developmental study of the defects of dental enamel in a group of post-medieval children from London. In: Mayhall, J. T. and Heikkinen, T. (eds.) *Dental Morphology '98: Proceedings of the 11th International Symposium on Dental Morphology*, pp. 102–111. Oulu: Oulu University Press.

Hillson, S. W. and Bond, S. 1997. Relationship of enamel hypoplasia to the pattern of tooth crown growth: A discussion. *American Journal of Physical Anthropology* 104:89–103.

Hillson, S. W. and Jones, B. K. 1989. Instruments for measuring surface profiles: An application in the study of ancient human tooth crown surfaces. *Journal of Archaeological Science* 16:95–105.

Hooijer D. A. 1948. Prehistoric teeth of man and of the orang-utan from central Sumatra, with notes on the fossil orang-utan from Java and southern China. *Zoologische Mededeelingen* 29:175–301.

Huda, T. F. J. and Bowman, J. E. 1995. Age determination from dental microstructure in juveniles. *American Journal of Physical Anthropology* 97:135–150.

Humphrey, L. T., Dean, M. C., and Jeffries, T. E., 2007. An evaluation of changes in strontium/calcium ratios across the neonatal line in human deciduous teeth. In: Bailey, S. E. and Hublin, J.-J. (eds.) *Dental Perspectives on Human Evolution: State of the Art Research in Dental Paleoanthropology*, pp. 303–319. Dordrecht: Springer.

Humphrey L. T., Dean, M. C., Jeffries, T. E., and Penn, M. 2008a. Unlocking evidence of early diet from tooth enamel. *Proceedings of the National Academy of Sciences* 105:6834–6839.

Humphrey, L. T., Dirks, W., Dean, M. C., and Jeffries, T. E. 2008b. Tracking dietary transitions in weanling Baboons (*Papio hamadryas anubis*) using Strontium/Calcium ratios in enamel. *Folia Primatologica* 79:197–212.

Irish, J. and Guatelli-Steinberg, D. 2003. Ancient teeth and modern human origins: An expanded comparison of African Plio-Pleistocene and recent world dental samples. *Journal of Human Evolution* 45:113–144.

Katzenberg, M. A., Herring, D. A., and Saunders, S. R. 1996. Weaning and infant mortality: Evaluating the skeletal evidence. *Yearbook of Physical Anthropology* 39:177–199.

Katzenberg, M. A., Oetelaar, G., Oetelaar, J., Fitzgerald, C., Yang, D., and Saunders, S. R. 2005. Identification of historical human skeletal remains: A case study using skeletal and dental age, history and DNA. *International Journal of Osteoarchaeology* 15:61–72.

Kay, R. F., Rasmussen, D. T., and Beard, K. C. 1984. Cementum annulus counts provide a means for age determination in *Macaca mulatta* (Primates, Anthropoidea). *Folia Primatologica* 42:85–95.

Keith, A. 1913. Problems relating to the teeth of the earlier forms of prehistoric man. *Proceedings of the Royal Society of Medicine* 6:103–113.

Kelley, J. 2008. Identification of a single birth cohort in *Kenyapithecus kizili* and the nature of sympatry between *K. kizili* and *Gripopithecus alpani* at Pasalar. *Journal of Human Evolution* 54:530–537.

King, T., Hillson, S., and Humphrey, L. T. 2002. A detailed study of enamel hypoplasia in a post-medieval adolescent of known age and sex. *Archives of Oral Biology* 47:29–39.

Lacruz, R. S., Dean, M. C., Ramirez-Rozzi, F., and Bromage, T. G. 2008. Megadontia, striae periodicity and patterns of enamel secretion in Plio-Pleistocene fossil hominins. *Journal of Anatomy* 213:148–158.

Rozzi, F. R., and Bromage, T. 2006. Variation in enamel development of South African fossil hominids. *Journal of Human Evolution* 51(6):580–590.

Le Cabec, A., Tang, N., and Tafforeau, P. 2015. Accessing developmental information of fossil hominin teeth using new synchrotron microtomography-based visualization techniques of dental surfaces and interfaces. *PLoS One* 10(4):e0123019.

Le Gros Clark, W. 1950. Hominid characters of the Australopithecine dentition. *Journal of the Royal Anthropological Institute* 80:37–54.

Leeuwenhoeck, A. 1677–1678. Microscopical observations of the structure of teeth and other bones: Made and communicated, in a letter by Mr. Anthony Leeuwenhoeck. *Philosophical Transactions* 12:1002–1003.

Lieberman, D. E. 1994. The biological basis for seasonal increments in dental cementum and their application to archaeological research. *Journal of Archaeological Science* 21:525–539.

Liversidge, H. M. 2003. Variations in modern human dental development. In: Thompson, J. L, Krovitz, G. E., and Nelson, A. J. (eds.) *Patterns of Growth and Development in the Genus Homo*, pp. 73–113. Cambridge: Cambridge University Press.

Macchiarelli, R., Bondioli, L., Debénath, A., Mazurier, A., Tournepiche, J.-F., Birch, W., and Dean, C., 2006. How Neanderthal molar teeth grew. *Nature* 444:748–751.

Marks, M., Rose, J., and Davenport, W. 1996. Technical Note: Thin section procedure for enamel histology. *American Journal of Physical Anthropology* 99:493–498.

Martin, S. A., Guatelli-Steinberg, D., Sciulli, P. W., and Walker, P. L. 2008. Brief communication: Comparison of methods for estimating chronology age at linear enamel formation on anterior dentition. *American Journal of Physical Anthropology* 135:362–365.

Moorrees, C. F. A., Fanning, E. A., and Hunt, E. E. 1963. Age variation of formation stages for ten permanent teeth. *Journal of Dental Research* 42:1490–1502.

Murphy, A. P. and McNeil, G. 1964. Precision Ultramicrotome of simplified design. *The Review of Scientific Instruments* 35:132–134.

Neal, R. J. and Murphy, A. P. 1969. Technique for sectioning human enamel. *Archives of Oral Biology* 14:135–139.

Nielsen-Marsh, C. M., Stegemann, C., Hoffmann, R., Smith, T., Feeney, R., Toussaint, M., Harvati, K., Panagopoulou, E., Hublin, J.-J., and Richards, M. P. 2009. Extraction and sequencing of human and Neanderthal mature enamel proteins using MALDI-TOF/TOF MS. *Journal of Archaeological Science* 36:1758–1763.

Nikiforuk, G. and Fraser, D. 1979. Etiology of enamel hypoplasia and interglobular dentin: The roles of hypocalcemia and hypophosphatemia. *Metabolic Bone Disease and Related Research* 2:17–23.

Olejniczak A. J., Grine, F. E., and Martin, L. B. 2007. Micro-computed tomography of the post-canine dentition: Methodological aspects of three-dimensional data collection. In: Bailey, S. E. and Hublin, J.-J. (eds.) *Dental Perspectives on Human Evolution: State of the Art Research in Dental Paleoanthropology*, pp. 103–116. Springer: Dordrecht

Peyrégne, S., Slon, V., Mafessoni, F., de Filippo, C., Hajdinjak, M., Nagel, S., Nickel, B., Essel, E., Le Cabec, A., Wehrberger, K., Conard, N. J., Kind, C. J., Posth, C., Krause, J., Abrams, G., Bonjean, D., Di Modica, K., Toussaint, M., Kelso, J., Meyer, M., Pääbo, S., and Prüfer K. 2019. Nuclear DNA from two early Neandertals reveals 80,000 years of genetic continuity in Europe. *Science Advances* 5:eaaw5873.

Reid, D. J., Beynon, A. D., and Ramirez Rozzi, F. V. 1998b. Histological reconstruction of dental development in four individuals from a medieval site in Picardie, France. *Journal of Human Evolution* 35:463–477.

Reid, D. J. and Dean, M. C. 2000. The timing of linear hypoplasias on human anterior teeth. *American Journal of Physical Anthropology* 113:135–139.

Reid, D. J. and Dean, M. C. 2006. Variation in modern human enamel formation Times. *Journal of Human Evolution* 50: 329–346.

Reid, D. J. and Ferrell, R., 2006. The relationship between number of striae of Retzius and their periodicity in imbricational enamel formation. *Journal of Human Evolution* 50:195–202.

Reid, D. J., Guatelli-Steinberg, D., and Walton, P. 2008. Variation in modern human premolar enamel formation times: Implications for Neandertals. *Journal of Human Evolution* 54:225–235.

Renz, H. and Radlanski, R. J. 2006. Incremental lines in root cementum of human teeth – a reliable age marker? *Homo* 57:29–50.

Reid, D. J., Schwartz, G. T., Dean, C., and Chandrasekera, M. S. 1998a. A histological reconstruction of dental development in the common chimpanzee, *Pan troglodytes*. *Journal of Human Evolution* 35:427–448.

Reynard L. M. and Tuross, N. 2015. The known, the unknown and the unknowable: Weaning times from archaeological bones using nitrogen isotope ratios. *Journal of Archaeological Science* 53:618–625.

Richards, M., Harvati, K., Grimes, V., Smith, C., Smith, T., Hublin, J. -J., Karkanas, P., and Panagopoulou, E. 2008. Strontium isotope evidence of Neanderthal mobility at the site of Lakonis, Greece using laser-ablation PIMMS. *Journal of Archaeological Science* 35:1251–1256.

Ritzman, T. B., Baker, B. J., and Schwartz, G. T. 2008. A fine line: A comparison of methods of estimating ages of linear enamel hypoplasia formation. *American Journal of Physical Anthropology* 135:348–361.

Rose, J. C., Armelagos, G. J., and Lallo, J. W. 1978. Histological enamel indicator of childhood stress in prehistoric skeletal samples. *American Journal of Physical Anthropology* 49:511–516.

Rose, J. J. 1983. A replication technique for scanning electron microscopy: Applications for anthropologists. *American Journal of Physical Anthropology* 62:255–261.

Rushton, M. A. 1933. On the fine contour lines of the enamel of milk teeth. *Dental Record* 53:170–171.

Schmidt, W. J. and Keil, A. 1971. *Polarizing Microscopy of Dental Tissues*. Oxford: Pergamon Press.

Schoeninger, M. J., Hallin, K., Reeser, H., Valley, J. W., and Fournelle, J. 2003. Isotopic alteration of mammalian tooth enamel. *International Journal of Osteoarchaeology* 13:11–19.

Schour, I. 1936. The neonatal line in the enamel and dentin of human deciduous teeth and first permanent molar. *Journal of the American Dental Association* 23:1946–1955.

Schwartz, G. T. and Dean, C. 2001. Ontogeny of canine dimorphism in extant hominoids. *American Journal of Physical Anthropology* 115:269–283.

Schwartz, J. H., Houghton, F., Macchiarelli, R., and Bondioli, L. 2010. Skeletal remains from Punic Carthage do not support systematic sacrifice of infants', *PLoS One* 5(2): e9177.

Schwartz, G. T., Reid, D. J., Dean, M. C., and Zihlman, A. L. 2006. A faithful record of stressful life events preserved in the dental developmental record of a juvenile gorilla. *International Journal of Primatology* 22:837–860.

Simpson, S. W. 1999. Reconstructing patterns of growth disruption from enamel microstructure. In: Hoppa, R. D. and Fitzgerald, C. M. (eds.) *Human Growth in the Past: Studies from Bones and Teeth*, pp. 241–263. Cambridge: Cambridge University Press.

Skinner, M. F. 1986. Enamel hypoplasia in sympatric chimpanzee and gorilla. *Human Evolution* 1:289–312.

Skinner, M. F. 1996. Developmental stress in immature hominines from late Pleistocene Eurasia: Evidence from enamel hypoplasia. *Journal of Archaeological Science* 23:833–852.

Skinner, M. F. and Anderson, G. S. 1991. Individualization and enamel histology: A case report in forensic anthropology. *Journal of Forensic Sciences* 36:939–948.

Skinner, M. F. and Hopwood, D. 2004. Hypothesis for the causes and periodicity of repetitive linear enamel hypoplasia in large, wild African (*Pan troglodytes* and *Gorilla gorilla*) and Asian (*Pongo pygmaeus*) apes. *American Journal of Physical Anthropology* 123:216–235.

Smith, B. H. 1991. Standards of human tooth formation and dental age assessment. In: Kelley, M. A. and Spencer Larsen, C. (eds.) *Advances in Dental Anthropology*, pp. 143–168. New York: Wiley-Liss.

Smith, T. M. 2006. Experimental determination of the periodicity of incremental features in enamel. *Journal of Anatomy* 208:99–114.

Smith, T. M. 2008. Incremental dental development: Methods and applications in hominoid evolutionary studies. *Journal of Human Evolution* 54:205–224.

Smith, T. M. 2013. Teeth and human life-history evolution. *Annual Review of Anthropology* 42:191–208.

Smith, T. M. and Boesch, C. 2015. Developmental defects in the teeth of three wild chimpanzees from the Taï forest. *American Journal of Physical Anthropology* 157:556–570.

Smith, T. M. and Reid, D. J. 2009. Temporal nature of periradicular bands ("striae periradicales") on mammalian tooth roots. In: Koppe, T., Meyer, G., Alt, K. W., Brook, A., Dean, M. C., Kjaer, I., Lukacs, J. R., Smith, B. H., and Teaford, M. F. (eds.) *Comparative Dental Morphology*, pp. 86–92. Basle: Karger Medical and Scientific Publishers.

Smith, T. M. and Tafforeau, P. 2008. New visions of dental tissue research: Tooth development, chemistry, and structure. *Evolutionary Anthropology* 17:213–226.

Smith, T.M., Austin, C., Green, D.R. Joannes-Boyau, R. Bailey, S., Dumitriu, D., Fallon, S., Grün, R., James, H.F., Moncel, M-H., Williams, I.S., Wood, R., and Arora, M. 2018. Wintertime stress, nursing, and lead exposure in Neanderthal children. *Science Advances* 4: eaau9483.

Smith, T. M., Harvati, K., Olejniczak, A. J., Reid, D. J., Hublin, J.-J., and Panagopoulou, E. 2009. Brief communication: Dental development and enamel thickness in the Lakonis Neanderthal molar. *American Journal of Physical Anthropology* 138:112–118.

Smith, T. M., Martin, L. B., Reid, D. J., de Bouis, L., and Koufos, G. D. 2004. Anexamination of dental development in *Graecopithecus freybergi* (= *Ouranopithecus macedoniensis*). *Journal of Human Evolution* 46:551–577.

Smith, T. M., Reid, D. J., Olejniczak, A. J., Tafforeau, P., Hublin, J.-J., and Toussaint, M. 2014. Dental development in and age at death of the Scladina 1-4A juvenile Neanderthal. In: Toussaint, M. and Bonjean, D. (eds.) *The Scladina I-4A Juvenile Neandertal (Andenne, Belgium) Palaeoanthropology and Context*, pp. 155–166. Liège: Études et Recherches Archéologiques de l' Université de Liège.

Smith, T. M.*, Tafforeau, P.*, Le Cabec, A., Bonnin, A., Houssaye, A., Pouech, J., Moggi-Cecchi, J., Manthi, F., Ward, C., Makaremi, M., and C. G. Menter 2015. Dental ontogeny in Pliocene and early Pleistocene hominins. *PLoS One* 10(2): e0118118. *These authors contributed equally to this work.

Smith, T. M., Tafforeau, P. T., Reid, D. J., Grün, R., Eggins, S., Boutakiout, M., and Hublin, J.-J. 2007c. Earliest evidence of modern human life history in North African early *Homo sapiens*. *Proceedings of the National Academy of Science of the United States of America* 104:6128–6133.

Smith, T. M., Tafforeau, P., Reid, D. J., Pouech, J., Lazzari, V., Zermeno, J. P., Guatelli-Steinberg, D., Olejniczak, A. J., Hoffman, A., Radovčić, J., Masrour, M., Toussaint, M., Stringer, C., and Hublin, J.-J. 2010. Dental evidence for ontogenetic differences between modern humans and Neanderthals. *Proceedings of the National Academy of Science of the United States of America* 107:20923–20928.

Smith, T. M., Toussaint, M., Reid, D. J., Olejniczak, A. J., and Hublin, J.-J. 2007a. Rapid dental development in a Middle Paleolithic Belgian Neanderthal. *Proceedings of the National Academy of Science of the United States of America* 104:20220–20225.

Sponheimer, M., Passey, B. H., de Ruiter, D. J., Guatelli-Steinberg, D., Cerling, T. E., and Lee-Thorp, J. A. 2006. Isotopic evidence for dietary variability in the early hominin *Paranthropus robustus*. *Science* 314:980–982.

Stringer, C. B., Dean, M. C., and Martin, R. D. 1990. A comparative study of cranial and dental development within a recent British sample and among Neandertals. In: De Rousseau, C. J. (ed.) *Primate Life History and Evolution*, pp. 115–152. New York: Wiley-Liss.

Tafforeau, P. 2004. *Phylogenetic and functional aspects of tooth enamel microstructure and three-dimensional structure of modern and fossil primate molars: Contributions of X-ray synchrotron microtomography*. Doctoral thesis, Universitè de Montpellier II.

Tafforeau, P., Boistel, R., Boller, E, Bravin, A., Brunet, M., Chaimanee, Y., Cloetens, P., Feist, M., Hoszowska, J., Jaeger, J.-J., Kay, R.F., Lazzari, V., Marivaux, L., Nel, A., Nemoz, C., Thibault, X., Vignaud, P., and Zabler, S. 2006. Applications of X-ray synchrotron microtomography for non-destructive 3D studies of paleontological specimens. *Applied Physics A-Materials Science and Processing* 83:195–202.

Tafforeau, P. T. and Smith, T. M. 2008. Nondestructive imaging of hominoid dental microstructure using phase contrast X-ray synchrotron microtomography. *Journal of Human Evolution* 54:272–278.

Thomas, R. F. 2003. *Enamel defects, well-being and mortality in a medieval Danish village*. Doctoral thesis, Pennslvania State University.

Toussaint, M. and Pirson, S. 2006. Neanderthal studies in Belgium: 2000–2005. *Periodicum Biologorum* 108:373–387.

Weidenreich, F. 1937. The dentition of *Sinathropus pekinensis:* A comparative odontography of the hominids. *Geological survey of China, new series D* 1: 1–180.

Wittwer-Backofen, U., Buckberry, J., Czarnetzki, A., Doppler, S., Grupe, G., Hotz, G., Kemkes, A., Larsen, C. S., D. Prince, Wahl, J., Fabig, A., and Weise, S. 2008. Basics in paleodemography: A comparison of age indicators applied to the early medieval skeletal sample of Lauchheim. *American Journal of Physical Anthropology* 137:384–396.

Wittwer-Backofen, U., Gampe, J., and Vaupel, J. W. 2004. Tooth cementum annulation for age estimation: Results from a large known-age validation study. *American Journal of Physical Anthropology* 123:119–124.

Witzel, C., Kierdorf, U., Schultz, M., and Kierdorf, H. 2008. Insights from the inside: Histological analysis of abnormal enamel microstructure associated with hypoplastic enamel defects in human teeth. *American Journal of Physical Anthropology* 139:193–203.

Wolpoff, M. H. 1971. *Metric Trends in Hominid Dental Evolution.* Cleveland: Case Western Reserve University Press.

Wood, B. A., Li, Y., and Willoughby, C. 1991. Intraspecific variation and sexual dimorphism in cranial and dental variables among higher primates and their bearing on the hominid fossil record. *Journal of Anatomy* 174:185–205.

9

Geometric Morphometrics

Philipp Gunz

The analysis of the three dimensional shape of objects as a means of classification and analysis, especially for human evolution studies.

1 INTRODUCTION

The ability to objectively compare shapes of skeletal remains, such as skulls and teeth, or artefacts, such as stone tools, is central to many questions in archeology and palaeoanthropology. Over the last decade, geometric morphometric (GMM) techniques have revolutionised the statistical analysis of shape and form. Statistical shape-analysis can be a helpful tool for answering many archeological questions. One might, for example, be interested in the population dynamics associated with changes in material culture. Studying the human skeletal remains from different archeological stratas using geometric morphometrics can provide insights into the population history. Based on artefacts alone it is often impossible to determine whether a cultural change was linked to the replacement of a local population, or whether this new set of behaviors and skills developed locally.

As well as introducing basic principles and providing an overview of geometric morphometrics in archaeology and palaeoanthropology, this chapter will explore some key examples of how these methods for quantifying shape and form differences can help researchers understand the archeological and fossil record.

Any geometric morphometric analysis starts by digitizing coordinates of measurement points (known as "landmarks") on every object of study (Figure 9.1). It is from these coordinates, placed at the same points on every sample, that information about each object's shape and size can be extracted. The *shape* of an object is defined as the information that is independent of position, orientation and scale.

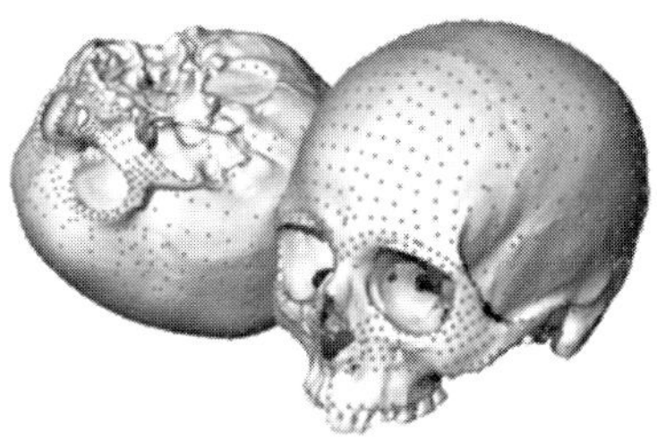

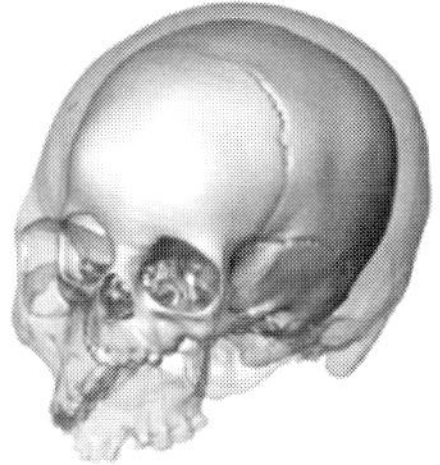

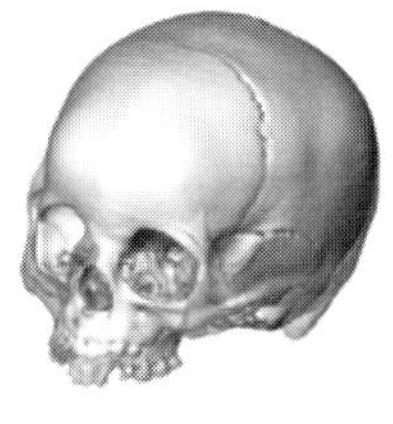

FIGURE 9.1 Procrustes superimposition. Left: Two crania (a modern human child and an adult) were measured using a surface scanner; 3D coordinates of homologous landmarks and semilandmarks (988 points in total) were digitised on either specimen. The raw coordinates still contain information about the position, orientation and size of the crania. Middle: The specimens are centered to standardise position. For clarity the landmarks are not shown, and the adult surface is drawn semitransparent. All computations however are based on the landmarks and semilandmarks, not the surface-vertices. Right: The crania in Procrustes orientation: position, orientation, and size are standardised; what remains are the shape differences between these two specimens. Data collected by Sarah Freidline

Form, on the other hand, comprises information about shape and size. Geometric morphometric (GM) studies employ multivariate statistics to analyse size and shape variables. GM methods, based on landmark coordinates, have three main advantages over traditional morphometric techniques, which are based on distances and angles: in GM (1) the spatial relationships among the landmarks are being preserved throughout the analysis; (2) it is possible to separate size information from shape information; and (3) the statistical results can be visualised and interpreted intuitively.

2 DESCRIPTION OF METHODS AND EQUIPMENT

Landmark Coordinates and Homology

Data collection starts by measuring a sequence of two-dimensional (x and y) or three-dimensional (x, y, and z) landmark coordinates. Landmarks are defined as homologous measurement points that can be identified on every specimen in the sample set. The underlying assumption of correspondence between these landmarks is critical for every GM analysis. If it is impossible to define reliable landmark points, it is also not possible to conduct GM analysis. For the quantification of curves and surfaces, *semilandmarks* may be used. When using semilandmarks, the respective curves and surfaces on which they are placed must be homologous among all specimens of study.

Data Sources

When conducting a two-dimensionional (2D) GM study, it is easy to digitise 2D landmark coordinates from digital pictures, or scans. However, given that the objects are usually not flat, one needs to pay attention to standardizing the original images, which are, after all, only two-dimensional projections of a three-dimensional object. The position and orientation of the object, its distance from the camera, the focal length of the lens and lens distortion, have to be taken into account. It is always useful to also include a scale – otherwise it will be hard, or even impossible, to extract the object's size information later.

For most applications it makes more sense to digitise three-dimensional coordinate data. One can either measure landmark coordinates directly, using a 3D digitiser (e.g., a Microscribe) connected to a computer, or measure landmarks on virtual objects from 3D surface scans or computed-tomographic (CT) scans. 3D surface scanners work with either laser technology or use a digital camera setup. They provide an accurate three-dimensional representation of the outer surface of an object. Some surface scanner models are portable and can be used in the field, others require a more elaborate setup in a dedicated lab. CT scanners yield three-dimensional x-ray images; it is therefore possible to also study hidden internal structures, for example, the inside of a skull.

As the relationship between the measurement points is preserved throughout the analysis, and because it is possible to quantify the morphology of curves and surfaces through the use of semilandmarks, GM methods can capture very subtle shape differences. This advantage comes at a price, however: usually the amount of work and effort required to collect landmark and semilandmark data suitable for GM analyses is significantly higher than for traditional morphometric approaches based on linear distances and angles. This usually results in smaller sample sizes for GM studies. Although the origin of the landmark coordinate does not affect the subsequent statistical analyses, if one pools measurements from different data sources (e.g., when a sample comprises specimens where some landmarks were measured on CT scans and others were measured directly on the original specimen), it makes sense to carefully check for potential biases prior to the analysis. The same applies to data collected by multiple observers.

3 CORE METHODS

Geometric morphometrics is built around two core methods: the *Procrustes superimposition*, and the *thin-plate spline*. The former converts the raw coordinate measurements into shape variables; the latter is a powerful tool for visualizing the results of a GM analysis. An overview of these methods is provided below, and further details can be found in Mitteroecker and Gunz (2009). An alternative methodological approach, called *Euclidean Distance Matrix Analysis* (EDMA), is based on distances among all landmarks (for a review see Richtsmeier et al. 2002).

Procrustes Superimposition

The raw landmark coordinates include information about the position of the measured object within the respective coordinate system. To convert these raw coordinates to shape variables, the information about position, orientation and scale has to be removed for every specimen. This is achieved using a Procrustes superimposition (Figure 9.1). The computation involves the following steps (for details see Rohlf and Slice 1990):

(a) The centroid of specimen is calculated by averaging all x, all y, (and all z if the data are three-dimensional) coordinates.
(b) Subtracting the respective centroid from all landmarks of a specimen translates it to the coordinate origin. This standardises the position.
(c) To remove the absolute size differences, each specimen is divided by its *centroid size* (CS). CS is defined as the square root of the summed squared distances of each landmark to the specimen's centroid. This step scales each specimen to unit centroid size, size related (allometric) effects on shape, however, remain.
(d) The final step removes the information about the rotation of the specimens. It is repeated several times until the differences between subsequent runs (iterations) are negligible. In the first iteration all specimens are rotated to first specimen in the dataset. The criterion for optimizing the fit between two specimens is that one rotates one specimen until the square root of the summed squared distances between homologous landmarks (the *Procrustes distance*) is minimised. A mean shape is then computed by averaging all superimposed homologous coordinates, and the fit of each specimen to this mean shape is optimised. This algorithm usually converges after a few iterations.

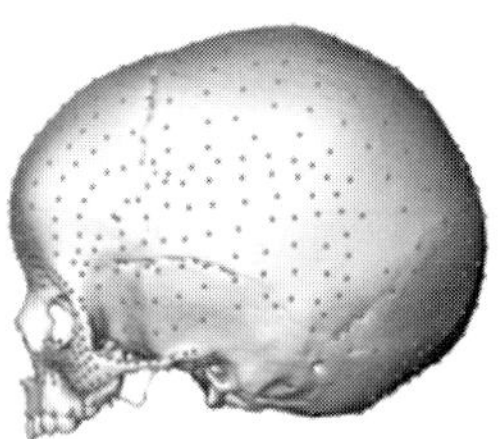

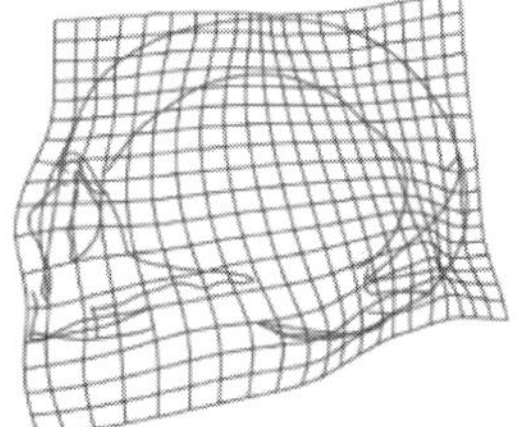

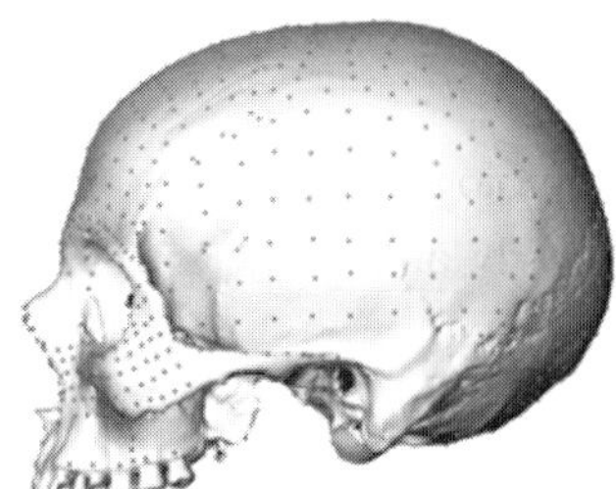

FIGURE 9.2 Thin-plate spline (TPS) interpolation. A TPS deformation grid drawn in the symmetry plane visualises the shape differences between the child on the left and the adult on the right. This visualises how one would have to "push and pull" an initially square grid to get from the left form to the right: the face is relatively larger in the adult than in the child, therefore the TPS grid bulges in the area of the upper jaw. The child's braincase is more globular than the more elongated adult; the TPS grid therefore appears "pinched in" in the posterior part of the skull.

Procrustes superimposition yields a matrix of shape variables and a size variable (CS) for each specimen.

Thin-Plate Spline Deformation

A powerful way to visualise the shape differences between two landmark configurations is computing a thin-plate spline deformation grid or TPS (Bookstein 1989; Bookstein 1991). These grids show how one would have to deform a reference configuration, to arrive at a target shape (Figure 9.2). TPS deformation grids rely on an interpolation function that is computed based on the landmarks of the reference and target shape; the space "in-between" the landmarks is interpolated. The notion of smoothness is approached by minimizing the so-called *bending energy* of the deformation – a scalar quantity computed as the integral of the squared second derivatives of that deformation. The TPS formalism is also central to the semilandmark algorithm and the estimation of missing data in morphometrics. It is worth noting that no prior superimposition of reference and target is required for computing a TPS. This is because position, orientation and scale are affine transformations (i.e., they affect all landmarks in exactly the same way), which do not affect the TPS.

Semilandmarks

Semilandmarks (Bookstein 1997; Gunz et al. 2005) are a GM technique for analysing curves and surfaces using coordinate-based statistics. Smooth curves and surfaces can be captured by placing the same number of points (semilandmarks) in homologous positions on every specimen (Figures 9.1, 9.2, and 9.4). The notion of homology employed here is one of geometric correspondence across a sample. Clearly observable curves on surfaces, such as ridges, should be treated as curves instead of surface points. In general, the sampling of semilandmarks depends on the complexity of curves or surfaces, and on the spatial scale of shape variation that is of interest.

To arrive at the same number of semilandmarks, and in the same order, on each specimen, it is convenient to begin with points equidistantly spaced along outline arcs, for example, through automatic resampling of a polygonal approximation to the curve. Techniques for surfaces differ substantially from those for curves in that, except for planes and cylinders, there is no straightforward analogue to the notion of "equal spacing." The algorithm developed by Gunz et al. (2005) starts by equidistant resampling of the curves, and by projecting a template mesh of surface semilandmarks onto every specimen via TPS. To remove the confounding effects of the arbitrary spacing, these semilandmarks are then allowed to slide along the curves and surfaces prior to the statistical analysis. Two alternative approaches to semilandmarks exist: one either optimises the bending energy between each specimen and the Procrustes average (Bookstein 1997; Gunz et al. 2005), or the Procrustes distance between each specimen and the Procrustes average (e.g., Frost et al. 2003). The statistical properties of these two different algorithms are discussed in detail in Mitteroecker and Gunz (2009). To linearise the minimisation problem, the semilandmarks do not slide on the actual curve or surface but along the tangent vectors to the curve or the tangent planes to the surface. After the sliding step, landmarks and semilandmarks can be treated the same in the subsequent multivariate analysis.

Statistical Analysis in Shape Space

The *Procrustes distance* between specimens is the metric of "shape-space." Procrustes distance measures the shape similarity between two objects based on the measured coordinates: it is zero when two objects are identical; if two objects have very different shapes, then the Procrustes distance is large. One can study the large-scale trends of shape variability in a dataset using *principal component analysis* (PCA); in the GM literature PCA is sometimes referred to as "*relative warps analysis.*"

To assess which dimensions of shape space best separate a priori defined groups one can compute a *linear discriminant analysis* (often called canonical variates analysis or CVA). These axes can then be used to classify unknown shapes to one of the prior groups. CVA can only be applied if there are more specimens than variables, which creates a serious problem for many GM applications. Given that each three-dimensional landmark has x, y and z coordinates (i.e., three variables), the number of variables often exceeds the number of specimens – especially in archaeological or palaeoanthropological samples where sample numbers may be very limited. It is possible to reduce the dimensions of the original data-matrix using principal component analysis first, and then compute the discriminant analysis in a lower dimensional subspace of the first few principal components (by using the PC scores as input variables for the CVA, rather than the original Procrustes shape variables). However, no fixed rules exist about how many principal components to use. The choice of subspace is therefore arbitrary, and may affect the classification results. It is therefore important to test the numerical stability of the results of a discriminant analysis (for more on this subject see Mitteroecker and Gunz 2009; Skinner et al. 2009b).

Statistical Significance Tests

In addition to more fundamental issues with statistical inference based on P values (Ziliak and McCloskey 2008), GM analyses are usually affected by the "large p, small N"-problem, as mentioned above (with p being the number of variables, and N being the number of specimens). Randomisation methods based on permutation and bootstrapping help overcome many of the limitations of parametric statistical testing (Good 2005). Using the power of modern personal computers one can design very complex test designs that do not require the data to be normally distributed. Randomisation methods therefore make it possible to go beyond simple tests of mean differences (although such test are possible too, of course), and can be used even when the number of variables exceeds the number of cases. Examples can be found in Bulygina et al. (2006), Gunz et al. (2009b), Mitteroecker et al. (2004), and Schaefer et al. (2006).

Estimating Missing Data

All GM methods require every specimen in the sample to have the same number of homologous landmarks and semilandmarks. These methods, therefore, do not

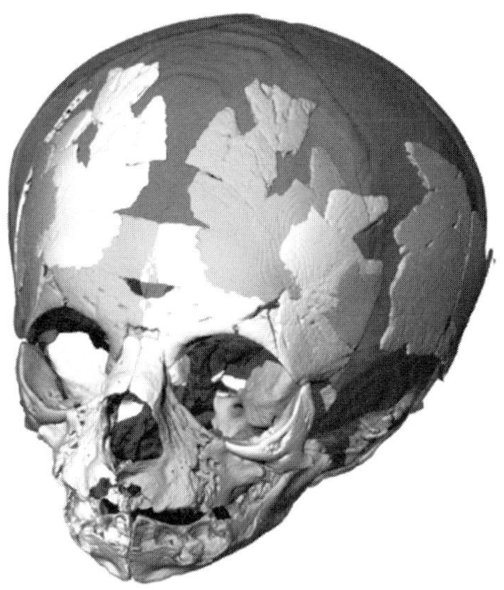

FIGURE 9.3 Virtual reconstruction of a Neanderthal newborn. Geometric morphometrics was used to estimate the missing parts of this partially preserved Neanderthal skull from Le Moustier, France (after Maureille 2002a,b). In the first step, the digital fragments were assembled based on anatomical criteria. If parts were missing on one side, or were better preserved on one side than the other, we reflected them across a midsagittal symmetry plane; mirrored parts are drawn in a darker shade. After mirror-imaging we digitised three-dimensional coordinates of landmarks and semilandmarks on Le Moustier 2, as well as on modern human and Neanderthal reference crania. Coordinates that could not be measured on Le Moustier 2 were estimated via a thin-plate spline interpolation between a reference cranium and the incomplete fossil; the estimated bone is drawn as a semitransparent surface. We could then estimate the endocranial volume of a Neanderthal at the time of birth based on a virtual endocast (darker shade). We found that the endocranial volumes of modern humans and Neanderthals were very similar around the time of birth. (Adapted from Gunz et al. 2010)

allow data to be missing. Archeological specimens, however, are often broken and incomplete. One can either restrict the analysis to the subset of landmarks and semilandmarks available on all specimens, or estimate the missing data. In many applications the first option is impractical, as the number of landmarks available on *all* specimens is often very small. Estimating missing data, on the other hand, is usually based on prior assumptions that will affect the results. Gunz et al. (2004; Gunz et al. 2009a,b) describe principles for the reconstruction of incomplete skulls, where, based on surface or CT scans of the original fragments, it can be possible to assemble the digital fragments on a computer like a three-dimensional jigsaw puzzle (Figure 9.3). Parts missing on only one side of the skull are then mirrored across a local midplane. Data that are missing on both sides, as well as missing data along the midsagittal plane of the skull, can then be estimated using GM methods. Gunz et al. (2004; 2009a,b) propose two algorithms with different statistical properties, one is based on multiple multivariate regression, the other on the thin-plate spline interpolation. In the latter, missing landmarks and semilandmarks are allowed to move freely so as to minimise the overall bending energy between the incomplete specimen and a complete reference configuration; this method has been shown to be particularly well-suited for estimating relatively smooth surfaces (e.g., on the braincase). Of course, the accuracy of such reconstructions depends upon the size of the defect and the number of coordinates that are recorded in the vicinity of the missing part such that reconstruction of a small defect with many adjacent coordinates will have greater accuracy.

4 EXAMPLE APPLICATIONS

Cranial and dental shapes preserve a broad population history signal but shape can also be adaptive. As bone is remodeled constantly, and reacts to mechanical strains such as the ones caused by bite-forces, many cranial features adapt to dietary changes. As diet and environmental stress during childhood have a direct relationship to body size, it is also essential to understand the relationship between cranial shape and overall size. As GM can statistically separate size from shape information, these methods are ideal for studies of such integrated shape changes. It has been shown that among modern humans, measurements of the braincase retain the population history signal best (Roseman and Weaver 2004; Roseman and Weaver 2007; von Cramon-Taubadel 2009; Weaver et al. 2007), whereas measurements of the face seem to be more strongly influenced by climatic and dietary variables (Harvati and Weaver 2006). If in one site or area of study we find continuity over time in measurements of the braincase, together with changes in the material culture such as stone tools, this supports the notion that a local population changed its behavior. These cultural innovations could either be invented locally, or acquired through contact with others. By contrast, if a change in material culture is associated with differences in braincase shapes, this supports arguments about population replacement. Sometimes the question is not whether an entire population was replaced, but pertains to the identity of a single individual. Based on analyses of skulls and teeth, GM can also help to identify outliers in a burial population. Together with evidence from isotopic-analyses of enamel, GM can therefore provide evidence about migration patterns and trade routes. In the absence of direct dates, phenetic affinities analysed using GM can also help determine whether a skeleton found in an Upper Palaeolithic layer was an intrusive, much younger, burial (Stansfield and Gunz 2010).

One big advantage of geometric morphometric methods over more traditional morphometric approaches based on linear distances and angles is that GM can pick up very subtle signals. Moreover, it is possible to study the influence of the overall size of an object on its shape. This covariation of size and shape is called *allometry*. If there is a temporal trend from more robust towards more gracile individuals, GM can help identify such a temporal relationship based on the regression of shape on centroid size. This regression models the direct influence of, for example, cranial size on cranial shape.

An increase in population density is usually associated with increased stress on the population, with disease and scarcity of food being among the most important factors. Individual body height is extremely sensitive to such stressors during development, and as living conditions get worse, the average body size of an entire population will decrease. Stynder et al. (2007) used GM to study the temporal trends in South African Khoe San based on directly dated crania. They used archeological evidence (e.g., the introduction of pottery vessels) to identify likely episodes of genetic discontinuity (i.e., population displacement). They could show, however, that the shape differences among crania of different periods covaried with size changes. These authors therefore suggested that a continuous population changed its size and thereby cranial shape over time, and that the changes of overall body size were related to climatic factors.

A population trend toward gracilisation of the skull might reflect an overall decrease of body size. This can easily be checked by looking at associated post-cranial elements, such as femoral head size, that strongly correlate with body size. Understanding the relationship between size and shape is also invaluable for understanding the domestication of animals. Paschetta et al. (2010) studied the influence of masticatory loading on craniofacial morphology based on crania of an extinct population from the middle and upper Ohio valley. Archeological evidence suggested that during the last 3000 years this population underwent a marked shift from hunting-gathering to extensive farming. These authors found localised shape differences in the masticatory apparatus between skulls from periods with different subsistence strategies. However, they could not confirm a general trend from more robust to more gracile skulls associated with the transition to farming.

Using hundreds of semilandmarks to compare the shape of the braincase between modern and fossil human adults, GM methods have been used to explore variability between modern humans and our extinct hominin relatives. These methods have revealed that modern humans are much more variable than

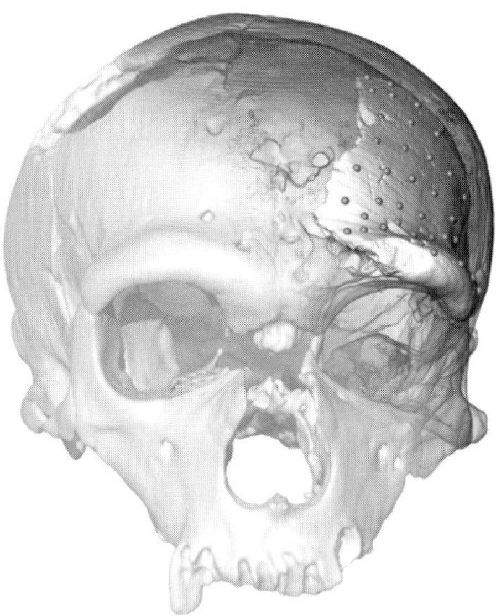

FIGURE 9.4 The Zeeland Ridges Neanderthal fragment. The frontal bone fragment, found in sediments from the North Sea, is compared here to the Neanderthal from La Chapelle-aux-Saints. Based on a comparative analysis using the semilandmarks shown here Hublin et al. (2009) were able to conclusively classify this fossil fragment as a Neanderthal. (Adapted from Hublin et al. 2009)

Neanderthals and other archaic humans (Gunz et al. 2009b). Interestingly, even higher levels of variation among *Homo sapiens* fossils that are up to 300,000 years old were found. This implied that today's phenotypic diversity is not a recent effect of the world's large population size, or a result of relaxed constraints in a modern culture but it is instead perhaps due to the migration pattern of *Homo sapiens* out of Africa being more complex than previously thought.

A GM analysis of a fairly small piece of a frontal bone (Figure 9.4) found in sediments extracted from the bottom of North Sea, a few kilometers off the coast of the Netherlands, confirmed that it belonged to a Neanderthal (Hublin et al. 2009). Using semilandmarks to capture the shape of the bone fragment, we assessed its phenetic affinities. To rule out that it was just an unusually robust modern human, the allometric relationship between supraorbital morphology and size within recent *Homo sapiens*, and Upper Palaeolithic humans, was examined. Whereas many of the shape differences between recent modern humans and Upper Palaeolithic *Homo sapiens* are related to allometric scaling (i.e., the shape differences can be attributed to differences in overall cranial size), it was shown that the cranial shape differences between modern humans and Neanderthals are mostly non-allometric.

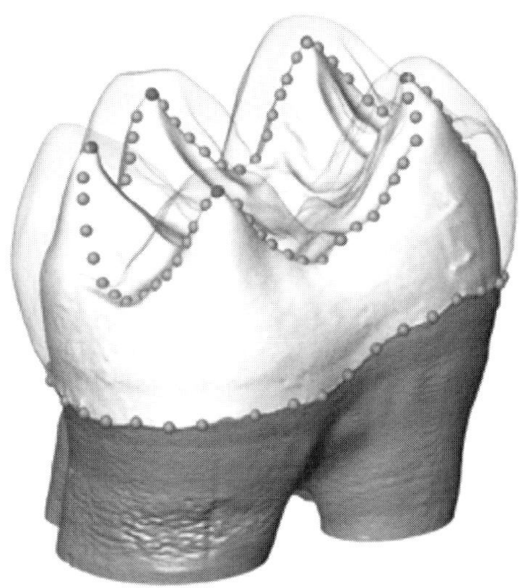

FIGURE 9.5 Landmarks and semilandmarks on the dentine crown of a tooth. Based on high resolution CT data the dentine crown can be quantified even in many heavily worn teeth. The tips of the dentine horns are treated as real landmarks; the two ridges are series of curve semilandmarks. The enamel crown is drawn as a semitransparent surface. Details on the measurement protocol can be found in Skinner et al. (2008; Skinner 2009a,b) and tooth data from Paul Tafforeau

To classify the fossil, log-likelihood ratios were computed: the fossil is >3,000 times more likely to be a Neanderthal than a recent modern human.

GM methods are not limited to measurements of bone; they have also been used to find patterns of shape variation among assemblages of stone tools (Cardillo 2010; Lycett et al. 2006). The algebra of landmarks and semilandmarks, as well as the multivariate statistical analytical tools are the same for a skull and a biface. However, it is important to keep in mind that in geometric morphometrics the landmark and semilandmark coordinates are analysed with the implicit assumption of homology. In growing, developing biological shapes, this notion of homology is rooted in the way organisms develop and evolve. Human-made objects, such as stone tools, often lack homologous structures. If the geometric homology cannot be expressed as point-to-point, curve-to-curve or surface-to-surface correspondence, then geometric morphometric analyses are not appropriate. The requirement for homology therefore must guide any landmark (and semilandmark) measurement protocol, for biological specimens as well as for artefacts.

Teeth provide a rich data resource that can be exploited using GM (Figure 9.5). If high-resolution CT data are available, it is possible to measure the internal structure of the tooth, the crown of the dentine rather than the enamel crown (Skinner et al. 2008; Skinner et al. 2009a,b). As dental wear changes the shape of the enamel crown during use, it is very hard to define homologous landmarks and curves on the enamel crown. Studies of the dentine crown, the enamel crown's developmental precursor, overcome this problem, as dentine can be quantified even in many heavily worn teeth. One expects that dietary changes of a population will affect the wear pattern of the enamel crown, whereas the population history signal recorded by the shape of the dentine crown stays the same. A GM analysis of the dentine crown combined with a study on enamel wear patterns can therefore elucidate dietary changes over time and distinguish dietary changes from population replacement.

ACKNOWLEDGMENTS

I would like to thank Mike Richards for inviting me to contribute this volume. I want to thank Jean-Jacques Hublin, Simon Neubauer (Max Planck Institute for Evolutionary Anthropology Leipzig), and Philipp Mitteröcker and Fred Bookstein (University of Vienna), as well as the late Dennis Slice (The Florida State University), for their support. The data used for Figures 9.1 and 9.2 were collected by Sarah Freidline. The scanning and reconstruction of the Le Moustier 2 specimen (Figure 9.3) has been made possible thanks to the support of J.-J. Cleyet-Merle (Musée National de Préhistoire Les Eyzies de Tayac) and Bruno Maureille (Université de Bordeaux); Andreas Winzer and Adeline Le Cabec scanned the specimen. The tooth shown in Figure 9.5 was scanned by Paul Tafforeau (European Synchrotron Radiation Facility).

REFERENCES

Bookstein, F. L. 1989. Principal warps: Thin-plate splines and the decomposition of deformations, *IEEE Transactions on Pattern Analysis and Machine Intelligence* 11(6):567–585.

Bookstein, F. L. 1991. *Morphometric Tools for Landmark Data: Geometry and Biology*. Cambridge: Cambridge University Press.

Bookstein, F. L. 1997. Landmark methods for forms without landmarks: Morphometrics of group differences in outline shape. *Medical Image Analysis* 1(3):225–243.

Bulygina, E., Mitteroecker, P., and Aiello, L. 2006. Ontogeny of facial dimorphism and patterns of individual development within one human population. *American Journal of Physical Anthropology* 131(3):432–443.

Cardillo, M. 2010. Some applications of geometric morphometrics to archaeology. In: Elews, A. M. T. (ed.) *Morphometrics for Nonmorphometricians*, pp. 325–341. Berlin: Springer.

Frost, S. R., Marcus, L. F., Bookstein, F. L., Reddy, D. P., and Delson, E. 2003. Cranial allometry, phylogeography, and systematics of large-bodied papionins (primates: Cercopithecinae) inferred from geometric morphometric analysis of landmark data. *The Anatomical Record. Part A, Discoveries in Molecular, Cellular, and Evolutionary Biology* 275(2):1048–1072.

Good, P. I. 2005. *Permutation, Parametric and Bootstrap Tests of Hypotheses.* New York: Springer.

Gunz, P., Bookstein, F. L., Mitteroecker, P., Stadlmayr, A., Seidler, H., and Weber, G. W. 2009a. Early modern human diversity suggests subdivided population structure and a complex out-of-Africa scenario. *Proceedings of the National Academy of Sciences of the United States of America* 106(15):6094–6098.

Gunz, P., Mitteroecker, P., and Bookstein, F. L. 2005. Semilandmarks in three dimensions. In: D. E. Slice (ed.) *Modern Morphometrics in Physical Anthropology*, pp. 73–98. New York: Kluwer Academic/Plenum Publishers.

Gunz, P., Mitteroecker, P., Bookstein, F. L., and Weber, G. W. 2004 Computer aided reconstruction of incomplete human crania using statistical and geometrical estimation methods. In: *Enter the Past: Computer Applications and Quantitative Methods in Archaeology*, pp. 92–94. BAR International Series 1227. Oxford: Archaeopress.

Gunz, P., Mitteroecker, P., Neubauer, S., Weber, G.W., and Bookstein, F. L. 2009b. Principles for the virtual reconstruction of hominin crania. *Journal of Human Evolution* 57(1):48–62.

Gunz, P., Neubauer, S., Maureille, B., and Hublin, J.-J. 2010. Brain development after birth differs between Neanderthals and modern humans. *Current Biology* 20(21):R921–R922.

Harvati, K. and Weaver, T. D. 2006. Human cranial anatomy and the differential preservation of population history and climate signatures. The Anatomical Record. *Part A, Discoveries in Molecular, Cellular, and Evolutionary Biology* 288(12):1225–1233.

Hublin, J.-J., Weston, D., Gunz, P., Richards, M., Roebroeks, W., Glimmerveen, J., and Anthonis, L. 2009. Out of the North Sea: The Zeeland Ridges Neandertal. *Journal of Human Evolution* 57(6):777–785.

Lycett, S. J., von Cramon-Taubadel, N., and Foley, R. A. 2006. A crossbeam co-ordinate caliper for the morphometric analysis of lithic nuclei: A description, test and empirical examples of application. *Journal of Archaeological Science* 33(6):847–861.

Maureille, B. 2002a. La redécouverte du nouveau-né néandertalien Le Moustier 2, *Paléo* (14):221–238.

Maureille, B. 2002b. A lost Neanderthal neonate found. *Nature* 419(6902):33–34.

Mitteroecker, P. and Gunz, P. 2009. Advances in geometric morphometrics. *Evolutionary Biology* 36(2):235–247.

Mitteroecker, P., Gunz, P., Weber, G. W., and Bookstein, F. L. 2004. Regional dissociated heterochrony in multivariate analysis. *Annals of Anatomy = Anatomischer Anzeiger: Official Organ of the Anatomische Gesellschaft* 186(5–6):463–470.

Paschetta, C., de Azevedo, S., Castillo, L., Martínez-Abadías, N., Hernández, M., Lieberman, D. E., and González-José, R. 2010. The influence of masticatory loading on craniofacial morphology: A test case across technological transitions in the Ohio valley. *American Journal of Physical Anthropology* 141(2):297–314.

Richtsmeier, J. T., DeLeon, V. B., and Lele, S. R. 2002. The promise of geometric morphometrics. *American Journal of Physical Anthropology*, Suppl 35:63–91.

Rohlf, F. J. and Slice, D. 1990. Extensions of the Procrustes method for the optimal superimposition of landmarks, *Systematic Zoology* 39:40–59.

Roseman, C. C. and Weaver, T. D. 2004. Multivariate apportionment of global human craniometric diversity. *American Journal of Physical Anthropology* 125(3):257–263.

Roseman, C. C. and Weaver, T. D. 2007. Molecules versus morphology? Not for the human cranium. *BioEssays: News and Reviews in Molecular, Cellular and Developmental Biology* 29(12):1185–1188.

Schaefer, K., Lauc, T., Mitteroecker, P., Gunz, P., and Bookstein, F. L. 2006. Dental arch asymmetry in an isolated Adriatic community. *American Journal of Physical Anthropology* 129(1):132–142.

Skinner, M. M., Gunz, P., Wood, B. A., Boesch, C., and Hublin, J.-J. 2009a. Discrimination of extant Pan species and subspecies using the enamel-dentine junction morphology of lower molars. *American Journal of Physical Anthropology* 140(2):234–243.

Skinner, M. M., Gunz, P., Wood, B. A., and Hublin, J.-J. 2008. Enamel-dentine junction (EDJ) morphology distinguishes the lower molars of Australopithecus africanus and Paranthropus robustus. *Journal of Human Evolution* 55(6):979–988.

Skinner, M. M., Gunz, P., Wood, B. A., and Hublin, J.-J. 2009b. How many landmarks? Assessing the classification accuracy of Pan lower molars using a geometric morphometric analysis of the occlusal basin as seen at the enamel-dentine junction. *Frontiers of Oral Biology* 13:23–29.

Stansfield Nee Bulygina, E. and Gunz, P. 2010. Skhodnya, Khvalynsk, Satanay, and Podkumok calvaria: Possible Upper Paleolithic hominins from European Russia. *Journal of Human Evolution* 60:129–144.

Stynder, D. D., Ackermann, R. R., and Sealy, J. C. 2007. Craniofacial variation and population continuity during the South African Holocene. *American Journal of Physical Anthropology* 134(4):489–500.

von Cramon-Taubadel, N. 2009. Congruence of individual cranial bone morphology and neutral molecular affinity patterns in modern humans. *American Journal of Physical Anthropology* 140(2):205–215.

Weaver, T. D., Roseman, C. C., and Stringer, C. B. 2007. Were neandertal and modern human cranial differences produced by natural selection or genetic drift? *Journal of Human Evolution* 53(2):135–145.

Ziliak, S. T. and McCloskey, D. N. 2008. *The Cult of Statistical Significance: How the Standard Error Costs Us Jobs, Justice, and Lives.* Ann Arbor: University of Michigan Press.

Part IV

Environmental Archaeology

10

Vertebrate Zooarchaeology

Beth Upex and Keith Dobney

The study of animal remains in archaeology, focusing on vertebrates like mammals, birds and fish.

1 INTRODUCTION

Our relationship with animals has a long and complex history, one that is as important today as in the past. However, while most of us interact with domesticated animals (and their by-products) daily, we rarely give this complex relationship (or its history) a second thought. We put milk or yoghurt on our breakfast cereal, eat cheese (and perhaps ham) sandwiches as snacks and consider roast chicken as a treat for Sunday lunch. Most of us wear shoes or other clothes made from animal products and sleep under down duvets. We take our dogs for walks, stroke (or chase away from our gardens) the neighbour's cat (whilst likely getting bitten by its fleas!), and – if we're very lucky – ride horses for pleasure. Our interactions with animals are not, however, always positive. Whilst we might encourage songbirds to our gardens by feeding them, we're less keen on sharing our living spaces with those animals considered pests, who can spread disease and (if given the opportunity) spoil our stored foods.

Our complex interactions with and reliance upon animals can be studied directly through their remains preserved on (and then excavated from) archaeological sites – a discipline known as zooarchaeology (or archaeozoology). These remains can be diverse (depending on preservation conditions), allowing us to investigate a huge range of topics; from key events in the human past – such as the begins of farming and animal domestication – to diet, living conditions, and the identity or social status of specific communities or even households in the past. Consequently, zooarchaeology is a broad and interdisciplinary subject, containing a huge array of questions, approaches and concepts embedded in a robust theoretical framework.

Zooarchaeology refers to the study of all animals, from snails and fleas to horses and whales. Here we focus on vertebrate zooarchaeology – the study of animals characterised by segmented spines – including mammals, birds, fish, reptiles and amphibians. The term archaeozoology is also often used in the literature – interpreted as "old zoology"– and does not necessarily (unlike the term zooarchaeology) emphasise the meaning of interpreting human behaviours through the study of animal bones. Although the discipline has a long history (the earliest zooarchaeological studies were conducted in the 1700s), the subject has grown dramatically over the last four decades along three complementary principal research trajectories: methodological, anthropological, and biological (Reitz and Wing 2008). Combined with complementary datasets from multiple sources such as palaeoecology archaeology and (where relevant) historical texts, we can achieve a degree of understanding of the bio-cultural evolution, consequences, and outcomes of past human-animal interactions.

2 HOW DID ALL THOSE BONES GET THERE?

The animal remains we recover from archaeological sites have been through multiple taphonomic (*from the Greek taphos = burial and nomos = law*) processes that affect how well the remains are preserved (if they have survived at all), the particular species we find, which parts of those animals are present and where on the site we find them. The process of archaeological excavation itself can also inherently impact the quantity and type of animal remains recovered. Therefore, it is important to study and understand these issues and to recognise that the remains we recover and study will likely not reflect the true range of animals, activities, and even human behaviours originally occurring at the site.

Killing, Cooking, and Disposing of Animals

It is rather rare on most archaeological sites to uncover the remains of animals that have died naturally – that is, one that has become part of the burial record where it fell and remained unchanged until excavated. Where this does occur, it is often animals such as rabbits, rodents, or amphibians that have died in their burrows or fallen into pits, where humans and other animals are unlikely to move or interfere with the carcass. In general, the vast majority of bones recovered from human settlements are from animals that have been deliberately killed, most commonly for food or other products. In some cases the actual killing or slaughter of the animal leaves visible marks on the bones – for example, a wild ass vertebra found with an embedded Levallois point from Umm el Tlell (Syria) (Boëda et al. 1999), or cut marks on the underside of the cervical (neck) vertebrae of caprines from the late Bronze Age site of Kamid el-Lo (also in Syria) interpreted as the animals having had their throats cut (Bartosiewicz 2006). Once animals have been slaughtered (unless an animal has been killed for deliberate or ritual burial – such as the complete horse burial from the fourth to seventh-century cemetery near Sindos, Greece (Antikas 2008) – the carcass is normally dismembered. Cuts of meat (with or without associated bones) may then be removed and distributed across different locations; heads, hooves and horns may be subject to specialised processing at separate locations or simply abandoned/disposed of at or away from the kill/slaughter site. Various preserving or cooking processes may also be applied (e.g., roasting, salting, boiling, and smoking) all of which can leave traces on the bones and which can, importantly, affect their preservation (e.g., Alen and Ervynck 2005; Enloe 1993; Lyman 1994a; Mateos 2005; Noe-Nygaard 1977; Outram 2005; Saint-Germain 2005; Zohar and Cooke 1997).

Depending on the geographic, temporal, and cultural context, carcass processing can also involve a range of secondary products related to specific craft or industrial activities (e.g., horn and bone working or the production of leather and glue). The potential, however, for these processes to provide confounding signals in the zooarchaeological record is clearly demonstrated by a study of the animal bone assemblage from the seventeenth–eighteenth century Royal Navy Victualling Yard in London (West 1995; cited in O'Connor 2000). Historical sources document the slaughter of 40 oxen per day to supply the Navy, yet evidence from the animal bones revealed only a small number of cattle remains present at the site. Although it is possible that waste from cattle processing may simply not have been disposed of at the site itself – most likely being dumped in landfill sites along the Thames, West suggests that an increase in the demand for furniture glue at this time may have seen the bones transported to other locations where such specialised industries flourished. Historical sources support this suggestion, demonstrating that even as late as 1910 the Netherlands imported 7,000,000 kg of bone a year for glue production (O'Connor 2000). Finally, once the bones have no further use, they have to be disposed of. Domestic refuse such as left over bones from dinner might be disposed of in specific rubbish dumps, or just thrown into the back yard. Once thrown away, the bones may become quickly buried, especially in contexts such as refuse pits where rubbish is regularly dumped, or they may lie around for a while becoming prime pickings for scavenging animals such as cats and dogs. If the bones remain unburied for longer periods of time they can then become worn from being moved around and weathered from exposure to the elements, with smaller more fragile elements crushed under foot or disintegrating completely.

How Bones Are Preserved

If bones make it into the burial environment of a site, they tend to survive in reasonable condition over time due to their high inorganic mineral content. As such, they are often some of the most abundant finds excavated from archaeological sites. However, this does not mean that further degradation does not occur, since there are a multitude of taphonomic process that continue to impact such remains. These can include (but are not limited too) soil pH and waterlogging; intrusion by insects, plant roots and fungi; changes in temperature; physical weathering erosion and re-deposition (e.g., Davis 1987; Klein and Cruz-Uribe 1984; Lyman 1994a; Reitz and Wing 2008). Not all skeletal elements will preserve in the same way – so-called differential preservation. The enamel of tooth crowns is much harder than bone and thus survives best in all but the most chemically hostile burial environments (although its low organic content renders it more brittle and thus more prone to shattering than bone). Skeletal elements (or parts of bones) that are porous or less well-calcified (especially juvenile bones or the articular ends) are more susceptible to degradation than those from adult individuals or those with more compact, less spongy bone. By understanding taphonomy, we can at least begin to mitigate to some degree the likely biases in our subsequent interpretations.

Recovering Bones

Once the bones have traversed their varied and potentially complex depositional and taphonomic journeys, there is still no guarantee that they will end up in assemblages studied by the zooarchaeologist. Many bones and teeth (as well as other important objects and small finds) are never recovered during excavations due to the lack of (or, where present, inadequate) systematic sampling and screening of the deposits. Such practices not only significantly lower the chances of recovering the remains of birds, fish and small mammals, but also even the bones and teeth of larger animals such as sheep and cattle. The importance of wet and dry sieving, optimal mesh size, and excavation/sampling protocols have been extensively tested and discussed (e.g., Clason and Prummel 1977; Dobney et al. 1992; Gordon 1993; Payne 1972; Shaffer 1992; Shaffer and Sanchez 1994; Wing and Quitmyer 1985). All clearly demonstrate the relationship between decreasing mesh size and increasing quantity, variety, and significance of materials recovered. It is, therefore, important that all involved in the excavation and subsequent analyses are aware of the sampling methods deployed and the possible biasing factors these may have introduced to any subsequent quantitative analyses of the animal bone assemblage.

3 WHAT CAN WE DO WITH ALL THOSE BONES?

Identifying and Recording

One of the first tasks of the zooarchaeologist is to identify the many bone fragments comprising the assemblage, a task undertaken over several steps and approaches. The first (and perhaps most straightforward) is identifying which skeletal element (bone or tooth) is present and whether it is from the left or right side of the body. This slightly counterintuitive step requires a basic to good working knowledge of skeletal anatomy. However, due to the fact that the functional attributes of specific bones and teeth are largely similar (e.g., a femur or tibia has essentially the same basic form in all vertebrates – except obviously fish), it is always much easier to first assign a bone fragment to a specific skeletal element than it is to a particular animal taxa. The next step is to identify a bone or tooth fragment to species. This is best achieved with the aid of a relatively comprehensive reference collection of modern comparative specimens of known identification, and a detailed knowledge of the local fauna of the region you are working in. With experience, even species that are very similar, such as sheep and goats, can be separated on the basis of their subtly different bone morphologies (Balasse and Ambrose 2005; Boessneck 1969; Payne 1969; Rowley-Conwy 1998). However, there are significant limitations to being able to identify particularly fragmented bones and teeth to species level that should not be underestimated. In many cases, significant parts of the assemblage may not confidently (or honestly) be assigned beyond genus, family, or even class (taxon) level.

Once a bone has been identified to element, sided, and assigned to a taxon, it must then be described through some kind of subjective or objective recording protocol. Often animal bones are very fragmented, normally as part of the complex taphonomic process they undergo before and after burial, making systematic recording less than straightforward. The use of widely used anatomical terms (e.g., the greater trochanter of the femur), along with schematic drawings highlighting the parts of each element present, goes some way to resolving this problem, although they can lack detail and make it difficult to accurately quantify and compare datasets across a site or sites (Reitz and Wing 2008). One method that systematically provides a high level of information divides every bone into a series of "identifiable zones" (Münzel 1988). A further level of accuracy can be added by only recording each zone if there is more than 50 percent of it present, meaning that there is never the risk of a zone being broken into two and, therefore, counted twice (Dobney and Reilly 1988). The use of different recording protocols by zooarchaeologists over the last decades renders much of the zooarchaeological record largely incomparable when attempting detailed quantitative comparisons between assemblages recorded using different methods. However, this can be achieved at a relatively basic level, when attempting general and broad assessments of the changing frequencies of animals (and skeletal elements) in time and space.

Counting Bones = Counting Animals?

There has been much debate about the best methods of quantifying animal bones from archaeological assemblages (e.g., Grayson 1984; Klein and Cruz-Uribe 1984: 25; Lyman 1994b; Nichol and Wild 1984; Reitz and Wing 2008: 167–168), with the general conclusion being that there is NO "best method!" (Peres 2010: 26). The most basic form of quantification is the Number of Identified Specimens Present (NISP), which provides a simple count of the number of fragments identified to each species. NISP can be used to estimate the relative frequency of species on the site, but thc data can be biased by a variety of factors. One of the most obvious of these is that some animals have more bones than others (instantly giving them a higher NISP value). Even in animals with similar numbers of elements, the bones themselves are not always equally identifiable. Of course fragmentation of larger bones, along with differential preservation and recovery methods, also impact such results. There are methods that attempt to correct these biases – such as dividing NISP by the number of identified elements per taxa in the assemblage

(Perkins 1973), or calculating fragmentation indices by dividing NISP by the number of unidentified fragments (Reitz and Wing 2008). However, NISP is generally considered a crude method for accurately assessing the relative frequencies of taxa present in an assemblage, so a number of other quantification methods are also used.

Probably the most common is calculation of the minimum number of individuals (MNI). Unlike NISP, which is a raw count of the number of identified specimens, MNI is an analytic product based on the smallest number of individuals required to account for all of the skeletal elements present. Again several methods can be used to calculate MNI (see Dobney and Reilly 1988; Klein and Cruz-Uribe 1984; White 1953;) and they can be adjusted to account for age, sex, skeletal element, and side (Bökönyi 1970). As with NISP, there are problems with MNI estimates, many of which are related to taphonomic processes, differential preservation, and recovery and thus can be mitigated by careful excavation and analysis. The multitude of other recording and quantification methodologies used in zooarchaeology, along with NISP and MNI, are discussed and compared in numerous publications (particularly Grayson 1984; O'Connor 2000; and Peres 2010; and Reitz and Wing 2008).

From Dry Bones Back to Living Animals

Once we have established which animals were present on a site, and what their relative frequencies were we can begin to explore their basic physical characteristics. To do this, zooarchaeologists traditionally measure bones and teeth to explore changes in size, shape and form, using standard measurements outlined by von den Driesch (1976) as a baseline. Using these raw measurements (and also applying various formulae based on modern comparative specimens) we can broadly reconstruct the form of the once living animal; for example, its withers height, its live body weight and how much meat it might have yielded (see Reitz and Wing 2008 for examples). Certain long bones (e.g., the metapodials and the astragalus) are particularly sexually dimorphic, meaning that measurements of their length and breadth can be plotted to provide an indication of sex and thus (importantly for reconstructing husbandry practices) the proportions of males and females (even castrates) within a herd.

Age at death can be established through the careful consideration of dental development and/or tooth wear, along with the fusion of articular ends of longbones. Growing longbones comprise several separate components – the shaft (diaphysis) and the articular ends (epiphyses) – joined throughout development by decreasing amounts of cartilage. These separate sections finally fuse once full growth of the particular element has been achieved – occurring in different chronological order depending on which skeletal element is involved. Therefore, by recording how many elements are unfused, fused, or actually in the process of fusing (which can be easily recognised) we can begin to reconstruct rough age-at-death profiles for the animals present on an archaeological site and, in doing so, begin to explore aspects of human decision-making and behaviour (e.g., Ruscillo 2005; Silver 1970; Schmid 1972: 74–75; Wilson 1978). This so-called "kill-off pattern" can be further refined (in mammals at least) using information from the teeth. Dental crowns grow and then erupt in well-studied sequential and chronological order, and involve first deciduous then permanent sets of dentition. The state of dental development, therefore, is perhaps the most accurate way of establishing actual chronological age. As with bone fusion, however, once development and growth is complete (normally at adulthood), then less accurate (relative) ways of ageing skeletal remains must be used. In zooarchaeology the most common is tooth wear, in which tooth crowns are worn down though mastication. Study of modern comparative specimens has shown that progressive tooth wear produces distinctive "wear-patterns" in the enamel and dentine which can be classified to (sometimes very specific) relative age groupings (see Grant 1982; Hillson 1986: 176–187; Payne 1973;).

4 WHAT CAN ALL THOSE BONES TELL US?

The basic data we record from animal bones provide the baseline information used to address a vast array of questions about both the animals themselves and the people with whom they shared their surroundings. Metric data can provide information on, for example, domestication (animals often get smaller when they become domesticated, e.g., Zeder 2006); climate change (wild animals in hot climates are generally smaller than their counterparts living in cold climates, e.g., Hill et al. 2008); hunting strategies (focus on large prime and/or male animals. e.g., Zeder 2008) or the selective breeding or importation of new improved stock (the introduction/breeding of larger cattle in Britain in the later Roman period, e.g., Albarella et al. 2008). By combining dental development and tooth wear patterns with bone fusion data, we can create "kill-off" profiles allowing us to make interpretations about the animal economy of a site (Payne 1973). Below we briefly explore some of these areas, and demonstrate that zooarchaeology is about far more than just what people ate or what pets they kept.

Settlements and Seasonality

The Ertebølle site of Ringkloster in Denmark provides a prime example of how zooarchaeological analysis can be used to reconstruct seasonal settlement occupation and hunting practices (Rowley-Conwy 1995). Wild boar remains from the site reveal animals killed at a series of different ages. If wild boar in Mesolithic Denmark shared a similar season of birth (March–April) and development rate to those found in northwest Europe today, these data indicate wild boar were hunted and killed between November and May and that occupation of the site was contemporaneous. This conclusion is corroborated by the red deer and roe deer remains from the site, which show similar kill-off patterns. Combining these with other data (such as skeletal elements present and butchery techniques), it has been argued that Ringkloster should be characterised as a seasonal hunting camp specialising in the procurement of meat, fur and skins used to provision coastal camps located approximately 15 km away.

Based on the location of structures known as desert kites (assumed to be used in the hunting of herd animals such as gazelles), local topography, early travelers accounts and zooarchaeological analyses, Legge and Rowley-Conwy (1987; Legge and Rowley-Conwy 2000) were able to reconstruct the prehistoric (early Holocene) migratory routes of gazelle in the Levant (modern day Jordan and Israel). The site of Abu Hureyra, in northern Syria, is located at the very northern extent of the gazelles' proposed migratory path, where they moved to escape the summer heat of the southern Levant and to give birth. Analyses of the kill-off patterns reconstructed from their remains excavated from epipalaeolithic levels at Abu Hureyra indicate that gazelles were only hunted and killed over a very short period of the year – that is, from late April to early May (Legge and Rowley-Conwy 1987; Legge and Rowley-Conwy 2000). The tightly clustered age groups of young gazelles from the site led the authors to conclude that the remains represent the earliest and most conclusive evidence of the seasonal mass killing of migrating gazelles in the region. More recent zooarchaeological analyses from two epipalaeolithic sites at the southern end of the gazelle migratory range (Kharaneh IV and Wadi Jilat 6, Jordan) show that the large number of juvenile gazelles were mostly killed between 8 and 11 months of age – that is, between late October and early February. This has led Martin et al. (2010) to suggest that these latter sites were occupied in the winter as people aggregated for the seasonal gazelle hunt.

Domestication and Herding

Potentially one of the most significant outcomes of the various human-animal relationships of the late Pleistocene and Holocene has been the domestication of certain animal species – all except one (the dog) have been associated with the beginnings and spread of farming. Although one of the key bio-cultural transitions in our own evolution, the processes involved are still little understood. Domestication has resulted in a range of similar traits in taxonomically diverse animals – a phenomenon first noted by Darwin (1868). Thus many domesticates have, for example, floppy ears, curly tails and coat colour variation never found in their wild counterparts. While such phenotypic traits can now be explored through the fast-developing field of ancient DNA (e.g., Lippold 2011) and advanced shape analyses (using 2D and 3D geometric morphometrics, e.g., Evin et al. 2015), traditional zooarchaeological approaches have been successfully used to reveal the classic morphological changes in size and shape (i.e., smaller body size and shorter faces) of the skeleton and teeth of animals undergoing domestication.

The process of domestication appears to be slow, occurring over several generations. Work by Ervynck and colleagues (2001) used tooth measurements and developmental defects in the enamel (thought to be linked to physiological stress) to assess the evidence for one of the earliest claims for pig domestication in western Asia at the early Neolithic site of Çayönü Tepesi in southeastern Turkey. Their analyses showed a gradual decrease in the size of *Sus scrofa* over approximately two millennia (specifically a shortening of the face) and an increase in the frequency of physiological stress – both assumed to be directly associated with domestication. This study clearly demonstrated that morphological changes linked with the domestication process occurred slowly over many generations. Similar conclusions were drawn from later studies of dental defects (Dobney et al. 2004; Dobney et al. 2005; Dobney et al. 2007; Rowley-Conwy and Dobney 2007) in *Sus* remains across Eurasia, where high frequencies of linear enamel hypoplasia in Neolithic domestic pig populations were interpreted as a direct consequence of early animal husbandry strategies.

Craft and Industry

Besides providing information on the animals themselves, along with their relationships with humans, the study of bones and teeth can also tell us about the industries and crafts that were dependent on animal products. Often we are only left with circumstantial (indirect) evidence for these crafts, such as butchery or processing marks suggesting horn working or skinning (Albarella 2003). However, occasionally exceptional preservation allows us to gain a more detailed insight into these industries. From Bruges in Belgium, over 80 large wooden barrels/tubs were excavated, containing lime, oak bark, cattle horn cores and over 30 preserved cow hides, all suggesting the presence of specialised horn and hide processing (Ervynck et al. 2003). Bone working is an industry obviously dependent on the animal's skeleton. The large worked bone assemblage from the Anglo-Scandinavian levels at Coppergate, York (containing worked bone in multiple stages from roughed out blanks to finished products) suggests the presence of local specialist workshops crafting bone combs and processing red deer antlers (MacGregor and Mainman 2001).

Moving away from localised craft and industry, bone assemblages can also inform us about provisioning on an industrial national, and even international, scale. For example, the growth and development of the North Atlantic stockfish trade can be traced across the region through the analyses of fishbone. Stockfish are air-dried, unsalted fish (commonly cod) and were an essential part of the diet in many northern regions during later medieval times and into the eighteenth century. Fish bone from Viking sites in Iceland have been used to trace the production, trade and consumption of this essential commodity. Perdikaris et al. (2007) demonstrate that Viking inland sites do not contain any *gadid* (cod family) premaxilla bones (a part of the head that is always removed in stockfish preparation), clearly marking them as consumer sites. In contrast, coastal sites of the same date have very high numbers of these bones, identifying them as sites that produced stockfish supplying inland sites.

Status and Identity

What you eat and when you eat it is not purely about consuming energy to survive and function. Food and its consumption forms part of a whole series of complex social, economic and cultural relationships within human groups and appears to have done so throughout our history and prehistory (see O'Day et al. 2004). The complex relationship between food consumption, status and identity can (although not always easily or conclusively) sometimes be pieced together by studying the bones and teeth of animals from archaeological sites. The concepts of status and identity are fraught with interpretational difficulties (see Ashby 2002). However, despite these difficulties, strong arguments have been made for the identification of both in the zooarchaeological record. For example, the remains of veal calves in medieval York have been used to suggest the presence of powerful/wealthy cattle owners, who could afford to kill their animals before they reached maximum body weight (Bond and O'Connor 1999). Historical documents often serve to reinforce interpretations of status relating to food consumption. For example, medieval legislation restricted the hunting of game animals such as deer and wild boar to the upper classes, which supports the zooarchaeological evidence indicating that these species were consumed more commonly at castle and palace sites than in towns or villages (Grant 1988a,b cited in Crabtree 1990). Cultural and/or religious identity can also be inferred through the study of animal remains. At Buda, in Hungary, remains from a fourteenth-century well were used to identify the previously unknown location of the early Jewish quarter of the town (Daróczi-Szabó 2002). In 1360, the Jewish population were expelled from the town and their houses reoccupied by Christians. This shift in religious/ethnic identity is clearly visible in the faunal stratigraphy of the well, particularly the presence or absence of pig remains and the differential represent of ungulate leg bones that is consonant with kosher dietary requirements.

Ritual and Religion

As discussed previously, animals play a variety of roles in society and these are not always purely functional. In many cultures animals are associated with ritual activities or religious status. As was the case with exploring possible signatures of status and identity, it is not always easy to draw conclusions about the use of animals for ritual and religious purposes from the zooarchaeological record. However, there are some cases where the evidence is substantive and obvious. For example, at the Saitic-Ptolemaic site of *Hermopolis Magna* (Tuna el-Gebel, Middle Egypt), over 245 mummified primates (along with other species such as Ibis) were discovered, relating to a temple complex (von den Driesch et al. 2004). The presence of these animals at this site is clearly not related to food or consumption, and their careful burial and preservation within the temple complex clearly links them to ritual activities.

A less conclusive – but still convincing – example comes from the late Bronze Age burial cave of Ara, Israel (Weissbrod and Bar-Oz 2002). Here, the human remains (MNI of 26 individuals) were heavily intermingled with those of animals. Several complete ceramic vessels also recovered from the site contained high numbers of amphibian (toad) bones. Interestingly, while toad limb bones were present in high numbers and generally complete, there was a complete absence of cranial elements and an underrepresentation of the pelves and extremities such as phalanges (finger and toe bones). Various possible scenarios for the presence of toads were discussed by the authors – including the possibilities that predators such as owls may have carried them into the cave, or that they may have simply died in the cave. Both these scenarios are very unlikely given the unusual skeletal element patterning. If the toads had died naturally, then all skeletal elements should be present, and if owls had eaten them there should also have been considerably more fragmentation and damage to the limb bones. The authors suggest that the unusual pattern of elements present, combined with the toads' association with ceramic vessels, are better explained as food offerings placed in the tomb. They even cite a Native American recipe for toads that calls for the complete removal of the head and skinning, explaining both the absence of skulls and phalanges.

5 SUMMARY

The study of vertebrate zooarchaeology is one that covers a huge array of topics and themes within the discipline of archaeology – one that can add a myriad of layers to our understanding of how animals were used and treated when both alive and dead by past human cultures. Its study requires diverse knowledge, for example, of the various uses and processes that bones can be subjected to before and after burial, as well as the anatomy of animals and the methods used to record them. It also requires a good deal of patience and methodological (as well as interpretative) rigour. As this short chapter has hopefully demonstrated, the time and effort involved in recording and analysing animal bone assemblages is rewarded by the fact that it allows us to investigate the complex and endlessly varied interactions that have taken place between humans and animals for millennia, and which are still ongoing. Zooarchaeology allows us to investigate these on a range of temporal and geographic scales – from the major bio-cultural transitions in human history to the local (even household) based questions about human behaviour. It is certainly about far more than just what people ate for their dinner!

REFERENCES

Albarella, U. 2003. Tawyers, tanners, horn trade and the mystery of the missing goat. In: Murphy, P. and Wiltshire, P. E. J. (eds.) *The Environmental Archaeology of Industry*, pp. 71–86. Oxford: Oxbrow Books.

Albarella, U., Johnstone, C., and Vickers, K. 2008. The development of animal husbandry from the Late Iron Age to the end of the Roman period: A case study from South-East Britain. *Journal of Archaeological Science* 35(7):1828–1848.

Alen, A. and Ervynck, A. 2005. The large scale and specialised late medieval urban craft of marrow extraction: Archaeological and historical evidence from Malines (Belgium), confronted with experimental work. In: Mulville, J. and Outram, A. K. (eds.) *The Zooarchaeology of Fats, Oils, Milk and Dairying*, pp. 193–200. Oxford: Oxbow Books.

Antikas, T. G. 2008. They didn't shoot horses: Fracture management in a horse of the 5th century BC from Sindos, Central Macedonia, Greece. *Veterinarija and Zootechnika* 42:24–27.

Ashby, S. 2002. The role of zooarchaeology in the interpretation of socioeconomic status: A discussion with reference to medieval Europe. *Archaeological Review from Cambridge* 18:37–59.

Bartosiewicz, L. 2006. Taphonomy and palaeopathology in archaeozoology. *Geobios* 41 (2008):69–77.

Balasse, M. and Ambrose, S. 2005. Distinguishing sheep and goats using dental morphology and stable carbon isotopes in C4 grassland environments. *Journal of Archaeological Science* 32:691–702.

Boëda, E., Geneste, J.-M., Griggo, C., Mercier, N., Muhesen, S., Reyss, J. L., Taha, A., and Valladas, H. 1999. A Levallois point embedded in the vertebra of a wild ass (Equus africanus): Hafting, projectile and Mousterian hunting weapons. *Antiquity* 73 (1999):394–402.

Boessneck, J. 1969. Osteological differences between sheep (Ovis aries Linné) and goats (Capra hircus Linné). In: Brothwell, D. and Higgs, E. S. (eds.) *Science in Archaeology*, pp. 331–358. London: Thames and Hudson.

Bökönyi, S. 1970. A new method for determining the number of individuals in animal bone material. *American Journal of Archaeology* 74:291–292.

Bond, J. M. and O'Connor, T. P. 1999. *Bones from Medieval Deposits at 16–22 Coppergate and Other Sites in York*. York: Council for British Archaeology.

Clason, A. T. and Prummel, W. 1977. Collecting, sieving, and archaeozoological research. *Journal of Archaeological Science* 4:171–175.

Crabtree, P. 1990. Zooarchaeology and complex societies: Some uses of faunal analysis for the study of trade, social status, and ethnicity. *Archaeological Method and Theory* 2:155–205.

Daróczi-Szabó, L. 2002. Animal bones as indicators of Kosher food refuse from 14th Century AD Buda, Hungry. In: Jones O'Day, S., Van Neer, W., and Ervynck, A. (eds.) *Behaviour*

Behind Bones: The Zooarchaeology of Ritual, Religion, Status and Identity, pp. 252–261. Oxford: Oxbow Books.

Darwin, C. 1868. *The Variation of Animals and Plants under Domestication*. 2 vols. London: John Murray.

Davis, S. J. 1987. *The Archaeology of Animals*. New Haven: Yale University Press.

Dobney, K., Anezaki, T., Hongo, H., Matsui, A., Yamazaki, K., Ervynck, A., Albarella, U., and Rowley-Conwy, P. 2005. The transition from wild boar to domestic pig as illustrated by dental enamel defects (LEH): A Japanese case study including the site of Torihama. *Torihama Shell Midden Papers* 4, 5:51–78.

Dobney, K., Ervynck, A., Albarella, U., and Rowley-Conwy, P. 2004. The chronology and frequency of a stress marker (linear enamel hypoplasia) in recent and archaeological populations of Sus scrofa in north-west Europe, and the effects of early domestication. *Journal of Zoology* 264:197–208.

Dobney, K., Ervynck, A., Albarella, U., and Rowley-Conwy, P. 2007. The transition from wild boar to domestic pig in Eurasia, illustrated by a tooth developmental defect and biometric data. In: Albarella, U., Dobney, K., Ervynck, A. and Rowley-Conwy, P. (eds.) *Pigs and Humans: 10,000 Years of Interaction*, pp. 57–82. Oxford: Oxford University Press.

Dobney, K., Hall, A. R., Kenward, H. K., and Milles, A. 1992. A working classification of sample types for environmental archaeology. *Circaea* 9:24–26.

Dobney, K. and Reilly, K. 1988. A method for recording information about mammal bones: The use of diagnostic zones. *Circaea* 5(2):79–96.

Enloe, J. G. 1993. Ethnoarchaeology of marrow cracking: Implications for the recognition of prehistoric subsistence organization. In: Hudson, J. (ed.) *From Bones to Behavior: Ethnoarchaeological and Experimental Contributions to the Interpretation of Faunal Remains*, pp. 82–100. Occasional Paper No. 21, Center for Archaeological Investigations, Southern Illinois University at Carbondale, Illinois.

Ervynck, A., Dobney, K., Hongo, H., and Meadow. R. 2001. Born free? New evidence of the status of pigs at Neolithic çayönü Tepesi Southeastern Anatolia, Turkey. *Palaeorient* 27:47–73.

Ervynck, A. Hillewaert, A. Maes, A., and Van Strydonck M. 2003. Tanning and horn working at late and post-medieval Bruges: The organic evidence. In: Murphy, P. and Wiltshire, P. E. J. (eds.) *The Environmental Archaeology of Industry*, pp. 60–70. Oxford: Oxbow Books.

Evin, A., Dobney, K., Schafberg, R., Owen, J., Strand Vidarsdottir, U., Larson, G., and Cucchi, T. 2015. Phenotype and animal domestication: A study of dental variation between domestic, wild, captive, hybrid and insular Sus scrofa. *BMC Evolutionary Biology* 15:6.

Gordon, E. A. 1993. Screen size and differential faunal recovery: A Hawaiian example. *Journal of Field Archaeology* 20(4):453–460.

Grant, A. 1982. The use of tooth wear as a guide to the age of domestic ungulates. In: Wilson, B., Grigson, C., and Payne, S. (eds.) *Aging and Sexing Animal Bone from Archaeological Sites*, pp. 91–108. BAR International series 109. Oxford: BAR.

Grant, A. 1988a. Animal resources. In: Astill, G. and Grant, A. (eds.) *The Countryside in Medieval England*, pp. 149–187. Oxford: Basil Blackwell.

Grant, A. 1988b. Food, status and religion in England in the Middle Ages: An archaeozoological perspective. In: Bodson, L. (ed.) *L'animal dans l'alimentation humaine: Les criteres de choix*, pp. 139–146. Actes du colloque international de Liège. Paris: HASRI.

Grayson, D. K. 1984. *Quantitative Zooarchaeology*. New York: Academic Press.

Hill, M. E., Hill, M. G., and Widge, C. G. 2008. Late Quaternary Bison diminution on the Great Plains of North America: Evaluating the role of human hunting versus climate change. *Quaternary Science Reviews* 27(17–18):1752–1771.

Hillson, S. 1986. *Teeth*. Cambridge: Cambridge University Press.

Klein, R. G. and Cruz-Uribe, K. 1984. *The Analysis of Animal Bones from Archaeological Sites*. Chicago: University of Chicago Press.

Legge, A. J. and Rowley-Conwy, P. 1987. Gazelle killing in Stone Age Syria. *Scientific American* 257(2):88–95.

Legge, A. J. and Rowley-Conwy, P. 2000. The exploitation of animals. In: Moore, G. C. Hillman, A. M. T., and Legge, A. J. (eds.) *Village on the Euphrates*, pp. 475–525. Oxford: Oxford University Press.

Lippold, S., Matzke, N. J., Reissmann, M., and Hofreiter, M. 2011. Whole mitochondrial genome sequencing of domestic horses reveals incorporation of extensive wild horse diversity during domestication. *BMC Evolutionary Biology* 11:328.

Lyman, R. L. 1994a. *Vertebrate Taphonomy*. Cambridge: Cambridge University Press.

Lyman, R. L. 1994b. Quantitative units and terminology in zooarchaeology. *American Antiquity* 59(1):36–71.

MacGregor, A. and Mainman, A. 2001. The bone and antler industry in Anglo-Scandinavian York: The evidence from Coppergate. In: Choyke, A. M. and Bartosiewicz, L. (eds.) *Crafting Bone: Skeletal Technologies through Time and Space. Proceedings of the 2nd meeting of the (ICAZ) Worked Bone Research Group, Budapest*, pp. 343–347. BAR International Series 937. Oxford: Archaeopress.

Martin, L., Edwards, Y., and Garrard, A. 2010. Hunting practices at an Eastern Jordanian Epipalaeolithic aggregation site: The case of Kharaneh IV. *Levant* 42(2): 107–135.

Mateos, A. 2005. Meat and fat: Intensive exploitation strategies in the Upper Palaeolithic approached from bone fracturing analysis. In: Mulville, J. and Outram, A. K. (eds.) *The Zooarchaeology of Fats, Oils, Milk and Dairying*, pp. 150–159. Oxford: Oxbow Books.

Münzel, S. C. 1988. Quantitative analysis and archaeological site interpretation. *Archaeozoologia* 2(1,2):93–110.

Nichol, R. K. and Wild, C. J. 1984. "Numbers of individuals" in faunal analysis: The decay of fish bone in archaeological sites. *Journal of Archaeological Science* 11(1):35–51.

Noe-Nygaard, N. 1977. Butchering and marrow fracturing as a taphonomic factor in archaeological deposits. *Paleobiology* 3:218–237.

O'Connor, T. P. 2000. Bones as evidence of meat production and distribution in York. In: White, E. (ed.) *Feeding a City: York. The Provision of Food from Roman Times to the Beginning of the Twentieth Century*, pp. 43–60. Devon, UK: Prospect Books.

O'Day, S. J., Van Neer, W., and Ervynck, A. (eds.) 2004. *Behaviour behind bones: The zooarchaeology of ritual, religion, status and identity. Proceedings of the 9th ICAZ Conference, Durham 2002*, Vol. 1. Oxford: Oxbow Books.

Outram, A. K. 2005. Distinguishing bone fat exploitation from other taphonomic processes: What caused the high level of bone fragmentation at the Middle Neolithic site of Ajvide, Gotland? In: Mulville, J. and Outram, A. K. (eds.) *The Zooarchaeology of Fats, Oils, Milk and Dairying*, pp. 32–43. Oxford: Oxbow Books.

Payne, S. 1969. A metrical distinction between sheep and goat metacarpals. In: Ucko, P. J. and Dimbleby, G. W. (eds.) *The Domestication and Exploitation of Plants and Animals*, pp. 295–305. London: Duckworth.

Payne, S. 1972. Partial recovery and sample bias: The results of some sieving experiments. In: Higgs, E. S. (ed.) *Papers in Economic Prehistory*, pp. 49–64. Cambridge: Cambridge University Press.

Payne, S. 1973. Kill-off patterns in sheep and goats. The mandibles from Asvan Kale. *Anatolian Studies* 23:281–303.

Perdikaris, S., Hambrecht, G., Brewington, S., and McGovern, T. H. 2007. Across the fish event horizon: A comparative approach. In: Plogmann, H. (ed.) *The Role of Fish in Ancient Time. Proceedings of the 13th Meeting of the ICAZ Fish Remains Working Group, August 2005, Basel*, pp. 51–62. Rahden: Leidorf.

Peres, T. M. 2010. Methodological issues in zooarchaeology. In: VanDerwarker, A. M. and Peres, T. M. (eds.) *Integrating Zooarchaeology and Paleoethnobotany: A Consideration of Issues, Methods, and Cases*, pp. 15–36. New York: Springer.

Perkins, D. 1973. A critique on the methods of quantifying faunal remains from archaeological sites. In: Matolcsi, J. (ed.) *Domestikationsforschung und Geschichte der Haustiere*, pp. 367–369. Budapest: Akadémiai Kiadö.

Reitz, E. J. and Wing, E. S. 2008. *Zooarchaeology*, 2nd ed. Cambridge: Cambridge University Press.

Rowley-Conwy, P. 1995. Meat, furs and skins: Mesolithic animal bones from Ringkloster, a seasonal hunting camp in Jutland. *Journal of Danish Archaeology* 12:87–98.

Rowley-Conwy, P. 1998. Improved separation of Neolithic metapodials of sheep (Ovis) and goats (Capra) from Arene Candide Cave, Liguria, Italy. *Journal of Archaeological Science* 25:251–258.

Rowley-Conwy, P. and Dobney, K. 2007. Wild boar and domestic pigs in Mesolithic and Neolithic southern Scandinavia. In: Albarella, U., Dobney, K., Ervynck, A., and Rowley-Conwy, P. (eds.) *Pigs and Humans: 10,000 Years of Interaction*, pp. 131–155. Oxford: Oxford University Press.

Ruscillo, D. (ed.) 2005. *Recent Advances in Ageing and Sexing Animal Bones. Proceedings of the 9th ICAZ Conference, Durham*. Oxford: Oxbow Books.

Saint-Germain, C. 2005. Animal fat in the cultural world of the native peoples of Northeastern America. In: Mulville, J. and Outram, A. K. (eds.) *The Zooarchaeology of Fats, Oils, Milk and Dairying*, pp. 107–113. Oxford: Oxbow Books.

Schmid, E. 1972. *Atlas of Animals Bones for Prehistorians, Archaeologists and Quaternary Geologists*. Amsterdam: Elsevier Science Publishers.

Shaffer, B. S. 1992. Quarter-inch screening: Understanding biases in recovery of vertebrate faunal remains. *American Antiquity* 57(1):129–136.

Shaffer, B. S. and Sanchez, J. L. 1994. Comparison of 1/8 and 1/4 mesh recovery of controlled samples of small-to-medium-sized mammals. *American Antiquity* 59(3):525–530.

Silver, I. A. 1970. The aging of domestic animals. In: Brothwell, D. R. and Higgs, E. S. (eds.) *Science in Archaeology: A Survey of Progress and Research*, 2nd ed., pp. 283–302. New York: Praeger Publishing

von den Driesch, A. 1976. *A Guide to the Measurement of Animal Bones from Archaeological Sites. Peabody Museum Bulletin 1.* Cambridge, Massachusetts: Harvard University Press.

von den Driesch, A., Kessler, D., and Peters, J. 2004. Mummified baboons and other primates from the Saitic-Ptolemaic animal necropolis of Tuna el-Gebel. Middle Egypt. *Documenta Archaeobiologicae: Conservation Policy and Current Research* 2:231–278.

Weissbrod, L. and Bar-Oz, G. 2002. Caprines and toads: Taphonomic patterning of animal offering practices in a Late Bronze Age burial assemblage. In: Jones O'Day, S., Van Neer, W., and Ervynck, A. 2002. *Behaviour behind Bones: The Zooarchaeology of Ritual, Religion, Status and Identity*, pp. 20–24. Oxford: Oxbow Books.

West, B. 1995. The case of the missing victuals. *Historical Archaeology* 29:20–42

White, T. E. 1953. A method for calculating the dietary percentage of various food animals utilized by Aboriginal people. *American Antiquity* 18(4):396–398.

Wilson, J. P. N. 1978. The interpretation of epiphysial fusion data. In: Brothwell, D. R., Thomas, K. D., and Clutton-Brock, J. (eds.) *Research Problems in Zooarchaeology*, pp. 97–101. Institute of Archaeology Occasional Publication 3. London: University of London.

Wing, E. S. and Quitmyer, I. R. 1985. Screen size for optimal data recovery: A case study. In: Adams, W. H. (ed.) *Aboriginal Subsistence and Settlement Archaeology of the Kings Bay Locality*, Vol. 2: *Zooarchaeology*, pp. 49–58. Reports of Investigations No. 2. Department of Anthropology, University of Florida, Gainesville.

Zeder, M. A. 2006. Archaeological approaches to documenting animal domestication. In: Zeder, M. A., Emshwiller, E., Smith, B. D., and Bradley D. G. (eds.) *Documenting Domestication*, pp. 171–180. Berkeley: University of California Press.

Zeder, M. A. 2008. Domestication and early agriculture in the Mediterranean Basin: Origins, diffusion, and impact. *Proceedings of the National Academy of Sciences* 105(33):11597–11604.

Zohar, I. and Cooke, R. G. 1997. The impact of salting and drying on fish bones: Preliminary observations on four marine species from Parita Bay, Panamá. *Archaeofauna* 6:59–66.

11

Invertebrate Zooarchaeology

Marcello A. Mannino

The analysis of invertebrate remains such as insects and molluscs from archaeological sites to reconstruct diet and environments.

1 INTRODUCTION

Invertebrates ("animals without backbones") constitute around 95 per cent of all existing fauna, and are therefore the majority of all living animals today. The remaining 5 percent of all animals are those from the sub-phylum Vertebrata that include fish, amphibians, reptiles, birds, and mammals (Barnes et al. 2001). Despite being present in most archaeological sites, invertebrates are often not adequately recovered or studied, partly due to the prevailing view among archaeologists that they are marginal for the understanding of past human behavior (Kenward 2009). Invertebrates (and their products) have been exploited throughout human history, not only as sources of food, but also for utilitarian purposes as tools, decorative objects, fibres, dyes, waxes, mastics, sealants, medicines, and poisons (Thomas and Mannino 2001). Detailed discussion of these uses by humans is not the scope of this chapter, which aims to highlight why the remains of these invertebrates hold great potential for archaeological science, as well as for reconstructing past environments beyond the scope of archaeology alone.

2 PRESERVATION, RECOVERY, AND QUANTIFICATION OF INVERTEBRATES IN ARCHAEOLOGY

With a few exceptions (e.g., molluscs such as giant squid, octopi, or clams) invertebrates are small (on the scale of millimeters to tens of millimeters) to microscopic in size. Many invertebrates have no mineralised or sclerotised (i.e., hardened) body parts (e.g., phyla Platyhelminthes, Nematoda, Rotifera, most Annelida), which means that they have little chance of surviving in the archaeological record, even in the most suitable depositional contexts. At the other end of the scale are soft-bodied animals with mineralised exoskeletons of calcium carbonate, such as those of sclerosponges or "hard sponges" (phylum Porifera, class Sclerospongiae), corals (phylum Cnidaria, class Anthozoa), some polychaete worms (phylum Annelida, class Polychaeta, family Serpulidae), molluscs (phylum Mollusca), and sea urchins (phylum Echinodermata, class Echinoidea). These calcareous exoskeletons are preserved at most sites, but surely in deposits with medium to high pH levels, thereby not acid (Davies 2008; Evans 1972). In between these two preservational extremes lie most invertebrate phyla, which include taxa with some hardened elements (e.g., structural elements found in sponges; mouthparts of cephalopods) and arthropods with sclerotised anatomical segments of chitin, such as those of insects (phylum Uniramia, class Insecta), or with carapaces, such as those of crustaceans (phylum Crustacea, class Malacostraca). Arthropod remains have stringent requirements for good preservation, as described in more detail below and by Elias (1994; 2010) and Kenward (2009), but are well-preserved in anoxic waterlogged deposits.

Although beyond the scope of this chapter, the techniques for the recovery of invertebrates from archaeological deposits are discussed for all invertebrates by Kenward (2009), for insects by Elias (1994; 2010) and for molluscs by Claassen (1998), Davies (2008), and Campbell (2017). The methods for estimating taxonomic abundances of invertebrate remains are similar to those for counting vertebrate remains (i.e., NISP, MNI), as discussed by Sutton (1995) and Kenward (2009) for insects, Davies (2008) for non-marine molluscs and Claassen (1998) for marine molluscs. It should be pointed out, however, that appropriate quantification of invertebrate remains (e.g., shells) depends on the research objectives pursued and on the taxonomic characteristics, taphonomic histories and depositional contexts of the remains (Thomas and Mannino 2017).

3 INSECTS

Insects (phylum Uniramia, sub-phylum Hexapoda, class Insecta) include about 1 million extant species (Price 1997), which is more than all other animal species put together. Insect remains of nine orders are normally found in archaeological deposits (Robinson 2001): dragonflies (Odonata), earwigs (Dermaptera), lice

(Phthiraptera), true bugs (Hemiptera), beetles (Coleoptera), fleas (Siphonaptera), flies (Diptera), caddis flies (Trichoptera), and bugs, wasps, and ants (Hymenoptera). The body structure of insects is formed by three segments (or *tagmata*): the head, the thorax, and the abdomen. These are structured by exoskeletal elements (sclerites) essentially of chitin, a polymeric polysaccharide $(C_8H_{13}NO_5)_n$. Adult insect body parts (i.e., head capsule, pronotum, elytra, male genitalia) and puparia (larval stage casings), survive well in anoxic sediments, such as natural waterlogged deposits (lake beds, peat bogs, etc.) or anthropogenic deposits below the water table, such as pits, wells, and ditches (Kenward 2009). Insect remains can survive in aerobic environments if the conditions are so cold (arctic/subarctic) or so hot and dry as to hinder or retard the action of chitin-decomposing microorganisms (bacteria and fungi). Chitin can also be preserved by calcium phosphate mineralisation, which occurs in presence of liquids rich in phosphate ions (e.g., sewage) against a background of calcium carbonate, as in cesspits with limestone lining (Robinson 2001). The following sections outline the topics of enquiry of studies on insects from archaeological sites or from natural deposits that might be associated with them: palaeoenvironmental reconstructions (*palaeoentomology*) and past human uses and interactions with insects (*archaeoentomology*).

Palaeoentomology

Insects are uniquely useful palaeoenvironmental indicators, not only because they are extremely sensitive to environmental change, but also because they (1) have great species diversity, recording data on almost all habitats, (2) have narrow ecological (*stenotopic*) or climatic (*stenothermic*) tolerances, providing detailed information on past environments, (3) have remained extant through epochs of archaeological interest, and (4) have been the object of detailed ecological studies (Elias 2010). The fact that most insect species have existed for millions of years allows us to use knowledge of their present-day biology and ecology when interpreting their remains for palaeoenvironmental reconstructions (*uniformitarianism*). Palaeoentomological studies of interest to archaeology are often based on insect assemblages from non-anthropic deposits (e.g., ponds, lakes, and peat bogs), close to archaeological sites and which accumulated during their occupation. The study of these insect remains is a source of a vast array of data on climatic and environmental conditions experienced by humans in the past (Elias 2010; Kenward 2009).

Insects, and carnivorous and scavenging beetles (class Coleoptera) in particular, have been invaluable in detecting rapid and intense climatic oscillations in mid- to high-latitude terrestrial environments (Elias 2010). Predatory coleopterans are the most reliable indicators for periods of extremely rapid climate changes, because they are the first to respond to such changes by colonizing newly deglaciated areas well before, and independently of, vegetation. Beetles have recorded sudden and intense climatic oscillations (e.g., the Quinton Cold Interlude in England during Marine Isotope Stage 11), which contemporary pollen data failed to detect (Coope and Kenward 2007). These palaeoclimatic reconstructions are based on the Mutual Climatic Range (MCR) method, introduced in the 1980s to obtain palaeotemperature estimates from fossil beetle assemblage data (Atkinson et al. 1986). This method requires the definition of the climatic range or "envelope" (corresponding to the interval between the mean temperatures of the warmest and coldest months of the year) of each predatory or scavenging beetle species in an assemblage. The climatic "envelopes" of the species are then put together to define the overlap in the respective climatic envelopes, which constitutes the *mutual climate range* of the assemblage. The highest and lowest mean temperatures of the mutual climatic range are the palaeotemperature estimates for the summer and winter seasons at the site in question.

In spite of the potentially confounding effects of human impacts on the environment and, therefore, on the invertebrate faunas during the Holocene after the adoption of agriculture, insects from historical-period natural and semi-natural deposits can be used for climatic reconstructions, provided that the factors that might have impacted on their ranges and abundances are evaluated in detail on a species by species basis (Kenward 2004).

Insects have also been used to reconstruct the environmental history of regions within which humans lived in the past. For instance, a study by Elias et al. (2009) on beetle assemblages from sites in the lower Thames valley has reconstructed the environmental changes that took place in that region from the Mesolithic to the Late Bronze Age. The increase in the proportion of open ground beetles (partly caused by land clearance), along with the appearance of beetle species associated with crops and of dung-feeding beetles, prove that agriculture and animal husbandry had become important economic activities in the lower Thames valley by the Early Bronze Age.

Insects have also been used to reconstruct forest history and human impacts on these environments. Studies on fossil ancient forest beetle fauna from sites in Britain and Ireland have demonstrated that humans started having an effect on woodlands by the Neolithic (Whitehouse 2006). A significant proportion of ancient woodland beetle species were extirpated by the end of the Bronze Age, mainly due to forest clearance and to habitat fragmentation.

Archaeoentomology

Insects were rarely introduced deliberately into archaeological contexts by humans, except when they were used by people for food (*entomophagy*) or for utilitarian purposes (Sutton 1995). Insects are a rich source of nutrients, exploited by humans throughout their evolutionary history. Entomophagy is not easy to prove archaeologically and has been demonstrated beyond doubt when insect remains have been recovered directly from human coprolites. As reviewed by Elias (2010), Anasazi coprolites from the site of Mesa Verde in Colorado (United States) were found to contain remains of cicadas and grasshoppers, the latter becoming a more frequent item in Anasazi diets following a local increase in shrub-grassland vegetation, which favored their populations. The use of insects for utilitarian purposes in archaeology is usually attested by the recovery of their products, rather than of their skeletal remains. Insect products are rarely unearthed in an unmodified form, as in the case of a lump of beeswax recovered at the site of Coppergate in York (Kenward and Hall 1995), but in the main they are found either adhering to textile fabrics in the case of dyes or as residues on pottery artefacts in the case of beeswax, mastics, and sealants. Gas chromatography-mass spectrometry or similar geochemical techniques are required for the identification of insect products preserved in the form of residues, as reviewed by Sutton (1995) and Thomas and Mannino (2001).

In most archaeoentomological studies, which are based on remains originating directly from deposits, it is necessary not only to evaluate the taphonomic dynamics that affected the assemblage, which might have led to the differential preservation of species, but also to assess how different taxa might have entered a deposit (Kenward 2009). The approach taken to investigate these issues is to study insect assemblages from modern analogues of the depositional environments present in archaeological contexts. While for many depositional contexts we have a good understanding of how insect assemblages might form (e.g., latrines, cesspits, roofs, corpses), for others such as "primitive" houses we do not have sufficient information. In these cases it might be necessary to study assemblages from recreated contexts, as was done by Kenward and Tipper (2008), who analysed the insects recovered in pitfall traps placed in reconstructed Anglo-Saxon houses at West Stow in England. This study confirmed that some of the insect taxa from the Anglo-Scandinavian site at Coppergate in York were correctly interpreted as "house fauna" characteristic of ancient buildings (Carrott and Kenward 2001). An unavoidable limitation of the study by Kenward and Tipper (2008) is that the reconstructed houses were not lived in and so they were not heated and did not contain food or other occupation debris, which would have led to the incorporation of a larger array of "household" insects (from the occupants, stored foods, litter, etc.) and "outdoor" insects (seeking suitable habitats, inadvertently imported by the occupants, etc.). In some cases, nevertheless, "unexpected insects" might be recovered from living quarters, which complicate interpretations of assemblages and might only be explained by the occurrence of unusual, or extreme, events for such contexts. For example, a high number of remains of the fly *Telomerina flavipes* and of carrion-feeding insects were found in contexts associated with the final phase of occupation even in the bedroom of a Norse farmhouse at Nipaatsoq in Greenland (Panagiotakopulu et al. 2007). The presence of these insects suggests that the occupants died in the bedroom, where carrion species fed on their corpses. It is worth highlighting here that insect remains offer great potential for reconstructing seasonality of death and conditions endured by human cadavers, for instance, whether they were left in open spaces (in which case colonisation by corpse-feeding fauna would be faster), indoors or buried (Vanin and Huchet 2017). The possibility of obtaining similar levels of information are rare archaeologically, given that human corpses rarely survive intact, but it should be noted that some insects, such as subterranean termites (Isoptera), beetles (Coleoptera), wasps (Hymenoptera), and some sarco-saprophagous fly larvae (Diptera) can cause osteolytic degradation, which can mimic damage produced to bone by degenerative or infectious pathologies.

Interpreting insect remains from urban deposits may be even more challenging, because assemblages are temporally mixed and contain insects from different communities, including species from the surroundings that did not live where the deposit formed and so do not reflect the local habitat. This problem can be tackled by establishing groups of co-occurring species, with analogous habitat requirements, each time an urban assemblage is investigated (Carrott and Kenward 2001). This has been done successfully in the case of the site of Coppergate in York, where evidence from insect remains has ascertained that urban living conditions were more hygienic in Roman than in medieval (Anglo-Scandinavian) times (Kenward and Hall 1995). Studies on insects from numerous other urban sites in northern Europe (e.g., Oslo, Gothenburg) have confirmed that living conditions in many medieval European towns were squalid (Elias 2010). People lived in houses with rotting timber frames, kept organic waste in the living quarters for long periods of time, ate infested foods and, not surprisingly, were parasitised by lice and fleas.

Insects associated with humans can be divided into two broad categories: *synanthropic* species, which benefit from living in close contact with humans, and in the artificial environments they create, and *parasitic* species, which are often disease vectors (Kenward 2009).

Synanthropic insects from archaeological deposits can provide us with data on a huge array of aspects of the human past, for example, on the destination of different areas within human settlements for waste disposal, stabling and sanitation, or living quarters of buildings for storage of foods or hay, and workspaces (e.g., Crabtree et al. 2017; Kenward 2009; Reilly 2012). Synanthropes can also inform us on human activities (butchery, crafts, funerary rituals, etc.) or living standards (sanitary conditions, health, etc.). The degree of synanthropy is potentially an indicator of intensity of occupation, as testified by the study of the Viking Age settlement of Kaupang in Norway (Barrett et al. 2007). A short-lived or intermittent occupation was hypothesised for this site, based on the species composition of its insect assemblage, which is characterised by a large proportion of facultative synanthropes (i.e., species common in natural and anthropic habitats), few typical synanthropes, and almost no obligate synanthropes. Another possible interpretation for similar, if not lower, levels of synanthropy has been proposed for assemblages from the Troitsky area at Novgorod, where the presence of raised wooden floors may have prevented the need for a build up of deep litter layers to the detriment of synanthropic insects such as *Aglenus brunneus* (Reilly 2012). These examples illustrate the potential of archaeoentomological reconstructions of site and structure use, but, as hinted above, their reliability depends on a good understanding of the ecological requirements of insect taxa recovered archaeologically and of assemblage taphonomy, as well as on adequate recovery. These issues were addressed by an actualistic study on live and recently dead beetle communities living in organic materials within and around traditional Icelandic barns and byres (Forbes et al. 2016). Stable manure in Iceland was found to support beetles associated with foul rotting matter, while no such species were recovered from stored hay. Moreover, the latter context contained not only taxa associated with decaying matter, but more ecologically diverse taxa, including non-synanthropic beetles from hayfields. The study by Forbes et al. (2016) thus represents a cautionary tale for the use of degrees of synanthropy as an interpretative tool and highlights the need for more actualistic studies.

Some synanthropic taxa, such as pests of stored foods, may indicate the existence of trade networks and provide valuable data on insect biogeography (e.g., King et al. 2014; Panagiotakopulu 2001; Panagiotakopulu and Buckland 2017). The most classic example of imported food pest is represented by the grain weevil *Sitophilus granarius*, a species never recorded outside of storage facilities (Plarre 2010). For this reason, and because *S. granarius* eveloved at the time of the development of agriculture, it has been argued that the initial spread of this flightless weevil was linked to the migrations of early Neolithic farmers (King et al. 2014; Panagiotakopulu and Buckland 2017). This represented the first expansion of food pests across Europe, which also occurred later in the Roman and medieval periods, when the grain weevil reached every corner of the continent traveling in sacks of traded cereals. Grain weevils were introduced to Great Britain by the Romans, but are extremely rare at sites on the island from the end of the Roman period to pre-Conquest times, attesting changes in trade networks during that time interval (Kenward 2009). Another example of insect pest introduced through trade in the past is the European species *Aglenus brunneus* recovered in a medieval farm at Reykholt in Iceland, its occurrence there only being explainable by its fortuitous importation in sacks of grain from Europe (Buckland et al. 2009).

Insects that parasitise humans include lice, fleas, and bed bugs and their remains have been recovered either within deposits or, frequently, in mummies (e.g., Kenward 2001; Kenward 2009; Mitchell 2017; Panagiotakopulu 2001). Commonly found ectoparasitic species from archaeological contexts are head lice (*Pediculus humanus capitis*), body lice (*Pediculus humanus corporis*), pubic lice (*Pthirus pubis*), fleas (*Pulex irritans*), and bed bugs (*Cimex lectularius*). Their presence can be indicative of poor hygiene (or conversely, hygiene practices, such as de-lousing) and can shed light on the sanitary conditions of past human populations. The earliest (possibly) archaeological remains of the genus *Cimex* are those from deposits excavated at the prehistoric site of Paisley Five Mile Point Cave in south-central Oregon, dating to between 11,000 and 9,500 calibrated years B.P. (Adams and Jenkins 2017). In the case of similar recoveries, association between cimicids and humans can only be postulated, given that members of the genus *Cimex* are obligate ectoparasites of vespertilionid bats. The latter live in caves, where Adams and Jenkins (2017) hypothesise that the relationship between cimicids and humans started, with infested bats acting as vectors. In the case of *Cimex* finds from living quarters and towns, more direct links between humans and ectoparasites can be hypothesised, as for the bed bugs (*C. lectularius*) and fleas (*P. irritans*) from Amarna in Egypt (Panagiotakopulu 2001). Positive associations between ectoparasites and human hosts can, however, only be fully established when there is a clear link between the two, as in the case of a highly infested Maitas Chiribaya mummy from Arica in Chile, the scalp and hair of which were covered by nits and adult head lice (Arriaza et al. 2012).

Remains of non-parasitic insects recovered in mummies can aid in reconstructing funerary rituals associated with mummification and even the last stages of life of an individual. In the study of a Chachapoya mummy from Perú (Nystrom et al. 2005), the adoption of forensic entomology techniques made it possible to ascertain that insect colonisation of the soft tissues began before death, which occurred 9 or 10 days after a lethal injury, and that the bundle was wrapped within two days of death.

Advances in the Study of Insect Remains

Studies on chitin preservation show that this protein can survive for millions of years and that archaeological sclerites are sufficiently stable chemically to be suitable for AMS radiocarbon dating, stable isotope, and ancient DNA analyses (Elias 2010). Advances in mass-spectrometry have made it possible to obtain radiocarbon dates from a few insect sclerites and stable isotope ratios from single sclerites. The possibility of dating insect fossils will surely improve the chronological accuracy of palaeoentomological studies. It has been known since the 1980s that carbon, nitrogen, oxygen, and hydrogen isotope analyses on chitin can provide data on arthropod diets, as well as on past environments and climates (Schimmelmann et al. 1986). However, with few exceptions these methods have practically been ignored for studies of archaeological samples.

A notable application is represented by an isotopic study on puparia of the so-called seaweed fly (*Thoracochaeta zosterae*), which commonly occurs in medieval and postmedieval cesspits in England (Webb et al. 1998). At present this fly breeds in decomposing seaweed, so it was suggested that seaweed was present in the cesspits in question. Archaeological and modern pupae of *T. zosterae* were sampled for carbon ($\delta^{13}C$) and nitrogen ($\delta^{15}N$) stable isotope analyses to test this hypothesis. The $\delta^{13}C$ values of the modern pupae from marine settings are typical of the isotopic ratios for marine invertebrates, while the $\delta^{13}C$ values from the archaeological specimens were found to be compatible with terrestrial grazing. This shows that puparia had been laid in a cesspit that did not contain seaweed and, hence, that cesspits were once a common habitat for *T. zosterae*.

More recently, King (2012) undertook carbon, nitrogen, and hydrogen ($\delta^{2}H$ = deuterium) isotope analyses on insect remains from Neolithic Linearbandkeramik sites in Germany to acquire high resolution data on past trophic webs and to reconstruct farming practices and trade of agricultural produce. Analyses conducted as part of the same study on modern beetles from the reconstructed *Grubenhaus* at West Stow in Sussex, however, suggest that the potential of such applications to detect the presence of *autochthonous* (originating from the locality of the sampled deposit) and *allochthonous* (originating from a different locality) materials at a site requires further actualistic research guided by detailed knowledge of the ecology of the species under investigation.

A study by King et al. (2009) has recovered ancient DNA from remains of grain weevil (*Sitophilus granarius*) of Roman and medieval date from northern England, opening new perspectives for palaeoentomology. In the case of synanthropic species, such as *S. granarius*, genetic studies should determine the origin of a taxon and whether its introduction into a region was the result of a single or multiple events. Ancient DNA studies could also be used to verify if the genomes of fossil insects differ from those of their modern counterparts and, if so, to evaluate the uniformitarian assumptions on which palaeoentomological studies are based (King et al. 2009).

4 MOLLUSCS

The phylum Mollusca includes taxa living in terrestrial, freshwater, and marine environments. Molluscs of the classes Polyplacophora, Scaphopoda, Gastropoda, and Bivalvia are frequently found at archaeological sites, in the form of their highly mineralised calcium carbonate ($CaCO_3$) exoskeletons, otherwise known as shells. In archaeology, the study of molluscs has recently been termed *archaeomalacology* (Bar-Yosef Mayer 2005). Shells are precious archives of past environments and human behaviors, because their morphology, shape, mineralogy, and chemical composition varies in relation to climate and ecology, as described below for molluscs from terrestrial and marine ecosystems (Allen 2017a).

Terrestrial and Freshwater Molluscs

Land and freshwater molluscs can be present in archaeological sites either because they occurred naturally in a deposit or because they were introduced by the human occupants to consume their flesh (Davies 2008) and/or, in the case of some freshwater taxa (e.g., *Margaritifera, Anodonta*), to use their shells as raw materials or as body ornaments (Claassen 1998). Shells of freshwater molluscs have been interpreted unambiguously as food refuse at most archaeological sites in which they have been found (Claassen 1998; Waselkov 1987). On the other hand, there is no unequivocal way of establishing whether land snails in an assemblage were eaten, as demonstrated by a study on shells of *Helix cincta* from Mesolithic levels at the Edera cave in Italy (Bonizzoni et al. 2009), which by using a suite of archaeometric techniques attempted to verify if the snails had been cooked.

As reviewed by Lubell (2004), the most convincing evidence for prehistoric land snail consumption is offered by some spectacular accumulations of shells of terrestrial molluscs in Capsian sites from Algeria and Tunisia. These sites are known as *escargotières* and the snails in them are considered as food refuse due to: (1) their sheer quantity, (2) their association with anthropic materials, and (3) the fact that the assemblage is overwhelmingly dominated by one (or few) herbivorous species suitable for human consumption (e.g., taxa of the family Helicidae). These criteria should be taken into account when evaluating whether a land snail accumulation is anthropogenic, although they are by no means conclusive. Numerous vertebrate taxa, including, for example, rodents and shrews, can accumulate sizeable middens, which usually contain nibbled shells with recognisable breakage patterns (e.g., Hunt and Hill 2017).

Taphonomic studies of snail accumulations in anthropogenic and natural deposits are needed to define more stringent criteria for the identification of the agents responsible for the presence of edible terrestrial molluscs in archaeological sites. To date, the most purposeful attempt at establishing the anthropic origin of a land snail accumulation was conducted by Fernández-López de Pablo et al. (2014) on specimens of the helicid *Iberus alonensis* from Cova de la Barriada in Spain. These researchers adopted a new analytical protocol, which included taphonomic, biometric, and micro X-ray diffractometric analyses on modern and archaeological specimens, to demonstrate that Gravettian hunter-gatherers likely introduced helicids to the cave for consumption.

Ethnoarchaeological investigations on the use of land snails in eastern Africa, and particularly of the Giant East African Land Snail *Achatina fulica*, warn those studying archaeological remains of terrestrial molluscs that these may have been used for more than mere consumption (Walz 2017: 94). Land snail shells from northeastern Tanzania are used by traditional peoples as subsistence tools (e.g., as latches to secure freshwater fish traps, to hoe agricultural fields, to cut stems and detach seeds from grain crops), as household tools (e.g., spoons, containers for salt), as landscape markers (e.g., to mark hunting traps, intersections between paths and boundaries between fields), as decorations (e.g., personal ornaments, adornments of graves), and as ritual implements (e.g., to call snakes by blowing, to conduct healing and witchcraft). Any of these activities is likely to leave specific taphonomic signatures on intact and fragmentary archaeological shells, so any study of remains of similar species should be conducted bearing such possibilities in mind.

Palaeoenvironmental Reconstructions

Naturally occurring shells of terrestrial and freshwater molluscs in sediments constitute a record of molluscs that lived, died, became buried, and survived as sub-fossils throughout the time in which the deposit accumulated (Davies 2008). An assemblage is thus rarely the relic of a single community, but represents the mixture of shells from communities that were present in the different periods over which a deposit formed. The correct interpretation of an assemblage depends on the understanding of the taphonomic processes that affected its formation (i.e., burial, mixing, sorting, and destruction processes) and on contextually targeted sampling (Allen 2017b). In a study on the taphonomy of shells in calcareous soils, Carter (1990) determined that mollusc assemblages in buried soils often have poor temporal resolutions, mainly containing data on short-term episodes rather than continuous records. To improve the temporal resolution of assemblages from buried soils it is necessary to adopt finer sampling strategies than is usually the case, ideally requiring the involvement of an archaeomalacologist during excavation.

Land snails can inform us on local habitat characteristics by determining the presence of grassland or woodland, sand dune habitats, rocky, rubbly, or scree deposits. To date, general terms such as "grassland" are still present in the literature, because we have not been able to distinguish between different grassland types due to a lack of progress in appropriate modern ecological work on open-country faunas (Davies 2008). Freshwater molluscs from natural deposits can be used to reconstruct lentic (i.e., bodies of still water, such as lakes and ponds) or lotic (i.e., flowing waters, such as those of streams and rivers) environments (Davies 2008). On the other hand, freshwater molluscs from archaeological sites are of little value for environmental reconstructions, because their taxonomic composition and representation is strongly biased by human selectivity in favor of food taxa.

Studies on land snails have proved particularly useful for palaeoenvironmental reconstructions in areas characterised by strongly oxidised sediments, in which insect and plant (e.g., pollen) remains do not survive, such as tufa deposits (i.e., limestone and chalkland regions), loess, hillwash, and so on. Land snail assemblages from tufa deposits are usually *autochthonous* and, therefore, useful for reconstructing the local palaeoecology (Evans 1972). Mollusc zonation schemes have been developed to reconstruct past environmental histories, with supporting chronological data from direct radiocarbon dating on shells or other organic materials. For example, a mollusc succession from Holywell Coombe in Folkestone (England) has been studied by Preece and Bridgland (1999), providing a record of environmental change through the past 13,000 radiocarbon years. The oldest stages of the sequence, corresponding to the Late Pleistocene, were characterised by cool temperate and cold conditions (as also confirmed by the application of the MCR method on beetle remains recovered from the same part of the deposit), while the Holocene was characterised by temperate conditions. The molluscs from Holywell Coombe testify that from the beginning of the Holocene there was a progressive development of forest, as indicated by the reduction in the presence of species intolerant of shade (e.g., *Pupilla muscorum*, *Vallonia pulchella*, *Vertigo geyeri*) and of heliophile species (*Vertigo angustior*), and by the increase in shade-demanding taxa (e.g., *Carychium tridentatum*). The first evidence for the thinning of the forest canopy is attested by a decline in shade-demanding snails during the late Mesolithic and Neolithic, possibly associated with land clearance by humans.

Studies of non-marine mollusca such as the one at Holywell Coombe (Preece and Bridgland 1999) are regrettably uncommon and most of them have been undertaken in Great Britain. A similar study has been conducted on successions from the upper Lena River in the Lake Baikal region (Siberia, Russia) by White et al. (2008). This investigation attested that the floodplain of the Lena River was characterised by alternating episodes of dryness and wetness. The methodological observations arising from the study by White et al. (2008) are that some of the species could not be identified with certainty, or could not be used for detailed palaeoecological reconstructions, due to poor knowledge of their present-day ecology (*neoecology*). The onus of studying the neoecology of poorly documented taxa to better interpret sub-fossil material might well be on archaeomalacologists, given the lack of interest for such studies by neoecologists (Davies 2008).

Geochemical Studies on Non-Marine Molluscs

Studies on modern terrestrial molluscs have shown that stable carbon ($\delta^{13}C$) and oxygen ($\delta^{18}O$) isotope ratios in their shells vary in relation to environmental and climatic factors (Colonese 2017; Goodfriend 1992; Leng and Lewis 2016; Thomas 2015a). Carbon isotope ratios in shell carbonate are primarily a function of the diet of snails and can be used to distinguish the consumption of plants with different photosynthetic pathways (C_3, C_4, or Crassulacean Acid Metabolism). Oxygen isotope ratios ($^{18}O/^{16}O$) in land snail carbonates reflect the oxygen isotope composition of meteoric waters and can, therefore, be used as a proxy for reconstructing past changes in rainfall and climatic conditions. Oxygen isotope analyses on freshwater mollusc shells can also be used to reconstruct past precipitation and climatic regimes (e.g., Davis and Muehlenbachs 2001).

An example of the application of isotope analyses on archaeological terrestrial molluscs (i.e., *Helix ligata*) is the study by Colonese et al. (2009), which investigates changes in rainfall patterns in Late Glacial and early Holocene southern Italy. This study shows that, for most of the time between the end of the Pleistocene and the early Holocene, environmental waters in the region of Grotta della Serratura had $\delta^{18}O$ values similar to present-day ones. Exceptions to this trend were recorded around 13.4 ka cal. BP, when shell carbonates had isotopically enriched values suggesting drier conditions (ca. 25 per cent less rainfall), and, around 7.4 ka cal BP, when carbonates had depleted values suggesting wetter conditions (ca. 50 per cent more rainfall).

Stable isotope analyses have also been successfully applied to specimens of the helicid *Helix melanostoma* recovered from the stratigraphic sequence at Haua Fteah in Libya (Prendergast et al. 2016). The $\delta^{18}O$ values track the short-term climatic oscillations that affected the northern hemisphere during the late Pleistocene and early Holocene (e.g., Heinrich events, Holocene climatic optimum), implying strong atmospheric teleconnections between the south-eastern Mediterranean and the Atlantic. The $\delta^{13}C$ values from the same shells have failed to detect significant vegetational changes, suggesting that the Gebel Akhdar in eastern Libya may have been a *refugium* for plants, animals and humans during the late Pleistocene (in Marine Isotope Stages 3 and 2).

It should also be pointed out that radiocarbon dating of non-marine molluscs is problematic (Goodfriend 1992; Thomas 2015a), due to the incorporation of ^{14}C-depleted (or "dead") carbon from limestone and other carbonate rocks during shell secretion, which is known as the "limestone effect" (Douka 2017). An additional problem linked to radiocarbon dating land snails is that their shells may end up in layers that are not contemporary with the life of the molluscs, either because they have moved into such contexts of their own accord or because they have been transported there by their predators (Hunt and Hill 2017).

Recent studies making use of amino acid racemisation, nevertheless, have demonstrated that non-marine molluscs can be invaluable geochronological archives.

An impressive example of this line of research is represented by a recent study by Penkman et al. (2013) who analysed a range of aminoacids that racemize at different rates within the intracrystalline protein of the calcitic opercula of freshwater gastropods of the genus *Bithynia*. The protocol devised by these researchers ensures that the geochronological estimates are based on well-preserved amino acids, allowing us to attain high-resolution aminostratigraphies of non-marine deposits for the whole of the Quaternary.

Marine Molluscs

The flesh of marine molluscs has been consumed by modern humans (*Homo sapiens*) since the Middle Pleistocene (Marean et al. 2007) and by archaic humans (*Homo neanderthalensis*) from around the same time, or just after (e.g., Colonese et al. 2011; Thomas 2015b). The earliest known example of the use of shell as a symbolic medium is a valve of the freshwater mussel *Pseudodon vondembuschianus* from Trinil on Java, which was incised with a zigzag pattern by a *Homo erectus*, who may thus have been capable of abstract thought (Joordens et al. 2015). Shells of marine molluscs have been utilised by modern humans as ornamental objects for at least the last 100 ka years (Vanhaeren et al. 2006), while Neanderthals might have started using them for the same purpose and as pigment containers around 50 ka years ago (Zilhão et al. 2010). For reviews on the role of marine molluscs in past human subsistence the reader is invited to consult Claassen (1998), Thomas (2015b), and Waselkov (1987). Other essential reading for those intending to work on the zooarchaeology of marine molluscs is the seminal book by Betty Meehan (1982): *Shell Bed to Shell Midden*. This ethnoarchaeological study of shellfish exploitation by the Anbarra people in northern Australia demonstrates that the role of marine molluscs in human diets does not lie merely in their protein contribution, which in most environments would relegate them by default to supplementary foods, but in their nutritional properties and dependability, as they are available year-round.

Midden Formation Processes and Shell Taphonomy

The issue that has to be settled at the outset of any study on marine molluscs from archaeological deposits is to establish if the shells were introduced to the site by humans or by natural agents. This question is particularly difficult to tackle when dealing with shell-bearing deposits close to present or past shorelines, as reviewed by Claassen (1998). Members of the so-called "Kitchen Midden Commissions" faced the same problems when they considered whether the large prehistoric accumulations of shells found along the shores of northern Jutland in Denmark were anthropogenic or not (Andersen 2000). Excavations at some key sites (e.g., Krabbesholm, Ertebølle) resulted in the observation that shells of marine molluscs (e.g., *Ostrea edulis, Cerastoderma edule*) constituted the matrix of the deposits, which contained clear evidence of human occupation (e.g., lithics, skeletal remains of hunted mammals and fish, charcoal, raw materials, pottery). The outcome of those early interdisciplinary investigations was to confirm that they dealt indeed with sites where Mesolithic hunter-gatherers had discarded astronomical numbers of shells following mollusc consumption, which is why they were named *køkkenmøddinger* (lit.: kitchen middens) or shell middens (Andersen 2000).

Since those early days, the study of middens has expanded to become practically a subfield in its own right, highlighting the diversity of environmental and cultural data that their high archaeological visibility allows us to obtain from them (Szabó 2017; Waselkov 1987).

Recently, shell middens have been singled out as "stratigraphic markers" for the Anthropocene, the proposed epoch that we live in and that is characterised by unprecedented human impact on the Earth's geology and ecosystems (Erlandson 2013). In this light, the widespread appearance of shell mounds globally, from the Terminal Pleistocene onward, is an important indicator of the expanding "human footprint" on natural environments, particularly in coastal regions.

Accumulations of marine molluscs in the Cape York Peninsula (Australia) have been interpreted as *shell middens* (i.e., deposits of shells discarded by humans after the consumption of mollusc flesh) by archaeologists (Bailey 1993) and as *cheniers* (i.e., natural shell mounds) by geomorphologists (Stone 1995). In order to identify shell accumulations as middens, shell-bearing deposits should contain: (1) marine molluscs of a few edible species (represented mainly by large specimens and devoid of marine taphonomic signatures inside their valves), (2) artefacts, (3) animal bones, (4) charcoal, and (5) other stratigraphic features typical of anthropogenic sites (Bailey 1993). Some of these characteristics might be shared with *cheniers* (Stone 1995) and, therefore, new methods need to be devised, or more in-depth studies of the contents of shell-bearing deposits undertaken, in order to distinguish between natural and anthropogenic deposits in particularly complex cases. This debate highlighted the importance of always having to ascertain the agent of accumulation, which is something that can be done only by combining different lines of evidence (including geoarchaeological observations) and intensive radiocarbon dating of the shell matrix to establish the mode of shell deposition (Szabó 2017: 774). It should be added that more work on modern shell middens can help us obtain vital information on how these anthropogenic deposits form, which was the objective of work undertaken on mounds in the Saloum Delta (Senegal) by Hardy et al. (2016). These researchers found that all mounds constantly changed through time, as a result of ongoing accumulation and on-site activities, just as the perception that people had of them also changed, from viewing them as dumps to living contexts, religious places, burial sites, or even monuments. Interestingly, Hardy et al. (2016) also noted that all archaeological and modern middens in the Saloum Delta essentially contained a single species, which is probably because they were not discarded for immediate consumption, but rather after processing for trade.

An additional approach to the problem of determining whether shell mounds (particularly those in close proximity to present and/or ancient shorelines) are natural or cultural in origin, is represented by a method developed by Rosendahl et al. (2007), who used tests (i.e., "shells") of foraminifera (= single-celled invertebrates that live in marine environments) recovered from the deposits for this purpose. In a study of natural and anthropogenic shell deposits along the coasts of eastern Australia, Rosendahl and colleagues demonstrated that *cheniers* contain significantly higher densities of foraminifera compared to middens formed as a result of human dumping.

Detailed taphonomic studies based on the comparison of anthropogenic shell assemblages with natural *thanatocoenosis* (i.e., natural death assemblages) can provide data that might help in settling the issue, even though this time-consuming research is rarely undertaken by zooarchaeologists (Bonomo and Aguirre 2009). Shell features that result from natural post-depositional processes include abrasion of surfaces, rounding and smoothing of margins, loss of original pigmentation and ornamentation. In addition, shells that have been lying postmortem on the surface of or in shallow-water coastal sediments are often encrusted by the calcareous exoskeletons of epibiotic invertebrates, such as polychaetes (phylum Annelida, class Polychaeta, genera *Pomatoceros* and *Spirorbis*), or perforated by clionid sponges (phylum Porifera, class Demospongiae, genus *Cliona*), which leave borings called *entobia*. Whenever these encrusting exoskeletons or perforations are present in the interior of gastropod or bivalve shells, it can safely be concluded that the marine mollusc in question entered a deposit only after its death (which in archaeological contexts implies the collection of an empty shell and not of a live mollusc), because during life molluscs prevent other organisms from settling inside their valves.

The interpretation of the agent responsible for the presence of marine molluscs in anthropic deposits should be carefully evaluated, even at sites that are distant enough from the coast to have been unaffected by marine physical natural agents (e.g., wave action, rising sea levels). In fact, shells at these sites might not necessarily have been introduced by humans, given that many mammals and birds are known to prey on molluscs and some birds accumulate shells for non-dietary purposes (Erlandson and Moss 2001). For example, clams and scallops have been found in condor nests up to 48 km away from the coast. However, shells that have been predated by animals more often than not have distinctive breakage patterns. Seabirds (e.g., oystercatchers, seagulls) are known to vigorously hammer shells until they break them open to access the mollusc, leaving behind diagnostic fragments (Zuschin et al. 2003). Human actions linked to the exploitation of shellfish can also produce identifiable taphonomic signatures during collection, processing to extract the flesh and cooking. When shells from archaeological deposits are intact, or have breakage patterns that are anthropogenic, it is usually assumed that they were taken back to the site by humans as food.

Archaeological Marine Shell Assemblages

Studies of archaeological marine shell assemblages yield data on many aspects of the human exploitation of shellfish (collecting habits, dietary preferences, and role, etc.), as well as on coastal environments and on the possible impacts of anthropic predation on mollusc populations and their ecological communities of origin (e.g., Bailey and Craighead 2003; Bosch et al. 2015; Dupont 2006; Faulkner 2009; Gutiérrez Zugasti 2009; Jerardino 1997; Jerardino and Marean 2010; Mannino and Thomas 2001; Schapira et al. 2009; Thakar 2011;). Shell middens contain fewer mollusc species than are present on nearby shores and their assemblages are usually biased in favor of taxa that are more abundant, easy to collect, palatable and/or preferred by humans for any number of cultural and dietary reasons. The activities connected to shellfish exploitation can also affect the fidelity of anthropogenic assemblages to the populations and communities from which the molluscs originated, operating as taphonomic filters against taxa that might be damaged, as a result of collection and processing, and taxa with weaker shells.

Systematic analysis of shell middens starting from their taxonomic composition and representation can, nevertheless, yield a wealth of information on the types of shores exploited by humans (i.e., rocky or soft-bottomed, which can be sandy or muddy) and on changes in past coastal environments (e.g., in shore morphologies or in sea surface temperatures). Given the durability of shells, which confers them "high archaeological visibility," these kinds of reconstructions can be attained even on assemblages from sites with some of the oldest evidence for shellfish exploitation. A case in point is the study by Jerardino and Marean (2010) on shells dating to around 170–90 ka BP from the Middle Stone Age cave site of PP13B (Pinnacle Point, South Africa), which constitute the earliest-known evidence for significant mollusc exploitation by modern humans. The taxonomic composition and representation of the assemblage from PP13B attests that humans at the site ate preferentially molluscs from the nearest shores, which alternated from being rocky, when brown mussel (*Perna perna*) was the dominant taxon, to sandy, when bean clam (*Donax serra*) was more abundant.

Taxonomic representation and quantification data can also be used to reconstruct past climatic shifts, for example, at sites that were close to geographic distributional limits of mollusc species. In the northern hemisphere, mollusc distributions change in response to cooling episodes by shifting southwards and to warming episodes by shifting northward (the reverse being true for the southern hemisphere). In northern Spain, numerous studies have demonstrated that the climatic amelioration that took place in the early Holocene (i.e., the "climatic optimum") was recorded by a change in the species composition of shell middens along the Cantabrian and Asturian coasts (e.g., Bailey and Craighead 2003; Gutiérrez Zugasti 2009). At these sites, the periwinkle *Littorina littorea*, which has a more northerly range (at present from the White Sea in Russia to the north of Spain), was replaced by the toothed topshell *Phorcus lineatus* (previously named *Osilinus lineatus* and *Monodonta lineata*), which has a more southerly range (from the British Isles to Morocco).

Shell Morphometrics

In nature, the shell size of marine molluscs is affected by many physical factors (e.g., temperature, salinity, exposure to wave action, water turbidity) and biological factors (e.g., food availability, predation) that characterise the environment in which they live (Vermeij 1993). Environmental changes can modify these physical and biological features of coastal habitats and, consequently, produce changes in the size, as well as in the availability, of molluscs at shores exploited by humans in the past. The systematic measurement of molluscs from archaeological assemblages has, therefore, the potential to reveal such changes in past environments through morphometric analyses of size (e.g., Bailey and Craighead 2003; Jerardino 1997).

However, given that middens are formed by humans and that for this reason they tend to have relatively low fidelity to their communities of origin, as mentioned above, changes in mean shell size of molluscs within anthropogenic assemblages do not necessarily reflect the occurrence of adverse environmental changes for the molluscan taxa. In fact, humans tend to collect molluscs, either inadvertently (simply because they are more visible) or willingly (e.g., in order to avoid predating all the reproductive members of a population) on the basis of their size, generally harvesting larger specimens before smaller ones (Waselkov 1987). When human exploitation at a shore is intensive and frequent enough, this will eventually result in a decline in the mean sizes of targeted taxa, as shown by studies on the effects of anthropic predation on modern populations of marine molluscs. As a result of these observations, researchers studying marine mollusc assemblages from archaeological sites, when confronted by a decline in shell size paralleled by an increase in the abundance (= harvesting frequency) of a species, hypothesise its overexploitation by humans.

This alone, however, is not sufficient evidence for attributing observed dimensional variations to human predation and, as a result, additional criteria have been proposed by Claassen (1998), who suggested, among other things, that there should also be an attendant decrease in age. This is not always ascertainable, because few molluscs can be aged by counting visible annual growth rings (e.g., Mannino and Thomas 2001). Most studies that have established or hypothesised human predation as the cause of attendant changes in mean shell size (e.g., Erlandson et al. 2008; Faulkner 2009; Jerardino 1997; Mannino and Thomas 2001) have done so by evaluating whether these decreases in size were contemporaneous to and compatible with climatic or environmental changes that might have taken place in the region. This can be done using data from offsite environmental proxies or, ideally, should be done by using both offsite and onsite data from independent sources (Bailey and Craighead 2003). Data from onsite proxies might be obtained from analyses of shell shape, growth and geochemistry, which will be discussed below, on the same molluscs that are the object of the biometric study. In the absence of adequate palaeoenvironmental data, it might be difficult to attribute changes in shell size to natural or anthropogenic impacts, as in the case of a study on the humped conch (*Strombus gibberulus*) from prehistoric shell middens on the Pacific island of Palau (Giovas et al. 2010). This study verified an *increase* in shell size attributable either to changes in human foraging practices, to environmental changes or to anthropogenic impacts. The removal of predators of the humped conch or the enhancement of its habitat by humans are just two of a number of possible explanations for the observed increase. Intensification of shellfish exploitation can, however, also result in increases in mean mollusc size through time, as demonstrated by Thakar (2011) in a study of Pismo clam (*Tivela stultorum*) shells from a midden on Santa Cruz Island (California). This researcher found that human predation depleted clam stocks in the intertidal, which resulted in the survival only of larger/older individuals that live in the subtidal, where they are less accessible and more labor-intensive for humans to acquire. It should, therefore, be concluded that, as suggested by Faulkner (2009), in order to evaluate hypotheses of overexploitation the biology and ecology of the species in question should be well known to the researcher. In fact, some species are more likely to be overexploited than others for intrinsic biological reasons and molluscs living on rocky shore intertidal zones are the most vulnerable to human predation, given the accessibility of this habitat.

The implications of studies of shell size go beyond simply establishing whether humans overexploited molluscs at a shore. In favorable cases, measuring shells from different multi-period middens within geographically confined areas, such as islands, can allow researchers to evaluate the intensity of shellfish exploitation during prolonged periods of time, in turn providing insights even on human population dynamics (Erlandson et al. 2008). Studies of variations in size or age structures can prove the adoption of sustainable exploitation strategies and the management of mollusc fisheries (Cannon and Burchell 2009; Whitaker 2008). Shells from middens can also yield invaluable information for investigating long-term impacts of humans on molluscs and marine ecosystems. The study by Schapira et al. (2009) on queen conch (*Strombus gigas*) from pre-Colombian and modern middens in the Los Roques Archipelago (Venezuela) is a case in point, which demonstrates the usefulness of archaeological data for understanding present-day molluscan ecology and conservation. Biometric analyses on *S. gigas* from 27 sites show that through time there were decreases in the number of juvenile individuals, in overall mean size and in adult mean size, which was taken to indicate that humans are responsible for present low densities in heavily exploited areas and that current conservation legislation is not effective. Following a similar line of biometric research, Rick et al. (2016) have investigated changes in the size of oysters (*Crassostrea virginica*) from middens around Chesapeake Bay in North America, over a time interval between the Terminal Pleistocene and the Modern Age. This investigation suggests that oysters were resilient to Native American harvest pressure, attesting that their fishery strategies were sustainable on a millennial scale and that hand-collecting from fringing reefs allows oyster populations to be maintained, because specimens living in deeper reefs are not impacted.

Shape is another feature of shells that "encodes" environmental data. In intertidal taxa it varies to allow molluscs to avoid desiccation, to cope with predation by crabs, or other predators, and to stay attached to rocky shore substrata in spite of wave action (Vermeij 1993). Neoecological studies have demonstrated that some intertidal gastropods have different shell shapes across shores (e.g., limpets) or between shores (e.g., limpets, dogwhelks) in relation to exposure to wave action. Limpets have been shown to be squatter (i.e., have flatter and wider shells) lower down the shore and more conical further up the intertidal zone on the same rocky shores. Bailey and Craighead (2003) used differences in limpet shapes to evaluate whether the molluscs from the prehistoric site of La Riera (northern Spain) were collected from the upper or lower parts of the intertidal zone and whether collection took place on exposed (squat shells) or sheltered shores (conical shells). Shells of the dogwhelk *Nucella lapillus* recovered from the Mesolithic shell middens of Oronsay (Scotland) were studied biometrically to determine the exposure of the shores and the intensity of wave action during the occupation of the sites (Andrews et al. 1985). The shell shape of the dogwhelks from the Oronsay middens was indicative of calmer seas than at present and, on the basis of knowledge on the past morphology of local shores, shellfish gathering zones were hypothesised. In spite of the potential offered by studies of shell shape from archaeological sites, this kind of research is seldom pursued, possibly because most archaeomalacologists are not willing to collect experimental data on living molluscs, indispensable for these studies.

Sclerochronology and Shell Carbonate Geochemistry

Mollusc shells are high-resolution and temporally aligned archives of past environmental and climatic conditions (Schöne 2008). Environments and climates are, however, not the only variables that affect shell growth and chemistry, because molluscs are complex biological organisms and the secretion of their shells is also influenced by metabolic processes (i.e., by their physiology). No species secretes shell material continuously, as slowing down or checks (i.e. stops) in growth occur on a daily or sub-daily basis (as a consequence of tidal regimes) or episodically when conditions become extenuating, such as during spawning or when animals are pushed to their physiological limits (e.g., yearly when temperature limits are reached). As a result of these adverse conditions, daily, fortnightly, or annual growth checks occur. When visualised in thin section under a microscope these checks can be used to establish the periodicity of growth and the timing of final growth seizure, which correspond to the death of the mollusc and, practically, to its collection. Stops in growth vary greatly between taxa from different habitats (intertidal, subtidal, etc.) and within the same species across its geographical distribution. It is, therefore, necessary to study shell growth in modern counterparts of the species that one intends to use as an environmental indicator, to verify whether it is a suitable taxon, before analysing archaeological specimens. The study of shell growth increments combined with targeted geochemical analyses of these accretionary structures is defined sclerochronology, a topic reviewed in detail by Andrus (2011).

During growth, shells record the chemical composition of seawater, including its oxygen isotope composition (Wefer and Berger 1991). Oxygen isotope ratios ($\delta^{18}O$) in shells of molluscs that live in fully marine conditions (i.e., not affected by freshwater outflows, which produce variations in sea surface salinities) and which secrete carbonates in (or near) isotopic equilibrium with seawater will reflect (and be negatively correlated to) sea surface temperatures. If these conditions are met, and provided that work on living analogues has demonstrated that the species in question lays down enough shell material in each season to be sampled, marine shells can be used to reconstruct not only past sea surface temperatures, but also the seasons of death of molluscs (Shackleton 1973).

In the context of archaeology, the study of shell growth (sclerochronology) and shell carbonate geochemistry (mainly oxygen isotope analysis) have been aimed chiefly at the determination of the season of mollusc collection (Andrus 2011; Thomas 2015b; Twaddle et al. 2016). Data on the timing of the exploitation of marine molluscs are essential in studies of past human subsistence, because they can help to establish the periodicity of resource scheduling, but also of site occupation, having the potential to provide otherwise hard-to-come-by data on human territoriality. Some of the first sclerochronological (e.g., Deith 1983) and isotopic (e.g., Deith 1986) studies in archaeology analysed few modern analogue specimens from single collections. After these initial applications, researchers undertook detailed studies of modern analogues by monitoring shell growth monthly for sclerochronological (e.g., Milner 2001; Quitmyer et al. 1997) and isotopic (e.g., Mannino et al. 2003; Mannino et al. 2007; Mannino et al. 2008; Prendergast et al. 2013) analyses. This contributed to accomplishing more accurate reconstructions of the seasonality of mollusc exploitation at sites in North America and Europe. In the last few years, studies of the seasonality of shellfish exploitation, more often than not based on oxygen isotope analyses (e.g., Burchell et al. 2013; Bosch et al. 2017; Culleton et al. 2009; Stephens et al. 2008), have been applied successfully to an increasing number of species and environmental contexts worldwide. In the case of middens, when large numbers of specimens are analysed for seasonality of mollusc collection and a solid chrono-stratigraphic framework has been established, reconstructions of shell mound accumulation dynamics are possible (Hausmann and Meredith-Williams 2017). This approach has the potential to differentiate shell dumping episodes associated with standard subsistence routines from short-term dumping at feasting events, which would result in very rapidly accumulated midden deposits.The highest possible sclerochronological resolution has been attained through detailed analyses of shell growth to guide the sampling of temporally defined growth increments, improving the estimates of the seasonality of shellfish exploitation and providing us with reliable archives of sea surface temperature and salinity change (e.g., Carré et al. 2005; Colonese et al. 2017; Hallmann et al. 2009). The study by Hallmann et al. (2009) managed to determine the timing of collection of living specimens of the bivalve *Saxidomus gigantea* to the actual day and tide of collection, which implies that the level of accuracy that can now be achieved is far higher than simply seasonal. Another implication of these advances is that oxygen isotope analyses, undertaken with the aid of sclerochronological studies, can provide high-resolution palaeotemperature and palaeoceanographic data (e.g., Carré et al. 2005). Through analyses with similar aims and methodologies on shells of the bivalve *Mesodesma donacium* from Peruvian archaeological middens, Carré et al. (2014) were able to reconstruct the dynamics of the El Niño Southern Oscillation (ENSO) during the past 10,000 years. This has allowed them to discover that ENSO was similar to today in the early Holocene, severely damped around 5–4 ka cal. BP and attaining its modern regime around 4.5–3 ka cal. BP. The study by Carré et al. (2014) suggests that ENSO is sensitive to external forcing, which is important information for researchers of present-day climate and a clear example of the usefulness of palaeoclimatic data generated by analysing archaeological shells.

At the more local scale, sclerochronologically calibrated mollusc species, such as the bivalve *Anomalocardia flexuosa* from southeastern Brazil, can be used to reconstruct changes in past lagoonal ecosystems. This was done in a study by Colonese et al. (2017) who, undertaking oxygen and carbon nitrogen isotope analyses on archaeological specimens from the shell midden (*sambaqui*) of Cabeçuda, were able to demonstrate that the Laguna estuarine system was more marine around 3 ka cal BP and less subject to changes in salinity than now, which has important implications for our understanding of coastal hunter-gatherer adaptations in Brazil during the Holocene.

It should be added that, as reviewed here, marine shells from archaeological sites are used primarily for oxygen isotope analyses, conducted alongside carbon isotope analyses, the data from which are frequently marginally considered or ignored altogether because their major controls are less well understood and their variations not easily interpretable (Leng and Lewis 2016). More work should thus be conducted on such geochemical issue, as well as on ^{14}C dating of marine shell carbonates. As reviewed by Douka (2017), advances in the absolute dating of shells have been achieved by improving sample pretreatments and reservoir effect corrections, but this remains a relatively under-researched, and potentially rewarding, subfield of study. Shells of marine molluscs, however, also contain other elements that can be analysed to reconstruct past environments and behavior both through isotope and trace element analyses, which are constantly being developed (e.g., Prendergast et al. 2017) and beyond the scope of this chapter. A recent new application by Black et al. (2017), however, shows that there are probably still major developments in shell geochemistry ahead of us. In this research, valves of *Crassostrea virginica* from the above-mentioned Chesapeake Bay estuary, and from sites around it (dating to the last 3200 years), were subject to nitrogen isotope ($\delta^{15}N$) analysis. These demonstrated that after ~AD 1800 there was a rapid rise in $\delta^{15}N$ values, indicating an ealier-than-expected anthropic impact caused by pollution in the form of increased sewage and nitrogen-rich fertiliser discharges. Studies such as the one by Black et al. (2017) are demonstrations of the practical usefulness of archaeological shells.

Shells as Ornaments and Tools

Shells have been used as ornaments and tools by humans for a very long time, as mentioned above, and studies of shell beads from archaeological sites have increased noticeably in the last years. This is because shell beads are a category of artefacts that can yield data on the evolution of modern human behavior (e.g., Vanhaeren et al. 2006), as well as on ethnolinguistic diversity of prehistoric human groups (Vanhaeren and d'Errico 2006). The association between bead types and cultural affinity is so strong that Rigaud et al. (2015) used it to evaluate to what extent farming economies from southwestern Asia had an impact on the hunter-gatherers of Europe. This study shows that in central and southern Europe, where agro-pastoralism spread rapidly and through migrational movements, there was a significant discontinuity in bead typology, characterised, for instance, by the inception of the trade of *Spondylus* shells. On the other hand, in northern Europe there was clear continuity in the bead types used, with shells playing a limited role both in the Mesolithic and Neolithic. The study by Rigaud et al. (2015) is an example of how beads, including those produced using mollusc shells, can provide us with additional sources of evidence on contacts between groups belonging to different cultures.

Archaeological shells with holes are usually interpreted as beads or ornaments, often without establishing convincingly the agent that produced the perforation. However, holes in shells can be natural, produced by wave action, or by invertebrate animals (Thomas and Mannino 2001). Shells perforated by the abrasion of wave action can easily be collected on beaches and used as beads or ornaments, as described by Taborin (1993) in a detailed synopsis of shell artefacts from Palaeolithic France. Invertebrate animals that perforate shells of marine molluscs include (Zuschin et al. 2003): boring sponges of the genus *Cliona* (phylum Porifera, class Demospongiae), boring annelid worms of the genus *Polydora* (phylum Annelida, class Polychaeta) and predatory gastropods (e.g., Muricidae, Naticidae). Regular-shaped holes produced by muricid and naticid gastropods can be confused with well-made artificial holes, especially if predated shells were later used by humans as beads, because the friction caused by the suspending medium can obliterate the diagnostic features of predatory holes.

In order to adequately investigate the agent responsible for a perforation, one should compare archaeological perforated specimens with shells of the same taxa from natural death assemblages. Regrettably this is often not done by archaeomalacologists and the studies by Vanhaeren et al. (2006) and Zilhão et al. (2010) represent two notable exceptions. These kinds of investigations are usually decisive in determining whether shells were perforated by humans or not. Sometimes, even these studies might not identify the agent responsible for a hole, although they might show that for some species (e.g., *Nassarius gibbosulus*) the probability of finding a naturally perforated shell is so unlikely that, if practiced, the collection of perforated shells must have been a deliberate, time-consuming, activity (probably more so than just perforating shells!).

Microscopic analyses on experimentally perforated modern shells can also offer insights into whether archaeological specimens were perforated by humans. Experimental studies are also useful to improve our understanding of the work involved in the production of shell ornaments and to identify the tools which might have been used to work shells. D'Errico et al. (2008) perforated shells of the marine gastropod *Afrolittorina africana* with tools (i.e., a lithic point, bone and wooden awls), a small crab claw and a pebble to verify if shells of the same species from the Middle Stone Age site of Sibudu Cave in South Africa were worked by humans. The comparison between the experimental and the archaeological shells, which required the use of a microscope, suggested that the holes in the archaeological specimens are consistent with an anthropogenic origin.

Establishing whether shells were used as tools can be difficult, because many ethnographically attested uses (e.g., as containers for water, or as spoons) do not leave traces. Some uses produce clear wear patterns on shell tools (e.g., adzes, pounders), making it possible to interpret them (Thomas and Mannino 2001). What might be unclear in these cases is why certain shell raw materials were used and not others. Szabó (2008) has pointed out that to understand the working of a raw material it is necessary to know the material itself. Archaeomalacologists studying shell objects should have detailed knowledge of shell structures, as this is the only way of understanding why some taxa and microstructures were not used for the production of artefacts, while others were. Clarifying issues of shell taphonomy and making use of knowledge on shell microstructure are both necessary in order to improve the quality of studies on worked shell. These investigations can also be useful in attempting to establish what taxa may have been used to produce highly worked and artificially shaped shell beads. In a recent study, nevertheless, Demarchi et al. (2014) have successfully developed a biomolecular approach, based on the use of the bulk amino acid composition of the intra-crystalline protein fraction, to refine the taxonomic attribution of anthropically modified shell materials attainable through morphological and micro-structural analyses.

Provenance Studies of Shells

Shell objects are extremely useful to archaeology, because they can provide direct evidence for exchange networks between localities along the coasts of origin and inland sites hundreds of kilometers away (e.g., Fitzgerald et al. 2005). Evidence for trade networks on far larger scales can be proven undisputedly when "exotic" species, originating from seas or oceans in biogeographical provinces different from the one in which the site is located, are found (e.g., Reese 1991).

When it is necessary to provenance shell objects more accurately than attributing them simply to their oceans of origin, geochemical studies of the oxygen isotope composition of their carbonates can provide an answer. The first application of this method dates back to 40 years ago, when Shackleton and Renfrew (1970) used oxygen isotope analyses to establish that shells of *Spondylus gaederopus* recovered from the Neolithic tell site of Goljanio Delschevo, near the coast in Bulgaria, originated from the Aegean Sea and not from the nearby Black Sea. Regrettably, this method has been largely ignored, with few exceptions (e.g., Bajnóczi et al. 2013). A detailed study of this kind has been conducted by Eerkens et al. (2005) to provenance the sources of purple olive snail (*Olivella biplicata*) shell beads found at prehistoric sites in California. This study has the merit of establishing a sound methodology for the determination of shell provenance based not only on oxygen isotopes but also on carbon isotopes, which can be used to increase the accuracy of the estimates of the area of origin.

Humans have frequently used fossil shells from deposits of geological age, and not only sub-fossil shells from contemporary beaches, for the production of body ornaments (e.g., Taborin 1993). In some cases it is possible to distinguish fossil from sub-fossil shells on taxonomic grounds or on the state of preservation. However, this distinction is not always possible, especially in the case of shell ornaments and objects that are heavily worked. Strontium isotope analyses on shell carbonates can be used as a relative dating technique and, hence, to separate fossil from sub-fossil shells, because the former should be considerably older than the latter. Again, after its first successful application by Shackleton and Elderfield (1990), this method has rarely been applied. A rare exception is the study on *Dentalium* shell beads from an Upper Palaeolithic burial of a child at La Madeleine in the Dordogne region (France) that demonstrated that the ornamental shells were collected from the beaches of the Atlantic Ocean, rather than from the nearer Miocene outcrops (Vanhaeren et al. 2004).

5 OTHER INVERTEBRATES

Some invertebrates that have had a significant role in human history are difficult to record archaeologically. These include protozoans such as those of the genus *Plasmodium* that cause malaria and those of the genus *Entamoeba* that cause amoebic dysentery. Even in the most suitable contexts (e.g., the Tyrolean Iceman's colon and instestine), targeted parasitological examination fails to trace remains of protozoa (Aspöck et al. 2000). The occurrence of these parasitic organisms is detectable by means of biomolecular methods (Sallares and Gomzi 2001) or by immunohistochemical analyses on mummified human tissues (Bianucci et al. 2008). King Tutankhamun and some members of his family were diagnosed with *malaria tropica* (the most severe form of malaria) following the detection of ancient DNA of the malarial parasite *Plasmodium falciparum* in their tissues (Hawass et al. 2010). These are the most ancient directly dated mummies for which such diagnosis has been made, although it should be noted that the assumption that this disease caused the death of Tutankhamun remains controversial.

Many invertebrate phyla, which supply environmental data or potentially help in reconstructing complex site formation processes (e.g., foraminifera, ostracods, mites, bryozoans) have been all too often ignored as sources of information. Invertebrates of many other phyla have provided information on human health (e.g., parasitic worms), past human environments (e.g., mites) and human subsistence and activities (e.g., sponges, corals, crustaceans, echinoderms). A brief account of the archaeological use of these taxa is given in the sections that follow.

Parasitic Worms

The phyla Platyhelminthes (flatworms) and Nematoda (roundworms) include numerous species of worms that parasitise the internal tissues of vertebrates. The study of the remains of parasitic worms from archaeological sites is called *archaeoparasitology*, which also includes the parasitic insects mentioned above (i.e., lice, fleas, bed bugs), and is considered a branch of palaeopathology. It is generally practiced by parasitologists, because it requires specialist knowledge on parasite identification and ecology (Reinhard and Araújo 2008), although its ultimate success rests on adequate recovery during excavation. The most resistant anatomical parts of parasitic worms are represented by their eggs, which have tough cases and are laid in their thousands within the host (i.e., the organism that harbors a parasite). These eggs or cysts survive especially well in water-lain or organic-rich archaeological deposits, such as cesspits, latrines, and middens, as well as in coprolites and mummies (Kenward 2009; Reinhard 1990).

Parasitic worms recovered in archaeological contexts (e.g., liver fluke, tapeworm, pinworm, hookworm, giant roundworm, whipworm) cause moderate to severe health risks for the humans and animals that host them and are indicators of overcrowding and poor hygiene conditions (Reinhard 1990; Reinhard and Araújo 2008). Most of these parasites live in different vertebrate hosts and recovery of their eggs from archaeological sediments does not necessarily indicate infestation in humans. In some cases, nematode eggs are actually proxies of the presence of livestock animals such as horse, sheep, goat and pig (Kenward 2009). Circumstanced reconstructions of past human infestations are easily achieved when parasite eggs are recovered from human coprolites or mummified body tissues (Reinhard and Araújo 2008).

Once humans started living in close contact, following the adoption of agriculture and of a sedentary way of life, parasitic infestations increased sharply. Large numbers of whipworm (*Trichuris trichiura*) eggs were recovered, for instance, during the parasitological examination of the Iceman's intestine (Aspöck et al. 2000). This is the oldest evidence for this endoparasite in a human corpse (5320–5060 years calibrated BP) and, although based on available evidence it is not possible to reach a conclusion on the level of infestation, it is proof that the Iceman's standards of hygiene were not impeccable. The lack of other endoparasites and of ectoparasites such as head lice, which were not found either on his body or in his cap, indicates that the Iceman probably had relatively good standards of hygiene and health for a prehistoric individual.

In prehistoric times, the endoparasites that most commonly infected people were zoonotic (i.e., those that are transmitted from animals to humans), while with increasing crowding, roundworms, whipworms, and *Entamoeba* (protozoa that cause dissentry) became dominant (Mitchell 2017). The latter was the case during the Roman period, despite the invention of latrines with flushing systems and personal hygiene practices. An alternative explanation to inadequate sanitary conditions could be that roundworm and whipworm infestations were common because human faeces were spread on fields as crop fertiliser, not having composted. Another widespread endoparasitic infestation typical of Roman times was that of the fish tapeworm (*Diphyllobothrium latum*), which was likely a consequence of eating uncooked fish sauce (*garum*), fermented in the sun and traded throughout the empire (Mitchell 2017).

During historic periods, human populations living in crowded towns and cities, with inadequate sanitation were subject to high levels of parasitism, as attested by the recovery of the eggs of giant roundworm (*Ascaris lumbricoides*), whipworm (*Trichuris trichiura*) and tapeworms (e.g., *Taenia solium*, *Taenia saginata*, *Diphyllobothrium latum*) at numerous sites worldwide (e.g., Leles et al. 2010; Mitchell et al. 2013; Yeh et al. 2014). Although eggs of these intestinal worms are probably the most commonly recovered parasite remains, careful screening of latrine and midden deposits can favour the recovery of a wide range of parasitic taxa that inform us on diseases that afflicted people in the past, as well as on the foods that may have ingenerated such health problems. This is the case, for instance, of a medieval latrine from Riga (Latvia) that contained thousands of eggs of the fish tapeworm (*Diphyllobothrium latum*), indicating not only that the inhabitants of the town were eating large amounts of uncooked fish, but also that they probably suffered from anemia (Yeh et al. 2014). Careful excavation and targeted sampling of burial contexts also yields archaeologically useful parasite remains, as in the case of King Richard III (Mitchell et al. 2013). Soil samples taken from his sacrum, where the intestines would have been, yielded roundworm (*A. lumbricoides*) eggs, suggesting either that even kings in medieval times did not wash thoroughly or, as discussed above for the Romans, that faeces were used as crop fertilisers. The lack of other endoparasites (e.g., beef, pork, and fish tapeworms) may indicate that Richard III consumed well-cooked meat.

Archaeological records of parasitic worms can also provide data on human migrations, as in the case of a study on hookworms (*Ancylostoma duodenale* and *Necator americanus*) in the Americas (Montenegro et al. 2006). By relating data on past climates with the biological requirements of hookworm, these researchers demonstrated that it is unlikely for the so-called Clovis people (i.e., the first immigrants into the Americas) to have introduced this parasite to the continent and to have been the only pre-Columbian immigrants. Archaeological evidence of past parasitic infestation in humans is already being used in attempts to distinguish so-called "heirloom parasites," which coevolved with our ancestors in Africa from so-called "souvenir parasites," which are those that humans picked up in the course of their global expansion (Mitchell 2013). In the near future, the study of parasite remains from archaeological contexts may help our understanding of the effects of parasitism on human evolution and, as a result, even improve our knowledge of the clinical epidemiology of parasites.

Mites

Arachnids belonging to the sub-class Acarina, commonly known as mites (Acari), represent an underutilised source of archaeological data (Baker 2009; Kenward 2009). Mites of the orders Oribatida and Mesostigmata are frequently preserved whole, and in high numbers, in natural and anthropic deposits due to their heavily sclerotised exoskeletons. Acari are excellent environmental indicators because they have adapted specifically to live in most habitats and their distributions have been largely unaffected by humans (Baker 2009). Mites can be used to reconstruct site formation processes, to establish if dung or plant refuse were introduced into deposits and to determine if the deposits at a site had been affected by marine incursions. When Acari that live in dung are recovered, their careful identification can verify whether the excreta were human or produced by livestock, and in the latter case, mites can help in determining the animal species of origin. In fact, a zoological study on living "dung mites" (order Gamasida) has shown that most predatory Acari only live in excrement of a single vertebrate species (Schelvis 1992).

Miscellaneous Aquatic Invertebrates (Sponges, Corals, Crustaceans, Echinoderms)

The group of phyla treated in this section includes aquatic invertebrates that mainly live in marine environments. Sponges (phylum Porifera) have low archaeological visibility and have been used by humans as cleaning tools, pottery fillers, and for other utilitarian purposes (Thomas and Mannino 2001). Corals (phylum Cnidaria) are often recovered from archaeological sites. They were used mainly for decorative purposes and can provide evidence of past trade networks (Skeates 1993).

Crustaceans (phylum Crustacea) are mainly represented by aquatic taxa of arthropods, most of which were introduced to archaeological sites by humans as food items, although rarely in high numbers. Archaeological evidence for the consumption of barnacles has been obtained from many sites and in some cases these animals constituted regularly exploited resources (Álvarez-Fernández et al. 2010; Moss and Erlandson 2010). The presence of the whale barnacle *Coronula diadema* at the Middle Stone Age site PP13B (Pinnacle Point, South Africa) has been taken as evidence for the exploitation by humans of beached humpback whales upon which this invertebrate lives (Marean et al. 2007). Lobsters and crabs are frequently recovered from archaeological deposits and were probably the most important crustacean foods (e.g., Jerardino and Navarro 2002; Losey et al. 2004).

Most echinoderms (phylum Echinodermata) are archaeologically invisible, but sea urchin spines are frequently recovered at coastal sites. Estimating MNIs on the basis of spines is practically impossible, and even when other body parts are recovered, painstakingly identified and quantified, as in the case of the Roman site at Baie de Lannion in Brittany (Campbell 2008), it is unlikely that their study will show that sea urchins were more than delicacies, as they are considered nowadays.

6 CONCLUDING REMARKS

The main reason for entitling this chapter "Invertebrate zooarchaeology" is that all the fields of study that this label embraces require similar methodological developments. They all need more studies of taphonomy, modern ecology, and geochemistry, requirements that can only be met if "invertebrate zooarchaeologists" adopt a more experimental approach to their research, which might entail regularly collaborating with scientists in other fields. For instance, studies on modern ecology, specifically targeted to solve research questions arising from zooarchaeological research, are necessary in all the fields described in this chapter (and possibly should be at the top of the research agenda, given the incessant reduction in "natural environments" that characterises the Anthropocene). As this cannot be done by "invertebrate zooarchaeologists" alone, collaborations should be set up with biologists and ecologists, who in turn would benefit by learning more about the historical ecology of the species they study (e.g., Schapira et al. 2009). In fact, data obtained from archaeological invertebrates hold great potential for studying past human impacts on environments and for establishing what natural ecosystems might have looked like before humans started impacting them (e.g., Black et al. 2017; Rick et al. 2016).

In conclusion, making sure that invertebrate remains are adequately recovered during excavation and adopting a more holistic research approach will enable the different subfields of archaeological science grouped here under the label of "invertebrate zooarchaeology" to be useful in addressing some of the grand challenges for archaeology (Kintigh et al. 2014). Invertebrates can, as reviewed above, allow us to acquire data relevant to these challenges, which include the reconstruction of the emergence of cognitive and cultural complexity, the resilience of past societies, the mobility of people in the past and, especially, the interaction between humans and environments.

REFERENCES

Adams, M. E. and Jenkins, D. L. 2017. An early Holocene record of *Cimex* (Hemiptera: Cimicidae) from western North America. *Journal of Medical Entomology* 54:934–944.

Allen, M. J. (ed.) 2017a. *Molluscs in Archaeology: Methods, Approaches and Applications*. Oxford: Oxbow Books.

Allen, M. J. 2017b. The geoarchaeology of context: Sampling for land snails (on archaeological sites and colluvium). In: Allen, M. J. (ed.) *Molluscs in Archaeology: Methods, Approaches and Applications*, pp. 30–47.Oxford: Oxbow Books.

Álvarez-Fernández, E., Ontañón-Peredo, R., and Molares-Vila, J. 2010. Archaeological data on the exploitation of the goose barnacle *Pollicipes pollicipes* (Gmelin, 1790) in Europe. *Journal of Archaeological Science* 37:402–408.

Andersen, S. H. 2000. 'Køkkenmøddinger' (shell middens) in Denmark: A survey. *Proceedings of the Prehistoric Society* 66:361–384.

Andrews, M. V., Gilbertson, D. D., and Mellars, P. A. 1985. Biometric studies of morphological variation in the intertidal gastropod *Nucella lapillus* (L): Environmental and palaeoeconomic significance. *Journal of Biogeography* 12:71–87.

Andrus, C. F. T. 2011. Shell midden sclerochronology. *Quaternary Science Reviews* 30:2892–2905.

Arriaza, B., Orellana, N. C., Barbosa, H. S., Menna-Barreto, R. F. S., Araújo, A., and Standen, V. 2012. Severe head lice infestation in an Andean mummy of Arica, Chile. *Journal of Parasitology* 98:433–436.

Aspöck, H., Auer, H., Picher, O., and Platzer, W. 2000. Parasitological examination of the Iceman. In: Bortenschlager, S. and Oeggl, K. (eds.) *The Iceman and his Natural Environment*, pp. 127–136. Vienna: Springer Verlag.

Atkinson, T. C., Briffa, K. R., Coope, G. R., Joachim, M., and Perry, D. W. 1986. Climatic calibration of coleopteran data. In: Berglund, B. (ed.) *Handbook of Holocene Palaeoecology and Palaeohydrology*, pp. 851–858. New York: Wiley.

Bailey, G. 1993. Shell mounds in 1972 and 1992: Reflections on recent controversies at Ballina and Weipa. *Australian Archaeology* 37:2–18.

Bailey, G. N. and Craighead, A. S. 2003. Late Pleistocene and Holocene coastal palaeoeconomies: A reconsideration of the molluscan evidence from Northern Spain. *Geoarchaeology* 18: 175–204.

Bajnóczi, B., Schöll-Barna, G., Kalicz, N., Siklósi, Z., Hourmouziadis, G. H., Ifantidis, F., Kyparissi-Apostolika, A., Pappa, M., Veropoulidou, R., and Ziota, C. 2013. Tracing the source of Late Neolithic *Spondylus* shell ornaments by stable isotope geochemistry and cathodoluminescence microscopy. *Journal of Archaeological Science* 40:874–882.

Baker, A. S. 2009. Acari in archaeology. *Experimental and Applied Acarology* 49:147–160.

Barnes, R. S. K., Calow, P., Olive, P. J. W., Golding, D. W., and Spicer, J. I. 2001. *The Invertebrates: A Synthesis*, 3rd ed. Oxford: Blackwell Science.

Barrett, J., Hall, A., Johnstone, C., Kenward, H., O'Connor, T., and Ashby, S. 2007. Interpreting the plant and animal remains from Viking-age Kaupang. In: Skre, D. (ed.) *Kaupang in Skiringssal*, pp. 283–310. Aarhus: Aarhus University Press and The Kaupang Excavation Project, University of Oslo.

Bar-Yosef Mayer, D. E. (ed.) 2005. *Archaeomalacology: Molluscs in Former Environments of Human Behaviour*. Oxford: Oxbow Books.

Bianucci, R., Mattutino, G., Lallo, R., Charlier, P., Jouin-Spriet, H., Peluso, A., Higham, T., Torre, C., and Rabino Massa, E. 2008. Immunological evidence of *Plasmodium falciparum* infection in an Egyptian child mummy from the Early Dynastic Period. *Journal of Archaeological Science* 35:1880–1885.

Black, H. D., Andrus, C. F. T., Lambert, W. J., Rick, T. C., and Gillikin, D. P. 2017. δ^{15}N values in *Crassostrea virginica* shells provides early direct evidence for nitrogen loading to Chesapeake Bay. *Scientific Reports* 7:44241.

Bonizzoni, L., Bruni, S., Girod, A., and Guglielmi, V. 2009. Archaeometric study of shells of Helicidae from the Edera cave (northeastern Italy). *Archaeometry* 51:151–173.

Bonomo, M. and Aguirre, M. L. 2009. Holocene molluscs from archaeological sites of the Pampean region of Argentina: Approaches to past human uses. *Geoarchaeology* 24:59–85.

Bosch, M. D., Mannino, M. A., Prendergast, A. L., Wesselingh, F. P., O'Connell, T. C., and Hublin, J.-J. 2017. Year-round shellfish exploitation in the Levant and implications for Upper Palaeolithic hunter-gatherer subsistence. *Journal of Archaeological Science: Reports.*

Bosch, M. D., Wesselingh, F. P., and Mannino, M. A. 2015. The Ksâr 'Akil (Lebanon) mollusc assemblage: Zooarchaeological and taphonomic investigations on Upper Palaeolithic shells. *Quaternary International* 390:85–101.

Buckland, P. C., Panagiotakopulu, E., and Sveinbjarnardóttir, G. 2009. A failed invader in the North Atlantic, the case of *Aglenus brunneus* Gyll. (Col., Colydiidae), a blind flightless beetle from Iceland. *Biological Invasions* 11:1239–1245.

Burchell, M., Hallmann, N., Martindale, A., Cannon, A., and Schöne, B. R. 2013. Seasonality and intensity of shellfish harvesting on the north coast of British Columbia. *Journal of Island and Coastal Archaeology* 8:152–169.

Campbell, G. 2008. Sorry, wrong phylum: A neophyte archaeomalacologist's experiences in analyzing a European Atlantic sea urchin assemblage. *Archaeofauna* 17:77–90.

Campbell, G. 2017. The collection, processing and curation of archaeological marine shells. In: Allen, M.J. (ed.) *Molluscs in Archaeology: Methods, Approaches and Applications*, pp. 273–288. Oxford: Oxbow Books.

Cannon, A. and Burchell, M. 2009. Clam growth-stage profiles as a measure of harvest intensity and resource management on the central coast of British Columbia. *Journal of Archaeological Science* 36:1050–1060.

Carré, M., Bentaleb, I., Blamart, D., Ogle, N., Cardenas, F., Zevallos, S., Kalin, R.M., Ortlieb, L., and Fontugne, M. 2005. Stable isotopes and sclerochronology of the bivalve *Mesodesma donacium*: Potential application to Peruvian paleoceanographic reconstructions. *Palaeogeography, Palaeoclimatology, Palaeoecology* 228:4–25.

Carré, M., Sachs, J. P., Purca, S., Schauer, A. J., Braconnot, P., Falcón, R. A., Julien, M., and Lavallée, D. 2014. Holocene history of ENSO variance and asymmetry in the eastern tropical Pacific. *Science* 345: 1045–1048.

Carrott, J. and Kenward, H. 2001. Species associations among insect remains from urban archaeological deposits and their significance in reconstructing the past human environment. *Journal of Archaeological Science* 28:887–905.

Carter, S. P. 1990. The stratification and taphonomy of shells in calcareous soils: Implications for land snail analysis in archaeology. *Journal of Archaeological Science* 17:495–507.

Claassen, C. 1998. *Shells*. Cambridge: Cambridge University Press.

Colonese, A. C. 2017. Stable isotope ecology of terrestrial gastropod shells. In: Allen, M. J. (ed.) *Molluscs in Archaeology: Methods, Approaches and Applications*, pp. 400–413. Oxford: Oxbow Books.

Colonese, A. C., Mannino, M. A., Bar-Yosef Mayer, D. E., Fa, D. A., Finlayson, J. C., Lubell, D., and Stiner, M. C. 2011. Marine mollusc exploitation in Mediterranean prehistory: An overview. *Quaternary International* 239:86–103.

Colonese, A. C., Netto, S. A., Francisco, A. S., DeBlasis, P., Villagran, X. S., de Almeida Rocha Ponzoni, R., Hancock, Y., Hausmann, N., Sunderlick Eloy de Farias, D., Prendergast, A., Schöne, B., William da Cruz, F., and Fonseca Giannini, P. C. 2017. Shell sclerochronology and stable isotopes of the bivalve *Anomalocardia flexuosa* (Linnaues, 1767) from southern Brazil: Implications for environmental and archaeological studies. *Palaeogeography, Palaeoclimatology, Palaeoecology* 484:7–21.

Colonese, A. C., Zanchetta, G., Fallick, A. E., Martini, F., Manganelli, G., and Drysdale, R. N. 2009. Stable isotope composition of *Helix ligata* (Müller, 1774) from Late Pleistocene-Holocene archaeological record from Grotta della Serratura (Southern Italy): Palaeoclimatic implications. *Global and Planetary Change* 71:249–257.

Coope, G. R. and Kenward, H. K. 2007. Evidence from coleopteran assemblages for a short but intense cold interlude during the latter part of the MIS11 Interglacial from Quinton, West Midlands, UK. *Quaternary Science Reviews* 26:3276–3285.

Crabtree, P. J., Reilly, E., Wouters, B., Devos, Y., Bellens, T., and Schryvers, A. 2017. Environmental evidence from early urban Antwerp: New data from archaeology, micromorphology, macrofauna and insect remains. *Quaternary International* 460:108–123.

Culleton, B. J., Kennett, D. J., and Jones, T. L. 2009. Oxygen isotope seasonality in a temperate estuarine shell midden: A case study from CA-ALA-17 on the San Francisco Bay, California. *Journal of Archaeological Science* 36:1354–1363.

Davies, P. 2008. *Snails: Archaeology and Landscape Change*. Oxford: Oxbow Books.

Davis, L. G. and Muehlenbachs, K. 2001. A Late Pleistocene to Holocene record of precipitation reflected in *Margaritifera falcata* shell $\delta^{18}O$ from three archaeological sites in the Lower Salmon River Canyon, Idaho. *Journal of Archaeological Science* 28:291–303.

Deith, M. R. 1983. Molluscan calendars: The use of growth-line analysis to establish seasonality of shellfish collection at the Mesolithic site of Morton, Fife. *Journal of Archaeological Science* 10:423–440.

Deith, M. R. 1986. Subsistence strategies at a Mesolithic camp site: Evidence from stable isotope analyses of shells. *Journal of Archaeological Science* 13:61–78.

Demarchi, B., O'Connor, S., de Lima Ponzoni, A., de Almeida Rocha Ponzoni, R., Sheridan, A., Penkman, K., Hancock, Y., and Wilson, J. 2014. An integrated approach to the taxonomic identification of prehistoric shell ornaments. *PloS One* 9(6):e99839.

d'Errico, F., Vanhaeren, M., and Wadley, L. 2008. Possible shell beads from the Middle Stone Age layers of Sibudu Cave, South Africa. *Journal of Archaeological Science* 35:2675–2685.

Douka, K. 2017. Radiocarbon dating of marine and terrestrial shell. In: Allen, M. J. (ed.) *Molluscs in Archaeology: Methods, Approaches and Applications*, pp. 381–399. Oxford: Oxbow Books.

Dupont, C. 2006. *La malacofaune de sites mésolithiques et néolithiques de la façade atlantique: contribution à l'économie et à l'identité culturelle des groupes concernés. British Archaeological Reports S1571*. Oxford: Archaeopress.

Eerkens, J. W., Herbert, G. S., Rosenthal, J. S., and Spero, H. J. 2005. Provenance analysis of *Olivella biplicata* shell beads from the California and Oregon Coast by stable isotope fingerprinting. *Journal of Archaeological Science* 32:1501–1514.

Elias, S. A. 1994. *Quaternary Insects and their Environments*. Washington D.C.: Smithsonian Institution Press.

Elias, S. A., 2010. *Advances in Quaternary Entomology*. Developments in Quaternary Sciences 12. Amsterdam: Elsevier.

Elias, S. A., Webster, L., and Amer, M. 2009. A beetle's eye view of London from the Mesolithic to Late Bronze Age. *Geological Journal* 44:537–567.

Erlandson, J. M. 2013. Shell middens and other anthropogenic soils as global stratigraphic signatures of the Anthropocene. *Anthropocene* 4:24–32.

Erlandson, J. M. and Moss, M. L. 2001. Shellfish feeders, carrion eaters, and the archaeology of aquatic adaptations. *American Antiquity* 66:413–432.

Erlandson, J. M., Rick, T. C., Braje, T. J., Steinberg, A., and Vellanoweth, R. L. 2008. Human impacts on ancient shellfish: A 10,000 year record from San Miguel Island, California. *Journal of Archaeological Science* 35:2144–2152.

Evans, J. G. 1972. *Land Snails in Archaeology*. London: Seminar Press.

Faulkner, P. 2009. Focused, intense and long-term: Evidence for granular ark (*Anadara granosa*) exploitation from late Holocene shell mounds of Blue Mud Bay, northern Australia. *Journal of Archaeological Science* 36:821–834.

Fernández-López de Pablo, J., Badal, E., Ferrer García, C., Martínez-Ortí, A., and Sanchis Serra, A. 2014. Land snails as a diet diversification proxy during the early Upper Palaeolithic in Europe. *PLoS One* 9(8):e104898.

Fitzgerald, R. T., Jones, T. L., and Schroth, A. 2005. Ancient long-distance trade in Western North America: New AMS radiocarbon dates from Southern California. *Journal of Archaeological Science* 32:423–434.

Forbes, V., Dugmore, A. J., and Ólafsson, E. 2016. The life and death of barn beetles: Faunas from manure and stored hay inside farm buildings in northern Iceland. *Ecological Entomology* 41:480–499.

Giovas, C. M., Fitzpatrick, S. M., Clark, M., and Abed, M. 2010. Evidence for size increase in an exploited mollusc: Humped conch (*Strombus gibberulus*) at Chelechol ra Orrak, Palau from ca. 3000–0 BP. *Journal of Archaeological Science* 37:2788–2798.

Goodfriend, G. A. 1992. The use of land snail shells in paleoenvironmental reconstruction. *Quaternary Science Reviews* 11:665–685.

Gutiérrez Zugasti, F. I. 2009. *La explotación de moluscos y otros recursos litorales en la región cantábrica durante el Pleistoceno final y el Holoceno inicial.* Santander: Ediciones de la Universidad de Cantabria.

Hallmann, N., Burchell, M., Schöne, B. R., Irvine, G. V., and Maxwell, D. 2009. High-resolution sclerochronological analysis of the bivalve mollusk *Saxidomus gigantea* from Alaska and British Columbia: Techniques for revealing environmental archives and archaeological seasonality. *Journal of Archaeological Science* 36:2353–2364.

Hardy, K., Camara, A., Piqué, R., Dioh, E., Guèye, M., Diadhiou, H. D., Faye, M., and Carré, M. 2016. Shellfishing and shell midden construction in the Saloum Delta, Senegal. *Journal of Anthropological Archaeology* 41:19–32.

Hausmann, N. and Meredith-Williams, M. 2017. Exploring accumulation rates of shell deposits through seasonality data. *Journal of Archaeological Method and Theory* 24:776–795.

Hawass, Z., Gad, Y. Z., Ismail, S., Khairat, R., Fathalla, D., Hasan, N., Ahmed, A., Elleithy, H., Ball, M., Gaballah, F., Wasef, S., Fateen, M., Amer, H., Gostner, P., Selim, A., Zink, A., and Pusch, C. M. 2010. Ancestry and pathology in King Tutankhamun's family. *Journal of the American Medical Association* 303:8–647.

Hunt, C. O. and Hill, E. A. 2017. Caves and molluscs. In: Allen, M. J. (ed.) *Molluscs in Archaeology: Methods, Approaches and Applications*, pp. 100–110. Oxford: Oxbow Books.

Jerardino, A. 1997. Changes in shellfish species composition and mean shell size from a Late-Holocene record of the west coast of Southern Africa. *Journal of Archaeological Science* 24:1031–1044.

Jerardino, A. and Marean, C. W. 2010. Shellfish gathering, marine paleoecology and modern human behavior: Perspectives from cave PP13B, Pinnacle Point, South Africa. *Journal of Human Evolution* 59:412–424.

Jerardino, A. and Navarro, R. 2002. Cape rock lobster (*Jasus lalandii*) remains from South African west coast shell middens: Preservational factors and possible bias. *Journal of Archaeological Science* 29:993–999.

Joordens, J. C. A, d'Errico, F., Wesselingh, F. P., Munro, S., de Vos, J., Wallinga, J., Ankjærgaard, C., Reimann, T., Wijbrans, J. R., Kuiper, K. F., Mücher, H. J., Coqueugniot, H., Prié, V., Joosten, I., van Os, B., Schulp, A. S., Panuel, M., van der Haas, V., Lustenhouwer, W., Reijmer, J. J. G., and Roebroeks, W. 2015. *Homo erectus* at Trinil on Java used shells for tool production and engraving. *Nature* 518:228–231.

Kenward, H. 2001. Pubic lice in Roman and Medieval Britain. *Trends in Parasitology* 17:167–168.

Kenward, H. 2004. Do insect remains from historic-period archaeological occupation sites track climate change in Northern England? *Environmental Archaeology* 9:47–59.

Kenward, H., 2009. *Invertebrates in Archaeology in the North of England. Environmental Studies Report. Northern Regional Review of Environmental Archaeology.* Research Department Report Series no. 12-2009. London: English Heritage.

Kenward, H. and Hall, A. R. 1995. *Biological Evidence from 16–22 Coppergate*. Archaeology of York Fascicule 14/7. York: York Archaeological Trust.

Kenward, H. and Tipper, J. 2008. Insect invaders of reconstructed Anglo-Saxon houses at West Stow, Suffolk, England. *Environmental Archaeology* 13:51–57.

King, G. A. 2012. Isotopes as palaeoeconomic indicators: New applications in archaeoentomology. *Journal of Archaeological Science* 39:511–520.

King, G. A., Gilbert, M. T. P., Willerslev, E., Collins, M. J., and Kenward, H. 2009. Recovery of DNA from archaeological insect remains: First results, problems and potential. *Journal of Archaeological Science* 36:1179–1183.

King, G. A., Kenward, H., Schmidt, E., and Smith, D. 2014. Six-legged hitchhikers: An archaeobiogeographical account of the early dispersal of grain beetles. *Journal of the North Atlantic* 23:1–18.

Kintigh, K. W., Altschul, J. H., Beaudry, M. C., Drennan, R. D., Kinzig, A. P., Kohler, T. A., Limp, W. F., Maschner, H. D. G., Michener, W. K., Pauketat, T. R., Peregrine, P., Sabloff, J. A., Wilkinson, T. J., Wright, H. T., and Zeder, M.A. 2014. Grand challenges for archaeology. *Proceedings of the National Academy of Sciences of the USA* 111:879–880.

Leles, D., Reinhard, K. J., Fugassa, M., Ferreira, L. F., Iñiguez, A. M., and Araújo, A. 2010. A parasitological paradox: Why is ascarid infection so rare in the prehistoric America? *Journal of Archaeological Science* 37:1510–1520.

Leng, M. J. and Lewis, J. P. 2016. Oxygen isotopes in molluscan shell: Applications in environmental archaeology. *Environmental Archaeology* 21:295–306.

Losey, R. J., Yamada, S. B., and Largaespada, L. 2004. Late-Holocene Dungeness crab (*Cancer magister*) harvest at an Oregon coast estuary. *Journal of Archaeological Science* 31:1603–1612.

Lubell, D. 2004. Are land snails a signature for the Mesolithic-Neolithic transition? *Documenta Praehistorica* 31:1–24.

Mannino, M. A., Spiro, B. F., and Thomas, K. D. 2003. Sampling shells for seasonality: oxygen isotope analysis on shell carbonates of the inter-tidal gastropod *Monodonta lineata* (da Costa) from populations across its modern range and from a Mesolithic site in southern Britain. *Journal of Archaeological Science* 30:667–679.

Mannino, M. A. and Thomas, K. D. 2001. Intensive Mesolithic exploitation of coastal resources? Evidence from a shell deposit on the Isle of Portland (Southern England) for the impact of human foraging on populations of inter-tidal rocky shore molluscs. *Journal of Archaeological Science* 28:1101–1114.

Mannino, M. A., Thomas, K. D., Leng, M. J., and Sloane, H. J. 2008. Shell growth and oxygen isotopes in the topshell *Osilinus turbinatus* (von Born): Resolving past inshore sea surface temperatures. *Geo-Marine Letters* 28:309–325.

Mannino, M. A., Thomas, K. D., Leng, M. J., Piperno, M., Tusa, S., and Tagliacozzo, A. 2007. Marine resources in the Mesolithic and Neolithic at the Grotta dell'Uzzo (Sicily): Evidence from isotope analyses of marine shells. *Archaeometry* 49:117–133.

Marean, C. W., Bar-Matthews, M., Bernatchez, J., Fisher, E., Goldberg, P., Herries, A. I. R., Jacobs, Z., Jerardino, A., Karkanas, P., Minichillo, T., Nilssen, P. J., Thompson, E., Watts, I., and Williams, H. M. 2007. Early human use of marine resources and pigment in South Africa during the Middle Pleistocene. *Nature* 449:905–908.

Meehan, B. 1982. *Shell Bed to Shell Midden*. Canberra: Australian Institute of Aboriginal Studies.

Milner, N. 2001. At the cutting edge: Using thin sectioning to determine season of death of the European oyster, *Ostrea edulis*. *Journal of Archaeological Science* 28:861–873.

Mitchell, P. D. 2013. The origins of human parasites: Exploring the evidence for endoparasitism throughout human evolution. *International Journal of Palaeopathology* 3:1–198.

Mitchell, P. D. 2017. Human parasites in the Roman World: Health consequences of conquering an empire. *Parasitology* 144:48–58.

Mitchell, P. D., Yeh, H.-Y., Appleby, J., and Buckley, R. 2013. The intestinal parasites of King Richard III. *Lancet* 382:888.

Montenegro, A., Araujo, A., Eby, M., Ferreira, L. F., Hetherington, R., and Weaver, A. J. 2006. Parasites, paleoclimate, and the peopling of the Americas. *Current Anthropology* 47:193–200.

Moss, M. L. and Erlandson, J. M. 2010. Diversity in North Pacific shellfish assemblages: The barnacles of Kit'n'Kaboodle Cave, Alaska. *Journal of Archaeological Science* 37:3359–3369.

Nystrom, K. C., Goff, A., and Lee Goff, M. 2005. Mortuary behavior reconstruction through palaeoentomology: A case study from Chachapoya, Perú. *International Journal of Osteoarchaeology* 15:175–185.

Panagiotakopulu, E. 2001. New records for ancient pests: Archaeoentomology in Egypt. *Journal of Archaeological Science* 28:1235–1246.

Panagiotakopulu, E. and Buckland, P. C. 2017. A thousand bites – Insect introductions and late Holocene environments. *Quaternary Science Reviews* 156:23–35.

Panagiotakopulu, E., Skidmore, P., and Buckland, P. 2007. Fossil insect evidence for the end of the Western Settlement in Norse Greenland. *Naturwissenschaften* 94:300–306.

Penkman, K. E. H., Preece, R. C., Bridgland, D. R., Keen, D. H., Meijer, T., Parfitt, S. A., White, T. S., and Collins, M. J. 2013. An aminostratigraphy for the British Quaternary based on *Bithynia* opercula. *Quaternary Science Reviews* 61:111–134.

Plarre, R. 2010. An attempt to reconstruct the natural and cultural history of the granary weevil, *Sitophilus ggranaries* (Coleoptera: Curculionidae). *European Journal of Entomology* 107:1–11.

Preece, R. C. and Bridgland, D. R. 1999. Holywell Coombe, Folkestone: A 13,000 year history of an English chalkland valley. *Quaternary Science Reviews* 18:1075–1125.

Prendergast, A. L., Azzopardi, M., O'Connell, T. C., Hunt, C., Barker, G., and Stevens, R. E. 2013. Oxygen isotopes from *Phorcus (Osilinus) turbinatus* shells as a proxy for sea surface temperature in the central Mediterranean. *Chemical Geology* 345:77–86.

Prendergast, A. L., Stevens, R. E., O'Connell, T. C., Hill, E. A., Hunt, C. O., and Barker, G. W. 2016. A late Pleistocene *refugium* in Mediterranean North Africa? Palaeoenvironmental reconstruction from stable isotope analyses of land snail shells (Haua Fteah, Libya). *Quaternary Science Reviews* 139:94–109.

Prendergast, A. L., Versteegh, E. A. A., and Schöne, B.R. 2017. New research on the development of high-resolution palaeoenvironmental proxies from geochemical properties of biogenic carbonates. *Palaeogeography, Palaeoclimatology, Palaeoecology* 484:1–6.

Price, P. W. 1997. *Insect Ecology*. New York: Wiley.

Reese, D. S. 1991. The trade of Indo-Pacific shells into the Mediterranean basin and Europe. *Oxford Journal of Archaeology* 10:159–196.

Reilly, E. 2012. Fair and foul: analysis of sub-fossil insect remains from Troitsky XI-XIII, Novgorod (1996–2002). In: Brisbane, M. A., Makarov, N.A., and Nosov, E. N. (eds.) *The Archaeology of Medieval Novgorod in Context. Studies in Centre/Periphery Relations*, pp. 265–282. Oxford: Oxbow Books.

Reinhard, K. J. 1990. Archaeoparasitology in North America. *American Journal of Physical Anthropology* 82:145–163.

Reinhard, K. J. and Araújo, A. 2008. Archaeoparasitology. In: Pearsall, D. M. (ed.) *Encyclopedia of Archaeology*, pp. 494–501. New York: Elsevier.

Rick, T. C., Reeder-Myers, L. A., Hofman, C. A., Breitburg, D., Lockwood, R., Henkes, G., Kellogg, L., Lowery, D., Luckenbach, M. W., Mann, R., Ogburn, M. B., Southworth, M., Wah, J., Wesson, J., and Hines, A. H. 2016. Millennial-scale sustainability of the Chesapeake Bay Native American oyster fishery. *Proceedings of the National Academy of Sciences of the USA* 113:6568–6573.

Rigaud, S., d'Errico, F., and Vanhaeren, M. 2015. Ornaments reveal resistance of North European cultures to the spread of farming. *PLoS One* 10(4):e0121166.

Robinson, M. 2001. Insects as Palaeoenvironmental Indicators. In: Brothwell, D.R. and Pollard, A. M. (eds.) *Handbook of Archaeological Sciences*, pp. 121–133. Chichester: John Wiley and Sons, Ltd.

Rosendahl, D., Ulm, S., and Weisler, M. I. 2007. Using foraminifera to distinguish between natural and cultural shell deposits in coastal eastern Australia. *Journal of Archaeological Science* 34:1584–1593.

Sallares, R. and Gomzi, S. 2001. Biomolecular archaeology of malaria. *Ancient Biomolecules* 3:195–213.

Schapira, D., Montaño, I. A., Antczak, A., and Posada, J. M. 2009. Using shell middens to assess effects of fishing on queen conch (*Strombus gigas*) populations in Los Roques Archipelago National Park, Venezuela. *Marine Biology* 156:787–795.

Schelvis, J. 1992. The identification of archaeological dung deposits on the basis of remains of predatory Mites (Acari; Gamasida). *Journal of Archaeological Science* 19: 677–682.

Schimmelmann, A., DeNiro, M. J., Poulicek, M., Voss-Foucart, M-.F., Goffinet, G., and Jeuniaux, C. 1986. Stable isotopic composition of chitin from arthropods recovered in archaeological contexts as palaeoenvironmental indicators. *Journal of Archaeological Science* 13:553–566.

Schöne, B. R. 2008. The curse of physiology – challenges and opportunities in the interpretation of geochemical data from mollusk shells. *Geo-Marine Letters* 38:269–285.

Shackleton, J. and Elderfield, H. 1990. Strontium isotope dating of the source of Neolithic European *Spondylus* shell artefacts. *Antiquity* 64:312–315.

Shackleton, N. J. 1973. Oxygen isotope analysis as a means of determining season of occupation of prehistoric midden sites. *Archaeometry* 15:133–141.

Shackleton, N. and Renfrew, C. 1970. Neolithic trade routes re-aligned by oxygen isotope analyses. *Nature* 228:1062–1065.

Skeates, R. 1993. Mediterranean coral: Its use and exchange in and around the Alpine region during the later Neolithic and Copper Age. *Oxford Journal of Archaeology* 12:281–292.

Stephens, M., Mattey, D., Gilbertson, D. D., and Murray-Wallace, C.V. 2008. Shell-gathering from mangroves and the seasonality of the Southeast Asian Monsoon using high-resolution stable isotopic analysis of the tropical estuarine bivalve (*Geloina erosa*) from the Great Cave of Niah, Sarawak: methods and reconnaissance of molluscs of early Holocene and modern times. *Journal of Archaeological Science* 35:2686–2697.

Stone, T. 1995. Shell mound formation in coastal northern Australia. *Marine Geology* 129:77–100.

Sutton, M. Q. 1995. Archaeological aspects of insect use. *Journal of Archaeological Method and Theory* 2:253–298.

Szabó, K. 2008. Shell as a raw material: Mechanical properties and working techniques in the tropical Indo-West Pacific. *Archaeofauna* 17:125–138.

Szabó, K. 2017. Shell middens. In: Gilbert, A. S. (ed.) *Encyclopedia of Geoarchaeology*, pp. 772–788. Dordrecht: Springer.

Taborin, Y. 1993. La parure en coquillage au Paleolithique. *Gallia Préhistoire, Supplement* 29.

Thakar, H. B. 2011. Intensification of shellfish exploitation: Evidence of species-specific deviation from traditional expectations. *Journal of Archaeological Science* 38:2596–2605.

Thomas, K. D. 2015a. Molluscs emergent, part I: Themes and trends in the scientific investigation of mollusc shells as resources for archaeological research. *Journal of Archaeological Science* 56:133–140.

Thomas, K. D. 2015b. Molluscs emergent, part II: Themes and trends in the scientific investigation of molluscs and their shells as past human resources. *Journal of Archaeological Science* 56:159–167.

Thomas, K. D. and Mannino, M. A. 2001. The exploitation of invertebrates and invertebrate products. In: Brothwell, D. R. and Pollard, A. M. (eds.) *Handbook of Archaeological Sciences*, pp. 427–440. Chichester: John Wiley and Sons, Ltd.

Twaddle, R. W., Ulm, S., Hinton, J., Wurster, C. M., and Bird, M. I. 2016. Sclerochronological analysis of archaeological mollusc assemblages: Methods, applications and future prospects. *Archaeological and Anthropological Sciences* 8:359–379.

Vanhaeren, M. and d'Errico, F. 2006. Aurignacian ethno-linguistic geography of Europe revealed by personal ornaments. *Journal of Archaeological Science* 33:1105–1128.

Vanhaeren, M., d'Errico, F., Billy, I., and Grousset, F. 2004. Tracing the source of Upper Palaeolithic shell beads by strontium isotope dating. *Journal of Archaeological Science* 31:1481–1488.

Vanhaeren, M., d'Errico, F., Stringer, C., James, S. L., Todd, J. A., and Mienis, H. K. 2006. Middle Paleolithic shell beads in Israel and Algeria. *Science* 312:1785–1788.

Vanin, S. and Huchet, J.-B. 2017. Forensic entomology and funerary archaeoentomology. In: Schotsmans, E. M. J., Márquez-Grant, N., and Forbes, S. L. (eds.) *Taphonomy of Human Remains: Forensic Analysis of the Dead and the Depositional Environment*, pp. 167–186. Chichester: John Wiley and Sons Ltd.

Vermeij, G. J. 1993. *A Natural History of Shells*. Princeton: Princeton University Press.

Walz, J. 2017. Toward an ethnoarchaeomalacology of *Achatina* in East Africa. *Ethnobiology Letters* 8:90–96.

Waselkov, G. A. 1987. Shellfish and shell midden archaeology. *Advances in Archaeological Method and Theory* 10:93–210.

Webb, S. C., Hedges, R. E. M., and Robinson, M. 1998. The seaweed fly *Thoracochaeta zosterae* (Hal.) (Diptera: Sphaerocidae) in inland archaeological contexts: δ^{13}C and δ^{15}N solves the puzzle. *Journal of Archaeological Science* 25:1253–1259.

Wefer, G. and Berger, W. H. 1991. Isotope paleontology: Growth and composition of extant calcareous species. *Marine Geology* 100:207–248.

Whitaker, A. R. 2008. Incipient aquaculture in prehistoric California? *Long-term productivity and sustainability vs. immediate returns for the harvest of marine invertebrates. Journal of Archaeological Science* 35:1114–1123.

White, D., Preece, R. C., Shchetnikov, A. A., Parfitt, S. A., and Dlussky, K. G. 2008. A Holocene molluscan succession from floodplain sediments of the upper Lena River (Lake Baikal region), Siberia. *Quaternary Science Reviews* 27:962–987.

Whitehouse, N. J. 2006. The Holocene British and Irish ancient forest fossil beetle fauna: implications for forest history, biodiversity and faunal colonization. *Quaternary Science Reviews* 25:1755–1789.

Yeh, H.-Y., Pluskowski, A., Kalējs, U., and Mitchell, P. D. 2014. Intestinal parasites in a mid-14th century latrine from Riga, Latvia: Fish tapeworm and the consumption of uncooked fish in the medieval eastern Baltic region. *Journal of Archaeological Science* 49:83–89.

Zilhão, J., Angelucci, D. E., Badal-García, E., d'Errico, F., Daniel, F., Dayet, L., Douka, K., Higham, T. F. G., Martínez-Sánchez, M. J., Montes-Bernárdez, R., Murcia-Mascarós, S., Pérez-Sirvent, C., Roldán-García, C., Vanhaeren, M., Villaverde, V., Wood, R., and Zapata, J. 2010. Symbolic use of marine shells and mineral pigments by Iberian Neandertals. *Proceedings of the National Academy of Sciences of the USA* 107:1023–1028.

Zuschin, M., Stachowitsch, M., and Stanton, R. J., Jr. 2003. Patterns and processes of shell fragmentation in modern and ancient environments. *Earth Science Reviews* 63:33–82.

12

Palaeoethnobotany

A. Catherine D'Andrea

The study of plant remains from archaeological sites for the analysis of past diets, economies, and environments.

1 INTRODUCTION AND THEORETICAL BACKGROUND

Palaeoethnobotany (or archaeobotany[1]) can be defined as the study of the interrelationships between ancient peoples and plants based on the identification and interpretation of plant remains recovered from archaeological sites (Ford 1979; Helbaek 1959). Archaeobotanical remains are often classified into two analytical groups: macro- and microbotanical remains. This distinction relates to whether or not botanical specimens are visible (macro) or invisible (micro) to the unaided eye. Studies of macrobotanical remains have typically focussed on seeds (and seed-like fruits), fruits, nuts, wood charcoal (e.g., Pearsall 2000: 11–247; Thiébault 2002), and roots/tubers/parenchyma (Hather 1993). The study of wood charcoal, or anthracology, is a multidisciplinary field involving archaeologists, palaeoecologists, and conservationists (e.g., Chabal 1997; Cabanis and Marguerie 2013; Théibault 2002; Vernet et al. 2001). Investigations of microbotanical remains have concentrated on pollen (e.g., Bryant and Holloway 1983; Bryant and Holloway 1996), phytoliths (e.g., Pearsall 2000: 355–496; Piperno 2006b; Piperno and Pearsall 1993), and starch (e.g., Loy 1994; Torrence and Barton 2006). Microbotanical

[1] "Palaeoethnobotany" and "archaeobotany" are considered synonymous herein. However, Ford (1979) defines "archaeobotany" as the recovery and identification of archaeological plant remains by any specialist while he reserves the term "paleoethnobotany" for the analysis and interpretation of archaeobotanical remains to examine interrelationships between plants and people.

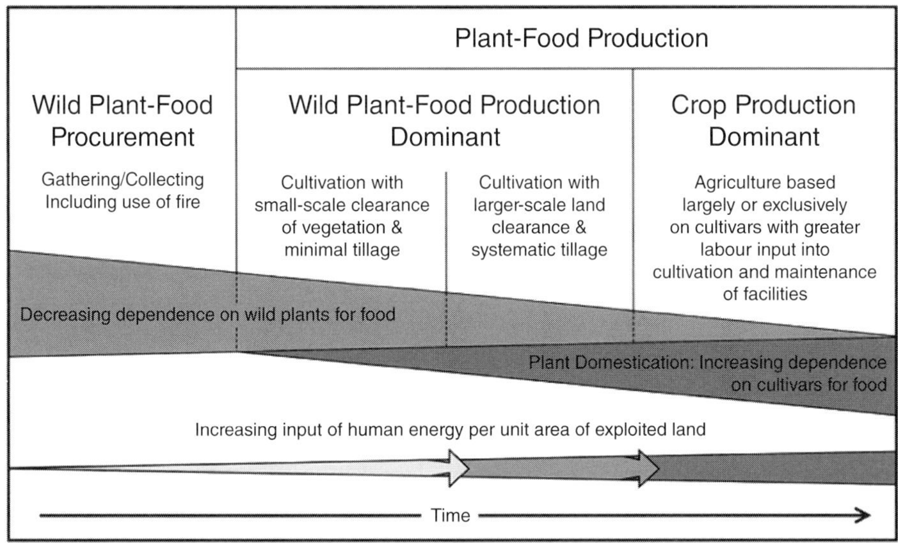

FIGURE 12.1 Spectrum of plant exploitation strategies. Adapted from Harris 1996 (figure: Vienna Chichi Lam)

remains can also include diatoms (Juggins and Cameron 1999) and biomolecular remains such as plant DNA (e.g., Brown et al. 2015; Schlumbaum et al. 2008), and lipids (e.g., Evershed 1993), however, these analyses are typically not completed by palaeoethnobotanists.

Human modification of plants exists in two overlapping spheres: at the plant community level (anthropogenesis) and at the species level (domestication). These interactions are dynamic and influenced by the environment, as well as other biological and cultural circumstances. Palaeoethnobotanists must keep the interplay of these aspects in mind when interpreting archaeologically preserved plant remains. A major aim of the palaeoethnobotanist is to interpret archaeologically preserved plant remains, which are the remnants of ancient human-plant interactions (Ford 1979). The spectrum of these relationships is very broad and illustrated in Figure 12.1. It includes the gathering of wild species with relatively little mutual interaction, to the cultivation of fully domesticated crops where humans have created new species and habitats (Harris 1996). Between these two extremes lies a vast "middle ground" (Smith 2001: 1) where ancient societies practiced food procurement or foraging, low level food production (with or without domesticates), and agriculture in various combinations. It appears that such mixed economies were quite common in the past.

Major themes of palaeoethnobotanical research include the study of subsistence and plant-based economies (e.g., Colledge 2001; Crawford and Smith 2003; Fairbairn et al. 2002; Jacomet 2009; Korstanje and Cuenya 2010; Liu et al. 2010; Madella et al. 2013; Mercuri 2008; Murray et al. 2007; Pearsall 1983; Rösch 2005; Valamoti et al. 2008; Weiss and Kislev 2004); anthropogenic impacts/environmental reconstruction (e.g., Clark and Royall 1995; Crawford 1997; Delcourt et al. 1998; Lentfer et al. 2002; Mercuri et al. 2013; Mercuri et al. 2015; Miller 1985; Morris et al. 2010; Piperno and Jones 2003; Riehl 2009; Thiébault 1997; Scheel-Ybert et al. 2014; Willcox 2002); technology (e.g., Barton et al. 1998; Perry 2004); social relations and identity (e.g., Fritz 1999; Hastorf 1991; Jamieson and Sayre 2010; Lentz 1991; VanDerwarker et al. 2007; Morehart and Eisenberg 2009; Watson and Kennedy 1991); political economy (e.g., Fuller and Stevens 2009; Hastorf 1990; Scarry and Steponaitis 1997; van der Veen 2011; Walshaw 2010; Weber 1999;); and ideology (e.g., Logan et al. 2012; Morales et al. 2011; Morehart et al. 2005; Palmer and van der Veen 2002). Additional themes include wild plant use/management/cultivation (e.g., Antolín and Jacomet 2015; Kahlheber 1999; Lepofsky et al. 2005; Logan and D'Andrea 2012; Piperno et al. 2004; Ramsey et al. 2017; Wasylikowa et al. 1997; Weiss et al. 2008; Willcox 2012; Wollstonecroft 2002); plant domestication and agricultural origins/spread (e.g., Colledge et al. 2004; Fuller 2007; Hillman and Davies 1990; Neumann 2005; Perry et al. 2007; Willcox et al. 2012; Zarrillo et al. 2008; Zeder et al. 2006; Zohary and Hopf 2000); ancient crop husbandry/processing practices based on traditional knowledge, ecological, and ethnoarchaeological models (e.g., Bogaard 2004; Charles et al. 1997; Charles 2002; D'Andrea 2008; D'Andrea and Mitiku 2002; Harvey and Fuller 2005; Hildebrand 2007; Hillman 1984; Jones 1984; Jones 1987; Jones et al. 2005; Moreno-Larrazabal et al. 2015; Peña-Chocarro et al. 2009; Reddy 1997; Rosen and Weiner 1994; Tsartsidou et al. 2008; Valamoti et al. 2011); foodways (e.g., Bogaard et al. 2009; Fowler and Rhode 2011; Fuller 2005; vanDerwarker and Detwiler 2002; Welch and Scarry 1995); and experimental archaeobotany (Abbo et al. 2008; Goette et al. 1994; Talay et al. 1984; Yang et al. 2014a).

Palaeoethnobotanical studies have been dominated by investigations of macrobotanical remains, but recently there has been an upsurge in studies focussing on microbotanical remains, in particular phytoliths and starches. Several overviews of the field are available (e.g., Dimbleby 1978; Dimbleby 1985; Fritz 2005; Gremillion 1997; Hastorf 1999; Hastorf and Popper 1988; Madella et al. 2014; Marston et al. 2014; Pearsall 2000; Pearsall 2015; Renfrew 1973; van Zeist and Casparie 1984; van Zeist et al. 1991).

2 METHODOLOGIES AND EQUIPMENT

Critical methodological issues in palaeoethnobotany relate to taphonomy, field sampling, sample processing, and identification.

Taphonomy

The archaeological preservation of plant materials is incomplete and palaeoethnobotanists must be content with developing a partial picture of plant use in the past. A key taphonomic factor in preservation has to do with innate features of plant tissues. Preserved macrobotanical remains tend to represent the tough or durable parts of plant materials that have survived various human, archaeological, and depositional taphonomic filters, the most significant of which is charring. Seeds are reproductive propagules of angiosperms made up of one or two seed coats, an embryo, and stored nutrients, including endosperm (Figure 12.2a). Strictly speaking, fruits are ripened ovaries and sometimes include accessory floral elements that contain and aid in the dispersal of seeds. The fruit wall is made up of the pericarp that is composed of three tissues: exocarp, mesocarp, and endocarp. There is a great deal of variation in the composition of these three layers (e.g., fleshy vs. dry fruits), which results in a multitude of fruit forms. Drupes are fleshy fruits bearing a fibrous or succulent mesocarp and hard endocarp surrounding a seed (Figure 12.2b). Nuts are dry fruits with hard pericarps surrounding an edible kernel (Hill et al. 1936: 245–268) (Figure 12.2c). The term "seed-like fruit" is used to denote specimens that are botanically defined as fruits but resemble seeds, such as maize and other cereal grains that are dry fruits where the pericarp and seed coat are fused (Figure 12.2a). Wood (Figure 12.2d) arises from woody plants that are perennial vascular plants with persistent stems bearing specialized conductive tissue including wood (xylem) and inner bark (phloem) (Panshin and de Zeeuw 1980: 11).

Macrobotanical remains are subject to several transformative processes in their mode of arrival at archaeological sites (e.g., Minnis 1981; van Vilsteren 1984), while in the hands of ancient peoples during food processing and other subsistence activities (e.g., Bottema 1984; Dennell 1976; Hillman 1984; Jones 1984; Kreuz 1990; Margaritis and Jones 2008; Théry-Parisot et al. 2010; van der Veen 2007;), and with deposition (e.g., Beck 1989; Braadbaart et al. 2009; Cappers 1993; Gasser and Adams 1981; Hally 1981). Perhaps the most significant taphonomic process is charring, which has both positive and negative impacts on preservation. Charring effectively eliminates the action of insects and microorganisms, making seeds, fruits, nuts, and woods resistant to decay on the order of thousands of years while preserving many morphological features (Figure 12.2d, Figure 12.3a, and 12.3b). At the same time, charring is a selective process, which results in a significant source of bias in the archaeological record. For example, if plants do not come into contact with fire, or if physically they do not char well, such as leaves and stems, they are not normally preserved in macrobotanical

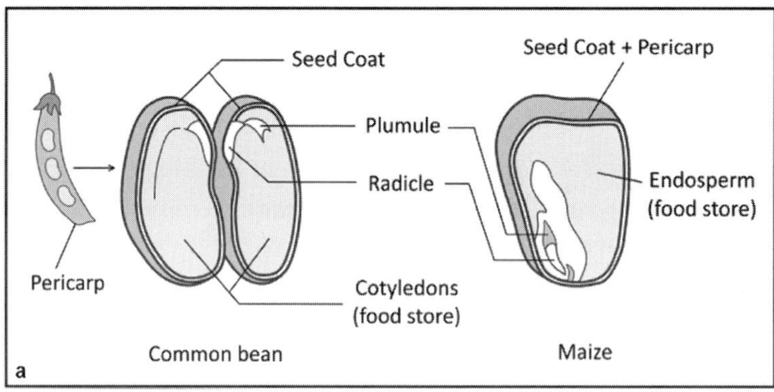

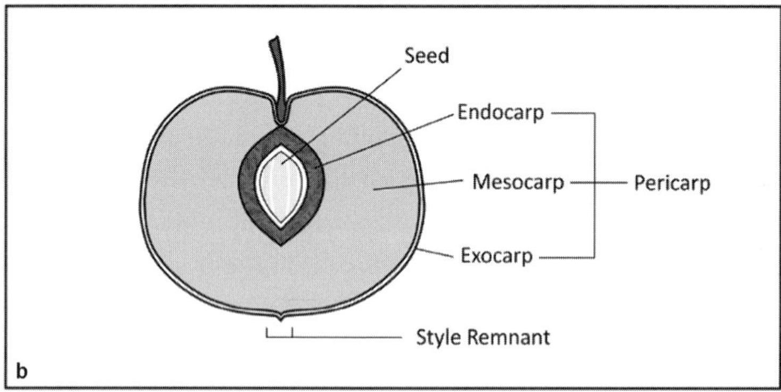

FIGURE 12.2 Macrobotanical remains. a. Comparative anatomy of monocot (maize) and dicot (bean) seeds. In grasses, endosperm carries stored nutrients for the developing embryo, while in beans stored food is held mainly in cotyledons (figure: Vienna Chichi Lam); b. A drupe, such as the peach (*Prunus persica*), is a fleshy fruit with a hard, stony endocarp surrounded by a succulent mesocarp and a leathery exocarp, all of which are clearly visible (figure: Vienna Chichi Lam); c. A botanically true nut, such as the acorn (*Quercus* spp.), is a dry fruit characterized by a hard pericarp (nutshell) surrounding an edible kernel (seed), where the exocarp, mesocarp, and endocarp are fused and not visible to the unaided eye (figure: Vienna Chichi Lam); d. Transverse section of black ash (*Fraxinus nigra*) reference charcoal from southern Quebec. From the collections of Centre D'Etudes Nordiques, Laval University (within Figure 12.2d: a = annual ring; b = springwood; c = summerwood). Scale bar = 100 microns. (Photo: Dominique Marguerie).

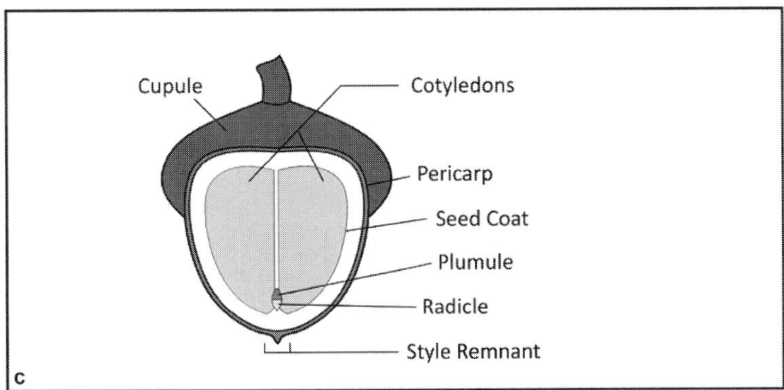

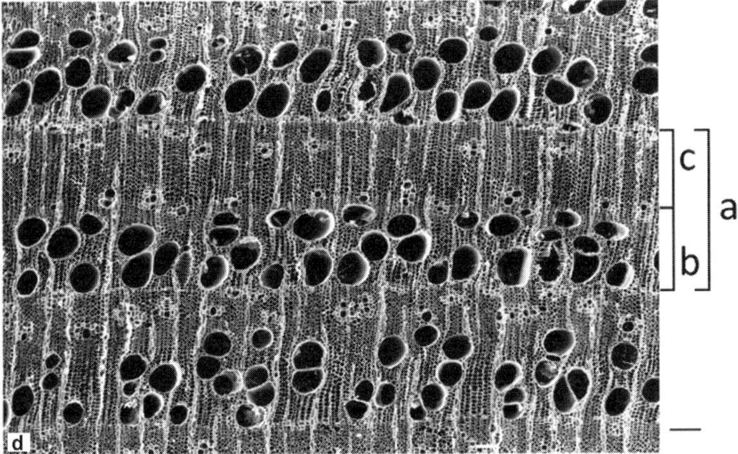

FIGURE 12.2 *(cont.)*

assemblages except in cases of exceptional preservation, such as waterlogging and extreme desiccation. Roots and tubers are also underrepresented for the same reason, however, these elements can survive charring under certain circumstances (Hather 1994). Charring also can also result in morphological changes that should be taken into account when identifying specimens. As such, charring has been the subject of numerous archaeobotanical investigations and experiments (e.g., Boardman and Jones 1990; Braadbaart and van Bergen 2005; D'Andrea 2008; Hubbard and al Azm 1990; Lopinot and Brussell 1982; Märkle and Rösch 2008; Nesbitt 2006; Szymanski and Morris 2015; Wright 2003; Wright 2008).

Microbotanical remains are affected by taphonomic factors that tend to differ from those acting on macroremains. This has the advantage that plants that are invisible

FIGURE 12.3 Charred macrobotanical remains (photos: Soultana Valamoti). a. Charred grains of emmer wheat (*Triticum dicoccum*) from an Early Neolithic burial (6590–6450 BCE) at the site of Mavropigi-Fylotsairi Kozanis, northern Greece (Valamoti 2011). Scale bar = 5 mm. b. Charred seeds of bitter vetch (*Vicia ervilia*) from the site of Agios Athanasios, Greece, dating to 2400–2100 BCE. Individual specimens are broken down into two halves (cotyledons) as the result of grinding (Valamoti et al. 2011). Scale bar = 1 cm.

because of destruction by charring or decomposition can be perceivable in the archaeological record as microbotanical remains such as starch, phytoliths, and pollen.

Starch

Starch is a complex carbohydrate found in varying quantities in plants. Storage starch occurs in seeds, fruits, tubers, roots, and stems where its main function is energy storage (Belitz et al. 2009; Tester et al. 2004). Storage starch granules

(Figure 12.4a) are able to survive after the plant has decomposed. They are taxonomically identifiable in the archaeological record, but are subject to damage or destruction during food processing (e.g., Del Pilar Babot and Apella 2003) and exposure to high temperatures in cooking (e.g., Crowther 2012; Henry et al. 2009). In addition, damage occurs in archaeological sediments the result of soil moisture, pH, and presence of enzymes, bacteria, and fungi (Haslam 2004).

Phytoliths

Phytoliths are inorganic silica bodies that form in leaves, stems, roots, and inflorescences of some plants, especially the monocotyledons (Figure 12.4b). They are durable and can survive in the archaeological record even when plant tissues in which they occur decompose or are destroyed by charring. Although not all plants produce phytoliths, many of those that do are identifiable to family, genus, or species (Pearsall 2000: 356–360; Piperno and Pearsall 1993). Phytoliths are deposited into soil following the decay of plant tissues and are subject to decomposition and movement through bioturbation, wind, and fluvial processes (Pearsall 2000: 392–395; Piperno 1991).

Palynology

Palynology is the study of pollen and spores, and is a discipline that has many applications beyond palaeoecology and archaeology. Pollen grains (Figure 12.4c) are produced in the anthers of flowers by specialized tissue. Upon maturity, the anther wall breaks, releasing the pollen so it can be transferred to the female reproductive parts of a flower. The outer layer of pollen (exine) is composed of sporopollenin, an organic substance that is resistant to decay under anaerobic conditions. Pollen grains can be diagnostic to family, genus, or species level (Faegri et al. 1989). Taphonomic factors in pollen preservation include pollen production, transfer, contribution to the pollen rain, the innate ability of different types of pollen grains to preserve and the depositional environment. A main source of bias in the pollen record lies in the vector of pollen transport. Anemophilous (wind pollinated) plants produce larger quantities of pollen and tend to be better represented in the pollen rain than zoophilous (animal pollinated) or hydrophilous (water pollinated) plants. Other taphonomic factors that can bias the pollen record include mechanical

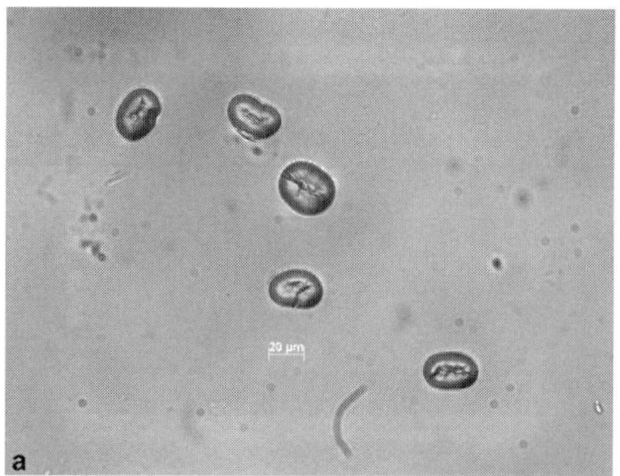

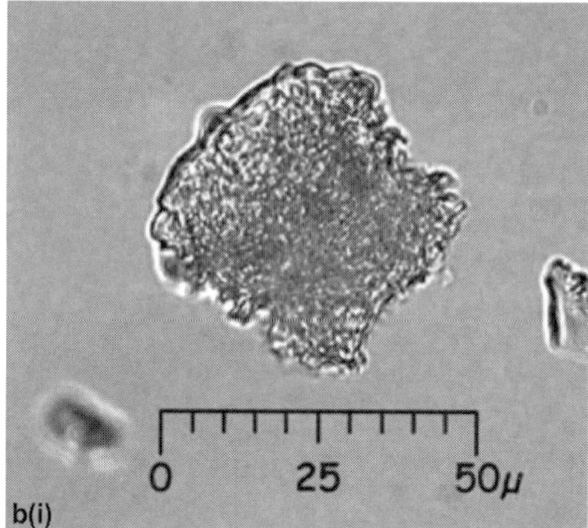

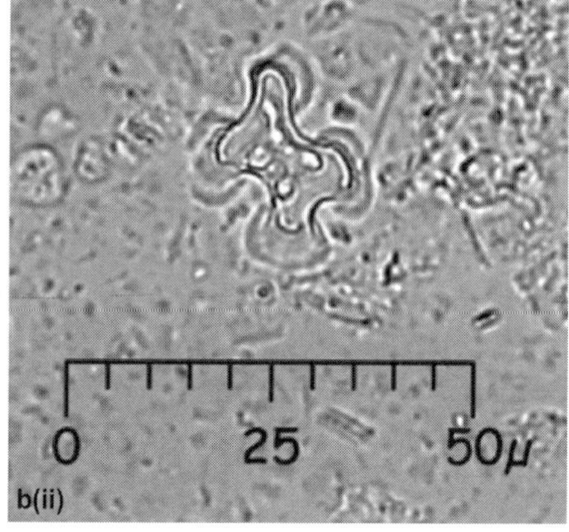

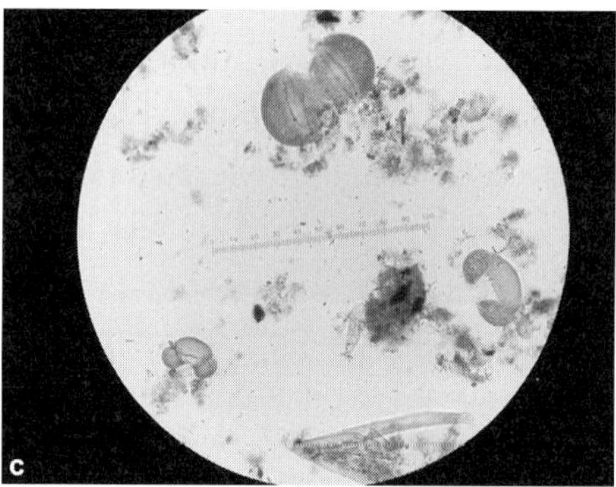

FIGURE 12.4 Microbotanical remains. a. Starch granules of tepary bean (*Phaseolus acutifolius*), a domesticate native to southwestern United States and Mexico (image: Linda Perry); b. Maize and lleren (*Calathea*) phytoliths from Real Alto, Ecuador, Valdivia 3 phase (2800–2400 cal. BCE). i. *Calathea* seed phytolith tip; ii. maize leaf extra-large Variant 1 cross (photos: Deborah M. Pearsall). c. Fossil pollen grains from the Pinaceae family from ~125-year old laminated sediment in Foy Lake, Montana, United States (Power et al. 2006). Pollen types include: spruce (*Picea*) top and right and pine (*Pinus*) bottom left. Images were captured at 400x and each unit on the scale bar equals 2.5 microns (photo: Mitchell J. Power).

turbation, soil pH, alternate wetting/drying of soils, and biotic forces that can abrade grains with thinner exines (Bryant 1989; Lebreton et al. 2010). The ideal preservation environments are acid-rich, anaerobic, waterlogged sediments and sediments in permanently arid conditions (Bryant and Holloway 1996; Dimbleby 1985).

Field Sampling

All classes of palaeoethnobotanical materials, including macro- and microbotanical remains, present a similar problem in field sampling. These remains are not normally visible during excavation, and consequently investigators may not know if sampling was successful in retrieving remains until after processing and examining samples in a laboratory setting. Because of these uncertainties, archaeobotanical sampling methodologies include judgemental (e.g., sampling burned areas with visible charcoal) and some combination of random and systematic sampling strategies. A general rule of thumb is to attempt to obtain a representative sample of each individual context on a site or at least one sample of each context type for every period of occupation: this is termed a "blanket strategy" (Pearsall 2000: 66). This method permits flexibility in the laboratory where it is possible to sub-sample specific contexts if necessary during analysis, for example, to random or systematically select 30 per cent of all hearths, pits, and middens for analysis. A problem with this strategy is that on larger sites it can produce a massive backlog of samples. In "pinch" or "composite" samples, small amounts of soil are taken throughout a large context and combined to represent the entire context. Column samples are taken from every stratigraphic unit in a sequence to provide information on chronological changes and "point sampling" involves taking samples in precisely measured locations, such as sampling a domestic floor using a 50 x 50 cm grid (Pearsall 2000: 69–75). It is also important to sample feature and non-feature contexts on a site to determine if features have diagnostic plant assemblages (Lennstrom and Hastorf 1995).

Methods used to sample archaeological soils for microbotanical remains are similar to those employed for macrobotanical assemblages. Both involve the taking of stratified samples to obtain chronological information and areal samples to investigate concentrations on ancient surfaces. Contamination from modern plants is a significant concern when working with microbotanical remains, and this necessitates the implementation of strictly controlled field collection and laboratory processing protocols (Pearsall 2000: 270–289, 399–411). Archaeological pollen has been sampled from ancient floor surfaces and sediments (e.g., Kelso et al. 2006).

In addition, palaeoenvironmental studies of pollen, which involve obtaining sediment cores from lakes and other deposits, can reflect anthropogenic activity (e.g., Bottema and Woldring 1990; Flenley 1994; Neff et al. 2006). Soil phytolith assemblages can reflect local vegetation and ancient plant processing activities (e.g., Tsartsidou et al. 2009) and they have been used to identify irrigation practices (e.g., Rosen and Weiner 1994). Starch grains also have been successfully sampled from soils (e.g., Horrocks 2005; Horrocks and Nunn 2007).

Apart from soils, microbotanical remains have been recovered from other archaeological contexts. Starch has been extracted from food residues (e.g., Boyd et al. 2006; Saul et al. 2012), dental calculus (e.g., Fox et al. 1996; Henry et al. 2011; Li et al. 2010; Perry et al. 2007; Piperno and Dillehay 2008), and artefact surfaces (e.g., Duncan et al. 2009; Loy et al. 1992; Loy 1994; Pearsall et al. 2004; Perry 2004; Yang et al. 2009; Yang et al. 2014b). Phytoliths also have been sampled from artefact surfaces (e.g., Pearsall 2000: 399–407; Pearsall et al. 2004; Saul et al. 2013). Archaeological pollen has been recovered from coprolites (e.g., Bryant and Dean 2006; Callen 1970; Reinhard et al. 1992) and artefact surfaces (Bryant and Murray 1982; Bryant and Morris 1986; Rösch 2005). Sampling methods to remove and study microbotanical remains from artefacts include the pollen wash technique (Loy 1994; Pearsall 2000: 281–282) while starch grains and phytoliths are removed from artefact surfaces through sonication and washing with distilled water (Pearsall et al. 2004).

Sample Processing

The investigation of macro- and microbotanical samples includes a diversity of plant parts and involves the extraction of plant remains from archaeological sediments, using mostly water in the case of macrobotanical remains (flotation) and various chemical agents in the case of microbotanical specimens.

Flotation was first employed at approximately the same time in Old and New World archaeology (Helbaek 1969: 385; Hole et al. 1969: 23–27; Struever 1968;). It is not an exaggeration to state that the development of field water recovery techniques for macrobotanical remains, also known as flotation or water separation[2] (Pearsall 2000: 11), was a main impetus in the development of palaeoethnobotany.

[2] The term flotation is used here in a broad sense to include manual and machine-assisted water flotation as well as water-separation.

This equipment was pivotal because it permitted the collection of sufficiently large samples of plant remains to enable a "revolution in recovery of data relevant to prehistoric subsistence" (Watson 1976: 79). Prior to this, plant remains were occasionally collected when visible, and because charred seeds, wood, and other botanical remains are not readily visible during excavation, assemblages were often small. Several works are available that detail the history of palaeoethnobotany and the development of recovery techniques (Ford 1979; Hastorf 1999: 55–58; Pearsall 2000: 3–10; Wagner 1988; Watson 1997; Yarnell 1970). Where flotation cannot be employed, such as in waterlogged plant remains and in arid conditions where the exposure of charred remains to water may result in their destruction (e.g., Cappers 2006; Hageman and Goldstein 2009) fine sieving can be used to extract macrobotanical specimens (Pearsall 2000: 80–93).

A great variety of water recovery methods have been employed to retrieve macrobotanical remains, the basic premise being that charred plants and other organic materials are buoyant, enabling their separation from excavated soils. The system selected depends upon water availability, size of site and samples, and sediment type. Methods can be divided into manual/bucket (Figure 12.5) and machine-assisted (Figure 12.6) techniques. Manual/bucket flotation methods are labor-intensive and best suited to smaller sample sizes (less than 8–10 liters). These techniques involve immersing archaeological soil in water, followed by agitation and pouring suspended organic remains into nested sieves (Figure 12.5) or scooping remains with a hand-sieve. The smallest standard mesh size used to capture light fractions is 250 microns. The resulting light fractions or flots constitute the main source of seeds, seed-like fruits, nutshell fragments, and charcoal. Sinking materials are processed by water screening, normally using a 1.0 or 1.5 mm mesh and are referred to as heavy fractions, which can include larger fragments of nutshell and charcoal, along with small bone, artefacts, and stones/sediments. The manual flotation system illustrated in Figure 12.5 has added the ability to recirculate water, which may be necessary when working in regions facing acute water shortages.

There are several types of machine-assisted flotation. Figure 12.6 illustrates a recirculating system based on the Ankara device (French 1971; Pearsall 2000: 49). This and other larger systems such as the SMAP (Shell Mound Archaeological Project) machine (Watson 1976) are capable of processing greater quantities of sediment, on the order of 100 liters per day or more, and are best suited for large-scale sampling. Archaeological sediments are poured into the upright tank and water pressure from below encourages organics to float to the surface. Floating materials are captured in nested sieves located beneath the overflow spout.

FIGURE 12.5 Bucket flotation of sediments from the Mezber site, northern Ethiopia. Soil is immersed in water and water with suspended material is slowly poured through nested sieves (1.00 mm and 250 microns). The spout is covered with fine scientific mesh (<150 microns) enabling water to be recirculated. (Photo: A. Catherine D'Andrea)

The remaining water is recirculated using a 1 or 2 hp pump after settling in two tanks. The light fraction flot is captured in nested sieves (smallest 250 micron) and the heavy fraction is contained by 1.0–1.5 mm mesh lining the upright tank.

While the extraction of macrobotanical remains takes place in the field using flotation, the separation of microbotanical samples from archeological soil takes place in a laboratory setting. This work involves the use of toxic chemicals and requires dedicated laboratory facilities and equipment, including centrifuge, fume hood, proper chemical disposal facilitics, and hot watcr bath (Pearsall 2000: 289, 411–416). While similar extraction methods can be used for starch and phytoliths, techniques employed for pollen tend to be different. The hydrofluoric acid and acetylation necessary in pollen extraction destroys silica-based phytoliths and starch granules (Horrocks 2005). Some workers have achieved success in separating pollen and phytoliths simultaneously (e.g., Chandler-Ezell and Pearsall 2003; Fredlund 1986; Lentfer and Boyd 2000), while others process samples separately

FIGURE 12.6 Machine-assisted flotation at Tel Tayinat, Turkey. (Photo: Molly Capper)

(Horrocks 2005: 1170). Detailed steps of pollen extraction from soils are available (e.g., Moore et al. 1991; Pearsall 2000: 289–302). Pearsall (2000: 426–443) describes procedures used in phytolith extraction, which requires heavy-liquid flotation, while starch and phytolith recovery procedures are presented by Horrocks (2005).

Identification

Identification of both macro- and microbotanical remains is a crucial step in analysis that requires access to well-organized comparative collections and explicit description of identification criteria. Descriptions of identification procedures for macrobotanical remains are available (e.g., Jacomet and Kreuz 1999; Pearsall 2000: 133–162).

Following flotation, light fraction flots are dried and normally sieved into several size categories. This is done to facilitate sorting, which takes place under a dissecting microscope with a range in magnification of 10–50x. Scanning Electron Microscopy (SEM) enables the study of small-scale morphological features and surface micro-topography that may aid in identification (e.g., Butler 1988; Butler 1996; D'Andrea et al. 2006; Fuller and Harvey 2006; Hilu et al. 1979; Nasu et al. 2007). Large light fractions can be sub-sampled using a riffle box sample splitter, which ensures a random subsample is taken. Fragment counts and weights (to nearest 0.01 g) are recorded on score sheets, which should be designed to include species expected in specific regions and can be linked to databases such as MS Access. Identification proceeds using seed reference collections, published manuals, and bibliographies (e.g., Beijerinck 1947; Berggren 1969; Berggren 1981; Cappers et al. 2006; Cappers et al. 2012; Hather 1993; Jacomet 2008; Martin 1946; Martin and Barkley 1961; Montgomery 1977; Nesbitt and Greig 1989; Panshin and de Zeeuw 1980; Schoch et al. 1988). In addition online sources are available to aid identification (e.g., Adams and Murray n.d.; Cappers et al. 2012; Fritz, n.d.; Nesbitt 2006;).

Identification of microbotanical remains requires mounting specimens on slides and the use of compound light microscopes with magnification on the order of 200–1000x with polarized light and dark field capability (Barton and Fullagar 2006: 47–48; Pearsall 2000: 414). Access to SEM enables detailed study of surfaces that can be useful to confirm identifications. Pollen grains are typically counted as relative or absolute counts (Moore et al. 1991; see Pearsall 2000: 302–311 for a discussion of various counting methods) and identification is based on exine morphology and surface features using comparative collections and regional print and digital-based identification keys (e.g., Colinvaux et al. 1999; Dupont et al. 2010; Kapp 1969; Langford et al. 1990). Archaeological phytoliths are identified based on morphometric analysis (e.g., Ball et al. 2016) but identification can be complicated because a single plant produces phytoliths of different shapes and different plants can produce similarly shaped phytoliths. Identifications can be made on the basis of phytolith assemblages and multivariate statistical methods, such as discriminate analysis, can be useful in identifying diagnostic types (Pearsall 2000: 375–392). Taxonomic identifications are also based on diagnostic individual phytoliths, for example, maize leaf phytoliths (Figure 12.4b). Phytolith identifications are made using reference specimens and published sources (e.g., Bowdery et al. 2001) and studies of phytolith morphotypes exist for specific regions and crop complexes (see summary in Pearsall 2000: 396; a few examples of recent studies include Gu et al. 2013; Fahmy 2008; Iríarte 2003; Novello and Barboni 2015; Out and Madella 2015;

Pearsall 2011; Piperno 2006a). Starch can be identified based on morphology of granules and also through chemical residues. The starch of some plants, such as rice, manioc, yams, and maize are identifiable to species (Torrence 2006a: 115–143). Analysts of archaeological starch aim to examine variation in assemblages of starch granules in a particular context, to identify the presence of species, and to examine the relative abundance of granules (for examples, see Fullagar 2006: 177–203; Torrence 2006b: 145–143).

In the study of both macro- and microbotanical remains, the availability of comparative collections is critical in obtaining reliable taxonomic determinations. In the case of macrobotanical remains, this involves the collection and identification of modern seeds, fruits, and woods usually in the vicinity of the archaeological site under investigation. Seeds and fruits can also be obtained from gene banks and herbaria, although it is good practice to doublecheck these identifications by obtaining samples from more than one source, coupled with field collections. Seed reference collections take many years to develop and effective management of these collections is critical (Nesbitt et al. 2003). In the case of phytoliths and starch granules, reference materials are processed from identified modern species in the laboratory (e.g., Field 2006: 95–113; Pearsall 2000: 435–443).

The quality of palaeoethnobotanical interpretation rests on accurate identifications, and as such the precision of identifications should be specified. Uncertainty should be clearly expressed with firm identifications distinguished from probable (preceded by "*cf.*") and questionable identifications (preceded by "?"). Although reference manuals and online sources are extremely useful in identifying specimens, firm identifications, in particular to the species level, ideally should be made by direct comparison with properly sourced reference collections.

3 GENERAL (THEORETICAL) EXAMPLES

Interpretations of palaeoethnobotanical assemblages have been situated for the most part within a theoretical framework of processual archaeology, and in particular cultural ecology (Steward 1959; Trigger 2006), as seen in some of the case studies presented below. Over the past 20 years, palaeoethnobotanists have adopted post-processual approaches, including gender (e.g., Hastorf 1991) and practice theory (Atalay and Hastorf 2006; Logan 2012). In addition, theoretical frameworks borrowed from the biological sciences have included evolutionary ecology and human behavioral ecology (HBE), including niche construction theory (NCT) (e.g., Gremillion 2002; Gremillion and Piperno 2009; Kennett et al. 2006; Marston 2011; Piperno 2006a; Rindos 1984; Smith 2007; Smith 2012; Smith 2015; Wollstonecroft 2011; Winterhalder and Goland 1997). These approaches have considerably broadened our perspective of the human past with respect to foraging, plant domestication, the transition to agriculture, agricultural risk management, and dietary choice. Two case studies are presented, each illustrating a different theoretical approach to palaeoethnobotanical data: one employing practice theory (Atalay and Hastorf 2006) and a second focusing on NCT (Wollstonecroft 2011).

Atalay and Hastorf (2006) investigate ancient food ways at Çatalhöyük, south-central Turkey in a study that provides a window into the social life of Neolithic inhabitants of the site (ca. 7200 BC). The research is undertaken from the perspective of practice theory (Bourdieu 1977), which is used as a framework to explain human behavior through the study of practice. A core concept of practice theory is *habitus*, which refers to the life ways of social groups that are constructed through everyday activities and experiences. Food preparation is described as the "ultimate *habitus* practice," more significant than others, because people prepare food each day (Atalay and Hastorf 2011: 283). It is argued that practice in all stages of preparing meals impacts the lives of the entire community and forms a core part of identity.

Archaeobotanical and other data sources are used to reconstruct plant and animal food resources available over an entire seasonal cycle. Analysis focusses on structural units and areas of the site where food preparation activities took place, including production and procurement, processing, cooking, presentation, and eating. Evidence of archaeological food practice is supplemented with ethnographic information obtained from nearby modern villages. Shifts in cooking practice are detected at the site, for example, a change from indirect boiling (placing heated clay balls into containers of food and stirring) to direct boiling in clay pots in later periods that would have freed cooks to complete other activities and enabled the preparation of new meals. The foods utilized remained constant, however, so that the shift reflected a change in cooking practice, time management, and cultural taste, but not a significant modification of cuisine. The detailed descriptions of food preparation practice offer a rich and varied picture of social life at Çatalhöyük through the lens of food studies (Atalay and Hastorf 2006).

In the second study, Wollstonecroft (2011) examines plant food processing and its role in human evolution, from the perspective of Niche Construction Theory (NCT). Niche Construction Theory posits that organisms are able to increase their potential to survive through reciprocal engagement with their environment, which results in long-term ecological changes. Such ecosystem engineering affects the species in question as well as other organisms. These actions result in the modification of selection pressures acting on organisms and their descendants. In this way, niche construction works in concert with natural selection in the evolution of organisms. Such behavior is known among many organisms, but is a particular feature of humans (Odling-Smee et al. 2003). Cultural niche construction (Laland et al. 2001) has been a significant factor in human evolution whereby humans are active agents in modifying evolutionary selection pressures through learning and the transmission of learned behaviors.

The concept of NCT is applied by Wollstonecroft (2011) to the postharvest processing of plant foods by humans. It is argued that food processing involves the transformation of plant and animal materials for human consumption by inducing physical and chemical changes to render them more palatable and nutritious. Activities include soaking, heating (cooking), grinding, fermentation, preservation, and storage, all of which involve specialized techniques and knowledge that can be culturally transmitted over generations. These actions increase the overall bioaccessibility and bioavailability of nutrients. Such practices have existed since 2 mya when early hominins began to use stone tools to acquire foods by pounding roots/tubers or cracking nutshells to obtain food. Ultimately, early human ancestors employed these technologies to broaden their diets by making plants more palatable and to obtain greater nutrition and energy from foods. This, in turn, led to changes in human evolutionary selection pressures, permitting humans to exploit new environments and resources that yielded nutritional and other benefits resulting in greater longevity, health, and higher survival rates.

4 CASE STUDIES

Four case studies are presented that illustrate contributions made by palaeoethnobotanical research in the study of early foraging societies (Revedin et al. 2010), complex chiefdoms (Scarry and Steponaitis 1997), urban populations (Walshaw 2010), and the ritual use of plants (Logan et al. 2012).

Microbotanical remains have incredible potential to elucidate the role of plants in early human diets where the lack of macrobotanical preservation precludes interpretation of ancient subsistence practices. An investigation conducted by Revedin et al. (2010) demonstrates that European Upper Palaeolithic diets included plants that were processed in complex ways. They identified several starch granule morphotypes recovered from grindingstones at three Upper Palaeolithic sites in Italy, Russia, and Czech Republic. Plants processed on grindingstones included grasses, cattails, and ferns, representing plant families with species that produce edible grains or rhizomes/roots. They conclude that some Upper Palaeolithic populations were not exclusively hunters, but participated in the intensive processing of plant foods by at least 30,000 years ago. Their work also suggests that the grinding of plant foods, including the production and cooking of flour-based foods, has a long history and would have afforded Upper Palaeolithic populations effective strategies to cope with seasonality in resource availability and other subsistence uncertainties.

Scarry and Steponaitis (1997) present a comprehensive study of plant macroremains recovered from Moundville, an important chiefdom that developed in the later prehistoric period (Mississippian Period, ca. AD 900–1250) in the southeastern United States. The work provides an example of how macrobotanical remains can reflect the movement of foods and food products across an emerging urban landscape. The authors examine social and economic relations between people living at the densely population centre of Moundville and those occupying farmsteads in the surrounding region. People inhabiting both areas appear to have had access to the same resources (maize, hickory nuts, and acorn), however, differences are found in resource abundance that are illustrated using box plots. Several interesting patterns emerge, for example, farmsteads are found to have larger quantities of corn cupules than Moundville and other larger sites and farmsteads appear to have been more involved in the production of nut resources. This suggests that occupants of farmsteads were involved in growing, producing, and initial processing of maize, the surplus production of which was transported in a more or less clean state to the elite centre of Moundville. These data are suggested to reflect economic and social relations between elite population centers and countryside. It is argued, with the support of ethnohistorical evidence, that the relationships between town and rural populations were governed by kinship networks and other sources of obligation such as taxes or tribute provided by commoners to elite centers.

The third case study demonstrates the potential of the archaeobotanical record to shed light on large-scale cultural processes, including urbanisation and religious transformation. Palaeoethnobotanical research on the island of Pemba, Tanzania (Walshaw 2010) has concentrated on sampling macrobotanical remains from two towns: Tumbe (seventh to tenth centuries AD) and Chwaka (eleventh to fifteenth centuries AD). The earliest urban communities along the Swahili coast develop between eighth and fifth centuries AD, and the first stonetowns are evident by the eleventh century AD. Swahili stonetowns functioned as key centers of international trade. Foreign merchants brought with them new commodities (including rice and other crops) and religious practices that resulted in the conversion of local populations to Islam. The archaeobotanical record documents a shift from a pearl millet-based agricultural economy at Tumbe to one dominated by Asian rice, cotton, and coconut at Chwaka. This shift is accompanied by the introduction of Islam and depopulation of the countryside, when many rural peoples migrated to stonetowns. Changes in ceramics also reflect modifications in cuisine, with jars and restricted bowls conducive to the preparation of millet beer and porridges being replaced by open bowls and wide-mouthed jars more amenable to the cooking and service of rice. Earlier levels of Tumba demonstrate the presence of rice, but it likely played an insignificant economic role. It is argued that despite risks involved in rice cultivation, introduced foodways based on rice were adopted by ancient Pembans because of the social advantages and their association with Islamic Middle Eastern culture. As such, the increasing involvement of the East African coastal peoples in oceanic trade networks left a signal in the palaeoethnobotanical record.

The fourth and final case study highlights the potential of archaeobotanical research to elucidate ritual/ceremonial uses of plants in the past (Logan et al. 2012). Analyses of phytolith and starch from four archaeological sites on the Taraco Peninsula of Bolivia demonstrate that during the initial introduction of maize to the Titicaca Basin (Middle Formative Period, 800–250 BC), it was consumed not as a grain food but in the form of *chicha* beer. *Chicha* played an immensely important role in Andean society, as is evident in both the archaeological and ethnohistorical records. It was consumed communally at feasts, used in expressing social hierarchies, and as payment for services/labor. *Chicha* also formed a significant component of ceremonial life and was included as offerings made to the gods and ancestors. During the initial appearance of maize in Middle Formative contexts, macrobotanical remains occur rarely while starch/phytoliths appear to be concentrated on artefacts and areas of ceremonial significance. Microbotanical remains were extracted from soils, charred cooking residues, grindingstones, burning vessels, and other artefacts, all of which were associated with ceremonial contexts such as courtyards, special food preparation areas, burning vessels, and the teeth of a human sacrificial victim. The rarity of charred macrobotanical remains of maize in numerous sites of this period suggests that maize processing took place without exposure to fire, which is consistent with the brewing of beer rather than the production of maize-based foods. In addition, recovered human skeletal remains do not carry significant C_4 isotopic signatures that would indicate the importance of maize in diets. It is concluded that maize consumption during the Formative was primarily in the form of small-scale production of *chicha* beer. This development was concurrent with a time of increasing sociopolitical complexity where *chicha* beer played an important role in communal ritual practices.

5 CONCLUSION

The study of ancient human-plant interactions through palaeoethnobotany forms a critical component of environmental archaeology and archaeological science. Palaeoethnobotanists tend to have multidisciplinary training in archaeology, botany and ethnobotany, but ideally they exploit synergies among these fields to create new and insightful interpretations about the human past. While macrobotanical remains once dominated research, in recent years studies of microbotanical remains, including phytoliths and starch grains, are making key contributions. Such investigations are demonstrating plant exploitation practices from archaeological sites inhabited in the remote past, where macrobotanical remains tend to be exceedingly few. Palaeoethnobotanists are now providing an unprecedented long-term view of human plant use that has revealed unexpected complexities in past lifeways.

REFERENCES

Abbo, S., Zezak, I., Schwartz, E., Lev-Yadun, S., and Gopher, A. 2008. Experimental harvesting of wild peas in Israel: Implications for the origins of Near East farming. *Journal of Archaeological Science* 35(4):922–929.

Adams, K. and Murray, S. S. n.d. Identification criteria for plant remains recovered from archaeological sites in the Central Mesa Verde Region. www.crowcanyon.org/researchreports/Archaeobotanical/Plant_Identification/plant_identification.asp (accessed July 9, 2019).

Antolín, F. and Jacomet, S. 2015. Wild fruit use among early farmers in the Neolithic (5400–2300 cal BC) in the north-east of the Iberian Peninsula: An intensive practice? *Vegetation History and Archaeobotany* 24(1):19–33.

Atalay, S. and Hastorf, C. A. 2006. Food, meals, and daily activities: Food *habitus* at Neolithic Çatalhöyük. *American Antiquity* 71(2):283–319.

Ball, T.B., Davis, A., Evett, R. R., Ladwig, J. L., Tromp, M., Out, W. A., and Portillo, M. 2016. Morphometric analysis of phytoliths: Recommendations towards standardization from the International Committee for Phytolith Morphometrics. *Journal of Archaeological Science* 68:106–111.

Barton, H. and Fullagar, R. 2006. Microscopy. In: Torrence, R. and Barton, H. (eds.) *Ancient Starch Research*, pp. 47–74. Walnut Creek, CA: Left Coast Press.

Barton, H., Torrence, R., and Fullagar, R. 1998. Clues to stone tool function re-examined: Comparing starch grain frequencies on used and unused obsidian artefacts. *Journal of Archaeological Science* 25(12):1231–1238.

Beck, W. E. 1989. The taphonomy of plants. In: Beck, W.E., Clarke, A., and Head, L. (eds.) *Plants in Australian Archaeology*. Tempus. Vol. 1. St. Lucia: University of Queensland Anthropology Museum.

Beijerinck, W. 1947. *Zadenatlas Der Nederlandische Flora*. Wageningen: H. Veenman and Zonen.

Belitz, H.-D., Grosch, W., and Schieberle, P. 2009. *Food Chemistry*, 4th ed. New York: Springer Verlag.

Berggren, G. 1969. *Atlas of Seeds and Small Fruits of North-West European Plant Species with Morphological Descriptions: Part 2. Cyperaceae*. Halmstad, Sweden: Berlings.

Berggren, G. 1981. *Atlas of Seeds and Small Fruits of North-West European Plant Species with Morphological Descriptions: Part 3. Salicaceae-Cruciferae*. Halmstad, Sweden: Academic Press.

Boardman, S. and Jones, G. 1990. Experiments on the effects of charring on cereal plant components. *Journal of Archaeological Science* 17(1):1–12.

Bogaard, A. 2004. *Neolithic Farming in Central Europe: An Archaeobotanical Study of Crop Husbandry Practices*. London: Routledge.

Bogaard, A., Charles, M., Twiss, K. C., Fairbairn, A., Yalman, N., Filipovic, D., Demirergi, G. A., Ertuğ, F., Russell, N., and Henecke, J. 2009. Private pantries and celebrated surplus: Storing and sharing food at Neolithic Çatalhöyük. *Antiquity* 83:649–668.

Bottema, S. 1984. The composition of modern charred seed assemblages. In: van Zeist, W. and Casparie, W. A. (eds.) *Plants and Ancient Man*, pp. 207–212. Rotterdam: Balkema.

Bottema, S. and Woldring, H. 1990. Anthropogenic indicators in the pollen record of the Eastern Mediterranean. In: Bottema, S., Entjes-Nieborg, G., and van Zeist, W. (eds.) *Man's Role in the Shaping of the Eastern Mediterranean Landscape*, pp. 231–264. Rotterdam: Balkema.

Bourdieu, P. 1977. *Outline of a Theory of Practice*. Cambridge: Cambridge University Press.

Bowdery, D., Hart, D. M., Lentfer, C., and Wallis, L. A. 2001. A universal phytolith key. In: Meunier, J. D. and Colin, F. (eds.) *Phytoliths: Applications in Earth Science and Human History*, pp. 267–278. Rotterdam: Balkema.

Boyd, M. C., Surette, C., and Nicholson, B. A. 2006. Archaeobotanical evidence of maize (*Zea mays*) consumption at the northern edge of the Great Plains. *Journal of Archaeological Science* 33:1129–1140.

Braadbaart, F., Poole, I., and van Brussel, A. A. 2009. Preservation potential of charcoal in alkaline environments: an experimental approach and implications for the archaeological record. *Journal of Archaeological Science* 36(8):1672–1679.

Braadbaart, F. and van Bergen, P. F. 2005. Digital imaging analysis of size and shape of wheat and pea upon heating under anoxic conditions as a function of the temperature. *Vegetation History and Archaeobotany* 14(1):67–75.

Brown, T. A., Cappellini, E., Kistler, L., Lister, D. L., Oliveira, H. R., Wales, N., and Schlumbaum, A. 2015. Recent advances in ancient DNA research and their implications for archaeobotany. *Vegetation History and Archaeobotany* 24(1):207–214.

Bryant, V. M., Jr. 1989. Botanical remains in archaeological sites. In: Mathewson, C. C. (ed.) *Interdisciplinary Workshop on the Physical-Chemical-Biological Processes Affecting Archaeological Sites*, pp. 85–115. Vicksburg, MI: Environmental Impact Research Program, Contract Report EL-89-1. Environmental Laboratory, US Army Engineer Waterways Experiment Station.

Bryant, V. M., Jr. and Dean, G. W. 2006. Archaeological coprolite science: the legacy of Eric O. Callen (1912–1970). *Palaeogeography, Palaeoclimatology, Palaeoecology* 237(1):51–66.

Bryant, V. M., Jr. and Holloway, R. G. 1983. The role of palynology in archaeology. In: Schiffer, M. B. (ed.) *Advances in Archaeological Method and Theory*, Vol. 6, pp. 191–223. New York: Academic Press.

Bryant, V. M., Jr. and Holloway, R. G. 1996. New frontiers in palynology: archaeological palynology. In: Jansonius, J. and McGregor, D. C. (eds.) *Palynology: Principles and Applications*, Vol. 3, pp. 913–917. Dallas: American Association of Stratigraphic Palynologists Foundation.

Bryant, V. M., Jr. and Morris, D. P. 1986. Uses of ceramic vessels and grinding implements: the pollen evidence. In: Morris, D. P. (ed.) *Archaeological Investigations at Antelope House*, pp. 489–500. Washington DC: National Park Service, US Department of the Interior.

Bryant, V. M., Jr. and Murray, R. E. 1982. Preliminary analysis of amphora contents. In: Bass, G. F. and van Doorninick, F. H., Jr. (eds.) *Yassi Ada*, Vol. 1: *A Seventh-Century Byzantine Shipwreck*, pp. 327–331. College Station: Texas A&M University Press.

Butler, E. A. 1988. The SEM and seed identification, with particular reference to the Vicieae. In: Olsen, S. L. (ed.) *Scanning Electron Microscopy in Archaeology*, pp. 215–224. Oxford: B.A.R.

Butler, E. A. 1996. Trifoleae and related seeds from archaeological contexts: Problems in identification. *Vegetation History and Archaeobotany* 5(1–2):157–167.

Cabanis, M. and Marguerie, D. 2013. Wood resources in the Clermont-Ferrand Basin from the Neolithic to the Roman Period based on dendro-anthracological analysis. *Quaternaire* 24(2):129–139.

Callen, E. O. 1970. Diet as revealed by coprolites. In: Brothwell, D. and Higgs, E. (eds.) *Science and Archaeology: A Survey of Progress and Research*, 2nd ed., pp. 235–243. New York: Praeger.

Cappers, R. T. J. 1993. Seed dispersal by water: A contribution to the interpretation of seed assemblages. *Vegetation History and Archaeobotany* 2(3):173–186.

Cappers, R. T. J. 2006. *Roman Foodprints at Berenike: Archaeobotanical Evidence of Subsistence and Trade in the Eastern Desert of Egypt*. Berenike Reports No. 6. Los Angeles: Cotsen Institute of Archaeology.

Cappers, R. T. J., Bekker, R. M., and Jans, J. E. A. 2006. *Digitale Zadenatlas van Nederland/ Digital Seed Atlas of the Netherlands*, 1st ed. Groningen: Barkhuis and Groningen University Library.

Cappers, R. T. J., Bekker, R. M., and Jans, J. E. A. 2012. *Digitale Zadenatlas van Nederland/ Digital Seed Atlas of the Netherlands*, 2nd ed. Groningen: Barkhuis and Groningen University Library. http://www.plantatlas.eu/ (accessed July 9, 2019).

Chabal, L. 1997. *Forêts et sociétés en Languedoc (Néolihique final, Antiquité tardive). L'anthracologie, méthode et paléoécologie*. Documents d'Archéologie Française 63, Paris: Editions de la Maison des Sciences de l'Homme.

Chandler-Ezell K. C. and Pearsall, D. M. 2003. "Piggy-back" microfossil processing: Joint starch and phytolith sampling from stone tools. *Phytolitharian Newsletter* 15(3):2– 8.

Charles, M., Bogaard, A., Jones, G., Hodgson, J., and Halstead, P. 2002. Towards the archaeobotanical identification of intensive cereal cultivation: Present-day ecological investigation in the mountains of Asturias, northwest Spain. *Vegetation History and Archaeobotany* 11(1–2):133–142.

Charles, M., Jones, G., and Hodgson, J. G. 1997. FIBS in archaeobotany: Functional interpretation of weed floras in relation to husbandry practices. *Journal of Archaeological Science* 24(12):1151–1161.

Clark, J. S. and Royall, P. D. 1995. Transformation of a northern hardwood forest by Aboriginal (Iroquois) fir: Charcoal evidence from Crawford Lake, Ontario, Canada. *The Holocene* 5(1):1–9.

Colinvaux. P., de Oliveira, P. E., and Moreno Patiño, J. E. 1999. *Amazon Pollen Manual and Atlas*. Amsterdam: Harwood Academic Publishers.

Colledge, S. 2001. *Plant Exploitation on Epipalaeolithic and Early Neolithic Sites in the Levant*. B.A.R. International Series 986. Oxford: British Archaeological Reports.

Colledge, S., Conolly, J., and Shennan, S. 2004. Archaeobotanical evidence for the spread of farming in the eastern Mediterranean. *Current Anthropology* 45:S35–S58.

Crawford, G. W. 1997. Anthropogenesis in prehistoric northeastern Japan. In: Gremillion, K. J. (ed.) *People, Plants, and Landscapes: Studies in Paleoethnobotany*, pp. 86–103. Tuscaloosa: University of Alabama Press.

Crawford, G. W. and Smith, D. G. 2003. Palaeoethnobotany in the Northeast. In: Minnis, P. (ed.) *People and Plants in Ancient Eastern North America*, pp. 172–257. Washington DC: Smithsonian Institution Press.

Crowther, A. 2012. The differential survival of native starch during cooking and implications for archaeological analyses: A review. *Archaeological and Anthropological Sciences* 4(3):221–235.

D'Andrea, A. C. 2008. *T'ef (Eragrostis tef)* in ancient agricultural systems of highland Ethiopia. *Economic Botany* 62(4):547–566.

D'Andrea, A. C., Logan, A. L., and Watson, D. J. 2006. Oil palm and prehistoric subsistence in tropical West Africa. *Journal of African Archaeology* 4(2):195–222.

D'Andrea, A. C. and Mitiku Haile. 2002. Traditional emmer processing in highland Ethiopia. *Journal of Ethnobiology* 22(2):179–217.

Delcourt, P. A., Delcourt, H. R., Ison, C. R., Sharp, W. E., and Gremillion, K. 1998. Prehistoric human use of fire, the eastern agricultural complex, and Appalachian oak-chestnut forests: paleoecology of Cliff Palace Pond, Kentucky. *American Antiquity* 63(2):263–278.

Del Pilar Babot, M. and Apella, M. C. 2003. Maize and bone: Residues of grinding in northwestern Argentina. *Archaeometry* 45(1):121–132.

Dennell, R. W. 1976. The economic importance of plant resources represented on archaeological sites. *Journal of Archaeological Science* 3(3):229–247.

Dimbleby, G. W. 1978. *Plants and Archaeology*, 2nd ed. New Jersey: Humanities Press.

Dimbleby, G. W. 1985. *The Palynology of Archaeological Sites*. London: Academic Press.

Duncan, N. A., Pearsall, D. M., and Benfer, R. A., Jr. 2009. Gourd and squash artifacts yield starch grains of feasting foods from preceramic Peru. *Proceedings of the National Academy of Sciences* 106(32):13202–13206.

Dupont, J., Nebout, N. C., Cazet, J.-P., Causse, F., and Lebbe, R. V. 2010. New key-tools for pollen identification in research and education. In: Nimis, P L. and Lebbe, R. V. (eds.) *Tools for Identifying Biodiversity: Progress and Problems*, pp. 383–387. Trieste: Edizioni Università di Trieste.

Evershed, R. P. 1993. Biomolecular archaeology and lipids. *World Archaeology* 25(1):74–93.

Faegri, K., Kaland, P. E., and Krzywinski, K. 1989. *Textbook of Pollen Analysis*, 4th ed. Chichester: John Wiley and Sons.

Fairbairn, A., Asouti, E., Near, J., and Martinoli, D. 2002. Macro-botanical evidence for plant use at Neolithic Çatalhöyük, south-central Anatolia, Turkey. *Vegetation History and Archaeobotany* 11(1–2):41–54.

Fahmy, A. G. 2008. Diversity of lobate phytoliths in grass leaves from the Sahel region, West tropical Africa: Tribe Paniceae. *Plant Systematics and Evolution* 270(1–2):1–23.

Field, J. 2006. Reference collections. In: Torrence, R. and Barton, H. (eds.) *Ancient Starch Research*, pp. 95–113. Walnut Creek, CA: Left Coast Press.

Flenley, J. R. 1994. Pollen in Polynesia: The use of palynology to detect human activity in the Pacific Islands. In: Hather, J. G. (ed.) *Tropical Archaeobotany*, pp. 202–214. New York: Routledge.

Ford, R. A. 1979. Paleoethnobotany in American archaeology. In: Schiffer, M. B. (ed.) *Advances in Archaeological Method and Theory*, pp. 285–336. New York: Academic Press.

Fowler, C. S. and Rhode, D. E. 2011. Plant foods and foodways among the Great Basin's Indigenous peoples. In: Smith, B. D. (ed.) *Subsistence Economies of Indigenous North American Societies*, pp. 233–270. Washington DC: Smithsonian Institution Scholarly Press.

Fredlund, G. 1986. Problems in the simultaneous extraction of pollen and phytoliths from clastic sediments. In: Rovner, I. (ed.) *Plant Opal Phytolith Analysis in Archaeology and Paleoecology. The Phytolitharian*, pp. 102–110. Occasional Paper No. 1. Raleigh: North Carolina State University.

French, D. H. 1971. An experiment in water-sieving. *Anatolian Studies* 21:59–64.

Fritz, G. 2005. Paleoethnobotanical methods and applications. In: Maschner, H. D. G. and Chippindale, C. (eds.) *Handbook of Archaeological Methods*, Vol. 1, pp. 771–832. Walnut Creek, CA: Altamira Press.

Fritz, G. n.d. Laboratory Guide to Archaeological Plant Remains from Eastern North America. http://artsci.wustl.edu/~gjfritz/ (accessed July 9, 2019).

Fritz, G. J. 1999. Gender and the early cultivation of gourds in Eastern North America. *American Antiquity* 64(3):417–429.

Fox, C. L., Juan, J., and Albert, R. M. 1996. Phytolith analysis on dental calculus, enamel surface, and burial soil: Information about diet and paleoenvironment. *American Journal of Physical Anthropology* 101(1):101–113.

Fullagar, R. 2006. Starch on artefacts. In: Torrence, R. and Barton, H. (eds.) *Ancient Starch Research*, pp. 177–203. Walnut Creek, CA: Left Coast Press.

Fuller, D. Q. 2005. Ceramics, seeds and culinary change in prehistoric India. *Antiquity* 79:761–77.

Fuller, D. Q. 2007. Contrasting patterns in crop domestication and domestication rates: Recent archaeobotanical insights from the Old World. *Annals of Botany* 100(5):903–924.

Fuller, D. Q. and Harvey, E. L. 2006. The archaeobotany of Indian Pulses: Identification, processing and evidence for cultivation. *Environmental Archaeology* 11(2):219–246.

Fuller, D. Q. and Stevens, C. J. 2009. Agriculture and the development of complex societies: an archaeobotanical agenda. In: Fairbairn, A. and Weiss, E. (eds.) *Ethnobotanist of Distant Pasts: Papers in Honour of Gordon Hillman*, pp. 37–57. Oxford: Oxbow Books.

Gasser, R. E. and Adams, E. C. 1981. Aspects of deterioration of plant remains in archaeological sites. *Journal of Ethnobiology* 1(1):182–192.

Goette, S., Williams, M., Johannessen, S., and Hastorf, C. A. 1994. Toward reconstructing ancient maize: Experiments in processing and charring. *Journal of Ethnobiology* 14(1):1–22.

Gremillion, K. J. 1997. *People, Plants, and Landscapes: Studies in Paleoethnobotany*. Tuscaloosa: University of Alabama Press.

Gremillion, K. J. 2002. Foraging theory and hypothesis testing in archaeology: An exploration of methodological problems and solutions. *Journal of Anthropological Archaeology* 21(2):142–164.

Gremillion, K. J. and Piperno, D. R. 2009. Human behavioral ecology, phenotypic (developmental) plasticity, and agricultural origins: Insights from the emerging evolutionary synthesis. *Current Anthropology* 50(5):615–619.

Gu, Y., Zhao, Z., and Pearsall, D. M. 2013. Phytolith morphology research on wild and domesticated rice species in East Asia. *Quaternary International* 287:141–148.

Hageman, J. B. and Goldstein, D. J. 2009. An integrated assessment of archaeobotanical recovery methods in the neotropical rainforest of northern Belize: Flotation and dry screening. *Journal of Archaeological Science* 36(12):2841–2852.

Hally, D. J. 1981. Plant preservation and the content of palaeoethnobotanical Samples: A case study. *American Antiquity* 46(4):723–742.

Harris, D. R. 1996. Domesticatory relations of people, plants and animals. In: Ellen, R. and Fukui, K. (eds.) *Redefining Nature*, pp. 437–463. Oxford: Berg.

Harvey, E. and Fuller, D. Q. 2005. Investigating crop processing using phytolith analysis: The example of rice and millets. *Journal of Archaeological Science* 32(5):739–752.

Haslam, M. 2004. The decomposition of starch grains in soils: Implications for archaeological residue analyses. *Journal of Archaeological Science* 31:1715–1734.

Hastorf, C. A. 1990. The effect of the Inka state on Sausa agricultural production and crop consumption. *American Antiquity* 55(2):262–290.

Hastorf, C. A. 1991. Gender, space and food in prehistory. In: Gero, J. M. and Conkey, M. W. (eds.) *Engendering Archaeology: Women and Prehistory*, pp. 132–159. Oxford: Blackwell.

Hastorf, C. A. 1999. Recent research in paleoethnobotany. *Journal of Archaeological Research* 7(1):55–103.

Hastorf, C. A. and Popper, V. S. 1988. *Current Paleoethnobotany*. Chicago: University of Chicago Press.

Hather, J. 1993. *An Archaeobotanical Guide to Root and Tuber Identification*. Vol. 1: *Europe and Southwest Asia*. Oxford: Oxbow Books.

Hather, J. 1994. *Tropical Archaeobotany: Applications and New Developments*. London: Routledge.

Helbaek, H. 1959. The domestication of food plants in the Old World. *Science* 130:365–372.

Helbaek, H. 1969. Plant collecting, dry-farming, and irrigation agriculture in prehistoric Deh Luran. In: Hole, F., Flannery, K. V., and Neeley, J. A. (eds.) *Prehistory and Human Ecology of the Deh Luran Plain*, pp. 383–426. Ann Arbor: Memoirs of the Museum of Anthropology, No. 1, University of Michigan.

Henry, A. G., Brooks, A. S., and Piperno, D. R. 2011. Microfossils in calculus demonstrate consumption of plants and cooked foods in Neanderthal diets (Shanidar III, Iraq; Spy I and II, Belgium). *Proceedings of the National Academy of Sciences* 108(2):486–491.

Henry, A. G., Hudson, H. F., and Piperno, D. P. 2009. Changes in starch grain morphologies from cooking. *Journal of Archaeological Science* 36(3):915–922.

Hildebrand, E. 2007. A tale of two tuber crops: How attributes of enset and yams may have shaped prehistoric human-plant interactions in southwest Ethiopia. In: Denham, T., Vrydaghs, L., and Iríarte, J. (eds.) *Rethinking Agriculture*, pp. 273–298. Berkeley: Left Coast Press.

Hill, B., Overholts, L. O., and Popp, H. W. 1936. *Botany*. New York: McGraw Hill.

Hillman, G. C. 1984. Interpretation of archaeological plant remains: Ethnographic models from Turkey. In: van Zeist, W. and Casparie, W. A. (eds.) *Plants and Ancient Man*, pp. 1–42. Rotterdam: Balkema.

Hillman, G. C. and Davies, M. S. 1990. Measured domestication rates in wild wheats and barley under primitive cultivation and their archaeological implications. *Journal of World Prehistory* 4(2):157–222.

Hilu, K. W., De Wet, J. M. J., and Harlan, J. R. 1979. Archaeobotanical studies of Eleusine coracana ssp. coracana (finger millet). *American Journal of Botany* 66(3):330–333.

Hole, F., Flannery, K. V., and Neely, J. A. 1969. *Prehistory and Human Ecology of the Deh Luran Plain*. Ann Arbor: Memoirs of the Museum of Anthropology, No. 1, University of Michigan.

Horrocks, M. 2005. A combined procedure for recovering phytoliths and starch residues from soils, sedimentary deposits and similar materials. *Journal of Archaeological Science* 32(8):1169–1175.

Horrocks, M. and Nunn, P. D. 2007. Evidence for introduced taro (*Colocasia esculenta*) and lesser yam (*Dioscorea esculenta*) in Lapita-era (c. 3050–2500 cal. yr BP) deposits from Bourewa, southwest Viti Levu Island, Fiji. *Journal of Archaeological Science* 34(5):739–748.

Hubbard, R. N. L. B. and al Azm, A. 1990. Quantifying preservation and distortion in carbonized seeds and investigating the history of *friké* production. *Journal of Archaeological Science* 17:103–106.

Iríarte, J. 2003. Assessing the feasibility of identifying maize through the analysis of cross-shaped size and three-dimensional morphology of phytoliths in the grasslands of southeastern South America. *Journal of Archaeological Science* 30(9):1085–1094.

Jacomet, S. 2008. *Identification of Cereal Remains from Archaeological Sites*, 3rd ed. Basel: University of Basel.

Jacomet, S. 2009. Plant economy and village life in Neolithic lake dwellings at the time of the alpine iceman. *Vegetation History and Archaeobotany* 18(1):47–59.

Jacomet, S. and Kreuz, A. 1999. *Archäobotanik. Aufgaben, Methoden und Ergebnisse vegetations- und agrargeschichtlicher Forschung*. Stuttgart: Ulmer.

Jamieson, R. W. and Sayre, M. B. 2010. Barley and identity in the Spanish colonial *Audiencia* of Quito: Archaeobotany of the 18th century San Blas neighborhood in Riobamba. *Journal of Anthropological Archaeology* 29(2):208–218.

Jones, G. 1984. Interpretation of archaeological plant remains: Ethnographic models from Greece. In: van Zeist, W. and Casparie, W. A. (eds.) *Plants and Ancient Man: Studies in Paleoethnobotany*, pp. 43–61. Rotterdam: Ballkema.

Jones, G. 1987. A statistical approach to the archaeological identification of crop processing. *Journal of Archaeological Science* 14(3):311–323.

Jones, G., Charles, M., Bogaard, A., Hodgson, J. G., and Palmer, C. 2005. The functional ecology of present-day arable weed floras and its applicability for the identification of past crop husbandry. *Vegetation History and Archaeobotany* 14(4):493–504.

Juggins, S. and Cameron, N. 1999. Diatoms and archaeology. In: Stoermer, E. F. and Smit, J. P. (eds.) *The Diatoms*, pp. 389–401. Cambridge: Cambridge University Press.

Kahlheber, S. 1999. Indications for agroforestry: archaeobotanical remains of crops and woody plants from Medieval Saouga, Burkina Faso. In: van der Veen, M. (ed.) *The Exploitation of Plant Resources in Ancient Africa*, pp, 89–100. New York: Kluwer Academic.

Kapp, R. O. 1969. *How to Know Pollen and Spores*. Dubuque, Iowa: Brown.

Kelso, G. K., Dimmick, F. R., Dimmick, D. H., and Largy, T. B. 2006. An ethnopalynological test of task-specific area analysis: Bay View Stable, Cataumet, Massachusetts. *Journal of Archaeological Science* 33(7):953–960.

Kennett, D. J., Voorhies, B., and Martorana, D. 2006. An ecological model for the origins of maize-based food production on the Pacific coast of southern Mexico. In: Kennett, D. J. and Winterhalder, B. (eds.) *Behavioral Ecology and the Transition to Agriculture*, pp. 103–136. Berkeley: University of California Press.

Korstanje, M. A. and Cuenya, P. 2010. Ancient agriculture and domestic activities: a contextual approach studying silica phytoliths and other microfossils in soils. *Environmental Archaeology* 15(1):43–63.

Kreuz, A. 1990. Searching for "single activity refuse" in Linearbandkeramik settlements. An archaeobotanical approach. In: Robinson, D. E. (ed.) *Experimentation and Reconstruction in Environmental Archaeology*, pp. 63–74. Symposia of the Association for Environmental Archaeology No. 9, Roskilde, Denmark. Oxford: Oxbow Books.

Laland, K. N., Odling-Smee, F. J., and Feldman, N. W. 2001. Cultural niche construction and human evolution. *Journal of Evolutionary Biology* 14:22–23.

Langford, M., Taylor, G. E., and Flenley, J. R. 1990. Computerized identification of pollen grains by texture analysis. *Review of Palaeobotany and Palynology* 64(1–4):197–203.

Lebreton, V., Messager, E., Marquer, L., and Renault-Miskovsky, J. 2010. A neotaphonomic experiment in pollen oxidation and its implications for archaeopalynology. *Review of Palaeobotany and Palynology* 162:29–38.

Lennstrom, H. A. and Hastorf, C. A. 1995. Interpretation in context: Sampling and analysis in paleoethnobotany. *American Antiquity* 60:701–721.

Lentfer, C. J. and Boyd, W. E. 2000. Simultaneous extraction of phytoliths, pollen and spores from sediments. *Journal of Archaeological Science* 27(5):363–372.

Lentfer, C., Therin, M., and Torrence, R. 2002. Starch grains and environmental reconstruction: A modern test case from West New Britain, Papua, New Guinea. *Journal of Archaeological Science* 29(7):687–698.

Lentz, D. L. 1991. Maya diets of the rich and poor: paleoethnobotanical evidence from Copan. *Latin American Antiquity* 2(3):269–287.

Lepofsky, D., Hallett, D., Washbrook, K., McHalsie, A., Lertzman, K., and Mathewes, R. 2005. Documenting precontact plant management on the Northwest Coast: An example of prescribed burning in the central and upper Fraser Valley, British Columbia. In: Deur, D. E. and Turner, N. J. *Keeping It Living: Traditions of Plant Use and Civilization on the Northwest Coast of North America*, pp. 218–239. Seattle: University of Washington Press.

Li, M. Q., Yang, X. Y., Wang, H., Wang, Q., Jia, X., and Ge, Q. S. 2010. Starch grains from dental calculus reveal ancient plant foodstuffs at Chenqimogou site, Gansu Province. *Science China Earth Sciences* 53(5):694–699.

Liu, L., Field, J., Fullagar, R., Bestel, S., Chen, X. C., and Ma, X. L. 2010. What did grinding stones grind? New light on early Neolithic subsistence economy in the Middle Yellow River Valley, China. *Antiquity* 84:816–833.

Logan, A. L. 2012. *A history of food without history: Food, trade, and environment in West-Central Ghana in the second millennium AD*. Doctoral thesis, Department of Anthropology, University of Michigan.

Logan, A. L. and D'Andrea, A. C. 2012. Oil palm, arboriculture, and changing subsistence practices during Kintampo times, 3900–3600 bp. *Quaternary International* 249:63–71.

Logan, A. L., Hastorf, C. A., and Pearsall, D. M. 2012. "Let's drink together": Early ceremonial use of maize in the Titicaca basin. *Latin American Antiquity* 23(3):235–258.

Lopinot, N. H. and Brussell, D. E. 1982. Assessing carbonized seeds from open-air sites in mesic environments: An example from southern Illinois. *Journal of Archaeological Science* 9(1):95–108.

Loy T. H. 1994. Methods in the analysis of starch residues on prehistoric stone tools. In: Hather, J. G. (ed.) *Tropical Archaeobotany: Applications and New Developments*, pp. 86–114. London: Routledge.

Loy T. H., Spriggs, M., and Wickler, S. 1992. Direct evidence of human use of plants 28,000 years ago: Starch residues on stone artefacts from the northern Solomon Islands. *Antiquity* 66:898–912.

Madella, M., Lancelotti, C., and Garcia-Granero, J. J. 2013. Millet microremains: An alternative approach to understand cultivation and use of critical crops in prehistory. *Archaeological and Anthropological Sciences* 8(1):17–28.

Madella, M., Lancelotti, C., and Savard, M. 2014. *Ancient Plants and People*. Tucson: University of Arizona Press.

Margaritis, E. and Jones, M. K. 2008. Olive oil production in Hellenistic Greece: The interpretation of charred olive remains from the site of Tria Platania, Macedonia, Greece (fourth–second century B.C.). *Vegetation History and Archaeobotany* 17(4):393–401.

Märkle, T. and Rösch, M. 2008. Experiments on the effects of carbonization on some cultivated plant seeds. *Vegetation History and Archaeobotany* 17 (Suppl 1):S257–S263.

Marston, J. M. 2011. Archaeological markers of agricultural risk management. *Journal of Anthropological Archaeology* 3(2):190–205.

Marston, J. M., Guedes, J. D., and Warinner, C. 2014. *Method and Theory in Paleoethnobotany*. Boulder: University Press of Colorado.

Martin, A. C. 1946. The comparative internal morphology of seeds. *American Midland Naturalist* 36(3):513–660.

Martin, A. C. and Barkley, W. D. 1961. *Seed Identification Manual*. Berkeley: University of California Press.

Mercuri, A. M. 2008. Plant exploitation and ethnopalynological evidence from the Wadi Teshuinat area (Tadrart Acacus, Libyan Sahara). *Journal of Archaeological Science* 35 (6):1619–1642.

Mercuri, A. M., Allevato, E., Arobba, D., Mazzanti, M. B., Bosi, G., Caramiello, R., Castiglioni, E., Carra, M. L., Celant, A., Costantini, L. Di Pasquale, G., Fiorentino, G., Florenzano, A., Guido, M., Marchesini, M., Lippi, M. M., Marvelli, S., Miola, A., Montanari, C., Nisbet, R., Pena-Chocarro, L., Perego, R,. Ravazzi, C., Rottoli, M., Sadori, L., Ucchesu, M., and Rinaldi, R. 2015. Pollen and macroremains from Holocene archaeological sites: a dataset for the understanding of the bio-cultural diversity of the Italian landscape. *Review of Palaeobotany and Palynology* 218:250–266.

Mercuri, A. M., Mazzanti, M. B., Florenzano, A., Montecchi, M. C., Rattighieri, E., and Torri, P. 2013. Anthropogenic pollen indicators (API) from archaeological sites as local evidence of human-induced environments in the Italian peninsula. *Annali di Botanica* 3:143–153.

Miller, N. F. 1985. Paleoethnobotanical evidence for deforestation in ancient Iran: A case study of urban Malyan. *Journal of Ethnobiology* 5(1):1–19.

Minnis, P. E. 1981. Seeds in archaeological sites: sources and some interpretive problems. *American Antiquity* 46(1):143–152.

Montgomery, F. H. 1977. *Seeds and Fruits of Plants of Eastern Canada and Northeastern United States*. Toronto: University of Toronto Press.

Moore, P. D., Webb, J.A., and Collinson, M. E. 1991. *Pollen Analysis*, 2nd ed. Oxford: Blackwell.

Morales, J., Navarro-Mederos, J. F., and Rodríguez-Rodríguez, A. 2011. Plant offerings to the gods: Seed remains from a pre-Hispanic sacrificial altar in La Gomera Island (Canary Islands, Spain). In: Fahmy, A. G., Kahlheber, S., and D'Andrea, A. C. (eds.) *Windows on the African Past: Current Approaches to African Archaeobotany*, pp. 67–78. Frankfurt: Africa Magna Verlag.

Morehart, C. T. and Eisenberg, D. T. A. 2009. Prosperity, power and change: Modeling maize at Postclassic Xaltocan, Mexico. *Journal of Anthropological Archaeology* 29(1):94–112.

Morehart, C. T., Lentz, D. L., and Prufer, K. M. 2005. Wood of the gods: The Ritual Use of Pine (*Pinus* spp.) by the Ancient Lowland Maya. *Latin American Antiquity* 16(3):255–274.

Moreno-Larrazabal, A., Teira-Brión, A., Sopelana-Salcedo, I., Arranz-Otaegui, A., and Zapata, L. 2015. Ethnobotany of millet cultivation in the north of the Iberian Peninsula. *Vegetation History and Archaeobotany* 2(4):541–554.

Morris, L. R., Ryel, R. J., and West, N. E. 2010. Can soil phytolith analysis and charcoal be used as indicators of historic fire in the pinyon-juniper and sagebrush steppe ecosystem types of the Great Basin Desert, USA? *The Holocene* 20(1):105–114.

Murray, M. A., Fuller, D. Q., and Cappeza, C. 2007. Crop production on the Senegal River in the early first millennium AD: Preliminary archaeobotanical results from Cubalel.

In: Cappers, R. (ed.) *Fields of Change, Progress in African Archaeobotany*, pp. 63–70. Groningen: Barkhuis Publishing.

Nasu, H., Momohara, A., Yasuda, Y., and He, J. 2007. The occurrence and identification of *Setaria italica* (L.) P. Beauv. (foxtail millet) grains from the Chengtoushan site (*ca*. 5800 cal B.P.) in central China, with reference to the domestication centre in Asia. *Vegetation History and Archaeobotany* 16(6):481–494.

Neff, H., Pearsall, D. M, Jones, J. G., Arroyo, B., Collins, S. K., and Friedel, D. E. 2006. Early Maya adaptive patterns: Mid-Late Holocene paleoenvironmental evidence from Pacific Guatemala. *Latin American Antiquity* 17(3):287–315.

Nesbitt, M. 2006. *Identification Guide for Near Eastern Grass Seeds*. London: Institute of Archaeology, University College London.

Nesbitt, M., Colledge, S. and Murray, M. A. 2003. Organization and management of seed reference collections. *Environmental Archaeology* 8(1):77–84.

Nesbitt, M. and Greig, J. 1989. A bibliography for the archaeobotanical identification of seeds from Europe and the Near East. *Circaea* 7(1):11:30.

Neumann, K. 2005. The romance of farming: plant cultivation and domestication in Africa. In: Stahl, A. B. (ed.) *African Archaeology*, pp. 249–275. Oxford: Blackwell.

Novello, A. and Barboni, D. 2015. Grass inflorescence phytoliths of useful species and wild cereals from sub-Saharan Africa. *Journal of Archaeological Science* 59:10–22.

Odling-Smee, F.J., Laland, K. N., and Feldman, M.W. 2003. *Niche Construction: The Neglected Process in Evolution. Monographs in Population Biology 37*. Princeton: Princeton University Press.

Out, W. A. and Madella, M. 2015. Morphometric distinction between bilobate phytoliths from *Panicum miliaceum* and *Setaria italica* leaves. *Archaeological and Anthropological Sciences* 8(3):505–521.

Palmer, C. and van der Veen, M. 2002. Archaeobotany and the social context of food. *Acta Palaeobotanica* 42(2):195–202.

Panshin, A. J. and de Zeeuw, C. 1980. *Textbook of Wood Technology*. New York: McGraw Hill.

Pearsall, D. M. 1983. Evaluating the stability of subsistence strategies by use of paleoethnobotanical data. *Journal of Ethnobiology* 3(2):121–137.

Pearsall, D. M. 2000. *Paleoethnobotany: A Handbook of Procedures*, 2nd ed. New York: Academic Press.

Pearsall, D. M. 2011. *Phytoliths in the Flora of Ecuador: The University of Missouri Online Phytolith Database*. http://phytolith.missouri.edu/ (accessed July 19, 2019).

Pearsall, D. M. 2015. *Paleoethnobotany: A Handbook of Procedures*, 3rd ed. Walnut Creek, CA: Left Coast Press.

Pearsall, D. M., Chandler-Ezell, K., and Zeidler, J. A. 2004. Maize in ancient Ecuador: Results of residue analysis of stone tools from the Real Alto site. *Journal of Archaeological Science* 31(4):423–442.

Peña-Chocarro, L. Peña, L. Z., Urquijo, J. E. G., and Estévez, J. J. I. 2009. Einkorn (*Triticum monococcum* L.) cultivation in mountain communities of the Western Rif (Morocco):

An ethnoarchaeological project. In: Fairbairn, A. S. and Weiss, E. (eds.) *From Foragers to Farmers: Papers in Honour of Gordon C. Hillman*, pp. 103–111. Oxford: Oxbow Books.

Perry, L. 2004. Starch analyses reveal the relationship between tool type and function: An example from the Orinoco valley of Venezuela. *Journal of Archaeological Science* 31(8):1069–1081.

Perry, L., Dickau, R., Zarrillo, S., Holst, I., Pearsall, D. M., Piperno, D. R., Berman, M. J., Cooke, R. G., Rademaker, K., Ranere, A. J., Raymond, J. C., Sandweiss, D. H., Scaramelli. F., Tarble, K., and Zeidler, J. A. 2007. Starch fossils and the domestication and dispersal of chili peppers (*Capsicum* spp. L.) in the Americas. *Science* 315:986–988.

Piperno, D. R. 1991. The status of phytolith analysis in the American tropics. *Journal of World Prehistory* 5(2):155–191.

Piperno, D. R. 2006a. The origins of plant cultivation and domestication in the Neotropics: A behavioural ecology perspective. In: Kennett, D. J. and Winterhalder, B. (eds.) *Behavioral Ecology and the Transition to Agriculture*, pp. 137–166. Berkeley: University of California Press.

Piperno, D. R. 2006b. *Phytoliths: A Comprehensive Guide for Archaeologists and Paleoecologists*. Lanham, MD: AltaMira Press.

Piperno D. R. and Dillehay, T. D. 2008. Starch grains on human teeth reveal early broad crop diet in northern Peru. *Proceedings of the National Academy of Sciences* 105:19622–19627.

Piperno, D. R. and Jones, J. G. 2003. Paleoecological and archaeological implications of a Late Pleistocene/Early Holocene record of vegetation and climate from the Pacific coastal plain of Panama. *Quaternary Research* 59(1):79–87.

Piperno, D. R. and Pearsall, D. M. 1993. The nature and status of phytolith analysis. In: Pearsall, D. M. and Piperno, D. R. (eds.) *Current Research in Phytolith Analysis: Applications in Archaeology and Paleoecology*, pp. 9–18. Philadelphia: University Museum of Archaeology and Anthropology, University of Pennsylvania.

Piperno, D. R., Weiss, E., Holst, I., and Nadel, D. 2004. Processing of wild cereal grains in the Upper Palaeolithic revealed by starch grain analysis. *Nature* 430:670–673.

Power, M. J., Whitlock, C., Bartlein, P. J., and Stevens, L. 2006. Fire and vegetation history during the last 3800 years in northwestern Montana. *Geomorphology* 75:420–436.

Ramsey, M. N., Rosen, A. M., and Nadel, D. 2017. Centered on the wetlands: Integrating new phytolith evidence of plant-use from the 23,000-year old site of Ohalo II, Israel. *American Antiquity* 84(2):702–722.

Reddy, S. N. 1997. If the threshing floor could talk: integration of agriculture and pastoralism during the Late Harappan in Gujarat, India. *Journal of Anthropological Archaeology* 16:162–187.

Reinhard, K. J., Geib, P. R., Callahan, M. M., and Hevly, R. H. 1992. Discovery of colon contents in a skeletonized burial: Soil sampling for dietary remains. *Journal of Archaeological Science* 19(6):697–705.

Renfrew, J. 1973. *Palaeoethnobotany: The Prehistoric Food Plants of the Near East and Europe*. New York: Columbia University Press.

Revedin, A., Aranguren, B., Becattini, R., Longo, L., Marconi, E., Lippi, M. M., Skakun, N., Sinitsyn, A., Spiridonova, E., and Svoboda, J. 2010. Thirty-thousand-year-old evidence of plant food processing. *Proceedings of the National Academy of Sciences* 107(44):18815–18819.

Riehl, S. 2009. Archaeobotanical evidence for the interrelationship of agricultural decizion-making and climate change in the ancient Near East. *Quaternary International* 19(1–2):93–114.

Rindos, D. 1984. *The Origins of Agriculture: An Evolutionary Perspective*. New York: Academic Press.

Rösch, M. 2005. Pollen analysis of the contents of excavated vessels: Direct archaeobotanical evidence of beverages. *Vegetation History and Archaeobotany* 14(3):179–188.

Rosen, A. M. and Weiner, S. 1994. Identifying irrigation: A new method using opaline phytoliths from emmer wheat. *Journal of Archaeological Science* 21(1):125–132.

Saul, H., Madella, M., Fischer, A., Glykou, A., Hartz, S., and Craig, O. E. 2013. Phytoliths in pottery reveal the use of spice in European prehistoric cuizine. *PLoS One* 8(8):1–5.

Saul, H., Wilson, J., Heron, C. P., Glykou, A., Hartz, S., and Craig, O. E. 2012. A systematic approach to the recovery and identification of starches from carbonised deposits on ceramic vessels. *Journal of Archaeological Science* 39(12):3483–3492.

Scarry, C. M. and Steponaitis, V. P. 1997. Between farmstead and center: the natural and social landscape of Moundville. In: Gremillion, K. J. (eds.) *People, Plants, and Landscapes: Studies in Paleoethnobotany*, pp. 107–122. Tuscaloosa: University of Alabama Press.

Scheel-Ybert, R., Beauclair, M., and Buarque, A. 2014. The forest people: landscape and firewood use in the Araruama region (Southeastern Brazil) during the late Holocene. *Vegetation History and Archaeobotany* 23(2):97–111.

Schlumbaum, A., Tensen, M., and Jaenicke-Després, V. 2008. Ancient plant DNA in archaeobotany. *Vegetation History and Archaeobotany* 17(2):233–244.

Schoch, W. H., Pawlik, B., and Schweingruber, F. H. 1988. *Botanische Makrorests/Botanical Macro-Remains/Macrorestes Botaniques*. Berne and Stuttgart: Paul Haupt.

Smith, B. D. 2001. Low Level Food Production. *Journal of Archaeological Research* 9(1):1–43.

Smith, B. D. 2007. Niche construction and the behavioral context of plant and animal domestication. *Evolutionary Anthropology* 16(5):188–199.

Smith, B. D. 2012. A cultural niche construction theory of initial domestication. *Biological Theory* 6(3):1–12.

Smith, B. D. 2015. A comparison of niche construction theory and diet breadth models as explanatory frameworks for the initial domestication of plants and animals. *Journal of Archaeological Research* 23(3):215–262.

Steward, J. H. 1959. The concept and method of cultural ecology. *Readings in Anthropology* 2:81–95.

Struever, S. 1968. Flotation techniques for recovery of small-scale archaeological remains. *American Antiquity* 33(3):353–362.

Szymanski, R. M. and Morris, C. F. 2015. Internal structure of carbonized wheat (*Triticum* spp.) grains: relationships to kernel texture and ploidy. *Vegetation History and Archaeobotany* 24(4):503–515.

Talay, L., Keller, D.A., and Munson, P. J. 1984. Hickory nuts, walnuts, butternuts, and hazelnuts: Observations and experiments relevant to their Aboriginal exploitation in eastern North America. In: Munson, P. J. (ed.) *Experiments and Observations on Aboriginal Wild Plant Food Utilization in Eastern North America*, pp. 338–359. Indianapolis: Prehistory Research Series, Vol. VI, No. 2. Indiana Historical Society.

Tester, R. F., Karkalas, J., and Qi, X. 2004. Starch: Composition, fine structure and architecture. *Journal of Cereal Science* 39(2):151–165.

Théry-Parisot, I., Chabal, L., and Chrzavzez, J. 2010. Anthracology and taphonomy, from wood gathering to charcoal analysis: A review of the taphonomic processes modifying charcoal assemblages in archaeological contexts. *Palaeogeography, Palaeoclimatology, Palaeoecology* 291:142–153.

Thiébault, S. 1997. Early Holocene vegetation and the human impact in central Provence (Var, France): Charcoal analysis of the Baume de Fontbrégoua. *The Holocene* 7(3):343–349.

Thiébault, S. (ed.) 2002. *Charcoal analysis: Methodological Approaches, Palaeoecological Results and Wood Uses.* Proceedings of the Second International Meeting of Anthracology. B.A.R. International Series 1063. Oxford: Archaeopress.

Torrence, R. 2006a. Description, classification, and identification. In: Torrence, R. and Barton, H. (eds.) *Ancient Starch Research*, pp. 115–143. Walnut Creek, CA: Left Coast Press.

Torrence, R. 2006b. Starch in sediments. In: Torrence, R. and Barton, H. (eds.) *Ancient Starch Research*, pp. 145–176. Walnut Creek, CA: Left Coast Press.

Torrence, R. and Barton, H. 2006. *Ancient Starch Research*. Walnut Creek, CA: Left Coast Press.

Trigger, B. G. 2006. *A History of Archaeological Thought*, 2nd ed. Cambridge: Cambridge University Press.

Tsartsidou, G., Lev-Yadun, S., Efstratiou, N., and Weiner, S. 2008. Ethnoarchaeological study of phytolith assemblages from an agro-pastoral village in northern Greece (Sarakini): Development and application of a phytolith difference index. *Journal of Archaeological Science* 35(3):600–613.

Tsartsidou, G., Lev-Yadun, S., Efstratiou, N., and Weiner, S. 2009. Use of space in a Neolithic village in Greece (Makri): Phytolith analysis and comparison of phytolith assemblages from an ethnographic setting in the same area. *Journal of Archaeological Science* 36(10):2342–2352.

Valamoti, S. M. 2011. Grain for the dead? Archaeobotanical evidence from Mavropigi-Fylotsairi Kozanis. In: Karametreou-Mentesidi, G. (ed.) *The Archaeological Work in Upper Macedonia* 1, 2009, pp. 245–256. Kozani: Archaeological Ergo in Ano Macedonia.

Valamoti, S. M., Moniaki, A., and Karathanou, A. 2011. An investigation of processing and consumption of pulses among prehistoric societies: Archaeobotanical, experimental and ethnographic evidence from Greece. *Vegetation History and Archaeobotany* 20(5):381–396.

Valamoti, S. M., Samuel, D., Bayram, M., and Marinova, E. 2008. Prehistoric cereal foods from Greece and Bulgaria: Investigation of starch microstructure in experimental and archaeological charred remains. *Vegetation History and Archaeobotany* 17 (Suppl. 1): S265–S276.

van der Veen, M. 2007. Formation processes of desiccated and carbonized plant remains: The identification of routine practice. *Journal of Archaeological Science* 34(6):968–990.

van der Veen, M. 2011. *Consumption, Trade and Innovation: Exploring the Botanical Remains from the Roman and Islamic Ports at Qudseir Al-Qadim, Egypt.* Frankfurt: Africa Magna Verlag.

VanDerwarker, A. M. and Detwiler, K. R. 2002. Gendered practice in Cherokee foodways: A spatial analysis of plant remains from the Coweeta Creek Site. *Southeastern Archaeology* 21(1):21–28.

VanDerwarker, A. M., Scarry, M., and Eastman, J. M. 2007. Menus for families and feasts: Household and community consumption of plants at Upper Saratown, North Carolina. In: Twiss, K. (ed.) *Archaeology of Food and Identity*, pp. 16–49. Carbondale: Centre for Archaeological Investigations, Southern Illinois University.

Van Vilsteren, V. T. 1984. The medieval village of Dommelen: A case study for the interpretation of charred seeds from postholes. In: van Zeist, W. and Casparie, W. A. (eds.) *Plants and Ancient Man*, pp. 227–235. Rotterdam: Balkema.

van Zeist, W. and Casparie, W. A. 1984. *Plants and Ancient Man: Studies in Palaeoethnobotany*. Rotterdam: Balkema.

van Zeist, W., Wasylikova, K., and Berhe, K.-E. 1991. *Progress in Old World Palaeoethnobotany*. Rotterdam: Balkema.

Vernet, J.-L., Ogereau, P., Figueiral, I., Machado Yanes, C., and Uzquiano, P. 2001. *Guide d'identification des charbons de bois préhistoriques et récents: Sud-Ouest de l'Europe: France, Péninsule Ibérique et Îles Canaries.* Paris: CNRS editions.

Wagner, G. E. 1988. Comparability among recovery techniques. In: Hastorf, C. A. and Popper, V. A. (eds.) *Current Palaeoethnobotany*, pp. 17–35. Chicago: University of Chicago Press.

Walshaw, S. C. 2010. Converting to rice: urbanisation, Islamization and crops on Pemba Island, Tanzania, AD 700–1500. *World Archaeology* 42(1):137–154.

Wasylikowa, K., Mitka, J., Wendorf, F., and Schild, R. 1997. Exploitation of wild plants by the early Neolithic hunter–gatherers of the Western Desert, Egypt: Nabta Playa as a case-study. *Antiquity* 71:932–941.

Watson, P. J. 1976. In pursuit of prehistoric subsistence: A comparative account of some contemporary flotation systems. *Mid-Continental Journal of Archaeology* 1(1):77–100.

Watson, P. J. 1997. The shaping of modern paleoethnobotany. In: Gremillion, K. J. (ed.) *People, Plants, and Landscapes: Studies in Paleoethnobotany*, pp. 13–22. Tuscaloosa: University of Alabama Press.

Watson, P. J. and Kennedy, M. C. 1991. The development of horticulture in the Eastern Woodlands of North America: Women's role. In: Gero, J. M. and Conkey, M. W. (eds.) *Engendering Archaeology: Women and Prehistory*, pp. 255–275. Oxford: Blackwell.

Weber S. A. 1999. Seeds of urbanism: Palaeoethnobotany and the Indus Civilization. *Antiquity* 73:813–826.

Weiss, E. and Kislev, M. E. 2004. Plant remains as indicators for economic activity: A case study from Iron Age Ashkelon. *Journal of Archaeological Science* 31(1):1–13.

Weiss, E., Kislev, M. E., Simchoni, O., Nadel, D., and Tschauner, H. 2008. Plant-food preparation area on an Upper Paleolithic brush hut floor at Ohalo II, Israel. *Journal of Archaeological Science* 35(8):2400–2414.

Welch, P. D. and Scarry, C. M. 1995. Status-related variation in foodways in the Moundville chiefdom. *American Antiquity* 60(3):397–419.

Willcox G. 2002. Evidence for ancient forest cover and deforestation from charcoal analysis of ten archaeological sites on the Euphrates. In: Thiébault, S. (ed.) *Charcoal Analysis. Methodological Approaches, Palaeoecological Results and Wood Uses*, pp. 141–145. BAR International Series 1063. Oxford: Archaeopress.

Willcox, G. 2012. Pre-domestic cultivation during the late Pleistocene and early Holocene in the northern Levant. In: Gepts, P., Famula, T. R., Bettinger, R. L., Brush, S. B., Damania, A. B., McGuire, P. E. and Qualset, C. O. (eds.) *Biodiversity in Agriculture: Domestication, Evolution and Sustainability*, pp. 92–109. Cambridge: Cambridge University Press.

Willcox G., Nesbitt, M., and Bittmann, F. 2012. From collecting to cultivation: Transitions to a production economy in the Near East. (Editorial). Special Issue The Origins of Agriculture in the Near East. *Vegetation History and Archaeobotany* 21(2):81–83.

Winterhalder, B. and Goland, C. 1997. An evolutionary ecology perspective on diet choice, risk, and plant domestication. In: Gremillion, K. J. (ed.) *People, Plants, and Landscapes: Studies in Paleoethnoboany*, pp. 123–160. Tuscaloosa: University of Alabama Press.

Wollstonecroft, M. M. 2002. The fruit of their labour: plants and plant processing at EeRb 140 (860 ± 60 uncal BP to 160± 50 uncal B.P.) a late prehistoric hunter-gatherer-fisher site on the southern Interior Plateau, British Columbia, Canada. *Vegetation History and Archaeobotany* 11(1–2):61–70.

Wollstonecroft, M. M. 2011. Investigating the role of food processing in human evolution: A niche construction approach. *Archaeological and Anthropological Sciences* 3(1):141–150.

Wright, P. J. 2003. Preservation or destruction of plant remains by carbonization? *Journal of Archaeological Science* 30(5):577–583.

Wright, P. J. 2008. Understanding the carbonization and preservation of sunflower and sumpweed remains. *Midcontinental Journal of Archaeology* 33(2):137–153.

Yang, X., Ma, Z., Li, Q., Perry, L., Huan, X., Wan, Z., Li, M., and Zheng, J. 2014a. Experiments with lithic tools: Understanding starch residues from crop harvesting. *Archaeometry* 56(5):828–840.

Yang, X., Ma, Z., Wang, T., Perry, L., Li, Q., Huan, X., and Yu, J. 2014b. *Chinese Science Bulletin* 59(32):4352–4358.

Yang, X. Y., Yu, J. C., Lu, H. Y., Cui, T. X., Guo, J. N., and Ge, Q. S. 2009. Starch grain analysis reveals function of grinding stone tools at Shangzhai Site, Beijing. *Science in China Series D, Earth Sciences* 52(8):1164–1171.

Yarnell, R. A. 1970. Paleo-ethnobotany in America. In: Brothwell, D. and Higgs, E. (eds.) *Science and Archaeology*, pp. 215–228. New York: Praeger.

Zarrillo, S., Pearsall, D. M., Raymond, J. S., Tisdale, M. A., and Quon, D. J. 2008. Directly dated starch residues document early formative maize (*Zea mays* L.) in tropical Ecuador. *Proceedings of the National Academy of Sciences* 105(13):5006–5011.

Zeder, M. A., Bradley, D. G., Emshwiller, E., and Smith, D. B. 2006. *Documenting Domestication: New Genetic and Archaeological Paradigms*. Berkeley: University of California Press.

Zohary D. and Hopf, M. 2000. *Domestication of Plants in the Old World*, 3rd ed. New York: Oxford University Press.

13

Geoarchaeology

Panagiotis Karkanas

The application of geoscience-based methods to archaeological sites to understand site formation processes and use.

1 INTRODUCTION

In its broadest definition, geoarchaeology is the study of the archaeological record using any geoscience-based technique, method, concept, or knowledge (Rapp and Hill 2006). However, since archaeometry is a well-defined field focusing on the application of physical sciences to archeological prospecting, dating, and provenance (Waters 1992), it could be proposed that geoarchaeology has a more narrow definition, actually closer to the original coining of the term (Renfrew 1976) and to its modern main application. In this approach, geoarchaeology is the discipline that studies site stratigraphy and site formation processes, and the interaction of human and nature in shaping the landscape (Butzer 1982; French 2003; Goldberg and Macphail 2006; Waters 1992;). The history of this approach goes back several hundred years, as can be seen in the 1863 monograph of Sir Charles Lyell: *Geological Evidences of the Antiquity of Man*. However, it was not until 1976 that Colin Renfrew introduced and defined the term "geoarchaeology" in the preface of an edited volume by Davidson and Shackley (1976). Indeed, Renfrew (1976) defined precisely what should be the main concern of geoarchaeology, concisely summed up by Goldberg and Macphail (2006: 3): "geoarchaeology provides the ultimate context of all aspects of archaeology from understanding the position of a site in a landscape setting to a comprehension of the context of individual finds and features."

That being so, the scale of practicing geoarchaeology varies from a regional perspective scale to that of a single site. Although a combination of offsite and on-site study will help with understanding the position of a site in the larger geomorphic system (Butzer 2008), there is usually a dichotomy between geoarchaeologists dealing with site formation processes and geoarchaeologists focusing on landscape studies. This does not imply that there are no integral perspectives or that there are no sites (e.g., early hominin sites) in which a mixed approach is always followed (see Ashley et al. 2009 and discussion in Butzer 2008; Quade et al. 2004). A possible distinction does exist and refers to whether we are looking for the context of the site as a whole or not. On-site geoarchaeology requires a range of expertise dictated by the infinitive repertoire of anthropogenic site-settlement activities, natural sedimentary facies that are not normally studied in larger scale projects (e.g., rain or sheetwash, ponding and very small-scale mass wasting and sediment gravity-flows) and site-specific post-depositional alterations and disturbances (e.g., trampling, dung decay, wood ash alteration). On the other hand, landscape geoarchaeology is a more straightforward application of geomorphology and environmental sciences. Nevertheless, both approaches are interdisciplinary and share the same ultimate goal, that is, the study of archaeological context. In addition, site-specific formation processes are not independent of the larger geomorphic system; therefore a good on-site geoarchaeological study needs to integrate the site processes into the surrounding landscape. Thus it appears that the aforementioned dichotomy never exists in reality but it can be theoretically accepted because it serves the specific objectives of archaeology.

The following summarises the main aspects of landscape and on-site geoarchaeology and provides some examples of their application.

2 LANDSCAPE GEOARCHAEOLOGY

The landscape approach dominates geoarchaeological research. It is mostly of regional perspective scale, aiming a) to reconstruct the landscape for understanding site locations, distributions and spatial changes, b) to recognise how natural and human-induced processes alter the landscape and c) to identify intentional manipulation of the environment (forest clearance, cultivation, manuring, irrigation systems, dams, land recreations, etc.).

The first objective is commonly associated with regional archaeological surveys, which attempt to locate unidentified sites and to trace changes in settlement pattern through time, often in relation to the distribution of natural resources. Geoarchaeological study aims to facilitate sampling strategies, prioritise survey regions, and provide an environmental framework for survey data interpretation (Wells 2001). In addition, a major goal is the prediction of the location of buried sites (Ferring 2001; Gladfelter 1985; Hassan 1985). In a first stage, the geoarchaeological survey requires the recognition of landform formations. In a later stage, the reconstruction of the palaeolandscape will show the relation of the settlements and land-use practices with the landscape during specific periods. According to Wells (2001), three distinct kinds of geomorphological data are needed to accomplish this goal: stability, chronology, and palaeoenvironment. The determination of the stability (stable, depositional, erosional, or mixed) of the geomorphological surfaces will show which artefacts have been reworked and explain why some surfaces are sterile (due to erosion or sedimentary burial). The age of the geomorphic surface will determine what parts of the landscape were extant during any particular period. Finally, the reconstruction of the palaeolandscape during a particular period will provide the ultimate context of the artefacts and sites. A good example is the geoarchaeology of the Great Plains in North America where the reconstruction of its geomorphic history was used to understand the presence and temporal distribution of Paleoindian sites and eventually contribute to the issue of peopling of the New World (Mandel 1992; Mandel 2000). Geomorphic, chronostratigraphic, and soil-stratigraphic data were used to predict buried sites for each cultural period in the river basins. It was shown that geological processes have affected the archaeological record by either removing or burying sites that date to certain cultural periods not presented in the area.

Furthermore, landscape geoarchaeology is concerned with setting a particular archaeological site in its immediate environment. It is interested in integrating the whole site into major landscape features and understanding what circumstances governed its location, and defined land-use practices, but also in investigating what affected its subsequent preservation over the longer term (e.g., Draut et al. 2008). This approach tries to put the archaeological site as a whole in its regional context and can be considered in its broader sense as site formation processes (Goldberg and Macphail 2006). For example, the geoarchaeological study of the alluviation history of the floodplain surrounding the medieval city of Alzira (Spain) illuminated its constructional and settlement history, such as expansion and shrink, and abandonment and occupation (Butzer et al. 1983). The geoarchaeological reconstruction of the past landscape and environment at the Neolithic Çatalhöyük (Turkey) was directly linked to the excavated on-site evidence for subsistence. It was shown that the bulk of the cereal agriculture was not carried out in the immediate vicinity of the site as the area was flooded each spring and thus would

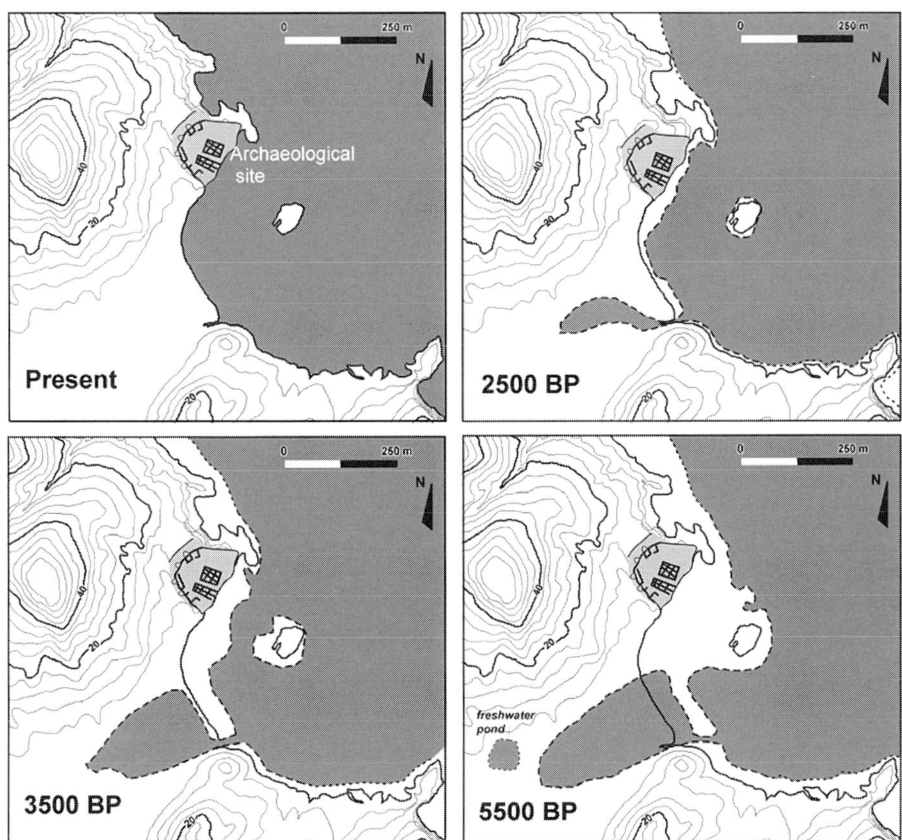

FIGURE 13.1 Palaeogeographical reconstruction of the coastal area in the Bay of Palamari, Skyros Island, Greece. Note that the extent of Palamari archaeological site during antiquity is not known in the presently submerged area (see Pavlopoulos et al. 2010).

have damaged any autumn-sown cereal crops (Roberts and Rosen 2009). Another example comes from the reconstruction of the palaeoenvironment and coastal evolution at the Bronze Age Palamari fortification in Skyros Island, Greece (Pavlopoulos et al. 2010). The flourishing of the settlement is probably related to the existence of a sheltered and protected lagoon connected to the sea between about 4000 and 1500 BC. The decline of Palamari might be related to geomorphological and environmental changes that rendered the embayment a restricted body of water (Figure 13.1).

The second objective of landscape geoarchaeology includes the documenting of all landform changes, such as tectonic and sea-level changes; aeolian and periglacial processes; erosional and alluvial events; and recognizing all the effects of humans in altering the environment. The ultimate goal is to differentiate natural from human-induced changes, find their interrelationships and understand how people managed such changes (Frederick 2001; French 2003). Intensive geoarchaeological research in the past decades has made considerable progress in assessing the impact of human activities in a naturally changing environment. The Mediterranean environment, for example, has witnessed several stages of erosion and formation of alluvial fill. Vita-Finzi (1969) in his pioneering classic investigation of Mediterranean alluviation introduced a general model of aggradation restricted to two well-defined time periods. Later, Wagstaff (1981) showed that the Holocene alluviation history of Greece was much more complicated than Vita-Finzi thought. Van Andel et al. (1986), in an intensive geoarcheological study of the Argolid peninsula, Peloponnese, Greece, suggested that the Pleistocene alluvial sediments could be a climatic result but the Holocene series was essentially the result of human impact. Van Andel and his team expanded their research further north to Thessaly, Greece, where they documented earlier erosional and depositional phases attributed to the clearance of the land by rising Neolithic farming populations (Van Andel and Runnels 1995). Although several other scholars have contributed to expanding the record of alluvial and erosion episodes in Greece, what is interesting is the ongoing debate on the causes of these episodes as to whether they are human induced, natural, or multi-causal (see discussion in Bintliff 2002 and Butzer 2005). At this point, close links between regional geoarchaeological research and basic research in climatic changes, tectonics, and geomorphology (to name a few) should be underlined. Although both types of research have their own agendas, in the last decades, geoarchaeological research has gained much from palaeoclimatology, for example; conversely it has also contributed to some degree in studying past climatic changes (see Karkanas et al. 2008; Karkanas et al. 2015).

The third objective, although of regional importance, is often based on smaller-scale studies. It is actually concerned with direct human impacts on the environment through a number of activities. Medium-scale land recreations are often encountered in urban archaeology. By using a scrics of cores, Ammerman (1996) was able to reconstruct the relief of the area of the ancient Agora at Athens. He demonstrated that a major transformation of the landscape was necessitated at the end of the sixth century BC to build the well-known complex of monuments and relocate the drainage system. In the same vein, the detailed sedimentological and stratigraphic work of Huckleberry (1995; Huckleberry 1999) on the prehistoric Hohokam agriculturalists (Arizona) that practised canal irrigation provided a detailed record of palaeofloods and channel changes. These were partly responsible for the changes in their settlement pattern.

Soil evidence identifying forest and woodland clearance, cultivation, and manuring have been found in several cases. Soil micromorphological features, charcoal analysis, pollen, phytoliths, and chemical changes are all used to provide evidence of soil disturbances associated with agricultural practices (Courty et al. 1989: 126–137; Davidson and Carter 1998; Goldberg and Macphail 2006: 193–210; Macphail et al. 1990). Disposal of urban waste in arable lands has also been successfully recognised (Davidson et al. 2006). In some cases, extensive soil modifications and deterioration of vast areas have been attributed to human impact (Macphail et al. 1987). The use of agricultural terracing is very well known in the Mediterranean area. Detailed stratigraphic, soil, and sediment analysis showed interesting implications for the preservation of the archaeological record; early agricultural landscapes and soils; and past land use, as well as for interpretation of local records of Holocene erosion and valley alluviation (Krahtopoulou and Frederick 2008).

Most of the studies related to landscape geoarchaeology employ traditional soil science, geological, and geomorphological methods. These include recognition and analysis of geomorphological features, which establish a sequence of landforms (morphostratigraphy), for instance an alluvial terrace sequence (Ferring 2001; Mandel 1992). Another method is the identification of alluvial facies bounded by discontinuities (allostratigraphic units). The latter connote a significant change in the depositional regime, caused by climatic changes; tectonic activity; or base level changes (Ferring 2001). Furthermore, identification of sequences of buried soils (Holliday 2004; Mandel and Bettis III 2001) could be a fundamental tool for stratigraphic correlations (pedostratigraphy) and dating the sediments (geochronology) will provide the necessary time framework. In addition, more detailed soil studies (pH, organic matter, cation exchange capacity, chemical analysis, etc.) and analysis of soil formation processes (soil micromorphology) can be used in landscape and climatic reconstruction (Angelucci et al. 2007; Macphail 1986). A variety of sedimentological analytical approaches (sedimentary structures, grain-size analysis, mineralogy, chemical analysis, magnetic parameters, etc.) are used to characterise the depositional environment and determine the source of the sediments (Woodward et al. 2001). In addition, palaeoenvironmental indices such as micro-charcoal, pollen, phytoliths, ostracods, and diatoms are employed for reconstructing the palaeolandscape (Glais et al. 2017; Pavlopoulos et al. 2006; Sadori et al. 2004).

3 ON-SITE GEOARCHAEOLOGY

Site geoarchaeology is more neglected, although it is now becoming of increasing importance in geoarchaeological investigations (Butzer 1981; Goldberg et al. 2007; Goldberg et al. 2009; Karkanas et al. 2007; Karkanas et al. 2015; Karkanas and Goldberg 2019; Karkanas and Van de Moortel 2014; Macphail et al. 1997; Macphail et al. 2017; Matthews et al. 1996; Mallol 2006; Mentzer et al. 2017; Milek and Roberts 2013; Miller et al. 2013; Shahack-Gross et al. 2005; Shillito and Matthews 2013; Weiner et al. 1993). It is concerned with the deposits found at a site, and with what people have left behind. This microscale approach is focused on the formation processes that built the site and actually deals with archaeological sediments *sensu stricto* (Goldberg and Macphail 2006).

In contrast to landscape geoarchaeology, the study of occupational deposits demands a nontraditional approach and analyses. Site microstratigraphy and microfacies analysis using microscopic techniques (Courty et al. 1989; Courty 2001) are combined with traditional bulk sedimentological methods (i.e., granulometry, bulk chemistry, see also above) focused on deciphering the special nature of anthropogenic deposits. In particular, such an approach involves micromorphology, the study of intact sediments and soils at a microscopic scale (Courty et al. 1989), and mineralogical, microchemical, or physicochemical analysis of soils and sediments using instrumental techniques (Goldberg and Macphail 2006: 335–367). By using this combination of techniques it is possible to unravel specific human activities, identify the use of a space and to understand the depositional context of all archaeological remains.

As opposed to architectural sites (e.g., urban centers), in non-constructed sites (e.g., palaeolithic sites) cultural deposits mainly consist of burnt and other organic remains. In these sites, the study of the microstatigraphy and microstructure of cultural deposits can unravel specific burning activities and use of space, such as *in situ* burning and dumping areas, or activities related to cleaning and modifying living sectors (Goldberg 2003; Goldberg et al. 2009; Karkanas and Goldberg 2019: 171–197; Meignen et al. 2007; Miller et al. 2013). Post-depositional alterations tend to obliterate combustion features, either by ash recrystallisation (Karkanas et al. 2007) or chemical alterations (Karkanas et al. 2000; Karkanas et al. 2002; Schiegl et al. 1996; Weiner et al. 1993). These post-depositional processes have serious implications for the preservation of all archaeological remains, since each type of archaeological material is stable under certain chemical conditions and can dissolve when found in a different geochemical regime (Karkanas et al. 2000). Organic matter, phytoliths, bone, chert or flint, wood ash, and sometimes even charcoal could be destroyed, thus impoverishing the archaeological record and even leading to erroneous interpretations. In some cases there are good indications, direct or indirect, of the past presence or absence of these materials (for a review see Karkanas 2010).

Natural sedimentary processes dominate at non-constructed sites. The superimposition of natural and cultural processes in the same depositional unit produces unique sedimentary structures and contents that cannot easily be identified by the naked eye. To disentangle these processes someone has to detect fine-scale grading, crude sorting, and orientation of particles, sometimes in mm-thick layers inside predominately anthropogenic deposits. All of the above are the result of a particular natural depositional regime that provides the basic framework for interpreting the context of the archaeological remains (Courty et al. 2001; Goldberg et al. 2007; Karkanas 2001; Karkanas et al. 2015; Karkanas and Goldberg 2019: 21–98; Macphail and McAvoy 2008; Mallol et al. 2011). Nonetheless, the type of processes can also be linked with the spatial patterning of the cultural remains at the specific site (Lenoble et al. 2008). Climatic signals have also been detected in archaeological sedimentary sequences. In particular, open caves and rockshelters have been proved to be very promising in revealing climatic changes (Courty and Vallverdu 2001; Karkanas et al. 2008; Karkanas et al. 2015; Woodward and Goldberg 2001) because caves act as sedimentary traps. The study of the cave sedimentary sequences has employed both traditional sedimentological analyses (Butzer 1981) and micromorphology (Goldberg et al. 2009; Karkanas et al. 2015; Karkanas and Goldberg 2013; Mallol et al. 2011; Miller et al. 2013; Shahack-Gross et al. 2014).

The Paleoindian site of Wilson-Leonard is an example of using on-site data to understand both the relation of the site to the changing palaeoenvironment (actually in the realm of landscape geoarchaeology), and the identification of human behaviors at the site. At this site, sedimentary facies and microfacies analyses and their vertical and lateral variations were used to reconstruct the site settlement and sediment history. Wilson-Leonard was occupied when a fluvial channel was abandoned by avulsion. Fluvial sediment continued to accumulate on the site from the nearby river but gradually became less important and covered the site only during major floods. Concomitantly the occupation of the site increased, along with the use of numerous burnt rock ovens and the production of fire-related organic matter that was mixed with colluvium material derived from the slopes behind the site (Goldberg and Macpail 2006: 33–37, and references therein).

One of the best examples of site geoarchaeology is the study of stabling activities in southern Europe where occupational deposits interchange in time and space, with stabling remains as a result of the complex (almost idiosyncratic) nature of human activities (Golberg and Macphail 2006). On the basis of differences in the nature of the components and the microstructure and arrangement of dung remains, it was possible to differentiate between animal species and possible food sources. Furthermore, specific human practices were identified, such as dung burning for clearing purposes and the construction of floors (Karkanas 2006; Macphail et al. 1997; Boschian and Montagnari-Kokelj 2000).

Site formation processes in urban and other architectural sites are even more complicated (Karkanas and Goldberg 2019: 199–221). Natural sedimentary features are not well expressed. These sites are dominated by small-scale gravity-based processes, rain wash, and aeolian activities (e.g., disintegration and gradual collapse of houses). Microscopic water-laid surface crusts, well-sorted wind-laid sands, and graded bedding in puddles are good indications of unroofed areas (Matthews and Postage 1994; Matthews 1995). Moreover, geoarchaeological studies of occupational sequences in tells have provided valuable information on social behavior, change and organisation (Karkanas and Efstratiou 2009; Karkanas and Van de Moortel 2014; Matthews 1995; Matthews et al. 1996). A set of sediment characteristics is related to different maintenance and discard practices and specific activities (Karkanas and Goldberg 2019: 138–148; Karkanas and Van de Moortel 2014; Matthews 1995). Evidence of dumping, trampling, sweeping, and food preparation, storage, and cooking were identified in several cases as the micro-content and, particularly, the fabric of the sediment are indicative of the different mechanisms involved in their formation (Courty et al. 1989; Ge et al. 1993).

In addition, petrographic, grain-size, mineralogical, and chemical analyses of architectural materials (mudbricks, plasters, mortars, constructed floors, etc.) has enabled identification of a range of natural and anthropogenic source materials and characterisation of different manufacturing techniques (Goren and Goldberg 1991; Karkanas 2007; Nodarou et al. 2008; Simpson et al. 2006). In particular, the study of spatial and temporal variation of floor sequences, and associated occupational debris, at the Neolithic site of Çatalhöyük has provided clues for the use of space and changes in use (Matthews et al. 1996). At the same site, micromorphology is used to infer how the deposits were formed, while phytolith, mineralogical, and residue analyses are used to analyse specific components in each thin layer of the micromorphology block. By integrating these microanalytical techniques, it was possible to infer cyclical patterns in deposits and activity types in the middens of the site (Shillito et al. 2011). Along the same lines, at a Neolithic tell site in northern Greece, Makri, the micromorphological study identified two types of floors. One type were the numerous informal floor surfaces that were prepared with recycled

FIGURE 13.2 Micromorphological sample (a) and a resin-impregnated slab of it (b) of a series of constructed floors in the Neolithic site of Marki, Greece. Photomicrographs of certain areas of the sample are shown in c, d, and e with plane polarised light: c. Articulated phytoliths (with arrow) on top of a floor that might represent a relic of matting; d. Red clay finishing coats (dark grey on the photo) on well-prepared lime floors. The upper one was laid on a replastering; e. Well-prepared lime floors showing lamina of debris (every-day dirt) entrapped in between them (see Karkanas and Efstratiou, 2009).

rubbish by the occupants. The others were formal floors, rich in lime plaster that had been relaid at regular intervals, indicating a communal decision (Karkanas and Efstratiou 2009). Both type of floors preserve anthropogenic remains on their surface, implying specific activities (Figure 13.2). At the Iron Age Tel Dor (Israel), the microscopic fabric and content enabled differentiation between constructional fills (i.e., those representing a single depositional episode) and occupational-accumulated fills (i.e., those slowly accumulating through continuous *in situ* habitation) (Shahack-Gross et al. 2005). The nature of the fills allowed a chronological and functional association between artefacts and fills, and the surrounding architecture. Such a microanalytical approach may also solve problems related to the general nature of the site. At the Iron Age settlements of the Negev highlands (Israel), based on the nature of the components and the microstructure and arrangement of dung remains, and corroborated by mineralogical and isotopic analyses, it was shown that the inhabitants were desert-adapted pastoralists, rather than garrisoned soldiers as it was long believed (Shahack-Gross and Finkelstein 2008).

Occupational deposits might have been exposed to high temperatures. Mineralogical and chemical analysis, corroborated by micromorphology, at Tel Dor identified different ways that heat-affected sediments were produced and accumulated (Berna et al. 2007). This type of analysis can be used to reconstruct fire-associated activities.

Finally, unintentionally left chemical imprints of daily activities provide important clues as to past practices and space use. Phosphorous and multi-element analyses have been applied to a range of occupational sequences with very promising results (King 2008; Middleton 2004). For example, a good correlation is found between high phosphorous concentrations in soils and food processing, consumption and disposal, whereas heavy metals are related to the use of mineral pigments and craft activities (Terry et al. 2004).

4 CONCLUDING REMARKS

Geoarchaeological research is an integral aspect of archaeological study. As Renfrew stated when he originally coined the term, "every archaeological problem starts as a problem in geoarchaeology" (1976: 2). This is not surprising if someone considers that all archaeological findings are buried in sediment or scattered on the landscape. Geoarchaeology provides the means for interpreting the context of all anthropogenic remains, either of a site or an individual artefact. In the realm of the site, geoarchaeology is of increasing importance, but a lot more has to be done to unravel the full suite of anthropogenic processes responsible for the formation of the archaeological deposits. Nevertheless, studies so far have clearly shown how powerful a tool geoarchaeology is in understanding the use of space and the nature of the human activities, or for reconstructing the palaeoenvironmental setting of a site. In studying the role of humans in changing past landscapes, geoarchaeology has made huge progress in the last few years. However, cause-and-effect relationships cannot rely only on natural science information but must also draw on social science approaches in an integrative and interdisciplinary methodology (Butzer 2005). Finally, one of the most successful applications of geoarchaeology is landscape reconstruction for finding new sites and understanding site locations, distributions and spatial changes. These kinds of studies are based on a much more solid body of geological, geomorphological and other environmental data, and – with an associated literature of far greater temporal history – have consequently more straightforward interpretations.

REFERENCES

Ammerman, A. J. 1996. The Eridanos valley and the Athenian Agora. *American Journal of Archaeology* 100:699–715.

Angelucci, D. E., Soares, A. M., Almeida, L., Brito, R., and Leitão, V. 2007. Neolithic occupation and mid-Holocene soil formation at Encosta de Sant'Ana (Lisbon, Portugal): A geoarchaeological approach. *Journal of Archaeological Science* 34:1641–1648.

Ashley, G. M., Tactikos, J. C., and Owen, R. B. 2009. Hominin use of springs and wetlands: Paleoclimate and archaeological records from Olduvai Gorge (~1.79–1.74 Ma). *Palaeogeography, Palaeoclimatology, Palaeoecology* 272:1–16.

Berna, F., Behar, A., Shahack-Gross, R., Berg, J., Boaretto, E., Gilboa, A., Sharon, I., Shalev, S., Shilstein, S., Yahalom-Mack, N., Zorn, J.R., and Weiner, S. 2007. Sediments exposed to high temperatures: Reconstructing pyrotechnological processes in Late Bronze and Iron Age Strata at Tel Dor (Israel). *Journal of Archaeological Science* 34:358–373.

Bintliff, J. 2002. Time, process and catastrophism in the study of Mediterranean alluvial history: A review. *World Archaeology* 33:417–435.

Boschian, G. and Montagnari-Kokelj, E. 2000. Prehistoric shepherds and caves in Trieste Karst (northeastern Italy). *Geoarchaeology: An International Journal* 15:332–371.

Butzer, K. W. 1981. Cave sediments, Upper Pleistocene stratigraphy and Mousterian facies in Cantabrian Spain. *Journal of Archaeological Science* 8:133–183.

Butzer, K. W. 1982. *Archaeology as Human Ecology*. Cambridge: Cambridge University Press.

Butzer, K. W. 2005. Environmental history in the Mediterranean world: Cross-disciplinary investigation of cause-and-effect for degradation and soil erosion. *Journal of Archaeological Science* 32:1733–1800.

Butzer, K. W. 2008. Challenges for a cross-disciplinary geoarchaeology: The intersection between environmental history and geomorphology. *Geomorphology* 101:402–411.

Butzer, K. W., Miralles, I., and Mateu, J. F. 1983. Urban geo-archaeology in Medieval Alzira (Prov. Valencia, Spain). *Journal of Archaeological Science* 10:333–349.

Courty, M. A. 2001. Microfacies analysis assisting archaeological stratigraphy. In: Goldberg, P., Holliday, V. T, and Ferring, C.R. (eds.) *Earth Sciences and Archaeology*, pp. 205–239. New York: Kluwer Academic/Plenum Publishers.

Courty, M. A., Goldberg, P., and Macphail, R. 1989. *Soils and Micromorphology and Archaeology, Cambridge Manuals in Archaeology*. Cambridge: Cambridge University Press.

Courty, M. A. and Vallverdu, J. 2001. The microstratigraphic record of abrupt climate change in cave sediments of the western Mediterranean. *Geoarchaeology: An International Journal* 16:467–500.

Davidson, D. A. and Carter, S. P. 1998. Micromorphological evidence of past agricultural practices in cultivated soils: The impact of a traditional agricultural system on soils in Papa Stour, Shetland. *Journal of Archaeological Science* 25:827–838.

Davidson, D. A., Dercon, G., Stewart, M., and Watson, F. 2006. The legacy of past urban waste disposal on local soils. *Journal of Archaeological Science* 33:78–783.

Davidson, D. A. and Shackley M. L. 1976. *Geoarchaeology: Earth Science and the Past*. London: Duckworth.

Draut, A. E., Rubin, D. M., Dierker, J. L., Fairley, H. C., Griffiths, R. E., Hazel, J. E., Jr., Hunter, R. E., Kohl, K., Leap, L. M., Nials, F. L., Topping, D. J., and Yeatts, M. 2008. Application of sedimentary-structure interpretation to geoarchaeological investigations in the Colorado River corridor, Grand Canyon, Arizona. *Geomorphology* 101:497–509.

Ferring, C. D. 2001. Geoarchaeology in alluvial landscapes. In: Goldberg, P., Holliday, V. T. and Ferring, C. R. (eds.) *Earth Sciences and Archaeology*, pp. 77–106. New York: Kluwer Academic/Plenum Publishers.

Frederick, C. 2001. Evaluating causality of landscape change. Examples from alluviation. In: Goldberg, P., Holliday, V. T., and Ferring, C. R. (eds.) *Earth Sciences and Archaeology*, pp. 55–76. New York: Kluwer Academic/Plenum Publishers.

French, C. A. I. 2003. *Geoarchaeology in Action: Studies in Soil Micromorpholgy and Landscape Evolution*. New York: Routledge.

Ge, T., Courty, M. A., Matthews, W., and Wattez, J. 1993. Sedimentary formation processes of occupation surfaces. In: Goldberg, P., Nash, D. T., and Petraglia, M. (eds.) *Formation Processes in Archaeological Context*, pp. 149–163. Monographs in World Archaeology, 17. Madison, WI: Prehistory Press.

Gladfelter, B. G. 1985. On the interpretation of archaeological sites in alluvial settings. In: Stein J. K. and Farrand, W. R. (eds.) *Archaeological Sediments in Context*, pp. 41–52. Peopling of the Americas, edited volume series: Vol. 1. Center for the Study of Early Man. Institute for Quaternary Studies, University of Maine at Orono.

Glais, A., Lespez, L., Vannière, B., and López-Sáez, J. A. 2017. Human-shaped landscape history in NE Greece: A palaeoenvironmental perspective. *Journal of Archaeological Science: Reports* 15:405–422.

Goldberg, P. 2003. Some observations on Middle and Upper Palaeolithic ashy cave and rockshelter deposits in the Near East. In: Goring-Morris, A. N. and Belfer-Cohen, A. (eds.) *More than Meets the Eye: Studies on Upper Palaeolithic Diversity in the Near East*, pp. 19–32. Oxford: Oxbow Books.

Goldberg, P., Laville, H., and Meignen, L. 2007. Stratigraphy and Geoarchaeological History of Kebara Cave, Mount Carmel. In: Bar-Yosef, O. and Meignen, L. (eds.) *Kebara Cave, Part 1*, pp. 49–89. Cambridge, MA: Peabody Museum of Archaeology and Ethnology Harvard University.

Goldberg, P. and Macphail, R. I. 2006. *Practical and Theoretical Geoarchaeology*. Malden: Blackwell Publishing.

Goldberg, P., Miller, C. E., Schiegl, S., Ligouis, B., Berna, F., Conard, N. J., and Wadley, L., 2009. Bedding, hearths, and site maintenance in the Middle Stone Age of Sibudu Cave, KwaZulu-Natal, South Africa. *Archaeological and Anthropological Sciences* 1(2):95–122.

Goren, Y. and Goldberg, P. 1991. Petrographic thin sections and the development of Neolithic plaster production in Northern Israel. *Journal of Field Archaeology* 18:131–138.

Hassan, F. A. 1985. Fluvial systems and geoarchaeology in arid lands: With examples from North Africa, the Near East and the American Southwest. In: Stein, J. K. and Farrand, W. R. (eds.) *Archaeological Sediments in Context*, pp. 53–68. Peopling of the Americas, edited volume series: Vol. 1. Center for the Study of Early Man. Institute for Quaternary Studies, University of Maine at Orono.

Holliday, V. T. 2004. *Soils in Archaeological Research*. Oxford: Oxford University Press.

Huckleberry, G. A. 1995. Archaeological implications of Late-Holocene channel changes on the Middle Gila River, Arizona. *Geoarchaeology: An International Journal* 10:159–182.

Huckleberry, G. A. 1999. Assessing Hohokam canal stability through stratigraphy. *Journal of Field Archaeology* 26:1–18.

Karkanas, P. 2001. Site formation processes in Theopetra cave: A record of climatic change during the Late Pleistocene and early Holocene in Thessaly, Greece. *Geoarchaeology: An International Journal* 16:373–399.

Karkanas, P. 2006. Late Neolithic household activities in marginal areas: The micromorphological evidence from Kouveleiki caves, Pelopennese, Greece. *Journal of Archaeological Science* 33:1628–1641.

Karkanas, P. 2007. Identification of lime plaster in prehistory using petrographic methods: A review and reconsideration of the data on the basis of experimental and case studies. *Geoarchaeology: An International Journal* 22:775–796.

Karkanas, P. 2010. Preservation of anthropogenic materials under different geochemical processes: A mineralogical approach. *Quaternary International* 210: 63–69.

Karkanas, P., Bar-Yosef, O., Goldberg, P., and Weiner, S. 2000. Diagenesis in prehistoric caves: The use of minerals that form in situ to assess the completeness of the archaeological record. *Journal of Archaeological Science* 27:915–929.

Karkanas, P., Brown, K. S., Fisher, E. C., Jacobs, J., and Marean, C. W. 2015. Interpreting human behavior from depositional rates and combustion features through the study of sedimentary microfacies at site Pinnacle Point 5–6, South Africa. *Journal of Human Evolution* 85:1–21.

Karkanas, P. and Efstratiou, N. 2009. Floor sequences in Neolithic Makri, Greece: Micromorphology reveals cycles of renovation. *Antiquity* 83(322):955–967.

Karkanas, P. and Goldberg, P. 2013. Micromorphology of cave sediments. In: Shroder, J. F. (Editor-in-chief) and Frumkin, A. (Volume Editor) *Treatise on Geomorphology*, Vol. 6, pp. 286–297. Karst Geomorphology, San Diego: Academic Press.

Karkanas, P., and Goldberg, P. 2019. *Reconstructing Archaeological Sites. Understanding the Geoarchaeological Matrix*. Chichester: Wiley-Blackwell.

Karkanas P., Rigaud J.-Ph., Simek J. F., Albert R. A., and Weiner S. 2002. Ash, bones and guano: A study of the minerals and phytoliths in the sediment of Grotte XVI, Dordogne, France. *Journal of Archaeological Science* 29:721–732.

Karkanas, P., Shahack-Gross, R., Ayalon, A., Bar-Matthews, M., Barkai, R., Frumkin, A., Gopher, A., and Stiner, M. 2007. Evidence for habitual use of fire at the end of the Lower Paleolithic: Site formation processes at Qesem Cave, Israel. *Journal of Human Evolution* 53:197–212.

Karkanas, P., Schepartz, L. A., Miller-Antonio, S., Wei, W., and Weiwen, H. 2008. Late Middle Pleistocene climate in southwestern China: Inferences from the stratigraphic record of Panxian Dadong Cave, Guizhou. *Quaternary Science Reviews* 27:1555–1570.

Karkanas, P. and Van de Moortel, A. 2014. Micromorphological analysis of sediments at the Bronze Age site of Mitrou, central Greece: Patterns of floor construction and maintenance. *Journal of Archaeological Science* 43:198–213.

King, S. M. 2008. The spatial organization of food sharing in Early Postclassic households: An application of soil chemistry in Ancient Oaxaca, Mexico. *Journal of Archaeological Science* 35:1224–1239.

Krahtopoulou, A. and Frederick, C. 2008. The stratigraphic implications of long-term terrace agriculture in dynamic landscapes: polycyclic terracing from Kythera Island, Greece. *Geoarchaeology: An International Journal* 23:550–585.

Lenoble, A., Bertran, P., and Lacrampe, F. 2008. Solifluction-induced modifications of archaeological levels: Simulation based on experimental data from a modern periglacial slope and application to French Palaeolithic sites. *Journal of Atmospheric Science* 35:99–110.

Macphail, R. 1986. Paleosols in archaeology: Their role in understanding Flandrian pedogenesis. In: Wright, V. P. (ed.) *Paleosols: Their Recognition and Interpretation*, pp. 262–290. Oxford: Blackwell.

Macphail, R. I. and McAvoy, J. M. 2008. A micromorphological analysis of stratigraphic integrity and site formation at Cactus Hill, an Early Paleoindian and hypothesized pre-Clovis occupation in South-Central Virginia, USA. *Geoarchaeology* 23:675–694.

Macphail, R. I., Courty, M. A., and Gebhardt, A. 1990. Soil micromorphological evidence of early agriculture in north-west Europe. *World Archaeology* 22:53–69.

Macphail, R., Courty, M. A., Hather, J., and Wattez, J. 1997. The soil micromorphological evidence of domestic occupation and stabling activities. In: Maggi, R. (ed.) *Arene Candide: A Functional and Environmental Assessment of the Holocene Sequences Excavated by L. Bernabò Brea (1940–1950)*, pp. 53–88. Roma: Memorie dell'Instituto Italiano di Paleontologia Umana.

Macphail, R. I., Graham, E., Crowther, J., and Turner, S. 2017. Marco Gonzalez, Ambergris Caye, Belize: A geoarchaeological record of ground raising associated with surface soil formation and the presence of a Dark Earth. *Journal of Archaeological Science* 77:35–51.

Macphail, R. I., Romans, J. C. C., and Robertson, L. 1987. The application of micromorphology to the understanding of Holocene soil development in the British Isles; with special reference to cultivation. In: Fedoroff, N., Bresson, L. M., and Courty, M. A. (eds.) *Soil Micromorphology*, pp. 669–676. Plaisir: Assosiation Française pour l' Étude du Sol.

Mallol, C. 2006. What's in a beach? Soil micromorphology of sediments from the Lower Paleolithic site of 'Ubeidiya, Israel. *Journal of Human Evolution* 51:185–206.

Mallol, C., VanNieuwenhuyse, D., and Zaidner, Y. 2011. Depositional and Paleoenvironmental setting of the Bizat Ruhama early pleistocene archaeological assemblages, Northern Negev, Israel: a microstratigraphic perspective. *Geoarchaeology* 26:118–141.

Mandel, R. D. 1992. Soils and Holocene landscape evolution in central and southwestern Kansas: Implications for archaeological research. In: Holliday, V.T. (ed.) *Soils in Archaeology*, pp. 41–100. Washington: Smithsonian Institution Press.

Mandel, R. D. 2000. *Geoarchaeology of the Great Plains*. Norman, OK: University of Oklahoma Press.

Mandel, R. D. and Bettis III, A. 2001. Use and analysis of soils by archaeologists and geoscientists: A North American perspective. In: Goldberg, P., Holliday, V. T., and Ferring, C. R. (eds.) *Earth Sciences and Archaeology*, pp. 173–204. New York: Kluwer Academic/Plenum Publishers.

Matthews, W. 1995. Micromorphological characterization and interpretation of occupation deposits and microstratigraphic sequences at Abu Salabick, Iraq. In: Barham, A. J. and Macphail, R. I. (eds.) *Archaeological Sediments and Soils: Analysis, Interpretation and Management*, pp. 41–74. London: Institute of Archaeology.

Matthews, W., French, C., Lawrence, T., and Cutler, D. 1996. Multiple surfaces: The micromorphology. In: Hodder, I. (ed.) *On the Surface: Çatalhöyük 1993–95*, pp. 301–342. Cambridge: The MacDonald Institute for Research and British Institute of Archaeology of Ankara.

Matthews, W. and Postage, J. N. 1994. The imprint of living in an early Mesopotamian city: Questions and answers. In: Luff, R. and Rowley-Conwy, P. (eds.) *Whither Environmental Archaeology?*, pp. 171–212. Monograph 38. Oxford: Oxbow Books.

Meignen, L., Goldberg, P., and Bar-Yosef, O. 2007. The hearths at Kebara Cave and their role in site formation processes. In: Bar-Yosef, O. and Meignen, L. (eds.) *Kebara Cave, Part 1*, pp. 91–122. Cambridge, MA: Peabody Museum of Archaeology and Ethnology Harvard University.

Mentzer, S. M., Romano, D. G., and Voyatzis, M. E., 2017. Micromorphological contributions to the study of ritual behavior at the ash altar to Zeus on Mt. Lykaion, Greece. *Archaeological and Anthropological Sciences* 9:1017–1043.

Middleton, W. D., 2004. Identifying chemical activity residues on prehistoric house floors: A methodology and rationale for multi-elemental characterization of a mild acid extract of anthropogenic sediments. *Archaeometry* 46:47–65.

Milek, K. B. and Roberts, H. M. 2013. Integrated geoarchaeological methods for the determination of site activity areas: A study of a Viking Age house in Reykjavik, Iceland. *Journal of Archaeological Science* 40:1845–1865.

Miller, C. E., Goldberg, P., and Berna, F. 2013. Geoarchaeological investigations at Diepkloof Rock Shelter, Western Cape, South Africa. *Journal of Archaeological Science* 40:3432–3452.

Nodarou, E., Frederick, C., and Hein, A. 2008. Another (mud)brick in the wall: Scientific analysis of Bronze Age earthen construction materials from East Crete. *Journal of Archaeological Science* 35:2997–3015.

Pavlopoulos, K., Karkanas, P., Triantaphyllou, M., Karymbalis, E., Tsourou, T., and Palyvos, N. 2006. Paleoenvironmental evolution of the coastal plain of Marathon, Greece, during the Late Holocene: Depositional environment, climate, and sea level changes. *Journal of Coastal Research* 22:424–438.

Pavlopoulos, K., Triantaphyllou, M., Karkanas, P., Kouli, K., Syrides, G., Vouvalidis, K., Palyvos, N., and Tsourou, T. 2010. Paleoenvironmental evolution and prehistoric Human environment, in the embayment of Palamari (Skyros Island, Greece) during Middle-Late Holocene. *Quaternary International* 216:41–53.

Quade, J., Semaw, S., Stout, D., Renne, R. P., Rogers, M., and Simpson, S. 2004. Paleoenvironments of the earliest stone toolmakers, Gona, Ethiopia. *Geological Society of America Bulletin* 116:1529–1544.

Rapp, G., Jr. and Hill C. L. 2006. *Geoarchaeology: The Earth-Science Approach to Archaeological Interpretation*, 2nd ed. New Haven: Yale University Press.

Renfrew, C. 1976. Archaeology and the earth sciences. In: Davidson, D. A. and Shackley, M. L. (eds.) *Geoarchaeology: Earth Science and the Past*, pp. 1–5. Boulder: Westview Press.

Roberts, N. and Rosen, A. 2009. Diversity and complexity in early farming communities of southwest Asia: New insights into the economic and environmental basis of Neolithic Çatalhöyük. *Current Anthropology* 50:393–402.

Sadori, L., Giraudi, C., Petitti, P., and Ramrath, A. 2004. Human impact at Lago di Mezzano (central Italy) during the Bronze Age: A multidisciplinary approach. *Quaternary International* 113:5–17.

Shahack-Gross, R., Albert, R. M., Gilboa, A., Nagar-Hilman, O., Sharon, I., and Weiner, S. 2005. Geoarchaeology in an urban context: The uses of space in a Phoenician monumental building at Tel Dor (Israel). *Journal of Archaeological Science* 32:1417–1431.

Shahack-Gross, R., Berna, F., Karkanas, P., Lemorini, C., Gopher, A., and Barkai, R. 2014. Evidence for repeated use of a central hearth at Pleistocene (300 ky ago) Qesem Cave, Israel. *Journal of Archaeological Science* 44: 12–21.

Shahack-Gross, R. and Finkelstein, I. 2008. Subsistence practices in an arid environment: a geoarchaeological investigation in an Iron Age site, the Negev Highlands, Israel. *Journal of Archaeological Science* 35:965–982.

Schiegl, S., Goldberg, P., Bar-Yosef, O., and Weiner, S. 1996. Ash deposits in Hayonim and Kebara caves, Israel: Macroscopic, microscopic and mineralogical observations, and their archaeological implications. *Journal of Archaeological Science* 23:763–781.

Shillito, L.-M. and Matthews, W. 2013. Geoarchaeological Investigations of Midden-Formation Processes in the Early to Late Ceramic Neolithic Levels at Çatalhöyük, Turkey ca. 8550–8370 cal BP. *Geoarchaeology* 28:25–49.

Shillito, L.-M., Matthews, W., Almond, M. J., and Bull, I. D. 2011. The microstratigraphy of middens: Capturing daily routine in rubbish at Neolithic Çatalhöyük, Turkey. *Antiquity* 85:1024–1038.

Simpson, I. A., Guttmann, E. B., Cluett, J., and Shepherd, A. 2006. Characterizing anthropic sediments in north European Neolithic settlements: An assessment from Skara Brae, Orkney. *Geoarchaeology: An International Journal* 21:221–235.

Terry, R. E., Fernández, F. G., Parnell, J. J., and Inomata, T. 2004. The story in the floors: chemical signatures of ancient and modern Maya activities at Aguateca, Guatemala. *Journal of Archaological Science* 31:1237–1250.

Van Andel, T. H. and Runnels, C. 1995. The earliest farmers in Europe. *Antiquity* 69:481–500.

Van Andel, T. H., Runnels, C. N., and Pope, K. O. 1986. Five thousand years of land use and abuse in the Southern Argolid, Greece. *Hesperia* 55:103–28.

Vita-Finzi, C. 1969. *The Mediterranean Valleys*. Cambridge: Cambridge University Press.

Wagstaff J. M. 1981. Buried assumptions: some problems in the interpretation of the "younger fill" raised by recent data from Greece. *Journal of Archaeological Science* 8:247–264.

Waters, M. R. 1992. *Principles of Geoarchaeology: A North American Perspective*. Tuscon: The University of Arizona Press.

Weiner, S., Goldberg, P., and Bar-Yosef, O. 1993. Bone preservation in Kebara Cave, Israel using on-site Fourier Transform Infrared spectrometry. *Journal of Archaeological Science* 20:613–627.

Wells, L. E. 2001. A geomorphological approach to reconstructing archaeological settlement patterns based on surficial artifact distribution. Replacing humans on the landscape. In Goldberg, P., Holliday, V. T., and Ferring, C. R. (eds.) *Earth Sciences and Archaeology*, pp. 107–141. New York: Kluwer Academic/Plenum Publishers.

Woodward, J. C. and Goldberg, P. 2001. The sedimentary records in Mediterranean rock-shelters and caves: Archives of environmental change. *Geoarchaeology: An International Journal* 16:327–354.

Woodward, J. C., Hamlin, R. H. B., Macklin, M. G., Karkanas, P., and Kotjabopoulou, E. 2001. Quantitative sourcing of slackwater deposits at Boila rockshelter: A record of late-glacial flooding and Palaeolithic settlement in the Pindus Mountains, Northern Greece. *Geoarchaeology: An International Journal* 16:501–536.

Part V

Materials Analysis

14

Ceramics

Andrew J. Shortland and Patrick Degryse

The various methods for understanding ceramic production and use in archaeology.

1 INTRODUCTION

Ceramics are the most abundant surviving material on almost all Neolithic and later archaeological sites. Their abundance and ubiquity is the result of several factors. Firstly, the raw materials that are used to create most ceramics are commonly available in a wide variety of areas. Most require very little in the way of specialised processing. This means that it is generally relatively inexpensive in terms of the time and energy required to gather and process the raw materials to create ceramics. Secondly, they tend to be fragile – if dropped they are easily broken. Thirdly, the broken ceramic sherds cannot easily be reused. Unlike metals, which can be sharpened or remelted, the fate of most broken ceramics is to be discarded. In contrast to the relative fragility of the complete vessel, sherds are remarkably resistant to further degradation in burial and diagenesis. This means that sherds tend to pass relatively unchanged into the hands of the archaeologist, where the reconstruction of the shape and material of the original vessel is possible. Ceramics, therefore, despite their fragility, can be extremely useful, both to the societies who have employed them, usually in great abundance, and to the scientists who study them.

What Is a Ceramic?

The definition of a ceramic tends to vary through time and between specialisms. However, in terms of archaeology, ceramics might be defined as objects made out of clay that has in some way been processed. Clay is a naturally occurring geological deposit usually formed from the weathering of rocks. It is made up of clay minerals with a greater or lesser amount of other minerals entrained within it. Clay minerals are hydrous aluminium phyllosilicates of various compositions and structures (e.g., Klein and Hurlbut 1998). Common clay minerals encountered in the clays used for archaeological ceramics include kaolinites, smectites, chlorities and illites. Naturally occurring clay bodies often combine a wide range of different clays within these groups. The different clay types confer slightly different properties on the ceramics which are made from them.

The simplest type of ceramic would be clay that has been shaped and dried, perhaps in the sun, or near a fire. This is sometimes termed 'baked clay', and makes up some of the earliest use of clay that survives in the archaeological record. One of the most important uses of this early baked clay is the manufacture of figurines, for example, the Palaeolithic Venus figurines of Dolní Věstonice (Vandiver et al. 1989). Somewhat later baked clay goes on to form a very important source of building material in many areas of the world. In arid climates, baked clay bricks are still the mainstay of architecture as they have been for many thousands of years. However, baked clay is vulnerable to damp, and rapidly turns back to clay when subjected to contact with water for any length of time. It was determined in the Neolithic material that not just baking, but *firing* clay was the best way for it to keep its shape (e.g., Amiran 1970). Fired clay can be used in cooking and storage vessels and is relatively unaffected by exposure to moisture and heat. The invention of firing allows ceramic to fulfil its full potential and this is what leads to its widespread use. The most commonly found ceramic is therefore fired clay (or 'earthenware'), combined with greater or lesser additions of other materials as discussed below.

What Questions Are Asked?

Due to the fact that ceramics are so widespread and common on archaeological sites, they have been used to answer a range of different questions of interest to the archaeologist and historian. These can be divided into perhaps three different groups. The first question concerns how the ceramic was made. The technology of producing ceramics, while in essence rather simple, in practice is extensively modified and refined by different societies. A complex *chaîne opératoire* (Bar-Yosef et al. 1992) of different technological methods and choices can often be defined. This can reveal important information about how ceramic production is carried out – the selection, sorting, refining and mixing of raw materials, the methods of shaping and moulding and the control of temperature and oxidation state of kilns. In more recent studies this often leads on to the discussion of the place of the production process and its workers within the society as a whole and how the decisions they are making both shapes and is shaped by the culture in which they are operating (Arnold 2008; Orton et al. 1993; Rye 1981).

The second major group of questions asked of ceramics is concerned with determining what they might have been used for. This can be attempted firstly by an examination of the ceramic itself. Traditionally, archaeological science has concentrated on a technical study of ceramics – how 'fit for purpose' are they? This has involved attempting to define failure points of vessels, especially those involved in specialist operations such as metallurgical crucibles, but also cooking vessels, for example. The relationship between the presence of minerals, their amounts, sizes and the performance characteristics of ceramics (e.g., thermal shock resistance, impact resistance and strength) may directly be linked with technological choices made by the potter. The magnitude of these stresses is affected by the thermal conductivity of the vessel body, bulk thermal expansion coefficient, and thickness of the wall and shape of the vessel (Tite and Kilikoglou 2002). Beyond this level, the identification and classification of decoration of various types and the complexity of the production process can help to define 'prestige wares' over utilitarian, and define broad groups of storage, cooking, serving, display and funerary wares amongst others. Recent work has shown that the idea of a single designed use of a ceramic is too simplistic. Hodder has referred to artefacts as part of a 'material culture language', a means of communicating information between individuals and groups (Hodder 1986). As such, ceramics may serve as transmitters of information about their producer, owner or user. Ceramics have a complex life history or 'biography', which can involve several periods of different uses and reuses more or less related to the purpose in the mind of the original manufacturer. Thus the evidence of several periods of use might be superimposed on each other in the ceramic. In addition to the study of the ceramic itself to determine use, there is also the possibility of looking at residues within the ceramic that might reflect what was held and how it was used.

The third major group of questions relate to both of the above, but go one stage beyond. This is the attempt to determine where a vessel might have been made by looking at its raw material components. Ethnographic studies of potters have shown that the raw materials of ceramic production tend to be gathered very close to the kiln site, usually within a day's journey there and back (Arnold 1985).

This means that the raw materials of local ceramics are derived very locally to the production site. Considering provenance, the use of misfired sherds is highly desirable, as these are often thrown away in situ, or in close proximity to the production site, after a failed firing process (Mommsen et al. 1988).

The identification and description of a rare imported, foreign vessel or sherd in a mass of locally produced wares is perhaps the most important and certainly the most frequently asked question of the scientific study of ceramics. Non-local ceramics, because of the opportunity they give for the plotting of ancient trade and exchange networks as well as the possibility of identifying high-status individuals or sites, are perhaps the most challenging and interesting parts of the analysis of this material.

2 ANALYSING CERAMICS

As with the study of many material types, ceramics can be studied using a range of different equipment, ranging from a hand lens costing only a few pounds to analytical equipment costing millions. The huge numbers of ceramics on many sites also in itself presents challenges that are not common in other, rarer, material. There tends therefore to be a hierarchy of techniques used in the analysis of ceramics, starting simply, cheaply and quickly with the bulk of the samples and selecting smaller numbers at each stage to be subjected to analysis by more lengthy and expensive techniques.

Hand Lens to Binocular Microscope

Most initial ceramic sorting is done by eye, assisted by low power hand lens or binocular microscope. This sorting attempts to characterise the ceramic, saying something of its internal composition, external makeup and shape. This is often done quite fast in order to organise sherds into groups. A key concept here that will be continued below is that of *fabric* (Peacock 1970; Peacock 1977). Fabric analysis of a ceramic is the study and classification of ceramics based on the characteristics of the clay paste used and also their inclusions. This includes the colour of the matrix, hardness, feel, nature of the fracture, firing process, production process, nature of the inclusions, size of the inclusions, amount of the inclusions and sorting of these inclusions. Fabrics are made up of the clay itself plus any other additions that have been deliberately, or accidentally, added to the clay. The most common deliberate addition to the clay is temper, a material added that changes the properties of the clay, especially during firing, but also during use. Temper can include sand, straw, rock fragments, ground up broken ceramics (known as grog) and others. The reason for the selection of a particular temper can be technological, for example, it improves the survivability of the ceramic when it is fired, but it can also be ritual, connected with tradition or religion. The appearance of the clay and temper can be moderated by the way the ceramic has been shaped. Ceramics vessels can be hand-modelled, coiled, slabbed, moulded and thrown on various sorts of wheels (Edwards and Jacobs 1986; Orton et al. 1993; Rice 1987; Rye 1981). Each of these has the potential of manifesting itself on the fabric, perhaps by the preferential orientation or non-homogeneous distribution of temper. These will be changed once again by the firing process, which can change the colour of the clay and develop glassy patches or matrices if very high.

The surface of the ceramics can be treated with different techniques to alter the material properties of the ceramic (Orton et al. 1993). Commonly seen are relief, slips and glazes. It is very common for the surface of vessels to be decorated with incised patterns. These might be scored into the ceramic as it is drying after forming with a knife or stick, or other shapes or materials might be pressed into the surface, for example, twine, to create a pattern. Another possibility is to wait until the ceramic is fully dry, but before it is fired, and to polish its surface, perhaps with a smooth pebble. This is known as burnishing and results in the smoother surface characteristic of this technique. This sort of decoration does not usually change the physical characteristics of the vessel very much, but does presumably make the vessel more pleasing to the eye of the manufacturer. Another possible surface technique is the application of a slip. A slip is a fine-grained clay, sometimes a finer version of the body clay and sometimes a different clay. This is either painted onto the surface or the ceramic is dipped into it. It creates a thin layer on the surface of the ceramic, which can look smoother than the main bulk of the body (Velde and Druc 1999). A 'wash' is a very thin slip layer that has been applied to the pottery, not necessarily homogenously. Therefore, in contradiction to a slip layer, a wash is not entirely coating. Slips can be contrasting colours and can also be painted with pigments to create polychrome vessels. The surface(s) of the ceramic can also be smoothed to create an even surface without any pores or mineral inclusions visible. The final possibility is the glaze, which is applied to the ceramic as a slurry and then fired to create a glassy surface layer. Glazes can be many colours, can be multilayered and can themselves be painted or enamelled – essentially a glass adhering to the surface of the ceramic.

The resulting macroscopic groups are often referred to as 'wares'. This term denotes 'a recurring combination of distinctive attributes including colour, temper, forming and finishing techniques, characteristic vessel forms and types of decoration' (Henrickson 1994: 115). After ceramics are sorted into groups by these relatively simple techniques, then the next stage is to try to characterise the groups. There are two different ways of doing this: mineralogical and chemical.

Mineralogical Approaches

Perhaps the traditional way of characterising a group of ceramics is to examine its mineralogy. This is a technique derived from the study and description of rocks or petrography, hence the term ceramic petrography is often used. The primary tool of the ceramic petrographer is the polarising light microscope (PLM). Fragments of sherds representing the different groups of ceramic on a site are glued to a microscope slide and polished down until they are only 0.03mm thick to create a thin section. At this thickness, most minerals in ceramics are translucent. The section is placed on the PLM, where it sits between two polarisers arranged at ninety degrees to each other. The minerals of the sample interact with the light, generating colours and other properties characteristic of the mineral involved. Prior to the thin section preparation, samples are often impregnated with an ultra-low viscosity resin. The resin especially fixates inclusions and pores within the clay body and improves the determination of the actual porosity (Oliveira et al. 1983).

As long as the ceramic is course grained enough for the minerals to be visible, this is a very good and very well established method for identifying minerals in the raw material mixture used, the clay as well as the temper. It can also give indications of firing temperature and oxidation states. Moreover, thin section petrography may add indications for studying the formation processes of the vessels, not visible by surface examination. The orientation/alignment of mineral inclusions (e.g., micas) and voids are frequently used to identify formation processes in thin section (Gibson and Woods 1997; Vaughan 1995). Many textbooks exist on the basics of thin section petrography (e.g., MacKenzie and Adams

1994); Reedy (2008) describes ceramics specifically. The description of thin sections of ceramic material is often based on a system provided by Whitbread (1995) on Greek transport amphora, later discussed by Josephs (2005), derived from soil micromorphology.

Thin section work by PLM is the main technique for the study of ceramics. It requires a sample large enough to be representative of the ceramic fabric as a whole, but the cost of the equipment needed is relatively low. What it does require is a good level of expertise and experience at looking at ceramic sections, which even to those geologically trained, can be difficult. To balance that, the number of minerals commonly found in ceramic sections is relatively low, certainly less than fifty, which makes their routine identification easier. Producing a qualitative estimate of the type and abundance of minerals can therefore be carried out in this way and this is often enough to distinguish different clay sources. However, applying a more quantitative approach, that is to say applying percentage values to the proportion of these different minerals, is rather more difficult. The first reason for this is a fundamental one as regards thin section work – how representative of the ceramic as a whole or the clay/temper source are the relatively few instances of these in the thin sections taken? The larger and more numerous the thin sections, the more likely they are to be representative, but the larger the sample taken has to be. Secondly, there is the problem of how to count the minerals in the sections. This is normally done by point counting, that is to say setting a grid across the thin section and assessing which mineral is present at each grid point. However, this once more means reducing the sample size – the entire section is not counted.

The second possibility for the assessing of the mineralogy of the sample is to use a polished section and a scanning electron microscope (SEM). The section is placed in the SEM and the minerals identified by a combination of morphology, contrast (the brighter the mineral the higher the average atomic number of the elements it contains) and using an attached energy dispersive spectrometer to compositionally analyse individual phases. This has the disadvantages of generally being slower than the thin section approach, and also it is more difficult to classify individual mineral grains using SEM than with PLM. However, it is an approach which seems to be increasingly used (e.g., Tite et al. 2001). It is possible to automate the identification of grains on the SEM, so that the whole section is mapped for different elements and then grains that are the same grouped together and counted. This can give good quantitative results for the mineral analysis of the ceramic or clay.

Neither of the mineralogical techniques is suitable when the ceramic becomes too fine, or too high fired, to have a recognisable mineralogy. In these cases at least, chemical approaches have to be resorted to

Chemical Approaches

The second approach to the analysis of ceramics is to go from the optical, hand specimen grouping to a bulk chemical analysis. There are several ways of doing this and, as techniques have been invented and refined, this has changed through time (e.g., Mommsen 2001; Rice 1987). The early approaches were to use wet chemical analysis, but this has now been completely superseded by other techniques, especially neutron activation analysis (NAA), X-ray fluorescence (XRF), atomic absorption spectroscopy (AAS), optical emission spectroscopy (OES) and inductively coupled plasma (ICP) techniques (e.g., Pollard and Heron 2008). It is likely that, with the price of equipment going down and their sensitivity going up, various types of ICP will be the future of the chemical analysis of ceramics. In most of the modern chemical techniques, the sample is ground up and dissolved in acid. In terms of ICPMS, the solution is then injected into the plasma chamber of the machine, ionised and the elemental composition determined by a sensitive mass spectrometer. ICPMS, in addition to giving bulk chemical analysis for almost all elements required, has detection limits for most elements down to parts per billion (ppb) or even parts per trillion (ppt), allowing analysis of rare earth elements, for example, which can give a very good signature of the clay source. The technique is therefore highly discriminatory, and combined with statistical approaches can be very good at grouping ceramics and determining outliers and imported wares. However, it does tend to hide the detail in a way that mineralogical approaches do not. Whilst it is easy to say that one group of ceramics is compositionally different to another in terms of certain elements, it can be difficult to say *why* that might be so. Could it be connected with different clays, different temper or amount of temper, clay processing, the post-depositional environment and alteration of mineral grains, or firing? The difficulty of chemical analysis is also directly related to the sedimentary processes at hand, which can result in an (un)even mix of all rocks found in the environment of the basin and thus may counteract chemical differentiation (Mason and Moore 1982). With a thin section this could be investigated relatively easily, with a chemical composition this can be much more difficult. However, in pottery studies it is believed that the chemistry of sediments (and ceramics) approximately reflects the main characteristics and the chemical properties of the rocks from which they were derived in the catchment area or river system which provided them.

Isotopic Approaches

Recent developments have also applied radiogenic isotope ratios to the analysis of pottery ($^{87}Sr/^{86}Sr$, $^{143}Nd/^{144}Nd$, $^{207}Pb/^{206}Pb$ etc.) (Guzowska et al. 2003; Li et al. 2006). So far, lead isotopes have hardly ever been applied to characterize the source materials of ceramics (Knacke-Loy et al. 1995; Renson et al. 2007, 2011). It needs to be stated, however, that these studies are best carried out only when no other technique provides sufficient data for answering research questions. Although providing a substantial amount of information on their own, the simultaneous use of all these methods provides a more robust framework for interpreting ancient potteries.

Unusual Ceramics

Whilst the vast majority of ceramics have a chemical composition that falls within a more or less continuous spectrum, there are other, specialised ceramics that have very unusual compositions. These are usually ceramics that have been developed to cope with particularly unusual conditions or requirements. Two different types are worth briefly noting here. The first are those developed for high temperature processes for example metalworking and refining. Crucible technology had to be developed in response to the desire to achieve and maintain higher and higher temperatures in the pursuit of particular alloys, perhaps especially in alchemical investigations. Clays were specially selected for their refractory characteristics, and high temperature mullite crucibles developed (e.g., Rehren 2003). The second, much larger, but related group, are the porcelains. These are pure kaolinitic clays that were high fired to produce a glazed ceramic that could have a brilliant white colour and very thin walls. These decorative vessels produced were extremely valuable and their study by SEM and ICPMS is ongoing.

When time and money permits, a combination of mineralogical and chemical approaches gives the best combination of information and is most likely to answer the archaeological questions posed (Degryse and Braekmans 2014). The very ubiquity of ceramic finds on the majority of archaeological sites really requires this investment in their careful study. They can reveal a wealth of information impacting on a whole range of archaeological and historical questions. A carefully constructed sampling strategy informed by clear questions and combined analytical techniques still has the potential to say as much about our past as any archaeological science technique.

REFERENCES

Amiran, R. 1970. *Ancient Pottery of the Holy Land: From Its Beginnings in the Neolithic Period to the End of the Iron Age*. New Brunswick, NJ: Rutgers University Press.

Arnold, D. E. 1985. *Ceramic Theory and Cultural Process*. Cambridge: Cambridge University Press.

Arnold, D. E. 2008. *Social Change and the Evolution of Ceramic Production and Distribution in a Maya Community*. Boulder, CO: University Press of Colorado.

Bar-Yosef, O., Vandermeersch, B., Arensburg, B., Belfer-Cohen, A., Goldberg, P., Laville, H., Meignen, L., Rak, Y., Speth, J. D., Tchernov, E., Tillier, A.-M. and Weiner, S. 1992. The excavations in Kebara Cave, Mt. Carmel. *Current Anthropology* 33(5):497–550.

Degryse, P. and Braekmans, D. 2014. Elemental and isotopic analysis of ancient ceramics and glass. In: Cerling, T. (ed.) *Treatise of Geochemistry*, Vol. 14: *Treatise on Geochemistry in Archaeology and Anthropology*, pp. 191–207. Amsterdam: Elsevier.

Edwards, I. and Jacobs, L. 1986. Experiments with stone pottery wheel bearings – notes on the use of rotation in the production of ancient pottery. *Newsletter. Department of Pottery Technology (University of Leiden)* 4:49–55.

Gibson, A. and Woods, A. 1997. *Prehistoric Pottery for the Archaeologist*. London: Leicester University Press.

Guzowska, M., Kuleff, I., Pernicka, E. and Satir, M. 2003. On the origin of Coarse Wares of Troia VII. In: Wagner, G. A., Pernicka, E. and Uerpmann, H. P. (ed.) *Troia and the Troad, Scientific Approaches*, pp. 233–249. Berlin-New York: Springer.

Henrickson, R. C. 1994. Continuity and discontinuity in the ceramic tradition of Gordion during the Iron Age. In: Çilingiroğlu, A. and French, D. H. (ed.) *Anatolian Iron Ages 3*, pp. 95–129. British Institute of Archaeology at Ankara Monograph 16, London.

Hodder, I. 1986. *Reading the Past: Current Approaches to Interpretation in Archaeology*. Cambridge: Cambridge University Press.

Josephs, R. L. 2005. Applying micromorphological terminology to ceramic petrology. *Geoarchaeology* 20(8):861–865.

Klein, C. and Hurlbut, C. S. 1998. *Manual of Mineralogy*. Chichester: John Wiley and Sons.

Knacke-Loy, O., Satir, M. and Pernicka, E. 1995. Zur Herkunftsbestimmung der bronzezeitlichen Keramik von Troia: Chemische und isotopengeochemische (Nd, Sr, Pb) Unterschungen. *Studia Troica* 5:145–175.

Li, B. P., Zhao, J. X., Greig, A., Collerson, K. D., Feng, Y. X., Sun, X. M., Guo, M. S. and Zhuo, Z. X. 2006. Characterisation of Chinese Tang sancai from Gongxian and Yaozhou kilns using ICP-MS trace element and TIMS Sr-Nd isotopic analysis. *Journal of Archaeological Science* 33:56–62.

MacKenzie, W. S. and Adams, A. E. 1994. *A Colour Atlas of Rocks and Minerals in Thin Section*. London: Manson Publishing.

Mason, B. and Moore, C. B. 1982. *Principles of Geochemistry*. New York: John Wiley and Sons.

Mommsen, H. 2001. Provenance determination of pottery by trace element analysis: Problems, solutions and applications. *Journal of Radioanalytical and Nuclear Chemistry* 247:657–662.

Mommsen, H., Kreuser, A. and Weber, J. 1988. A method for grouping pottery by chemical composition. *Archaeometry* 30:47–57.

Oliveira, L., Burns, A., Bissalputra, T. and Yang, K. C. 1983. The use of an ultra-low viscosity medium (VCD/HXSA) in the rapid embedding of plant cells for electron microscopy. *Journal of Microscopy* 132:195–202.

Orton, C., Tyers, P. and Vince, A. 1993. *Pottery in Archaeology: Cambridge Manuals in Archaeology*. Cambridge: Cambridge University Press.

Peacock, D. P. S. 1970. The scientific analysis of ancient ceramics: A review. *World Archaeology* 1:375–89.

Peacock D. P. S. 1977. *Pottery and Early Commerce. Characterization and Trade in Roman and Later Ceramics*. London: Academic Press.

Pollard, A. M. and Heron, C. 2008. *Archaeological Chemistry*. Cambridge: The Royal Society of Chemistry.

Reedy C. L. 2008. *Thin-Section Petrography of Stone and Ceramic Cultural Material*. London: Archetype Publications Ltd.

Rehren, Th. 2003. Crucibles as reaction vessels in ancient metallurgy. In: Craddock, P. and Lang, J. (Eds.) *Mining and Metal Production through the Ages*, pp. 207–215. London: British Museum Press.

Renson, V., Coenaerts, J., Nys, K., Mattielli, N., Åström, P., and Claeys, P. 2007. Provenance determination of pottery from Hala Sultan Tekke using lead isotopic analysis: Preliminary results. In: Åström, P. and Nys, K. (eds.) *Hala Sultan Tekke 12. Tomb 24, Stone Anchors, Faunal Remains and Pottery Provenance*, pp. 53–60. Studies in Mediterranean Archaeology 45(12). Sävedalen: Paul Åströms förlag.

Renson, V., Coenaerts, J., Nys, K., Mattielli, N., Vanhaecke, F., Fagels, N. and Claeys, P. 2011. Lead isotopic analysis for the identification of Late Bronze Age pottery from Hala Sultan Tekke (Cyprus). *Archaeometry* 53:37–57.

Rice, P. 1987. *Pottery Analysis. A Sourcebook*. Chicago: University of Chicago Press.

Rye, O. S. 1981. *Pottery Technology. Principles and Reconstruction*. Washington: Taraxacum.

Tite, M. and Kilikoglou, V. 2002. Do we understand cooking pots and is there an ideal cooking pot? In: Kilikoglou, V., Hein, A. and Maniatis, Y. (eds.) *Modern Trends in*

Scientific Studies on Ancient Ceramics, pp. 1–8. BAR International Series 1011. Oxford: Archaeopress.

Tite, M., Kilikoglou, V. and Vekinis, G. 2001. Strength, toughnes and thermal shock resistance of ancient ceramics, and their influence on technological choice. *Archaeometry* 43:301–324.

Vaughan, S. J. 1995. Ceramic petrology and petrography in the Aegean? *American Journal of Archaeology* 99(1):115–117.

Vandiver, P. B., Soffer, O., Klima, B. and Svoboda, J. 1989. The origins of ceramic technology at Dolni Věstonice, Czechoslovakia. *Science* 246:1002–1008.

Velde, B. and Druc, I. C. 1999. *Archaeological Ceramic Materials*. Berlin: Springer-Verlag.

Whitbread, I. K. 1995. *Greek Transport Amphorae: A Petrological and Archaeological Study*. Fitch Laboratory Occasional Paper 4. Athens: British School at Athens.

15

Glass

Andrew J. Shortland and Thilo Rehren

The scientific analysis of glass as found in archaeological contexts, including methods of production.

1 INTRODUCTION

Human produced glass was first regularly produced in Egypt and the Near East in the sixteenth century BC. It is often brightly coloured and was of high value, rating as a precious stone. As such, its study has the potential to not only give valuable information about technological ability and transfer, but also to map out exchange networks, especially if the sites where the glass was made can be identified and characterised. Therefore, glass is an important part of the archaeological assemblage, and an increasing amount of work has been devoted to it, especially over the last twenty or so years (Rehren and Freestone 2015).

Glass is formed when a hot molten material is cooled rapidly. The rapid cooling does not allow time for the atoms within the liquid to order themselves into a crystalline structure, but instead they solidify where they are (Paul 1990; Zachariasen 1932). This means that glass is a homogeneous solid without 'long range order', that is to say it lacks the regular, repeating structures of crystalline materials (Doremus 1994; Paul 1990). The different elements in a glass have different roles in its structure. After oxygen, the most common element in glasses is usually the *network former*, which is more or less linked into a continuous structure by *bridging oxygens*. Bridging oxygens sit between two network forming elements, and bind them together, raising the melting temperature of the glass and its other working properties. The most common network forming element in historical, and indeed modern, glass is silicon.

Other network formers can be aluminium and in certain circumstances lead, amongst others (Zachariasen 1932). Bridging oxygens in silicate glasses sit between two silicon atoms: Si-O-Si, with each silicon being linked to four bridging oxygens in a tetrahedral arrangement to form a three-dimensional network. The structure created by the network formers is changed by the inclusion of other elements acting as *network modifiers*. There are two groups that are important in early glasses: the alkali metals and the alkali earths. The alkali metals, particularly sodium and potassium, disrupt the network structure, creating *non-bridging oxygens*. Some of the Si-O-Si bridges change to $Si{-}O^{-}(Na^{+})(Na^{+})O^{-}{-}Si$, having the effect of lowering the melting point and general stability of the glass (Paul 1990). Alkali earths, especially calcium, usually counteract this effect to a certain extent, forming new bridges: $Si\text{-}O^{-}(Ca^{2+})O^{-}{-}Si$, and therefore act as a *network stabiliser* in the glass. Almost all historical glasses are alkali-lime-silicate glasses and are therefore made up of these as the most common elements in the glass (Turner 1956a).

It is normal in the analysis of ancient glasses to refer to the percentage of soda (Na_2O), potash (K_2O) and lime (CaO) as opposed to sodium, potassium and calcium respectively. This is partly for historical reasons, since these words are connected with those used by early glassmakers for different raw materials, but also reflects the fact that glass analyses are normally quoted as oxide weight percent rather than elemental percent.

The raw materials of glassmaking change through time, but there remains a commonality in the roles that the different raw materials play. The first raw material has to be a source of the silica, which could be river or beach sand, or hydrothermal vein quartz, amongst others (Caley 1962; Turner 1956b). The silica-rich sources have very high melting points, quartz for example melts at around 1700°C, well in excess of the capability of historical furnaces. The network modifiers, as a raw material called a *flux*, are therefore added to reduce the melting temperature. Fluxes have varied through time, and include certain plant ashes or specific minerals rich in either of the alkali metals, discussed above or, rarely, lead oxide (Sayre and Smith 1961; Turner 1956c). The calcium can come as a natural component from either the silica source (lime-rich sand), or the flux (plant ash), or might be added separately (shells, limestone; Turner 1956b; Turner 1956c; Brill 1970a). Finally, colorants, decolorants and/or opacifiers were frequently added to change the colour or optical properties of the glass; these are typically oxides of transition metals such as copper, cobalt or manganese, or of heavy metals such as lead, tin or antimony.

2 GLAZES AND ENAMELS

Glass is found not only in objects made entirely of the material, such as beads, inlays, vessels and window panes, but also as decorative or functional layers on other types of material. The most common of these is a *glaze*, which is a glassy layer on the surface of ceramic or stone (Tite 1987; Tite and Bimson 1986; Vandiver 1982; Vandiver 1998). Glazes are perhaps the most common form in which glass is seen in the archaeological record of most periods, and since their raw materials, internal structure and properties are very similar to glasses, so they are discussed here, too. Less commonly the raw materials of glass or glass itself are ground up and applied onto other materials, most commonly metal, glazed ceramic or other glasses, and fired. This is an *enamel*, and is used for decorative effect, especially on medieval metalwork and later ceramics (Freestone 2002; Freestone et al. 2003a). Once again, this is essentially a glass-type composition.

3 ANALYSING GLASS

The types of questions asked that lead to the analysis of glass are similar to those asked of other inorganic materials. Analysis attempts to identify the raw materials of the glass and then say something of production technology: the furnace type required, firing duration and temperature and so on. Very similar to metals (but unlike ceramics), glassmaking and glass working require very different skills and are often carried out historically by different workers, in different facilities on different sites (Freestone et al. 2002a, 2002b; Pusch and Rehren 2007). Glassmaking is the conversion of raw materials into 'raw glass', which can then be transported, perhaps in the form of ingots or cullet (broken glass fragments), to glassworking sites, where it is made into finished objects. Analyses of waste materials and other finds related to these activities provide information about the different processes and activities that were performed at a given site. However, of at least equal interest is the attempt to identify where glass objects might have been made. The reason for this is that in the early periods, certainly the second millennium BC in Egypt and the Near East and maybe the mid first millennium BC as well, and later than this in Europe and elsewhere, glass was regarded as a valuable material and classified along with precious stones such as lapis lazuli and turquoise (Nicholson 2007; Pusch and Rehren 2007). Even after glass became a mass commodity and used across Europe, the Middle East, South Asia and beyond, in the first millennium, its production remained highly centralised and restricted to a few areas in northern Egypt, the Levant and a few sites in India. From there it was traded and exchanged across vast distances, and the tracking of such exchange, often between wealthy courts and individuals, can reveal very interesting information about contacts and political activities in the period (Degryse and Shortland 2009; Freestone et al. 2003b;).

Glass presents special challenges to the analyst. Most significantly, because it forms from a rapidly cooled molten substance, it usually does not have any structure or mineralogy that is accessible to most techniques. Except for deliberately added opacifiers and bubbles, and accidentally entrained or preserved raw materials (which are generally rare), glass is a homogeneous whole. This means that those structural, optical and imaging techniques used to study ceramics and metals, such as X-ray diffraction, polarising light microscopy and scanning electron microscope imaging, give relatively little information about glass. Instead, analysis of the chemical composition of the glass and its interpretation is the primary source of evidence for raw materials, technology and provenance. Secondly, glass is vulnerable to weathering, particularly to the surface loss of mobile elements by dissolution in water (see Figure 15.1). This can make the reconstruction of the initial glass composition very difficult, especially if for curatorial reasons only analysis of this weathered surface layer is possible.

The chemical analysis of glass started as early as the nineteenth century and expanded greatly in the mid-twentieth century (Caley 1962; Forbes 1957; Sayre and Smith 1961). There is now a well-established series of methodologies that allow a very complete picture of the composition of the glass to be acquired. The first aim of analysis usually carried out on a glass is to determine its major and minor element composition. For the last two to three decades, two techniques were most often used for this: the scanning electron microscope with attached energy dispersive spectrometer (SEM-EDS) and the electron probe micro-analyser (EPMA or microprobe). Compared to traditional chemical methods of analysis, these have the advantage that they provide images of the glass as well as analyses (see Figures 15.1–15.3), and SEM-EDS is relatively widely available and easy to use. However, it has the major disadvantage that the peak resolution of the technique is not high, which means that where two elements have similar X-ray energies it can be difficult to quantify them. One of the most important examples for glass of overlapping energies is cobalt (Kα peak) and iron (Kβ), which are very similar and make the analysis of cobalt difficult when there is significant iron. Although SEM-EDS has been successfully used in the major and minor element analysis of glasses

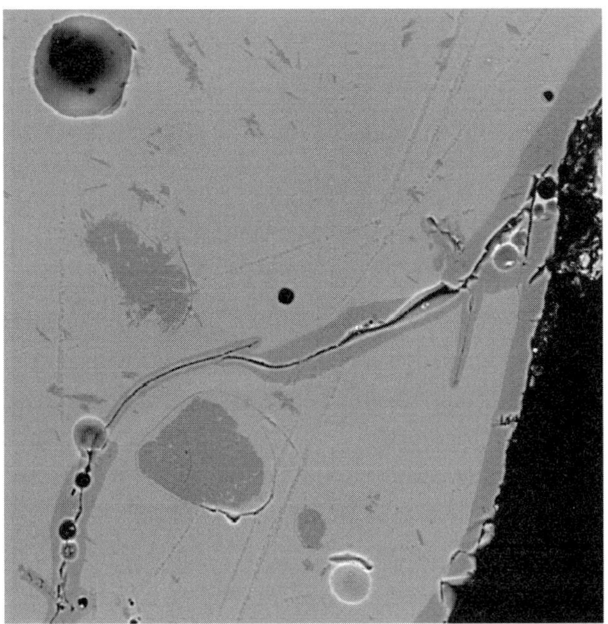

FIGURE 15.1 SEM micrograph showing a section through a piece of glass. The unweathered glass is mid grey in BSE mode, but shows a darker grey weathered layer at the surface to the right and running along cracks. Vesicles (black), and other remnant features and secondary phases are also present (image ~1 mm across). (Adapted from Ruckstuhl and Shortland 2004)

(Tite 1987), because of its greater peak resolving power, better calibration and lower detection limits down to 100 ppm for many elements, microprobe analysis is perhaps the preferred technique (Henderson 1988a) despite its higher cost and much slower operation. It is usual for the microprobe to analyse for around 20 elements in a glass, which would include all the major elements and many of the minor ones too. Either SEM-EDS or microprobe can give the sort of compositional information that is required in order to place a glass in the correct compositional group and say something of the raw materials used in its production. More recently, the significance of trace element analysis for more refined interpretations of group association and geological origin has been recognised. With the emergence of laser ablation inductively coupled plasma mass spectrometry (LA-ICPMS) as a quasi-non-invasive analytical method providing reliable data in the single ppm range, this is likely to become the analytical standard approach for the foreseeable future.

4 GLASS COMPOSITIONS AND RAW MATERIALS

Almost all ancient and historical glasses are silicate based – the most common element in their composition after oxygen being silicon. The silicate network is moderated by the presence of sodium, potassium, magnesium and calcium and the various ratios of these elements in the glass are characteristic of the raw materials used in the formation of the glass. The most common glass type contains silica, soda and lime as the most abundant oxides and hence is known as a soda-lime-silicate glass (Sayre and Smith 1961; Turner 1956b). This is still by far the most common glass type in modern glass, just as it has been dominant in early glasses. Two fundamentally different soda-lime-silicate glasses can be identified (Sayre and Smith 1961).

The first human-made glass from the sixteenth century BC onwards has this soda-lime-silicate composition, but also has significant potash and magnesia, both of the order of a few percent (Brill 1970a; Sayre and Smith 1974). Within a century, this glass composition spread across the Near East, Egypt and the Eastern Mediterranean. It continues in use in these areas until the very early first millennium BC, when it is superseded by another glass type (Sayre and Smith 1961; Turner 1956a). This second type of glass has the same soda-lime-silicate basic composition, but instead it has very little potash or magnesia, usually less than 1 per cent of each. This glass composition is typical of Iron Age, Hellenistic and Roman glasses in the Mediterranean world and continues in use through the Roman period until the decline of the Roman Empire in the mid-first millennium in northern Europe (Jackson 2005), and throughout the Byzantine period in the mid- and late first millennium in eastern Europe, western Asia and the Levant. In Mesopotamia and Central Asia, however, the traditional composition rich in magnesia and potash continues to be used throughout the Iron Age, Roman, Byzantine and Islamic periods, suggesting a separation of glassmaking traditions along major geographical lines.

The two key glass compositional groups reflect the use of different raw materials in the glass production. Specifically, they reflect the use of different fluxes and, to a lesser extent, silica sources. The low magnesia and potash compositions of the Roman glasses suggest that these were made of a flux that is correspondingly low in these two elements. The usual interpretation of this is that they were made using a mineral form of soda (Sayre and Smith 1967; Turner 1956b). The most likely source for such a mineral is evaporitic lakes, where chlorides, sulphates and most importantly carbonates of sodium and other elements are found (Shortland 2004). The sodium carbonates, particularly trona and natron, of the evaporite deposits such as the Wadi Natrun in Western Egypt are thought to be the major source of soda for the production of glass with this low magnesia, low potash composition (Forbes 1957). This glass is therefore often called 'soda glass' or 'natron glass' after one of the carbonate minerals that may be involved and is usually thought to have been mixed with beach sand to create the basic composition. The mineral natron is thought to be chemically very consistent, resulting in glass with very consistent chemical flux signatures. However, the beach sands impart their particular geochemical signature to the glass; so far, at least six major compositional glass groups have been identified among the Roman and Byzantine natron glass, suggesting that during this period glassmaking was concentrated in a small number of places along the eastern Mediterranean coast, all using mineral natron from Egypt but drawing on their particular local sand sources (Freestone et al. 2002b).

The other glass composition, characterised by higher magnesia and potash, shows a source of flux that is higher in these elements than the natron flux. The most likely source for this is the ashes of halophytic desert plants, which can tolerate living in saline conditions and include significant amounts of soda in their structure (Brill 1970a). They also accumulate other elements as well, such as phosphorous, which are incorporated into the glass on melting (Barkoudah and Henderson 2006; Tite et al. 2006). In the medieval and later periods, the ash of these plants was a valuable export from desert areas, especially the Levant, and was used in some of the major western glass factories, in particular in Venice, where glass of plant ash composition was dominant (Silvestri et al. 2005). Shiploads of ash where brought into Europe from the Levant through the port of Venice and elsewhere and fed a major glass industry in Italy and up through Central Europe (Verità and Zecchin 2009). Local recipes were produced and exploited and there was much exchange of both glassmaking knowledge and the glassmakers themselves, both voluntarily and by industrial espionage. Glass was an important commodity for the production of jewellery, where deliberate copying of precious stones was carried out, echoing Late Bronze Age production of nearly 3000 years before (Putzgruber et al. 2012).

'Natron glass' and 'plant ash glass' compositions are used quite widely through millennia for the production of glass in different areas (Sayre and Smith 1961).

However, there are also other glass compositions that are more temporally and/or geographically restricted, reflecting a more unusual choice of raw materials. These often occur in wetter areas, for example, Europe, where evaporitic lakes and desert plants were not readily available as a source for flux and ashes of trees or ferns were used instead. The same is true of regions where different sand sources result in fundamentally different glass compositions, such as the alumina- and potash-rich glasses of southern India, and of the chemically rather complex and diverse wider Southeast Asian glassmaking traditions (Dussubieux et al. 2010; Lankton et al. 2008). Indian glassmaking in particular focussed almost exclusively on beads (Francis 1991) and bangles, and developed into a highly sophisticated village-based industry producing many millions of beads annually which enter much of SE Asia's maritime trade as far north and east as Taiwan.

From the mid-first millennium onwards, glass beads play an important role in sub-Saharan African social and economic relations. Almost all of the beads were imported, either from the Egyptian production centres along trans-Saharan trade routes, or from India through the Indian Ocean trade with major entry points on the Red Sea and Swahili coast; from the mid-second millennium European glass beads begin to dominate the trade both in Africa and in North America (e.g., Hancock et al. 1999). Linking these beads back to their production centres, and tracing their way beyond the European and Arab coastal entrepôts is a major field of research utilising chemical analyses of the glass. For several centuries glassmaking flourished in southern Nigeria (Babalola et al. 2017; Lankton et al. 2006), producing beads visually indistinguishable from those imported from elsewhere but using local raw materials. The origin of this seemingly indigenous technology, and its demise at some point after the seventeenth century, remains enigmatic.

Chinese glass represents a unique and relatively short-lived phenomenon of roughly half a millennium on either side of the BC/AD transition, and restricted mostly to the Great Plains occupied by the Han population, and their immediate neighbours (Brill et al. 1991; Gan 2005). Here, glassmaking was based on lead and barium oxide or a mix of lead oxide, barium oxide and potash as the main fluxes. This particular lead- and barium-rich compositional pattern is mirrored in the contemporary Chinese faience and pigments such as lead white, Han blue and Han purple, demonstrating that the various vitreous materials are technologically linked to each other by the common use of uncommon raw materials.

Different compositional glass groups are sometimes known by acronyms that abbreviate the key elements of their composition. Examples of these include 'mixed alkali' glass, with similar high levels of soda and potash in the flux, sometimes known as 'low magnesium high potassium' (LMHK) glass, which occurs in Europe in the Bronze and Iron Ages (Brill 1992; Henderson 1988a; Henderson 1988b). Later in the same area 'wood ash' (also known as 'beech ash') glass or 'forest glass' occurs, which has high potash, but low soda levels, giving it the further name 'potash glass' (Jackson et al. 2005). This is the glass that is used predominantly in the windows of

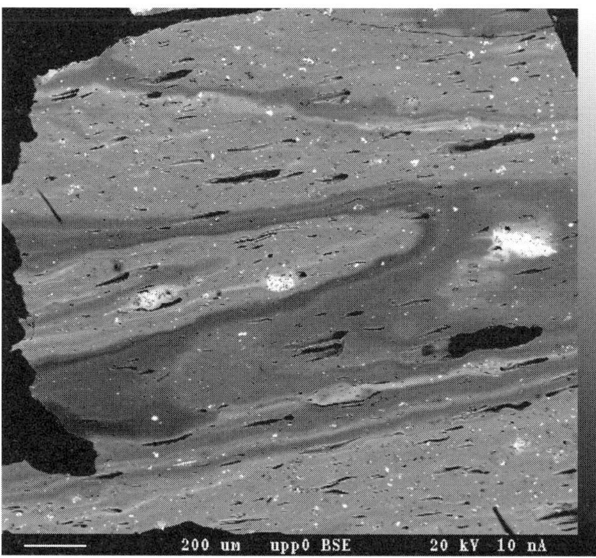

FIGURE 15.2 SEM micrograph of deliberately added lead antimonate phases in a Late Bronze Age Egyptian glass – the varying swirls of the glass reflect the poor mixing of lead in the glass. (Adapted from Shortland 2002)

the great medieval cathedrals of Western Europe (Cox and Gillies 1986; Wedepohl 1997). A further compositional group was developed in the late seventeenth and eighteenth centuries, which was once again used extensively in window glass of churches and cathedrals. This was 'High-Lime, Low-Alkali' glass, HLLA, often with levels of lime greater than 20 per cent CaO (Scott et al. 2012), and using an alkali source that is still debated.

Glass of many periods is deliberately coloured or opacified, almost always to resemble precious stones. Minor and trace element analytical techniques can give important information about the colouring elements used (Weyl 1951). The most important colorants through glass history include copper and cobalt for blues, manganese for blacks and pinks, and iron or copper for reds. Opacity is added to glasses either by adding particulate matter (Figure 15.2), or by causing crystals to precipitate out in the melt, see Figure 15.3 (Freestone 1987). A range of lead-tin and antimony compounds was used in different periods to do this for opaque white and yellow glasses (Shortland 2002; Turner and Rooksby 1959). In addition, glass was frequently palely coloured even if a colorant is not used, due to the range of other elements, especially iron, accidentally included in the melts through the use of impure raw materials. If true 'colourless' glass was required, this would need to be

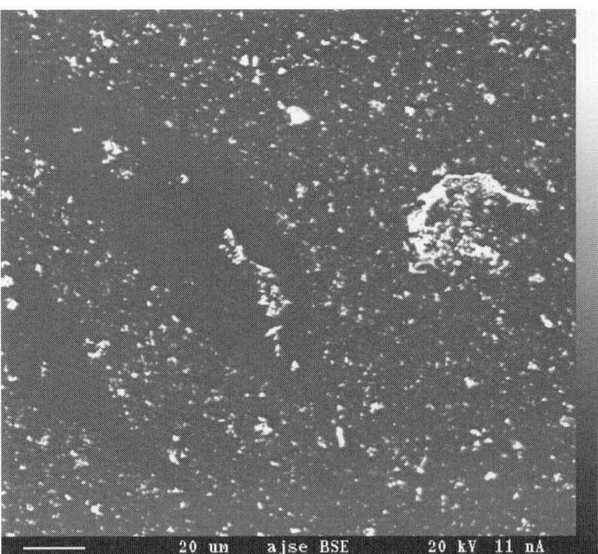

FIGURE 15.3 SEM micrograph of calcium antimonate phases that have precipitated in Late Bronze Age Egyptian glass. (Adapted from Shortland 2002)

tackled, leading to the inclusion in glass recipes of 'decolourising' elements, particularly manganese and antimony (Henderson 1985; Sayre and Smith 1961), which could give a truly colourless glass despite the impurities. Glass colorants can act as a good indicator of the age of the glass, just as the use of varying fluxes discussed above. While some colorants, such as copper, have been used for millennia, others are relatively modern discoveries. Attempts first by alchemists and later by the first true chemists to discover more about how substances interacted and changed led to the discovery of a whole range of new elements such as chromium, selenium and uranium. Many of these very quickly began to be used for their colouring properties in the glass and glaze industries in the nineteenth and early twentieth centuries (Bertini et al. 2016).

5 TRACE ELEMENTS AND PROVENANCING GLASS

Major and minor element compositions give valuable information about the raw materials of glassmaking and allow compositional groups to be determined. Where different compositions are used simultaneously in adjacent areas, they can also lead to the provenancing of the glass that is made into objects to one area or another. However, where all the glass of a period is of one compositional type, it is often very difficult to tell from these elements alone where the glass has been made if production is known or suspected in a number of areas. With the objective of provenancing the glass, a range of more recent techniques have been used to push the understanding of glass compositions beyond the circa twenty elements most often analysed for by microprobe. The most common technique being used for this work is LA-ICPMS (Gratuze 1999; Gratuze 2013). This has been selected, firstly, because it can be carried out on exactly the same polished blocks used for the microprobe analysis of the glass. It can even analyse complete objects such as beads, or fragments of larger vessels, if they are small enough to fit in the ablation chamber. Secondly, it has very low detection limits. For most elements this might be measured in parts per million (ppm) or parts per billion (ppb), several orders of magnitude better than that of the microprobe. Glasses produced in different areas can have different trace element compositions, caused by the raw materials being sourced ultimately in different geological zones, or by subtly different processing. This difference can be quantified by LA-ICPMS and glass compositions sub-divided into different manufacturing areas (Dussubieux et al. 2008; Shortland et al. 2007). Recent successes in this application include the differentiation between Mesopotamian- and Egyptian-made glass among the numerous glass beads that have been excavated in Greece (Polikreti et al. 2011; Walton et al. 2009), and which are typologically Mycenaean; it seems that in Greece, only imported glass was being worked into artefacts (Rehren 2014).

Perhaps one of the most important new areas for the analysis of glass and determination of glass provenance is the use of isotopic techniques. Yellow glasses and other glasses with high lead contents have been subjected to lead isotope analysis with some success (Brill et al. 1974; Lilyquist and Brill 1993; Shortland et al. 2000). Oxygen isotope measurements have also been utilised, with the aim of determining the source of the silica in the glass (Brill 1970b). However, recently two new isotopic systems, both developed in the geological sciences, have been applied for the first time in the assessment of glass provenance – strontium and neodymium. Strontium is incorporated into the glass with the lime component, since strontium commonly substitutes for calcium in crystal lattices (Freestone et al. 2003a). The amount of strontium and its $^{87}Sr/^{86}Sr$ ratio varies depending on whether the source of the calcium is modern shell or limestone and the geological age of limestone involved (Degryse et al. 2010b). This can give provenancing information that is not available to the trace element techniques, which can suffer from fractionation of elements in production and weathering. Neodymium is a rare earth element and its isotopes vary between different crustal formation episodes. Analysing the $^{144}Nd/^{143}Nd$ ratio of a glass can give strong evidence of where it was made, and is now being applied to ancient glasses, with very promising results (Degryse et al. 2010a; Degryse et al. 2010b).

6 GLASSMAKING TECHNOLOGIES

In addition to the analysis of finished glass, there are rare survivals of the debris of the glassmaking process – crucibles, furnaces, waste debris, failed batches and so on. This sort of debris is rare because glassmaking does not leave much waste compared, for instance, to the abundant slag heaps of ancient metallurgy. However, it is important for a number of reasons. Firstly, it is virtually the only sort of evidence apart from historical texts that can positively identify a glassmaking workshop. An example of this is the identification of Qantir-Pi-Ramesse and Amarna in Egypt as sites of primary glass production during the Late Bronze Age (Rehren 1997; Rehren and Pusch 2005; Smirniou and Rehren 2011), when previously pictorial and textual evidence only pointed to glassmaking in Mesopotamia (Oppenheim et al. 1970; Shortland 2012). Secondly, only such debris can reveal important information about how glassmaking was being carried out, as in Hellenistic Rhodes (Rehren et al. 2005) or LBA Egypt (Pusch and Rehren 2007), which then, in turn, can inform laboratory-based experiments to address specific technical details (Merkel and Rehren 2007; Shugar and Rehren 2002; Tanimoto and Rehren 2008). Such debris is frequently analysed by SEM-EDS, which gives the opportunities for both informative images and compositional information.

In addition to the bulk chemical analysis of glasses described above, glass formation processes have been investigated by other techniques. This is especially true of those glasses that contain a deliberately added particulate phase as an opacifier (Mason and Tite 1997; Molera et al. 1997). The way these opacifiers form (and under what temperature or compositional parameters) has been investigated to determine the degree of control of kilns historical glassmakers might have had and their recipes. The techniques used have included Raman and XRD to closely identify phases. However, it is synchrotron based XRD (X-Ray Diffraction), especially involving hot stages, which seems to be giving the most interesting results (Tite et al. 2008).

7 CONCLUDING COMMENT

Glass is unique among the artificial materials in that it is chemically highly complex and much more variable than most metals and alloys, and still entirely artificial, as opposed to the similarly chemically complex ceramics, which are predominantly representing raw geological materials. Where metals are made by extracting just one or two elements from complex ores while leaving behind a large amount of waste slag, glass is made by the complete fusion of various raw materials rich in silica and flux, with hardly any production remains surviving archaeologically. The scientific analysis of glass has to consider this combination of complex and often exotic raw materials and the effects of very specific technical processes, by combining major, minor and trace elemental analysis with the study of production and manufacturing methods. For a long time, glass analyses focussed on characterising and defining compositional groups and identifying the raw materials used in the production of these glass groups. Only recently has it become possible to provenance some of these glass groups to their geological origins, complementing the typological origin of the artefacts as determined by art historical study, and the archaeological origin given by excavation or find spot. This enables us today to trace the flow, often over considerable distances, of raw glass from the primary production centres to the secondary workshops where artefacts were made to local tastes, and for onwards shipment to the final consumers. In this effect, a glass object often has three different origins, and the interpretation of the geographical differences between these three can provide unparalleled insights into the life history of the artefact in question, and more generally into past patterns of trade and exchange of this most mobile and colourful material.

REFERENCES

Babalola, A. B., McIntosh, S. K., Dussubieux, L. and Rehren, Th. 2017. Ife-Ife and Igbo Olokun in the history of glass in West Africa. *Antiquity* 91:732–750.

Barkoudah, J. and Henderson, J. 2006. Plant ashes from Syria and the manufacture of glass: Ethnographic and scientific aspects. *Journal of Glass Studies* 48:297–321.

Bertini, M., Verveniotou, E., Lowe, M. and Miller, C. G. 2016. Laser ablation inductively coupled plasma mass spectrometry investigation of late 19th century Blaschka marine invertebrate glass models. *Journal of Archaeological Science: Reports* 6:506–517.

Brill, R. H. 1970a. The chemical interpretation of the texts. In: Oppenheim, A. L., Brill, R. H., Barag, D. and Von Saldern, A. (eds.) *Glass and Glass-Making in Ancient Mesopotamia*, pp 105–128. Corning, NY: Corning Museum of Glass.

Brill, R. H. 1970b. Lead and oxygen isotopes in ancient objects. *Philosophical Transactions of the Royal Society, London* 269:143–164.

Brill, R. H. 1992. Chemical analyses of some glasses from Frattesina. *Journal of Glass Studies* 34:11–22.

Brill, R. H., Barnes, I. L. and Adams, B. 1974. Lead isotopes in some ancient Egyptian objects. In: Bishay, A. (ed.) *Recent Advances in the Science and Technology of Materials*, pp. 9–27. New York, NY: Springer.

Brill, R. H., Tong, S. S. C. and Dohrenwend, D. 1991. Chemical analyses of some early Chinese glasses. In: Brill, R. H. and Martin, J. H. (eds.) *Scientific Research in Early Chinese Glass*, pp. 31–58. Corning, NY: Corning Museum of Glass.

Caley, E. R. 1962. *Analysis of Ancient Glass*. Corning, NY: Corning Museum of Glass.

Cox, G. A. and Gillies, K. J. S. 1986. The X-ray fluorescence analysis of Medieval durable blue soda glass from York Minster. *Archaeometry* 28:57–68.

Degryse, P., Boyce, A., Erb-Satullo, N., Eremin, K., Kirk, S., Scott, R., Shortland, A. J., Schneider, J. and Walton, M. 2010a. Isotopic discriminants between Late Bronze Age glasses from Egypt and the Near East. *Archaeometry* 52:380–388.

Degryse, P., Freestone, I. C., Schneider, J. and Jennings, S. 2010b. Technology and provenance study of Levantine plant ash glass using Sr-Nd isotope analysis. In: Drauschke, J. and Keller, D. (eds.) *Glass in Byzantium: Production, Usage, Analyses*, pp. 83–91. Mainz: Römisch-Germanisches Zentralmuseum.

Degryse, P. and Shortland, A. J. 2009. Trace elements in provenancing raw materials for Roman glass production. *Geologica Belgica* 12:135–143.

Doremus, R. H. 1994. *Glass Science*. New York, NY: John Wiley.

Dussubieux, L., Gratuze, B. and Blet-Lemarqand, M. 2010. Mineral soda alumina glass: occurence and meaning. *Journal of Archaeological Science* 37:1646–1655.

Dussubieux, L., Kusimba, C. M., Gogte, V., Kusimba, S. B. and Oka, R. 2008. The trading of ancient glass beads: New analytical data from South Asian and East African soda-alumina glass beads. *Archaeometry* 50:797–821.

Forbes, R. J. 1957. Glass. In: Forbes, R. J. (ed.) *Studies in Ancient Technology*. Leiden: Brill.

Francis Jr, P. 1991. Beadmaking at Arikamedu and beyond. *World Archaeology* 23:28–43.

Freestone, I. C. 1987. Composition and microstructure of early red glasses. In: Bimson, M. and Freestone, I. C. (eds.) *Early Vitreous Materials*, pp. 173–191. London: British Museum Occasional Papers 56.

Freestone, I. C. 2002. The relationship between enamelling on ceramic and on glass in the Islamic World. *Archaeometry* 44:251–255.

Freestone, I. C., Greenwood, R. and Gorin-Rosen, Y. 2002a. Byzantine and early Islamic glassmaking in the Eastern Mediterranean: Production and distribution of primary glass. In: Kordas, G. (ed.) *Hyalos-Vitrum-Glass. History, Technology and Conservation of Glass and Vitreous Materials in the Hellenic World, 1st International Conference*, pp. 167–174. Athens: Glasnet Publications.

Freestone, I. C., Leslie, K. A., Thirwall, M. and Gorin-Rosen, Y. 2003b. Strontium isotopes in the investigation of early glass production: Byzantine and early Islamic glass from the Near East. *Archaeometry* 45:19–32.

Freestone, I., Ponting, M. and Hughes, M. J. 2002b. The origins of Byzantine glass from Maroni Petrera, Cyprus. *Archaeometry* 44:257–272.

Freestone, I. C., Stapleton, C. P. and Rigby, V. 2003a. The production of red glass and enamel in the Late Iron Age, Roman and Byzantine periods. In: Entwistle, C. (ed.) *Through a Glass Brightly — Studies in Byzantine and Medieval Art and Archaeology Presented to David Buckton*, pp. 142–154. Oxford: Oxbow Books.

Gan, F. X. 2005. Evolution of the chemical composition and the origin of making technology of Chinese ancient glass. In: Gan, F.X. (ed.) *Development of Chinese Ancient Glass*, pp. 220–240. Shanghai Scientific and Technical Publishers (in Chinese).

Gratuze, B. 1999. Obsidian characterisation by laser ablation ICPMS and its application to prehistoric trade in the Mediterranean and the Near East. *Journal of Archaeological Science* 26:869–891.

Gratuze, B. 2013. Glass characterisation using laser ablation inductively coupled plasma mass spectrometry methods. In: Janssens, K. (ed.) *Modern Methods for Analysing Archaeological and Historical Glass*, pp. 201–234. Chichester: John Wiley and Sons.

Hancock, R., Aufreiter, S., Kenyon, I. and Latta, M. 1999. White glass beads from the Auger Site, southern Ontario, Canada. *Journal of Archaeological Science* 26:907–912.

Henderson, J. 1985. The raw materials of early glass production. *Oxford Journal of Archaeology* 4:267–291.

Henderson, J. 1988a. Electron microprobe analysis of mixed alkali glasses. *Archaeometry* 30:77–91.

Henderson, J. 1988b. Glass production and Bronze Age Europe. *Antiquity* 62:435–451.

Jackson, C. M. 2005. Making colourless glass in the Roman Period. *Archaeometry* 47:763–780.

Jackson, C. M., Booth, C. A. and Smedley, J. W. 2005. Glass by design? Recipes and compositional data. *Archaeometry* 47:781–795.

Lankton, J., Dussubieux, L. and Rehren, Th. 2008. A study of mid-first millennium CE southeast Aian specialized glass beadmaking traditions. In: Bacus, E., Glover, I. and Sharrock, P. (eds.) *Interpreting Southeast Asia's Past*, pp. 335–356. Chicago, IL: University of Chicago Press.

Lankton, J., Ige, A. and Rehren, Th. 2006. Early primary glass production in southern Nigeria. *Journal of African Archaeology* 4:111–138.

Lilyquist, C. and Brill, R. H. 1993. *Studies in Ancient Egyptian Glass*. New York, NY: Metropolitan Museum of Art.

Mason, R. B. and Tite, M. S. 1997. The beginnings of tin opacification in pottery glazes. *Archaeometry* 39:41–58.

Merkel, S. and Rehren, Th. 2007. Parting layers, ash trays and Ramesside glassmaking: An experimental study. In: Pusch, E. and Rehren, Th. (eds.) *Hochtemperatur-Technologie in der Ramses-Stadt, Rubinglass für den Pharao*, pp. 201–221. Hildesheim: Gerstenberg Verlag.

Molera, J., Vendrall-Saz, M., Garcia-Valles, M. and Pradell, T. 1997. Technology and colour development of Hispano-Moresque lead-glazed pottery. *Archaeometry* 39:23–39.

Nicholson, P. T. 2007. *Brilliant Things for Akhenaten*. London: Egypt Exploration Society.

Oppenheim, L., Brill, R., Barag, D. and von Saldern, A. 1970. *Glass and Glassmaking in Ancient Mesopotamia*. Corning, NY: Corning Museum of Glass.

Paul, A. 1990. *The Chemistry of Glasses*. London: Chapman and Hall.

Polikreti, K., Murphy, M. A., Kantarelou, V. and Karydas, A. G. 2011. XRF analysis of glass beads from the Mycenean palace of Nestor at Pylos, Peloponnesus, Greece: New insight into the LBA glass trade. *Journal of Archaeological Science* 38:2889–2896.

Pusch, E. and Rehren, Th. 2007. *Hochtemperatur-Technologie in der Ramses-Stadt, Rubinglas für den Pharao. Teil 1, Text, Teil 2, Katalog*. Hildesheim: Gerstenberg Verlag.

Putzgruber, E., Verità, M., Uhlir, K., Frühmann, B., Grießer, M. and Krist, G. 2012. Scientific investigation and study of the sixteenth-century glass jewellery collection of Archduke Ferdinand II. *Studies in Conservation* 57 (Supplement 1):217–226.

Rehren, Th. 1997. Ramesside glass colouring crucibles. *Archaeometry* 39:355–368.

Rehren, Th. 2014. Glass production and consumption between Egypt, Mesopotamia and the Aegean. In: Pfälzner, P., Niehr, H., Pernicka, E., Lange, S. and Köster, T. (eds.) *Contextualising Grave Inventories in the Ancient Near East* (Qatna Studien Supplementa 3), pp. 217–223. Wiesbaden: Harrassowitz.

Rehren, Th. and Freestone, I. C. 2015. Ancient glass: From kaleidoscope to crystal ball. *Journal of Archaeological Science* 56:233–241.

Rehren, Th. and Pusch, E. 2005. Late Bronze Age Egyptian glass production at Qantir-Piramesses. *Science* 308:1756–1759.

Rehren, Th., Spencer L. and Triantafyllidis, P. 2005. The primary production of glass at Hellenistic Rhodes. In: Cool, H. (ed.) *Annales du 16e Congres de l'Association Internationale pour l'Histoire du Verre*, pp. 39–43. Nottingham: AIHV.

Ruckstuhl, B. and Shortland, A. J. 2004. Glassperlen. In: Bauer, I. (ed.) *Die spätbronzezeitlichen Ufersiedlungen von Zug-Sumpf. Band 3: Die Funde der Grabungen 1923–37*, pp. 306–314. Zug, Switzerland: Kantonales Museum für Urgeschichte.

Sayre, E. V. and Smith, R. W. 1961. Compositional categories of ancient glass. *Science* 133:1824–1826.

Sayre, E. V. and Smith, R. W. 1967. Some materials of glass manufacturing in antiquity. In: Levey, M. (ed.) *Archaeological Chemistry*, pp. 279–311. Philadelphia, PA: University of Pennsylvania Press.

Sayre, E. V. and Smith, R. W. 1974. Analytical studies in ancient Egyptian glass. In: Bishay, A. (ed.) *Recent Advances in the Science and Technology of Materials*, pp. 47–70. New York, NY: Springer.

Scott, R. B., Shortland, A. J. and Power, M. 2012, The interpretation of compositional groupings in 17th century window glass from Christ Church Cathedral, Oxford. In: Ignatiodou, D. and Antonaras, A. (eds.) *Annales du 18e Congrés de l'Association Internationale pour l'Histoire du Verre*, pp. 425–429. Thessaloniki: AIHV.

Shortland, A. J. 2002. The use and origin of antimonate colorants in early Egyptian glass. *Archaeometry* 44:517–531.

Shortland, A. J. 2004. Evaporites of the Wadi Natrun: Seasonal and annual variation and its implication for ancient exploitation. *Archaeometry* 46:497–516.

Shortland, A. J. 2012. *Lapis Lazuli from the Kiln: Glass and Glassmaking in the Late Bronze Age.* Studies in Archaeological Science. Leuven: Leuven University Press.

Shortland, A. J., Nicholson, P. T. and Jackson, C. M. 2000. Lead isotopic analysis of 18th dynasty Egyptian eyepaints and lead antimonate colorants. *Archaeometry* 42:153–159.

Shortland, A. J., Rogers, N. and Eremin, K. 2007. Trace element discriminants between Egyptian and Mesopotamian Late Bronze Age glasses. *Journal of Archaeological Science* 34:781–789.

Shugar A. and Rehren, Th. 2002. Formation and composition of glass as a function of firing temperature. *Glass Technology* 43C:145–150.

Silvestri, A., Molin, G. and Salviulo, G. 2005. Roman and Medieval glass from the Italian area: Bulk characterisation and relationships to production technologies. *Archaeometry* 47:797–816.

Smirniou, M. and Rehren, Th. 2011. Direct evidence of primary glass production in Late Bronze Age Amarna, Egypt. *Archaeometry* 53:58–80.

Tanimoto, S. and Rehren, Th. 2008. Interactions between silicate and salt melts in LBA glassmaking. *Journal of Archaeological Science* 35:2566–2573.

Tite, M. S. 1987. Characterisation of early vitreous materials. *Archaeometry* 29:21–34.

Tite, M. S. and Bimson, M. 1986. Faience: an investigation of microstructures associated with the different methods of glazing. *Archaeometry* 28:69–78.

Tite, M. S., Pradell, T. and Shortland, A. J. 2008. Discovery, production and use of tin-based opacifiers in glasses, enamels and glazes from the Late Iron Age onwards: a reassessment. *Archaeometry* 50:67–84.

Tite, M. S., Shortland, A. J. and Maniatis, Y. 2006. The composition of soda-rich and mixed alkali plant ashes used in the production of glass. *Journal of Archaeological Science* 33:1284–1292.

Turner, W. E. S. 1956a. Studies in ancient glasses and glass making processes. Part III. The chronology of glass making constituents. *Journal of the Society of Glass Technology* 40:39–52.

Turner, W. E. S. 1956b. Studies in ancient glasses and glass making processes. Part V. Raw materials and melting processes. *Journal of the Society of Glass Technology* 40:277–300.

Turner, W. E. S. 1956c. Studies in ancient glasses and glass making processes. Part IV. The chemical composition of ancient glasses. *Journal of the Society of Glass Technology* 40:162–184.

Turner, W. E. S. and Rooksby, H. P. 1959. A study of opalising agents in ancient opal glasses throughout three thousand years. *Glasstechnische Berichte* 32K:17–28.

Vandiver, P. 1982. Technological change in Egyptian faience. In: Olin, J. S. and Franklin, A. D. (eds.) *Archaeological Ceramics*, pp. 167–180. Washington DC: Smithsonian Institution.

Vandiver, P. 1998. A review and the proposal of new criteria for the production technologies of Egyptian faience. In: Colinart, S. and Menu, M. (eds.) *La couleur dans la peinture at l'émaillage de L'Égypte ancienne*, pp. 121–142. Ravello: Centro Universitario Europeo.

Verità, M. and Zecchin, S. 2009. Thousand years of Venetian glass: The evolution of chemical composition from the origins to the 18th century. In: Janssens, K. H. A. (ed.) *Annales du 17e Congrès de l'Association Internationale pour l'Histoire du Verre*, pp. 602–613. Antwerp: University Press Antwerp.

Walton, M.S., Shortland, A. J., Kirk, S. and Degryse, P. 2009. Evidence for the trade of Mesopotamian and Egyptian glass to Mycenean Greece. *Journal of Archaeological Science* 36:1496–1503.

Wedepohl, K. H. 1997. Chemical composition of medieval glass from excavations in West Germany. *Glastechnische Berichte / Glass Science and Technology* 70:246–255.

Weyl, W. A. 1951. *Coloured Glasses*. Sheffield: Society of Glass Production.

Zachariasen, W. H. 1932. The atomic arrangement of glass. *Journal of the American Chemical Society* 54:3841–3851.

16

Metals

Thilo Rehren

The importance of metals in archaeology and methods to determine how metals were first developed and how they were used in the past.

1 INTRODUCTION

Metals have always fascinated humans, for reasons ranging from practical through aesthetic to philosophical considerations. More than for other materials, this fascination can be seen to cover both the production of metals and their use. In most societies, ceramics play a much more fundamental and ubiquitous role than metals, but it is only the high-end varieties, such as porcelain, terra sigillata or colourful glazed wares, that attract particular attention. Few people, past and present, philosophise about the transformational processes involved in changing the plastic, pliable clay into a hard and rigid water-resistant ceramic. Interest in wool, linen and other fibres is almost entirely restricted to our obsession with fashion and the social expressions it allows, but the production processes involved are a minority interest and outside the general folklore. In contrast, metals play not only a role in many societies' mythology and moral narrative, assigning notions of nobility, strength and value to them, but even their production forms the basis for many metaphors, tales and symbolic expressions. The phrase 'trial by fire' makes direct reference to cupellation, an obscure and specialised metallurgical operation in which the quality of gold or silver is tested for any debasement by copper – but as a metaphor it already appears in the Old Testament, and is still understood today. 'Brass' evokes a very different connotation from 'gold' when talking about values and appearances. Prospects of a 'mother lode' or 'bonanza' resonate with many people even if they are not metal prospectors. In archaeology, metals not only make a disproportionately high contribution to structuring major periods of cultural development and evolution, but archaeometallurgists specialising in the study of their production have even been referred to as a 'priesthood' trying to exploit secret knowledge and driving hidden agendas, potentially not in the best interest of the wider scholarly community (Doonan and Day 2007); a charge that to the best of my knowledge has not been levelled against any other science-based discipline within archaeology, such as archaeo-botany or -zoology, or ceramic petrography. Clearly, metals fascinate humans, whether it is for the right or wrong reasons.

2 THE BEGINNINGS

Native Metals as Stones

Humans' fascination with metals can be traced back well into periods predating the emergence of metallurgy, when naturally occurring pieces of metal first attracted attention (e.g., Aldenderfer et al. 2008 and Binford 1962 for the New World; Roberts et al. 2009 and Roberts 2009 for the Old World), as just another type of interesting stone. Often, their use as pieces of personal adornment seems to emerge from and run parallel to that of colourful minerals, such as pigments and bead material (e.g., Rehren et al. 2013). In the case of native copper, this may well be due to the close geological association among the various secondary copper minerals, of which native copper is often found near malachite. It is thus easily imaginable how the exploitation of malachite led to the discovery of native copper, another relatively rare mineral with different, but similarly interesting properties, and suitable for jewellery production. Where the traditional colourful and rare precious stones could only be broken, ground and polished to take the desired shape and surface finish, this one could be hammered and plastically deformed, enabling the production of thin sheet that could be rolled into interesting shapes. In addition, copper has a particular colour and a higher density, setting it further apart from more ordinary stones. While these properties, in particular its malleability, toughness and high specific gravity, were to underpin copper's future use in tools and weapons, they initially only facilitated the production of novelty items among a much wider range of rare and at times exotic materials that were used for beads and pendants.

Heat Treatment as Neolithic Technology

This use of selected minerals for adornment or practical use goes hand in hand with the emergence of the regular application of fire to alter the properties of certain stones; most notably of flint and chert, for the purposes of improving their mechanical properties for ease of knapping (Domanski and Webb 1992). In Neolithic China, jade was regularly heat-treated during working, improving both hardness and appearance (Wen and Jing 1992). In pre-dynastic Egypt, soft steatite was carved into beads and then fired to harden, as well as to take a fuel ash glaze (Tite and Bimson 1989). The heat treatment of steatite and agate beads to enhance their visual quality is also well documented for the Harappan culture in NW India and Pakistan (Miller 2007). The colours of red and yellow pigments based on iron oxides were improved through firing, possibly as early as the Palaeolithic (Salomon et al. 2015). Copper metal hardens when it is hammered and deformed, to the point where it loses its unique malleability and becomes prone to cracking. Heating such work-hardened copper to moderate temperatures, a process called annealing, leads to a re-softening of the metal, facilitating further hammering and shaping without cracking; this has been used by Woodland Period cultures in North America (Chastain et al. 2011), as well as in late Neolithic Anatolia (Yalcin and Pernicka 1999). Thus, within the spectrum of firing stones and minerals, the heat treatment of native copper falls closer to that of flint, chert and steatite, constituting a functional step within the manufacture of an artefact to facilitate its shaping or hardness, rather than improving its appearance, as is the case for agate or the iron-based pigments. Conceptually, it is firmly part of this established Neolithic tradition of applying heat to stones and minerals, in that a particular desirable property is enhanced, without fundamentally altering the material. This heat treatment is therefore much less drastic or visible than the transformational effects long known from food processing, or those from pottery production, which emerged side by side with the heat treatment of stones and which changed the properties of the clay in a much more fundamental way. From a modern perspective, what all three (cooking food, firing pottery and heat-treating stones) have in common is a primary emphasis on the two-dimensional application of heat. The only dimensions that matter and therefore need to be controlled to enable a predictable outcome are the intensity and the duration of the firing.

Defining Metallurgy

The combination of mineral selection, routine application of fire to modify these properties, and the modern need to classify and categorise both materials and human activities is key in the discussion about the origins of metallurgy. Many of the minerals exploited early on for their beauty, such as haematite, malachite or galena, happen to be used later primarily as metal ores, giving rise to some confusion in the archaeological literature regarding terminology. We define an ore as a rock or mineral from which metal can be profitably extracted. Differences in technological ability, as well as economic fundamentals across time, space and cultures mean that the term 'ore' is highly context-dependent, and must not be used as an absolute term, tacitly assuming current situations as being universally valid. Thus, it is inappropriate to term any mineral an 'ore' in the context of a culture that does not make metal from this mineral, even if in modern understanding this same mineral can be an ore. The malachite that was used to produce beads is not and never was a copper ore; it is a stone that just happened to contain copper. Other green stones do not contain copper, and were still used for bead making, often alongside malachite (e.g., Affonso and Pernicka 1997; Bar-Yosef Mayer and Porat 2008).

The desire to define the 'beginning' of metallurgy has been a major driving force in archaeological and archaeo-metallurgical research. However, this desire is again an ill-placed reflection of modern concepts onto prehistoric situations, and probably irrelevant for the mindset of the people who actually 'invented' metallurgy. In reality, there was most likely a continuum of activities covering the exploitation of a wide range of materials and ways of modifying their properties, through a number of actions, including mechanical processing, such as grinding, mixing and shaping, and the application of heat. Within this broad spectrum of fashioning jewellery, producing pottery and making tools, the serendipitous discovery occurred that the application of heat to certain (mostly green) minerals transformed them into copper metal. Such an occurrence required conditions where access of air to the heat source was limited to the extent that the fire operated under predominantly reducing conditions. Two closely related cognitive events therefore set metallurgy apart from the other high-temperature crafts, and only their mastery can be seen as the genuine beginning of metallurgy. These are the realisation that this additional dimension, the control of air flow or air supply within the fire that contained the ore, was necessary to effect the transformation of a stone into a metal, followed by the development of a sequence of actions that allowed ancient craftsmen to predictably repeat this effect. In modern language, it is the routine control of redox conditions that made possible the routine production of metal, and it is this less tangible technological dimension that I take as the defining criterion for the emergence of metallurgy as a discrete craft, as opposed to the simple application of heat to some raw material – regardless of whether the latter may have resulted in the serendipitous formation or structural modification of metal at one point or another.

Multiple Origins of Metallurgy?

Based on current knowledge, metallurgy has evolved several times in human history. Metallurgy in South America is clearly an independent development, not aided or affected by developments in the Old World. For Africa, the debate is still raging – see the debate in part 1 of volume 8 of the *Journal of African Archaeology* – and hinges very much on issues of dating rather than technology. For the Old World, the debate between those favouring a single point of origin and subsequent spread of the idea (Roberts et al. 2009) and others who argue for multiple independent regions of discovery has recently gained new momentum following the discovery of unambiguous smelting evidence securely dated to ca. 5,000 BC in Serbia (Radivojević et al. 2010). This suggests that in the Balkans metallurgy is contemporary with or even predates much of the available evidence for smelting in Iran, another 'heartland of metallurgy' (Pigott 1999; Thornton 2009). The distance between these two regions is simply too large to seriously contemplate diffusion of metallurgical technology from one to the other, within just one hundred years or so. For half a century, much depended on the date and nature of the evidence from Çatalhöyük in Turkey, roughly halfway between Iran and Serbia and said to have smelted metal as early as ca. 6,500 BC (Cessford 2005; Neuninger et al. 1964). Recent reanalysis of the original material unambiguously identified the 'slag' from Çatalhöyük as a burnt piece of malachite pigment, from a destructive fire and not related to metallurgy at all (Radivojević et al. 2017). For China and Southeast Asia, the available dates for the emergence of metallurgy point to relatively late developments, and in view of well-established cross-continental contacts, it seems unlikely that these regions invented metallurgy all by themselves; however, the details of any transmission of technology are not well understood (see Mei et al. 2015 and Thornton et al. 2010 for brief summaries of the debate).

3 METALLURGICAL PRACTICE

The development of metallurgy is often seen as forming part of a much wider package, including craft specialisation, social stratification and major changes in lifestyle (e.g., Renfrew 1978 or Smith 1981, and literature therein). The following text cannot do justice to the manifold expressions and variations of metallurgical developments across space and time, and will have to focus on some core concepts. From a modern perspective, metallurgy can be divided into two main sets of operations or practices, and I will argue that this division is widely applicable from a relatively early period onwards. The primary production consists of ore prospection, mining, beneficiation and smelting, and is completed with the production of metal in a form suitable for transport or storage. It requires specialist skills in what we would call economic geology, mining technology and extractive metallurgy, including analytical chemistry and process technology. In contrast, the manufacture of artefacts includes operations such as alloying, melting, casting, hammering, annealing and a wide range of surface treatments. The skills here fall into the modern categories of craft production, artisanal casting and design, all grounded in a practical understanding of the control of fire and some practical materials science, coupled with strong aesthetic and artistic skills. It is these fundamentally different skill sets, which for me justify seeing these two branches of metallurgy as conceptually different, providing a logical structuring element. What is more, for much of developed metallurgy, these two sets of activities take place in clearly separated socioeconomic contexts; mining and smelting are often carried out in remote mountainous areas where ore and fuel are plentiful, while manufacturing often takes place in settlements and near the patrons who ultimately consume the finished objects. This spatial division is overcome by means of transport and trade, involving third parties with no technical or specialist knowledge of metallurgy, often acting as a barrier or filter stripping the metal of its original narrative and metadata about its origin and production, and providing it with another legend, often more based on marketing than observation. It is sensible to apply this division also to the archaeological study of metallurgy, even though, particularly in the very early phases, both branches were often in the hands of the same person or groups of people.

Primary Production: Mining and Beneficiation

Mining significantly predates metallurgy. Stones, salt and pigments have all been mined for tens of thousands of years, using a combination of surface and underground techniques. Some of the best known are the Neolithic flint mines of Grimes Graves (Russell 2000), while salt was mined as well as extracted from brine through evaporation in many different parts of Europe, Africa, Asia and the Americas well before the beginnings of metallurgy (e.g., Marro et al. 2010; Weller 2002).

Metal mining, in contrast, can be expected to postdate the inception of metallurgy, which in many areas is assumed to have started using small quantities of ore collected from the surface or from outcrops exposed by rivers and rockfalls. However, the double function of the mineral malachite, acting both as a raw material for pigment and bead making, and as a copper ore, meant that fully developed late Neolithic mines such as Rudna Glava in Serbia (Jovanović 1982) could have initially served as sources for bead malachite before becoming mines for copper ore. The difference is purely semantic, with no change in technology; at the level of mining, metal ores are no different from other rocks valued for some specific properties.

The archaeology of ancient mining has significantly expanded over the last 30 years, with major case studies documenting underground mines in the Middle East (e.g., Rothenberg 1988; Weisgerber 2006; Weisgerber and Hauptmann 1988;), Europe (e.g., Cech 2007; O'Brien 2004; Pittioni 1948), and elsewhere. Even in the early phases, however, rarely was the ore so pure that it could have been smelted directly as mined. Typically, the rich ore mineral is intergrown with a variety of other minerals and host rock, necessitating a further mechanical separation before the charge can be smelted. This beneficiation is archaeologically hard to document, but plays a central role in ensuring consistent properties of the charge – a crucial factor when aiming to achieve predictable results. The best-documented beneficiation landscape in archaeology is the Lauriotiki in eastern Attika in Greece (Conophagos 1980), source of the lead-silver ore that underpinned the rise in the fifth and fourth centuries BC of Athens to cultural and military dominance in the eastern Mediterranean. The ore was crushed for the rich mineral particles to be mostly liberated from their host rock. The ground material was then subjected to a washing operation that separated the minerals by their different specific gravities, exploiting the different response of grains of similar size but different specific gravity to the flow of water down a carefully textured work surface; the heavier particles were retained and concentrated in little grooves, while the lighter ones were washed further down and discarded as tailings (Rehren et al. 2002). The close relationship among mining shafts, road networks, beneficiation workshops and water management installations demonstrate the central role that water played in this process. Technically very similar installations are known from New Kingdom to Ptolemaic Egypt, where they served to separate gold from crushed quartz (Klemm and Klemm 1994).

Primary Production: Smelting Metal

Smelting is the chemical separation of a metal from its mineral compound, typically an oxide. This requires heat to facilitate the reaction to proceed at a reasonable speed, as well as the excessive presence of carbon monoxide that has a higher affinity for oxygen than the metal itself, necessary to reduce the metal oxide to pure metal. Heat is generated through combustion of fuel, such as wood, charcoal, dung or mineral coal. This much was practised for millennia in open fires, loosely contained mostly for convenience and safety. In metallurgy, the need to produce carbon monoxide rather than the more typical combustion product, carbon dioxide, requires first the limiting of the access of air to the fuel, and then the containment of the gaseous carbon monoxide for long enough together with the ore charge to facilitate the reaction to take place. In practice, enclosed spaces such as crucibles and later furnaces provided this controlled environment, with air supplied initially by blowpipes and later by bellows or natural draft channelled through ceramic tubes known as tuyères. The incomplete combustion to carbon monoxide provides only about one third of the thermal energy compared to full combustion to carbon dioxide, and the smelting reaction itself is endothermic; thus, the need to generate carbon monoxide as a specific agent to facilitate smelting came at the expense of the ability to generate heat to smelt and melt the charge. Therefore, the walls of these reaction vessels were designed to be thermally insulating, so as to contain the heat as much as possible. Early smelting crucibles are invariably fired from above and the inside, with relatively thick and porous walls, similar in principle to the furnaces that replaced them at some time during the Early Bronze Age (Rehren 2003; Thornton et al. 2010). Heating crucibles from the outside only became a viable option once sufficiently refractory ceramics were available, which did not routinely become the case prior to the late Iron Age. By this time, smelting took place in furnaces, while crucibles were primarily used for melting, a physical process that did not require the charge to be in direct contact with carbon monoxide (Martinón-Torres and Rehren 2014).

Ore minerals can be divided into those with sulphur as the main nonmetallic element, and those where oxygen is the key bonding element. All ores benefit from some initial heat treatment, often referred to as roasting if it is carried out as a separate process; otherwise, it happens almost inevitably within the upper parts of a furnace. This heat treatment, at temperatures below the melting point of the charge and done under oxidising conditions, removes most of the sulphur and replaces it with oxygen, and breaks down most of the oxide-rich complexes. Thus, the ore reaches the reaction zone as cracked and porous lumps composed of relatively simple metal oxides with a large surface area. The actual smelting then reduces the oxide to pure metal by the action of carbon monoxide gas. Other compounds present in the furnace charge, mostly host rock or gangue remaining after the beneficiation, together with the fuel ash and any fused clay from the furnace structure, combine to form a slag. Slag is not only of interest to archaeometallurgists; it plays a central role in coalescing the forming metal to larger prills and particles, and preventing its reoxidation in front of the air inlet. The mechanical separation of metal and slag requires that at least one of them is present in liquid form; this determines the minimum operating temperature of the system. Depending on the actual composition of the charge, an additional component can be added to aid in the formation of a low-melting slag; such fluxes include silica, iron oxide, limestone or lead-rich compounds. However, most ores smelted in antiquity are thought to have been self-fluxing, and sound evidence for intentional fluxing is restricted to the Middle Ages (e.g., Eckstein et al. 1994). For most metals, smelting takes place at around 1100–1250°C, at the upper end of temperatures achievable with charcoal and simple bellows. In China, superior bellows design led to the early development of furnaces operating at higher temperatures, probably reaching 1350 to 1400°C, as early as the first millennium BC (Wagner 2008); in Europe, this did not happen until the early to mid-second millennium.

Copper Smelting

The earliest well-dated evidence for copper smelting currently comes from Belovode, a Vinča-culture site in Serbia (Radivojević et al. 2010), closely radio-carbon dated to c. 5000 BC. Two aspects are particularly significant. One is the lack of crucibles or furnaces among the metallurgical remains; a simple hole in the ground, lined with broken pottery, may have served as the smelting installation, as documented in Chalcolithic eastern Bulgaria (Rehren et al. 2016). Remelting the smelted metal in order to cast it into artefacts such as the heavy axes that survive in large numbers from the fifth millennium BC across the Balkans would certainly have required crucibles and moulds; these, however, have not yet been found. The other interesting aspect is the complex network of materials that already at this very early phase spans across the Balkans. Chemical and lead isotope analyses by E. Pernicka have shown that at Belovode malachite bead making used a different mineral source from copper smelting, suggesting some degree of specialisation. Furthermore, the copper smelted at Belovode has the same chemical and isotopic signature as a group of 16 chalcolithic copper implements found along the River Danube as far east as Bulgaria, indicating that Belovode copper served a considerable market along the main communication route. Finally, analysis of a set of typologically similar artefacts from the site of Pločnik in southern Serbia demonstrates that the copper here comes from at least six different sources, indicating that a single site consumed copper from multiple producers (Radivojević et al. 2010).

Smelting rich oxidic ores such as malachite leaves little waste and can therefore be difficult to detect archaeologically, in particular when the scale of production was limited. However, the emergence in the Bronze Age of large-scale smelting of chalcopyrite, a sulphidic ore containing as much iron as copper, resulted in the deposition of large quantities of slag. For each kilogram of copper extracted from pure chalcopyrite, at least two, and more likely three kilograms of slag were generated (see Maldonado and Rehren 2009), together with a considerable amount of furnace debris. Large-scale copper smelting, such as documented from the Late Bronze Age and Iron Age in Austria, China, Cyprus, Italy, Jordan, Oman, Spain, Thailand, Turkey and elsewhere, was only feasible in relatively stable societies with a sufficient infrastructure to organise production and distribution, and is likely to have had a considerable impact not only on the economy, but also on the environment, at least in areas of marginal vegetation cover.

Copper itself is a relatively soft metal, suitable for decorative items, but as a tool material inferior to many stones. Only the combination of copper with other metals, such as arsenic, tin or zinc, produced sufficiently hard and tough alloys to make it the material of choice for most tools and weapons. The scientific analysis of these alloys for chemical composition and microstructure enables us to gain insight into the actions of ancient metal smiths, in terms of metal selection and control over alloy design, and the ability to manipulate the internal structure of the metal through hammering and careful heat treatment during manufacturing.

Lead, Silver and Gold

Lead and silver are geologically and metallurgically intimately connected, and both metals occur very early in the archaeological record. The main lead mineral is galena, lead sulphide, which is shiny-silvery and was used early on for bead making, for instance in Late Neolithic Çatalhöyük (Sperl 1990). Metallic lead, clearly a smelted material since native lead is virtually unknown in nature, has been widely used to produce jewellery, for instance in Early Bronze Age Scotland (Hunter and Davis 1994) or Mesopotamia (Moorey 1994), even though it is not particularly appealing for modern tastes. In later periods, lead continues to be used for cheap decorative items, but its main function is in architecture for pipes and roofs, and to encase iron cramps holding stones together. Further uses for lead are for sling shot and other missiles, seals, net sinkers and weights. In metallurgy it is a necessary component for the production, refining and recycling of silver, and an alloying component in bronze, particularly for cast objects. However, we know little about the technology and economy of lead production, despite its versatility and importance as a practical and auxiliary material, which is archaeologically reflected in the significant number of LBA, Roman and medieval lead ingots recovered, witnessing the economic importance of this strategic metal. Of particular interest is the analysis of lead metal for its trace element content, which can indicate whether it had been desilvered or recycled (Rehren and Prange 1998).

Silver and gold occur as native metals and in a variety of rich minerals from which they are easily smelted. However, throughout history most silver was extracted from lead minerals, which often contain up to 0.5 wt% silver, but may have been much richer as well (e.g. Schultze et al. 2009). In addition to their aesthetic appeal, gold and silver are primarily metals of economic importance, used as a means to store and exhibit wealth in the form of tableware, jewellery or ingots, and as a medium to facilitate economic transactions, as minted currency. The latter function often gave rise to close administrative control over their production, use and purity. The compositional analysis of gold and silver for fineness and trace elements therefore informs about economic as well as technological practices (Ramage and Craddock 1999).

Iron

The earliest use of iron is from meteoritic metal, characterised by its nickel content and other diagnostic trace elements (Jambon 2017). It was used for jewellery and prestige items, such as the Early Bronze Age beads from Gerzeh in Egypt or the LBA iron dagger with gold sheath from Tutankhamen's tomb. Iron remained a rare and high-status metal until the end of the Late Bronze Age (Waldbaum 1999), and became commonly used only during the Iron Age. Two main traditions dominate iron smelting. The bloomery or direct process operates at around 1200–1300°C and produces a lump of solid iron with a relatively low carbon content and interspersed with slag inclusions, called bloom. The bloom is directly useable for the production of artefacts and needs only mechanical cleaning through smithing to remove slag and charcoal remains. This was the dominant process of iron production throughout the Middle East and Europe until the Middle Ages, and remained in use in Africa and North America until the early twentieth century. In contrast, cast iron production operates at significantly higher temperatures, reaching 1450°C, and produced liquid iron alloyed with several percent by weight of carbon, and small quantities of silicon, manganese and other siderophil elements. It developed in Europe during the high Middle Ages, and was called the indirect process because it required the cast (or pig) iron to be decarburised in order to obtain useful steel. It depended on water-powered bellows to provide a very strong air blast into the furnace to ensure the higher combustion rates and temperatures and more strongly reducing conditions necessary to produce liquid cast iron (Rostoker and Bronson 1990). In China, blast furnaces emerged much earlier, powered by sophisticated box bellows, and cast iron production dominated from the mid-first millennium BC. Based on a highly developed tradition of bronze castings, cast iron objects were the tools of choice wherever possible. In parallel, Chinese smiths developed sophisticated methods to forge cast iron, partly decarburising it to steel, so that both hard and brittle cast iron and softer but tougher steel were available (Wagner 2008). Crucible or damascene steel, also known as *wootz* or *pulad*, is a high-quality iron-carbon alloy produced in Central Asia, Iran, India and Sri Lanka from the tenth to nineteenth century. Most crucible steel was made by melting bloomery iron in closed crucibles with carbonaceous matter and fluxes, although other methods are also said to have been used, such as the decarburisation of cast iron or the co-fusion of cast and bloomery iron (Alipour and Rehren 2014; Allan and Gilmour 2000).

Iron and its alloys are of limited temptation for most analytical chemists. The main information about manufacture, function or quality is in the carbon content and the microstructure of the metal; both are best determined and interpreted through classical metallography. Trace element contents and isotope ratios have so far proved difficult to use for provenancing iron, which was widely traded both in ingot and artefact form; only recently do we see some progress in this field (Brauns et al. 2013; Schwab et al. 2006). For bloomery iron, which even after careful smithing retains small slag inclusions, the analysis of those can provide some relevant information about the nature of the ore from which the metal was smelted, and hence its likely geological origin (Pages et al. 2011).

Quantifying Production

Undeniably, metals play an important role in the economy of most developed societies. Quantifying their use, however, is fraught with difficulties. In addition to the uncertainty of depositional survival and biased recovery rates that are common to all archaeological materials, metals are prone to extensive recycling, hoarding, and long-distance trade, all of which distort the picture. For the early metal use in the Balkans, Taylor (1999: 26) estimated that the roughly 4.7 tons of archaeologically known metal artefacts from the fifth millennium BC represent ca. 0.01 per cent of the total metal in use throughout that time, while assumptions used by Pernicka et al. (1997) put this figure nearer to 0.1 per cent. Despite this difference, it is clear that significant amounts of metal were in circulation during this early period, whatever the actual archaeological recovery rate may be.

Another approach to quantifying the use of metal is to quantify its production, which at least broadly should be in the same order of magnitude. The presence of slag enables us to estimate the amount of metal produced, provided we can determine the average or typical slag composition, and estimate the average richness of the ore that was smelted. Total metal production can only be reasonably quantified for smelting sites where full recovery – or at least full quantification – of slag is possible. Using mass balance calculations, it is then possible to identify to which extent other materials contributed to the slag formation, particularly furnace wall material. It is then possible to calculate the theoretical amount of metal produced per unit of slag (e.g., Maldonado and Rehren 2009; Veldhuijzen and Rehren 2007, and literature therein). This depends to a large extent on the richness of the ore; for bloomery iron smelting, the ratio of metal to slag can vary from 0.1 to 10.

4 ARCHAEOMETALLURGY: WHY AND HOW

Metals have been used for four main reasons: decorative (jewellery, inlays), military (arms and armour), domestic (tools, general implements), and economic (ingots and coins). These relate to different characteristics that were perceptible in antiquity, such as colour, density, malleability, hardness or rarity. In contrast, modern interest in archaeological metal objects is either curatorial, that is to describe and preserve the objects, or academic, that is to extract archaeologically relevant information from them within curatorial, practical and economic constraints. The analysis of metal objects can help to understand whether for a given object certain properties have been exploited or modified, indicating levels of metallurgical knowledge and the relative importance of these parameters to the person or society producing the object. Reconstructing the techniques used to smelt and process metals from the waste left behind is a closely related field. Still focussing on the ancient mindset are analyses meant to determine the functionality of objects, for example, whether they were made for display only or for real use; this can be a question for funerary or dedicatory objects. More indirectly relevant archaeological information is obtained by identifying the geological origin of a given object, typically combining chemical with isotopic analysis (Pernicka 2014), and thus mapping the movement of raw materials and finished objects as a reflection of economic interactions and cultural connections.

The curatorial desire for archaeometric analysis of metal objects combines the basic curiosity to classify objects by material types and to identify similarities and differences in composition in order to form groups, with the necessity to identify the most suitable conservation methods. Thus, different research fields prevail in the analysis of archaeological metal objects: determining their composition and current condition; defining compositional groups; reconstructing metallurgical practice; and locating the geological origin of the metal. Of these four research fields, the first two are predominantly descriptive and the latter two mostly interpretative; the first and the third are absolute in that they consider only the material at hand, while the second and fourth are relative, as they require data about comparative material. This has major ramifications for the analytical practice; research requiring comparative data will depend on, and have to match the type of, existing data when conducting new analyses.

Analytical Practice

Metallurgical analysis in archaeology draws from the entire range of materials science methods of analysis; however, for metal objects, several approaches have been particularly successful and therefore more widely adopted. Traditionally, we distinguish between methods that do not alter the physical integrity of the objects and those that require a sample to be removed and processed. More recent developments blur this distinction, using methods that remove a minute amount of material without leaving damage visible to the naked eye.

In contrast to the wide array of physico-chemical methods used for the analysis of metal objects, archaeological slag analysis draws almost exclusively from Earth science methods. Often, this combines fully quantitative multi-element chemical methods with optical or electron microscopy.

Ideally, the choice of analytical method and instrument is governed primarily by the particular research questions under consideration, moderated only by curatorial constraints. In reality, costs of analysis and ease of access to or availability of instruments often play a decisive role. For all quantitative methods, it is imperative to monitor and report data quality (accuracy and precision) through publishing results for analysis of certified reference materials along with the unknown samples, in order to be able to combine data from different laboratories.

Two important considerations are sample size and location. Archaeological metals are often heterogeneous, with grain sizes up to several millimetres; intentional surface treatments such as gilding or patination, or unintentional alterations through corrosion or conservation treatments, can result in major differences in composition between the surface and the body of an object. Sampling and analytical methods have to take account of this, allowing, for instance, for invasive sampling to characterise both the surface and the body. A balance between the curatorial desire to minimise the sampling impact and the analytical need for a representative or meaningful sample is sometimes difficult to achieve.

Identifying Composition and Condition

The analytical emphasis in identifying the composition of nonferrous metals is on the main constituents down to about one percent by weight. Components below that level have only a limited effect on the properties of the main metal, and their presence or absence will not have resulted in perceptible changes in properties that could be linked to archaeologically relevant alloy selection for particular types of objects or specific purposes. Correct alloy identification for categorisation purposes or conservation treatment also does not require more detailed analyses. This type of information is easily available from a range of analytical techniques, most recently through portable X-ray fluorescence (pXRF) instruments that operate without the need for invasive sampling. Surface analysis only requires a small area to be cleaned to expose fresh metal, and can be done in conjunction with normal conservation treatment.

Establishing Compositional Groups

Beyond identifying the broader metal and alloy types, much information regarding distribution and circulation of metals between societies can be gained from a more detailed analysis of minor and trace elements. This enables forming chemically defined groups, informing on metal supply in a given society and adding an independent dimension to artefact groups defined by stylistic criteria. It requires comparing data from different laboratories and thus needs both precise and accurate data. Establishing compositional groups now often includes isotopic characterisation and provenancing (see below), but remains an important line of enquiry of its own.

Reconstructing Metallurgical Practice

Chemical analysis of metal artefacts informs about alloying and refining practices, heterogeneity of complex objects (soldering, surface treatments, repairs, etc.), and possible corrosion effects. Analytical practice depends on the metal or alloy in question, and considers main components as well as trace elements and nonmetallic inclusions. The best analytical approach combines chemical and microscopic analysis to understand the spatial distribution of chemical components within an object. Electron microscopy offers this combination in one instrument, using only one sample.

Locating Geological Origin

Provenancing follows on from the formation of compositional groups and compares their chemical and isotopic signature to ore deposits or production sites. The most widely used method entails determining the isotope ratio of the four stable lead isotopes in a series of artefacts, and comparing it to the isotope ratios of known ore fields or smelting sites. The minute lead content present in most nonferrous metals is sufficient to determine these ratios, enabling lead isotope analysis (LIA) for almost all metals and alloys. A mismatch between a potential source field and an artefact demonstrates that the respective object does not come from that source. A match between source field and artefact is not on its own proof of origin, but requires further supporting evidence, such as contemporary mining activity at and cultural contact with the potential source region. The lead isotope ratio of a source is determined by its geological history; thus any source with the same geological history will have the same isotope signature, resulting in widespread overlap between geologically contemporary ore sources. Provenancing by LIA relies on high-precision and high-accuracy measurements and the availability of substantial comparative geological data, even for remote and very small ore sources.

Interpretation of Data

Any data interpretation necessitates discussion of analytical error, accuracy and precision. The interpretation of the chemical composition of artefacts requires understanding the effects of the different metallurgical processes involved in their production. Smelting, refining, alloying and recycling or corrosion all influence the chemical composition of the metal; identifying their respective signatures and effects as the result of the production history of an object is at the core of archaeo-metallurgical analysis. Understanding which signatures and effects are determined by natural processes and governed by the laws of physics eventually enables the identification of those that are due to human activity and choice. Bringing these into the open is the ultimate purpose of metallurgical analysis in archaeology.

5 CONCLUDING COMMENTS

As argued in more detail elsewhere (Rehren and Pernicka 2008), archaeometallurgy is historically a very broad and diverse academic field, and draws from a very wide range of scholarly and analytical methods of study. Since metals play a fundamental role in the social, economic and technological fabric of almost all post-Neolithic societies but are in their technical complexity not easily covered by traditional archaeological approaches to artefacts, it is not surprising that they feature centrally in many analytical programmes. The study of ancient metal production and manufacturing, of the trade in raw metal and finished metal objects, and of their use, deposition and recycling, includes such diverse approaches as optical microscopy, physical, chemical and isotopic analysis and experimental reconstruction. There is no standard method or instrument that could be prioritised over all others; the range of questions is too diverse and the pace of instrumental and intellectual development too fast to settle for routine or textbook approaches. Several trends, however, emerge from a broader review of past and current practice.

Firstly, there is a strong sense of 'fascination' with metals, as opposed to their mere 'use' – this is visible in the early use of all metals first for ostentation and jewellery (e.g., the use in 1858 of aluminium for tableware and jewellery at the court of Napoleon III; Bourgarit and Plateau 2007), before they become the material of choice for weapons or tools. To a large degree this is certainly driven by the inherent rarity of the 'earliest' or 'first' metal as it makes its appearance in a society, and to a considerable extent also by their distinct and often appealing appearance. However, a part of this fascination may also originate from the contrast between seeing what happens during smelting while not being able to really understanding it. This not only gives the resulting material a mystical aura but also prevents successful copying, since the process was dependent on too many invisible factors, such as redox conditions, or sensory aspects, such as details of sound or smell that are not easily communicated or recognised as important by the casual (or probing) observer.

Secondly, metal production is in many respects linked to power, both economic and military, and connotations related to this are often found in the public perception and literature. This sets metals apart from the other main staples of materials in the past (and present) – food, cloth, building materials, ceramics. Only glass, an archaeologically much younger and in its production and working even more enigmatic material, reaches a similar level of fascination: but more for its aesthetics than for its power (e.g., Beretta 2009).

Thirdly, modern science-based studies of metals typically fall into several main and rarely connected categories – studies of production technology, drawing much from Earth sciences and process engineering; alloy and manufacturing studies, drawing from traditional metallurgical methods such as bulk determination of composition and microstructural investigation by metallography; and provenance studies, almost exclusively developed out of geochemical ideas and using advanced methods of analytical chemistry.

The main challenges for the future are in combining these three broad streams of science-based approaches to ancient metals, first with each other to reach a more holistic and less fragmented approach to archaeometallurgy, and then to relate the results in a meaningful manner to the archaeological and anthropological questions and theoretical frameworks that ideally should be driving the whole endeavour. Achieving this, in the face of ever-increasing specialisation, requires not only an enormous amount of goodwill and tolerance, but also a high level of diplomacy and translation skills.

REFERENCES

Affonso, M. T. C. and Pernicka, E. 1997. INAA analysis of late pre-pottery neolithic rings from Basta. In: Gebel, H. G. K., Kafafi, Z. and Rollefson, G. O. (eds.) *Prehistory of Jordan II. Perspectives from 1997*, pp. 641–650. Studies in Early Near Eastern Production, Subsistence, and Environment 4. Berlin: Ex Oriente.

Aldenderfer, M., Craig, N. M., Speakman, R. J. and Popelka-Filcoff, R. 2008. Four-thousand-year-old gold artifacts from the Lake Titicaca basin, southern Peru. *Proceedings of the National Academy of Sciences* 105:5002–5005.

Alipour, R. and Rehren, Th. 2014. Persian Pūlād Production: Chāhak Tradition. *Journal of Islamic Archaeology* 1:237–267.

Allan, J. W. and Gilmour, B. J. 2000. *Persian Steel: The Tanavoli Collection*. Oxford: Oxford University Press.

Bar-Yosef Mayer, D. E. and Porat, N. 2008. Green stone beads at the dawn of agriculture. *Proceedings of the National Academy of Sciences* 105:8548–8551.

Beretta, M. 2009. *The Alchemy of Glass – Counterfeit, Imitations, and Transmutation in Ancient Glassmaking*. Sagamore Beach, MA: Watson Publishing.

Binford, L. R. 1962. Archaeology as anthropology. *American Antiquity* 28:217–225.

Bourgarit, D. and Plateau, J. 2007. When aluminium was equal to gold: Can a 'chemical' aluminium be distinguished from an 'electrolytic' one? *Historical Metallurgy* 41:57–76.

Brauns, M., Schwab, R., Gassmann, G., Wieland, G. and Pernicka, E. 2013. Provenance of Iron Age iron in southern Germany: A new approach. *Journal of Archaeological Science* 40:841–849.

Chastain, M., Deymier-Black, A., Kelly, J., Brown, J. and Dunand, D. 2011. Metallurgical analysis of copper artifacts from Cahokia. *Journal of Archaeological Science* 38:1727–1736.

Cech, B. 2007. *Spätmittelalterliche bis frühneuzeitliche Edelmetallgewinnung in den hohen Tauern*, 2 vols. Monographies of the Römisch-Germanisches Zentralmuseum 70. Mainz.

Cessford, C. 2005. Absolute dating at Çatalhöyük. In: Hodder, I. (ed.) *Changing Materialities at Çatalhöyük: Reports from the 1995–99 Seasons*, pp. 65–100. Cambridge/London: McDonald Institute Monographs/British Institute at Ankara.

Conophagos, C. 1980. *Le Laurium Antique et la technique grecque de la production de l'argent*. Athens: Ekdotike Hellados.

Domanski, M. and Webb, J. A. 1992. Effect of heat treatment on siliceous rocks used in prehistoric lithic technology. *Journal of Archaeological Science* 19:601–614.

Doonan, R. and Day, P. 2007. Mixed origins and the origins of mixing: alloys and provenance in the Early Bronze Age Aegean. In: Day, P. and Doonan, R. (eds.) *Metallurgy in the Early Bronze Age Aegean*, pp. 1–18. Sheffield Studies in Aegean Archaeology 7. Oxford: Oxbow Books.

Eckstein, K., Rehren, Th. and Hauptmann, A. 1994. Hochmittelalterliches Montanwesen im sächsischen Erzgebirge und seinem Vorland – Die Gewinnung von Blei und Silber. *Der Anschnitt* 46:122–132.

Hunter, F. and Davis, M. 1994. Early Bronze Age lead – a unique necklace from southeast Scotland. *Antiquity* 68:824–830.

Jambon, A. 2017. Bronze Age iron: meteoritic or not? A chemical strategy. *Journal of Archaeological Science* 88:47–53.

Jovanović, B. 1982. *Rudna Glava, najstarije rudarstvo bakra na centralnom Balkanu* [Rudna Glava, the oldest copper metallurgy in the Central Balkans]. Beograd, Bor, Arheološki Institut, Muzej rudarstva i metalurgije.

Klemm, D. and Klemm, R. 1994. Chronologischer Abriss der antiken Goldgewinnung in der Ostwüste Ägyptens. *Mitteilungen des Deutschen Archäologischen Instituts, Abteilung Kairo* 50:189–222.

Maldonado, B. and Rehren, Th. 2009. Early copper smelting at Itziparátzico, Mexico. *Journal of Archaeological Science* 36:1998–2006.

Marro, C., Bakhshaliyev, V. and Sanz, S. 2010. Archaeological investigations on the salt mine of Duzdagi (Nakhchivan, Azerbaijan). *TÜBA-AR*, Vol. 13, Ankara.

Martinón-Torres, M. and Rehren, Th. 2014. Technical ceramics. In: Roberts, B. and Thornton, C. (eds.) *Archaeometallurgy in Global Perspective*, pp. 107–131. London: Springer.

Mei, J., Wang, P., Chen, K., Wang, L., Wang, Y. and Liu, Y. 2015. Archaeometallurgical studies in China: Some recent developments and challenging issues. *Journal of Archaeological Science* 56:221 232.

Miller, H. 2007. Associations and ideologies in the locations of urban craft production at Harappa, Pakistan (Indus Civilization). *Archeological Papers of the American Anthropological Association* 17:37–51.

Moorey, P. R. S. 1994. *Ancient Mesopotamian Materials and Industries: The Archaeological Evidence*. Oxford: Clarendon Press.

Neuninger, H., Pittioni, R. and Siegl, W. 1964. Frühkeramikzeitliche Kupfergewinnung in Anatolien. *Archaeologia Austriaca* 35:98–110.

O'Brien, W. 2004. *Ross Island: Mining, Metal and Society in Early Ireland*. Galway: Department of Archaeology, National University of Ireland.

Pages, G., Dillmann, Ph., Fluzin, P. and Long, L. 2011. A study of the Roman iron bars of Saintes-Maries-de-la-Mer (Bouches-du-Rhône, France). A proposal for a comprehensive metallographic approach. *Journal of Archaeological Science* 38:1234–1252.

Pernicka, E. 2014. Provenance determination of archaeological metal objects. In: Roberts, B. and Thornton, C. (eds.) *Archaeometallurgy in Global Perspective*, pp. 239–268. London: Springer.

Pernicka, E., Begemann, F., Schmitt-Strecker, S., Todorova, H. and Kuleff, I. 1997. Prehistoric copper in Bulgaria. Its composition and provenance. *Eurasia Antiqua* 3:41–180.

Pigott, V. 1999. A heartland of metallurgy: Neolithic/Chalcolithic metallurgical origins on the Iranian Plateau. In: Hauptmann, A., Pernicka, E., Rehren, Th. and Yalcin, Ü. (eds.) *The Beginnings of Metallurgy*, pp. 109–122. *Der Anschnitt* 9. Bochum: Deutsches Bergbau-Museum.

Pittioni, R. 1948. Recent researches on ancient copper-mining in Austria. *Man* 48:120–122.

Radivojević, M., Rehren, Th., Farid, Sh., Pernicka, E., Camurcuoğlu, D. 2017. Repealing the Çatalhöyük extractive metallurgy: the green, the fire and the 'slag'. *Journal of Archaeological Science* 86:101–122.

Radivojević, M., Rehren, Th., Pernicka, E., Šljivar, D., Brauns, M. and Borić, D. 2010. On the origins of extractive metallurgy: New evidence from Europe. *Journal of Archaeological Science* 37:2775–2787.

Ramage, A. and Craddock, P. T. 1999. *King Croesus' Gold. Excavations at Sardis and the History of Gold Refining*. British Museum Press in association with Archaeological Exploration of Sardis.

Rehren, Th. 2003. Crucibles as reaction vessels in ancient metallurgy. In: Craddock, P. and Lang, J. (eds.) *Mining and Metal Production through the Ages*, pp. 207–215. London: British Museum.

Rehren, Th., Belgya, Th., Jambon, A., Káli, G., Kasztovszky, Zs., Kis, Z., Kovács, I., Maróti, B., Martinón-Torres, M., Miniaci, G., Pigott, V., Radivojević, M., Rosta, L., Szentmiklósi, L. and Szőkefalvi-Nagy, Z. 2013. 5,000 years old Egyptian iron beads made from hammered meteoritic iron. *Journal of Archaeological Science* 40:4785–4792.

Rehren, Th., Leshtakov, P. and Penkova, P. 2016. Reconstructing Chalcolithic copper smelting at Akladi cheiri, Chernomorets, Bulgaria. In: Nikolov, V. and Schier, W. (eds.) *Der Schwarzmeerraum vom Neolithikum bis in die Früheisenzeit (6000–600 v. Chr.)*, pp. 205–214. Rhaden/Westfalen: Leidorf.

Rehren, Th. and Pernicka, E. 2008. Coins, artefacts and isotopes: Archaeometallurgy and Archaeometry. *Archaeometry* 50:232–248.

Rehren, Th. and Prange, M. 1998. Lead metal and patina: A comparison. In: Rehren, Th., Hauptmann, A. and Muhly, J. (eds.) *Metallurgica Antiqua, In Honour of Hans-Gert Bachmann and Robert Maddin*, pp. 183–196. *Der Anschnitt* 8. Bochum: Deutsches Bergbau-Museum.

Rehren, Th., Vanhove, D. and Mussche, H. 2002. Ores from the ore washeries in the Lavriotiki. *Metalla (Bochum)* 9:27–46.

Renfrew, C. 1978. Varna and the social context of early metallurgy. *Antiquity* 52:199–203.

Roberts, B. W. 2009. Production networks and consumer choice in the earliest metal of western Europe. *Journal of World Prehistory* 22:461–481.

Roberts, B. W., Thornton, C. P. and Pigott, V. C. 2009. Development of metallurgy in Eurasia. *Antiquity* 83:1012–1022.

Rostoker, W. and Bronson, B. 1990. *Pre-industrial Iron – Its Technology and Ethnology*. Archeomaterials Monograph 1. Philadelphia.

Rothenberg, B. 1988. *The Egyptian Mining Temple at Timna: Researches in the Arabah*, Vol. 1, London: The Institute for Archaeo-Metallurgical Studies.

Russell, M. 2000. *Flint Mines in Neolithic Britain*. Stroud: Tempus.

Salomon, H., Vignaud, C., Lahlil, S. and Menguy, N. 2015. Solutrean and Magdalenian ferruginous rocks heat-treatment: Accidental and/or deliberate action? *Journal of Archaeological Science* 55:100–112.

Schultze, C., Stanish, C., Scott, D., Rehren, Th., Kuehner, S. and Feathers, J. 2009. Direct evidence of 1,900 years of indigenous silver production in the Lake Titicaca Basin of Southern Peru. *Proceedings of the National Academy of Sciences* 106:17280–17283.

Schwab, R., Heger, D., Höppner, B. and Pernicka, E. 2006. The provenance of iron artefacts from Manching: A multi-technique approach. *Archaeometry* 48:433–452.

Smith, S. C. 1981. On art, invention and technology. In: Smith, S. C. (ed.) *A Search for Structure*, pp. 325–331. Cambridge, MA: MIT Press.

Sperl, G. 1990. Zur Urgeschichte des Bleies. *Zeitschrift für Metallkunde* 81:799–801.

Taylor, T. 1999. Envaluing metal: Theorizing the Eneolithic 'hiatus'. In: Young, S. M. M., Pollard, A. M., Budd, P. and Ixer, R. A. (eds.) *Metals in Antiquity*, pp. 22–32. BAR International Series 792. Oxford: Archaeopress.

Thornton, C. P. 2009. The emergence of complex metallurgy on the Iranian Plateau: Escaping the Levantine paradigm. *Journal of World Prehistory* 22:301–327.

Thornton, C. P., Golden, J., Killick, D., Pigott, V. C., Rehren, Th. and Roberts, B. W. 2010. A Chalcolithic error: Rebuttal to Amzallag 2009. *American Journal of Archaeology* 114:305–315.

Tite, M. and Bimson, M. 1989. Glazed steatite: An investigation of the methods of glazing used in ancient Egypt. *World Archaeology* 21:87–100.

Veldhuijzen, A. H. and Rehren, Th. 2007. Slags and the city: Early iron production at Tell Hammeh, Jordan, and Tel Beth-Shemesh, Israel. In: La Niece, S., Hook, D. and Craddock, P. (eds.) *Metals and Mines: Studies in Archaeometallurgy*, pp. 189–201. London: Archetype.

Wagner, D. 2008. Science and civilisation in China. Vol. 5: Chemistry and chemical technology. Part 11: *Ferrous metallurgy*. Cambridge: Needham Research Institute.

Waldbaum, J. 1999. The coming of iron in the Eastern Mediterranean: Thirty years of archaeological and technological research. In: Pigott, V. C. (ed.) *The Archaeometallurgy of the Asian Old World*, pp. 27–57. MASCA Research Papers in Science and Archaeology 16. Philadelphia, PA: University of Pennsylvania.

Weisgerber, G. 2006. The mineral wealth of ancient Arabia and its use I: Copper mining and smelting at Feinan and Timna: Comparison and evaluation of techniques, production, and strategies. *Arabian Archaeology and Epigraphy* 17:1–30.

Weisgerber, G. and Hauptmann, A. 1988. Early copper mining and smelting in Palestine. In: Maddin, R. (ed.) *The Beginning of the Use of Metals and Alloys*, pp. 52–62. Cambridge, MA and London: The MIT Press.

Weller, O. 2002. The earliest rock salt exploitation in Europe: A salt mountain in the Spanish Neolithic. *Antiquity* 76:317–318.

Wen, G. and Jing, Z. 1992. Chinese neolithic jade: A preliminary geoarchaeological study. *Geoarchaeology* 7:251–275.

Yalcin, Ü. and Pernicka, E. 1999. Frühneolithische Metallurgie von Asikli Höyük. In: Hauptmann, A., Pernicka, E., Rehren, Th. and Yalcin, Ü. (eds.) *The Beginnings of Metallurgy*, pp. 45–54. *Der Anschnitt* 9. Bochum: Deutsches Bergbau-Museum.

17

Lithics

Shannon P. McPherron

The various methods used to study the manufacture and use of stone tools in archaeology.

1 INTRODUCTION

Lithic analysis is primarily about understanding the factors that lead to variability in stone tool assemblages. These include properties of the raw materials used to make stone tools and the ways the sources for these raw materials were managed; the techniques and strategies used to reduce these materials into useable tools; the functional needs these tools were designed to meet; and stylistic preferences. Underlying these factors is fracture mechanics, the basic physical laws, which make stone knapping possible. Through the study of these various factors and how they each contribute to formation of a lithic assemblage, archaeologists hope to say something about prehistoric behavior.

Recently there have been a number of substantial treatments of how lithic analysis is done (see, for instance, Andrefsky 2005; Kooyman 2000; Odell 2000; Odell 2001; Odell 2004). These cover the range of techniques and approaches used in lithic studies with examples of how they are applied. From a technique perspective, the majority of lithic analysis is done by observing and measuring stone tool attributes thought to be sensitive to the factors just outlined with no more equipment than a hand lens, a pair of calipers, a scale, and sometimes a goniometer. There are, however, a number of areas where lithic analysis relies heavily on techniques of measurement and analysis that derive from outside the field itself. Some of these are discussed here in the fields of fracture mechanics, raw material studies, functional studies, and morphometrics.

2 FRACTURE MECHANICS

Fracture mechanics, the study of how rock responds to applied force, is fundamental to understanding variability in stone tools. It plays, for instance, a key role in determining what kinds of rocks can be worked and how they will respond; in the relationship between flaking techniques and flake morphology; and in how various materials will respond to use with regard to polish formation, edge damage, and so on. Fracture mechanics, however, are still poorly understood from an archaeological perspective.

Most work in this area is done through experimental replication. By varying the techniques of manufacture, for instance, changing the type of hammer stone used to remove a flake or changing how the hammer and stone are held when struck, archaeologists can gain some insights into the relationship between how stone fractures and the attributes they are recording on actual archaeological specimens. Replication experiments provide insights into what can be accomplished without explaining how it is accomplished. Thus an alternative to the replicative approach is to look at the first principles involved in fracture mechanics using physics (Cotterell and Kamminga 1979; Cotterell and Kamminga 1987; Speth 1972). While intuitively this would seem the most sensible approach, it has not been very successful and has had a very limited impact on the discipline. As summarised by Dibble and Rezek (2009), this is in part because physicists do not yet agree among themselves on the best approach to modelling fracture mechanics and in part because the models do not tend to translate well to the concerns of archaeologists. Given a particular model, for instance, it is unclear how varying the hardness of the hammer or characteristics of the striking platform will affect the resulting flake.

Certainly one aspect of physical modelling of fracture mechanics is controlled experimentation, and this is where most of the progress in archaeological fracture mechanics has taken place. It differs from experimental replication in that laboratory techniques are applied to achieve greater independent control and quantification of each tested variable than is possible when a person flintknaps. Thus, in the last forty years there have been a number of studies in fracture mechanics using primarily some variant of metal ball-bearings dropped on glass (Dibble and Rezek 2009 and citations within; Lin et al. 2013; Magnani et al. 2014; Rezek et al. 2011). These experiments have allowed archaeologists to investigate under controlled conditions the effects of variables such as force, mass, angle of blow, platform thickness, and core surface morphology on flake size and to some extent shape. These experiments produced highly quantifiable data, but their greater applicability to the archaeological record was limited by the nature of the materials in the experiment, most of which have relied on striking a piece of plate glass on its edge. The resulting flakes are thus unlike the majority of pieces found in archaeological assemblages.

More recent experimental designs (Dibble and Rezek 2009) now produce flakes and cores similar to archaeological ones, but the raw material remains glass. Determining the applicability of principles derived from these glass experiments and the magnitude of measured effects when applied to more common archaeological raw materials, such as chert, is a high priority for making these results more applicable in lithic analysis. Advances in material and manufacturing sciences may make it possible to overcome most if not all of the previous experimental limitations. In particular, the ability to use computer aided design (CAD) software to create prototypes that can then be machined from archaeologically relevant raw materials (e.g., chert, basalt, obsidian) should allow much better experiments into fracture mechanics from an archaeological perspective. These prototypes can be designed to look more like lithics found in the archaeological record but have the advantage of being both replicable and variable in a control manner.

3 RAW MATERIALS

An important factor in structuring variability in stone tool assemblages is the quality, availability, size, and shape of raw materials from which tools are made. Not all rocks can be knapped into stone tools. Generally rocks that can be knapped are made largely of silica in the form of quartz (e.g., obsidian, chert, basalt). How much quartz a rock contains, the size of the quartz crystals, and the size and type of other crystals in the rock all affect its quality. Quality generally refers to two aspects of the material: workability and suitability for its intended use. A highly workable material is one that fractures when struck by the knapper in a controlled, predictable manner. In general, high-quality materials are homogeneous, brittle, elastic and isotropic (Braun et al. 2009). A brittle material breaks at or near yield stress meaning that a flake can be removed when the material is struck with enough force. An elastic material can be deformed or undergo a reversible change meaning that the rock does not simply shatter when struck. Isotropic materials distribute force uniformly rather than, for instance, along specific vectors or faults in the material meaning that flakes will follow from the direction the rock was struck. Homogenous materials have these properties throughout and do not have flaws or locations where these other properties are locally quite poor. To some extent raw material type, as identified by archaeologists or geologists, is associated with variability in these properties; however, there is considerable variability within raw material types and separate types can have similar qualities.

Frequently, quality is assessed subjectively (e.g., "good" and "poor" quality materials) through experimental replication of artefacts found in the archaeological record using similar raw materials found in proximity to the site. Though archaeologists have become quite familiar with the qualities of various raw materials in this way, these kinds of categorisations do not lend themselves to statistical assessment. More recently attempts have been made to quantify raw material quality assessments, and this is becoming more standard in both studies of archaeological materials and in replication experiments. Brantingham et al. (2000), for instance, look at the effects of crystalline structure, crystal size, and especially the frequency of impurities on fracture predictability and relate this to lithic reduction strategies. Similarly, Stout et al. (2005) assess quality by the percentage of phenocryst per unit area, phenocryst size, and groundmass texture. Braun et al. (2009) examine the effects of rebound hardness measured with a Schmidt Hammer and impurity frequency rates to raw material selection patterns in early hominins. Noll (2000) measured Schmidt and Shore rebound hardness in addition to quantifying the strength of materials with a uniaxial compression test, again in the context of understanding the criteria early hominins used in raw material selection and management. In a replication setting, Eren et al. (2014) categorise the properties of raw materials by examining grain size and distribution and quantitatively by apply the rebound hardness test and a measure of biaxial flexure. In each of these instances, quantitative measures of raw material properties were tested for correlations with attributes such as the relative frequency of the material in an archaeological assemblage, intensity/kinds of tool production, tool shapes, intensity of lithic reduction, type of reduction strategy, and so on.

Aside from the workability of the stone, another important aspect of quality must include the suitability of the stone for its intended use. The sharpness of the edge and its durability, the ability of the edge to resist degradation during use, may have been important factors in raw material selection. Though durability can be quantified using Moh's hardness scale, it is difficult to apply in archaeological contexts, in part because rocks used to make stone tools fall within a limited range on this scale. Alternatively, Noll (2000) applies the Taber abrasion hardness test, Braun et al. (2009) use the American Standard Abrasion Hardness test, and Yonekura (2015) uses the Vickers microhardness test. In some contexts our incomplete knowledge as to which stones in an assemblage were actually used and what tasks particular tools might have been used for makes it difficult to assess and quantify suitability.

Aside from issues of raw material quality, the main area where archaeological sciences have been applied to lithic studies is in identifying raw material sources. By identifying the source, the movements of prehistoric peoples across the landscape and trade and exchange networks they may have participated in can be studied. Raw material sourcing is a critical component in evaluating raw material availability, which in turn affects variability in raw material size and shape. All of these are important factors in structuring variability in lithic assemblages.

Raw material sourcing is generally done through macroscopic observation (colour, texture, fossil inclusions, impurities, surface weathering, etc.) and through geochemical analysis (see reviews by Shackley 1998; Shackley 2008). When geochemical techniques have been used to test the reliability of visual observations, the results have shown the latter to be only about 50 per cent accurate (Odell 2000: 313). These latter techniques are used to identify the elemental composition of lithics and particularly to identify proportions of elements that are specific to particular formations so that archaeological finds can be matched with their sources on the landscape. Trace elements, elements with concentrations less than 0.02 per cent, can be particularly useful in uniquely identifying raw material sources. Raw materials vary at the geochemical level in how easily they can be characterised and sourced. Obsidians, for instance, are often spatially restricted, can contain a wide variety of mineral components, and are also more homogenous at a particular source. As a result they are more easily characterised and have been used in numerous raw material sourcing studies since the 1960s. Similar principles apply to other igneous rocks, though they have been sourced less frequently. Cherts are formed sometimes over quite large regions, can be quite variable within a source, and at the same time have a more limited overall range of minerals they can contain. As a result, sourcing cherts using geochemical techniques has proven more difficult.

Techniques for geochemical analysis include X-ray fluorescence spectrometry (XRF), particle induced X-ray emission analysis (PIXIE), and particle induced gamma ray emission analysis (PIGME), electron microprobe analysis (EMPA), neutron activation analysis (NAA), inductively coupled plasma mass spectroscopy (ICP-MS), atomic absorption spectroscopy (AAS), and X-ray diffraction (XRD) (Andrefsky 2005; Odell 2004; Shackley 1998; Shackley 2008). These techniques vary in whether they are non-destructive, whether they measure the whole artefact or a small portion, and what elements they are able to identify.

XRF is generally a non-destructive methodology. The surface of the sample is irradiated with X-rays, which excite electrons into higher energy states. When the electrons return to their normal state they emit characteristic X-rays that can be used to determine element composition and concentration. Surface irregularity and sample heterogeneity can decrease precision and accuracy, and in some cases samples must be taken from the rock and crushed before being analysed (Andrefsky 2005: 44). Portable XRF machines (pXRF) now offer the possibility to record data directly in the field.

PIXIE is like XRF in that it involves irradiating a sample to excite electrons, which then release characteristic X-rays or, in the case of PIGME, characteristic gamma rays. It differs from XRF in that the particle beam can be focused on a small area of the sample. The analysis is faster but also more costly. Like XRF, it also works better on smoother surfaces.

EMPA is also similar to XRF. It can be used to examine single crystals in the source material non-destructively. An electron beam is focused on the material, which then emits secondary X-rays that are measured and analysed using the same techniques as XRF. Because it works on such a small scale, it is best applied to homogenous materials such as chert and obsidian where a sample from a limited region of the piece is more likely representative of the whole piece as well.

NAA involves irradiating the sample with a beam of electrons in a nuclear reactor. The resulting radionuclides decay into gamma-rays that are characteristic of the elements present. NAA can detect and measure precisely a very wide range of elements and in this way exceeds XRF and ICP-MS (Shackley 2008). It does not measure Ba, Sr, and Zr (which can be extremely important in obsidian analysis) as accurately as other methods (Shackley 1998; Shackley 2008). Additionally, theoretically the technique is non-destructive, however, the sample may remain radioactive for an extended period of time (Odell 2004: 33) and because NAA machines require a nuclear reactor, they are not widely available.

An ICP-MS creates a gas plasma into which the sample is introduced as an aerosol. The plasma converts the sample atoms into ions that are then extracted from the plasma and put through a mass-spectrometer and counted. Laser ablation (LA) is often combined with ICP-MS such that very small areas can be precisely targeted. Besides requiring only a very small sample, ICP-MS has the advantage being able to measure a very wide range of elements in trace quantities. Though ICP-MS is destructive, the sample sizes are sufficiently small (<0.05 grams) as to go virtually unnoticed on the original artefact.

X-ray diffraction (XRD) analysis is also applied to raw material sourcing. This method is able to identify and quantify the mineral constituents of rocks based on the principle that crystals have characteristic spacing between lattice planes in their three-dimensional structures (Odell 2004: 38; Pretola 2001). Analysis requires grinding a portion of the sample into a powder. XRD has been used in the analysis of ceramics, metals, and bone, but has seen fewer applications in lithic raw material sourcing. XRD has also been used to show internal structural changes to flint as a result of heat treatment (see below; Domanski et al. 2009; Domanski and Webb 1992). Heat treatment alters the size and structure of the crystals that can be measured by XRD.

AAS is a destructive technique requiring approximately 1 gram of material. The sample is put into solution, vaporised, and passed through a flame. Light of a wavelength characteristic of the element under investigation is also passed through the flame and a detector measures the amount of light not absorbed by the sample. In this way the concentration of particular elements can be calculated. AAS is highly sensitive, relatively inexpensive, and useful for targeting specific elements not covered by the other techniques listed here.

Most studies combine several of these geochemical methods to take advantage of the strengths of each, particularly with regard to which elements they can measure, and to generally increase the number of different elements that can be measured. The differences in the precision and accuracy of the techniques are not sufficient to outweigh more practical considerations of cost and access to equipment (Shackley 2008).

The data generated by these methods typically do not provide an exact match. Where particularly diagnostic trace elements are present, matching a source to an archaeological artefact may be straightforward. Otherwise statistical treatment of the data is needed and matches have an attached probability (Shackley 1998; Shackley 2007). Another important concern is source sampling. Locating raw material sources on the landscape can require significant fieldwork. Care has to be taken to identify primary and secondary sources and to characterise each. Care also has to be taken to sufficiently sample each source to establish its internal variability. Shackley (1998) stresses that although there is no agreement on the numbers of samples required for this analysis, he recommends at least five.

4 HEAT TREATMENT

Heat treatment is a technique used to improve the quality of a raw material, typically chert, by making flaking more predictable (see Domanski and Webb

2007 and Schmidt 2011 for overviews and models of heat treatment research). An understanding of exactly how heating improves the material is still evolving (Domanski et al. 2009; Odell 2000: 311; Schmidt 2011; Schmidt et al. 2012), but as a result the material becomes more brittle and more isotropic or homogeneous (Whittaker 1994: 72–73). Heat treating has been shown to increase measures of rebound hardness in silcrete (Brown et al. 2009) meaning the material is stiffer and more isotropic. It has also been shown to decrease the resistance to fracturing (more brittle) in cherts (Domanski et al. 2009). Heating increases the Young's modulus of elasticity (Odell 2000: 311).

As it is typically understood, heat treatment involves slowly heating raw materials, sometimes in a sand filled pit over which are placed fire heated rocks, and then letting them slowly cool. This process can take many hours to days. A slow, even distribution of heat is sought, and direct contact with the heat source is avoided (Domanski and Webb 2007). However, it is clear that the speed of the heating process is a function of material size (Mercieca and Hiscock 2008; Schmidt et al. 2012), its internal structure (Schmidt et al. 2012) and the material itself (e.g., flint versus silcrete; Schmidt et al. 2013). Some silcretes, for instance, can be very quickly heated in an open fire (Schmidt et al. 2013), whereas other silcretes require slower, indirect heating (Wadley and Prinsloo 2014).

The resulting heat-treated material has improved flaking qualities but can be difficult to recognise visually. Excessive heating can leave clearly visible traces on the material including crazing (small cracks in the material), pot-lids (round spalls removed from the surface of the material), and discolourations. Stones that show these attributes, particularly cherts, are potential candidates for thermoluminescence (TL) dating. With heat treated flints there can be some discolouration (brighter and redder) but this is known to be unreliable (Domanski and Webb 2007). The most widely used criteria is a smooth, glossy texture to the material. This texture is not visible on the outside of the heated material but is visible on any subsequent flake removals. However, postdepositional site formation processes can both mimic and obscure this character of the material (Schmidt et al. 2013).

Whether an artefact comes from a heat-treated stone can also be tested (Domanski and Webb 2007; Rowney and White 1997). One method is through palaeomagnetic analysis (Borradaile et al. 1993; Brown et al. 2009; Rowney and White 1997), which looks at both the natural and thermally induced magnetic signature in the stone. Rocks heated above the Curie point for the remnant magnetic carrying minerals in the material will acquire a thermo-remnant magnetisation or a partial thermo-remnant magnetisation if heated below the Curie point.

By heating the rock in a series of steps in a controlled magnetic environment, the thermomagnetic history of the sample can be measured including the maximum temperature to which it was heated.

Another method more widely applied is based on the principle of thermoluminescence (TL) (see Bailey (Chapter 19), and Aitken 1985; Alperson-Afil et al. 2007; Richter 2007). When raw materials such as chert are subject to ionizing radiation (from radioactive nuclides in the surrounding matrix, those in the materials itself, and ionizing radiation from cosmic rays), electrons in the crystal lattice of minerals are moved to higher energy states and are held there in faults or traps for extended periods. In a naturally formed rock all of these traps are filled, but heating the material opens these traps and frees the electron emitting a photon in the process. Thus to test for heat treating, the material is heated in the laboratory and its luminescence is measured across a range of temperatures. Additionally, the thermoluminescent response of the material to additional radioactive doses is measured across a range of temperatures. The response of materials that have not been previously heated to additional radioactive doses will differ from those that have been recently heated and, therefore, have empty traps that can absorb the additional radiation. By examining the ratio of these two doses as well as the shape and position of the peak in the curves, it can be determined whether the sample was heated and, to a limited extent, the temperature to which it was heated.

More recently, Schmidt et al. (2013; see also Schmidt 2011) outlined a method for detecting heat treatment using Fourier transformed infrared spectrometry. This method is based on the chemical transformation that occurs within the rock as it is heated. In flint, starting at about 200°C, water in the form of chemically bound hydroxyl or silanole (SiOH) is transformed into new Si – O – Si bonds, resulting in both a mechanical transformation and a loss of porosity, both of which improve the knapping qualities of the stone. Near infrared spectrometry can then be used to detect heated flints by measuring this chemical transformation and computing a ratio between two energy absorption peaks in the SiOH band. Similarly, Weiner et al. (2015) propose using the relationship of two other peaks in the Fourier transformed infrared spectrum to detect heating based on this same chemical transformation and suggest that the responsiveness of different absorption energy peaks may vary by raw material type.

Note that a potential limiting factor to the TL test for heat treatment is that it requires destroying a non-negligible portion of the sample. Measuring the palaeomagnetic properties of stone does not require destroying the sample but equipment related limitations in sample size may require that the sample is cut. The FTIR techniques, however, are fast and inexpensive, can be non-destructive, and access to this type of equipment is more easily obtained. Note too that determining that a stone has been heated does not necessarily imply controlled heat treating. Stones can become inadvertently heated through proximity to fire of both natural and cultural origin. Demonstrating controlled heat treatment requires establishing a systematic pattern, for instance, in the spatial distribution of heated lithics or in the manufacture of particular tool types from heated lithics (e.g., Price et al. 1982), perhaps combined with a demonstration of an absence of fires which could have inadvertently heated the lithics in the same deposit (e.g., Brown et al. 2009).

5 FUNCTION

Use-wear studies on stone tools date to the pioneering studies of Semenov (1964) in the 1960s, and became quite popular in the 1970s as a method for understanding the roll of function in structuring stone tool variability (see reviews in Odell 2001; Odell 2004). Use-wear on stone tools consists of edge damage (removal of material from the edge as result of use), rounding of edges and flake ridges, polish (removal of material from the tool surface), and surface striations (Figure 17.1). Use-wear analysis was generally divided into two approaches based on equipment: low-powered and high-powered. This distinction, however, is not clear-cut, particularly with recent advances in microscopy, and involves factors other than magnification. Most practitioners today use a combination of approaches. In general, lower-powered studies use stereomicroscopy with external lighting at magnifications between 6x and 160x. High-powered studies use metallurgical microscopes with incident lighting that strikes the object at either a 90 degree angle or a 45 degree

FIGURE 17.1 An example of edge damage on a Levallois flake from Amalda Cave (Level VII). The image was taken at 10x magnification and the piece has been treated with magnesium smoke powder. This damage is consistent with contact with a hard material such as bone and likely represents butchery. (Photo: Joseba Rois Garaizar)

angle. Magnifications are typically between 100x and 500x. SEM is also sometimes used in use-wear studies though, because of the technical difficulty of placing large objects into an SEM and the spatially limited view of the surface it provides, it tends to be used more in experimental studies of use-wear formation.

In part whether one uses a low- or a high-powered approach relates to the relative importance of polishes. While polishes can sometimes be identified with low-powered approaches, they are more easily identified with high-powered equipment. The trade-off has been that high-powered instruments do not produce a three-dimensional image and have a limited depth of field, making the identification and interpretation of other features such as edge damage, rounding and striations more difficult. Advances in microscopy are eliminating these issues, with some newer microscopes able to achieve 500x magnification with a stereoscopic image (Banks and Kay 2003).

Of the use-wear traces, polishes are considered the only method for determining the type of material worked (e.g., bone, wood, dry hide, meat). Low-powered approaches are unable to determine the material type but instead rank the worked material by hardness. At the same time, polishes have proven problematic in a number of ways. There has been considerable debate as to the exact mechanisms behind polish formation, including whether they are only abrasive or whether there is an additive agent as well (Evans and Donahue 2005; Odell 2001). Techniques such as PIXIE, Rutherford backscattering, SEM, and LA-ICP-MS have been used to examine whether polishes include added residues (see Evans and Donahue 2005). Polishes have also been difficult to document and describe in objective terms that can be evaluated and replicated by others. Attempts to quantify polish attributes using digital image analysis techniques have had mixed results (González-Urquijo and Ibáñez-Estévez 2003; Grace 1996) and have led some to question the accuracy of the high-powered approach. Alternatively, these efforts may have failed because they over-emphasised the importance of the "look" of the polish and did not fully capture the range of variables analysts use in interpreting a polish, such as its placement on the tool and its relationship with the surface morphology (Bamforth 1988).

High-powered studies of polish are especially sensitive to postdepositional surface residues. Initial techniques employed by Keeley involved extensive cleaning including use of white spirits, ammonia-based cleaners, and HCl and NaOH solutions (Odell 2004: 151). Subsequent experiments showed flint surface alteration and degradation as a result (Unrath et al. 1986) and current cleaning protocols avoid chemical solutions. Evans and Donahue (2005) have used

LA-ICP-MS to find trace quantities of residues even after using harsh cleaners, suggesting that polish formation has an additive component. This leaves open the possibility that this technique may be useful for identifying the type of material worked. Residues are themselves a subject of analysis for the identification of plant remains (starches and phytoliths) and for the identification of animal species (animal tissues including blood).

In considering use-wear, attention must also be paid to the effects of post-depositional alterations that can both obscure traces and create traces that can be mistaken for use-wear (Burroni et al. 2002; Levi-Sala 1986; Shea and Klenck 1993). Raw-material colour variability and patinas can also affect the identification and interpretation of polishes. High-resolution casting has been used to mitigate colour and patina issues (Banks and Kay 2003). Casting is also advantageous when the archaeological material cannot be brought to the microscope.

Experimentally derived referential collections are an essential part of use-wear studies. Most studies create referential collections using the same raw materials found in the archaeological collection. Care must be taken to control and document these experimental studies. Finally, blind-tests are performed on these materials to test methodology and to determine limits of interpretation.

A series of blind-tests published in the late 1970s and in the 1980s tested the accuracy of both low- and high-powered techniques (see Evans 2014 for an overview of blind-testing). Initial results showed the efficacy of the respective techniques (Odell 2004). High-powered techniques were shown to accurately determine the presence of wear, the tool motion, and the type of material worked (Bamforth et al. 1990; Keeley and Newcomer 1977). Low-power techniques were shown to accurately determine the location of wear and the tool motion (Odell and Odell-Vereecken 1980). However, two blind-tests published in the mid-1980s suggested that both high- and low-powered techniques were less accurate than previously suggested (Newcomer et al. 1986; Unrath et al. 1986). Despite criticisms of the experimental design in the low-power study, the perceived failure of these blind-tests negatively impacted the field and the acceptance of use-wear results by the larger archaeological community (Odell 2004). Nevertheless, the result has been improved methodological rigor, and a search for more quantitative methods to characterise changes in surfaces due to use (e.g., MacDonald 2014; Stemp 2014). Use-wear studies are still very much a part of lithic analysis, are widely applied, and are perhaps currently increasing in popularity. The current consensus view is that multiple approaches (low- and high-powered) are best (Kooyman 2000; Odell 2001).

6 ANALYSING SHAPE

More recently, data collection and analysis techniques for the analysis of shape in fossil materials are being applied to lithic analysis including, in particular, the application of three-dimensional morphometrics (e.g., Archer 2015; Clarkson et al. 2006; Ioviță 2009; Lycett et al. 2006). Stone tools are, of course, three-dimensional objects and while traditional caliper measurements can capture some aspects of variability quite easily (e.g., length, width, and thickness) other aspects of shape and orientation in particular are more difficult to quantify (e.g., the convexity of the core surface, flake scar patterning, or regularities in the shape of retouched edges).

Generally, three-dimensional landmark data form the basis of the analysis. These data are either captured directly from the lithics using a 3D point digitiser or are taken in 3D space from rendered images of three-dimensional scanned objects. Advances in computer technology have made the two approaches equally feasible from a technical (i.e., primarily issues of portability) and cost perspective, though recent advances in photogrammetry and particularly structure from motion (SfM) have made 3D scanning the more popular approach. Scanning offers several advantages, including the ability to archive a complete representation of each piece that can be used for additional data collection without reference to the original object. Scanning also produces a dataset that can be printed in 3D dimensions to produce actual artefact replicates, and yields a dataset amenable for automated feature detection and analysis. Scanning data can also be used for other types of non-landmark three-dimensional analysis. Alternatively, direct 3D point digitizing is more efficient and less time-consuming if only landmarks are required.

While there are clearly advantages to these approaches, there are still a number of methodological challenges. In comparison to fossils, stone artefacts have a limited number of clearly defined and widely recognised landmarks that can be used to orient and standardise artefacts in three-dimensional space. Typically, too, lithic attribute analysis involves assemblages with large sample sizes making the extra time and storage a limiting factor in, especially, artefact scanning. Both methodological and technological advances, however, will likely reduce or eliminate these concerns.

Efforts have been made to 3D scan lithic artefacts and analyse their shape to find refits. Refits are cases where two or more artefacts can be put together as they were before they were flaked apart. Refitting requires substantial skill, an excellent knowledge of the material at hand, and substantial amounts of time, but the effort can produce important insights into techniques of stone tools manufacture and into the state of preservation of the level from which they derive. Automated refitting analysis is an effort to reduce the time it currently takes to do refit analysis. Currently these efforts have not succeeded as measured against traditional techniques (Riel-Salvatore et al. 2002). Another approach has been to use predictive modelling tools built into GIS to combine standard lithic attributes with spatial information to predict which pieces have a higher potential to refit. In one study, success rates were better than random but still quite low (Cooper and Qiu 2006).

7 CONCLUSIONS

While it is still true that most lithic analysis is done with simple direct observations and measurements with tools no more complicated than calipers, scales and goniometers, the archaeological sciences are increasingly contributing additional insights into the drivers of variability we see in archaeological assemblages. The main areas of research have been highlighted here. Overall, there is a general trend in science wherein the instruments needed to make fast, precise measurements are costing less and are more portable or require less space. As a result, they are becoming more accessible to archaeologists, and so there is greater experimentation in what these new techniques can do to achieve a better understanding of prehistoric peoples. While the basics of lithic analysis will probably remain unchanged, it is clear that the archaeological sciences will continue to play a greater role in the future.

REFERENCES

Aitken, M. 1985. *Thermoluminescence Dating*. London: Academic Press.

Alperson-Afil, N., Richter, D., and Goren-Inbar, N. 2007. Phantom hearths and the use of fire at Gesher Benot Ya'aqov, Israel. *PaleoAnthropology* 2007:1–15.

Andrefsky, W. 2005. *Lithics: Macroscopic Approaches to Analysis*. Cambridge: Cambridge University Press.

Archer, W., Gunz, P, van Niekerk, K. L., Henshilwood, C. S., and McPherron, S. P. 2015. Diachronic change within the Still Bay at Blombos Cave, South Africa. *PLoS One* 10(7): e0132428.

Bailey, R. M. in press. Luminescence dating. In: Richards, M. P. and Britton, K. (eds.) *Archaeological Science*. Cambridge: Cambridge University Press.

Bamforth, D. 1988. Investigating microwear polishes with blind tests: The Institute results in context. *Journal of Archaeological Science* 15:11–23.

Bamforth, D., Burns, G., and Woodman, C. 1990. Ambiguous use traces and blind test results: New data. *Journal of Archaeological Science* 17:413–430.

Banks, W. and Kay, M. 2003. High-resolution casts for lithic use-wear analysis. *Lithic Technology* 28:27–34.

Bienenfeld, P. 1995. Duplicating archaeological microwear polishes with epoxy casts. *Lithic Technology* 20:29–39.

Borradaile, G., Kissin, S., Stewart, J., Ross, W., and Werner, T. 1993. Magnetic and optical methods for detecting the heat treatment of chert. *Journal of Archaeological Science* 20:57–66.

Brantingham, P., Olsen, J., Rech, J., and Krivoshapkin, A. 2000. Raw material quality and prepared core technologies in northeast Asia. *Journal of Archaeological Science* 27(3):255–271.

Braun, D., Plummer, T., Ferraro, J., Ditchfield, P., and Bishop, L. 2009. Raw material quality and Oldowan hominin toolstone preferences: evidence from Kanjera South, Kenya. *Journal of Archaeological Science* 36(7):1605–1614.

Brown, K., Marean, C., Herries, A., Jacobs, Z., Tribolo, C., Braun, D., Roberts, D., Meyer, M., and Bernatchez, J. 2009. Fire as an engineering tool of early modern humans. *Science* 325(5942):859–862.

Burroni, D., Donahue, R. E., Pollard, A. M., and Mussi, M. 2002. The surface alteration features of flint artefacts as a record of environmental processes. *Journal of Archaeological Science* 29(11):1277–1287.

Clarkson, C., Vinicius, L., and Lahr, M. 2006. Quantifying flake scar patterning on cores using 3D recording techniques. *Journal of Archaeological Science* 33(1):132–142.

Cooper, J. and Qiu, F. 2006. Expediting and standardizing stone artifact refitting using a computerized suitability model. *Journal of Archaeological Science* 33(7):987–998.

Cotterell, B. and Kamminga, J. 1979. The mechanics of flaking. In: Hayden, B. (ed.) *Lithic Use-Wear Analysis*, pp. 97–112, New York, NY: Academic Press.

Cotterell, B. and Kamminga, J. 1987. The formation of flakes. *American Antiquity* 52(4):675–708.

Dibble, H. and Rezek, Z. 2009. Introducing a new experimental design for controlled studies of flake formation: Results for exterior platform angle, platform depth, angle of blow, velocity, and force. *Journal of Archaeological Science* 36(9):1945–1954.

Domanski, M. and Webb, J. 1992. Effect of heat treatment on siliceous rocks used in prehistoric lithic technology. *Journal of Archaeological Science* 19:601–614.

Domanski, M. and Webb, J. 2007. A review of heat treatment research. *Lithic Technology* 32(2):153–194.

Domanski, M., Webb, J., Glaisher, R., Gurba, J., Libera, J., and Zakościelna, A. 2009. Heat treatment of Polish flints. *Journal of Archaeological Science* 36(7):1400–1408.

Eren, M. I., Roos, C. I., Story, B. A., von Cramon-Taubadel, N., and Lycett, S. J. 2014. The role of raw material differences in stone tool shape variation: An experimental assessment. *Journal of Archaeological Science* 49:472–487.

Evans, A. A. 2014. On the importance of blind testing in archaeological science: the example from lithic functional studies. *Journal of Archaeological Science*, 48:5–14.

Evans, A. A. and Donahue, R. E. 2005. The elemental chemistry of lithic microwear: An experiment. *Journal of Archaeological Science* 32(12):733–1740.

González-Urquijo, J. E. and Ibáñez-Estévez, J. J. 2003. The quantification of use-wear polish using image analysis. First results. *Journal of Archaeological Science* 30(4):481–489.

Grace, R. 1996. Review article use-wear analysis: The state of the art. *Archaeometry* 38(2):209–229.

Ioviţă, R. 2009. Ontogenetic scaling and lithic systematics: Method and application. *Journal of Archaeological Science* 36(7):1447–1457.

Keeley, L. and Newcomer, M. 1977. Microwear analysis of experimental flint tools: a test case. *Journal of Archaeological Science* 4(1):29–62.

Kooyman, B. 2000. *Understanding Stone Tools and Archaeological Sites*. Albuquerque, NM: University of New Mexico Press.

Levi-Sala, I. 1986. Use wear and post-depositional surface modification: A word of caution. *Journal of Archaeological Science* 13(3):229–244.

Lin, S. C., Rezek, Z., Braun, D., and Dibble, H. L. 2013. On the utility and economization of unretouched flakes: The effects of exterior platform angle and platform depth. *American Antiquity* 78(4):724–745.

Lycett, S., von Cramon-Taubadel, N., and Foley, R. 2006. A crossbeam co-ordinate caliper for the morphometric analysis of lithic nuclei: A description, test and empirical examples of application. *Journal of Archaeological Science* 33(6):847–861.

Macdonald, D. A. 2014. The application of focus variation microscopy for lithic use-wear quantification. *Journal of Archaeological Science* 48:26–33.

Magnani, M., Rezek, Z., Lin, S. C., Chan, A., and Dibble, H. L. 2014. Flake variation in relation to the application of force. *Journal of Archaeological Science* 46:37–49.

Mercieca, A. and Hiscock, P. 2008. Experimental insights into alternative strategies of lithic heat treatment. *Journal of Archaeological Science* 35(9):2634–2639.

Newcomer, M., Grace, R., and Unger-Hamilton, R. 1986. Investigating microwear polishes with blind tests. *Journal of Archaeological Science* 13:203–217.

Noll, M. 2000. *Components of Acheulean lithic assemblage variability at Olorgesailie, Kenya*. Doctoral thesis, University of Illinois at Urbana-Champaign, IL.

Odell, G. 2000. Stone tool research at the end of the millennium: Procurement and technology. *Journal of Archaeological Research* 8(4):269–331.

Odell, G. 2001. Stone tool research at the end of the millennium: Classification, function, and behavior. *Journal of Archaeological Research* 9(1):45–100.

Odell, G. 2004. *Lithic Analysis*. New York, NY: Plenum Pub Corp.

Odell, G. and Odell-Vereecken, F. 1980. Verifying the reliability of lithic use-wear assessments by'blind tests': The low-power approach. *Journal of Field Archaeology* 7(1):87–120.

Pretola, J. 2001. A feasibility study using silica polymorph ratios for sourcing chert and chalcedony lithic materials. *Journal of Archaeological Science* 28(7):721–739.

Price, T., Chappell, S., and Ives, D. 1982. Thermal alteration in Mesolithic assemblages. *Proceedings of the Prehistoric Society* 48:467–485.

Rezek, Z., Lin, S., Ioviţă, R., and Dibble, H. L. 2011. The relative effects of core surface morphology on flake shape and other attributes. *Journal of Archaeological Science* 38(6):1346–1359

Richter, D. 2007. Advantages and limitations of thermoluminescence dating of heated flint from Paleolithic sites. *Geoarchaeology: An International Journal* 22(6):671–683.

Riel-Salvatore, J., Bae, M., McCartney, P., and Razdan, A. 2002. Palaeolithic archaeology and 3D visualization technology: recent developments. *Antiquity* 76(294):929–930.

Rowney, M. and White, J. 1997. Detecting heat treatment on silcrete: Experiments with methods. *Journal of Archaeological Science* 24(7):649–657.

Schmidt, P. 2011. *Traitement Thermique Des Silicifications Sédimentaires : Un Nouveau Modèle Des Transformations Cristallographiques et Structurales de La Calcédoine Induites Par La Chauffe.* Paris: Muséum national d'histoire naturelle. http://www.theses.fr/2011MNHN0008 (accessed July 9, 2019).

Schmidt, P., Léa, V., Sciau, Ph., and Fröhlich, F. 2013. Detecting and quantifying heat treatment of flint and other silica rocks: A new non-destructive method applied to heat-treated flint from the Neolithic Chassey culture, southern France. *Archaeometry* 55(5):794–805.

Schmidt, P., Masse, S., Laurent, G., Slodczyk, A., Le Bourhis, E., Perrenoud, C., Livage, J., and Fröhlich, F. 2012. Crystallographic and structural transformations of sedimentary chalcedony in flint upon heat treatment. *Journal of Archaeological Science* 39(1):135–44.

Semenov, S. 1964. *Prehistoric Technology*. London: Cory, Adams and Mackay.

Shackley, M. 1998. Gamma rays, X-rays and stone tools: Some recent advances in archaeological geochemistry. *Journal of Archaeological Science* 25(3):259–270.

Shackley, M. 2008. Archaeological petrology and the archaeometry of lithic materials. *Archaeometry* 50:194–215.

Shea, J. and Klenck, J. 1993. An experimental investigation of the effects of trampling on the results of lithic microwear analysis. *Journal of Archaeological Science* 20:175–194.

Speth, J. 1972. Mechanical basis of percussion flaking. *American Antiquity* 37(1):34–60.

Stemp, W. James. 2014. A review of quantification of lithic use-wear using laser profilometry: A method based on metrology and fractal analysis. *Journal of Archaeological Science* 48:15–25.

Stout, D., Quade, J., Semaw, S., Rogers, M., and Levin, N. 2005. Raw material selectivity of the earliest stone toolmakers at Gona, Afar, Ethiopia. *Journal of Human Evolution* 48(4):365–380.

Unrath, G., Owen, L., Van Gijn, A., Moss, E., Plisson, H., and Vaughan, P. 1986. An evaluation of use-wear studies: A multi-analyst approach. In: Owen, L. and Unrath, G. (eds.) *Technical Aspects of Microwear Studies on Stone Tools*, pp. 117–176. Early Man News. Tübingen: Institut für Urgeschichte.

Wadley, L. and Prinsloo, L. C. 2014. Experimental heat treatment of silcrete implies analogical reasoning in the Middle Stone Age. *Journal of Human Evolution* 70:49–60.

Weiner, S., Brumfeld, V., Marder, O., and Barzilai, O. 2015. Heating of flint debitage from Upper Palaeolithic contexts at Manot Cave, Israel: Changes in atomic organization due to heating using infrared spectroscopy. *Journal of Archaeological Science* 54:45–53.

Whittaker, J. 1994. *Flintknapping*. Austin, TX: University of Texas Press.

Yonekura, K. 2015. Rock properties and material selection for blade manufacture in Upper Paleolithic Japan. *Lithic Technology* 40(2):85–93.

Part VI

Absolute Dating Methods

18

Radiocarbon Dating

Simon Blockley

The use of radiocarbon dating in archaeology, including sample selection calibration and quality control recommendations.

1 INTRODUCTION

The radiocarbon (^{14}C) method underpins most chronologies for the last 50,000 years, due to the accuracy and ubiquity of the technique, suitable for organic material and some carbonates, with uncertainties in the tens to hundreds of years. It is used widely in archaeology, and in studies of past environmental change, but there have been problems to overcome. This chapter outlines the basic principles and examines some of the key developments in the technique.

2 PRINCIPLES

^{14}C is an unstable isotope of carbon. Two stable isotopes ^{12}C and ^{13}C occur naturally and make up respectively ^{12}C 98.89 per cent, ^{13}C 1.11 per cent and 0.0000000001 per cent ^{14}C (Aitken 1989). ^{14}C is formed in the upper atmosphere through subatomic nuclei, themselves products of cosmic ray interaction with atoms. During production free neutrons interact with ^{14}N and add a neutron to the nucleus in exchange for a proton:

$$^{14}N + n \rightarrow {}^{14}C + p$$

^{14}C has a half-life of 5730 + 40 years (Aitken 1989), although originally calculated by Libby as 5568 + 30 (Arnold and Libby 1949; Libby 1955). Radiocarbon decays back to stable nitrogen in the reaction:

$$^{14}C \rightarrow {}^{14}N + e^{-} + \nu_e$$

Production is controlled by cosmic ray flux, which is influenced by solar wind and the strength of the Earth's magnetic field. There is substantial variability in the cosmic ray flux and thus radiocarbon production.

3 RADIOCARBON AGES AND RESERVOIRS

^{14}C is rapidly incorporated into the carbon cycle as $^{14}CO_2$, entering the atmosphere, and oceans (Aitken 1989). Radiocarbon enters the biosphere through plant photosynthesis and is ingested by animals through the food chain. The terrestrial biosphere is usually in equilibrium with atmospheric $^{14}CO_2$ and while living, organisms have the same radiocarbon isotope ratio as other parts of the biosphere. Upon death the organism ceases to be in equilibrium and radioactive decay reduces the radiocarbon content and therefore isotope ratio.

In marine organisms there is an added complication due to the residence time of carbon in the oceans. The deep ocean is the largest carbon reservoir and there is a long residence time. Upwelling of deep water means that old carbon is mixed with younger carbon leading to an upper mid ocean radiocarbon *reservoir effect* (R) of 400 years too old. There are regional variations in R (ΔR) of tens to hundreds of years. Due to past changes in ocean circulation there is also variation in ΔR over time. Changes in ΔR over time can be hundreds to over a thousand years (Eiriksson et al. 2004; Siani et al. 2000;). Dating marine samples, or human remains with a marine dietary component, may be difficult. Localised ΔR values have also been recorded in deep lakes or in lakes where there is input from geological carbon.

4 RADIOCARBON MEASUREMENT

In the early experiments Libby (1955) and co-workers used modified Geiger counters. This was followed by a technique where samples were either combusted or evolved to CO_2 and then analysed in gas proportional *beta* counters, with the activity being proportional to the ^{14}C in a sample. This technique requires large samples, leaving many archaeological samples unavailable for dating. The next development involved liquid scintillation counters (Polach 1987), using liquid compounds that fluoresce during exposure to ionising radiation. Each fluorescence event is proportional to a *beta* emission. The benzene has the chemical formula C_6H_6 meaning most of the sample is carbon. A sample is initially converted to CO_2 and then into benzene, then placed in vials in a liquid scintillation counter. Activity is measured using photomultiplier spectrometers. Liquid scintillation reduces sample size and many laboratories still use scintillation counters.

For archaeology a key development was accelerator mass spectrometry (AMS) dating in the 1980s. This approach directly measures the proportion of carbon isotopes in a sample (see Aitken 1989). Samples are initially converted to CO_2 and then to graphite. In an accelerator, graphitised samples are sputtered using a suitable gun, ionised and accelerated towards a high voltage source. The ion beam enters an ion stripper, which breaks up any remaining molecules, and also strips electrons from the outer shells of the ions, reversing their charge. The now oppositely charged ions accelerate away from the source as they continue along the accelerator, where they are then separated by mass using magnets. This allows the proportion of ^{12}C, ^{13}C and ^{14}C to be measured with a significant increase in instrument sensitivity and reduction in sample size. This has made radiocarbon dating suitable for a wide range of artefacts, most famously the Turin Shroud (Damon et al. 1989).

5 COUNTING ERROR

Despite the sample size differences, laboratories are capable of reporting similar measurement errors (a function of sample size, concentration, counting statistics, measurement time and instrument sensitivity). Errors are reported as a mean age with a Gaussian uncertainty one degree of freedom (1σ; or 68 per cent confidence). Early radiocarbon measurement errors were often large but precise estimates with errors of 10–50 years are now possible, even for older samples (e.g., Jacobi and Higham 2009).

6 FRACTIONATION CORRECTION

Natural isotopic fractionation occurs during exchange between carbon reservoirs and within organisms, which requires correction as it would produce an incorrect age. To do this most laboratories use mass spectrometers to measure the ratio of ^{12}C to ^{13}C in a sample, compared to a standard ($\delta^{13}C$). Due to the abundance of these isotopes, this does not require accelerator spectrometry. This fractionation is

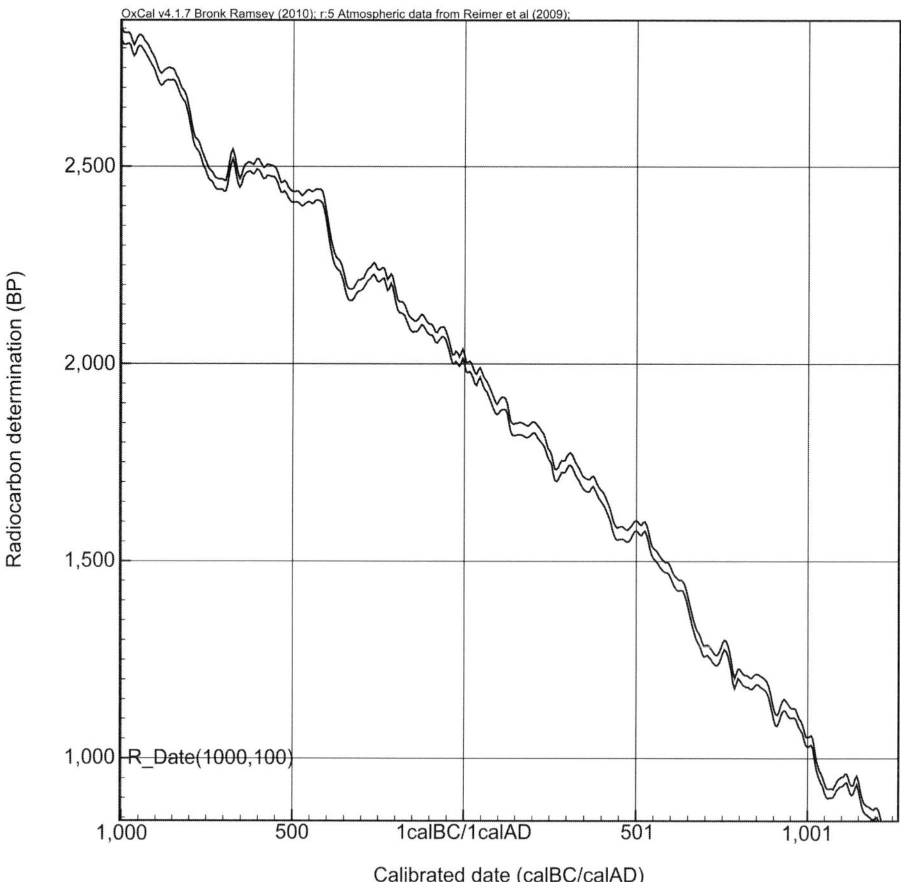

FIGURE 18.1 The tree-ring based radiocarbon calibration curve for the last 1000 years from IntCal09 (Reimer et al. 2009) showing the fluctuations in the production of radiocarbon production over time. (Adapted from Reimer et al. 2009)

mass dependent and, as the masses for all three isotopes are known, $\delta^{13}C$ can be used to correct for ^{14}C fractionation. The expected $\delta^{13}C$ ranges for most types of samples are also known so $\delta^{13}C$ is used to check for obvious contamination.

7 RADIOCARBON CALIBRATION

The production of radiocarbon in the atmosphere varies significantly. This means that the radiocarbon timescale is non-linear. Figure 18.1 shows the variation in radiocarbon production in the last few thousand years. Radiocarbon dates thus require calibration against samples of known age. For part of radiocarbon time there is a well established European and North American tree-ring chronology that can be used. Tree rings vary in width due to climatic and local environmental conditions and trees can be matched statistically by their pattern of ring widths. This has been used to generate a master record to 12,400 BP (years before 1950; Reimer et al. 2009). Since the 1970s there have been attempts to use radiocarbon dated tree rings to provide radiocarbon calibration (e.g., Suess and Clarke 1976). As atmospheric CO_2 equilibrates rapidly, calibration using these data should be effective for the Northern Hemisphere at least. Moreover, as the uncertainty on tree-ring dating is very small, it is possible to produce high resolution calibration curves. Hundreds of radiocarbon measurements have been taken from the tree-ring archive with radiocarbon counting errors as low as 10–15 years. Since the 1980s attempts to produce internationally accepted curves have been undertaken, with several radiocarbon laboratories using agreed methodological protocols. The first of these provided calibration for the last 6000 years (Stuiver and Kra 1986). Successive curves have extended the tree-ring based calibration further back (Stuiver et al. 1993) and it now extends to 12,400 BP in the IntCal 09 curve (Reimer et al. 2009). In addition to the northern Hemisphere tree-ring calibration, a curve for the last 1000 years has been developed for samples that require precise dating in the Southern Hemisphere (McCormac et al. 2004).

Radiocarbon can be measured 40,000–50,000 radiocarbon years, leading to efforts to calibrate beyond the tree ring limit. In the early 1990s, IntCal93 was extended to ~19,000 Cal BP (calibrated BP; Stuiver et al. 1993) using paired $^{234}U/^{230}Th$ and ^{14}C dates on corals. The first of these extensions, while important, was of low resolution and more coral data were included in IntCal 98. Additional resolution in the IntCal 98 and later IntCal04 and 09 curves (Reimer et al. 2004; Reimer et al. 2009; Stuiver et al. 1998) came via radiocarbon dates on a high resolution marine core from the Cariaco basin, off the coast of Venezuela (Hughen et al. 1998). Samples of planktonic foraminifera were ^{14}C dated and an absolute timescale was derived by comparing climate data from the core to the climate record from Greenland GISP2 ice core. The records were aligned assuming a synchronous relationship climatic record between the two sequences and the layer counted GISP2 chronology was transferred onto the Cariaco record (Hughen et al. 2004). From the end of the tree-ring limit to 26,000 Cal BP there was sufficient agreement between calibration data for a consensus calibration curve to be agreed, beyond this limit consensus broke down. This was resolved to a degree when Cariaco was realigned to climate data from $^{234}U/^{230}Th$ dated speleothems from Hulu Cave, China, which brought the Cariaco curve into line with the coral data (Hughen et al. 2007). This, along with the addition of significantly more coral data points, formed IntCal09, allowing consensus calibration to 50,000 Cal BP.

Despite the success of IntCal09 there were problems. Firstly, marine-based curves have a constant reservoir offset applied (Reimer et al. 2009). Attempts to compare the Cariaco radiocarbon data with other cosmogenic isotopes (^{10}Be) from the Greenland ice cores suggested one or more shifts in ΔR at Cariaco (Muscheler et al. 2008; Reimer et al. 2009). While this problem was addressed to a degree in IntCal09 by not using some sections of Cariaco, some researchers suggested a terrestrially-derived calibration is required. Potential data are available from either speleothems, or through long annually laminated lake records, such as Suigetsu, Japan (Nakagawa et al. 2012). These records also have their own issues, however, such as reservoir effects in carbonate rocks or years of missing annual laminations in lakes. Archaeological interpretations based on calibrated radiocarbon dates must, thus, always take a degree of caution, whether using IntCal09 or subsequently published curves (e.g. IntCal13, IntCal19) that incorporate additional datasets. However, it is far better to attempt calibration than not. Since the development of the first calibration curves the implications for archaeology have been significant in changing ideas and allowing radiocarbon-based chronologies to be compared to other records such as ice cores and absolute radiometric techniques.

8 AGE MODELLING

Calibration adds an additional uncertainty to radiocarbon-based age models. The probability distributions of calibrated dates are affected by the shape of the curve as can be seen in Figure 18.2. It is normal to express calibrated uncertainties at 95 per cent confidence and the variability in the shape of the calibration curve means dates with the same radiocarbon error can have different final 95 per cent ranges. The non-Guassian probabilities of calibrated dates have led to significant advances in age modelling techniques. Where measurements have Guassian distributions there are a range of classical statistical techniques available. While such approaches, particularly regression, have been used to examine radiocarbon dates (e.g., Lowe et al. 1995) these are rarely statistically appropriate. One exception to this is the use of the Chi-squared test for the combination of radiocarbon dates from the same organism (Bronk Ramsey 2009). An alternative approach is the use of Bayesian

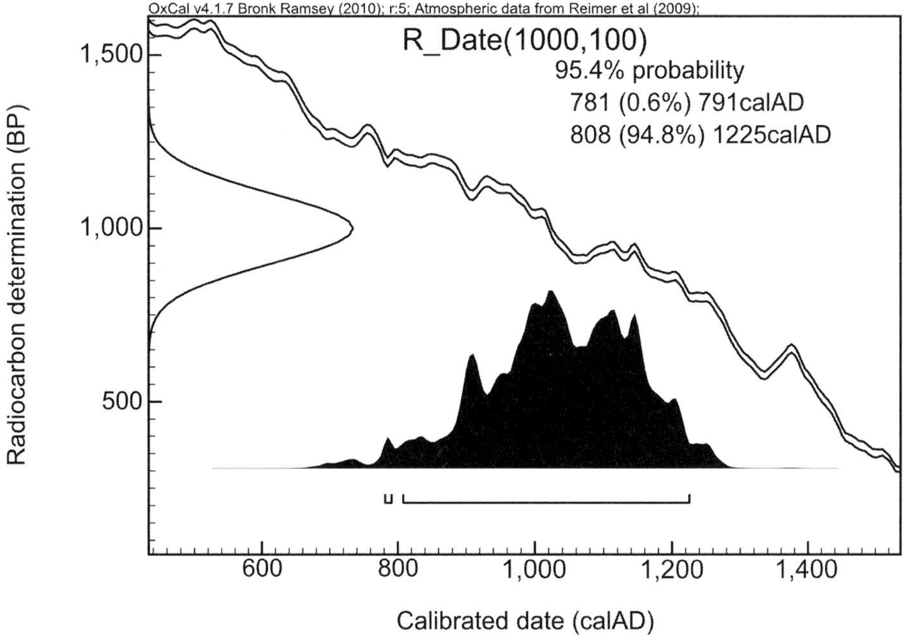

FIGURE 18.2 Calibration of a radiocarbon date and the impact of the calibration curve on the probability distribution of the final age.

analyses using complex probability matrices. This approach, pioneered in radiocarbon dating for archaeology by Buck and colleagues (Buck et al. 1991; Buck et al. 1992), has been very successful in generating useful age models and is now widely applied (e.g., Blockley and Pinhasi 2011; Buck et al. 1996) with a range of Bayesian calibration programmes freely available (e.g., OxCal, Bronk Ramsey [2008]; BCal, Buck et al. [1999]).

The Bayesian approach is based on the incorporation of prior information to constrain likelihood in a posterior highest likelihood density function. The prior consists of the radiocarbon data, the calibration curve, stratigraphy and any rules imposed, such as the uniform prior, where within set constraints any outcome has equal likelihood, see Bronk Ramsey (2008) and Buck et al. (1996). Models include dates in sequence, where the constraints are that age must not decrease with depth, and more advanced Poisson distribution models of sediment formation (Bronk Ramsey 2008). These methods have been used successfully in a range of settings including caves (Jacobi and Higham 2009) and lakes (Blockley et al. 2004; Blockley et al. 2008b). Other models include phases, which are unordered groups useful for modelling multiple phases of occupation at a site.

9 PRETREATMENT AND QUALITY ASSURANCE

Quality assurance can be broken down into the following questions: (1) are the age of the sample and the event of interest the same; (2) is there the potential for contamination during the time of burial; are there effective protocols to (3) remove and (4) avoid contamination in the laboratory?

1) Are the Age of the Sample and the Event of Interest the Same?

This question relates to the care taken during field investigations. The importance of correct sampling and the choice of suitable materials cannot be overstressed. For example, many archaeological sites are dated by charcoal samples often from hearth deposits. It is essential to know how this fits into the stratigraphy of the site and to have the charcoal identified to plant species, as wood from some trees can be hundreds of years old at the time of burning. In some areas this led to a programme of dating human, animal bone or bone artefacts. While archaeologically sound, this strategy raises further problems relevant to questions 2 and 3, as bone is a complex material with significant potential for contamination. Some environmental remains give good dating results but care has to be taken in establishing secure context and determining there is no reworking. A careful strategy based on a large data set from different types of suitable samples is often seen as the way forward (Lowe et al. 1995).

2) Is There the Potential for Contamination during the Time of Burial?

This is a significant issue in radiocarbon dating. In most archaeological contexts charcoal is relatively robust with a straightforward pretreatment process. While this does not always hold, charcoal is often the sample of choice, but wood and most macrofossils also give good results. Bone is prone to *in situ* contamination and extensive pretreatments have been developed. In environmental samples, macrofossils, such as seeds or plant material are often seen to be less prone to contamination than other options. However, movement within a profile is not uncommon for such material. On the other hand, taking samples from bulk peat, while stratigraphically more secure, is open to a much wider range of contamination including percolation of humic acids down a profile or in-wash of dissolved dead carbonate.

3) Are There Effective Protocols to Remove Contamination in the Laboratory?

Most material that is routinely dated has suitable pretreatment strategies. For many archaeological sites that date within the last 10,000 years, samples such as wood or charcoal will receive effective pretreatment. Radiocarbon laboratories have developed some important steps such as $\delta^{13}C$. There has, however, been a long-running debate over effective pretreatment for archaeological bone, and to a lesser extent old charcoal. Effective bone dating started in the 1980s with access to accelerators, allowing laboratories to date collagen, the main protein in bone (Hedges and van Klinken 1992). Even then, despite major dating programmes in the early to mid-1990s (Housley et al. 1991; Housley et al. 1997), important samples were problematic. Recently some laboratories have specialised in producing bone ages. This involves testing for viable collagen using the carbon/nitrogen ratio of the organic component (Brock et al. 2007) and using ultrafilters to remove and discard material other than large collagen strands (Higham et al. 2006).

Charcoal is usually pretreated by heating and cleaning in acids and bases (ABA). For old samples this is not necessarily reliable (see Bird et al. 1999 and Chappell et al. 1996) and some laboratories have developed a harsher pretreatment by aggressive oxidation of samples to remove organic contamination (ABOX; Turney et al. 2001). While not yet as routinely used as ultrafiltration, such techniques have the potential to refine the chronologies of older sites.

4) Are There Effective Protocols to Avoid Contamination in the Laboratory?

Radiocarbon laboratories test reliability using known standards as well as international comparison exercises, where samples are sent to them as part of the exercise and used to test measurement reliability, error estimation, and pretreatment protocols (Scott et al. 1998). Despite this rigour, radiocarbon dating is challenging due to minimal natural ^{14}C concentration and the difficulty of removing younger or older carbon contamination.

Quality Assurance Procedures

In order to use and understand radiocarbon dating it is important to follow good practice. As a guide, below are some of the common criteria used by internationally accepted studies.

1) Good security of association between sample and dated event, considering reworking and long-lived species.
2) Good understanding of the depositional context, including problems such as ^{14}C reservoirs.
3) Rigorous removal of contamination (Brock et al. 2007; Brock et al. 2010a; Brock et al. 2010b; Higham et al. 2006).
4) An internationally agreed calibration curve is available and calibration uncertainties are accounted for.
5) Statistical manipulation of the radiocarbon data should account for the non-normal probability densities (e.g., Buck et al. 1991; Buck et al. 1992).

10 CASE STUDIES: KEY TRANSITIONS IN HUMAN HISTORY

A prevailing question in archaeology is how and when major transitions occur. One example is the colonisation of Europe by anatomically modern humans (AMH) and the apparent replacement of the Neanderthals (*H. neanderthalensis*). Despite debates over hybridisation (Duarte et al. 1999; Tattersall et al. 1999) and recent genetic evidence for limited interbreeding (Green et al. 2010), there is a clear pattern of a disappearance of the Neanderthals as a distinct species and a transition from Middle to Upper Palaeolithic tools some time around 40,000 years ago (Joris and Street 2008) or later. This pattern is based on a large database of radiocarbon ages, of varying quality. An added interest is the role of climate change, as around this time cold episodes known as Heinrich (H) events are recognised in a variety of archives, including Greenland (Svensson et al. 2008). One of these episodes, H4, dates to around 40,000 BP, and is suggested by some as being significant in the AMH replacement of Neanderthals (Fedele et al. 2008). It has also been suggested by d'Errico and Sanchez-Goni (2003) that H4 delayed AMH arrival into southern Iberia, as the reduced biomass of arid southern Iberia may have limited their ability to occupy this region, creating a Neanderthal refuge.

If the available radiocarbon dates are taken and simply calibrated, using IntCal09, then there is significant overlap in many regions between late Neanderthals and early AMH. Indeed in some regions the raw data suggest many thousands of years of overlap. This has contributed to the idea of some cultural and possibly genetic admixture. Evidence for this idea comes from transitional tool industries, such as the French Châtelperronian, which has both Upper Palaeolithic and Midddle Palaeolithic affinities, but is thought to be a Neanderthal industry.

Gravina et al. (2005) and later Mellars et al. (2007) suggested intrastratification of Châtelperronian and Aurignacian levels, suggesting sequential periods of use by Neanderthal and AMH groups. Others, however, see Neanderthal extinction as very rapid (Fedele et al. 2008) and linked directly to the H4 event and possibly to a very large volcanic eruption known as the Campanian Ignimbrite (CI) from the Campanian volcanic province, Italy, at 39,282 ± 110 BP (de Vivo et al. 2001).

There is a problem of radiocarbon chronological control over this important research area. An example of the problem is the age of the iconic human remains of the Red Lady of Paviland. This male Palaeolithic burial comes from the Gower peninsula, Wales. Initial dating in the 1980s using early AMS facilities suggested that the burial occurred around 18,000 radiocarbon years ago. Recent re-dating using more advanced pretreatment put the date back to 26,350 ± 550 BP (Aldhouse-Green and Pettitt 1998). Further re-dating using the ultrafiltration technique, has moved the burial back to between 28,870 ± 180 to 29,490 ± 210 (Jacobi and Higham 2008). In this case the type of pretreatment has made 10,000 years difference in the reported age, and is much more acceptable on archaeological grounds. If we consider that the radiocarbon database for the Middle/Upper Palaeolithic contains hundreds of dates on bone (Joris and Street 2008), with few using ultrafiltration, then the difficulties of studying this period are apparent.

In addition to bone, many of the available dates for the Middle to Upper Palaeolithic transition are also based on charcoal, and old charcoal dates may be problematic. As mentioned above, at this time there is a major volcanic eruption know as the CI, that is very well dated by non-radiocarbon methods. Ash from this eruption is widespread and is found in archaeological sites as far afield as Italy and Russia (Pyle et al. 2006). Ash deposition can be treated under normal circumstances as a geologically instantaneous event and thus be used to link the chronologies of numerous sites. Blockley et al. (2008a) used this fact to test the available radiocarbon chronologies for Palaeolithic sites where this ash occurred. They combined the IntCal 09 calibration data, and the available radiocarbon dates for the sites containing the CI ash, the $^{40}Ar/^{39}Ar$ ages for the CI from the volcano and a Bayesian model to order the stratigraphy of the sites. This study revealed that in all of the Middle to Upper Palaeolithic archaeological sites where the ash was reported all but one of the radiocarbon dates were too young to support the model. This suggested that, firstly, these sites required re-dating using ABOX pretreatments, and that all charcoal ages for this time period had to be suspect. Subsequently Higham et al. (2009) re-dated samples from this time period at the important site of Grotta di Fumane, Italy, using the refined acid-base-oxidation/stepped combustion (ABOX-SC) method for charcoal pretreatment and demonstrated that this method systematically produced older and more reliable ages than the traditional ABA pretreatment.

What is clear is that one of the most important transitions in European history is currently poorly understood and that this is the result of problems with the available radiocarbon database. New work is showing that significant improvements can be made but it is now important for the relevant archaeological community to drive research forward by a European wide re-dating programme.

Another major transition in European and Near Eastern history is the onset of agriculture (e.g., Childe 1951), starting in the Fertile Crescent and the southern Levant. This has been seen as a three-stage process with the adoption of a fully sedentary lifestyle by Natufian hunter-gatherers; followed by a process of innovation in the Pre-Pottery-Neolithic PPNA-C (Bar-Yosef 1998; Kuijt and Goring-Morris 2002). This occurs roughly between ~17,000 BP and ~9000 BP, and coincides with climatic upheavals at the end of the last ice age. There is a long period of cool, and in the Levant dry, conditions, followed by a sudden warming at the start of the late glacial period (~14,700 BP), with a rapid return to cold conditions during the Younger Dryas (12,800–11,700), before warmer stable conditions return into the Holocene (11,700 BP; Rasmussen et al. 2006). It has been argued that these conditions induced fluctuations between cooler/dryer and warmer/wetter conditions in the southern Levant, influencing human populations. In this model, late glacial Natufian hunter-gatherers adopted a fully sedentary lifestyle, but are forced adopt a more open mobile lifestyle by the Younger Dryas (the Late Natufian), and that this may have been the earliest onset of horticulture, before a transition to early agriculture in the PPNA (Bar-Yosef 2001; Bar-Yosef and Belfer-Cohen 2002).

From an environmental perspective this is sound as there is good evidence from speleothem records in Israel of a pattern similar to the record from the Greenland ice cores (Bar-Matthews et al. 1999; Bar-Matthews et al. 2000). However, all of the important sites in this period have chronologies based on radiocarbon dating. In order to investigate the chronological aspects in more detail, Blockley and Pinhasi (2011) took the existing radiocarbon database for the southern Levant (Pinhasi et al. 2005), and examined it on quality assurance grounds. One of the most interesting results was that, from a database of 149 samples, only 84 were deemed suitable (based on internationally accepted criteria) and 9 of the most important sites had no reliable dates covering this transition. Importantly, rejection was not based on any prior idea of what a correct age should be but simply the application of basic quality assurance approaches.

11 CONCLUSION

This chapter has aimed to outline the key principles, advantages and challenges of radiocarbon dating. This method is at the heart of archaeological chronologies and thus deserves the careful attention of archaeologists and archaeological scientists. When archaeological interpretation is undertaken without sufficient attention to chronological problems, it is very easy for poor interpretations, or at least confusion, to be the result. The method is powerful and applicable to a range of sites and samples, but care and attention is required from the sample selection stage through to the final interpretation of dates, or of large radiocarbon databases, to ensure accurate and meaningful dating of archaeological events.

REFERENCES

Aitken, M. J. 1989. *Science-Based Dating in Archaeology*. London: Longman.

Arnold, J. R. and W. F. Libby. 1949. Radiocarbon from pile graphite: Chemical methods for its concentrations. *Argonne National Laboratory, United States Department of Energy (through predecessor agency the Atomic Energy Commission).*

Aldhouse-Green, S. and Pettitt, P. 1998. Paviland Cave: Contextualizing the "Red Lady." *Antiquity* 72:756–772.

Bar-Matthews, M., Ayalon, A., and Kaufman, A. 2000. Timing and hydrological conditions of Sapropel events in the Eastern Mediterranean, as evident from speleothems, Soreq cave. *Israel Chemical Geology* 169:145–156.

Bar-Matthews, M., Ayalon, A., Kaufman, A., and Wasserburg, G. 1999. The Eastern Mediterranean paleoclimate as a reflection of regional events: Soreq cave, Israel. *Earth and Planetary Science Letters* 166:85–95.

Bar-Yosef, O. 1998. The Natufian culture in the Levant: Threshold to the origins of agriculture. *Evoutionary Anthropology* 6:159–177.

Bar-Yosef, O. 2001. From sedentary foragers to village hierarchies: The emergence of social institutions. In: Runciman, G. (ed.) *The Origin of Human Social Institutions*, pp. 1–38. Oxford: Oxford University Press.

Bar-Yosef, O. and Belfer-Cohen, A. 2002. Facing environmental crisis. In: Cappers, R. T. J. and Bottema, S. (eds.) *The Dawn of Farming in the Near East: Studies in Early Near Eastern Production, Subsistence, and Environment*, pp. 55–66. Berlin: Ex Oriente.

Bird, M. I., Ayliffe, L. K., Fifield, L. K., Turney, C. S. M., Cresswell, R. G., Barrows, T. T., and David, B. 1999. Radiocarbon dating of "old" charcoal using a wet oxidation, stepped-combustion procedure. *Radiocarbon* 41:127–140.

Blockley, S. P. E. and Pinhasi, R. 2011. A revised chronology for the adoption of agriculture in the Southern Levant and the role of Lateglacial climatic change. *Quaternary Science Reviews* 30:98–108.

Blockley, S. P. E., Lowe, J. J., Walker, J. J., Asioli, A., Trincardi, F., Coope, G. R., Donahue, R. E., and Pollard, A. M. 2004. Bayesian analysis of radiocarbon chronologies: Examples from the European Lateglacial. *Journal of Quaternary Science* 19:159–175.

Blockley, S. P. E., Ramsey, C. B., and Higham, T. 2008a. The Middle to Upper Palaeolithic transition: Dating, stratigraphy and isochronous markers. *Journal of Human Evolution* 55:764–771.

Blockley, S. P. E., Ramsey, C. B., Lane, C. S., and Lotter, A. F. 2008b. Improved age modelling approaches as exemplified by the Revised Chronology for the Central European Varved Lake, Soppensee. *Quaternary Science Reviews* 27:61–71.

Brock, F., Bronk Ramsey, C., and Higham, T. F. G. 2007. Quality assurance of ultrafiltered bone dating. *Radiocarbon* 49:187–192.

Brock, F., Higham, T., Ditchfield, P., and Ramsey, C. B. 2010a. Current pretreatment methods for AMS radiocarbon dating at the Oxford Radiocarbon Accelerator Unit (ORAU). *Radiocarbon* 52(1):103–112.

Brock, F., Higham, T., and Ramsey, C. B. 2010b. Pre-screening techniques for identification of samples suitable for radiocarbon dating of poorly preserved bones. *Journal of Archaeological Science* 37(4):855–865.

Bronk Ramsey, C. 2008. Deposition models for chronological records. *Quaternary Science Reviews* 27:42–60.

Bronk Ramsey, C. 2009. Bayesian analysis of radiocarbon dates. *Radiocarbon* 51:337–360.

Buck, C. E., Cavanagh, W. G., and Litton, C. D. 1996. *The Bayesian Approach to Interpreting Archaeological Data*. Wiley: Chichester.

Buck C. E., Christen J. A., and James G. N. 1999. BCal: An on-line Bayesian radiocarbon calibration tool. *Internet Archaeology* 7. http://intarch.ac.uk/journal/issue7/buck/ (accessed July 19, 2019).

Buck, C. E., Kenworthy, J. B., Litton, C. D., and Smith, A. F. M. 1991. Combining archaeological and radiocarbon information – a Bayesian-approach to calibration. *Antiquity* 65:808–821.

Buck, C. E., Litton, C. D., and Smith, A. F. M. 1992. Calibration of radiocarbon results pertaining to related archaeological events. *Journal of Archaeological Science* 19:497–512.

Chappell, J., Head, J., and Magee, J. 1996. Beyond the radiocarbon limit in Australian archaeology and Quaternary research. *Antiquity* 70:543–552.

Childe, V. G. 1951. *Man Makes Himself*. London: Watts.

Damon, P. E., Donahue, D. J., Gore, B. H., Hatheway, A. L., Jull, A. J. T., Linick, T. W., Sercel, P. J., Toolin, L. J., Bronk, C. R., Hall, E. T., Hedges, R. E. M., Housley, R., Law, I. A., Perry, C., Bonani, G., Trumbore, S., Woelfli, W., Ambers, J. C., Bowman, S. G. E., Leese M. N., and Tite M. S. 1989. Radiocarbon dating of the Shroud of Turin. *Nature* 337:611–615.

Duarte, C., Mauricio, J., Pettitt, P. B., Souto, P., Trinkaus, E., van der Plicht, H., and Zilhaom, J. 1999. The early Upper Paleolithic human skeleton from the Abrigo do Lagar Velho (Portugal) and modern human emergence in Iberia. *Proceedings of the National Academy of Sciences of the USA* 96:7604–7609.

d'Errico, F. and Sanchez-Goni, M. F. 2003. Neandertal extinction and the millennial scale climatic variability of OIS 3. *Quaternary Science Reviews* 22:769–788.

de Vivo, B., Rolandi, G., Gans, P. B., Calvert, A., Bohrson, W. A., Spera, F. J., and Belkin, H. E. 2001. New constraints on the pyroclastic eruptive history of the Campanian volcanic Plain (Italy). *Mineralogy and Petrology* 73:47–65.

Eiriksson, J., Larsen, G., Knudsen, K. L., Heinemeier, J., and Simonarson, L. A. 2004. Marine reservoir age variability and water mass distribution in the Iceland Sea. *Quaternary Science Reviews* 23:2247–2268.

Fedele, F. G.,Giaccio, B., and Hajdas, I. 2008. Timescales and cultural process at 40,000 BP in the light of the Campanian Ignimbrite eruption, Western Eurasia. *Journal of Human Evolution* 55:834–857.

Gravina, B., Mellars, P., and Ramsey, C. B. 2005. Radiocarbon dating of interstratified Neanderthal and early modern human occupations at the Chatelperronian type-site. *Nature* 438:51–56.

Green, R. E., Krause, J., Briggs, A. W., Maricic, T., Stenzel, U., Kircher, M., Patterson, N., Li, H., Zhai, W., Fritz, M. H.-Y., Hansen, N. F., Durand, E. Y., Malaspinas, A.-S., Jensen, J. D., Marques-Bonet, T., Alkan, C., Prüfer, K., Meyer, M., Burbano, H. A., Good, J. M., Schultz, R., Aximu-Petri, A., Butthof, A., Höber, B., Höffner, B., Siegemund, M., Weihmann, A., Nusbaum, C., Lander, E. S., Russ, C., Novod, N., Affourtit, J., Egholm, M., Verna, C., Rudan, P., Brajkovic, D., Kucan, Ž., Gušic, I., Doronichev, V. B., Golovanova, L. V., Lalueza-Fox, C., De La Rasilla, M., Fortea, J., Rosas, A., Schmitz, R. W., Johnson, P. L. F., Eichler, E. E., Falush, D., Birney, E., Mullikin, J. C., Slatkin, M., Nielsen, R., Kelso, J., Lachmann, M., Reich, D., and Pääbo, S. 2010. A draft sequence of the Neandertal genome. *Science* 328:710–722.

Hedges, R. E. M. and van Klinken, G. J. 1992. A review of current approaches in the pre-treatment of bone for radiocarbon dating by AMS. *Radiocarbon* 34(3):279–291.

Higham, T. F. G., Jacobi, R. M., and Bronk Ramsey, C. 2006. AMS radiocarbon dating of ancient bone using ultrafiltration. *Radiocarbon* 48:179–195.

Higham T., Brock F., Peresani M., Broglio A., Wood R., and Douka K. 2009. Problems with radiocarbon dating the Middle to Upper Palaeolithic transition in Italy. *Quaternary Science Reviews* 28:1257–1267.

Housley, R. A. 1991. AMS dates from the Late Glacial and early Postglacial in north-west Europe. In: Barton, R. N. E, Roberts, A. J., and Roe, D. A. (eds.) *The Late Glacial in North-West Europe: Human Adaptation and Environmental Change at the End of the Pleistocene*, pp. 227–233. London: Council for British Archaeology.

Housley, R. A., Gamble, C. S., Street, M., and Pettitt, P. 1997. Radiocarbon evidence for the Lateglacial human recolonisation of northern Europe. *Proceedings of the Prehistoric Society* 63:25–54.

Hughen, K., Lehman, S., Southon, J., Overpeck, J., Marchal, O., Herring, C., and Turnbull, J. 2004. ^{14}C activity and global carbon cycle changes over the past 50,000 years. *Science* 303:202–207.

Hughen, K. A., Overpeck, J. T., Lehman, S. J., Kashgarian, M., Southon, J., Petersen, L. C., Alley, R. B., and Sigman, D. M. 1998. Deglacial changes in ocean circulation from an extended radiocarbon calibration. *Nature* 391:65–68.

Hughen, K., Southon, J., Lehmanc, S. Bertrand, C., and Turnbull, J. 2007. Marine-derived 14C calibration and activity record for the past 50,000 years updated from the Cariaco Basin. *Quaternary Science Reviews* 25:3216–3227.

Jacobi, R. M. and Higham, T.F.G. 2008. The "Red Lady" ages gracefully: new ultrafiltration AMS determinations from Paviland. *Journal of Human Evolution* 55:898–907.

Jacobi, R. M. and Higham, T. F. G. 2009. The early Lateglacial re-colonization of Britain: New radiocarbon evidence from Gough's Cave, southwest England. *Quaternary Science Reviews* 28:1895–1913.

Joris, O. and Street, M. 2008. At the end of the C-14 time scale – the Middle to Upper Paleolithic record of western Eurasia. *Journal of Human Evolution* 55:782–802.

Kuijt, I. and Goring-Morris, N. 2002. Foraging, farming, and social complexity in the pre-pottery Neolithic of the Southern Levant: A review and synthesis. *Journal of World Prehistory* 16:361–440.

Libby, W. F. 1955. *Radiocarbon Dating*, 2nd ed. Chicago, IL: University of Chicago Press.

Lowe, J. J., Coope, G. R., Sheldrick, C., Harkness, D., and Walker, M. J. C. 1995. Direct comparison of UK temperatures and Greenland snow accumulation rates, 15,000 to 12,000 years ago. *Journal of Quaternary Science* 10:175–180.

McCormac, F. G., Hogg, A. G., Blackwell, P. G., Buck, C. E., Higham, T. F. G., and Reimer, P. J. 2004. SHCal04 Southern Hemisphere Calibration 0–1000 cal BP. *Radiocarbon* 46:1087–1092.

Mellars P., Gravina B., and Ramsey, C. B. 2007. Confirmation of Neanderthal/modern human interstratification at the Chatelperronian type-site. *Proceedings of the National Academy of Sciences of the United States of America* 104:3657–3662.

Muscheler, R., Kromer, B., Björck, S., Svensson, A., Friedrich, M., Kaiser, K. F. K., and Southon, J. 2008. Tree rings and ice cores reveal 14C calibration uncertainties during the Younger Dryas. *Nature Geoscience* 1:263–267.

Nakagawa, T., Gotanda, K., Haraguchi, T., Danhara, T., Yonenobu, H., Brauer, A., Yokoyama, Y., Tada, R., Takemura, K., Staff, R. A., Payne, R., Bronk Ramsey, C., Bryant, C., Brock, F., Schlolaut, G., Marshall, M., Tarasov, P., Lamb, H., and Suigetsu 2006 Project Members. 2012. SG06, a fully continuous and varved sediment core from Lake Suigetsu, Japan: Stratigraphy and potential for improving the radiocarbon calibration model and understanding of late Quaternary climate changes. *Quaternary Science Reviews* 36:164–176.

Polach, H. A. 1987. Perspectives in radiocarbon dating by radiometry. *Nuclear Instruments and Methods B* 29:415–423.

Pyle, D. M., Ricketts, G. D., Margari, V., van Andel, T. H., Sinitsyn, A. A., Praslov, N. D., Nicolai, D., and Lisitsyn, S. 2006. Wide dispersal and deposition of distal tephra during the Pleistocene "Campanian Ignimbrite/Y5" eruption, Italy. *Quaternary Science Reviews* 25:2713–2728.

Rasmussen, S. O., Andersen, K. K., Svensson, A. M., Steffensen, J. P., Vinther, B. M., Clausen, H. B., Siggaard-Andersen, M. L., Johnsen, S. J., Larsen, L. B., Dahl-Jensen, D., Bigler, M., Röthlisberger, R., Fischer, H., Goto-Azuma, K., Hansson, M. E., and Ruth, U. 2006. A new Greenland ice core chronology for the last glacial termination. *Journal of Geophysical Research* 111, D06102.

Reimer, P. J., Baillie, M. G. L., Bard, E., Bayliss, A., Beck, J. W., Bertrand, C. J. H., Blackwell, P. G., Buck, C. E., Burr, G. S., Cutler, K. B., Damon, P. E., Edwards, R. L., Fairbanks, R. G., Friedrich, M., Guilderson, T. P., Hogg, A. G., Hughen, K. A., Kromer, B., McCormac, G., Manning, S., Ramsey, C. B., Reimer, R. W., Remmele, S., Southon, J. R., Stuiver, M., Talamo, S., Taylor, F. W., van der Plicht, J., and Weyhenmeyer, C. E. 2004. IntCal04 terrestrial radiocarbon age calibration, 0-26 cal kyr BP. *Radiocarbon* 46:1029–1058.

Reimer, P. J., Baillie, M. G. L., Bard, E., Bayliss, A., Beck, J. W., Blackwell, P. G., Bronk Ramsey, C., Buck, C. E., Burr, G. S., Edwards, R. L., Friedrich, M., Grootes, P. M., Guilderson, T. P., Hajdas, I., Heaton, T. J., Hogg, A. G., Hughen, K. A., Kaiser, K. F., Kromer, B., McCormac, F. G., Manning, S. W., Reimer, R. W., Richards, D. A., Southon, J. R., Talamo, S., Turney, C. S. M., van der Plicht, J., and Weyhenmeyer, C. E. 2009. IntCal09 and Marine09 radiocarbon age calibration curves, 0–50,000 years cal BP. *Radiocarbon* 51:1111–1150.

Scott, E. M., Harkness, D. D., and Cook, G. T. 1998 Interlaboratory comparisons: lessons learned. *Radiocarbon* 40:331–340.

Siani, G., Paterne, M., Arnold, M., Bard, E., Metivier, B., Tisnérat, N., and Bassinot, F. 2000. Radiocarbon reservoir ages in the Mediterranean Sea and Black Sea. *Radiocarbon* 42:271–280.

Stuiver, M. and Kra, R. S. (eds.) 1986. Calibration issue, proceedings of the 12th International 14C conference. *Radiocarbon* 28:805–1030.

Stuiver, M. and Reimer, P. J. 1993. Extended 14 C data base and revised CALIB 3.0 14 C age calibration program. *Radiocarbon* 35(1):215–230.

Stuiver, M., Reimer, P. J., Bard, E., Beck, J. W., Burr, G. S., Hughen, K. A., Kromer, B., McCormac, G., van der Plicht, J., and Spurk, M. 1998. INTCAL98 Radiocarbon Age Calibration, 24000–0 cal BP. *Radiocarbon* 40:1041–1083.

Suess, H. and Clarke, M. 1976. *Calibration curve for radiocarbon-dates Antiquity* 50:61–63.

Svensson, A, Andersen, K. K., Bigler, M., Clausen, H. B., Dahl-Jensen, D., Davies, S. M., Johnsen, S. J., Muscheler, R., Parrenin, F., Rasmussen, S. O., Röthlisberger, R., Seierstad, I., Steffensen, J. P., and Vinther, B. M. 2008. A 60 000 year Greenland stratigraphic ice core chronology. *Climates of the Past* 4:47–57.

Turney, C. S. M., Bird, M. I., Fifield, L. K., Kershaw, A. P., Cresswell R. G., Santos, G. M., di Tada, M. L., Hausladen, P. A., and Youping, Z. 2001. Development of a robust C-14 chronology for Lynch's Crater (north Queensland, Australia) using different pretreatment strategies. *Radiocarbon* 43:45–54.

19

Luminescence Dating

Richard M. Bailey

The use of optical and thermal luminescence methods to date objects and sediments from archaeological sites.

1 INTRODUCTION

The range of chronological methods described by the term "luminescence dating" provides a rich set of tools for dating many types of events relevant to archaeological research. These include assessing the depositional age of sediments (the time elapsed since those sediment were deposited by, for example, water, wind, or human activity), and estimating the time since pottery, casting cores, or stones were last fired/heated. Following an initial suggestion by Daniels et al. (1953), luminescence dating methods were introduced into the archaeological context by Aitken et al. (1964) with the thermoluminescence (TL) dating of pottery. Since then, considerable improvements in understanding the basic underlying physical mechanisms have been translated into significant methodological breakthroughs. Notable among these was the development of optically stimulated luminescence (OSL) methods (Huntley et al. 1985) and the improved confidence in dating sedimentary material that this brought. A more recent technologically driven advance was the dating of individual sand grains (so-called single-grain dating), allowing more in-depth assessments of dating reliability and widening the applicability of OSL dating (also referred to as "optical dating").

Luminescence methods are now widely used in both geological/environmental and archaeological settings, alongside more established methods such as radiocarbon dating. Two possible reasons may account for its success: (i) the ability to date nonorganic material: the use of quartz and feldspar minerals is well-developed and these materials are effectively ubiquitous in terrestrial sediments; (ii) the datable timescale: reliable ages have been reported for samples with ages as young as decades (e.g., Madsen et al. 2005; Stokes et al. 2004) and as old as several hundreds of thousands of years (e.g., Wang et al. (2006) provided accurate dates on independently dated loess up to almost 800 ka). Indeed, comparisons of luminescence dating results to those obtained from independent methods provides compelling evidence of its reliability (e.g., Murray and Olley 2002). Examples of archaeological applications cover a broad range of general topics, and include the dating of sediments containing lithic cultures (e.g., Tribolo et al. 2006); cultural and developmental markers (e.g., Henshilwood 2002); the spread of modern humans away from Africa (e.g., Bowler et al. 2003; Feathers et al. 2006); and the evolution of our own (e.g., Grine et al. 2007) and other hominin species (Morwood et al. 2004).

2 THE PHYSICAL BASIS OF THE METHOD

Luminescence-based dating methods work by estimating two quantities: the rate at which radiation is being absorbed by a sample, and the total amount of radiation that has been absorbed since the event of interest. The radiation here is the relatively low-level natural "background" radiation field present due to the decay of naturally occurring radioisotopes (predominantly ^{40}K, ^{235}U, ^{238}U, ^{232}Th, and their associated daughter products). Archaeological materials (e.g., sediments, pottery sherds) are exposed to this radiation field during burial, and luminescence measurements provide estimates of total radiation exposure. The duration of this exposure (the "age" of the sample) can be calculated if the dose rate (the amount of radiation absorbed per year) is known.

Why is it called "luminescence" dating? During irradiation (the burial period), electrons are dislodged from parent atoms that make up crystalline minerals within the sample (typically quartz and/or feldspar are used for dating). The freed electrons diffuse through the crystal and a fraction become trapped at positively charged defects within the crystal. As this process continues (during the burial period), the population of trapped electrons grows. After collection, the refined sample is stimulated by either heat or illumination, and a part of the trapped-electron population returns to positions equivalent to their "starting conditions" on parent atoms. During this return to the "original state," energy is emitted as light and heat, and the intensity of the light (once calibrated) is used to provide a measure of the total absorbed radiation dose (see below). Following stimulation, the sample may be referred to as having been "reset" and is capable of recording subsequent radiation doses. Emissions stimulated with heat are referred to as "thermoluminescence" (TL) and those stimulated by illumination, "optically stimulated luminescence" (OSL).

Detailed descriptions of the physical mechanisms upon which luminescence methods rest can be found in several other sources (e.g., Bailey and McKeever 2009; McKeever 1988; McKeever and Chen 1997).

3 HOW IT WORKS IN THE NATURAL ENVIRONMENT: AN IDEALISED EXAMPLE

Here we take an idealised scenario, for illustrative purposes, in which sediment was transported in the past by wind in to a point of deposition, leading to sediment accumulation (see also Figure 19.1). During aeolian transport, individual grains are exposed to daylight for a sufficient period (a few 10s of seconds) such that each was fully reset (see previous section) prior to deposition. During burial the deposited grains are irradiated at a constant rate by radionuclides present in the sediment. A sediment sample is subsequently taken for optical dating and OSL measurements are made (see following section), which indicate the sample has received a total dose of 3 Gy (Gray, Gy, is a standard unit of radiation, with 1 Gy = 1 Joule of absorbed energy per kg of mass; the estimate of the absorbed dose is the "equivalent dose," D_e). The rate at which the radiation was absorbed by the sample (D', typically described in units of Gy per thousand years, Gy/ka) depends on the concentration of U, Th, K in the sediment. In our scenario, these concentrations are measured and a value determined for the dose rate of 1.5 Gy/ka (D'=1.5 Gy/ka). The burial period, the "depositional age" of the sample, is therefore estimated as 3 Gy divided by 1.5 Gy/ka, yielding an age of 2 ka (age = D_e/D'). Due to expected statistical variation in the measurements, and uncertainty in some of the factors used in calculating the dose rate, age estimates have an associated uncertainty (an "error bar") usually within the range 5–15 per cent (discussed below). In our worked example, a typical result would be 2 $\pm$ 0.16 ka (an 8 per cent error). The usual convention is to report 1-sigma errors, which in the present example would be interpreted as a 68 per cent chance that the true burial age is within the range 1.84–2.16 ka.

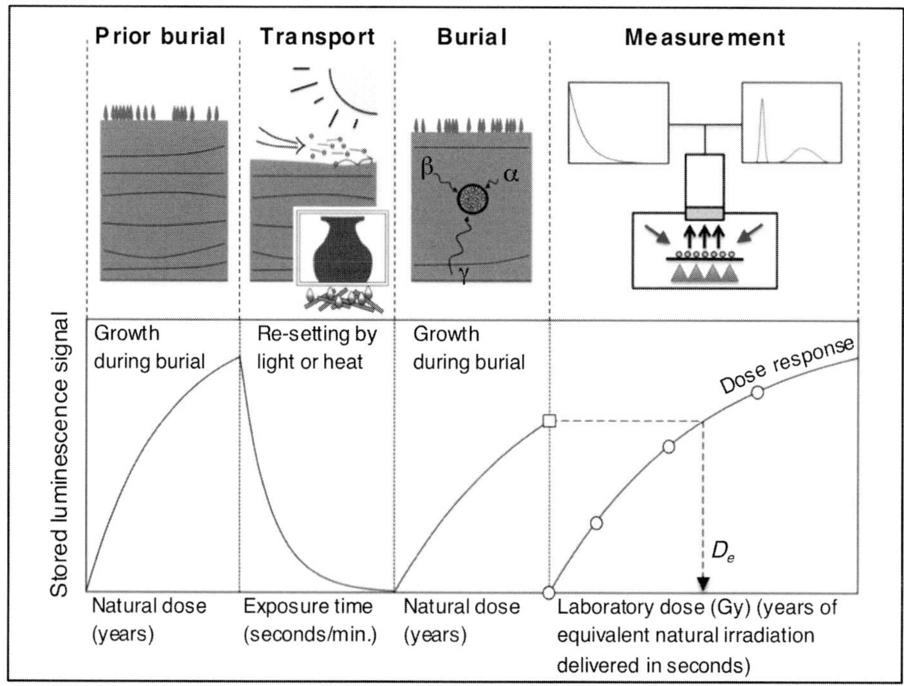

FIGURE 19.1 This figure depicts events described in the idealised example of luminescence dating given in the main text. The bottom panels show the progressive change in the magnitude of stored luminescence signal as a sample goes through the events described in the upper panels. α, β, and γ refer to the radiogenic components of *D'*. During measurement, luminescence can be stimulated by light or heat and typical resultant signal forms (OSL and TL respectively) for quartz are indicated by the blue and red plots (plotted with time and temperature respectively). In the lower right panel, the square represents the "natural luminescence" (resulting from the burial dose) and the circles (which define the dose response) are the result of administered laboratory doses. D_e (the "equivalent dose") is the estimate of the burial dose.

4 PRACTICALITIES

Sampling

A broad range of materials can be dated with luminescence methods (Table 19.1). Effective sampling of these materials requires consideration of the relationship between the resetting event and the archaeological event under investigation, the appropriateness of the material (with respect to signal-resetting postdepositional disturbance, for example) and certain practical points described below. Ideally, luminescence dating samples should not be taken from within 30 cm of a

Table 19.1 *Luminescence dating in a nutshell.*

Event dated: last exposure of material to daylight or to temperatures above ~350°C[a]
Materials: grains of quartz and feldspar, in size range 5–300 μm; burnt flint

Contexts:

Archaeological sediments (e.g., burial sediments), aeolian, fluvial, alluvial, colluvial, glacial, marine, lacustrine, coastal

Other: fired pottery, heated stones, casting cores, furnace lining

Approximate age range: 10–400,000 years[b]
Precision: best ~5%[c] of age; typically 8–12% of age

[a] There is an equivalence of temperature/time, such that the time required for resetting grows exponentially as temperature is reduced (e.g., minutes at 300°C, but hours to days at 200°C, for adequate resetting);
[b] See main text for discussion of increased range;
[c] The lower limit is set by the need to put relatively large uncertainties on factors that cannot presently be measured, and are subject to educated guesses (e.g., mean water content during burial), together with unavoidable statistical uncertainty on factors such as laboratory source calibrations, radiation absorption coefficients, and D_e estimates.

sedimentary boundary/surface and the sediment matrix should be homogeneous within a 20–30 cm sphere of the sampling point. Locations close to irregularities, such as uncharacteristically large stones/boulders, breaks in sedimentary unit, surfaces, or cave walls should be avoided as this can significantly complicate the calculation of *D'*. If avoiding such discontinuities is not possible, a full record of the context is necessary and samples of nearby sedimentary units may be required (consulting with a specialist would be necessary in this case). For the collection of samples from unconsolidated sedimentary material, opaque tubes may be forced into the sediment face (typically several cm in diameter, black plastic or metal, with the outward pointing end securely covered and "light-tight"). The minimum sample volume required depends on the relative concentration of the desired mineral (quartz/feldspar), but would ideally yield >1 cm^3 of refined grains (significantly smaller samples can be used, but this may limit the final precision/accuracy of the date). If the sediment is highly consolidated, removal of intact blocks of sediment is advisable and sufficient volume should be taken such that the outer ~1 cm of each light-exposed face can be removed (under controlled lighting). There is no requirement to control light-exposure during collection of pottery sherds or burnt flints/stones, as the outer face of each is discarded during the preparation procedure (removing light-exposed material and also simplifying the dose rate calculation). This requirement to remove outer material sets a practical limit on the preferred minimum size of object that can be dated. A more detailed discussion of sampling considerations is given in Aitken (1985; Aitken 1998).

Laboratory Preparation

This is necessary to isolate the target mineral grains (typically quartz and/or K-feldspar) of known size ("fine grains" are typically 5–15 μm, "coarse grains" are in most cases taken from relatively narrow ranges within the 90–250 μm band). The details of the refinement process are adjusted depending on the target grain-type, and involve treatments with reagents aimed at removing unwanted mineral and organic content, density separation and isolation of the required grain size. Sample preparation is undertaken in specialist facilities under low-intensity red/orange lighting. Relevant procedures are described in most applied luminescence papers (see, for example, Aitken 1997).

Estimating the Total Absorbed Dose (D_e)

This estimate involves comparing the magnitude of the "natural" luminescence signal (the signal due to radiation received by the sample during burial) to that from a known laboratory dose. This calibration process allows estimates of light emission to be converted to estimates of absorbed radiation dose and in practice is achieved using a series of laboratory irradiations that define a "dose response" function, against which the natural luminescence is compared. D_e can be measured from a range of materials (see Table 19.1), the choice of which depends on the context. In recent years a much-favored approach has been to use quartz OSL methods and this is in part related to problems of age underestimation (due to signal instability), which have complicated many dating attempts based on infrared-stimulated luminescence (IRSL) signal from some feldspar and polymineral samples (although recent advances may have significantly improved this situation – see following section). Toward the end of the last century, the established "multiple aliquot" procedures for estimating D_e (see Aitken 1985; Aitken 1997) were replaced, in the case of quartz OSL, by newer "single aliquot" methods. A review of the most recent of these methods (single-aliquot regenerative-dose, SAR, applicable to quartz OSL) is given by Wintle and Murray (2006). The SAR method has improved dating accuracy and precision considerably and, along with the ability to measure single grains (e.g., Duller 2008), as compared to multi-grain aliquots, provides well-tested procedures for assessing the internal consistency and applicability of the methods on a sample-by-sample basis. The usual practice is to take sub-samples (single sand grains or aliquots composed of tens to thousands of grains) and to measure D_e for each. In the simplest case the variation between each aliquot is due only to combined random uncertainties (e.g., counting statistics from OSL measurement) and the best estimate of the burial dose is an error-weighted estimate of the central value (e.g., the *Central Age Model* of Galbraith et al. 1999). Over-dispersion of the D_e values (where the spread of the D_e values is greater than that expected from random (statistical) variation alone) can be suggestive of problems, and some of these are discussed in the following section.

Estimating the Environmental Dose Rate (D')

The environmental dose rate (D') can be estimated using a wide range of techniques. Two classes of methods widely used in the luminescence community are: (i) those which involve the measurement of radionuclide concentration in dating samples (using standard techniques such as inductively coupled plasma mass spectrometry and neutron activation analysis) and a calculation of *D'* based on their known decay rates and emission energies (Adamiec and Aitken 1998); and (ii) measurement of the beta- and/or gamma-radiation field either at the sampling location (using portable gamma-spectrometry equipment) or from the recovered sample using laboratory-based beta- and gamma-spectrometry. Beyond measurement of the present-day dose rate, account must also be made for the moisture content of the sediment during the burial period (water absorbs radiation that would otherwise reach the dating sample) and the (usually minor) contribution of cosmic radiation (see Aitken 1985; Wintle 2008 for more detailed discussion). Given the uncertainties in factors affecting *D'* and the measurement of D_e, it is generally not possible to reduce the combined uncertainty in the overall age estimate to below ~6 per cent in all but exceptional circumstances.

5 SOME POTENTIAL DIFFICULTIES AND POSSIBLE SOLUTIONS

This section describes some of the problems that may hamper attempts to date archaeological material with luminescence methods, and some of the solutions (where they exist) that have emerged over the past few years.

Exceeding the Maximum Age Range

The maximum limit on dating is set by two factors: signal saturation and signal stability. Figure 19.1 shows an idealised response of a luminescence signal to laboratory irradiation. As the defects capable of trapping freed electrons become increasingly occupied (see above), the signal ultimately saturates. The amount of dose required to reach saturation is, however, sample-dependent (and also grain-dependent within each sample), as is the rate at which the dose is delivered to the sample (*D'* is sampling-location-dependent). Saturation of the quartz OSL signal typically occurs under natural burial conditions over timescales of hundreds of thousands of years. While it is not possible to obtain a finite age for a saturated sample, an estimate of the minimum possible age can be obtained from the dose response data by calculating the minimum dose necessary for the natural luminescence signal to reach "within errors" of the saturation intensity. Further progress may be made by choosing individual grains with higher saturation doses (Yoshida et al. 2000), selectively focusing on quartz OSL signals with higher saturation doses (Bailey 2000; Wang et al. 2006) or minerals (e.g., K-feldspar) with higher saturation doses. Problems with signal stability occur when, for example, the electrons captured on defects during the burial period escape prior to measurement (analogous to a bucket accumulating drips of water, with a hole in the base). The measured signal will, in this case, underestimate the length of the burial period. This "fading" of the signal has hampered attempts to date using feldspar grains, although recent methodological advances (e.g., Lauer et al. 2011; Thomsen et al. 2011) provide some hope that this problem may be soluble.

Daylight Resetting

Factors that reduce the absorption of daylight by mineral grains during natural transport processes (e.g., attenuation of daylight by water/sediment, grain coatings) can reduce the efficiency of bleaching. In the worst case, residual signals remain at the time of deposition, and the age subsequently calculated will overestimate the burial age of the sediment. The problem of incomplete resetting is often referred to in the luminescence literature as "partial bleaching." It is unlikely in such cases that all transported grains would be "partially bleached" to the same degree, and a distribution of residual signal magnitudes (and therefore ages) would be expected under such circumstances. Where significant, incomplete, and heterogeneous preburial bleaching leaves a signature in the distribution of D_e values measured from single grains (or aliquots containing relatively small numbers of grains) (e.g., Bailey and Arnold 2006; Duller 2008; Olley et al. 1998). Statistical procedures designed specifically for such cases (e.g., the Minimum Age Model of Roberts et al. 1999) are capable of providing accurate ages estimates in such cases (e.g., Olley and Pietsch 2004). An additional source of information on the efficacy of predepositional bleaching is the nature of the (multicomponent) signal (in the case of quartz OSL). The constituent components are reset (under illumination) at different rates and incomplete complete bleaching can be inferred if the ages increase for the more slowly bleaching components (Bailey et al. 1997; Bailey et al. 2003; Singarayer et al. 2005).

Dose Rate

Under some circumstances, it is possible for the environmental dose rate (*D*') to vary temporally, over the burial period. Time-dependence in *D*' can be identified under some circumstances through the measurement of the activity of daughter products in the Th and U decay chains (see Olley et al. 1996 for discussion). Corrections can be made if the evolution of *D*' over time can be confidently estimated (e.g., Grine et al. 2007), or limits put on the additional uncertainty in the age due to incomplete knowledge of *D*'. In addition to the temporal variation, *D*' varies spatially, over all scales, due to the heterogeneous distribution of relatively active (strongly emitting) and inactive (strongly absorbing) material in samples and their surrounding environment. For example, the presence of highly radioactive minerals such as zircon and/or low-activity carbonate nodules produces considerable spatial variation in the beta component of *D*' (Burrough et al. 2009; Nathan et al. 2003). Each grain effectively has its own *D*', but only the volumetrically averaged value is known (*in situ* spatial variation in beta dose-rate is technically very difficult to measure). The effect is to widen the measured D_e distribution and ultimately to reduce the precision of the age estimate.

Post-Depositional Mixing

In what are most probably relatively rare circumstances, a range of effects have the potential to mix sediment grains and other archaeological material within the sediment column during the burial period. These effects include the action of plants, animals or insects ("bioturbation"); the growth of ice ("cryoturbation") (e.g., Bateman 2003; Bateman et al. 2007); and direct human activity (e.g., burials/ excavations). The mixing together of grains of different depositional ages potentially reduces dating precision and accuracy by disassociating the apparent sediment age from the event of interest being dated and the expression of this event in the sediment. Post-depositional mixing of grains with different ages can potentially be detected by dating single grains and the use of statistical methods to identify discrete age populations (Galbraith and Green 1990; Sivia et al. 2004). An example of the successful use of such an analysis is the re-dating of the Jinmium rock shelter (Australia) by Roberts et al. (1999). Here, the problematic effects of incorporated poorly bleached material (e.g., directly weathered and non-bleached material) were identified and removed through the application of single-grain methods and appropriate statistical methods, reducing the body of dates from >50 ka to <10 ka.

6 EXAMPLE APPLICATIONS IN ARCHAEOLOGICAL CONTEXTS

The breadth of applications of luminescence methods in archaeological settings is considerable and it is possible only to give a brief taster of this body of work. Luminescence-based methods have been much used in dating evidence of hominid/ hominin evolution, often in combination with other independent corroborating methods. For example, Morwood et al. (2004) in their dating of the eastern Indonesian *Homo floresiensis* specimen used a combination of methods, including radiocarbon, U-series, and luminescence, to date this hitherto unknown hominin species. Luminescence dates based on both quartz and feldspar were used to confirm the species existed from >38 ka until at least 18 ka. The dating of the Hofmeyr skull (Grine et al. 2007) is a further example. Here, carbonate-cemented sediment within the cranium was dated using a combination of OSL and uranium-series methods, the latter being combined with CT scan data to model the spatial and temporal evolution of the dose rate. The date of 36 ± 3 ka confirmed the specimen as the first cranial evidence in support for the genetics-based theory that modern humans evolved in sub-Saharan Africa. The chronology of the expansion of modern humans beyond Africa is another key research area where luminescence methods have contributed significantly. Examples include dating the early appearance of modern humans in Europe (Anikovich et al. 2007), parts of the Middle East (Mercier and Valladas 2003), Australia (e.g., Bowler et al. 2003) and North America

(Waters et al. 2011). Much debate surrounds the effects of recently arrived modern humans on the landscapes and ecosystems of the past, notably on extinctions of large vertebrates. In contributing to this debate, Roberts et al. (2001) dated 28 Australian sites, yielding a mean extinction age of ca. 46 ka, the date of which is consistent with the most likely date for the arrival of modern humans (50±5 ka; David et al. 2007), although this debate continues. Luminescence methods have also been used to date evidence of cultural and technological aspects of the archaeological record, with examples including the early appearance of symbolic art (Blombos Cave, South Africa; dated by Henshilwood et al. [2002] to ~77 ka) and examples of early pottery production in the Russian Far East to before 10 ka (Kuzmin et al. 2001). Indeed, there is no shortage of examples of luminescence dating applications in archaeological contexts, and the pace at which new studies are being published shows no sign of slowing.

7 CONCLUSIONS

Luminescence dating has made an invaluable contribution to archaeological science, in many cases providing dating control where no other technique is applicable, and in providing corroborating evidence for other independent techniques. The rate of technical and methodological development of luminescence methods over the past couple of decades has been considerable, providing a rich set of tools for further extending chronological control in archaeological contexts. Challenges remain, however, particularly in gaining greater confidence in estimates of the dose rate; in correctly interpreting the causes of scatter in D_e estimates; and in extending the age range limits ever further back in time. Beyond the references cited in this chapter, additional up-to-date information on developments in these methods can be found in the proceedings of the tri-annual Luminescence and Electron Spin Resonance Dating (LED) conference, published in dedicated editions of the journals *Quaternary Geochronology* and *Radiation Measurements*, and in a host of other archaeological science and Quaternary-focused periodicals.

REFERENCES

Adamiec, G. and Aitken, M. J. 1998. Dose rate conversion factors: Update *Ancient TL* 16:37–49.
Aitken, M. J. 1985. *Thermoluminescence Dating*. Academic Press: London.

Aitken, M. J. 1989. Luminescence dating: A guide for non-specialists. *Archaeometry* 31:147–159.

Aitken, M. J. 1997. Luminescence dating. In: Taylor, R. E. and Aitken, M. J. (eds.) *Chronometric Dating in Archaeology*, pp. 183–216. Boston, MA: Springer.

Aitken, M. J. 1998. *An Introduction to Optical Dating*. Oxford: Oxford University Press.

Aitken, M. J., Tite, M. S., and Reid, J. 1964. Thermoluminescent dating of ancient ceramics. *Nature* 202:1032–1033.

Anikovich, M. V., Anikovich, M. V., Sinitsyn, A. A., Hoffecker, J. F., Holliday, V. T., Popov, V. V., Lisitsyn, S. N., Forman, S. L., Levkovskaya, G. M., Pospelova, G. A., Kuz'Mina, I., and Burova, N. D. 2007. Early Upper Paleolithic in Eastern Europe and implications for the dispersal of modern humans. *Science* 315(5809):223–226.

Bailey, R. M. 2000. The slow component of quartz optically stimulated luminescence. *Radiation Measurements* 32(3):233–246.

Bailey, R. and Arnold, L. 2006. Statistical modelling of single grain quartz De distributions and an assessment of procedures for estimating burial dose. *Quaternary Science Reviews* 25(19–20):2475–2502.

Bailey, R. M. and McKeever, S. W. S. 2009. The physical basis of luminescence dating. In: Krbetschek, M. (ed.) *Luminescence Dating: An Introduction and Handbook*. Berlin: Springer.

Bailey, R. M., Singarayer, J. S., Ward, S., and Stokes, S. 2003. Identification of partial resetting using De as a function of illumination time. *Radiation Measurements* 37(4–5):511–518.

Bailey, R. M., Smith, B. W., and Rhodes, E. J. 1997. Partial bleaching and the decay form characteristics of quartz OSL. *Radiation Measurements* 27(2):123–136.

Bateman, M. 2003. Investigations into the potential effects of pedoturbation on luminescence dating. *Quaternary Science Reviews* 22(10–13):1169–1176.

Bateman, M. D., Boulter, C. H., Carr, A. S., Frederick, C. D., Peter, D., and Wilder, M. 2007. Detecting post-depositional sediment disturbance in sandy deposits using optical luminescence. *Quaternary Geochronology* 2(1–4):57–64.

Bowler, J. M., Johnston, H., Olley, J. M., Prescott, J. R., Roberts, R. G., Shawcross, W., and Spooner, N. A. 2003. New ages for human occupation and climatic change at Lake Mungo, Australia. *Nature* 421(6925):837–840.

Burrough, S. L, Thomas, D. S. G., and Bailey, R. M. 2009. Mega-Lake in the Kalahari: A Late Pleistocene record of the Palaeolake Makgadikgadi system. *Quaternary Science Reviews* 28:1392–1411.

David, B., Roberts, R. G., Magee, J., Mialanes, J., Turney, C., Bird, M., White, C., Fifield, L. K., and Tibby, J. 2007. Sediment mixing at Nonda Rock: Investigations of stratigraphic integrity at an early archaeological site in northern Australia and implications for the human colonisation of the continent. *Journal of Quaternary Science* 22:449–479.

Duller, G. A. T. 2008. Single-grain optical dating of Quaternary sediments: Why aliquot size matters in luminescence dating. *Boreas* 37(4):589–612.

Daniels, F., Boyd, C. A., and Saunders, D. F. 1953. Thermoluminescence as a research tool. *Science* 117:343–349.

Feathers, J. K., Rhodes, E. J., Huot, S., and Mcavoy, J. M. 2006. Luminescence dating of sand deposits related to late Pleistocene human occupation at the Cactus Hill Site, Virginia, USA. *Quaternary Geochronology* 1(3):167–187.

Galbraith, R. F. and Green, P. F. 1990. Estimating the component ages in a finite mixture. *Nuclear Tracks and Radiation Measurements* 17:97–206.

Galbraith, R. F., Roberts, R. G., Laslett, G. M., Yoshida, H., and Olley, J. M. 1999. Optical dating of single and multiple grains of quartz from Jinmium rock shelter, Northern Australia: Part I, experimetal design and statistical models. *Archaeometry* 41(2):339–364.

Grine, F. E., Bailey, R. M., Harvati, K., Nathan, R. P., Morris, A. G., Henderson, G. M., Ribot, I., and Pike, A. W. 2007. Late Pleistocene human skull from Hofmeyr, South Africa, and modern human origins. *Science* 315(5809):226–229.

Henshilwood, C. S. 2002. Emergence of modern human behavior: Middle Stone Age engravings from South Africa. *Science* 295(5558):1278–1280.

Huntley, D. J., Godfrey-Smith, D. I., and Thewalt, M. L. W. 1985. Optical dating of sediments. *Nature*, 313(5998):105–107.

Kuzmin, Y. V., Hall, S., Tite, M. S., Bailey, R., O'Malley, J. M., and Medvedev, V. E. 2001. Radiocarbon and thermoluminescence dating of the pottery from the early Neolithic site of Gasya (Russian Far East): Initial results. *Quaternary Science Reviews* 20:945–948.

Lauer, T., Krbetschek, M., Frechen, M., Tsukamoto, S., Hoselmann, C., and Weidenfeller, M. 2011. Infrared radiofluorescence (Ir-Rf) dating of middle pleistocene fluvial archives of the Heidelberg Basin (Southwest Germany). *Geochronometria* 38(1):23–33.

Madsen, A. T., Murray, A. S., Andersen, T. J., Pejrup, M., and Breuning-Madsen, H. 2005. Optically stimulated luminescence dating of young estuarine sediments: a comparison with ^{210}Pb and ^{137}Cs dating. *Marine Geology* 214(1–3): 251–268.

McKeever, S. W. S. 1988. *Thermoluminescence of Solids*. Cambridge: Cambridge University Press.

McKeever, S. W. S. and Chen, R. 1997. Luminescence models. *Radiation Measurements* 27(5):625–661.

Mercier, N. and Valladas, H. 2003. Reassessment of TL age estimates of burnt flints from the Paleolithic site of Tabun Cave, Israel. *Journal of Human Evolution* 45:401–409.

Morwood, M. J., Soejono, R. P., Roberts, R. G., Sutikna, T., Turney, C. S., Westaway, K. E., Rink, W. J., Zhao, J. X., van den Bergh, G. D., Due, R. A., and Hobbs, D. R. 2004. Archaeology and age of a new hominin from Flores in eastern Indonesia. *Nature* 431(7012):1087–1091.

Murray, A. and Olley, J. M. 2002. Precision and accuracy in the optically stimulated luminescence dating of sedimentary quartz: A status review. *Geochronometria* 21:1–16.

Nathan, R. P., Thomas, P. J., Jain, M., Murray, A. S., and Rhodes, E. J. 2003. Environmental dose rate heterogeneity of beta radiation and its implications for luminescence dating:

Monte Carlo modelling and experimental validation. *Radiation Measurements* 37:305–313.

Olley, J., Caitcheon, G., and Murray, A. 1998. The distribution of apparent dose as determined by Optically Stimulated Luminescence in small aliquots of fluvial quartz: implications for dating young sediments. *Quaternary Science Reviews* 17(11):1033–1040.

Olley, J. M., Murray, A., and Roberts, R. 1996. The effects of disequilibria in the uranium and thorium decay chains on burial dose rates in fluvial sediments. *Quaternary Science Reviews* 15(7):751–760.

Olley, J. M. and Pietsch, T. 2004. Optical dating of Holocene sediments from a variety of geomorphic settings using single grains of quartz. *Geomorphology* 60:337–358.

Roberts, R. G., Flannery, T. F., Ayliffe, L. K., Yoshida, H., Olley, J. M., Prideaux, G. J., Laslett, G. M., Baynes, A., Smith, M. A., Jones, R., and Smith, B. L. 2001. New ages for the last Australian megafauna: Continent-wide extinction about 46,000 years ago. *Science* 292(5523):1888–1892.

Roberts, R., Galbraith, R., and Olley, J. 1999. Optical dating of single and multiple grains of quartz from Jinmium rock shelter, northern Australia: Part II, results and implications. *Archaeometry* 41(2):365–395.

Singarayer, J. S., Bailey, R. M., Ward, S., and Stokes, S. 2005. Assessing the completeness of optical resetting of quartz OSL in the natural environment. *Radiation Measurements* 40(1):13–25.

Sivia, D. S., Burbidge, C., Roberts, R. G., and Bailey, R. M. 2004. A Bayesian approach to the evaluation of equivalent doses in sediment mixtures for luminescence dating. *AIP Conference Proceedings* 735:305–311.

Stokes, S. 2004. Optical dating of aeolian dynamism on the West African Sahelian margin. *Geomorphology* 59(1–4):281–291.

Stokes, S., Bailey, R. M., Fedoroff, N., and O'Marah, K. E. 2004. Optical dating of aeolian dynamism on the West African Sahelian margin. *Geomorphology* 59(1–4):281–291.

Thomsen, K. J., Murray, A. S., and Jain, M. 2011. Stability of IRSL signals from sedimentary K-feldspar samples. *Geochronometria* 38(1):1–13.

Tribolo, C., Mercier, N., Selo, M., Valladas, H., Joron, J. L., Reyss, J. L., Henshilwood, C., Sealy, J., and Yates, R., 2006. Tl dating of burnt lithics from Blombos Cave (South Africa): Further evidence for the antiquity of modern human behaviour. *Archaeometry* 48(2):341–357.

Wang, X., Lu, Y., and Wintle, A. 2006. Recuperated OSL dating of fine-grained quartz in Chinese loess. *Quaternary Geochronology* 1(2):89–100.

Waters, M. R., Forman, S. L., Jennings, T. A., Nordt, L. C., Driese, S. G., Feinberg, J. M., Keene, J. L., Halligan, J., Lindquist, A., Pierson, J., and Hallmark, C. T. 2011. The Buttermilk Creek complex and the origins of Clovis at the Debra L. Friedkin site, Texas. *Science* 331(6024):1599–1603.

Wintle, A. 2008. Luminescence dating: Where it has been and where it is going. *Boreas* 37:471–482.

Wintle, A. and Murray, A. 2006. A review of quartz optically stimulated luminescence characteristics and their relevance in single-aliquot regeneration dating protocols. *Radiation Measurements* 41(4):369–391.

Yoshida, H., Roberts, R. G., Olley, J. M., Laslett, G. M., and Galbraith, R. F. 2000. Extending the age range of optical dating using single "supergrains" of quartz. *Radiation Measurements* 32:439–446.

INDEX